BARRON'S

SAT* SUBJECT TEST
WORLD HISTORY

2ND EDITION

William V. Melega, M.Ed., NBPTS
Chapel Hill High School
Chapel Hill, North Carolina

BARRON'S

Now Available!

Go to
barronsbooks.com/TP/SAT/world/
to take a free SAT World
History practice test, complete
with answer explanations
and automated scoring.

Note: You'll need your copy of *SAT Subject Test in World History*,
2nd Edition, handy to complete your online registration.

All inquiries should be addressed to:
Barron's Educational Series, Inc.
250 Wireless Boulevard
Hauppauge, New York 11788
www.barronseduc.com

ISBN: 978-1-4380-1000-7

Library of Congress Control Number: 2017941657

PRINTED IN THE UNITED STATES OF AMERICA

9 8 7 6 5 4 3 2 1

10%
POST-CONSUMER
WASTE
Paper contains a minimum
of 10% post-consumer
waste (PCW). Paper used
in this book was derived
from certified, sustainable
forestlands.

Contents

3.2 MILLION B.C.E.–3000 B.C.E.

3500 B.C.E.–500 B.C.E.

1500 B.C.E.–350 C.E.

1800 C.E.–1881 C.E.

1900 C.E.–1949 C.E.

1500 C.E.–1947 C.E.

1800 C.E.–1918 C.E.

Introduction

Welcome to the Barron's SAT World History Review. I am a veteran high school teacher with 22 years of classroom experience, and this book encompasses exactly what I teach my students to prepare them for the SAT World History exam.

LATERAL HISTORY AND GLOBAL CONNECTIONS

In many textbooks and review books, history is broken down into five time periods.

- Ancient History (3600 B.C.E.–500 C.E.)
- Postclassical Era (500 C.E.–1500 C.E.)
- Early Modern Period (1500 C.E.–1750 C.E.)
- Mid Modern Period (1750 C.E.–1914 C.E.)
- Contemporary Period (1914 C.E.–present)

These designations are accurate, but this review book does not break down history into these sections.

This book features lateral history. At times, several civilizations are doing nearly the same thing at the same time. You can see patterns of history develop and see where historical concepts can overlap and be applied to several different areas of the world. Viewing history laterally (moving across dates) instead of linearly (guided strictly by dates in a straight line) will help you understand the global connections of world history.

WHY STUDY WORLD HISTORY?

World history can be a guide to your future. Within our global, interconnected world, the ability to understand the historical and cultural backgrounds of others can help you grow and mature. It is exciting to see how history is becoming a growing discipline within the academic community.

We are going to review 52,000 years of history around the world. This book is a condensed version of material covered in most world history classes and textbooks.

If you have completed your world history course and are using this book to prepare for the SAT, give yourself around 50 days to prepare for the exam.

If you are using this book at the same time you are taking your world history course, review each unit as you cover it in your class. You can also go back and hit any areas that you struggled with during the year.

Online Practice Test
Visit *barronsbooks.com/TP/SAT/world/* to take a free online practice test.

To use the book most effectively, start by taking the diagnostic test beginning on page 7. Answer each of the questions, and then tally up your score. This should give you an idea of your strengths and also indicate what sections of world history you need to review. This is the best way to plan your review sessions.

After you've finished the review portion of the book, take one of the practice tests, see how you scored, and then continue reviewing the sections with which you struggled. Repeat the process until you are comfortable with the material. Doing a little every day will help you retain the information.

The chapters are set up in such a way as to focus on the "what happened," the "why it happened," and the important result, instead of just stating and memorizing a fact and a date.

References connecting the events in a specific chapter to other civilizations are included and are called "Global Connections." The goal is that you will begin to see the developing patterns of global connections as well as understand and synthesize the material, instead of just gaining basic knowledge and memorizing facts.

As a high school teacher, I have been using this format of teaching for more than 20 years, and I truly believe that you will master these historical concepts to achieve a successful score on the SAT World History test.

TEST FORMAT

The SAT Subject Test in World History is made up of 95 multiple-choice questions. For each question you will have five answer choices from which you are to select the BEST answer. The test is 60 minutes in length with no breaks given. One point is given for each correct answer, and ¼ point is deducted from the total for each incorrect answer. Answers left blank receive zero points.

The College Board, who administers the test, stresses that you can achieve the maximum score of 800 without completing all of the questions in the allotted time. It is also not necessary to get every question correct to achieve the highest score.

Test topics include historical themes from prehistory through present day. The historical themes include social, economic, cultural, political, and intellectual. Test questions will have multiple formats. You will need to be able to

- Analyze cause and effect relationships throughout history
- Understand geography and interpret maps, graphs, and/or charts
- Analyze political statements, cultural and artistic images, and/or quotations from important historical figures or literature in the context of history
- Know facts and terms
- Understand and analyze major historical developments in all civilizations

The content of the SAT World History test is broken down into the following percentages:

■ Global or comparative material	25%
■ Europe	25%
■ Southwest Asia	10%
■ South and Southeast Asia	10%
■ East Asia	10%
■ Africa	10%
■ The Americas (typically not including the United States)	10%

The questions are also broken down by chronological periods to ensure understanding throughout the development of world history.

- Prehistory through civilization development to 500 C.E.   25%
- 500–1500 C.E.   20%
- 1500–1900 C.E.   25%
- 1900 C.E.–present day   20%
- Cross-chronological   10%

This review guide is designed to mirror these percentages in order to prepare you as fully as possible for the SAT Subject Test in World History.

STUDY TIPS

Knowing the format of the test is important, but there are some other important strategies you can use to maximize your effectiveness on the test.

Some of these study tips may sound funny, but in my years of teaching high school students, these are tried and true techniques.

Before you begin each chapter, I suggest you look at the chapter title and do what I call a "brain dump." Write down everything you can possibly remember about the chapter. You'll be able to see how much (or how little) you remember about that specific topic. In this way, you can focus your direction of study on the specific chapter.

When taking the practice tests, I suggest timing yourself as if you were taking the actual test. You have 60 minutes to answer 95 questions, so pacing yourself properly is crucial. Knowing the level of your reading ability is important. Typically, the interpretation of the maps and the primary documents will take longer, so you'll need to make up time on the factual questions.

This book is designed to help you look at and analyze historical material over time. When you come to a question, stop and think. If you are not sure of the correct answer, there are several things you can do.

- First and foremost, read the question again.
- Second, think of other parts of history: Did something similar ever happen somewhere else?
- Finally, apply your knowledge about a similar civilization to the question that you are having trouble with. History happens laterally, so don't just get hyper-focused on one specific point in history.

This review book is different from many of the textbooks you've used. Having a source or perspective different from what you are accustomed to can be helpful. Getting two or three different perspectives on the same historical situation will help you prepare for the test as it will teach you to analyze and interpret the historical situation so you can identify the correct answer.

PRACTICE TESTS

Taking practice exams is an integral part of your review while preparing for the SAT World History test. In addition to the Diagnostic Test and three full-length practice exams in this book, you can get even more practice by taking a *FREE* online practice exam at *http://barronsbooks.com/TP/SAT/world/*. You will need to have your copy of *SAT World History*, 2nd Edition, handy to complete your online registration. As you progressively work through each exam, you will be able to pinpoint your strengths and the areas you still need to work on.

10 THINGS TO REMEMBER BEFORE TAKING THE TEST

1. Keep your same sleep schedule. Many people stay up late studying for the test or try to sleep in on the day of the test. Either way, this causes your internal clock to be out of sync. Stick with your normal sleep routine, or do very little to change it.

2. On the night before the test, do your best to relax. *Do anything but study world history*. Ask your parents to cook your favorite dish or maybe have some friends over for pizza and a movie. Put your feet up, relax, and get ready for the next day.

3. On the day of the test, eat a good breakfast, even if you normally don't eat breakfast. Your body and your mind are going to be working overtime and they need fuel. If you are not used to coffee, don't drink it. However, if you are a coffee addict, make sure you drink it the day of the exam so your body isn't craving it when you're taking the test.

4. Wear comfortable clothes. If you are particularly worried, you can dress up a little bit to make yourself feel better, but choose something comfortable. You are taking a very long test, and you want to be comfortable in your seat. Wear clothes in layers. It may be really hot or really cool in the testing room.

5. While you are studying for the test, feel free to listen to music *without* words. Studies show that classical music heightens brain activity. However, if you listen to music *with* lyrics, it forces your brain to concentrate not only on *what you are studying but on the lyrics as well*. Therefore, soft, melodic classical music is the best choice to increase your brain activity without distracting your attention.

6. Along with listening to music, make sure you move around often while studying. Don't lay on a couch or your bed to study. When you are sedentary, your body uses less energy and begins to shut down. When you're moving, everything is working at optimal level. Also, talk to yourself. Speak the material out loud, just as you would if you were preparing to give a speech. In this way, you are reinforcing the material several different ways: you are thinking it, you are reading it, and you are processing it as you say it out loud.

7. Have at least two or three No. 2 pencils sharpened and ready to go (or mechanical pencils with extra lead) when you take your exam.

8. Get to your testing location a little early. Plan to get there 15 to 20 minutes ahead of time, so you can take your time finding parking and locating the testing room. If you are overly stressed, being late will make things even worse.

9. When taking a multiple-choice test, some questions will require you to choose the *best possible answer*. Sometimes, it will be easy to find the best possible answer, and it will be clear which answers are totally incorrect. However, in many questions, there will be an eyecatcher, which is an answer that looks right, but if you read carefully, you"ll find that it is actually incorrect. When you see an eyecatcher, start by eliminating the answers that you are sure are incorrect. Then, see what you are left with and analyze them. When faced with several possible options, choose the one that set everything else in motion. Ask yourself, "Is there an answer that, *without its inclusion*, none of the other answers could have happened?" Most likely, that is your answer.

10. Take time to go back and look at your answers. If you're not sure of an answer, leave it blank, but REMEMBER TO GO BACK TO IT. Make sure you didn't make any bubbling errors.

Relax and good luck! This is just a test. You have taken many exams of this magnitude before. If you've studied, I believe you will be pleased with the results.

ANSWER SHEET
Diagnostic Test

1. Ⓐ Ⓑ Ⓒ Ⓓ Ⓔ
2. Ⓐ Ⓑ Ⓒ Ⓓ Ⓔ
3. Ⓐ Ⓑ Ⓒ Ⓓ Ⓔ
4. Ⓐ Ⓑ Ⓒ Ⓓ Ⓔ
5. Ⓐ Ⓑ Ⓒ Ⓓ Ⓔ
6. Ⓐ Ⓑ Ⓒ Ⓓ Ⓔ
7. Ⓐ Ⓑ Ⓒ Ⓓ Ⓔ
8. Ⓐ Ⓑ Ⓒ Ⓓ Ⓔ
9. Ⓐ Ⓑ Ⓒ Ⓓ Ⓔ
10. Ⓐ Ⓑ Ⓒ Ⓓ Ⓔ
11. Ⓐ Ⓑ Ⓒ Ⓓ Ⓔ
12. Ⓐ Ⓑ Ⓒ Ⓓ Ⓔ
13. Ⓐ Ⓑ Ⓒ Ⓓ Ⓔ
14. Ⓐ Ⓑ Ⓒ Ⓓ Ⓔ
15. Ⓐ Ⓑ Ⓒ Ⓓ Ⓔ
16. Ⓐ Ⓑ Ⓒ Ⓓ Ⓔ
17. Ⓐ Ⓑ Ⓒ Ⓓ Ⓔ
18. Ⓐ Ⓑ Ⓒ Ⓓ Ⓔ
19. Ⓐ Ⓑ Ⓒ Ⓓ Ⓔ
20. Ⓐ Ⓑ Ⓒ Ⓓ Ⓔ
21. Ⓐ Ⓑ Ⓒ Ⓓ Ⓔ
22. Ⓐ Ⓑ Ⓒ Ⓓ Ⓔ
23. Ⓐ Ⓑ Ⓒ Ⓓ Ⓔ
24. Ⓐ Ⓑ Ⓒ Ⓓ Ⓔ
25. Ⓐ Ⓑ Ⓒ Ⓓ Ⓔ

26. Ⓐ Ⓑ Ⓒ Ⓓ Ⓔ
27. Ⓐ Ⓑ Ⓒ Ⓓ Ⓔ
28. Ⓐ Ⓑ Ⓒ Ⓓ Ⓔ
29. Ⓐ Ⓑ Ⓒ Ⓓ Ⓔ
30. Ⓐ Ⓑ Ⓒ Ⓓ Ⓔ
31. Ⓐ Ⓑ Ⓒ Ⓓ Ⓔ
32. Ⓐ Ⓑ Ⓒ Ⓓ Ⓔ
33. Ⓐ Ⓑ Ⓒ Ⓓ Ⓔ
34. Ⓐ Ⓑ Ⓒ Ⓓ Ⓔ
35. Ⓐ Ⓑ Ⓒ Ⓓ Ⓔ
36. Ⓐ Ⓑ Ⓒ Ⓓ Ⓔ
37. Ⓐ Ⓑ Ⓒ Ⓓ Ⓔ
38. Ⓐ Ⓑ Ⓒ Ⓓ Ⓔ
39. Ⓐ Ⓑ Ⓒ Ⓓ Ⓔ
40. Ⓐ Ⓑ Ⓒ Ⓓ Ⓔ
41. Ⓐ Ⓑ Ⓒ Ⓓ Ⓔ
42. Ⓐ Ⓑ Ⓒ Ⓓ Ⓔ
43. Ⓐ Ⓑ Ⓒ Ⓓ Ⓔ
44. Ⓐ Ⓑ Ⓒ Ⓓ Ⓔ
45. Ⓐ Ⓑ Ⓒ Ⓓ Ⓔ
46. Ⓐ Ⓑ Ⓒ Ⓓ Ⓔ
47. Ⓐ Ⓑ Ⓒ Ⓓ Ⓔ
48. Ⓐ Ⓑ Ⓒ Ⓓ Ⓔ
49. Ⓐ Ⓑ Ⓒ Ⓓ Ⓔ
50. Ⓐ Ⓑ Ⓒ Ⓓ Ⓔ

Diagnostic Test

1. During the Paleolithic Age, humans would be associated with which of the following practices?

    A. Advancement in art by using it as a type of communication
    B. Quickly settling in permanent villages for defense and abundant resources
    C. Living in small groups and moving to new areas as food became insufficient or the herds moved to a new location
    D. Worshipping one god
    E. Crafting precious metals into usable tools

2. The Neolithic Revolution is a significant point in history as humans

    A. developed a complex religion.
    B. mastered the creation of fire.
    C. buried the dead with great care, including carvings of a fertility goddess.
    D. developed and used stone tools and other advanced technology.
    E. began to form permanent settlements and developed agriculture.

3. Which Chinese dynasty sponsored travels at sea by a large flotilla to demonstrate the power of the Chinese empire and to increase its trade routes and partners?

    A. Tang
    B. Manchu
    C. Ch'in
    D. Qing
    E. Ming

4. In medieval Spain, Abd al-Rahman I and III were known for which contribution to world society and culture?

    A. Encouraging mosaic artwork to be used throughout the Middle East
    B. Building the Alhambra castle and mosque to further education in the region
    C. Starting the trade network out of Europe and linking it to the trans-Sahara trade route
    D. Providing Henry the Navigator with the basis to begin creating navigational instruments
    E. Halting the violence after the Reconquista

5. During the Old Kingdom of Egypt, Egyptians constructed pyramids for which of the following reasons?

   A. To leave behind a record of their accomplishments
   B. To affirm their belief in the afterlife as a resting place for their pharaohs
   C. To indicate to invaders the wealth and power of the Egyptian Kingdom
   D. To control their large number of slaves by keeping them working on public works projects
   E. To plot points to help the Egyptians map the movements of the planets and determine when the Nile would flood

6. Why are objects such as the Behistun Rock, the Rosetta Stone, and the Vedas important in the study of history?

   A. To understand the spoken dialect of ancient languages
   B. To decipher the legal codes and how they applied to ancient societies in terms of the social hierarchy
   C. To understand and decipher ancient writing systems or give insight into the values and belief systems of ancient societies
   D. To fully understand the governmental organization and hierarchies of these ancient societies
   E. To further define the religious beliefs and practices of each River Valley civilization

7. Greek philosophers differed from other ancient people because they taught which of the following ideas that advanced human thinking and the acquisition of knowledge?

   A. Every citizen should submit to the needs of their polis.
   B. The gods alone control the universe.
   C. The sun is the center of the universe—the heliocentric theory.
   D. Mathematics should be the foundation behind every decision made for the polis.
   E. Reason and observation are the only things needed to understand the workings of the universe.

8. The teachings of Confucius, which were used to explain how to achieve an efficient moral government, were written down in which document?

   A. Analects
   B. Greek philosophy
   C. Vedas
   D. *Mahabharata*
   E. The Middle Path

9. The Zhou/Chou Dynasty used this concept to justify the overthrow of the Shang Dynasty.

   A. Daoism
   B. Legalism
   C. Vedas
   D. Mandate of Heaven
   E. The Middle Path

10. The concept of Pax Romana can best be characterized as a period of

    A. constant warfare and tension.
    B. a period of peace and prosperity in Rome, allowing for achievements in art, architecture, and technology.
    C. stagnation due to the size of the empire and the successive barbarian attacks.
    D. great expansion.
    E. war with the Carthaginian Empire, creating Mare Nostrum.

11. Alexander the Great created an empire that combined the knowledge of Greek, Egyptian, Persian, and Indian culture known as?

    A. Orthodox philosophy
    B. Carolingian minuscule
    C. Macedonian association
    D. Liberal arts curriculum
    E. Hellenistic culture

12. Which commonality was shared by both the Aztec Empire in Mexico and the Incan Empire in South America?

    A. Both were closely linked to the Mayan civilization.
    B. Both were long distance traders whose materials have been found from the Pacific Islands to the Mississippi Delta.
    C. Both acquired vast empires by military conquest.
    D. Neither had writing systems, so much is left open to speculation or bias from conquistadors.
    E. Both simultaneously discovered the use of iron for tools and weapon-making technology.

13. Why is the Olmec civilization considered the "mother culture" of all Mesoamerican civilizations?

    A. The Olmec was the founding civilization in the region.
    B. The Olmecs wrote down and diffused their civilization throughout the area.
    C. The Olmec gods were worshipped throughout Mesoamerica.
    D. The Mayan civilization developed simultaneously but did not have a lasting impact.
    E. All Mesoamerican dynasties descended from Olmec royalty.

14. During the Ch'in/Qin Dynasty, the government instituted strict laws with harsh penalties that were the result of which Chinese political philosophy?

    A. Daoism
    B. Legalism
    C. Isolationism
    D. Confucianism
    E. Buddhism

15. The Maurya Dynasty of India was the first Indian empire to accomplish which Indian achievement?

    A. Building of the Taj Mahal
    B. Uniting much of the Indian subcontinent
    C. Encouraging the exportation of cash crops
    D. Expanding the empire through peaceful negotiation, not conquest
    E. Encouraging the people to participate in the election of officials

16. Which best describes the primary goal of the Crusades?

    A. To bring unification within the church
    B. To show the dominance of the Pope over the patriarch of Constantinople
    C. To forcibly convert Muslims and polytheists to Christianity
    D. To reclaim the Holy Land from the Muslims
    E. To expand the borders of the Byzantine Empire

17. As Islam spread throughout the world, the sharia was created for which of the following reasons?

    A. To preserve the writings and precedents of the prophet Muhammad
    B. The ulama and Islamic scholars wrote down their discussions and ideas over a period of time, creating a work that outlines all aspects of Muslim life
    C. To create the doctrine of Islamic expansion and treatment of newly conquered peoples
    D. To provide a guide for Christian men who became new converts to Islam
    E. To regulate the ever-increasing Arabic trade networks

18. The Islamic civil war that was fought over who would become the successor of Muhammad resulted in which of the following?

    A. Led to the Islamic schism and the splitting of Sunni and Shiite sects of Islam
    B. Was settled peacefully by Abu Bakr
    C. Was able to further unify followers of Islam
    D. Created a European and Arabic caliphate
    E. Ended with converts from Mecca achieving victory

19. The East African kingdom of Axum was able to thrive as a trading empire because of which factor?

    A. Easy access to the Silk Road route heading into Asia Minor
    B. Location along the Mediterranean, which allowed it to trade with the Mediterranean empires of Greece, Rome, and Carthage, as well as those in Asia
    C. Its advanced technology
    D. Importance of the growing gold trade with Europe
    E. Location on the Red Sea, which was well suited for participating in and controlling trade with the Middle East

20. The West African kingdom of Ghana was able to acquire vast amounts of wealth because of its ability to

    A. dominate the smaller kingdoms along the Niger River.

    B. connect the trans-Sahara trade network to the Silk Road.

    C. negotiate favorable trade treaties with Arab merchants during the expansion of Islam.

    D. establish a monopoly on the trading of gold and salt throughout the region.

    E. control the European trade along the Atlantic Coast.

21. Under the rule of the Song Dynasty, the Confucian civil service exam was re-instituted to determine what about a candidate applying to become a Confucian advisor?

    A. Overall academic ability

    B. Literacy and handwriting ability as the bureaucracy was becoming bogged down due to inefficiency

    C. Understanding of key Confucian principles necessary for a governmental minister to have before working in the Chinese bureaucracy

    D. Diplomatic ability as the Silk Road was expanding into territory beyond China's knowledge

    E. Understanding of key turning points in Chinese history to avoid repeating mistakes

22. A major result of the Golden Horde conquering Russia along the Volga River was

    A. missionaries gained wide acceptance among the Mongols and brought Christianity to East Asia.

    B. that the Mongol conquest facilitated trade between Asia and different parts of Europe that had been previously unattached to a major trade route.

    C. that Mongol culture was absorbed into the advanced civilization in Russia and eventually vanished altogether.

    D. that the country was closed to all foreigners.

    E. increased warfare along the European frontier, which caused further suffering among peasants.

23. Charlemagne, who created an empire in Western Europe in the late 700s, is also known for

    A. dividing Europe into manageable kingdoms as a way to replace feudalism.

    B. leading of the First Crusade into the Holy Land.

    C. his rivalry with Emperor Justinian of the Byzantine Empire.

    D. his interest in exploration of the New World.

    E. his determination to bring education back into Europe as a way to create advisors who would make ruling his vast empire more efficient and uniform.

24. Which Islamic leader was able to defeat Richard the Lionheart during the Third Crusade and recapture much of the territory taken by the European crusaders?

    A. Harun al-Rashid

    B. Ibn Battuta

    C. Saladin

    D. Abu Bakr

    E. Muhammad al-Razi

25. Which definition would best fit the political and economic system developed in the Middle Ages between lords and the peasants that depended on a reciprocal relationship?

A. Serfdom
B. Manoralism
C. Catholicism
D. Castle mentality
E. Monasticism

26. How did the Aztec civilization choose to govern their newly conquered territories?

A. The Aztecs placed selected governors to transition the conquered people toward Aztec ideals.
B. Aztecs only required conquered people to give tribute and left them to self-govern.
C. The new territories were assigned to an Aztec military district, controlled by an Aztec elder and proven general.
D. Newly conquered territories had to acknowledge Aztec authority and pay the required tribute. After that, they left the territory alone, and the local governmental system remained intact.
E. The conquered territories were absorbed into the calpulli system and became, in effect, a suburb of Tenochtitlan.

27. The Renaissance began in Italy for which of the following reasons?

A. It housed a large literate population left over from the Roman Empire.
B. It contained the vast resources of the Roman Catholic Church.
C. Italy contained many large cities that had large accumulations of money due to trading within the Mediterranean.
D. Hellenistic culture had deep roots in Italy.
E. Increased trading in the Mediterranean was a result of the Crusades.

28. Why did religious reformer Martin Luther nail his *95 Theses* to the door of the church in Wittenberg, Germany?

A. He was angry at the direction of the Protestant Reformation.
B. Martin Luther felt the selling of indulgences was a deviation from the church's true mission.
C. The people near Wittenberg began to leave the church as they turned toward humanism and had no need for the church.
D. King Henry VIII's creation of the Church of England led to another splintering of the faith, and Martin Luther's *Theses* were geared to prevent that from happening.
E. The Papal Decree included in the Edict of Worms did not align with Martin Luther's philosophy.

29. Why were the European explorers able to travel, explore, and conquer further distances in their sailing expeditions after 1450?

    A. European explorers adapted new technology that they learned about in China to use in their trading fleets.
    B. European explorers encountered very little opposition to their conquests.
    C. Muslim merchants had already begun to plot and map these newer trade routes.
    D. European governments supported and financed these explorations, beginning with Portugal's Prince Henry the Navigator. Inventions allowed sailors to plot their course and sail for greater distances.
    E. Europeans had vastly superior weapons technology, allowing them to create faraway empires.

30. As the Spanish conquistadors began to exploit the riches of the New World, which labor practice employed by the Spanish is closely related to the mita system used by the Incan Empire?

    A. Casa de Contratación
    B. Flotilla system
    C. Encomienda
    D. Indentured servitude
    E. Calpulli

31. During the Cold War, this area was the first "hot spot" of the era, and where a state of war exists to this day.

    A. Korea
    B. China
    C. Vietnam
    D. Poland
    E. India

32. During the era of decolonization after World War II, the continent of Africa faced many challenges. Which of the following problems was NOT a direct result of European rule?

    A. Independence and separatist movements were led by minority groups inside the new countries.
    B. Governments were run by a western-educated elite who governed without the consent of the greater population.
    C. The development of governments was based on the military rule of generals to organize the state.
    D. Warfare and genocide were based on religious differences.
    E. Tribal ties were stronger for their locality rather than for the nation as a whole.

33. The quotes "L'etat, c'est moi" and "People? What are people? I have subjects" are indicative of what period of world history?

    A. Nationalism
    B. Imperialism
    C. Feudalism
    D. Industrialization
    E. Absolutism

34. Why did the Ming Dynasty emperors decide to adopt a policy of isolation?

   A. The Ming emperors did not like the behaviors and growing influence of European merchants and wanted to maintain China's ancient traditions.
   B. The Ming emperors felt they had learned all they could from outsiders and wanted time to adopt what they had learned to fit specific Chinese needs.
   C. They did not want to divert attention from building the Great Wall.
   D. The growing power of the Mughal and Sassanid dynasties forced China to stay within its borders so as not to provoke a war with a more technologically advanced empire.
   E. The amount of money spent on Zheng He's voyages had bankrupted the Ming treasury.

35. Which of the following was Russian Czar Peter the Great's main objective after returning from his tour of Western Europe?

   A. Subjecting the boyars
   B. Extending the current trade networks and creating new ones as outlets for the growing Russian economy
   C. Reforming the inefficient Russian bureaucracy by creating a new Russian legislature
   D. Pursuing a policy of modernization and industrialization for Russia
   E. Punishing the streltsy for abuses of power during his absence

36. The works of the Enlightenment philosophers had a great influence on this document, which built the cornerstones of democracy?

   A. The Magna Carta
   B. The Halifax Accords
   C. The U.S. Constitution
   D. The English Bill of Rights
   E. Thomas Paine's *Common Sense*

37. The primary cause of the French Revolution can be traced to which factor affecting France in the 1780s?

   A. A lack of clear and decisive leadership
   B. The government clearly lacked support from the church
   C. There was a distinct and sizable gap in French society between a small upper class and the masses of French people
   D. The Estates General was planning its first meeting as a legislature
   E. Many generals were mustering support in the military for a coup

38. What was the main factor that changed the world during the Industrial Revolution?

   A. Production changed from being powered by animal or human power to one that was driven by mechanical power, leading to production being done in factories.
   B. The conflict grew between migrants moving into the cities looking for work and the urban poor hoping to monopolize new factory jobs.
   C. Great Britain was able to create and maintain higher rates of production.
   D. Towns were more easily created as feudal lords were no longer needed.
   E. Skilled artisans and other urban guilds resisted the Industrial Revolution.

39. When Karl Marx and Thomas Engels wrote *The Communist Manifesto*, which best describes their vision of socialism and the factors of production?

A. Governments should sponsor the private ownership of industrial property.

B. Governments should be the controlling factor on quotas and the production of industrial goods.

C. All governments should seek to expand their exports to developing countries.

D. The community as a whole will regulate and control the production and distribution of goods.

E. Companies should stop competing and merge resources.

40. Which of the following statements would be the best description of the Japanese archipelago before 1853?

A. The Japanese had a working knowledge of the west from Portuguese missionaries.

B. The samurai formed a separate level of society and held vast power and privileges.

C. There was no clear, defined effective governmental leader.

D. Marxism and Socialism had made its way into society along the Silk Road and defined the Meiji Restoration.

E. Japan existed in a state of isolation that was deemed as such by governmental policy.

41. Which movement was created to combat problems such as famine and overpopulation in developing countries after World War II?

A. Asian Independence

B. the Green Revolution

C. Pan-Arabism

D. the Developing Nations wing of the United Nations and the World Bank

E. the creation of the World Health Organization

42. By 1917, in the middle of World War I, which factor was the major cause of unrest in Russia?

A. The loss of property at the hands of the invading German Army

B. Russian Czar Nicholas II calling for an increase in his dictatorial powers

C. Repeated losses in World War I and the growing need for reforms

D. Weakening economy due to the influx of refugees fleeing the fighting

E. The Slavic countries of Eastern Europe, whom the Russians said they would protect by signing an armistice with Germany

43. Of the many factors that combined to cause World War I, which factor would qualify as the most immediate trigger or cause of the outbreak of war?

A. The growing threat to the spector of communism

B. The assassination of the Archduke Franz Ferdinand

C. The firing of Chancellor Otto von Bismarck by Kaiser Wilhelm I

D. The complicated and intricate tangle of alliances that existed before the war

E. The growing competition between European countries for lands to colonize

44. The Treaty of Versailles signed at the end of World War I, which brought an end to the conflict, was immediately controversial for which of the following reasons?

   A. Germany was forced to make heavy reparation payments.
   B. The treaty declared the end of the war was an armistice, or cease-fire; thus, it did not declare a defined victor.
   C. Germany and the Soviet Union were absent from the peace conference.
   D. Not all countries ratified the new League of Nations charter.
   E. Both A and C

45. Twentieth-century leaders Joseph Stalin, Benito Mussolini, and Adolf Hitler followed/favored which governmental ideology?

   A. Each leader believed in slow and steady decolonization of colonial territories.
   B. All believed in forming defensive alliances, such as the Warsaw Pact, to defend against aggression from Western Europe.
   C. Each man believed in running authoritarian and totalitarian governments.
   D. All wanted to spread the growing ideology of communism.
   E. All had won a democratic election that legally placed them in power.

46. In South Africa, the Afrikaner National Party instituted a policy of separation based on race that was known to the world as

   A. populism.
   B. Jim Crow.
   C. Nuremberg laws.
   D. apartheid.
   E. internment.

47. After World War II, which factor had the largest influence on the economy of South Korea as it grew into an economic superpower?

   A. The collapse of the Korean economy after Mao Tse-tung occupied North Korea
   B. The competition for influence between China and the Soviet Union
   C. The splitting of the Korean Peninsula into two halves with capitalism in the South and communism in the North
   D. The dominance of the American economic presence in Japan, which stifled much of Korea's growth
   E. The devastation caused by the Japanese invasion during World War II

48. The Cold War, which dominated world political events for much of the second half of the 20th century, came to an end following which event?

   A. The Serbian civil war and genocide led by Slobodan Milosevic
   B. The collapse and break up of the Soviet Union
   C. The election of former Polish Cardinal Karol Wojtyla to the office of the pope
   D. The success of the Hungarian Revolution
   E. The United States launching the Star Wars defensive shield in the 1980s

49. Why does Western culture have such a heavy influence on world culture?

    A. The defeat of the Soviet Union by the United States in the Cold War

    B. The domination of Western media over worldwide mass media and entertainment

    C. The uniting of the economies of Western Europe with the creation of the European Union

    D. The appeal of major sports marketing of teams and personalities

    E. The creation of the World Wide Web, allowing transactions to happen faster and safer

50. Why was the United States asked to intervene and lead a multinational coalition into the Middle East in 1991?

    A. To liberate the country of Kuwait and protect the kingdom of Saudi Arabia from aggression by Iraq

    B. To pursue the "war on terror," which was underway after the attacks on September 11, 2001

    C. To keep the Suez Canal open and running after the devastating earthquake that hit the eastern Mediterranean and Persian Gulf

    D. To defend against the increased frequency of Somali pirate attacks

    E. To carry out part of President Reagan's plan to further weaken the Soviet Union during its war in Afghanistan

ANSWER KEY
Diagnostic Test

1.	C	14.	B	27.	C	40.	E
2.	E	15.	B	28.	B	41.	B
3.	E	16.	D	29.	D	42.	C
4.	B	17.	B	30.	C	43.	B
5.	B	18.	A	31.	A	44.	E
6.	C	19.	E	32.	C	45.	C
7.	E	20.	D	33.	E	46.	D
8.	A	21.	C	34.	A	47.	C
9.	D	22.	B	35.	D	48.	B
10.	B	23.	E	36.	C	49.	B
11.	E	24.	C	37.	C	50.	A
12.	C	25.	B	38.	A		
13.	A	26.	D	39.	D		

ANSWER EXPLANATIONS

1. **(C)** Paleolithic clans were nomadic as they moved from place to place following herds of game or when available resources ran out.

2. **(E)** The Neolithic Revolution marked the beginning of permanent settlements and villages that no longer had to move in search of food. Instead, they began to farm and domesticate animals, leading to the eventual creation of cities.

3. **(E)** The Ming Dynasty sent Admiral Zheng He on voyages throughout the Pacific Ocean and Indian Ocean in the early 1400s to increase China's trade network and demonstrate the power and glory of the Chinese empire.

4. **(B)** Abd al-Rahman I and III built the mosque and castle to house a university where both Muslim and Christian students could study.

5. **(B)** The Great Pyramids of Giza, built during the Old Kingdom, were built as houses for the dead pharaohs, who were seen as living gods to the people of Egypt.

6. **(C)** The Behistun Rock and Rosetta Stone allowed the writing systems of Mesopotamia and Egypt to be deciphered. The Vedas give us an explanation of the values and beliefs of the Vedic Age in India.

7. **(E)** Beginning with the philosopher Thales, Greek philosophers taught that the world is rational and knowable. They believed that, through observation, all things can be known and explained and that the gods control the workings of the universe.

8. **(A)** Students of Confucius wrote down his philosophies and teachings in the Analects, which were used as a model for governing officials in China. They were fully accepted in the Han Dynasty from 206 B.C.E. to 220 C.E.

9. **(D)** The Zhou/Chou used the Mandate of Heaven to explain that as a dynasty ages, it becomes corrupt and neglects its duties. When this happens, the gods will remove their approval of the dynasty, allowing it to be overthrown. Then, a new dynasty receives their blessing.

10. **(B)** Pax Romana, beginning with the reign of Augustus Caesar, is seen as the Golden Age of Rome. Pax Romana was a time of peace and prosperity with cultural and technological achievements.

11. **(E)** During his conquests from Greece to Egypt to the Indus River Valley, Alexander combined the learning of the ancient world, which is referred to as Hellenistic culture. The name is based on Helen of Troy, who was "the face that launched a thousand ships."

12. **(C)** Both Aztecs and Incas had large powerful militaries that were used to conquer and acquire territory.

13. **(A)** The Olmecs were the oldest civilization in Mesoamerica, and as a result, they formed the foundation that all other Mesoamerican civilizations were built upon.

14. **(B)** Shi Huang Di and his ministers felt that people were by nature bad. Since people liked rewards and disliked punishments, strict and swift punishments were instituted to bring uniformity to China.

15. **(B)** The Maurya Dynasty was able to bring initial unity to the large and diverse subcontinent of India.

16. **(D)** The primary goal of the Crusades was to drive the Arabic Muslims out of the Holy Land and the city of Jerusalem.

17. **(B)** The sharia is made up of the interpretations of the ulama and governs the economic, commercial, social, and political aspects of a follower of Islam.

18. **(A)** The Umayyad and Abbasid civil war resulted in the splitting of Islam into two different branches, based on differing views on who should be the leader, or caliph.

19. **(E)** Axum's location on the East African Coast along the Red Sea allowed it to have easy access to the trade networks coming out of the Middle East.

20. **(D)** Ghana became a wealthy empire by establishing a monopoly on the trading of salt (an essential mineral) and gold (which was used as currency) with overland traders. As a result, Ghana was able to acquire vast amounts of wealth.

21. **(C)** The civil service exam tested a student's knowledge of Confucian principles that were necessary for one to master before getting assigned a role in the government. Officials had to be good men as they were role models for the Chinese people to follow.

22. **(B)** As a result of the conquests of the Mongol Golden Horde, new trade routes were opened up as contact increased between northern Europeans and people in Asia and the Byzantine Empire, creating greater cultural diffusion.

23. **(E)** Although not literate himself, Charlemagne hired Alcuin of York to create a school to train students to become governing officials to help unify his empire.

24. **(C)** Saladin, the great Islamic warrior, was able to briefly unite the Arabic tribes and push back the crusaders to reclaim territory captured by the European knights.

25. **(B)** Manoralism is a political, economic, and social system in which peasants were tied to a lord in medieval Europe, creating a small self-sufficient estate.

26. **(D)** As the Aztecs conquered a territory, they required the subjected people to acknowledge their leadership and pay heavy tribute. After that, the community was left alone so they could rebuild their population, as the Aztecs would periodically return for sacrificial victims.

27. **(C)** Italy had wealthy cities like Venice, Genoa, Naples, and Florence due to trading with the Middle East and up into the Black Sea region. This gave them surplus capital to become patrons of the arts.

28. **(B)** Martin Luther witnessed the selling of indulgences, or money paid for the forgiveness of sins of dead relatives so they would gain entrance into heaven. The money was being used to fund a new cathedral in Rome, and Luther decided that the church had deviated from its true mission. Reform was needed so Luther outlined the 95 problems that he felt needed to be addressed.

29. **(D)** Governments such as Spain and Portugal began to finance and support sailing missions. The sailing school of Prince Henry the Navigator helped to develop tools

like the astrolabe and sextant, allowing for the voyages of Columbus, Vasco de Gama, and Magellan to take place.

30. **(C)** The encomienda was a practice where an agent of the Crown in the New World was given a set number of natives to work for a set period of time. The Incas required all citizens to work a set number of days each year on public works projects.

31. **(A)** The Korean War began in 1950 along the 38th Parallel. When the war ended in 1953, the 38th parallel was again the border dividing the country into nearly two even halves. Today, the Demilitarized Zone is one of the most heavily guarded borders where a state of war exists to this day.

32. **(C)** Many African countries looked to military rulers to bring structure and organization to their new governments in the postcolonial era.

33. **(E)** Louis XIV's "I am the State" and Austrian Emperor Franz Joseph's "I have subjects" would be indicative of the age of absolutism where kings and emperors had, or sought, absolute and total power in their countries.

34. **(A)** The Chinese government decided to close off China to the outside world because they were angry at the behavior of foreign sailors and wanted to limit European influence on the people of China. Instead, they wanted to focus on traditional Chinese values.

35. **(D)** After his return from Western Europe, Peter began to immediately pursue policies for the rapid industrialization and modernization of the Russian economy to compete with Western Europe.

36. **(C)** The thoughts of many of the Enlightenment philosophers were directly incorporated into the creation of the U.S. government and written in the U.S. Constitution, such as the separation of powers and the responsibility of the government to the governed.

37. **(C)** The first two Estates (the clergy and the nobility) comprised the smallest percentage of French society. However, they controlled nearly all the wealth and property, and they dominated the decision-making process as they always outvoted the Third Estate (French citizens) in a vote of 2 to 1.

38. **(A)** With inventions such as the water frame and steam engine, industrial power became mechanical. It changed the workforce by relocating labor from rural towns to new cities, changing the world and workforce forever.

39. **(D)** Marx and Engels believed that capitalism would always lead to corruption and poverty. They advocated for society or the community as a whole to control the factors of production and the distribution of goods in a classless society.

40. **(E)** Being within the shogunate of Tokugawa Ieyasu, the Japanese felt they had learned all they could from outsiders. Thus, they turned inward to reflect on themselves and believed they were the most civilized country in the world.

41. **(B)** The Green Revolution sought to make India a self-sufficient country in terms of food production by experimenting with new hybrid seeds and fertilizers that, if successful, could be used in other countries as well.

42. **(C)** The many losses during World War I, especially at Tannenberg, coupled with the already poor conditions of the peasants, enabled Vladimir Lenin to call for the overthrow of the czar.

43. **(B)** Many factors led to the outbreak of World War I; however, the cause or factor that brought about the conflict was the assassination of Archduke Franz Ferdinand in Sarajevo.

44. **(E)** The Treaty of Versailles drew heavy criticism because Germany and the Soviet Union had not been invited, and because the reparation payments with which Germany would be burdened were enormous.

45. **(C)** All three leaders are known for their authoritarian and totalitarian regimes that affected much of the history of the 20th century.

46. **(D)** In 1948, South Africa instituted the policy of apartheid, or racial separation, where the white minority ruled over a larger black majority.

47. **(C)** The splitting of the Korean Peninsula into two halves left Korea with a communist, totalitarian country in the north and a democratic, capitalist country in the south. Being a capitalist country has allowed South Korea to develop its economy into one that has become an economic superpower throughout the world.

48. **(B)** The Cold War came to a sudden end on December 25, 1991, when the Soviet Union was dissolved.

49. **(B)** Western countries dominate mass media, social media, and entertainment around the globe, giving Western countries a great deal of influence over the habits, ideas, and beliefs of people around the globe.

50. **(A)** The United States was asked to lead the coalition forces against Saddam Hussein's army, which invaded Kuwait and was threatening worldwide oil shipments.

Prehistory and Paleolithic Man to the Emergence of Human Civilization

1

GEOGRAPHY

One of the most important factors in studying history is understanding the geography of where things happen. In its most basic form, geography is the environment in which a group of people live and the resources available to them. People have to look at their location, assess where they are, and then decide what is actually available for them to use.

Early on, people had to migrate. They were nomadic, meaning they had to stay on the move in order to have enough food. There are many reasons for migration throughout history, but warfare, natural disasters, and some type of persecution top the list of reasons why early peoples were nomadic and migrated to stay alive. All of this migration led to cultural diffusion and, eventually, populated the whole of the earth.

EARLIEST HUMANS IN EAST AFRICA

In 1960 in the Olduvai Gorge in Tanzania, Africa, scientists Louis and Mary Leakey found some of the oldest human remains. Dr. Donald Johanson found the oldest human skeleton in Ethiopia in 1974. By starting at these locations and then moving outward from these points, students of history can follow the migration of people. Migration allowed the human species to populate all corners of the earth.

PALEOLITHIC AGE

"Paleolithic" is another name for the "Old Stone Age." *Paleo* means "old" and *lithic* means "stone." This section of human life is known as prehistory, or history that existed before human writing. The Paleolithic Age started circa 2.5 million years ago. There is evidence of humans and their lives, but not much is known about prehistory because there are no written records. Many historical texts use the term *circa*, which means "around" or "about." The term *circa* is used by historians in these situations because they are not sure about the specific date.

Currently, two new headings are used to delineate historical dates. B.C.E. stands for "before common era." C.E. stands for "common era." Most people now use B.C.E. and C.E. Older history textbooks may still use the designations of B.C. and A.D.

> **DINNER TABLE TALK**
>
> Think about the process of feeding people. When you host Thanksgiving dinner, how much work is it to feed an entire extended family for just one day? Imagine feeding all of these people on a continual basis. How difficult would that become during cold weather? Rainy weather? Dry weather?

Nomads

For the most part, humans in Paleolithic times were nomads. They moved in search of food, following herds of game like elk or woolly mammoths. They gathered fruits, nuts, and berries. These nomadic clans traveled in bands of up to 30 people. These people did not have permanent shelters and lived in caves or a lean-to. The maximum number possible in these groups was 20–30 people. With more than 30 people, it became too difficult to feed or move the group.

Gender Relations

At this time, everyone was expected to contribute to the group to make sure everyone survived. The men hunted and fished to provide food for the tribe. The women and young children gathered the fruits, nuts, and berries, plus they did much of the cooking and making of clothing. The jobs were divided into separate categories, but it is important to note that there was no distinction between men and women when it came to gender equality. Neither was superior over the other. These Paleolithic people had to work together, and each one was dependent upon the others as equals in order for the entire clan to survive.

Technological Advancements

At some point during the Paleolithic Age, simple tools were developed, and the first human technological advancements were achieved. These simple tools were digging sticks or spears made from wood or bone and eventually stone.

Also during the Paleolithic Age, people developed the ability to produce spoken language. It is most likely that spoken language was developed for cooperation during a hunt. As the Paleolithic people encountered large animals, they needed a way to simply ask for help or to coordinate a trap in order to catch large game. It was much easier to catch one large animal—a woolly mammoth, for example—that would feed the entire clan for weeks and also help make clothing or living quarters than it was to catch many smaller animals. Paleolithic clans used every piece of the game they caught. They used the animal hide for clothing and shelter, the bones for tools and weapons, and even the bladders as containers for water and other precious liquids. They maximized every single bit of the resources they had at their disposal.

Circa 1.5 million years ago, Paleolithic man also achieved the ability to create and control fire, another life-changing development for humans.

Religious Beliefs

Since Paleolithic people were dependent upon the forces of nature, their religious beliefs developed along those same lines.

Early human beings practiced polytheism. *Poly* means "many" and *theism* means "gods." According to Paleolithic beliefs, many gods controlled the forces of nature. There was the god of the sun, the god of the rain, the god of the river, the god of the earth, and so on. Evidence of Paleolithic people believing in gods and goddesses is found in their burial mounds. They were buried with great care, and they were buried with many tools and foodstuffs, showing that Paleolithic people believed in an afterlife.

MIGRATION OF HUMANS ACROSS THE EARTH

Interaction Between Continents

One of the most common misconceptions in world history classes is that people on different continents were cut off from one another throughout much of world history. This is simply not true.

It is especially erroneous when discussing the continents of Europe, Africa, and Asia, which are all interconnected. Evidence of interaction is seen in cave paintings in North Africa and the southern coast of Spain and France. The paintings of humans hunting large animals show amazing similarities. Some of these similar paintings also exist in South America. These paintings also show amazing similarities in the things Paleolithic people used to protect themselves from the spirits that inhabited the world. They drew them on the walls of caves for help and protection. These paintings are evidence that since the early days of human existence, there has always been contact between these continents.

Migration from East Africa

Using Tanzania, Africa, the location of the oldest known human skeleton, as the origin point of humanity, the development of the nomadic Paleolithic people can be seen in their migration. They followed herds of game and spread northward and westward into Africa. They spread eastward into the Middle East and Asia, and eventually up into Europe. They continued to spread farther east into Southeast Asia, China, the Korean peninsula, and Siberia. As humans continued to spread out over these three continents, the environment of the Paleolithic people slowly began to change. It began to get progressively colder and colder. This was the beginning of the Ice Age, which marks the end of the Paleolithic Age, circa 10,000 B.C.E. The ice that covered much of the northern hemisphere helped create a land bridge known as the Bering Strait between Asia and North America. Today, the remnants of this land bridge are the Aleutian Islands off the coast of Alaska. This land bridge allowed herds of game to cross the continents from Asia to the Americas. As the herds of game moved, people followed them, called Paleo-Indians. People came from Africa, the Middle East, and Eastern Asia to follow the herds across the Bering Strait into the Americas, allowing North and South America to be populated.

Ice Age and Cultural Diffusion in the Americas

Circa 10,000–9000 B.C.E., the Ice Age slowly began to end and recede. The Bering Strait collapsed, ending its use as a continuous land bridge between the two continents. When this happened, North America and South America were cut off from Africa, Europe, and Asia. This, in turn, prevented them from sharing in the cultural diffusion between the other three continents.

Cultural diffusion is extremely important. It is the sharing of ideas, beliefs, and technology between people. It usually happens as a result of trade, migration, or warfare, all of which allow people to share ideas and technology over a large area.

Being cut off from this cultural diffusion did not prevent advancements from being made by the Paleo-Indians of the Americas. They will develop some of the exact same technology as Africa, Europe, and Asia, and they will add some unique inventions of their own over time. However, at times, being separated does put the Americas slightly behind in the development of technology as compared to Africa, Europe, and Asia. For example, technological advancements that were developed in ancient Egypt, such as pyramid architecture, will also be developed in the Americas, but the Mesoamerican pyramids are thousands of years younger than the Egyptian pyramids.

This tells historians that people develop in much the same way. While the Americas were completely cut off from cultural diffusion between Africa, Europe, and Asia, people still created and duplicated the same ideas.

NEOLITHIC REVOLUTION

After the Ice Age , one of the greatest quantum leaps forward occurred among human civilization. Many consider it the biggest accomplishment of all humanity. This incredible breakthrough was farming.

Farming began to occur around the globe. Whether humans discovered farming when they dropped seeds in the ground by accident or when they saw plants growing in the rich soil left by the receding glaciers, people today will never know. Nonetheless, human beings started producing their own food. The result was that people could remain in one place. No longer were they dependent upon migrating herds of game for food. Since they could stay in one place, they began to develop civilizations and new skills and tools were needed.

New skills and tools were developed in what is called the Neolithic Age, or the New Stone Age. Neolithic humans planted seeds, cultivated crops, and began to domesticate animals, such as dogs, sheep, and goats.

Farming allowed them to have a surplus of food. This was an important fact. A surplus is having more than you can use. Whenever there was more food, it allowed two things to happen.

1. It allowed for a baby boom. Throughout history, whenever there was a surplus of food, there were always more people produced.
2. It gave people leisure time. During leisure time, people had time to think and invent labor-saving devices.

With these new inventions and food surplus, people did not need to work constantly to survive. The clans and tribes started expanding above the maximum of 30 people since they were not constantly on the move anymore. Labor-saving inventions and food became more readily available, and with more people and greater technology, there became an increased interaction among people and between tribes. This eventually allowed for the growth of villages. Neolithic Age villages were the foundation for modern-day society.

The development of farming and labor-saving tools may sound like small developments compared to what is seen today. Nonetheless, the developments of the Neolithic Age laid the foundation for today's societies around the planet, as many of the everyday interactions and institutions that we are familiar with emerged in their basic forms during the Neolithic Age.

Gender Status Changes

As the Neolithic Age continued, society underwent a change as well. Up to this point, the division of labor had been divided equally between the genders. The work continued to be divided between men and women, but the status of women began to slowly decline. At this point, men became dominant in the family, in economics, and in the political life of each village.

Villages and the Creation of Government

Now that societies were staying in one location, villages were created. With any established community comes the necessity of forming a government. The first governments were led by the heads of each family. Most likely, the older men formed a council of elders. They had been alive for a long time, and they understood the change of seasons—when to plant a crop, when to harvest—as well as the migration of animals. Their knowledge enabled them to be leaders. There was no blueprint for these early governmental leaders to follow. They had to figure out how to ensure a steady food supply for their growing population.

Over time, priests or medicine men formed a theocracy. These were men who were able to observe the signs of nature. For example, they noted that the river flooded every spring and summer and that the leaves changed every fall. They were a little bit smarter than their fellow villagers. The priests assumed a leadership role as they claimed to be able to please the gods who controlled the forces of nature. Since these priests were able to control the gods of nature through different prayers and elaborate rituals designed to ensure the survival of their villages, they became the leaders.

Even with a surplus of food, times of scarcity still occurred. Whether by drought, famine, or warfare between villages, it became necessary to defend the resources in the villages. Village warriors were able to gain prestige in battle and also began to control the villages.

Every leader in the Neolithic Age—the council of elders, the priests and medicine men, and the village warriors—had to create the laws of their society as well as collect taxes, organize systems of defense, and organize public works projects as these villages turned into cities. The jobs became increasingly more complex. Early rulers created the world's first bureaucracies, with priests heading some of the major departments. These societies grew so large and complex that their religious beliefs were added to the society governmental system. Neolithic man believed that the forces of nature not only controlled their lives in this world but also ruled them in the afterlife.

Global Connections

Having a warrior as a leader was a recurring event throughout history. At many different times in many different civilizations, leaders came from a military background. When you had resources and you built a village or civilization, you had to be able to defend it.

Social Classes

Now that people were living in permanent villages, they began to accumulate personal property and wealth. Some people appeared to be wealthier than their neighbors. However, at this point, there were still no large social class divisions.

Job Specialization

Circa 5000 B.C.E., some people began to specialize, becoming good at one particular job, craft, or skill. As a result, they no longer worked in the fields but became artisans or skilled craft workers such as blacksmiths, potters, tailors, bricklayers, and even soldiers. Some of these people developed the ability to work with early metals such as copper or bronze. This job specialization made people become more interdependent on each other for survival. A bartering economy developed. An example of bartering would be a farmer trading some of his crops to a blacksmith in return for a shovel or rake.

> **FUN FACT**
>
> Merchants and artisans did not have to toil in the sun like farmers. They could work early in the day or later in the evening when temperatures were cooler, thus they were regarded with higher standing than a simple farmer. However, in China, merchants were seen as the lowest class because they sold their goods based on the hard labor of other people.

As job specialization became more widespread, social classes developed. People became ranked according to their jobs. At the top of the social ladder were the king, the chief priests, and the other wealthy nobles. Next came the small class of wealthy merchants and skilled artisans. Below them was the majority of the population: the peasants, who were mostly farmers and did most of the labor for the city. At the bottom level were slaves, captured prisoners, or debt slaves, who were people who had to sell themselves into slavery to pay off their debts.

Invention of Writing

Circa 3000 B.C.E., another one of the most important developments in human history was created: writing. The art of writing was most likely developed by priests to record important prayers and rituals.

Global Connections

Throughout most of history, peasants are always the majority of the population and do almost all of the work.

Writing was used to record the amount of grain that was harvested, how much was collected in taxes, which taxes were being paid, and who was married and had children. Census records using this early writing were made up of pictograms or drawings to show or express ideas. Families volunteered their young men to go to school/temples to learn how to read, write, and become scribes. Their job was to record rituals for the priests, and later on, they worked for merchants to record business transactions. These were highly sought-after positions. Once a scribe came to work at a temple, he and his family moved from the fields to live and work within the temple compound. Even early in world history, education was the key to social mobility.

Creation of Monumental Architecture

As some villages got bigger and bigger, the creation of art and architecture became important. The buildings built by early civilizations, such as their temples and palaces, expressed the beliefs and values of the people.

As the Neolithic Age came to an end circa 3000 B.C.E., civilization was being created. People of the first civilizations built vast public works projects that continued to grow as their cities and civilization expanded. Some of these projects rival modern-day cities. The projects included road networks, bridges that spanned rivers, defensive walls that covered all types of terrain, irrigation projects to water crops, and living quarters for the citizens of that population.

Creation of Empires

As ancient rulers began to maximize their resources and territory, they began to look for other necessary resources outside of their land area. Some ambitious rulers used their warriors to conquer territory beyond their city. This expansion gave rise to the city-state. A city-state and its surrounding farmland operated as its own individual country. All citizens were required to give a portion of their earnings to support the city-state. If they did not have earned income, they gave crops or, in some cases, labor. Eventually, more powerful or ambitious leaders conquered multiple city-states, forming the world's first empires.

CULTURAL DIFFUSION

The survival of Paleolithic and Neolithic people was dependent upon land, environmental changes, and even disasters. Each of these factors had an immediate and long-lasting impact on their lives. In times of trouble, people were forced to migrate from one area to another and trade with other people. This is cultural diffusion: the spreading of ideas, beliefs, and technology from one people to another through trade, migration, and warfare. Cultural diffusion led to the first encounters by different peoples, thus beginning the spread of culture and history.

Circa 3000 B.C.E., history was nearing the emergence of the four river valley civilizations. Historians agree that there are eight factors that indicated the beginning of a civilization.

1. Formation of a city
2. Well-organized government
3. Complex religion
4. Job specialization
5. Social classes
6. Public works projects
7. Creation of monumental art and architecture
8. Writing

TIMELINE REVIEW

3.2 million years ago	Lucy
2.5 million years ago	Paleolithic Age begins.
	• Use of stone and wood tools
	• Ability to speak
	• Control of fire
30,000 B.C.E.	Cave paintings begin to appear.
22,000 B.C.E.	Bering Strait
10,000 B.C.E.	Ice Age ends and the Bering Strait collapses.
10,000–9000 B.C.E.	Neolithic Age begins.
	• Farming
	• Animals are domesticated.
	• Villages and governments are formed.
9000 B.C.E.	Permanent settlements begin to appear.

*All are rough estimates, or circa, as the exact dates are not known.

Early River Valley Civilizations: Egypt, Mesopotamia, India, and China, Plus Australia

2

EGYPT

The first civilizations developed in the river valleys of Africa and Asia circa 3000–500 B.C.E. *Egypt* means "gift of the Nile River" and the *Nile River* means "the river of life." The Nile flooded every summer, dropping rich, fertile soil for five miles on either side of the river. Beyond this was harsh desert, which formed natural barriers to protect the Egyptians from outside invasion. The Arabian Desert and the Nubian Desert, plus the Mediterranean Sea and the Red Sea, formed a barrier around Egypt, allowing the Egyptians to create their advanced civilization.

Geography

Ancient Egypt had two distinct regions. There was Upper Egypt in the south and Lower Egypt in the north. The Nile River flows northward, beginning in the interior of the country from Lake Victoria to the Mediterranean Sea, which is why Lower Egypt is in the north and Upper Egypt is in the south.

Both Upper and Lower Egypt were of the same ethnic group, and they both developed along the banks of the Nile River. There were six large cataracts, or waterfalls, that prevented the civilizations from linking up. Upper Egypt ranged from the first cataract to about 120 miles south of the Mediterranean Sea. From that point, Lower Egypt covered the rest of the river all the way to the Nile Delta region. The Delta was a triangular-shaped area formed by the rich deposits of silt by the mouth of the river.

Unification

In 3100 B.C.E., King Menes, Egypt's first strong ruler, conquered Upper Egypt, leading to the unification of Egypt. King Menes used the Nile River as a highway to build unity.

It is at this point that Egypt's history is divided into three time periods.

- The Old Kingdom—2702–2200 B.C.E.
- The Middle Kingdom—2050–1800 B.C.E.
- The New Kingdom—1552–1100 B.C.E.

Each kingdom was ruled by a dynasty, or ruling family, where the kingship was passed from father to son.

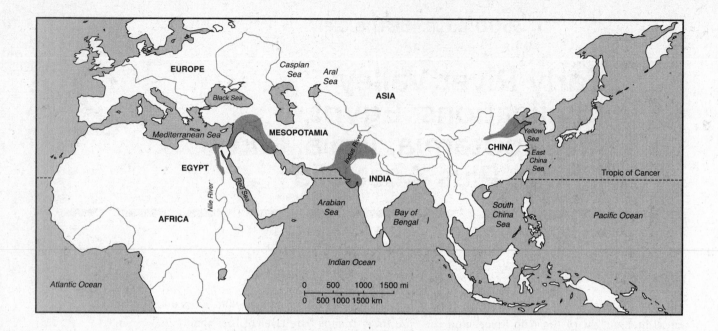

The Old Kingdom: 2702–2200 B.C.E.

During the Old Kingdom, pharaohs ruled the land. This was the iconic age of Egypt that most people think of when asked about Egypt. The pharaohs were some of the most powerful monarchs in world history. They had divine right to rule and were actually viewed as living representations of the sun god on Earth. A powerful monarch, such as the pharaoh, wanted to choose a powerful symbol to represent them. The sun, the largest, most powerful physical object seen in the universe, was normally what has been used throughout world history to symbolize a monarch's absolute power. The pharaoh's power was so absolute that there was no personal property in Egypt.

> ### 🍽 DINNER TABLE TALK
>
> The pharaohs owned everything, from the house you lived in to the cereal bowl and spoon you used for breakfast. In your house, what can you imagine being owned by someone else? How would it affect you?

As a divine being, the pharaoh's job was to preserve justice and order. To carry out the many responsibilities, a pharaoh depended upon chief advisers or ministers to supervise the operation of the government, collection of taxes, farming conditions, and the all-important irrigation networks. The ministers had to report to the pharaoh, who wanted to know everything. Thousands of scribes—who were educated young men—were used to carry out his orders.

The Old Kingdom is also known as the Pyramid Age because it was at this time that three great pyramids were built on the Giza plain. Though there are hundreds of pyramids in Egypt, the three pyramids of Giza get the most attention because of their size: Cheops, Khafre, and Menkaure. Each of them was built during the Old Kingdom. They were built for a grandfather, his son, and a grandson to preserve the bodies of these dead rulers and give them everything that they needed in the afterlife.

Thousands of workers had to quarry stone blocks and then move them 600 miles down the Nile River. Workers lifted stone blocks weighing 2.5 tons each, using no iron tools or the wheel, to make each pyramid. More than two million stone blocks were used to build the Great Pyramid of Cheops, which took nearly 30 years to complete.

Here are three important facts about the building of the pyramids of the Old Kingdom:

1. Old Kingdom pyramids were built by the Egyptian workers. The Hebrew slaves did not come to Egypt until the New Kingdom.
2. Pyramids demonstrated the power of the pharaoh. The pyramids had to be completed before the pharaoh died. Workers had only six months a year to work on the pyramids since the other six months were spent planting and harvesting the crops.
3. It showed the organization and planning skills of the pharaoh's central government. It was an enormous task to house and feed the workers. They made sure that the stone blocks, which had to be transported 600 miles down river from the quarry, arrived at the worksite on time.

Ironically, the Old Kingdom declined because the cost of the pyramids was too high, pharaohs became greedy, and there was a series of crop failures with no surplus left to support the people.

Global Connections

Other building projects that eventually caused the collapse of other empires include the Palace of Versailles in France, the Taj Mahal in India, and the Forbidden City in China.

The Middle Kingdom: 2050–1800 B.C.E.

After a century of disarray, new pharaohs reunited the land. It was still a time of corruption and turbulence, but a few strong rulers were able to make improvements. They created more farmland along the Nile Delta as the flooding of the Nile was not as regular as it had once been. Egypt also conquered Nubia in the interior of Africa and began developing new ideas and technologies.

However, disaster struck in 1700 B.C.E. when a group of invaders from the Middle East known as the Hyksos conquered the region. Being isolated by geography, the Egyptians had not developed a modern military or weapons technology, but the Hyksos had horse-drawn chariots and iron weapons. The Egyptians fought with copper or bronze and were easily defeated.

Up to this point in world history, whenever outside invaders conquered a larger, more sophisticated opponent, the culture of the conquering army was required to be followed by the conquered peoples. However, when the Hyksos saw the amazing Egyptian civilization, they decided to stay in Egypt and follow the rules of Egyptian society and Egyptian culture.

After 100 years of Hyksos rule, the Egyptian nobles outsmarted the Hyksos. They asked to be trained on the chariot and the manufacture of iron weapons. When they mastered that knowledge, the Egyptian nobles rebelled and drove the Hyksos out of Egypt circa 1600 B.C.E. This ended the Middle Kingdom and gave rise to the New Kingdom of Egypt.

The New Kingdom: 1552–1100 B.C.E.

The New Kingdom is known as the age of conquest. After driving the Hyksos from Egypt, there were a series of powerful and ambitious pharaohs. They created a larger empire that served as a buffer zone, or defensive area, between Egypt and the Middle East. They conquered territory all the way to the Euphrates River in Mesopotamia. This brought them into greater contact with the Middle East and Asia and began the process of cultural diffusion.

There were several pharaohs of the New Kingdom, but three significantly impacted world history.

1. **QUEEN HATSHEPSUT.** In 1473 B.C.E., she was the first woman ruler and reigned for 22 years as pharaoh. She was an effective ruler. Under her rule, Egypt traded with

Global Connections

Are there any other conquered peoples that followed the way of Egypt, and rose up and kicked out the conquering army? (See Rome in Chapter 5 and China in Chapter 18 for other examples.)

peoples as far away as Somalia. She also gave Egyptian women rights and privileges that women had never experienced.

2. **KING TUTANKHAMEN.** More often known as King Tut, he ruled circa 1332–1323 B.C.E. King Tut was the boy-king ruler whose tomb was found by Howard Carter in 1922. His tomb is the only tomb that has been found completely intact in the Valley of the Kings. From him, people have been able to learn much about the power of the pharaohs.

3. **KING RAMSES II.** He ruled from 1279–1213 B.C.E. and is famous from the Hebrew Torah and the Old Testament of the Christian Bible as he was the pharaoh on the throne when the Hebrew slaves left Egypt. However, Egyptians loved King Ramses II. He spent much of his 67 years as a pharaoh reviving the empire. He recorded the first-ever written peace treaty. Unlike previous pharaohs, he successfully defended the borders of the Egyptian empire from the Hittites and other Mesopotamian invaders.

The empire slowly declined after King Ramses II as there were no strong, dominant leaders like him. Power faded, and Egypt could not hold off invaders from Syria and Persia. However, this does not negate the amazing accomplishments that the Egyptians created.

Egyptian Religion

Egyptian religion was complex and polytheistic. The Egyptians worshipped the gods and goddesses of nature. The chief god was Amun Ra, who was the god of the sun. Osiris was god of the underworld and his wife, Isis, was the guardian and goddess of the Nile. When people died, they went down to Osiris to be judged. Their hearts would be placed on a scale with a feather. If they were good and kind people, they would pass into the "Happy Valley of Food." However, if their hearts were heavier than a feather, it meant they were bad, and they would be eaten by a fiery crocodile. This was the Egyptian scenario of "heaven and hell."

The Egyptian belief of the afterlife in the Happy Valley of Food was that it would be just like your life on earth, so people were buried with everything they would need. They were buried with food, jewels, and tools. Pharaohs were even buried with their favorite wives, pets, and servants. So the soul could use the body in the afterlife, the Egyptians perfected mummification. They removed organs from the body and then dried them out and wrapped the body.

Women

Under Queen Hatshepsut, women enjoyed a high status and greater independence in Egyptian society. They were now able to inherit property, conduct business, serve as doctors, enter the priesthood, and hold positions in commerce. However, the most important jobs still went to men.

Writing

Egyptian writing is significant. The Egyptians invented hieroglyphics, or picture writing, circa 3200 B.C.E. They wrote on stone temples, obelisks, and papyrus paper. Scribes used writing to record important religious ceremonies, tax amounts, prayers, and rituals. While earlier writing was done on stone, Egyptians learned to make a paper-like material out of papyrus. Papyrus was a reed that grew on the banks of the Nile River.

Egyptian writing can be read today because of the discovery of the Rosetta Stone, found by Napoleon's soldiers. It contained Egyptian hieroglyphics and Greek writing. The Rosetta

Stone was translated by Jean François Champollion in 1822, and when he was finished, historians could read and translate hieroglyphics.

Scientific Achievement

The Egyptians were very medically advanced. Due to the process of mummification, they were able to learn a lot about the human body. They learned to observe symptoms for sicknesses and the results of different medicines. They were able to set broken bones with casts and were even able to perform complex back surgery.

The Egyptians created a calendar with 12 months, with each month having 30 days. The calendar was divided into three seasons: flooding, planting, and harvesting. They also developed advanced skills in astronomy, charting the movements of the planets and the heavens.

The Egyptians were also highly advanced mathematically. Not only did they achieve great engineering feats by building the pyramids, but they were also excellent surveyors. They could redraw property lines and field boundaries after the flooding season was over.

MESOPOTAMIA

Mesopotamia means "the land between two rivers." The two rivers were the Tigris and the Euphrates. This area was known as the Fertile Crescent, or the crossroads of the world, as it connected three different continents: Europe, Africa, and Asia. The narrow strip of land between the rivers provided plentiful rich, dark soil, thus the name Fertile Crescent, as the rivers form a crescent running from the Persian Gulf heading northwest and arching into modern Turkey.

Unlike Egypt, this area had few natural barriers, making it the most conquered territory in the ancient world. As a result of its openness, many nomadic hunters settled in different groups. Each of these groups had different physical characteristics, ethnic backgrounds, religious philosophies, and languages. The interactions of these groups created a turbulent atmosphere. However, each group that settled in Mesopotamia offered different contributions to the civilization, many of which impact today's world.

Geography

Civilization in ancient Mesopotamia began on the banks of the Tigris River and the Euphrates River, in what is today modern-day Iraq. The city of Baghdad is possibly the oldest actual city in the world. Nomads eventually settled down and became farmers. Again, the food surpluses that were achieved created a sizable population growth.

River Problems

The Tigris and Euphrates acted just like the Nile River in Egypt, flooding and bringing good soil. Flood control was important. Unlike the Nile, the sources of the Tigris and Euphrates were in the temperate mountains of modern-day Turkey. The flooding was due to the amount of snow that fell, and when the spring thaw came, the people had no idea when the rivers were going to flood. Flash floods could wash away topsoil as well as huts along the riverbank. However, the destruction caused by these floods was the single biggest factor for the warring villages to work together. Under the direction of priests, who were able to study the flood season, the people built an intricate and elaborate series of dams and dikes to prevent the farmland from washing away. Without plentiful building material like wood and stones, the ancient Mesopotamians invented brick-making technology. Many of the ovens that harnessed the heat of the sun to bake the bricks are still in existence today.

Cities

Mesopotamian cities were perfectly rectangular, built in a grid pattern with all road systems running north, south, east, and west. The two roads leading to the center of the city were wider than the normal roads to accommodate victory parades and religious processions. Each city was surrounded by a city wall to keep out as many invaders as possible. Due to the lack of natural barriers, invaders were constantly sweeping through the area.

Monumental Architecture

Global Connections

What other societies developed pyramidal architecture, and was it due to cultural diffusion or natural development of humanity? (See Mesoamerica in Chapter 13 for examples.)

The centerpiece of every Mesopotamian city was the ziggurat. A ziggurat was a giant stone temple erected to honor the chief god or goddess of the city. They were similar to the Egyptian pyramids. Instead of having smooth sides, they were shaped like steps. They looked like giant stairs reaching up toward the heavens. On top of each ziggurat was a temple to house the god or goddess of the city. When the god of the city chose to take human form, he or she could walk down the steps and commune with the mortal worshippers. Ziggurats also had meaning for the social hierarchy. The higher a person's social class, the higher they could climb on the ziggurat to worship. The king and the high priest could worship on the top step, just below the temple. The nobles would worship on the next step down, artisans and lesser nobles on next, the peasants (who were the bulk of the population) came next, and slaves worshipped on the last step or on the ground.

Outside Contact

Mesopotamia is called the bridge of ancient civilizations as it was in a unique position to connect the three different continents. With few natural barriers to prevent travel and commerce, Mesopotamian merchants brought riches, information, and technological inventions from around the ancient Middle East. This led to increased commercial travel, and the Mesopotamian civilization of Sumer made use of the first wheeled vehicle. They did not invent the wheel, but they were the first to attach the wheel to an axle to carry larger, heavier loads. It allowed them to traverse vast amounts of territory and the deserts.

Mesopotamian Government

Throughout Mesopotamian history, people lived in independent city-states that were led by the priest-kings or a strong warrior male. Eventually, this leadership role became hereditary as it passed from father to son. The job of each king was to maintain the defensive walls, ensure the irrigation systems were always working, and enforce the laws. The king also worked with the high priest to perform certain religious duties, such as leading ceremonies to help ensure the gods would favor them. Once again, as in Egypt, as the size of each city grew, the king began to depend on a vast system of educated scribes to run the growing bureaucracy that differed from city-state to city-state.

Role of Women

In most Mesopotamian cities, women enjoyed special powers and privileges that were not seen in most ancient societies and were not seen again anywhere around the globe for thousands of years. Not only could women own property and conduct business, but they also had certain legal rights. However, as in most societies, their main job was to run the household, take care of the children, and manage the slaves (if they were wealthy), but just as in ancient Egypt, Mesopotamian women had a high level of rights and responsibilities.

Religion and the Afterlife

Mesopotamians, just like the Egyptians, were polytheistic, believing in the many forces of nature. However, the Mesopotamians had a unique twist on how they saw their gods. To them, gods acted like people and had human-like weaknesses and vices. They could eat, drink, get married, and even have families. The gods favored truth and justice; however, making them angry would cause violence and suffering. For example, if the people made them angry, the gods could cause flash floods, a drought, or an invasion. As a result, the Mesopotamians had a much bleaker view of the afterlife than the Egyptians. In Mesopotamia, everyone—good or bad—journeyed to a dark cave where they spent eternity eating mud. Nice and yummy! This dark view of the afterlife was most likely due to the violent and unpredictable floods plus their lifestyle of living between two rivers with the only fertile land in the area constantly under threat of invasion by a conquering army. Living in these harsh conditions affected their view of the afterlife.

Writing

The biggest contribution made by the Mesopotamian people was the invention of the first known form of writing, circa 3200 B.C.E. Mesopotamians used a sharp stick known as a stylus (very similar to a pencil) to write on a wet clay tablet. This writing was known as cuneiform. The Sumerians of Mesopotamia were the first to use cuneiform. They made pictograms that expressed a thought or an idea. Scribes went through years of strict schooling to learn how to write in cuneiform. This was a prestigious job, as scribes worked for the royal household, the high priest in the temple, or wealthy merchants. These were good jobs for a peasant's son. However, the training was very strict. If you wrote sloppily or without permission, you were beaten on the hands because you cannot just erase or delete a mistake on a clay tablet!

> **GLOBAL CONNECTIONS**
>
> As in Egypt, not only did Mesopotamian scribes get to live in the palace or temple, but their family got to come along with them. The entire family was lifted out of poverty and back-breaking labor in the fields. In what other civilizations did this occur? (See China in Chapter 6.)

Mesopotamia had schools attended mostly by boys, but some wealthy girls were allowed to attend. Particularly gifted students were taught an early form of the liberal arts curriculum: religion, medicine, math, and literature. When it comes to literature, Mesopotamia created the oldest known poem, *The Epic of Gilgamesh*. *The Epic of Gilgamesh* tells the Mesopotamian story of creation. This poem shows their belief in the relationship and interactions between humans, gods, and the forces of nature.

Civilization of Sumer in Mesopotamia

Sumer was a civilization in what is today Baghdad, Iraq. They made great advances in mathematics with their knowledge of algebra and geometry. They based their number system on six

and came up with the concept of the 60-second minute, the 60-minute hour, and the 360° circle. As a result, they were advanced in astronomy and could even predict eclipses. The many different armies that conquered the region spread the knowledge and accomplishments of the Sumerians across the Middle East, into Greece, and even into ancient Rome.

Additional Civilizations, Empires, and Achievements of Ancient Mesopotamia

Invasion and conquest were commonplace in the Middle East as warfare and advancing culture went hand in hand. Nomadic peoples frequently conquered Mesopotamian cities to loot the riches of the Fertile Crescent. Many powerful leaders from other civilizations saw the benefits of the resources in the area and created large, well-organized empires.

The Babylonians

In 1790 B.C.E., the Babylonian king Hammurabi brought most of Mesopotamia under his control by uniting the empire and publishing a remarkable set of laws. Known as the Code of Hammurabi, these laws were given to Hammurabi by their chief god, Marduk, on top of a mountain. This was the first known set of uniform laws. Hammurabi wanted all the people to know the 300 laws, so they were carved on different obelisks (pillars) for all to see. Their purpose was to allow justice to prevail in the land.

Global Connections

Hammurabi received this code in much the same way that the Hebrew named Moses received the Ten Commandments from the God of the Israelites.

While this was the first unified code of law, and many people like to quote its "eye for an eye" law, penalties were harsher for poor people and for women. Despite Hammurabi's good intentions, women and the poor were still unequal, providing a good example of the social divide of ancient Babylonia.

Another Babylonian king is Nebuchadnezzar, who ruled from 605–562 B.C.E. King Nebuchadnezzar set the standard for other conquerors. He was a ruthless warrior, but he allowed his conquered people to live more fairly. They were able to keep their own local government, customs, and religion. All they had to do was acknowledge Nebuchadnezzar as their king, pay taxes, and supply men for his army. If these things were done, the tribes were left alone. If not, Nebuchadnezzar would enforce quick destruction of the tribe with his powerful army. At its height, Nebuchadnezzar's empire stretched from the Persian Gulf to the Mediterranean Sea. Even though Nebuchadnezzar was less destructive than other conquerors (since he knew whatever he destroyed he would have to rebuild), he showed no mercy for the Hebrews. Located in the area of modern-day Israel, the Hebrews did not receive any of the fair treatment that other people of the ancient Middle East received. He enslaved all of the Hebrews circa 582 B.C.E.

Nebuchadnezzar was also known for building the Hanging Gardens of Babylon, one of the seven ancient wonders of the world.

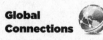

Global Connections

Alexander the Great (see Chapter 4) followed in Nebuchadnezzar's footsteps, treating his conquered subjects fairly.

The Persians

Persia was one of the longest-lasting empires of the ancient Middle East. Their king, Cyrus the Great (ruled from 559 B.C.E. to 530 B.C.E.), and his successors created the largest empire ever seen up to that time, stretching from Asia Minor in modern-day Turkey to India. They had a successful long-lasting kingdom because they were tolerant of the people they conquered and allowed them to keep their own religion, style of government, and customs, much like King Nebuchadnezzar.

Unification of the Persian Empire came under Emperor Darius between 522 B.C.E. and 486 B.C.E. He was a great organizer and knew the empire was so big that he could not control it alone, so he skillfully divided the empire into provinces called satrapies, which were ruled by a governor, or a satrap. These satraps had to collect taxes, ensure justice for the people, and make sure the people were fed. Emperor Darius used special investigators to check on the governors to keep them honest.

Darius also created a single code of laws. He wanted unification and standardization throughout his empire. To encourage unity, he had hundreds of miles of road built to speed communication and troop movements. This road was called the Great Royal Road, and it was 1600 miles long, reaching from the Persian Gulf to Asia Minor.

To improve trade and economics, Darius created a common system of weights and measures. He also used a single currency that made trade easier in the different parts of his large empire. Darius made simple changes to the transportation system, making sure that ruts in the road were easy to repair, requiring the same axle length on all chariots to speed repairs, and creating only one set of roads to follow and maintain. As a result, Persia had greater economic prosperity and longevity as compared to some of the other ancient city-states.

The Phoenicians

The Phoenicians are called the carriers of civilization. They were famous traders and sailors. They were the first people to sail long distances. Their empire was on the Mediterranean Sea near modern-day Lebanon. They traded everything available in the Mediterranean: papyrus, olive oil, and artifacts. They traded with people as far away as England, so they helped with cultural diffusion by taking one nation's goods or information and then trading it or selling it. For example, the Phoenicians would have traded Greek olive oil in Italy, Italian wine in Egypt, and Egyptian geometry and wheat in England.

The Phoenicians formed a quick, flexible form of writing to make trading simpler. It consisted of a 22-letter alphabet of all consonants, which is the basis of modern-day phonics. The Greeks would later add vowels to it, and it became the basis of our modern language. The Phoenicians were important to the spread of information, technology, and cultural diffusion around the Mediterranean Sea.

The Assyrians

The Assyrians were a savage, warlike people from the upper Tigris River. They controlled the region and terrorized it for over 500 years. They used terror and intimidation to keep conquered people in line and to frighten their enemies. They were often brutal in their treatment of conquered people.

The most famous Assyrian king was Ashurbanipal from 668 B.C.E. to 627 B.C.E. He was responsible for much of the terror, intimidation, and violence. His actions gave the Assyrian people a reputation as the most violent and warlike people of ancient Middle East. However, in stark contrast to his brutality, he built the world's first library in Nineveh. Eventually, the strict, oppressive rule of the Assyrians caused their subjects to rebel.

Global Connections

The Great Royal Road had a delivery system very similar to the Pony Express system in the early days of the United States. It could cover the entire distance of the Great Royal Road in 10 days.

The Hitties

The Hittites, who came from Asia Minor, adopted the use of coined money, but they were much less advanced than other peoples of Mesopotamia. However, they learned how to extract iron from ore, most likely by building a large fire next to rocks. Then, they shaped the metal that melted out of the pores of the rock. Using the iron, the Hittites were able to create stronger weapons, enabling them to defeat many people. Unfortunately, even though they tried to keep it a secret, eventually the word got out about how to make iron.

INDIA

Geography

The geography of India played a large role in its development. India was the third river valley civilization, and it developed along the banks of the Indus River in 2500 B.C.E. India is protected by many natural barriers: the Hindu Kush mountains to the west, the mighty Himalayas to the north, and the Indian Ocean. All of these protected early India from outside invasion in a way that was similar to ancient Egypt.

The Indian Subcontinent

Due to its vast size and difficult terrain, India was difficult to unite into one stable kingdom. It is a subcontinent that juts out from a larger continent. Today, it is one of the most populated regions on the planet.

India is divided into three main regions.

Global Connections

When picturing the Northern Plain of India, think of the Great Plains of the United States. Looking eastward from the Rocky Mountains, the majority of food grown in the United States is found in the Great Plains.

1. The Northern Plain lies at the southern end of the Himalaya mountain chain and is well watered by three rivers: the Indus, the Ganges, and the Brahmaputra. The Northern Plain is a large fertile area.
2. The Deccan Plateau is the most recognized region of India. It is the large triangular area located in the middle of the country. It is a large, dry, unproductive desert.
3. The eastern and western Ghats, or coastlines.

Monsoons

India was the only river valley civilization that did not depend on the yearly flooding of a river to bring the soil that was necessary for survival. Instead they depended on *monsoons*, meaning "a season wind."

Monsoons, which still occur seasonally today, are not just a long period of rain. In October, the winter monsoon blows from the northeast to southwest, blowing hot, dry air, which dries out the crops and the land. In May, the monsoons switch directions and blow from the southwest, bringing moist air from the Indian Ocean. When the monsoons make landfall, they deliver drenching downpours that replenish the land.

These monsoons shaped Indian life because the people were dependent on these rains for survival. If the monsoons came too late, it meant famine and starvation. If they came too early, they could produce flash floods that washed away all the crops.

Religion

The Indus River Valley people were polytheistic and worshipped the many gods of nature, with a mother goddess of creation and the two sacred river gods of the Indus and Ganges. The ancient Indians also worshipped many sacred animals, like the bull, which have influenced Indians throughout their history. Even today, cows are still sacred.

The Twin Cities of Harappa and Mohenjo-daro

In the river valley civilization of India circa 2500 B.C.E., there were twin capital cities located 100 miles apart: Harappa and Mohenjo-daro. These cities were nearly identical, like modern-day "cookie cutter" neighborhoods. Both were designed in a large grid pattern. They were among the first to use city blocks to organize layout. The houses and some shops were equipped with sewer systems and indoor plumbing with drains and water chutes than ran into sewer drains underneath the city. The houses were also uniformly built in square or rectangular shapes. Merchants used a standard system of weights and measures in both cities to make systems of exchange accurate throughout both of them.

CENTRAL PLANNING

Having two cities located 100 miles apart but built identical to each other demonstrated a high level of central authority. Whether it was priests or some other monarch, it took good organization, central planning, and power over the people to ensure a steady stream of building materials to two different locations. In addition, they had to provide housing, food, and construction supervision for not just one large city, but two cities simultaneously.

While Harappa was slightly larger, the population of both of these cities numbered in the tens of thousands. The precision found in the construction of the twin cities demonstrates that the people of the early Indus civilization had a great knowledge of complex mathematics. Around 1500 B.C.E., however, the people suddenly vanished, and the cause is unknown to this day.

ACCOMPLISHMENTS

Along with building the twin cities of Harappa and Mohenjo-daro, the early Indus River Valley people were farmers. They grew wheat, barley, melons, and dates. The biggest contribution made by the ancient Indians was the cultivation of cotton to be used as cloth. Cotton has remained the mainstay of Indian agriculture throughout history. This also led to trading by the early Indians with civilizations and empires from Mesopotamia.

Aryans

The Aryans are the second civilization of the Indus River Valley. In 1500 B.C.E., the Aryans, nomads from southern Russia, began to migrate through Asia with their herds of sheep, goats, and cattle looking for pastureland for their large herd. They eventually found their way into the northern plain of the Indus River Valley. They settled down in this open pastureland and

---

GLOBAL CONNECTIONS

There are monsoons all over the world. In America, there are the Santa Ana winds in Southern California that blow super-heated winds that dry out valleys around Los Angeles, causing many forest fires. Lake effect snow blows from Canada across the Great Lakes, picking up moisture, and as it makes landfall and cools off, heavy, wet snow falls, often measuring in multiple feet.

started their own civilization along the Ganges River. However, these early Aryans did not build any large cities or monumental works of architecture, and, initially, they did not have a writing system.

The Vedas

What we know of the ancient Aryans comes from the Vedas, a collection of religious prayers, rituals, and hymns. Priests had to memorize these Vedas, recite them perfectly, and then pass them down orally to their descendants. The Vedas oral history continued for around 1000 years, from 1500 B.C.E. to 500 B.C.E. By 500 B.C.E., it was acceptable to write down the Vedas, which were written in four massive volumes.

The Vedas described how the Aryans divided their population in terms of occupation. Though the Vedas were the beginning of what would become early religion, they also served as a way to justify social class structure.

There were four basic groups of Aryan society:

1. **BRAHMANS, OR PRIESTS:** they served as the elite upper class of Aryan society.
2. **KSHATRIYAS, OR WARRIORS:** they occupied the second rung of society.
3. **VAISYAS:** farmers, artisans, and merchants. This was the largest part of society.
4. **THE NON-ARYAN PEOPLE:** poor day laborers and slaves. They occupied the lowest levels of society and would eventually become known as the Untouchables in the caste system.

GOVERNMENT

Unlike the other ancient river valley civilizations who had priest-kings as their first leaders, the prophetic Aryan civilization started with strong warrior males. Since the Aryans were cut off from most external enemies, the warrior leaders gave way to priest-kings.

This development is the opposite of most other civilizations. In the other river valley civilizations, priest-kings rose to power because they were the only ones able to conduct the ceremonies to placate their gods. Then, when a civilization was threatened from an outside invading army, the priest-king and his leadership were replaced by strong warrior males.

SOCIETY

During this Vedic Age, social class divisions became intertwined and reflected the social and economic roles in society. These changes had nothing to do with racial differences but were based on a complex system of castes.

Castes are a social group into which a person is born. It is very difficult, if not impossible, to move from one caste to another. People cannot marry out of their caste, and social mobility is just about out of the question during a person's lifespan. Obeying the rules of your caste will eventually evolve into a religion known as Hinduism (see Chapter 3). The caste system justified social class structure in ancient Aryan society.

RELIGIOUS MOVEMENTS

Early priest leaders in society were called Brahmans. They offered sacrifices to the many polytheistic gods of nature, because of their belief that proper sacrifices could provide health and safety. Some Brahmans began to believe in a spiritual power higher than both the gods and the Vedas. It was called Brahman, or the spiritual power that existed in all things and bound them together. As Hinduism developed, one goal became the ability to achieve a union with Brahman and become part of the force that bound the universe together. This took many lifetimes to achieve.

The values, ideals, and morals of the Vedic Aryan society were transmitted through a series of heroic tales in the *Mahabharata*, which is very similar to the Mesopotamian story, *The Epic of Gilgamesh*.

CHINA

Geography

The Chinese were by far the most isolated of the first four civilizations. Long distances and physical barriers separated them from Egypt, Mesopotamia, and India. The barriers to the outside world included the Tian Shan Mountains to the west; the mighty Himalayas to the southwest; the dense, thick jungles of southeast Asia; the vast Pacific Ocean to the east; and the Gobi Desert and Siberia to the north. As a result, it was difficult for China to come into contact with anyone else. The Chinese called themselves "the Middle Kingdom" since they were not aware of any other civilization. They felt that they were the center of the universe.

The Yellow River

The main concentration of people developed along the Yellow River, or the Huang He, which gets its name from the fine, windblown soil that blows off the Gobi Desert and into the river. The Yellow River is also called the River of Sorrows because peasants were constantly laboring to build and repair dams and dikes to keep the river from overflowing. Each year, heavy rains caused it to flood and overflow, leading to disaster and mass starvation.

Chinese Civilization Takes Shape

In 1650 B.C.E., the Shang Dynasty began to dominate this north-central region of China, and the first Chinese civilization took shape.

The Shang government, unlike other empires, built many palaces in small areas. The original Shang kings rose to power by leaving warriors in certain areas to drive off invading nomads from the Gobi Desert as well as a few other peoples with whom the Chinese had contact.

By building many palaces in these small areas, it allowed

1. the people to see their emperor. Most emperors lived in a far-off palace where the normal people could not see them. By traveling to these palaces, it allowed more of the empire to see who was their emperor.
2. the emperor to keep check on his people. He could visit his people and check on his local governors.

Social Classes

The social class system of ancient China is similar to the other social classes of the first four river valleys. It had four basic levels:

Global Connections

China saw their emperor as a father figure. What other leaders in world history were considered father figures? (See Chapter 7.)

1. **THE ROYAL FAMILY:** these included the emperor, his sons and daughters, and other close family members.
2. **THE NOBLE WARRIORS:** these were aristocrats who had enough money to afford leather, armor, and other weapons.
3. **ARTISANS, LESSER NOBLES, AND SOME MERCHANTS:** they produced goods for the nobility.
4. **THE PEASANTS:** this was the bulk of the Chinese population. These peasants lived clustered together in farming villages. Their houses, made of mud covered by wood and bamboo, were built below ground. They led grueling lives working in the fields, preparing the irrigation systems, and even fighting in wars.

China had the greatest disparity between the rich and the poor when compared to all of the ancient river valley civilizations.

 GLOBAL CONNECTIONS

The idea of ancestor worship is not unique to China. Roman Catholics don't pray to their ancestors, but they pray to the various saints worshipped in Catholicism. Depending on your need, you would ask a saint to intervene on your behalf. Since you cannot pray for yourself 24 hours a day, you can ask a saint to do that for you!

Religion

The religion of ancient China was complex with many gods of nature. Ancient Chinese saw heaven and earth as a single plane without a distinct difference between the two. While the gods were important to the Chinese, they added something that the other river valley civilizations did not. They practiced ancestor worship, where people prayed to their ancestors who had gone on before them, and thus were closer to the Lord of Heaven. They prayed to ensure a good harvest or to bring fortune to the family. It was believed that a Chinese king or emperor started this practice, but then eventually the entire civilization joined in.

Yin and Yang

The Chinese believed in keeping the world in balance, and this is displayed in the Yin and Yang symbol. Imagine there are two forces: the earth/darkness and heaven/light. Yin would be the symbol for earth/darkness and is female. From Mother Earth—Yin—comes life. That must be balanced with Yang, which in this example is heaven/light and male. There must be a balance between heaven and earth, light and dark, male and female, for things to run smoothly. This is evidenced in the Yin and Yang symbol. The black teardrop has a white dot in it and the white teardrop has a black dot in it because both genders have a little bit of each other, forming balance and harmony.

Chinese Writing

Chinese writing has always been very complex. Their writing took shape nearly 4000 years ago, and what made it difficult was that Chinese writing consisted of tens of thousands of different characters expressing words or ideas. It was not easy to learn because in its most simplistic form, changing the angle or the slant of a character could turn a positive into a negative or a compliment into an insult. Students had to memorize these 10,000 different symbols, and as a result, it created an elegant handwriting system known as calligraphy. Eventually, it became famous as an art form. While the people spoke in different dialects, it was the unified writing system that allowed the people to communicate. Even if they could not speak to each other, they could all read and write the same language.

The Mandate of Heaven/The Dynastic Cycle

The Shang Dynasty lasted from 1650 B.C.E. until about 1027 B.C.E., which was when they were overthrown by the Zhou, or Chou, family. They formed the Zhou Dynasty, which lasted until 256 B.C.E. The Shang kings had become greedy and corrupt, and the Zhou family promoted the idea of the Mandate of Heaven.

The Mandate of Heaven claimed the emperor had a divine right to rule. He was blessed by the gods, all of whom gave him permission to rule. The Zhou claimed the last Shang kings were so cruel, oppressive, and out of touch with the people that the gods grew so angry, they removed the mandate, or divine blessing, from the dynasty.

The Mandate of Heaven

The Mandate of Heaven was cyclical and followed the same pattern throughout Chinese history.

1. In the Mandate of Heaven, a new dynasty came to power where the emperor restored peace from chaos. He appointed loyal, honest officials to govern his kingdom, and land was given to the peasants. The emperor oversaw the building of roads and irrigation canals, and he built up their defenses. He "rolled up his sleeves" and worked with the people.
2. The emperor, his son, and his grandson all did this. By the time five generations of the dynasty had gone through the cycle, the dynasty began to age. These great-great-grandsons did not have to do any of the hard work. They inherited a kingdom that was running smoothly and lived off the riches.
3. The aging dynasty was the complete opposite of the new dynasty. The emperor neglected his duties, and he ignored the corruption of his officials. The provinces rebelled or dissolved, and the defenses decayed. The emperor, out of touch with his people, imposed heavy taxes to pay for his lavish lifestyle. It was at this point that the gods became furious, and the dynasty collapsed.
4. The aging dynasty had lost the Mandate of Heaven, and the gods withdrew the divine right from the emperor to rule. That dynasty was over.
5. Punishments from the gods caused problems. The Yellow River flooded, and there was mass famine or other natural disasters, like earthquakes. The peasants revolted, leading to chaos.
6. Out of this chaos, someone rose, maybe a peasant, maybe a military general. It was a "person of the people" who knew what the people needed. He began the new dynasty.

Six Steps of the Chinese Dynastic Cycle

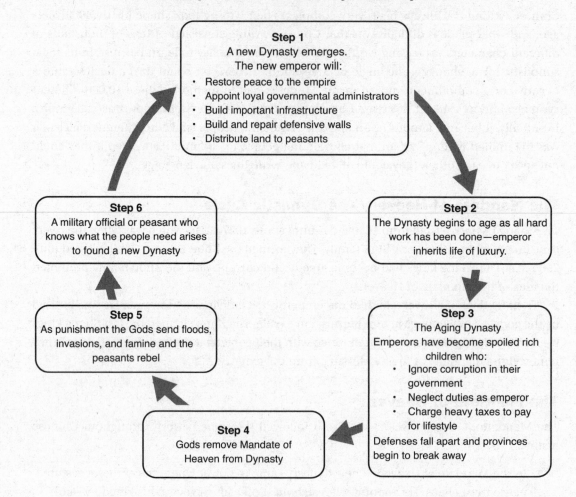

Step 1
A new Dynasty emerges.
The new emperor will:
- Restore peace to the empire
- Appoint loyal governmental administrators
- Build important infrastructure
- Build and repair defensive walls
- Distribute land to peasants

Step 2
The Dynasty begins to age as all hard work has been done—emperor inherits life of luxury.

Step 3
The Aging Dynasty
Emperors have become spoiled rich children who:
- Ignore corruption in their government
- Neglect duties as emperor
- Charge heavy taxes to pay for lifestyle
Defenses fall apart and provinces begin to break away

Step 4
Gods remove Mandate of Heaven from Dynasty

Step 5
As punishment the Gods send floods, invasions, and famine and the peasants rebel

Step 6
A military official or peasant who knows what the people need arises to found a new Dynasty

GLOBAL CONNECTIONS

A modern-day application of the Dynastic Cycle can be seen in the Goldman Sachs investment corporation. The guys who started the investment company more than 100 years ago worked hard, managed their money, got better investors, and earned better returns. However, as Goldman Sachs grew, it got too big and arrogant. It was not watching or managing its investments wisely, and the economic recession of 2006 led to the total collapse of Goldman Sachs. It will take 30 years of selling its assets to pay its creditors.

The great Chinese scholar Confucius validated the idea of the Mandate of Heaven around 500 B.C.E. The Mandate of Heaven ran its course 31 times throughout Chinese history. Some dynasties, like the Han, lasted a very long time. Some dynasties, like the Ch'in, lasted a very short time. The last of the 31 Chinese dynasties fell a little more than 100 years ago in 1911.

The Zhou Government

The governmental style used by the Zhou Dynasty was a little different than the other dynasties of China. As they began to rule, they used a system that became known as feudalism. Under feudalism, a king, or emperor, owned the land. He gave some of that land to local lords or nobles to govern it for him. In exchange for governing his land, the military of the king or emperor policed and protected the land. Since the king/emperor could not be everywhere when his people needed him, he used the local lords or nobles to maintain obedience among the people.

Economy

Chinese economy was always based in agriculture, and when they developed iron-based farming technology, it helped them to create very protein-rich crops, such as soybeans. As a result, China experienced a population boom, allowing it to be one of the most densely populated countries in world history.

Early Chinese Accomplishments

The ancient Chinese were known for advancements in astronomy. They created an accurate calendar of 365 1/2 days, very similar to the calendar used today in the United States. They developed the wheel and attached it to a wheelbarrow to help them move heavy loads.

The most valuable export of China was silk. It brought power and prestige to the Chinese empire, and it helped facilitate and name the most famous trading route in the history of the world: The Silk Road. The Silk Road ran from the Pacific Ocean all the way to Rome. Since silk making was so profitable and important, the Chinese tried to keep the process a secret.

The Chinese also invented the first books. They covered them with thin strips of bamboo, creating hardback protection. In these books, they recorded historical events and religious ceremonies.

AUSTRALIA

Geography

Australia is the world's smallest continent. It is located between the Pacific Ocean and Indian Ocean, south of Southeast Asia. Australia is about half the size of the continent of Europe. The geography is diverse, moving from vast deserts in the west to the central and the eastern portions of the continent, containing lowlands and highlands. Australia is one of the driest continents on the planet, and it is very temperate with very few cold weather zones.

The Aborigines

For most of Australia's history, the flat, arid landscape was home to only a few native inhabitants known as aborigines. After arriving in Australia from southern Asia thousands of years ago, they were a relatively peaceful people. The aborigines were nomadic and had almost no Neolithic development. No evidence has been found of domestic agriculture or job specialization. Aborigines were food gatherers and hunters. While they hunted with sharp weapons, like spears and arrows, they also showed no evidence of practicing warfare.

When the British captain James Cook first scouted the continent in 1770, only about 300,000 aborigines were living on the entire continent. In 1788, when the British returned to Australia, they had no trouble occupying the lands of the aborigines, who knew nothing about warfare. All of the British conquest was peaceful, but the aborigines fell victim to diseases and sickness brought by the British, which had a devastating effect on the local population.

3200 B.C.E	Writing in Sumeria
2700 B.C.E	• Old Kingdom of Egypt
	• Pyramids are built.
2500 B.C.E	Twin Cities in India: Harappa and Mohenjo-daro
2050 B.C.E	• Middle Kingdom Egypt
	• Hyksos invade Egypt.
1790 B.C.E.	Hammurabi's Code
1750 B.C.E.	Harappa and Mohenjo-daro disappear.
1700 B.C.E.	Hyksos rule Egypt.
1650 B.C.E.	Shang Dynasty rules China.
1550 B.C.E.	New Kingdom Egypt
1500 B.C.E.	• Hittites Iron
	• Aryans migrate to India.
1482 B.C.E.	Queen Hatshepsut rules Egypt.
1224 B.C.E.	Ramses II empire
1027 B.C.E.	Zhou/Chou Dynasty
1000 B.C.E.	Israel
900 B.C.E.	King David
612 B.C.E.	Nebuchadnezzar rules Babylonia.
600 B.C.E.	Phoenicia
522 B.C.E.	King Darius in Persia
500 B.C.E.	The Vedas are written.

GLOBAL CONNECTIONS

Mesoamerica

1400 B.C.E.—Olmecs in Mexico

850 B.C.E.—Chavín in South America

700 B.C.E.—Hopewell Mound Builders in North America

500 B.C.E.—City-state of Monte Albán

Africa

1500 B.C.E.—Start of the Great Bantu migrations

750 B.C.E.—Kingdom of Nubia

Egypt

2700 B.C.E.—Old Kingdom with Egyptian pyramids

2050 B.C.E.—Middle Kingdom

1550 B.C.E.—New Kingdom

Mesopotamia

3200 B.C.E.—Writing in Sumer

1790 B.C.E.—Hammurabi's Code

Circa 1100 B.C.E.—Ashurbanipal in Assyria

India

2500 B.C.E.—Twin cities in India: Harappa and Mohenjo-daro

1500 B.C.E.—Harappa and Mohenjo-daro disappear

500 B.C.E.—Vedas recorded

China

Circa 2200 B.C.E.—Writing in China

1650 B.C.E.—Shang Dynasty

1027 B.C.E.—Zhou Dynasty

1500 B.C.E.–350 C.E.

Advances in Religion and Philosophy in Asia

3

From 800 B.C.E. to 300 B.C.E., there were great advancements in religion and philosophy, all of which helped shape the history of the world. The initial advancements in religion, philosophy, and thought had several things in common.

1. They began in the ancient river valley civilizations, as these were the most sophisticated and advanced cultures in the world.
2. Any advancements or breakthroughs to these ideas stayed within the traditional framework. New ideas were added to them, and they evolved. An example of this would be Judaism, which was the first monotheistic faith. Judaism was the foundation, and built on its framework were Christianity and then Islam. Both Christianity and Islam can trace their roots back to Judaism.
3. The ideas spread across the globe. Interactions due to trade, migration, and cultural diffusion spread these ideas, crossing wide-ranging areas from the Pacific to the Atlantic and eventually to the Americas.
4. Each of these advancements was born of necessity to solve some type of problem. The old traditional ways of doing things were no longer working. Ancient civilizations needed to develop a code of behavior in order for the people to survive and govern themselves. Order needed to be restored and maintained.

CHINA

The Philosophy of Legalism

As China developed, the Zhou Dynasty (1027–221 B.C.E.) became a period of religious and philosophical advancement. As the dynasty progressed and began its spiral downward, China had entered the end of a dynastic cycle and began a period known as the warring states era. A new dynasty, the Ch'in, began to rule.

The Ch'in were concerned about ending the wars that had been plaguing China. The Ch'in Dynasty was the shortest in ancient Chinese history, ruling from 221 B.C.E. to 206 B.C.E. The Ch'in enacted the concept known as legalism. The developer of this new philosophy was Han Fei Tzu.

In legalism, it was believed that a unified country would be a strong country. The Ch'in did this by using military power.

As a legalist, Han Fei Tzu said China did not need to look back at the Shang Dynasty for help. He also believed that the Zhou Dynasty could not help China either, saying that conditions in the present were different than they were in the past. Legalists also did not look to the heavenly virtues of the polytheistic gods for answers.

Han Fei Tzu believed good and bad were human-based. He said that humans were evil and driven by greed, but humans also liked rewards and disliked punishments. If what

Global Connections

The Ch'in were like the Assyrians from the river valley civilization of Mesopotamia: fierce and ruthless.

strengthened a state was rewarded and what weakened a state was punished, then a strong state would occur. Laws should be sincere and impartial. Ch'in legalists put human laws above everything else. The emperor should be strong by swiftly rewarding good people and swiftly punishing those who did wrong.

EMPEROR SHI HUANG DI

Shi Huang Di was the emperor that put legalism into practice. He was the emperor famous for linking the various sections of the Great Wall of China into one massive wall. In the short term, he did help China. The military trained hard under Shi Huang Di, attaining order through violence and dominance. To Shi Huang Di, a ruler's greatest asset was his strength, and so for a very short period of 30 years, Shi Huang Di brought unity to China.

Unfortunately, many of his actions hurt China as well. Shi Huang Di ordered the burning of books containing various Chinese schools of thought. He kept only ones containing ideas of which he approved. With only his thoughts or philosophies being taught, his reign could not be questioned.

LEGALISTIC ACCOMPLISHMENTS

As rough as legalism was, Shi Huang Di was able to accomplish many things.

1. The amount of land that could be farmed increased, and food production increased.
2. The Great Wall sections were linked to form one giant wall.
3. The Chinese writing system was unified.
4. Axle lengths on carts were made the same so any ruts that were made were the same size.

Global Connections

The Romans also made their axle sizes the same to aid in the construction and repair of the road system.

With some of these benefits also came cruel penalties and increased punishments for criminals. The faces of criminals were tattooed black and they became workers along the Great Wall for the rest of their lives. High taxes were levied to fill the granaries to be prepared for times of famine, but the taxes were oppressive.

Shi Huang Di was also known as the famous emperor that built the terra-cotta warriors. He was going to rule the afterlife just as he did his earthly life, so he had his artisans make carbon copies of his soldiers to protect him and his tomb inside a pyramid.

END OF THE CH'IN DYNASTY

Unfortunately for Shi Huang Di, his changes happened too quickly. People needed to experience change over time. Too much change, coupled with a period of famine, brought about the end of the Ch'in Dynasty.

Global Connections

Remember Hester Prynne who wore the Scarlet Letter to let others know of her disgrace? The tattooed faces of criminals in China were the same. It meant that there was no escape, and there was nowhere that you could go.

Confucian Philosophy

One of the schools of thought that survived Shi Huang Di's purge was the idea of the great Chinese scholar Confucius. His ideas, known as Confucianism, began around 521 B.C.E.

Confucius wanted to be a royal advisor, but he had a bad habit of always telling the truth. Even today, when a person is an advisor to a ruler, government, or prince, sometimes the rulers do not want to hear what their advisors really think. Confucius did not think he was doing his job if he was anything but honest. As a result, he was fired a lot, and he became a teacher. He looked for ways to spread his ideas, and what better way to spread his ideas than to teach others.

Confucius did not write anything down. His students collected his works and sayings, writing them down in manuscripts called the Analects. Confucianism was eventually accepted by the people and the rulers during the Han Dynasty (see Chapter 6), and throughout its long history, whenever China had trouble, they would always look back at Confucius. They would ask themselves, "What would Confucius do? What did Confucius say about this particular trouble?"

CONFUCIUS'S ADVICE TO CHINA

Confucius saw himself not as an inventor or creator but rather as a good steward of Chinese tradition. He was a broadcaster of information that was already there. Confucius saw the top of the dynastic cycle for both the Shang and Zhou as the Golden Age of China. These dynasties had great leaders of virtue, who "rolled up their sleeves" and worked with the people. Different from the legalists, Confucius was not an innovator. He focused on relaying the good things that the early rulers of Shang and Zhou Dynasties did for their people. Confucius felt that China could resolve the current turmoil by returning to what the Zhou did.

FILIAL PIETY

Confucius broke things down into five basic relationships.

1. Ruler to subject
2. Father to son
3. Husband to wife
4. Older brother to younger brother
5. Friend to friend

Of all of these relationships, only one was equal: friend to friend. Confucius believed that people could be more honest with a friend than a family member.

The others were all considered a dual relationship. There was a superior (someone to teach and help), and there was an inferior (someone who must listen and be subservient). Confucius believed if everyone adhered to these responsibilities, harmony would prevail as an unbroken chain, starting with the emperor and continuing down to the poorest peasant. Confucius said to throw out the old social class system and modify some of the old ways of doing things.

The brilliance of what Confucius did was that he took the old meaning of being an aristocrat (someone rich by birth) and channeled it into something that any educated person could achieve. This meant that people could become truly noble not because of their birth and inherited title but because they were humane and righteous and did the right thing instead of the popular thing. An aristocrat was someone who understood this, whereas a commoner did not. However, a commoner could be made to follow a role model, so for Confucius, government officials needed to be role models for society to follow.

Other Types of Chinese Political Thought

Confucius had two contemporaries. First was the great military leader Sun Tzu. Sun Tzu said people were bad by nature. It was this desire that led to social conflict. He reasoned that the government needed to use a system of harsh punishments and lavish rewards to get the people to do what the government wanted them to do.

Confucius's second contemporary was Mencius, who held the opposite point of view. He said people tended to be good and that the government needed to provide education that cultivated this goodness.

Taoism

Taoism (or Daoism) is the most difficult part of Chinese philosophy to understand. A student of Western culture needs to let go of his Western ideals when looking at Taoism. It was created by Lao Tzu between 300 B.C.E. and 200 B.C.E., and it offered different levels of social responsibilities.

Tao translated means "the way," and "the way" was a mysterious concept. A person could not see it, touch it, or name it, but it was the creator of the universe on a large scale. And so to the believers of Tao, heaven and earth were almost cruel in their ruthlessness. People or animals were treated as "straw dogs," which in ancient China was a creature so insignificant that if the animal was gone, nobody would miss it. It was meaningless. Since that was the way the Tao treated the people of the earth, a perfect sage king or ruler should do so as well.

Keep in mind that this was a very turbulent period in China, so people were coming up with different thoughts and philosophies on how to stop chaos, how to run a government, and how to create a unified country.

If the sage king treated his people poorly, how did he become the person at the top of the dynastic cycle? The top of the cycle indicated rebirth and goodness. The answer was that the sage king must return to the original fundamentals of ruling.

To the Tao, purposely trying to acquire knowledge was bad because this created a distinction that one person was smarter or richer than another, which could have interfered with "the way." People needed to learn to live without anything beyond the basic needs: food, water, shelter, and clothing.

GOVERNMENTAL APPLICATION

If the sage king treated his people as straw dogs, if he was beyond morality, then he was, in fact, saving his people. He was in harmony with the unseen, unnamed Tao. A person who actually strived to be a sage king could not achieve harmony with the Tao. Ingenuity needed to be exterminated because anything that required thinking would upset the flow of things. People needed to make do with what they had because this would reduce crime.

The political philosophy in Taoism was that a sage king was ruling by not actually ruling. If the sage king or government was constantly helping the people, giving them a hand up, or relieving a crisis, then the people would become dependent upon the government. Every time there was a crisis, people would wait until the government showed up. As hard as it was, the sage king would not act. The people would have to figure things out, do things for themselves, and not become dependent upon governments.

INDIA

The Vedic or Brahmanic Age in India

Up until 500 B.C.E., the priest-kings of the Indus River Valley used a very elaborate magical approach when practicing their religious rituals. This practice was so intense that it soon became impossible for anyone to make sacrifices and practice the religion except the wealthiest people. Most people did not have access to the sacrifices that were required. It was too

Dinner Table Talk

One philosophy used today by some humanitarian aid groups is this: If you give a man fish to eat, then he'll eat for a day. But if you teach a man to fish, then he'll eat for a lifetime!

burdensome for the poorer people as they needed their food and their livestock for survival. They could not offer it as a sacrifice.

Around 500 B.C.E., India received the Vedas (see Chapter 2). The Vedas were a large collection of hymns, prayers, and rituals. The Vedas spoke out against the necessity of sacrifice and the elaborate, very expensive rituals that only the wealthy could afford. The newest Veda said that people could acquire power and union with Brahman through knowledge alone, not the ritual. People could escape from existence and be in union with the all-knowing, all-powerful Brahman without the rituals.

Hinduism

In 400 B.C.E., a new social and religious order developed in India: the Hindu Indian religion. It was different from the Vedic-Aryan or Brahmanic Age that had existed since the Aryans in 1500 B.C.E. and migrated into India around 500 B.C.E. Despite India's large size, diversity, and foreign rule for 1000 years, the Hindu Indian religion began to take shape. Things like the transmigration, the sacredness of the cow, and the belief in Shiva and Vishnu became accepted. The caste system became an institution.

The key thing to remember is that not all Indians were Hindu. Hindu was the largest main belief system; there was also the tremendous diversity to consider. When different kinds of foreign people mix, different branches of the same religion develop. As a result, many Hindus created their own visuals for the different Hindu gods. Many forms of worship also developed.

Despite this, all Hindus had the same basic belief. There was an unchanging, all-powerful spiritual force called Brahman. Since this was difficult for people to understand or visualize, people made different visuals of gods, trying to give Brahman a concrete, visual form. Underneath the all-encompassing Brahman, there were several other gods that were subject to Brahman's power. The main gods besides Brahman the Creator were Vishnu the Preserver and Shiva the Destroyer.

UPANISHADS

The Upanishad texts stated that knowledge was more important than any ritual. The goal was to achieve a real, permanent existence with Brahman, not live in the moment. Rituals were just an act of "going through the motions" without meaning. It was the knowledge of what the ritual was trying to accomplish that was important.

THREE PLANES OF EXISTENCE

In Hinduism, there were three planes of existence:

1. The earthly world, occupied by humanity
2. Heaven, occupied by the gods
3. Unity with Brahman, the all-powerful, all-knowing force, which humanity and the gods were both trying to achieve

In order to achieve unity with Brahman, the goal was to escape existence in earthly or heavenly form, which was not easy.

HOW TO ACHIEVE OR REACH UNITY WITH BRAHMAN

The Upanishads, and followers of Hinduism, tried to focus on the individual soul, or atman, and its relation to the ultimate plane of existence with Brahman.

Even gods were subject to the laws of existence. A person or god was going to have to live many lifetimes to achieve unity with Brahman. Death and rebirth was known as the transmigration, or the samsara. Hindus could pray to the gods for help; however, achieving unity with Brahman was not based on rituals or prayer but instead on mental decisions made by a believer. The only way for a believer to get to Brahman was really through himself or herself. The believer held the key: not a ritual and not a god. The problem was that a believer could not see or describe Brahman. Brahman was present in everything, but a person could not touch it, smell it, or hear it; nevertheless, it was there.

For Hindus, the key to understanding themselves was recognizing that they could not worry about their current mortal existence. This belief eventually formed into a justification for the social hierarchy of India.

LIFE AFTER DEATH

Hindus believed in a life after death, but with six caveats.

1. Existence was a constant, endless cycle of death and rebirth.
2. Believers had to accept their place in society: class, gender, and caste.
3. Since the goal was to achieve union with Brahman, believers should focus on themselves.
4. Understand that rebirth in heaven was probably the best a person could accomplish.
5. Believers were going to be born again, which was known as the transmigration, or the samsara.
6. Existence was liberating, yet burdensome, knowing that you were going to be born again.

KARMA

These may be familiar phrases: "You've got bad karma" or "You've got good karma." Essentially, karma meant that work was the key to breaking the transmigration. It was the individual work that a person did that mattered. Every action had an effect on the soul. Therefore, good deeds would have had good effects, but a person needed to remember that everything was temporary.

For an individual to achieve Brahman, or at least attain a higher life in the next round of rebirth, there were two basic things to do:

1. Maximize good actions
2. Minimize bad actions

By doing this, people could achieve the best possible result in their next life.

DHARMA

Dharma was the religious, moral, and social duty of the individual. It was different for everyone based on class, occupation, and gender. Dharma could be defined as social responsibility: what a person was supposed to do. It was simply the way people were supposed to conduct themselves in their political, religious, commercial, and social lives in order to achieve a next round of higher rebirth.

Living life following dharma meant several different things.

1. It required Hindus to understand that the transmigration was required and necessary.
2. It required Hindus to accept the responsibilities of their caste, their gender, and their social class. This was a way to maintain power within the social classes at this time.
3. It was acceptable for Hindus to look out for themselves first and foremost. The self-interest of Hindus was legitimized, and they only had to worry about themselves. Hindus did not have the communal aspect of a large church, so how they interacted and treated others was not a priority.
4. All things were subject to change. For most people, the best they would ever do was achieve rebirth in heaven, which was acceptable. Only a select few would ever achieve union with Brahman.

Global Connections

Dharma and the Islamic sharia have similar ideas in governing the social aspects of the separate religions.

MOKSHA

Moksha was the liberation from existence. When a person achieved moksha, they achieved union with Brahman, and could free themselves from existence. However, due to selfish human desire, few could achieve this in one lifetime, but it could be done. Achieving moksha meant escaping all karmic effect and all action.

Hinduism is similar to other religions like Judaism, Christianity, and Islam in that followers still need to act a certain way toward others. Followers must strive to be good people, in public and private, and maximize their good actions. This practice will be followed by the majority of Hindus, including the Jains and other offshoots of Hinduism, plus the followers of Buddhism.

The Jains and Mahavira

Between 540 B.C.E. and 468 B.C.E., the beliefs of the great hero named Mahavira entered the scene. He created the Jains, which was a sect of Hinduism. Mahavira was a teacher who found a way that Hindus could remove themselves from the bonds of the material world. He was trying to find an "Everyman's way" to get to Brahman.

To the Jains, there was the transmigration, or endless cycle of death and rebirth. Where the Jains differ was that karma took on material form. Think of the soul as being a magnet. When karma took material form, everything a person did (thoughts, actions, words, etc.) attracted karmic matter to the soul and weighed it down. Negative thoughts and actions weighed more, preventing a person from rising higher up. To the Jains, the path to escape existence was to eliminate many of these evil deeds, especially those that were harmful to others.

Mahavira taught his followers that the bad actions weigh the most, so when it came to karma, a person should not perform that action. Things that Mahavira cited as bad were

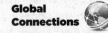

Global Connections

There is some similarity between Mahavira's list of bad actions for the Jains and the Israelites's Ten Commandments received by Moses.

- Killing
- Stealing
- Sexual promiscuity
- Lying
- Ownership of goods or property so a person was not corrupted (this was an extreme form of the Jains' belief system)

When Mahavira was 72 years old, he wanted to show the people that he really believed in the Jains. He went out to the wilderness and fasted himself to death in 527 B.C.E. to achieve union with Brahman.

Buddhism

Buddhism is one of the great Universalist forms of faith that exists in the world today. Most people believe it originated in China, but that is not true. It began in India but has since faded from that area. Buddhism has a wide appeal as it is adaptable.

SIDDHARTHA GAUTAMA

For many years in India, there was a single, larger-than-life hero named Siddhartha Gautama, who eventually became known as Buddha, or the Enlightened One. Depicted in many forms over a wide area in India, Siddhartha Gautama was born in 563 B.C.E. and grew up extremely wealthy. He never wanted or needed for anything. When he was 29 years old, he went outside of his palace for the first time. He saw three things that he did not know how to process: a poor man, a sick man, and a dying man. It changed his life. He could not process any of it because in his privileged world, everyone lived exactly like he did. He immediately left his family on a quest to find answers to the transmigration, or the endless cycle of existence, and how people could get out of the transmigration.

BECOMING THE BUDDHA

Siddhartha wandered, and he began to meditate underneath a pipal tree in India. He fell into some sort of trance, and during the trance, he was hit with an epiphany. He saw all of his past lives and every round of birth he had gone through. He saw what he did good and what he did bad, so now he knew how to stop the flow of karma. He knew the secret to getting out of the transmigration. As of 530 B.C.E., he was no longer Siddhartha Gautama, but was instead Buddha, or the Enlightened One.

He pledged to use his last life to help others achieve the release from transmigration. His goal was to teach this to others, which became known as Buddha's Middle Path.

FOUR NOBLE TRUTHS

To follow the Middle Path, one needed to understand the four noble truths that were the core of what Buddha was trying to teach.

> ### DINNER TABLE TALK
>
> Have you ever heard the phrase, "Keeping up with the Joneses"? This is what Buddha was warning about: people are never happy with "stuff." They want a nicer car, a bigger house, a higher paying job, and even the greenest lawn in the neighborhood!

1. Understand that all life was suffering. Life was hard.
2. The source of suffering was the desire to acquire material goods, or "stuff."
3. People needed to learn to end their selfishness, greed, and desire. When this ended, suffering stopped, and the transmigration would end.
4. Buddha's eightfold path would teach people how to stop desiring.

THE EIGHTFOLD PATH

For people to teach themselves how to end their desire, they had to focus their minds on what Buddha wanted them to think about.

- Right understanding
- Right thought
- Right speech
- Right action
- Right livelihood
- Right effort
- Right mindfulness
- Right concentration

THE DUKKHA

An essential part of Buddhist existence was the dukkha, which translated to "permanent suffering." Buddhists needed to understand that all life encompassed the dukkha: suffering. Nothing was permanent except suffering.

Buddha said to focus on the eightfold path. Those eight things were the right way to live. Be compassionate to all things, and Buddhists could take the "shortcut" to nirvana. Achieving union with nirvana was the same thing as achieving union with Brahman, just under a different name.

Buddha also made union with nirvana available for anybody, not just the wealthy or devout. If people did not have time to meditate but lived according to the eightfold path, they would skip the transmigration and achieve nirvana. It pulled people away from the rigidity of the caste system.

Global Connections

The eightfold path can also be compared to the Christian Ten Commandments and the tenants of Mahavira and Jains Hindus.

MESOPOTAMIA

Creation of Judaism and the Religion of the Israelites

In Mesopotamia, there was the religion of the people of Israel. The Israelites were different because of their worship of their one God, Yahweh. They were often abused as they lived in an area rich in polytheism, but the Israelites had a great impact on the world as they created the foundation for the three monotheistic faiths.

MONOTHEISM

Simply defined, monotheism is faith in one single, all-powerful, all-knowing god. Israelites did not need polytheistic gods. Their god did it all. For the first time in religious history, there was an emphasis placed on the moral demands and responsibilities to the community, not just the individual.

OLD TESTAMENT

The Old Testament was the historical narrative of the Israelite people, where the founder Abraham migrated from the Persian Gulf region to Palestine sometime between 1900 B.C.E. and 1600 B.C.E. Abraham became the symbolic founder, and he formed the first covenant with God. A covenant was a binding contract of the ancient world with reciprocal responsibilities. God told Abraham that if he served him and believed in him, he would bless Abraham's descendants and make them as numerous as the "stars in the sky or the sands on the seashore."

MOSES

Judaism has many prophets, which are inspired messengers sent to call people back to God when they stray. One of the most important was Moses. Moses brought about the idea of the supremacy of God, or Yahweh. He said that God was superior to all others and would help the Israelites win victory over the inhabitants of what is today the Middle East. Moses led the Hebrew slaves out of Egypt during the reign of Ramses II circa 1250 B.C.E.

Journeying through the desert, Moses received God's laws—the Ten Commandments and the Torah—on the top of Mount Sinai. The Torah was the rulebook for Hebrews and also promised God's protection as long as the people kept their covenant with him. This was an exciting moment in world history as the Israelite people began to see themselves as God's chosen people as God said that through them, all people would be brought to him.

PROPHETS

Since prophets were inspired messengers from God, they were sent to call people back to God. They helped God consolidate and purify this new faith. When the kingdom was falling apart and when people began to stray, God sent a prophet to the Israelites. Some other prophets of Judaism included:

- Joseph, who was sold into slavery and became the assistant to the Egyptian pharaoh
- King David, the warrior king and unifier
- King David's son Solomon, known for his wisdom

TWO CENTERPIECES OF JUDAIC MONOTHEISM

1. **GOD HAD A DIVINE PLAN.** He knew what people were going to do before they did it. When people experienced trouble, it was God's punishment for breaking the duties of the covenant. The purpose behind this was not a negative. It was not just the punishment that was important but the purpose behind it. Through Israel's suffering, they would eventually purify other nations and bring them to God. Judaism was the original foundation of the monotheistic faith, and with the addition of Christianity and Islam, God's divine plan was that everybody would be brought to God.

2. **THE ESSENCE OF GOD WAS IDEAL, PURE JUSTICE AND GOODNESS.** God expected this same righteousness from his people. When his believers strayed, he punished them, but that punishment was meant to bring them back to him. God would always take back a sinner. This belief created a key moment in history, when a monotheistic religion intersected with an ethical, moral code of behavior. The Israelite people became a nation that was not recognized or famous for a dynasty, for a new language, or where they were located, but they were recognized for a lasting faith and their practice of it.

JERUSALEM

Eventually between 1,000 B.C.E. and 900 B.C.E., the great King David unified the 12 tribes of Israel. An enormous capital was built in Jerusalem, and David's son Solomon built a temple. However, there was a constant round-robin of conflict in the ancient Middle East. The

Assyrians conquered Jerusalem in 722 B.C.E., and for a time, the unity of the Israelites was broken up, with only the kingdom of Judah and the capital of Jerusalem remaining.

While the Israelites did not have a kingdom or an empire, their faith lasted. It spread slowly across the globe.

GREECE

Greek Philosophy

Around 700 B.C.E., long after the founding of the four ancient river valley civilizations, the people of Greece began an individual examination of the physical world. They studied the place of human beings in the world, and this was eventually called philosophy. *Philosophy* means simply "the love of wisdom."

Due to their location on the Mediterranean Sea, Greece came into contact with the Eastern world and Mesopotamia. The Greeks had their own polytheistic gods living on Mount Olympus: Zeus, Apollo, Athena, and so forth.

The first philosopher was a man named Thales. Circa 600 B.C.E., he was sitting by stream one day, and he saw the river change course when sediment built up. He realized that the world changed on its own. It was not a god or goddess of the stream; it was not Poseidon that made the river move. It was the earth itself. The discovery that the world could be governed by rational thought and reason developed into a political and a moral philosophy.

The three most famous philosophers of ancient Greece were Socrates, Plato, and Aristotle.

Socrates (469–399 B.C.E.)

Socrates looked at the social and political ideals of the Greek city-state. Socrates felt that knowledge about human affairs could be revealed at its deepest core when they were repeatedly questioned. This is called the Socratic Method. Socrates believed people should seek improvement through academic knowledge.

Socrates did like the idea of the city-state, and he liked the idea of citizens helping in its defense and obeying its laws. However, he asked that leaders based their decisions on logic and reason. Socrates grew troubled as the city-state of Athens was being governed by a democracy. Socrates was angry because when he would ask somebody what they were doing, or why they were doing it, the answer was always the same. They could not tell him why they were doing it!

Socrates, a man very similar to Confucius in that he was a teacher, began to teach his students to question the gods and governmental leaders. However, Socrates did not like democracy because he felt people might not make informed decisions. How can a democracy make a decision for the people if they did not understand why they did it? Socrates taught his students to not be disrespectful but to ask the leaders why they made the decisions that they did. The governing leaders of Athens did not like it. The Socratic Method made people angry, so Socrates was eventually sentenced to death.

Plato (428–347 B.C.E.)

Plato was the best student of Socrates. He was upset that his teacher was killed, and he left Athens in search of the perfect form of government. He wanted to be a politician until his beloved teacher was killed.

Plato also believed in the city-state and that the values of harmony and justice in a polis could produce good people. However, Plato said there were only a few philosophers whose training, character, and intelligence allowed them to see the big picture. These people would prefer a life of thinking, study, and contemplation, but they would accept their role as philosopher kings.

Global Connections

Plato's belief is similar to Confucius's belief in filial piety creating nobles by being righteous and the legalist view of richly rewarding people to create a good society.

PLATO'S PERFECT GOVERNMENT

Plato claimed to find the perfect government: a Greek caste system in the mythological city of Atlantis. He said everyone had a specialized role, leading to the creation of a formulaic individual. People needed to subordinate themselves to the good of the community. Each person should do the things to which each was most suited in order to serve the country or city-state. Plato believed this would reduce internal stress and erase class struggles.

Plato's perfect government had three classes:

1. The philosopher king to govern the society
2. The warriors to protect society
3. Everyone else to farm the land

According to Plato, economic prosperity was essential, and he said the philosophy should be to destroy anything that stood in the way of what the city-state needed. Gods were not important as it was human logic and reason that put people in their proper place in society.

Aristotle (384–322 B.C.E.)

Aristotle was Plato's best student. He disagreed with his teacher. He said the purpose of most people could be found by just observing their behavior. They would eventually reveal their true nature. Aristotle preached moderation and common sense. People did not have to subordinate themselves to the will of society. When it came to wealth, moderate wealth was okay. Moderate comfort was fine. People should be happy for the success of others, but they should not get carried away.

Aristotle also said the problem with many societies was that they had not separated their religious philosophy from their governmental philosophy. Society should not marry religion and politics. The government should not tell people what to believe or dabble in their religion.

Aristotle said the perfect governmental philosophy should seek to allow individuals to be self-sufficient, but help could be provided to those in need (unlike in Taoism). Aristotle said it was okay to help people to become self-sufficient.

Aristotle also believed that people should not be locked into a caste system like his teacher Plato believed. If people wanted to climb the social ladder and do better for themselves, then help them achieve it. He believed this would create the best state and the best government possible. This would provide justice and stability for the majority.

TIMELINE REVIEW

1500 B.C.E.	Vedas were recited.
1300 B.C.E.	Moses leads Israelites from Egypt.
1000 B.C.E.	King David
961 B.C.E.	King Solomon
722 B.C.E.	Defeats by Assyrians
624–546 B.C.E.	Thales Greek philosopher
551 B.C.E.	Confucius is born.
530 B.C.E.	Siddhartha Gautama becomes the Buddha.
500 B.C.E.	Vedas were written.
468 B.C.E.	Mahavira
430 B.C.E.	Socrates
400 B.C.E.	Hindu tradition forms.
399 B.C.E.	Plato leaves Athens.
330 B.C.E.	Aristotle
321 B.C.E.	Chandragupta Maurya Dynasty
300 B.C.E.	Taoism
268 B.C.E.	Ashoka converts to Buddhism.
221 B.C.E.	Shi Huang Di unites China: Ch'in dynasty.
100 C.E.	Buddhism arrives in China.
320 C.E.	Guptas

GLOBAL CONNECTIONS

Mesoamerica

1400 B.C.E.—Olmecs in Mexico

700 B.C.E.—Hopewell Mound Builders in North America

200 B.C.E.—Pyramid of the Sun in Teotihuacan

100 C.E.—Moche in South America

300 C.E.—Mayan Civilization

Africa

900 B.C.E.—Great Zimbabwe

750 B.C.E.—Kingdom of Nubia

350 C.E.—Kingdom of Axum

Rome

770 B.C.E.—Romulus and Remus found Rome

500 B.C.E.—Roman Republic is formed

31 B.C.E.—Pax Romana

180 C.E.—Pax Romana ends

350 C.E.—Huns arrive in Italy

Greece

1250 B.C.E.—Trojan War

750 B.C.E.—Rise of city-states

490 B.C.E.—Persian Wars begin

334–326 B.C.E.—Alexander the Great invades Persia and India

China

141 B.C.E.—Han Wu Ti leads Han Dynasty

105 C.E.—Invention of paper

220 C.E.—Han Dynasty collapses

Korea

300 C.E.—Korean kingdoms of Koguryo, Paekche, and Silla

Quick Quiz: Chapters 1–3

1. This country in Eastern Africa is the starting point for human migration.

   A. Ethiopia
   B. Tanzania
   C. Sudan
   D. Egypt

2. Understanding this discipline is important when it comes to historians studying ancient cultures and civilizations and how they interacted with their environment.

   A. Geography
   B. Writing systems
   C. Physical remains
   D. Religion

3. Which of the following is the term for a group of people moving in search of food or following game?

   A. Paleolithic
   B. Clans
   C. Cro-Magnon man
   D. Nomads

4. As people in the Neolithic Age began to settle down in permanent villages, what did living in these villages make it necessary for the people to create?

   A. Farming
   B. Early forms of government
   C. Religious temples
   D. Trade routes

5. What is the term that describes the spreading of ideas, beliefs, and technology, which is one of the main recurring features in overall history?

   A. Trade routes
   B. Cultural diffusion
   C. Conquest
   D. Migration

6. The three kingdoms of ancient Egyptian civilization were governed by which of the following?

   A. Oligarchies
   B. Aristocracies
   C. Dynasties
   D. Bureaucracies

7. Which of the following are the rivers that brought life to ancient Mesopotamia?

   A. Ganges and Indus
   B. Nile and Yellow
   C. Euphrates and Danube
   D. Tigris and Euphrates

8. Nebuchadnezzar, who built the Hanging Gardens and was a fair ruler of conquered people except for the Hebrews, was king of which of the following Mesopotamian empires?

   A. Babylonia
   B. Persia
   C. Assyria
   D. Hittite

9. These ancient people of the Middle East were known as the carriers of civilization as they spread ideas and culture throughout the Mediterranean world.

   A. Carthaginians
   B. Phoenicians
   C. Lydians
   D. Hebrews

10. The civilization of ancient India depended upon which of the following for its survival?

    A. Snowfall in the mountains
    B. Monsoon seasons
    C. River flooding
    D. Soil replenished by mountain runoff

11. What do the building of the twin cities Harappa and Mohenjo-daro tell us about the ancient Indus River Valley civilization?

    A. They were polytheistic.
    B. We are not sure as we don't know what happened to them.
    C. Their building demonstrates strong central government and careful central planning.
    D. The early people were nomadic as they kept moving in search of resources.

12. Due to their geographic location in respect to the other river valley civilizations, what did the early Chinese civilization call themselves?

   A. Blessed by the gods
   B. The Middle Kingdom
   C. Near the river of sorrows
   D. Classically civilized

13. What common feature found in Egypt, Mesopotamia, and China greatly aids historians in studying these ancient river valley societies?

   A. Writing systems that we have the ability to translate
   B. Long-standing physical ruins
   C. Written records describing the accomplishments of each civilization
   D. Their religious systems

14. The concept of legalism was practiced by this Chinese emperor.

   A. Wang Mang
   B. Han Wu Ti
   C. Kublai Khan
   D. Shi Huang Di

15. In which early religion are even the gods subjected to the will of the lord of the universe?

   A. Dharma
   B. Buddhism
   C. Zoroastrianism
   D. Hinduism

16. Which religious leader wanted to teach other people to escape the process of the trans-migration?

   A. Mahavira
   B. Thales
   C. Buddha
   D. Muhammad

17. Which religion or culture created the first long-lasting form of monotheism?

   A. Judaism
   B. Buddhism
   C. Hinduism
   D. Jainism

18. Which civilization believed in its polytheistic gods but created philosophy, believing that the laws of the universe could be known and studied closely?

   A. Taoists
   B. Legalists
   C. Ancient Greeks
   D. Zoroastrians

Quick Quiz Answers

1. B; **2.** A; **3.** D; **4.** B; **5.** B; **6.** C; **7.** D; **8.** A; **9.** B; **10.** B; **11.** C; **12.** B; **13.** A; **14.** D; **15.** D;
16. C; **17.** A; **18.** C

Ancient Greece

4

CULTURES OF ANCIENT GREECE

The Minoans

The Minoan civilization (circa 2050–1400 B.C.E.) on the island of Crete was mostly known for the ancient King Minos. He was the mythological king that kept the Minotaur under his palace. The palace at Knossos contained more than 800 rooms and was renowned for its beauty. In it, there were many frescoes (paintings) that showed the daily life of the ancient Minoans. One thing it did not show was any type of defenses of the island. Crete was a peaceful island, and they possibly believed that it was sheltered from any attack. The Minoans lived in peace until they were conquered by the Mycenaeans in 1400 B.C.E., who assimilated the Minoans into their empire.

The Mycenaeans

The Mycenaeans were Indo-Europeans, but they lived on the mainland. They had an empire that lasted from 1400 B.C.E. to 1200 B.C.E. The Mycenaeans wrote about all of their travels and experiences. They were most famous for taking part in the Trojan War.

The Trojan War was fought between the Mycenaeans from Europe and the city of Troy in Asia Minor, in what is today Turkey. The war was most likely fought for control of trading routes in the Black Sea region. The Trojans controlled the trading routes, and the warlike Mycenaeans wanted control.

> ### 🍽 DINNER TABLE TALK
>
> The legend of the Trojan War is that a Trojan prince, Paris, captured Helen, the wife of the Greek king Menelaus. The Greeks went to war to get Helen back. The war lasted for 10 years, but after returning home, King Agamemnon and the Mycenaeans were so weakened that they were quickly taken over by another ancient Greek civilization, the warlike Dorians. For most of world history, the Trojan War was thought to be a myth. In 1870 C.E., a German mining-engineer-turned-amateur-archaeologist named Heinrich Schliemann found the ancient city of Troy, proving that the Trojan War myth was true.

The Dorians

The Dorians were a barbarian group of people, and they quickly defeated the Mycenaeans. This is the so-called "dark ages" of Greece, the first time in human history that learning actually came to a standstill or regressed. The Dorians did not read or write so much of the history was passed down orally through the dark ages of Greece. The Dorian Empire lasted from 1100 B.C.E. to 800 B.C.E. What is known about the Greek dark ages comes from the great epics *The Iliad* and *The Odyssey*. The blind storyteller Homer was given credit for these epics. Around 750 B.C.E., Greece eventually emerged from the dark ages.

It is these three groups—the Minoans, the Mycenaeans, and the Dorians—that formed what was known as ancient Greek culture, one of the classic ages of history.

THE FORMATION OF GREEK CITY-STATES

Geography and Greek City-states

The geography of Greece was very harsh. The rugged mountains and valleys made it difficult to move around, so the Greeks built many small city-states, known as poleis. The city-states were cut off from one another by land and water. These city-states and the surrounding farmland operated as their own separate individual countries with different laws, different currencies, and different governments. They were all Greek in culture, but each city-state developed a passionate loyalty to their polis. This led to jealousy, rivalry, and frequent warfare.

Due to the difficult geography, it was the Mediterranean Sea that provided a vital link to the outside world. With hundreds of bays and islands on the Aegean Sea and the Mediterranean Sea, the Greeks became expert sailors. They carried goods like olive oil, marble, and wine to Egypt and the Middle East in exchange for grain and metal.

The Layout of the Greek City-state

Greek city-states were split into levels. In the middle, they had an Acropolis, a city on a hill. On top of the Acropolis were the temples to the chief god or goddess of the city and a granary. It also had a defensive wall behind which people could retreat in times of warfare.

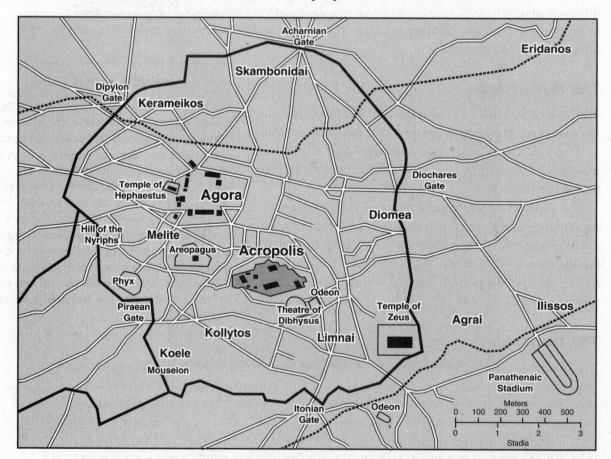

On the lower level, located on flatter ground, was a common area where the people went to the market to shop and to the theaters for entertainment. The city-state was walled on all four sides. All of this helped to further unify the people as they spent a lot of time outdoors interacting in this common area.

Early Government

Between 758 B.C.E. and 500 B.C.E., most city-states were run by a king and a monarchy. Greece was different than most ancient civilizations in that Greek warfare required weapons and armor made of bronze and chariots pulled by horses, both of which were not affordable or available to the working class. It was the nobles who served as the backbone of the army, and they realized that the king needed them more than they needed the king. Using that advantage, they were able to win political power for themselves.

Phalanx

As iron weapons replaced bronze, it allowed more people to enter combat. The Greek phalanx is a battle formation that changed warfare. The phalanx was a triangle-shaped battle formation that required a lot of precision and practice. Some city-states, like Athens, began to require mandatory military service. This had a positive effect as rich people and poor people were forced to work together to make the phalanx work. They had to eat together, sleep in the same barracks, and practice together. This broke down social class barriers and led to the creation of the two most prominent city-states of Greece: Sparta, with its militaristic discipline, and Athens, which wanted to exemplify individuality and focus on political rights.

Greek Phalanx

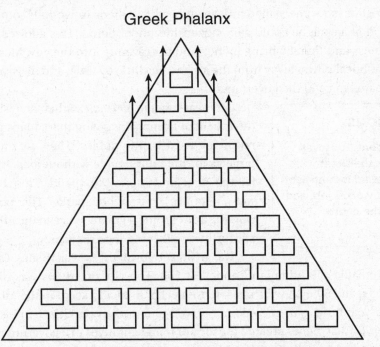

The Greek phalanx was a triangle-shaped battle formation. It required many hours of drills and maneuvers as the tip, or point, needed to face your opponent at all times. The interlocking shields protected the Greek soldiers on the sides, while allowing the Greeks to inflict maximum damage to their opponents.

Athens

SLOW ROAD TO DEMOCRACY IN ANCIENT ATHENS

The city-state of Athens gained a lot of wealth and power under the rule of the monarchy and the aristocracy, yet common people—artisans and merchants—began to get angry as they were kept out of the political process. The rich were able to buy out small farmers and business owners, putting them out of work, which forced these citizens to sell themselves into what is called debt slavery. Debt slavery is when one works simply to pay off debt, acquiring no personal income. This practice made for a slow road to democracy in ancient Athens.

ATHENIAN POLITICAL REFORMERS

The Athens city managers, who ran the day-to-day operations of the city, began to implement reforms, moving Athens on the path to democracy.

In 621 B.C.E., a reformer named Draco codified the Athenian law. He deemed that Athenian law applied equally to both rich and poor. With this, no matter what your social class, you were subject to the same laws and punishments. On the surface, it did not seem like a big move forward, but back in ancient Greece, this was a huge step toward equality in Athens.

Solon was a reformer around 594 B.C.E. He did several things to reform Athens. He outlawed the practice of debt slavery, and he freed those who were already in debt. He opened the high governmental offices to more citizens, and he granted citizenship to some selected foreigners. Remember that Greek city-states were passionately loyal to each other, and it was rare that a person would leave his city-state for another. However, Athens was a large and wealthy city-state, so some skilled artisans moved to Athens to work. If someone was particularly good at a skill, he could gain citizenship under Solon. This allowed the person to open a business and thereby bring money and tax revenue into the city. Most importantly, Solon took political power away from the aristocracy little by little, and he gave the common person a greater voice in the government.

GLOBAL CONNECTIONS

This is the same idea that President Roosevelt used in the United States during the Great Depression. Even Julius Caesar used it in ancient Rome! Give people who want to work a job, and it will have a positive effect on the entire economy.

Fifty years later in 550 B.C.E., Athenian Pisistratus helped the Athenian farmers by giving them loans and extra land not being used by the nobles. Then, he created building projects for the poor people without jobs. It provided jobs for the poor and money to spend. They built defensive walls, temples, and public parks. The poor were now working and earning a greater voice in the Athenian assembly, further weakening the aristocracy.

The greatest reformer was Cleisthenes. Circa 508 B.C.E., Cleisthenes created the Athenian Council of 500. The city of Athens was divided into 10 voting districts, and 50 men were chosen from each district to serve in the Athenian assembly for a one-year term. A man could not serve again until every citizen in his district had a chance to serve. Cleisthenes created the idea of representatives in a government. He created voting districts and term limits, allowing more people than ever to participate in the Athenian government.

Citizenship was highly prized in all Greek city-states but maybe the most so in Athens. To be a citizen in Athens, a man had to be a freeborn man of freeborn parents, who were both native Athenians (until Solon began granting citizenship to foreigners). The men had to go through two years of military training, and then they would become citizens at the age of 20. At this time, they could take part in the Athenian assembly. While men had these rights, and Athens was on the road to democracy, it was only for men. Women were forbidden from working in governmental service, and there were still thousands of slaves who had no rights at all.

	Athens	**Sparta**
Education	Educationally curious. Were taught grammar, music, and rhetoric. Learned about religious beliefs, history, and values of the ideal warrior.	Learned how to read and write. Discussion was discouraged. When a boy was asked a question, he had to answer in as few words as possible.
Citizenship	Free men born of free parents and native-born in Athens.	At 30 years old, men became citizens and took their place in the assembly.
Politics	Loved open discussion and debate.	Discouraged new ideas and forbade travel outside of Spartan lands.
Military	Went through two years of military training, then became full citizens at age 20.	At age 7, boys left home to live in a military barracks. Brutal discipline as they had to fend for themselves.

Sparta

Sparta was the complete opposite of Athens in many ways. It was an isolated city-state in southern Greece that began to take over the surrounding city-states. Spartans were outnumbered by their slaves, known as helots, by a ratio of 20:1.

The goal in Sparta was to have strong warriors. To prepare strong warriors, boys would leave their home at the age of 7 to prepare for life in the military. The boys were subjected to brutal discipline. Although they were permitted to marry at the age of 20, they continued to live in the barracks for another 20 years. Spartans became citizens at the age of 30.

Unlike Athens, which was fond of education, art, and literature, Sparta forbade art or literature. They discouraged new ideas because it could lead to questioning of the government. Sparta also forbade outside travel without permission.

PERSIAN WARS

By 500 B.C.E., Athens had become the largest and wealthiest city-state in ancient Greece. However, due to their geography, the ancient Greeks did not have much room to expand their empire. They began to settle colonies around the Mediterranean Sea and on the west coast of Asia Minor, now known as Turkey. However, this caused problems as Asia Minor was part of the Persian Empire.

The land of Persia was very fertile and located relatively close to ancient Athens. The people of Athens considered themselves superior and powerful, so they did not ask King Darius of Persia if they could settle the land. They simply took it. When King Darius found out, he was angry and demanded that the Greek colonies pay taxes on the food they were growing in his empire. However, the Athenian colonists could not send grain back to Athens, and keep enough for themselves, plus pay taxes to King Darius, so they refused.

In 492 B.C.E., King Darius sent his messengers to ask the Athenian colonists to surrender; otherwise, he planned to destroy these colonies. Athens sent ships and weapons, but no extra men to fight King Darius, so he easily conquered the Athenians. Still angry, King Darius decided he would conquer all of Greece. Many city-states in Greece agreed to surrender to him, but Athens and Sparta did not.

Marathon

The first battle of the Persian War on Greek soil was fought on the beaches of Marathon in 490 B.C.E. King Darius sent a huge invasion force across the Aegean Sea, and when they landed at Marathon, the Greeks were outnumbered. They asked the Spartans to help, but the Spartans were in the middle of an important religious festival. They said they would provide assistance at the conclusion of the festival.

In the meantime, King Darius attacked, and using the Greek phalanx formation, the Greeks won an upset victory over Persia at Marathon. This forced King Darius to flee back to Persia. The soldiers at Marathon sent a soldier to run to Athens to tell the Athenians that they did not need to evacuate the city. Marathon was 26 miles from Athens, and the soldier ran the entire distance. This is where the modern-day 26-mile marathon comes from. When Sparta showed up for the battle at Marathon, the Athenians mocked them for not showing up until the battle was over. The strong warriors of Sparta were humiliated and angry, and they returned to Sparta.

FUN FACT

One legend has it that the soldier began to stagger as he neared Athens, and the goddess Nike put her winged sandals on his feet, propelling him to Athens. This legend inspired one shoe company to name themselves "Nike"!

King Darius and King Xerxes

When King Darius arrived in Persia after the loss at Marathon, he was assassinated on the way to his daughter's wedding. Darius's son, Xerxes, was made the new king. Xerxes had two immediate objectives: to avenge his father's loss at Marathon and to secure the western edge of his empire, meaning he had to defeat all of the Greeks.

King Xerxes amassed an impossibly large army to conquer all of Greece. Athens knew it needed to ask Sparta for help, but after their poor treatment of the Spartans at Marathon, the Athenians knew they might refuse to help. However, the Spartans agreed to fight, but they demanded control over the entire land army because of the disrespectful treatment they received at Marathon.

Thermopylae

The Persians and King Xerxes landed in northern Greece as they wanted to trap Athens against the sea. However, by landing in northern Greece, the only way to enter the heart of Greece was through a narrow mountain pass near the town of Thermopylae.

In 480 B.C.E., King Leonidas of Sparta and his 300 best warriors rushed to Thermopylae to meet the Persian army. Their goal was to slow down the Persians and block their route through the mountain pass to give Athens time to evacuate its citizens and organize the Athenian army.

This famous battle lasted for three days. Eventually, King Leonidas and all of his men were killed, but they accomplished their goal and delayed Xerxes. As the Persian army finally made its way through the mountain pass, Xerxes sent men ahead to Athens. He wanted it looted and burned to the ground. He also planned to enslave the men, women, and children.

When Xerxes arrived in Athens, he found it deserted. The Athenians were on the small island of Salamis, just off the coast of ancient Athens. There was a narrow inner rocky channel between the mainland and the island, making it very easy for ships to run aground. Xerxes sent his army out to Salamis in big Persian ships, which was when the Athenian navy sprung their trap. The Athenian navy sailed out from the back of the island, and sunk the slow, lumbering Persian ships that could not navigate the tricky channel. The Athenians forced Xerxes to flee back to Persia. The remnants of the Persian army tried to walk back to Persia, but they were surrounded and destroyed in the final battle at Plataea.

When the Persian Empire was defeated by the underdog Greeks in 479 B.C.E., it was a very important turning point in world history. After the Greeks won, the city-state of Athens created the world's first working democracy.

The Delian League

After the victory over the Persian Empire, a defensive alliance called the Delian League was formed in 478 B.C.E. to the protect Greece from further Persian attack. Member city-states agreed to join a defensive alliance, meaning that if any one of them were attacked by Persia, the other city-states would come to their aid. A treasury was set up in a temple on the island of Delos, and city-states joined by paying money or providing ships and weapons. Athens became the head of the Delian League.

Pericles and the Golden Age of Athens

After the Persian war, a Greek general-turned-statesman named Pericles took over. From 460 B.C.E. to 429 B.C.E., his leadership ushered in the Golden Age of Athens. Athens became a direct democracy.

In a direct democracy, a large number of males take part in the operation of the city, and when issues are voted upon, it is an open vote and the majority vote wins. The outcome is immediate, and each person knows who voted "yes" and who voted "no."

GLOBAL CONNECTIONS

The United States Congress, consisting of the Senate and the House of Representatives, runs on a direct democracy as the voting in Congress is open with the majority vote winning. Here's an example in its most simplistic form: If I asked 30 students who wanted pepperoni on their pizza, and 20 students raised their hand, we know we are ordering pepperoni, and we know the 10 students who don't like it!

Athenian citizens believed that Athenian people bore a special responsibility to their city. To have a successful democracy, people needed to be passionate about it. They felt that people who took no interest in their city-state and government were not harmful but useless.

Pericles used money from the Delian League to rebuild Athens. He hired the best architects and sculptors to expand the city-state, rebuild the Athenian Acropolis, and build a defensive wall. Pericles increased jobs and prosperity for artisans and workers in the city. Athens looked outstanding, and Pericles was so good at accomplishing tasks for the good of the people, they let Pericles do everything for them.

Athenian Domination

After a while, members of the Delian League began to resent Athenian domination. Athens was taking money from the Delian League treasury to rebuild Athens. Athens's rationale for using the Delian League money was that it was their city that was destroyed by Persia. In addition, Athens provided the majority of the men and ships to fight, so they believed they could do whatever they wanted. Other city-states rebelled, saying that Persia was not coming back anyway, so they refused to pay any more into the Delian League. Athens threatened them, bullied them, and even subjugated their people, saying that city-states were never allowed to leave the Delian League. This made many city-states uneasy, especially in the south of Greece. Sparta was watching this happen, and they began to fear Athenian domination of the entire country of Greece. They formed a counteralliance known as the Peloponnesian League to defend against Athenian aggression.

Global Connections

This is similar to actions taken by the United States and the Soviet Union during the Cold War in the 1950s. The United States led NATO and the Soviet Union led the Warsaw Pact. You had two big countries leading alliances with smaller satellite members.

PELOPONNESIAN WAR

In 431 B.C.E., the Peloponnesian War broke out between Athens and Sparta. Athens won a few victories at sea, so Sparta decided to take the war inland. They laid siege to Athens, but Athens was able to get supplies in and out due to the defensive wall Pericles had built. However, after years of being locked inside the city, a plague broke out inside of Athens, killing one-third of the population, including Pericles.

After his death, the leadership of Athens was in turmoil. Successors were not very good, and there was a constant power struggle over who was going to be the next Pericles. No one knew how to lead because Pericles was so good at it that the people had just let him do everything. The great philosopher Socrates spoke up, asking why Athenians were fighting each other when the enemy was outside the gates.

Sparta used this time to gain an important ally: Persia. They asked the Persian navy to block the Athenian seaport in order to force Athens to surrender. Persia agreed, seeing a chance to have its revenge against Athens. Athens was eventually forced to surrender in 404 B.C.E., losing its power and its prestige. Soon, Thebes, from the Delian League, attacked and defeated Sparta, which cost Greece their empire.

GREEK CULTURE AND ARTISTIC ACHIEVEMENTS

During the classical age of Greece from 500 B.C.E. to 300 B.C.E. (but occurring after the Persian and Peloponnesian Wars), three important Athenian philosophers influenced Greek culture and thought. Philosopher means "a lover of wisdom" and the Big Three philosophers in Greece were Socrates, Plato, and Aristotle.

Socrates (469–399 B.C.E.)

Socrates was a teacher very similar to Confucius (see Chapter 3). Socrates wrote nothing down, and he taught his students to question everything. He told them not to accept the simple answer, particularly when it came to the government and to keep asking questions to get to the barest element of truth. Today, this is known as the Socratic Method, used by politicians and lawyers.

However, because of Athenian failures during the Peloponnesian War, Socrates was branded a traitor, and the law stated that he must be executed. However, the Athenian assembly gave him a way out. They let Socrates choose execution or banishment from Athens. He would be ostracized and kicked out of the city, but he would live. Socrates knew the law stated that someone convicted of his sentence had to be put to death, and he always taught his students that the laws of a polis are binding. Rather than be a hypocrite, he chose death.

Plato (428–347 B.C.E.)

Plato was the best student of Socrates. He focused on the importance of reason and rational thinking. Using rational thought, Plato said one could develop perfect ethical values, leading to perfect idealistic beauty and the creation of the perfect society.

However, Plato was so upset at the death of Socrates, he left Athens and wandered, looking for the perfect place. During this time, he believed he found the mythical city of Atlantis. He also wrote 26 political essays during this time, the most famous of which are *Republic* and *Allegory in a Cave*. Plato said the perfect society would be divided into three different categories, with philosopher kings as rulers. These would be the wisest people and even women could be included to run the city. The next category would be soldiers and warriors to protect the city. The final category would be the rest of society: peasants, farmers, artisans, and merchants. Plato believed the best society possible was the one where the people subordinated themselves for the good of the community. He rejected democracy as it killed his favorite teacher, Socrates.

Aristotle (384–322 B.C.E.)

Aristotle was Plato's most famous student. Aristotle developed his own ideas about government. He looked at every single type of government, from monarchy to oligarchy to aristocracy and even democracy. Aristotle believed that by looking at anything, one could find positives and negatives in each. After studying the different types of government, he came to the conclusion that the best government was one that helped people achieve the highest level possible in society. Aristotle said people needed to exercise moderation in all things, including government, which is why he advocated for the middle class to have the power in government. With middle-class rulers, the power could more easily bring the lower classes up and the upper classes down, so everyone is brought together.

Aristotle set up a school in Athens to study the liberal arts curriculum. Later universities were modeled after Aristotle's school, and as a result, Aristotle was taken to Macedonia to be the tutor of Alexander the Great.

Greek Art

Along with the philosophical works of Socrates, Plato, and Aristotle, these three men also influenced art, for which Athens was also famous. Plato said that everything existed in an idealistic form, so Greek artists and architects tried to exemplify this in their work. In ancient Greece, all statues showed people in their best, most perfect form. If a person was short, tall, fat, or skinny, it did not matter. They were shown as thickly muscled with a thin waist and broad shoulders with no scars or blemishes. An example of this would be the Discobolus, now one of the symbols of ancient Greece. Ancient Greek art had a simple, beautiful elegance reflecting Greece at its very best.

Greek Architecture

Greek architecture followed Plato's thinking as well. The most famous building in Greece is the Parthenon, the temple to Athena located at the top of the Athenian Acropolis. The builders wanted to convey a sense of perfect balance and harmony, and so when the people saw it from far away (as most Greeks did), it looked like a perfectly square building. In reality, it was not. The back was taller than the front, and it was not built with perfect 90° square angles. The columns in the center bowed outward. When light would hit the Parthenon, it looked bigger and brighter than it actually was. It was a great example of an optical illusion, which was what the Greeks were after. They strived for simple, tasteful perfection.

Greek Hubris and the Development of the Theater

During the classical age of Greece, there was a worry about individual pride. People were striving for perfection, but they had to be careful about how proud they were of their accomplishments and achievements. To the Greeks, the idea of excessive pride is known as hubris.

The Greeks were fond of festivals that were religious in nature, honoring the gods. They performed outdoors, and all of the actors were men. They wore elaborate masks. The Greek smiling/frowning masks that exemplified comedy and tragedy are the symbol of the theater today.

The Greek Playwrights of Tragedy

There are three playwrights that used the idea of tragedy to warn people about excessive pride. Aeschylus was the father of the tragedy and served as a model for others to follow. Euripides was a social movement activist, and he championed the rights of slaves and women, trying to raise their status and prominence in society through theater. Sophocles was probably the most famous of the Greek playwrights. He wrote 123 plays but only seven of them have survived. Sophocles's plays were specifically written to warn against what happens when you become full of too much pride.

ARISTOPHANES: THE KING OF THE GREEK COMEDY

Even though Aeschylus, Euripides, and Sophocles were great playwrights, the Greek people got tired of the depressing tragedies, and a new playwright named Aristophanes rose to fame. Aristophanes invented the comedy. His plays contained humorous satire-like comedy that made fun of people and customs. However, the Greek leaders were offended by his comedy because they were often the target of his satire. The politicians did not like Aristophanes, but the people loved him. Eventually, he was so popular that if Aristophanes was not making fun of you, then you were not doing your job.

HERODOTUS AND THUCYDIDES: THE KINGS OF HISTORICAL DRAMA

When it came to the writing of history, Herodotus was known as the father of history. He mixed fact with fiction and legend. As he chronicled the Persian Wars, whatever he could not prove or corroborate with eyewitnesses, he filled in himself. Following him was a man named Thucydides, who was more factual. He wrote reports that had no bias, and if he could not corroborate what happened with an eyewitness, he did not write it.

AGE OF ALEXANDER

Alexander the Great was the son of King Philip of Macedon in Greece. King Philip lived through the Persian War, and afterward, he became very upset with how Greece was governed. In 338 B.C.E., the Greeks were defeated at the battle of Chaeronea by King Philip and his son Alexander. They conquered the Greeks to save them from their corrupt and inefficient government. When King Philip was murdered on the way to his daughter's wedding (just like King Darius), young Alexander the Great assumed the throne at the age of 20. Alexander the Great ruled from 336–323 B.C.E.

Alexander was seen by many people as a barbarian, but being educated in Greece, he loved and admired Greek culture. So after the Peloponnesian War, Alexander quickly assumed control of Greece. He had a plan to invade Persia to punish them for destroying Athens and to take back some artistic achievements stolen by Persia. In 334 B.C.E., he attacked Persia and quickly won a series of victories. He conquered Egypt to set up a supply line for his troops, and then he decided to completely destroy the Persian Empire. He surrounded the armies of the Persian emperor, Darius III, and in 331 B.C.E., Alexander captured the capital city of

Babylon. Going eastward, Alexander crossed the Hindu Kush Mountains into northern India in 326 B.C.E. Along the way, Alexander never lost a battle but upon closing in on the Indus River, Alexander's troops wanted to go no farther. They wanted to return home. Over 10 years, they had marched close to 11,000 miles, so Alexander was forced to return to Babylon to relax and refit his army. While in Babylon, Alexander died at the age of 32 in 323 B.C.E. Alexander the Great created one of the largest empires the world had seen up to that point.

The Legacy of Alexander in the Hellenistic World

Alexander the Great was more than just a conqueror. He had an insatiable thirst for knowledge. Being tutored by Aristotle nurtured Alexander's love of learning, so he ended up creating what was known as Hellenistic culture.

Hellenistic culture was a combination of Greek, Egyptian, Persian, and Indian culture. As Alexander the Great moved through the land conquering civilizations, he brought botanists, zoologists, and linguists to capture plants, animals, and languages of the civilizations that he conquered. Everything was brought back to a city of almost one million people that Alexander founded in 331 B.C.E., located on the coast of Egypt and appropriately named Alexandria. In Alexandria, Alexander the Great had the Pharos Lighthouse built to aid navigation at sea. Standing at 440 feet tall, the lighthouse stands eight feet shorter than the Great Pyramid at Cheops, which Alexander did out of respect for the ancient Egyptians.

While in Alexandria, he created a museum called the House of Muses, named for the muses, ancient Greek goddesses of learning. This museum had laboratories, lecture halls, and a library that housed 10,000 scrolls of ancient learning. Everything learned by the Egyptians, the Mesopotamians, and the Indians was brought to the library in the House of Muses, where people could go to study.

Many advancements in math and science were made in the House of Muses. Pythagoras created the idea of the right triangle: $a^2 + b^2 = c^2$. Another mathematician, Euclid, did not create geometry, but he took the knowledge of geometry from Egypt and shared it with the known world. Euclid wrote a step-by-step geometry book called *The Elements*. Many students in high school use materials written by Pythagoras and Euclid.

Archimedes studied ideas of physics and came up with the use of simple machines like the lever, the pulley, the inclined plane, and the measurement of volume. Archimedes said, "If you give me a long enough lever in a firm place to stand, I can move the world."

The astronomer Aristarchus came up with the heliocentric theory, which states that the earth revolves around the sun, but he would not be believed for many years. He also calculated the circumference of the Earth at the widest point and was off by only a few miles.

The physician Hippocrates studied the causes of illnesses, and he looked for the cures. He searched for medicine that would alleviate symptoms, and he opened a school to train other men and women how to cure and treat illnesses and injuries. He made his students take an oath of ethical standards that they would not intentionally harm any patient, so today doctors, nurses, dentists, and others who work in the medical field must take the Hippocratic Oath.

GLOBAL CONNECTIONS TO INDIA

During the rise of ancient Greece, there was a new dynasty in India taking shape, called the Maurya Dynasty. It developed at nearly the same time as ancient Greece and was also when the growth of Hinduism took off.

The Vedic Age

Aryan invaders had come into India's river valley and began what was known as the Vedic Age, which lasted from 1500 B.C.E. to 500 B.C.E. There were limited changes at this time, however, as northern India turned into a battleground. Rival chiefs and Rajahs fought for control of the Ganges River Valley until 322 B.C.E.

Maurya Dynasty and Chandragupta Maurya

In 322 B.C.E., a young man named Chandragupta Maurya formed the first great Indian empire by unifying northern India. Chandragupta Maurya conquered northern India by building a large vast army, which was located very close to that of Alexander the Great's empire.

Chandragupta Maurya created Pataliputra, a large, prosperous city with state-owned schools and factories. The largest city in the world at the time, it had a well-organized bureaucracy as royal officials supervised everything from roads to harbors. All labor and work was designed to benefit trade. The people of India thought the emperor should have a job like everyone else, so Chandragupta Maurya enforced the laws and made sure there was justice for everyone. Chandragupta Maurya instituted a very harsh ruling system with a secret police force, but society ran fairly efficiently.

Ashoka

However, it was the son and grandson of Chandragupta Maurya (Bindusara and Ashoka) who were probably the most famous rulers of this new Indian dynasty.

After Ashoka became emperor in 268 B.C.E., he witnessed slaughter on a battlefield where nearly 100,000 people were killed. Afterward, he converted to Buddhism to promote nonviolence and tolerance. He ruled by setting a moral example to follow.

Ashoka built a road system that rivaled that of the famous Roman Empire. He was famous for setting stone pillars with the heads of four lions on top of the governmental buildings. Ashoka announced that once people entered beyond the pillars, they would find a righteous and good government.

He took steps to improve the infrastructure of India. He built hotels for travelers and helped pave the way for commerce. Ashoka had water wells dug, fruit trees planted, and missionaries sent throughout India to spread the ideas of Buddhism throughout the civilization.

The Maurya Dynasty formed trade contracts with the ancient Greeks, expanding the Silk Road, which came from China, through India, and continued into Europe.

Alexander the Great and the Maurya Dynasty both craved cultural diffusion, so while Alexander the Great moved eastward, the Maurya Dynasty moved westward. In northern India, Indian merchants traded with Africans and other Asian peoples plus the Greeks and Romans. India enjoyed a golden age of decent prosperity and began to make cultural achievements.

The civilizations of Greece and India stayed separated until Ashoka died in 232 B.C.E. At this point, there was a political vacuum with no strong ruler, leading to many years of turmoil and subsequent invasions by Greeks, Persians, and Central Asians.

1600 B.C.E.	Minoan civilization high point
1300 B.C.E.	Mycenaean civilization
1250 B.C.E.	Trojan War
1100 B.C.E.	Dorian invaders
750 B.C.E.	Rise of city-states
730 B.C.E.	Age of Homer
700 B.C.E.	Athenian aristocracy
629 B.C.E.	Start of Spartan rise to power
620 B.C.E.	Draco codifies law
594 B.C.E.	Solon's reforms
546 B.C.E.	Pisistratus
507 B.C.E.	Cleisthenes Council of 500
490 B.C.E.	Persian Wars begin, Battle of Marathon
480 B.C.E.	Thermopylae and Salamis
470 B.C.E.	Delian League
460 B.C.E.	Age of Pericles
431 B.C.E.	Peloponnesian War
409 B.C.E.	Acropolis
406 B.C.E.	Euripides
400 B.C.E.	Hippocrates
390 B.C.E.	Aristophanes
359 B.C.E.	King Philip of Macedon
334 B.C.E.	Alexander invades Persia.
326 B.C.E.	Alexander in India
323 B.C.E.	Alexander dies.

GLOBAL CONNECTIONS

Mesoamerica

1400 B.C.E.—Olmecs in Mexico

700 B.C.E.—Hopewell Mound Builders in North America

200 B.C.E.—Pyramid of the Sun in Teotihuacan

Africa

900 B.C.E.—Great Zimbabwe

750 B.C.E.—Kingdom of Nubia

Rome

770 B.C.E.—Romulus and Remus found Rome

500 B.C.E.—Roman Republic is formed

China

551 B.C.E.—Confucius is born

India

530 B.C.E.—Siddhartha Gautama becomes the Buddha

Ancient Rome

5

GEOGRAPHY

Unlike the geography of ancient Greece, the geography of ancient Rome was almost perfectly suited to the development of an empire. The location and geography allowed Rome to control land on three continents.

The country of Italy juts out into the Mediterranean Sea. Along the west coast of the Italian peninsula is the city of Rome, centrally located in an area that was perfect for uniting and controlling the entire peninsula. Rome was also located along the Tiber River, seven miles inland from the sea, so it was difficult to attack. Also unlike Greece, Italy was relatively easy to travel through, with the coasts of the peninsula giving the people easy access to each other and the sea, making them easier to unite.

Running down the center of the peninsula, like a spinal column, are the Apennine Mountains, which offered some protection and are much less formidable than the mountains in Greece. On either side of the Apennines there are long, flat plains of rich volcanic soil, making the climate perfect for agriculture. This resulted in an exploding population.

The city of Rome was founded by brothers Romulus and Remus and is situated across seven hills, making it a natural acropolis.

THE EARLY REPUBLIC OF ROME TAKES SHAPE

Located north of Rome were the Etruscans and in the south were the Greeks. While serving as subjugated people to the Etruscans and the Greeks, the Romans learned vital survival and development skills. From the Etruscans, they learned about engineering and architecture. They took the knowledge and perfected the design of the arch (now known as the Roman arch). From the Greeks, they learned about agriculture and farming. After three centuries of being enslaved, the Romans rebelled as they had grown from a small group of settlers into their own civilization.

After their successful rebellion, the Romans vowed to never again be ruled by a king. They created a new government, which they called a republic. *Republic* means "a thing of the people." With a republic, the Romans thought they would prevent any one individual from gaining too much power. The Roman Republic lasted from 509 B.C.E. to 133 B.C.E. Rome's government was extremely adaptive, changing as needed as it grew from a new civilization into a massive worldwide empire.

> **DINNER TABLE TALK**
>
> The founding fathers of the United States studied the office of the Roman consul when creating the office of the president of the United States. The similarities include:
>
> - Both were elected.
> - Both had term limits.
> - Both were commander-in-chief of the army.
> - Both had veto power.
> - There is a president and vice president in the United States, whereas Rome had two equal consuls.

Early Government

The early Roman government was run by a powerful entity known as the Senate. The Senate of Rome contained 300 members who were able to serve for life. These senators came from the wealthy landowning class, known as patricians. Two members of the Senate were elected every year to serve as a consul. Being a consul was a very important job as it was the consul's job to supervise the business of government. They had to carry out the day-to-day operations of the city and were in command of the Roman military. They had to be able to work collaboratively with the senators, they had to be elected, and they could serve only one-year terms. The expectation was that the two consuls would meet constantly with the Senate, forcing them to remember to be responsible to the people.

In the event of a national emergency, the Senate was able to elect a dictator, who had unlimited power for a maximum of six months until the crisis was solved. The most famous is the Roman dictator named Cincinnatus. Cincinnatus was a patrician, but was a hands-on landowner who would farm his own land. During national emergencies in Rome in 458 B.C.E. and 439 B.C.E., the senators sought him out as he was plowing his fields. After being informed of the emergencies, Cincinnatus assumed the role of dictator and solved the crisis. He then gave up his power and, within a short period of time, was back plowing his fields. He was the role model for many other great Roman leaders, such as Julius Caesar.

SOCIAL CLASSES

Other than patricians, the majority of the people in Rome belonged to the plebeian social class. Plebeians included everyone from farmers and merchants to skilled artisans. If a person was not a patrician, he could not serve in the government, no matter how highly skilled. The plebeians started what was to be a very long journey in order to gain political representation. The first breakthrough came in 450 B.C.E. with the writing of the Twelve Tables. Many plebeians were upset that citizens did not know the laws, and so they wrote the Twelve Tables, which contained the laws of Rome. For the first time, laws were made that afforded women equal treatment. Women could appeal a judgment handed down by a patrician judge, some of which were very harsh, similar to the Code of Hammurabi.

Eventually, the plebeians saved the Senate from an attack by barbarians, and they gained the right to elect their own officials to the Senate. The plebeians were allotted 10 tribunes, who were looking out for plebeian interests. They had the ability to veto or deny any laws that could prove harmful to the plebeians.

Over a slow 200-year period, the plebeians received more and more access to Roman government. In 367 B.C.E., the first plebeian was elected as a consul, and in 287 B.C.E., a new law was passed that made the plebeian assembly the Roman equivalent of what is today our House of Representatives. Now wealthy plebeians were afforded the same privileges and lifestyle that had once belonged only to Roman patricians.

ROMAN EXPANSION

As Rome grew and expanded throughout Europe, it successfully moved against the Greek city-states. Rome's successful expansion was due to a couple of reasons.

1. The Romans were very savvy and skillful diplomats.
2. They had an extremely disciplined army. The basic Roman unit was called a legion, consisting of roughly 5,000 soldiers. Roman soldiers were given lavish rewards for bravery and daring during battle, and they were given harsh punishments for failures.

Rome conquered their neighbors in Greece by 338 B.C.E. Some Greeks were given Roman citizenship, which was highly prized in ancient Rome. These Greeks were able to self-govern and gained trade rights with Romans; however, they were not allowed to enter politics. They could be Roman citizens, but they could not serve in the government.

Each civilization conquered by Rome was required to give men for the Roman army. It became a Roman tradition that what was conquered with the legion, the men in the legion got to keep. This created permanent colonies of Roman army veterans in foreign lands who would keep the peace. They kept raiders and barbarians out of the area, and the soldiers were made rich and wealthy. Instead of getting a few acres of land in Rome, they got thousands of acres in conquered territory, so it was very popular with the legions.

Rome built a defense network of retired legionnaires on the outskirts of Rome, so if anyone attacked the city, they would have to fight battle-trained Roman legionnaires. This gave Rome a sense of peace, safety, and security.

THE PUNIC WARS (264–146 B.C.E.)

Rome's conquest of the Italian peninsula brought them into contact with an enemy very close to their shores. On the northern coast of Africa on the Mediterranean Sea, there was an old Phoenician trading outpost: the city of Carthage.

Carthage had an empire throughout North Africa so as Rome began to spread around the Mediterranean Sea, it came into contact with Carthage. This resulted in a series of wars lasting 120 years (264–146 B.C.E.).

The first Punic War was won by Rome, and Carthage was forced to surrender the Mediterranean islands of Sicily, Corsica, and Sardinia. However, Rome brutally humiliated Carthage's general and leader, Hamilcar. Hamilcar made his son, Hannibal, promise to be an enemy of Rome forever, leading to the second Punic War 20 years later.

In 218 B.C.E., Hannibal commanded a large, multicultural army on a daring expedition from southern Spain, up over the Pyrenees Mountains. Hannibal made his men and war elephants march over the tall mountain peaks—14,000 feet high. For the next 15 years, Hannibal moved across Italy from the north, destroying crops and large villas owned by patricians and defeating one Roman army after another. However, when a Roman army was sent to destroy Carthage, Hannibal returned to defend his homeland. After being gone for 15 years, Hannibal's army was exhausted, and Hannibal's army was defeated by the Romans.

Even though it had been necessary for Rome to fight Carthage twice already, they offered terms of peace to Hannibal. Hannibal could live in Carthage and even serve as a Roman governor, but Carthage had to pay tribute to Rome. Hannibal accepted these terms publicly but secretly began to rebuild his army to attack Rome. When Rome found out, it sent soldiers to arrest him. Rather than be humiliated and surrender to his enemy (like his dad Hamilcar), Hannibal took poison and killed himself in 190 B.C.E.

Even with Hannibal dead, the Romans were still afraid of the Carthaginians. In 146 B.C.E., at the request of Roman senator Cato, a Roman army general named Scipio destroyed Carthage. All of the Carthaginian people were killed or sold into slavery. To send a clear message to their remaining enemies, the Romans covered all of the Carthaginian farmland with salt, permanently poisoning the soil. At this time in world history, salt was more valuable than gold, which let other civilizations know just how rich and powerful Rome was. The message was clear: if Rome could waste salt (and money) to destroy the people and poison the land of the mighty Carthage, it could do this to anyone.

ROME BECOMES AN EMPIRE

Now that Rome had conquered Carthage, it inherited the massive Carthaginian Empire. Rome moved from being a powerful, regionally based civilization in Europe to a massive empire that controlled lands in three continents: Africa, Europe, and Asia. This changed how the empire was ruled.

Ruling a large, multinational empire is different from ruling a regional civilization. Rome began to call the Mediterranean Sea *Mare Nostrum*, which means "Our Sea." These newly conquered provinces were treated differently from those in northern Italy and Europe, which were ruled by retired Roman legionnaires. They were subjugated provinces, with appointed governors sent from Rome to rule. The governors had no limits on their power as Rome was a long way away. The conquered people had to pay tribute to Rome. A tribute is tax money on what they made or what they grew. They were required to give tribute to Rome, whether it was grain from Egypt or salt from North Africa.

Roman citizenship became more highly restricted. Rome continued to conquer the Hellenistic world, and so much tribute was pouring into Rome that Roman citizens did not have to pay taxes. Everyone thought this was a good idea at first. Governors ruled conquered lands and generals and their armies were still given conquered territory, which served as their reward for serving the state.

Rome was now the center of the ancient world. It controlled busy trade routes and vast amounts of riches flowed into Rome. Generals, politicians, and merchants amassed vast fortunes, which everyone thought was great. However, it led to many problems later on.

Consequences of Expansion

As a result of increased trading and tribute, a new class of Romans was created: the merchant class. They started building large estates and filled them with tribute collected from the conquered territories. These estates increased in size, and they were eventually called latifundia.

Latifundia were staffed by slave labor. Using slaves hurt small business owners, farmers, and shopkeepers. Latifundia owners were getting grain for free as it was pouring in as tribute, plus they could produce as much food as they needed for a cheaper price using their slaves. This drove the price of grain down so much that it became worthless. Farmers and shopkeepers began to lose their land and businesses. Even today, when a farmer loses his land, he normally goes to a large city looking for work.

In Rome, there was now a large group of unemployed people looking for work, and the gap between rich and poor grew. Greed began to replace the old Roman mantra of "work for the good of the city." Hard work and working for the good of Rome no longer mattered. Romans became selfish.

Reformers

Between 150 B.C.E. and 121 B.C.E., two brothers, Gaius and Tiberius Gracchus, tried to make some reforms. They saw the problems plaguing Rome and wanted to fix them before it was too late. Tiberius and his brother Gaius were patricians, and they decided to quit the Senate so they could focus on reform. They both ran for the office of Tribune, which required being elected. They were both elected, with Tiberius being elected more than once.

In 133 B.C.E., Tiberius proposed to the Senate to limit the size of the largest estates and give some of that land to the unemployed farmers. This idea made sense as there was a land-owning requirement to serve in the Roman army. The more people who owned land, the more soldiers would be available to serve Rome. Rome was weakened, and this would help alleviate that problem. However, due to his popularity with the plebeians, the Senate assassinated Tiberius and 300 of his followers in 133 B.C.E.

Roughly 10 years later in 123 B.C.E., Tiberius's younger brother Gaius ran for Tribune. He promoted land reform that would take the unemployed people from Rome and resettle them in North Africa. The Senate agreed that this was a feasible plan, and Gaius began to suffer from hubris. He believed that since he got one idea passed through the Senate, he could get anything passed. Gaius asked that the price of grain be lowered and citizenship be extended to more people to make them allies of Rome. The plebeians loved Gaius's reforms, while the Senate once again became fearful of his popularity. The Senate had Gaius and 3,000 of his followers killed in 121 B.C.E.

The assassination of the Gracchi brothers set a dangerous precedent. Everyone knew that the Senate was involved in the assassinations, but the only people who could investigate the crimes were the senators, who were the ones who actually committed the crime!

Over the next hundred years, there were many upheavals that divided Rome. However, the assassination of the Gracchi brothers made it acceptable to assassinate your political enemies in order to accomplish your political goals.

The Fall of the Republic

In 87 B.C.E., a man named Lucius Cornelius Sulla, a general from an old Roman family, had become an impoverished patrician. He put down a small rebellion in a Roman province, and since he had performed well, he was elected as a consul. Sulla was eventually appointed dictator, and he tried to reorganize the Roman empire. He was a traditionalist who believed in the Roman Republic and wanted the Senate back in power. After Sulla solved all of Rome's problems as dictator, he restored the greedy, corrupt Senate and gave them back their power over the people.

THE RISE OF THE FIRST TRIUMVIRATE (60–53 B.C.E.)

After putting down a large slave rebellion, three ambitious young men managed to arrest power from senatorial control: Marcus Crassus, Gnaeus Pompey, and Julius Caesar. They took over with equal power divided among them.

Having three rulers with equal power is never a good idea, and the Triumvirate quickly fell apart. Marcus Crassus was killed in Asia Minor in 53 B.C.E. Pompey was then offered a seat in the Senate if he would help get rid of Julius Caesar.

After conquering Spain, Caesar returned to Gaul (today's France) to complete his conquest. However, Pompey had the Senate order Caesar to return to Rome where he was to be tried for treason. He was ordered to come alone and not bring his army. If his army came with him, they would be held as traitors. Caesar's army followed anyway. This series of events led to the Roman Civil War starting in 49 B.C.E. Caesar chased Pompey to Egypt, where Pompey was killed in 48 B.C.E. Now, Caesar was the sole dictator of Rome.

Caesar's dictatorship was actually good for Rome. Caesar passionately cared about Rome as he was Roman to the core. He really wanted to help Rome, and even though the Senate tried to have him killed, they ended up naming him dictator for life.

Caesar's Reforms

Between 48 B.C.E. and 44 B.C.E., Caesar instituted five reforms aimed at solving many of Rome's problems.

1. He launched public works projects, much like Pisistratus of ancient Greece. People who wanted to work were put to work to make Rome look better. The people felt good about themselves, and they put the money they earned back into the economy.

2. He reorganized the government and the provinces, placing his military commanders in charge. These men knew Caesar and knew the way he liked to get things done. There was clear chain of command, making the leadership streamlined, militaristic, and organized.

3. He granted citizenship to more people to secure the borders of the empire. These people had skills that could help Rome, and Caesar secured them as allies by offering them citizenship.

4. He raised the pay of soldiers, which raised their social class and status. They were no longer treated as secondary citizens, and more men were willing to volunteer to serve.

5. He introduced a new calendar based on Egyptian astrology. In the new calendar, he made a new month for himself called July.

Surprisingly, the problem with these reforms was that they worked too well. The ills that were plaguing Rome were cured, and everything was running smoothly. Caesar was practically elevated to the status of a demigod by the people of Rome. The Senate knew that if they did not act swiftly, Caesar could declare himself a god, and they would never get their power and prestige back. So on the Ides of March (March 15, 44 B.C.E.), Julius Caesar was assassinated on his way to the Roman Forum. The government assassination of the Gracchi brothers came back to haunt Caesar, as now the great Julius Caesar was dead.

SECOND TRIUMVIRATE (43–33 B.C.E.)

Julius Caesar had taken measures that should anything happen to him, his young nephew Octavian was going to take over, even though he was very young.

Octavian formed the Second Triumvirate with two of Julius Caesar's most trusted aides, Mark Antony and Marcus Lepidus. These three tracked down and killed the assassins of Caesar, and they divided the empire into thirds. Marcus Lepidus ruled North Africa, Mark Antony ruled the eastern part of the empire, and Octavian controlled the Western part of the old Roman Empire.

Octavian began to receive reports that Mark Antony and Cleopatra, the Egyptian princess, were planning to take over Octavian's empire. Mark Antony was angry at being overlooked for the top job by Julius Caesar, so he started another civil war. In 31 B.C.E., Octavian defeated Antony and Cleopatra. At the age of 32, Octavian was the sole master of the Mediterranean world.

This signaled the end of the 500-year-old republic, as Octavian was no longer a boy, and the Senate was terrified of his power. Octavian was given the title of Augustus, meaning "exalted one."

Augustus reigned from 31 B.C.E. to 14 C.E. He ushered in a new age: the age of Imperial Rome and Pax Romana, meaning "Roman peace." The government that Octavian had set up ushered in the Augustan Principate, which carried Rome for the next 200 years into its Golden Age of governing and culture.

Pax Romana

Octavian, now named Augustus, added some reforms aimed at helping Rome recover from their civil wars. In doing so, he actually destroyed the foundation for a stable government.

1. He left the Senate in place, but he also created an efficient, well-trained civil service program. Now, men of ability, regardless of social class, had access to high-level jobs in the government.
2. He ordered a census to get the population of the Roman Empire, so he would know how taxes should be levied on the people.
3. He cemented ties with the provinces by building smaller versions of Rome. This was the "make the world Rome" policy. Roman technology and culture were followed throughout the empire.
4. Augustus created a postal service and issued a new currency with his picture on it. Everyone in the empire could use only this new type of currency, making trade more efficient and easier throughout his new empire.
5. Augustus also kept up his uncle Caesar's idea of putting the people to work. Unemployed people and soldiers began to build a series of all-weather roads connecting Rome with the other parts of the empire.

Global Connections

Roman men who wanted to serve in the Senate had to take an exam. At the same time in Han Dynasty China, the men who wanted to serve in the Han Dynasty government had to pass a rigorous exam.

The government developed by Augustus allowed Rome to reach the pinnacle of its power and allowed it to function well for more than 200 years. Eventually, Augustus created a plan for who would replace him upon his death. Up to this point in Roman history, no one had passed on the title of emperor from father to son, but Augustus made this the law. Augustus began sharing power with his son, Tiberius. He brought Tiberius to business meetings and governing meetings and showed him how to run the government. As Tiberius became more active in politics, Augustus pulled back, farther and farther into the background. When Augustus died in 14 C.E., there was a smooth transition of power, and Tiberius officially declared that rule of the Roman Empire was hereditary.

Pax Romana allowed Rome to achieve great feats and make contributions to the modern world. Pax Romana ended in 180 C.E. during the reign of Marcus Aurelius. During Pax Romana, there was peace, order, and unity within the empire that stretched from the Euphrates River in the Middle East to modern-day England. Roman legions protected the borders, and road networks broadened and connected with the Silk Road from China. During Pax Romana, the Roman people thought that every day was better than the one before.

Roman Achievements During the Age of Augustus

During the age of Augustus, Rome pursued the "make the world Rome" policy. Small versions of Roman cities and towns were built throughout the empire. These new citizens were afforded the same rights and privileges as if they were living in Rome. This enabled the emperor to enlist the upper classes in governing the provinces. These provinces could self-rule until they became too efficient or profitable, and then the emperors would assimilate them into their central administration as a new source of revenue. It was during this time that Augustus tried to beautify Rome and glorify his reign. Rome borrowed a lot of its culture from Greece and the Hellenistic civilization created by Alexander the Great.

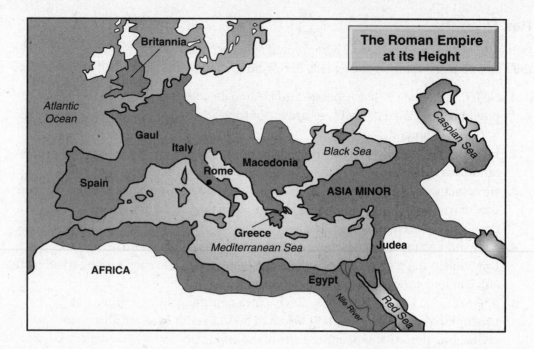

The Roman Empire at its Height

Art and Architecture

The Romans felt they could never equal or further the idealistic art and simplistic beauty of Greek art, so Roman art was more realistic. It showed the imperfection of humanity: a scar, a vein, a person's fat or lack thereof.

Whereas Greek architecture aimed for a simple elegance, Roman architecture aimed to show off Rome's power. Roman architecture emphasized grandeur in everything that was built. Aqueducts were monuments of the power of Rome, an empire spanning three continents. To build these structures, the Romans improved and perfected the use of the arch to build bridges and aqueducts that spanned rivers and canyons.

The Romans invented concrete, allowing them to build stable structures. Plumbing was so advanced that there was hot and cold running water in some patrician homes. Most patrician houses also had an elaborate sewer system to carry waste far underground and away from the cities. The Romans also specialized in roads, extending out from Rome like spokes on a wheel. The roads heralded in an age of quick communication, trade, and troop movements throughout the empire.

WEAKENING AND COLLAPSE OF THE EMPIRE

By the second century C.E., Romans had enjoyed a life of luxury. Unfortunately, greed and corruption began to erode traditional Roman values. No one wanted to work jobs that, at one time, were highly sought after and valued as good for the community. Emperors had to force unwilling members of the upper classes to hold public office and take governmental jobs, but people had made so much money off of slave labor that they did not want to work anymore. The emperors held the patricians responsible for the shortages in governmental revenue. At this time in history, the city of Rome had a sustained population of over one million people. It took a lot of money and resources to run the city and the bureaucracy.

Emperor Trajan saw that Rome was beginning to have trouble. Rome existed off the tribute that came from its conquered territories, and the people were beginning to run out of resources. In order to gain more tribute, Trajan needed to conquer more territory. He expanded the empire to its greatest size during his reign from 98 C.E. to 117 C.E. as he pushed over the mighty Danube River that bisects Europe. Unfortunately, he overextended the empire and upset a large group of new barbarians in the process.

Another problem was too much prosperity. By the end of the Second Triumvirate, Rome had received a massive inflow of wealth from Egypt and Middle Eastern spice trade routes. Near 150 C.E., the revenue slowly began to taper off. Once again, people began to lose their jobs and homes. To keep the people happy, emperors resorted to entertaining them at the Coliseum and the Circus Maximus. The emperors would throw bread to the people in the Coliseum to keep them happy. However, to pay for all this free entertainment, there was an increasing need for money. The easiest way to get it was to simply print it! This has happened time and time again throughout history. When governments need more money and think that printing more will solve their problems, it causes massive inflation. Prices for normal products skyrocket, and the people are trapped in the middle.

All of these events signaled the beginning of the end for ancient Rome, which began a very long, but steady, irrevocable decline until Rome finally collapsed in 476 C.E.

Emperors—Good and Bad

Even though some of Julius and Augustus Caesar's successors were strong, able rulers, others were more incompetent. They did terrible damage to Rome; nevertheless, the foundation laid by Augustus was able to break the dynastic cycle for a time (see Chapter 3).

The most famous terrible Roman emperor is Caligula. Caligula came to power in 37 C.E. after his mother poisoned Caligula's father to make sure the crown did not go to the son that Caligula's father had with his new wife. Caligula's mother believed that her son would allow her to rule with him. She was very quickly disappointed as Caligula had his entire family killed so they would not be rivals for his power. He then shocked and embarrassed everyone by appointing his horse as a consul of Rome. Caligula would talk to it and ask it questions when making decisions. Not surprisingly, he was quickly assassinated.

Another bad emperor was Nero. Ruling from 54 C.E. to 68 C.E., Nero had some strange habits. At night for fun, he liked to dress as a peasant and then beat up and rob poor Romans. He viciously persecuted the new growing movement of Christianity and burned down part of the city where they worshipped. He considered himself a great actor, singer, and musician, and he would interrupt performances by taking the lead role, killing anyone who protested.

Eventually, a man named Vespasian, a nonaristocrat, emerged from this chaos and started a new dynasty: the Flavian dynasty, which ruled from 69 C.E. to 79 C.E. In order to control and entertain the mobs of people, Vespasian started construction of the famous Coliseum in ancient Rome.

Emperor Hadrian ruled from 117 C.E. to 138 C.E. and made the first set of laws designed to unite the entire empire. He attempted to build a new miniature "Great Wall of China" around the whole of the Roman Empire.

Effects of Christianity

There was a new religion growing in a remote Roman province that the emperors and government blamed for the worsening situation in Rome: the concept of Christianity.

The messages of Christianity were appealing to the poor people of Rome, even though they were heavily persecuted if they believed in Jesus of Nazareth as the Son of God. The

FUN FACT

Picture the Roman Empire as a balloon. As Trajan conquered more and more territory, he overinflated the Roman balloon. What happens to a balloon that is overinflated? It pops!

teachings of Jesus are written down in four books called the Gospels. They serve as a reminder that Jesus's purpose was to free humanity, and for Christians, the resurrection of Jesus was proof of these teachings.

Whether people believe in Jesus as a religious entity or not, Jesus was a historical character who died circa 32–35 C.E. He had a heavy influence on what happened in ancient Rome. With his new message to abandon sin and worldly concerns, plus the idea that love, charity, humility, and a belief in him promised a better life, Jesus won a great following among the poor. This popularity scared the upper classes and the established religious structure in Jerusalem, and the Christians began to be seen as revolutionaries that had to be stopped.

PAUL OF TARSUS

Paul of Tarsus was a Roman citizen and a zealous member of a Jewish sect known as the Pharisees. The Pharisees strictly adhered to Jewish law, and Paul was famous as a relentless persecutor of Christians.

One day on the way to Damascus, Paul converted to Christianity circa 36 C.E. He became a great missionary for Christianity as he preached the word of Jesus to the Gentiles (non-Hebrew people) around the Mediterranean. Paul was able to convert huge numbers of people to Christianity.

As hard as the Roman government tried to get rid of the Christians, their numbers grew. In 200 C.E., Christians began to organize the creation of bishops, who were overseers of Christian groups around the Roman Empire. As the number of Christians grew, these bishops were elected to lead by their congregation or group of followers. Their authority became almost monarchical. It was their job to communicate with other Christian groups to prevent splintering. In order to stay unified, they formed councils to discuss their orthodoxy (what you believe). This was necessary because pagan Rome did not trust the early Christians. Their refusal to worship the emperor was considered treason, and it was a crime to become a Christian.

This persecution had a positive effect for the early church as it weeded out the weak from the faithful. A hardened core of Christians remained, and no matter what was done to them, they would not break. They stayed unified. This led to the creation of Catholicism and the Canon law. In the Christian religion, Canon law is comprised of the Old Testament, the four Gospels, and the writings of Paul. Throughout the persecution of the Christians, Rome itself had become the center of the Christian religion. The two main apostles of Christianity—Paul and Peter—were both martyred in Rome.

For years, Rome focused on trying to get rid of the Christians. However, at the start of the third century C.E., Rome was about to experience many other problems from outside their borders. They were so focused internally that they did not notice the other problems that were coming.

Military Difficulties

The pressure on Rome's borders became massive, wearing down the empire. In China, the Han Dynasty had gone on a massive campaign against the Mongols. As they drove the Mongols out of China, they were so relentless in their pursuit that the Mongols turned westward, moving across Asia and into Europe. The Mongols pushed other barbarian groups—like the Huns, the Visigoths, and the Vandals—in front of them like a snowplow, pushing them directly toward the Roman Empire.

The Romans spread themselves out to defend the empire, but there was simply too much borderland to cover. It was through one of these weak points that the German barbarians broke through into the Roman Empire in 350 C.E. The German barbarians were enticed by the technology and wealth of Roman border towns, and they followed the many roads that eventually led them to Rome.

Economic Difficulties

Economic difficulties also contributed to the collapse of Rome. Inflation reached massive proportions. In order to get soldiers into the army, their pay was doubled, leading to an increase in taxes to pay them. To move more men into the army quickly, their training was cut short. Roman discipline had become extremely lax, and the army was just not as good as it had once been.

The barbarian attacks also reduced agricultural production because imports coming in as tribute from the conquered areas were cut off. This also forced a stoppage on exports due to the increased threat of piracy. After sustaining itself for years off of tribute, Rome was beginning to crumble.

Along with everything else, there was the debasement of coins, the governmental currency of the emperor. The government began to confiscate property, which could no longer be used for private business. Many of the people were living day to day, hand to mouth.

Social Difficulties

The once-proud Senate—the leaders of the Roman community—was decimated by economic instability and insane emperors. Rome suffered enormous losses when it lost the Senate. Society was now being driven by military men who liked organization and hierarchy. These generals began to limit the upward social mobility of people, giving them little chance to better themselves. All freedom and private initiatives were beginning to slip away. Merchants were the only ones surviving, as they had to try to fill the economic needs of the state.

Civil Difficulties

From 268 C.E. to 275 C.E., several rebellions forced the emperors to fortify and build walls around Rome and their palaces to protect themselves. They brought their best troops home to defend the city, which left poor-quality soldiers trying to stop invasions from increasing hordes of barbarians.

In 50 years, there were 25 different emperors. This instability demonstrated four distinct problems that the empire needed to face.

1. Rome had lost its authority. When Caesar was emperor, Rome was cutting off the right hands of defeated warriors and salting the earth of cities like Carthage. People were no longer afraid of Rome. Rome was seen as old and weak.
2. Rampant corruption had weakened the civil service beyond the point of inefficiency. People were looking out only for themselves. They were selfish and greedy. They did not worry about the greater empire but instead just took what they could get.
3. The trade routes were disrupted from the increasing wars with barbarians. There was no more tribute or money coming into the Roman treasury.
4. Printing more money had devalued Roman currency to the point of worthlessness.

Diocletian

In 284 C.E., a general named Diocletian became emperor. He instituted several harsh laws meant to strengthen the Roman Empire.

1. He divided the empire in half. He moved the government to the eastern city of Byzantium (modern-day Istanbul, Turkey), and Diocletian ruled from there.
2. Diocletian reorganized the civil service along the lines of Julius Caesar and made officers directly responsible to him in the chain of command.
3. He trained a new division in the army, the cavalry. Meant to instill pride, the cavalry was full of true Romans, sitting high up on their horses. It gave the army and the people a feeling of prestige and honor.
4. In order to curb the rampant inflation, he set pricing limits. Every item was given a maximum cost not to be exceeded anywhere throughout the empire until inflation was curbed.
5. Until the empire was stabilized, people had to continue in their current occupations.

> **GLOBAL CONNECTIONS**
>
> Much the same thing occurred in Rome as occurred in China when Chairman Mao Tse-tung became the Communist leader of China. The wealthy Romans fled from the collapsing economy in Rome, while many affluent Chinese citizens and scholars fled to Hong Kong and Taiwan to escape the harsh rules of Communism.

These laws worked well while Diocletian was alive, and many wealthy patricians and merchants moved from Rome eastward to the city of Byzantium, bringing their wealth with them. Unfortunately, after his death, many of Diocletian's reforms were disbanded as his subordinates fought for the throne.

Constantine

In 312 C.E., Emperor Constantine briefly halted the fall of the empire as he reconnected and united both halves of the empire. However, the official capital of the empire was no longer the city of Rome. He chose Byzantium, which he renamed Constantinople. He did this because Constantinople was close to the commercial centers of the Middle Eastern trade routes, the Silk Road from China, and the Spice Road from India. Constantinople was also very defensible as it could only be attacked from one direction. Constantine reinstated Diocletian's reforms, and, once again, the collapse was slowed, but it was not stopped.

Collapse of the Empire

After the death of Constantine in 337 C.E., the empire was again split in half. This time, it was due to differences in religion.

The Eastern half of the empire was flourishing, with its defensible borders, good rulers, and economic prosperity. The Western half of the empire collapsed. With the ever-advancing hordes of barbarians, the few wealthy patricians left in Rome moved into the heartlands of Europe. They built small, self-sufficient fortresses, where they tried to stay out of sight so they would not be captured.

Christians were once again blamed for the collapse of Rome and were persecuted for the disasters that befell Rome. However, Christianity offered the belief in an all-powerful, all-knowing God who kept believers safe and prosperous in this world and in the next. The movement gained even more followers. This was key as the church will become the sole governing institution in Western Europe after the fall of the Roman Empire, which officially collapsed in 484 C.E.

INDIA DURING THE ROMAN EMPIRE

In India, the Gupta Dynasty lasted from 320 C.E. to 550 C.E. During this time, India enjoyed a Golden Age where they created and organized a strong central government that ensured peace and prosperity. Their reign was looser than that of Rome as individual villages controlled themselves. City governments were elected by merchants and artisans.

During the Gupta Dynasty, there were tremendous gains and advances in learning as students were educated in religious schools. In Hindu and Buddhist schools, learning was not limited to just religion. Students were taught mathematics, medicine, literature, and concepts of physics. They were taught to be multilingual, speaking different languages. Gupta mathematicians devised a simple numbering system, which today is called the Arabic numerical system. It was Arabs who carried the numbering system from India to the Middle East and eventually to Europe. Indian mathematicians came up with the concept of the zero, and they developed the decimal system based on the number ten, which is used today.

Indian physicians used herbs and other remedies to treat illnesses, and surgeons became so skilled, they could set bones and do simple plastic surgery. They began vaccinating people against smallpox, which was more than 1000 years earlier than when it was done in Europe.

While the Roman Empire was dominating the Mediterranean world, the Gupta Dynasty of India was doing many great things. This time period marked the growth of Hinduism, including the very complex rules of the caste system from Chapter 3, which India is still working within to this very day. The caste system was integrated into Indian life to ensure spiritual purity.

800 B.C.E.	Small villages
770 B.C.E.	Romulus and Remus found Rome.
500 B.C.E.	• Etruscan and Greeks are defeated.
	• Roman Republic is formed.
494 B.C.E.	Creation of Tribunes
450 B.C.E.	Twelve Tables of Law
270 B.C.E.	Rome conquers all of Italy.
264 B.C.E.	Punic Wars with Carthage start.
218 B.C.E.	Hannibal invades.
202 B.C.E.	Carthage is defeated.
146 B.C.E.	Carthage is destroyed.
133 B.C.E.	• Roman Empire/*Mare Nostrum*
	• Tiberius Gracchus
123 B.C.E.	Gaius Gracchus
53 B.C.E.	First Triumvirate
48–44 B.C.E.	Caesar's reforms
31 B.C.E.	• Octavian Augustus
	• End of the Republic
	• Beginning of Pax Romana
32 C.E.	Christianity begins.
106 C.E.	Emperor Trajan
138 C.E.	Hadrian
180 C.E.	• Marcus Aurelius
	• End of Pax Romana
200 C.E.	Long decline begins.
284 C.E.	Diocletian moves to Byzantium.
312 C.E.	• Constantine reunites the empire.
	• Christianity is the main religion.
350 C.E.	Huns arrive when they are displaced from Asia by the Mongols.
378 C.E.	Visigoths
476 C.E.	The fall of Rome

GLOBAL CONNECTIONS

Mesoamerica

500 B.C.E.—City-state of Monte Albán

200 B.C.E.—Pyramid of the Sun in Teotihuacan

50 C.E.—Natchez Native Americans in North America

300 C.E.—Mayan civilization

Africa

900 B.C.E.—Great Zimbabwe

750 B.C.E.—Kingdom of Nubia

350 C.E.—Kingdom of Axum

China

206 B.C.E.—Han Dynasty begins

100 C.E.—Buddhism arrives in China

220 C.E.—Han Dynasty collapses

Mesopotamia

612 B.C.E.—Nebuchadnezzar, King of Babylonia

522 B.C.E.—King Darius leads Persia

Han China

6

THE HAN DYNASTY (206 B.C.E.–220 C.E.)

The Han Dynasty of China was an exciting dynasty that developed parallel to the great culture of the ancient Roman Empire. The Han Dynasty was one of the golden ages of China in terms of culture and advancement. The previous dynasty, the Ch'in, had the strong, dominant Emperor Shi Huang Di. After the Ch'in collapsed, a new leader, Liu Bang, took the title Emperor Gaozu and set about restoring justice to the empire.

The internal wars that plagued China after the collapse of the Ch'in Dynasty ended with China's unification as Gaozu assumed the title and claimed the Mandate of Heaven. Gaozu was a plebeian, a peasant, which the people saw as proof that heaven wanted somebody to be emperor who could bring unity to China.

For the first 60 years of the Han Dynasty (during the top of the dynastic cycle), Gaozu and his immediate successors were very careful in how they consolidated their power. They moved slowly but steadily. They made the intentional decision to stay away from any action that reminded people of the Ch'in Dynasty. Part of the Ch'in Dynasty's problem was that things changed very rapidly, almost overnight in some cases. The Han Dynasty emperors made incremental changes, so people could adjust to each change before the implementation of something else new.

The Han Dynasty scaled back severe punishments for crimes. They put resources into the economy, which replenished itself. They were very smart by collecting large reserves of cash.

The Ch'in Dynasty was successful in unifying parts of China, building of the Great Wall, building road systems, and digging canals, but all of this took a lot of money, so the people were heavily taxed. When the Han Dynasty wanted to continue construction on the Great Wall, it used its large reserves of cash to pay for the project upfront so another heavy tax burden would not be put on the peasants.

FUN FACT

Han Wu Ti is what I call a Jedi Emperor. He was able to accurately predict the distant future and how his actions would reciprocate throughout time to aid his people.

The Reign of Han Wu Ti

Han Wu Ti was the next emperor of the Han Dynasty, and it was named after him. He was 16 years old when he came to power in 141 B.C.E., and he reigned for 54 years. Han Wu Ti brought stability to China. He also built on the prosperity of his predecessors. He expanded China, building a canal linking the Yellow River to the capital at Xian. This canal allowed a highway to be built that linked to large economic regions of the northern part of China.

Ever-Level Granaries

Han Wu Ti's rule resulted in a policy known as "the ever-level granaries." Han Wu Ti built large silos, or granaries, that were to be filled with surpluses from bumper crops. The silos were rotated every so often to keep the food fresh and stable. Now, in times of famine, flood, or other scarcity, the Chinese people had enough food to eat.

To pay for ever-level granaries, taxes needed to be collected. Merchants were heavily taxed to collect the needed funding. Merchants were low on the social scale as they were seen as people who made money on other people's labor, so they were required to pay the most taxes.

Another way that Han Wu Ti gained money was by reestablishing government-run monopolies so he could regulate them. He chose businesses that made products the people needed the most: copper, salt, iron, and liquor. The people used copper for tools and cooking. Salt was used to preserve food throughout the ancient world. Iron was used to build farming tools and implements. Han Wu Ti also wanted to control the iron so that the people did not have iron to build weapons. Last but not least was liquor, which was not a necessity but was highly coveted by the people. The Ch'in Dynasty actually started these monopolies, and the reestablishment of them by Han Wu Ti led to a great debate among royal advisers.

SALT AND IRON DEBATES

The Salt and Iron Debates took place in 81 B.C.E. They were between legalistic ministers, who served during the Ch'in Dynasty, and Confucian scholars, who became the hallmark of the Han Dynasty.

Legalists said the Chinese government should keep profits from the sale of salt, iron, copper, and liquor products, and it was natural for the government to make money off of these. The Confucians countered, saying these four items should be left in private hands to keep the moral purity of government officials. Money will corrupt them, Confucian scholars said, and by running this governmental monopoly, the government was no better than a merchant (who was seen as a low-class citizen). Confucian scholars were able to claim victory.

These debates coincided with the period of Roman expansion, and the Han Dynasty was very similar to the Pax Romana seen in Rome.

Expansion

Han Wu Ti aggressively expanded Chinese borders, and he was determined that the Han Dynasty would represent the best of all strong Chinese dynasties. He expanded southward to Vietnam and eastward into the Koreas. On the northern border, he also fought the Hsiung-nu Mongols from the Gobi Desert starting in 133 B.C.E. Han Wu Ti hired southern barbarians as mercenaries to fight for control of their northern cousins. To cement relationships, he became allies with some of these southern barbarians and allowed them to trade with Chinese merchants. To some, he gave some royal title, and he even sent them Chinese brides in order to cement relationships.

Han Wu Ti also relocated 100,000 trained Chinese soldiers to live on the Chinese steppes, destroying Mongol power in the southern part of the Gobi Desert. His plan was to have a defensive force to block the path of the Mongols. If they were going to attack, they would have to go through the Chinese army.

Global Connections

The Romans also hired southern Germanic barbarians to fight as mercenaries against northern German tribes.

Han Wu Ti then relocated 700,000 Chinese civilians to the steppes, building a city north of the Great Wall to show off Chinese cultural achievements. Now, he had 800,000 people—a major force of Chinese—who worked together to destroy the Mongol power base. The eventual defeat of the Mongols in 89 C.E. allowed people to safely travel along the Great Wall. The

Silk Road was extended to the Koreas, past the Jade Gate of western China, and all the way to ancient Rome. By the time the Han Dynasty was finished, China had an empire about the size of the continental United States.

Han Government

The Han Dynasty was brilliant in their government. They kept most of the framework of the Ch'in central bureaucracy. It was the same governmental structure, just under a different name.

One of the things that made the Han Dynasty so successful over a long period of time was that governing officials were organized by grade. Scholars were sent to Confucian schools, and the men had to take a civil service test. Their grades on this test determined where they worked. An average grade placed a worker in a Chinese village. An above-average grade would place a worker into a fairly large-sized city. The men with the top grades would work in a large metropolitan area or even advise the emperor.

The test score was not the only determining factor for governing officials. A man also had to be sponsored or recommended by another governing official. This was extremely important because if a man was sponsored and failed at his job, not only would the new worker lose his job but so would the worker who sponsored him. This was what allowed the Han Dynasty to last for 400 years. The government survived even during periods when there were bad or weak emperors because the men in the government were well trained and well selected.

Confucian Officials

About 120,000 Confucian scholars became government officials during the Han Dynasty, which had about 60 million people at this time in history. Confucian officials had justified the Mandate of Heaven so it made them useful. There was a large amount of record keeping necessary in the government, so the Confucian classics became the standard for education in Han China. The philosophy was that Confucian education would create moral men who would be good role models and, therefore, good officials. They would be honest and trustworthy, and they would do the right thing, not the popular thing (see Chapter 3). As a result, a Confucian government would be led by virtuous and talented men who stayed away from the problems that plagued other dynasties in China.

Han Governmental Functions

Han Wu Ti was a dominant, hands-on emperor. He liked to know everything that was going on, so his governmental bureaucracies were small and limited in function. The government had five main duties.

1. Keeping a current census to aid in the collection of taxes. With accurate census figures, the government knew which areas were consuming the most resources. The more resources the area consumed, the more taxes that area paid. This process allowed the flexibility to adjust taxes in times of famine or scarcity.
2. Administering laws. Having laws that were uniform, codified, and applied to everyone was a priority. Punishment was fairly and quickly carried out. The Chinese people knew what was right, what was wrong, and the punishments.

3. Training military forces. Han Wu Ti was a warrior emperor, so he wanted to know everything about his military: the current strength of the army, the location of his army, the training of soldiers, and any external threats to China.

4. Managing public works projects. The government made sure irrigation canals were working, crops were being watered, and trading canals and roads were maintained and repaired.

5. Maintaining the royal household. Keeping the palace and empire running required a whole governmental bureaucracy all by itself. Outlying districts or provinces were left in the hands of local nobles who handled local problems. The Chinese empire was too big for Han Wu Ti to be involved in the nitty-gritty details of government, so giving day-to-day control to provincial nobles was one of the things that made Han Wu Ti successful. He and his government maintained the royal household in order to focus on the country of China as a whole.

Cultural Achievements and Advances

The Han Dynasty was one of the golden ages of China. Many technological advancements were made at this time. The Han developed a way to make long-lasting, durable paper from the pulp of wood, aiding in writing and record keeping. To further grow water travel, they developed the stern-post ship rudder, which gave them greater steering control. They invented stirrups for balance and stability on a horse and helped develop suspension bridges to cross vast spans.

Medically, the Han were highly advanced. They developed herbal remedies for sicknesses, and they began to develop anesthesia to relieve pain when treating illnesses and/or broken bones.

Their most valued achievement was the creation of silk. Silk was such a highly sought after substance that the method of silk making was to be kept a secret under threat of pain or death. Silk making brought China a lot of power and prestige.

After Han Wu Ti

Eventually, military expenses exceeded the tax revenues, so cutbacks were implemented in the military. Economic monopolies were loosened, and large landowners used their influence to avoid paying taxes. With this loss in governmental revenue, peasants had to shoulder the burden. Peasants revolted under an emperor named Wang Mang, while the Hsiung-nu Mongols invaded from north of the Gobi Desert, and the Yellow River flooded. Interestingly enough, as the Han Dynasty was experiencing this recession, Rome was experiencing the height of Pax Romana.

However, even with all of these problems, distant cousins of Han Wu Ti were able to revive the Han Dynasty for about 200 years more. From 8 B.C.E. to 220 C.E., these new emperors and their successors went back to the policies of Han Wu Ti. They organized a strong central government that had more laws and a fair economy with no governmental monopolies. These policies had an immediate impact as agricultural surpluses rebounded and the population exploded. All things considered, this second revival of the Han Dynasty was even better off than its predecessor.

Keeping true to Han Wu Ti's policies, military expansion began into South China and Southeast Asia. Some problems with the Hsuing-nu Mongols allowed the Chinese to cement alliances with other southern tribes. When the Chinese army defeated the Hsuing-nu in the

Gobi Desert in 89 C.E., the defeat had a reciprocal effect. Because the Han victory was so devastating to the Mongols, they began to migrate westward across the Chinese and Russian steppes. Acting like a snowplow, the Mongols pushed multiple barbarians into the Roman Empire: Attila the Hun, the Ostrogoths, and the Visigoths. A major cause of the fall of the Roman Empire in 476 C.E. was the defeat of the Mongols on the other end of Eurasia by the Han Dynasty.

The expansion of China allowed merchants to raise their social status as trading was encouraged. The great Silk Road advanced during this time, traveling more than 4,000 miles across China, Asia, the Fertile Crescent of Mesopotamia, Iran, Palestine, and all the way to ancient Rome. In exchange for silk, traders brought back ideas like Buddhism from India and products like glass from Rome.

The Silk Road also brought the Han Dynasty into contact with diseases for which the Chinese people had no immunity. Along the Silk Road, several viruses were spread: smallpox, measles, and the bubonic plague. Historians always make reference to the bubonic plague, also known as the Black Death, as decimating the European continent in the 14th century C.E.; however, it affected Asia as well, killing millions.

COLLAPSE OF THE HAN DYNASTY

When the Han Dynasty arrived at the bottom of the dynastic cycle, the fall was much quicker and more rapid than that of ancient Rome. However, other than the differences in length of time, the fall of China and the fall of Rome are extremely similar.

1. Large Chinese landowners became more and more independent due to the large physical distance between them and the Han rulers. China had gotten so big that the emperors could not get out and see their people anymore.
2. Wealthy Chinese landowners built their own private armies, forcing smaller farmers to serve the wealthy. It was very similar to enslavement in the United States or serfdom of Europe.
3. Chinese landowners used their power and influence to avoid paying taxes, placing the burden on the working class. This caused a mass migration of poor Chinese to flee southward. The few remaining landowners ended up paying extreme monetary and labor taxes. This was also seen in Rome when the taxation fell heavily on the people.
4. By the mid-180s C.E., rebellions were breaking out. The Han Dynasty generals did exactly the same thing that Constantine and Diocletian did: They tried to quell the rebellions through violence.

In 220 C.E., the last Han emperor was overthrown after 400 years of great unity.

BUDDHISM

One of the positive aspects of the fall of the Han Dynasty was the spread of Buddhism from Central Asia into mainland China. Missionaries brought Buddhism to China along the Silk Road, and as the Han Dynasty began to crumble, Buddhism took root and spread rapidly.

TIMELINE REVIEW

206 B.C.E.	Han Dynasty begins with Emperor Gaozu.
141 B.C.E.	Han Wu Ti becomes emperor.
87 B.C.E.	Han Wu Ti dies.
81. B.C.E.	Salt and Iron Debates
23 C.E.	Wang Mang is killed.
100 C.E.	Buddhism makes it to China.
105 C.E.	Invention of paper
220 C.E.	Han Dynasty collapses.

GLOBAL CONNECTIONS

Rome

146 B.C.E.—Carthage destroyed

31 B.C.E.—Pax Romana begins

32 C.E.—Christianity begins

180 C.E.—Pax Romana ends

Mesoamerica

220 B.C.E.—Pyramid of the Sun in Teotihuacan

100 C.E.—Moche in South America

Quick Quiz: Chapters 4–6

1. This ancient civilization was the city-state in ancient Greece that was written about in Homer's *The Odyssey*.

   A. Mycenaea
   B. Sparta
   C. Troy
   D. Minoa

2. Pisistratus, the ancient Greek leader of Athens, can be compared to which United States president?

   A. George Washington
   B. Franklin Roosevelt
   C. Abraham Lincoln
   D. Herbert Hoover

3. Why did the city-state of ancient Sparta need to become so militaristic in its nature?

   A. They were outnumbered 20:1 by their slaves.
   B. Their location close to the coast made them susceptible to attack.
   C. They were ostracized by the other Greek city-states.
   D. They had to guard their many valuable natural resources.

4. Under the statesman Pericles in Athens, what type of democracy was used where the outcome of a vote and your decision in that vote was known publicly and immediately?

   A. Representative democracy
   B. Direct democracy
   C. Republican democracy
   D. Indirect democracy

5. The ancient Greek playwrights developed the concept of a tragedy to prevent or warn the Athenians from having this negative trait in ancient Athens.

   A. Jealousy
   B. Hubris
   C. Arete
   D. Selfishness

6. What is the name of the college or library built by Alexander the Great in Egypt?

    A. Pharos lighthouse
    B. House of Muses
    C. Persopolis
    D. Thebes

7. By building a large army, which of the following individuals was able to unify northern India for the very first time?

    A. Chandragupta
    B. Ashoka
    C. Tamerlane
    D. King Maurya

8. Which event led to Ashoka's conversion to Buddhism?

    A. Witnessing 100,000 soldiers slain in battle
    B. The destruction caused by the flooding of the Indus River
    C. Siddhartha Guatama's conversion to becoming the Buddha
    D. The collapse of Shi Huang Di's Ch'in Dynasty

9. Which other empire existed simultaneously with India's Maurya empire that also facilitated a high level of cultural diffusion?

    A. Roman
    B. Han China
    C. Empire of Alexander the Great
    D. Athenian

10. Which office of the ancient Roman Republic is used as the model for office of the United States president?

    A. Patrician
    B. Censorate
    C. Plebeian
    D. Consul

11. Rome became a massive worldwide empire after defeating which of the following enemies?

    A. Carthage
    B. Ostrogoths
    C. King Phyrrus
    D. Ptolemy in Egypt

12. Which of the following is the term for a large land plantation owned by the wealthy aristocracy of ancient Rome?

    A. Latifundia
    B. Helot
    C. A benefice
    D. A parcel

13. This Roman leader enacted reforms that helped revive the corrupt and weakening Roman Empire?

    A. Marcus Aurelius
    B. Caligula
    C. Trajan
    D. Julius Caesar

14. This is the term that describes the 200 years of peace created by Augustus Caesar.

    A. Pax Romana
    B. Latifundia
    C. Veni-vidi-vici
    D. Princeps

15. This Roman emperor divided the empire in half in an effort to stabilize the weak government, economy, and empire.

    A. Constantine
    B. Trajan
    C. Diocletian
    D. Hadrian

16. During this dynasty's Golden Age in India (which occurred simultaneously with the growth of the Roman Empire), they made major advances in learning, where most people were multilingual, and developed the concept of the zero and using decimal points.

    A. Maurya
    B. Gupta
    C. Ashokan
    D. Aryan

17. What is the major difference between the reforms of the Han Dynasty and that of the Ch'in Dynasty in China?

    A. The Han made slow and incremental change, whereas the Ch'in tried to reform China rapidly.
    B. The Han followed the practices set by earlier dynasties, whereas the Ch'in followed the pattern set by the Shang Dynasty.
    C. The Ch'in did not make any radical reforms, whereas the Han tried to reform China totally from top to bottom.
    D. There was no major difference as they both followed similar patterns in different points of Chinese history.

18. Which Han emperor set the pattern of aggressively expanding China's borders?

    A. Kublai Khan
    B. Wang Mang
    C. Han Wu Ti
    D. Li Ssu

19. Which would be the biggest achievement of the Han Dynasty?

    A. Expanding its borders
    B. Setting up an efficient government
    C. Breaking the dynastic cycle
    D. Recovering many of the ancient texts of learning that were destroyed by the Ch'in Dynasty

20. In which area did the Han Dynasty create new technologies that allowed them to trade farther distances than ever before?

    A. Creating the compass and attaching the stern post rudder to ships
    B. Mapping the Silk Road
    C. Creating cultural diffusion with India
    D. Mapping the different constellations to understand the seasons to know when it was safe to travel

21. During the Han Dynasty, which religion became deeply integrated into Chinese society because of its entrance to China via the Silk Road?

    A. Shintoism
    B. Buddhism
    C. Jainism
    D. Confucianism

22. When the Mongols were conquered and driven out of their traditional homeland by the Han Dynasty, what effect did it have throughout the rest of Asia and Europe?

    A. It allowed further expansion of the Silk Road.
    B. It created an era of peace and safety.
    C. It forced the Mongols westward, resulting in the displacement of other barbarian groups, some of which were forced into ancient Rome, hastening its fall.
    D. As the Mongols migrated farther northward, they began to settle Scandinavia and would eventually become the warlike Vikings.

Quick Quiz Answers

1. A; **2.** B; **3.** A; **4.** B; **5.** B; **6.** B; **7.** A; **8.** A; **9.** C; **10.** D; **11.** A; **12.** A; **13.** D; **14.** A; **15.** C; **16.** B; **17.** A; **18.** C; **19.** D; **20.** A; **21.** B; **22.** C

100 B.C.E.–1598 C.E.

Korea and Japan

7

KOREA

During the Han Dynasty, the location of Korea played an important role in its development. The Korean Peninsula borrowed many of its cultural and technological achievements from China, their powerful neighbor, but kept the Korean language separate and unique. This allowed Korea to serve as a cultural bridge, linking China and Japan. Korea adapted and adopted Chinese traditions and then eventually passed them over to Japan.

Geography of Korea

The Korean geography, in some ways, is very similar to ancient Greece, with intersecting and continuous mountains and valleys, making it difficult to move around.

Three Kingdoms of Korea and Unification

Between 300 C.E. and 600 C.E., there were three separate kingdoms in Korea, each forged by their three powerful local rulers.

1. Koguryo—located in the northern portion of Korea
2. Paekche—located in the southwestern section of the country
3. Silla—located in eastern Korea

Despite having the same basic culture and the same language, these kingdoms often fought with each other.

Global Connections

The kingdoms in Korea developed after Rome fell, at the beginning of the Dark Ages in Europe.

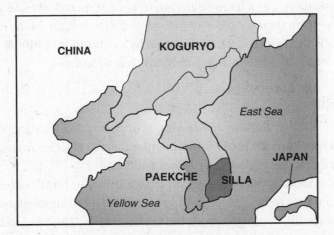

Unlike its Chinese neighbors, Korea only had three ruling dynasties. From 668 C.E. to 918 C.E., the Silla Kingdom became the sole ruling dynasty and unified Korea. Under the Silla, Korea became a tributary state of China.

The Koryo Dynasty ruled Korea from 918 C.E. to 1392 C.E. During this dynasty, the Korean people began to improve and perfect the ideas that were taken from China. They had very high standards and aimed for perfection. Buddhism also gained widespread acceptance in Korea during this period.

The Choson was the longest dynasty in Korea, lasting from 1392 to 1910. After driving the Mongols out of Korea and resisting Japanese expansion into their country, the Choson developed the Korean language of Hangul. Hangul was created to replace the Chinese characters that had been used in Korea until this point. The Choson were removed from power in 1910 during the Japanese occupation of Korea.

Throughout its history, Korea often looked at itself as the "younger brother" of China. However, the Korean Peninsula, especially the Paekche Kingdom, played an important role in the formation of Japan.

JAPAN

Geography of Japan

Japan is an *archipelago*, meaning "a series of islands." The Japanese geography was, and is today, unusually intense, resembling ancient Greece. It was very difficult to travel overland for the people who lived along the seashore; thus, they became expert sailors to travel up and down the Japanese archipelago.

Unification

Japan was in a state of constant power struggle at the same time Korea was dealing with its three-way power struggle.

Rich Japanese families ruled through a series of lesser aristocrats, who had authority over the people that answered to their king. The Yamato family was an ally of the Korean kingdom of Paekche, who gave them iron weapons. With this technology, they were able to bring unity to Japan in the mid-500s C.E. The Yamato family expanded its power by using its social status as a bridge of influence. The Paekche gave the Yamato family iron weapons, which increased its strength.

Also at this time, there was a large migration of Korean merchants and artisans to Japan. They had a monopoly on their goods, which increased their wealth. Many established themselves as aristocratic families. The Paekche served as a conduit for Chinese culture, bringing everything from Confucianism, writing, and Buddhism to Japan.

FUN FACT

Japanese gods are forces of nature. Examples of Japanese gods would have included natural, powerful, or unusual natural forces, like a large waterfall, a bizarrely growing tree, an oddly shaped rock, or a mountain.

Yamato Family

The Yamato family claimed the sun goddess as its ancestor. The sun goddess was the most powerful physical being seen in the sky, and the members of the Yamato family were seen as living gods, direct lineal descendants of the sun goddess.

What makes the Yamato family important is that it is the world's oldest single-running royal family still in power today. The current emperor of Japan, although not worshipped as a living god, can trace his ancestry back to the Yamato family. The Yamato family is the only single-family dynasty in world history!

Shintoism

The religion of Japan was polytheistic. Similar to many other cultures, they worshipped the forces of nature. *Shinto* means "the way of the gods."

UJI, OR "CLAN"

When it came to extended family, or uji (clan), Shintoism was important in Japan. Each uji had its own myth that centered on a force of nature, which the family claimed to be the original family ancestor. Today, Japanese families have elaborate genealogical trails that trace their descendants from this natural object.

The original family ancestor was very important when proclaiming political authority inside of Japan. By choosing a powerful force of nature, a Japanese family could set themselves apart from everyone else.

Shintoism was also important because of the location of Japan. Being part of an archipelago, they were isolated from most of the world for much of world history. Choosing something powerful—the sun or Mount Fuji—as a family's original ancestor gave the family political clout and power that lasted for thousands of years.

JAPAN'S RELATIONSHIP WITH KOREA AND CHINA

Because Japan was geographically isolated, they had experienced very little cultural diffusion. By the early 600s C.E., some Japanese students—mostly aristocratic young men—left Japan to study in China and Korea. They studied everything from art and architecture to science and language. When they returned to Japan, they assumed roles in the government so they could share their knowledge with the Yamato family. These men brought back knowledge of technology, legal systems, and Tang Dynasty governmental systems (see Chapter 14), and they explained it to the Yamato family.

The cultural diffusion that took place was an important part of Japanese history. Most of it took place during the Tang Dynasty of China from 618 C.E. to 907 C.E., and the Japanese had to decide whether or not they would adopt portions of higher Chinese civilization. Throughout its history, Japan was famous for adopting ideas from other people and making them fit better for Japan.

Problems with Chinese Philosophy

Japan experienced some growing pains during this time because it was hard for the Yamato court to understand some of the Chinese philosophy and how to match it up with Japanese culture.

The Yamato family borrowed the Tang Dynasty policy of giving loyal supporters rank and title, as well as surveying the land and taking a census to better gauge tax payments to the government. Although the Japanese loved many Chinese thoughts, philosophies, and inventions, they took only what they needed to fill an immediate and specific Japanese need.

Nara, Japan

In 710 C.E., the city of Nara was built. Nara was a carbon copy of the Tang Dynasty capital of Chang'an. The villagers lived in thatched-roofed, peasant shacks, while there was a beautiful capital center with pillared architecture and Buddhist-style pagodas. Nara was a brand-new modern Japanese city. However, the royal officials in Nara had more power than did their

Confucian contemporaries in China, and powerful Japanese clans, or ujis, were influencing the emperor. Every aristocrat in Nara who knew somebody important got a governmental job. With no external enemies to worry about, a lot of local government stayed in the hands of the local clans.

In China, there was very rarely tension between the emperor and his bureaucracy because of the civil service exam. Everyone knew that the workers in Chinese government deserved to be in power because of their scores on the civil service exam. However, in Japan, family ties meant more than grades. All aristocrats were educated, but the social status of the family and the ties the family had with other powerful families were most important. Unlike the great Confucian scholars of China, Japanese rulers in Nara were not based on merit but on family ties.

The End of Chinese Influence

The Japanese kept up the policy of selective borrowing from China until 839 C.E. Japan believed they had taken all that they needed from China and began to assimilate all of the Chinese information into the Japanese culture, which took about 350 years.

Heian, Japan

The Heian period was from 794 C.E. to 1185 C.E., and a new capital was built. Heian is the present-day city of Kyoto.

During this time, Japan experienced problems with rules that they borrowed from China. The census required a great deal of attention, and the land and tax system from China did not work as a form of taxation in Japan. It was a very complex system that required a lot of record keeping as land boundaries kept shifting. Also at this time, tax quotas could only be paid in foodstuff or local products. To make this system work in China, the Chinese government redistributed land every six years to ensure everyone could pay taxes. Unfortunately, in Japan, landholdings were hereditary instead of distributed, so the poor had no way to ever increase their landholdings or pay taxes. The landholding survey system as a way to collect taxes collapsed during the Heian Dynasty.

This brought about a big change in Japan as taxation was converted to a new system of payment. The new system ushered in Japanese feudalism. Paying taxes with foodstuffs or other monetary payment was very hard for the smaller landowners and the poor. Therefore, the powerful, rich nobles created free estates, or manors. Free, independent farmers began to sell their land and give their service to these large landowners so they would not have to pay taxes. The already-rich landowner had plenty of means to pay taxes, but for the small landowners, it was cheaper to serve as a serf on a manor than to pay taxes. The rich became richer, and the poor worked as serfs to the manor.

JAPANESE FEUDALISM (790–1800s C.E.)

Feudal society in Japan was a mirror image of the European feudal society of the 7th through 11th centuries, with some small changes in rank and title.

1. The emperor held the highest rank in society. The emperor could also be a figurehead, giving the executive authority to his second in command.
2. The shogun was the chief military officer who served as the actual ruler when the emperor served as a figurehead.

3. The daimyo was a large landowner. The land of the daimyo was ruled by samurai warriors.

4. Samurai warriors were loyal to the daimyo, and they clearly understood that they were underneath the emperor, shogun, and daimyo.

5. The peasants represented the remaining 75 percent of the population and included everyone from artisans, merchants, peasants, and day laborers.

Global Connections

In European terms, a daimyo was comparable to a lord, who was a large landowner.

This is how Japan was governed from 790 C.E. to 1185 C.E.

In the early Heian Dynasty, the army changed from a system of mandatory drafting. They switched to a professional horse-mounted cavalry made up of official government troops who did not have to pay taxes in return for their military service. The cavalry men were called "samurai," meaning "one who serves."

Much like knights in Europe, it was very expensive to be a samurai. A samurai had to own his own horse, procure his weapons and armor, as well as train for long periods of time. However, by 900 C.E., samurai training paid off for the Heian Dynasty. Military factions began to form throughout Japan whenever a regional governor did not like the required tax amount. A refusal to pay taxes was the same as rebelling against the emperor, so the samurai were sent to control the rebellions and swiftly put them down.

Late Heian Government

By the late Heian period, the elaborate bureaucracy and ideas that were brought to Japan from China were no longer working, so government functions were scaled down to three main ministries.

1. The auditors. They were governors who rotated periodically. They reported on monetary accounts and were responsible for tax collection.

2. The archivists. They processed and recorded all laws. They could also carry out the executive function of the court of the emperor.

3. The police commissioners. They enforced laws and made sure there was law and order in and around the capital. They became military officers as well.

All of these offices were controlled by the emperor and his court.

Fujiwara Family

In feudal Japan, powerful families could exert influence over the emperor. One of the most famous was the Fujiwara family. They knew they could never become the emperor, but from 858 C.E. to 1156 C.E., they were dominant players at court. They succeeded in marrying their young daughters to Yamato sons as a way to control and gain a lock on all-important governmental posts. Eventually, the Fujiwara family lost much of their power as the young Yamato emperor Shirakawa and other noble families began to get angry at Fujiwara control.

GLOBAL CONNECTIONS

Emperor Shirakawa reasserted imperial control at a very young age, but at age 33, he stepped back. He remained involved in the background as a retired emperor, much like Augustus Caesar did in ancient Rome, so he could help his successor.

JAPANESE LITERATURE

Chinese influence can be seen in Japanese literature, especially poetry, which always included the strong connection to nature. Since Japan did not have its own writing system, they had borrowed the Chinese system. Because the spoken Japanese language contained words and expressions that did not exist in the Chinese writing system, they needed to create their own.

In 951 C.E., Empress Amida wanted to read poems in Japanese, so she had scholars invent a new writing system called the Kana. This allowed the most important cultural flowering of the Heian Dynasty.

Japanese Women and Literature

Even though women were very repressed in Japanese society, it was the empress who came up with the Japanese written language. The main authors of much of Japanese literature during the Heian Dynasty were women. *The Pillow Book*, written by Sei Shonagon in 1002 C.E., showed a god who described court life in a satirical fashion so as not to get trouble. *The Tale of Genji*, written by Lady Murasaki Shikibu circa 1021 C.E., was the first Japanese novel. It was the life story of the main character, Genji, and talked about the successes, failures, loves, and sorrows throughout his life.

Feudalism Becomes Entrenched

By 1185 C.E., there was a change from governmental rule by a civilian aristocracy to that of a dominant military society where there was no influence of Chinese government. This was implemented by the shogun, the chief military official of the emperor. The shogun held the executive authority in the government and was tired of Chinese influence and weak emperors. All of the shoguns changed society and governmental organization.

Minamoto Yoritomo

Minamoto Yoritomo became the first official shogun of Japan in 1192 C.E. He won total control over Japan when he put down multiple rebellions as a samurai. He was so powerful that samurai from all over Japan wanted to become his samurai. Since his leadership was very much based on his military experience, Yoritomo did not want to fall to the corruption in the lavish Kyoto court, so he moved his capital to a place called Kamakura, where he set up a new government called bakufu. *Bakufu* meant "tent government." In simple terms, the capital was wherever the shogun pitched his tent.

Global Connections

Much like Julius Caesar, Yoritomo sent his subordinate military officers out to govern his provinces.

Minamoto Yoritomo set up three offices in his new military government to streamline the chain of command:

1. An office that handled the affairs and responsibilities of samurai
2. An office that carried out his laws
3. An office that organized the legal bureaucracy to hear arguments and solve problems

Even though Yoritomo implemented military authority over national problems, it was the emperor's court that still ruled for all provinces. The Japanese people still thought of the emperor as the head of Japan. However, in 1192 C.E. when Yoritomo received the title of shogun, he handled large problems while local problems were left in the hands of the nobles. When Yoritomo died in 1199 C.E., the policies that he set forth became institutionalized, and things ran well in Japan for an extended period of time.

Mongol Invasions

In 1266 C.E., Kublai Khan, emperor of China, demanded Japanese surrender. Kublai Khan had expanded his Mongol Empire to the north, south, and west of China, and the only direction left to conquer was east toward Japan. Japan refused. In 1274 C.E., Kublai Khan sent troops to conquer Japan. If his troops had landed in Japan, the Japanese would have been absorbed into the Chinese empire. However, a kamikaze—a divine wind—blew up on the Sea of Japan and sunk Kublai Khan's invasion fleet. In 1281 C.E., Kublai Khan tried again, sending a larger invasion force this time. But once again, a hurricane blew up on the Sea of Japan, sinking much of the fleet. It was at this point in Japanese history that they began to believe that they were a most-favored nation and that the gods were blessing them.

Ashikaga Era (1338–1573 C.E.)

In 1331 C.E., as Europe began to enjoy the Renaissance, Japan began to experience problems. The land plots of the daimyo and samurai were getting smaller and smaller, meaning the samurai were getting progressively poorer. At this time, the Japanese emperor led a revolt against his own shogun as he felt he should be in charge. A samurai named Ashikaga was sent by the shogun to end the rebellion in 1338 C.E. Instead, he joined the emperor as he wished to restore order to Japan with simple government offices. Ashikaga used the same three offices originally formed by Yoritomo in 1192 C.E.

At this point, Japanese history becomes cyclical. Japan will stabilize, reach a high point, and as it begins to fall apart, it will return to the same three offices or ministries to repair and reorganize itself once again.

1. An office for dealing with affairs of the samurai
2. An office for land records and legal record keeping
3. An office with a judicial board to settle disputes

As the new shogun, Ashikaga filled these offices with his most trusted vassals and daimyo. He gave them the power to set tax limits as well as have military and judicial authority in their domains.

Ashikaga also changed the economy. Skilled artisans were no longer required to produce their best products for the emperor and his court officials. They were able to sell them on a large scale in an open market. Some samurai families, like the Hondas and the Toyotas, had skilled artisans working for them. This new policy allowed them to become not only powerful military families but powerful economic families as well.

The Dark Ages of Japan (1603–1853 C.E.)

This is how Japan maintained itself for the next several hundred years. As long as there was a strong shogun or a strong emperor, society ran smoothly. Japan cut itself off from the outside world, thinking that it had everything it needed. Nothing could be better than what was available in Japan.

This era is sometimes referred to as the Japanese Dark Ages, as Japan was cut off from the rest of the world. The administrative leadership of Japan was almost exclusively military. Japan began to create a separate Japanese culture. The Chinese influences of the Tang and Song Dynasties were almost gone from Japanese society except for Buddhism, which began to have a heavy influence on Japan.

BUDDHISM

FUN FACT

Yoritomo's rule of Japan was similar to other absolute monarchs in history: Louis XIV, Suleiman the Magnificent, and many of the Ming emperors.

Buddhism was attractive to Japan because the samurai enjoyed the repetition and deep meditation. For others, meditation and a repetition of tasks provided salvation, as students would focus on peace, simplicity, and love. These Buddhist traits can be seen today in Japanese gardening with the trimming of the bonsai tree and the famous tea ceremony. Buddhism took a deep root in Japan at this time.

JAPANESE CULTURAL FLOWERING

Japan made advancements in the culture with the creation of Noh plays, which were dramas or mysteries performed outdoors on a large wooden stage. These were very similar to the tragedies and comedies of ancient Greece. All actors were male, and the actors wore large masks to demonstrate beauty and facial movements. Eventually the movements and the dances were a language of their own and told the history of Japan through moral themes. Noh plays were also fairy tales, stories about magic, and history of the battles of Minamoto Yoritomo.

TIMELINE REVIEW

100 B.C.E	Large mainland migration to Japan
300 C.E.	Korean Kingdoms: Koguryo, north; Paekche, southwest; Silla, east
450 C.E.	Shintoism
500 C.E.	Yamato family dominant
668 C.E.	Korean Silla
710 C.E.	• Capital of Nara
	• Tang Chinese practices are adopted.
794 C.E.	Capital of Heian
800 C.E.	Chinese borrowing declines.
900 C.E.	Development of the Kana
918 C.E.	Koryo, Korea
1010 C.E.	*The Tale of Genji*
1192 C.E.	Yoritomo becomes shogun.
1200 C.E.	Bushito develops.
1274–1281 C.E.	Kublai Khan invasions fail.
1338 C.E.	Warring States Era
1392 C.E.	Choson, Korea
1590 C.E.	Hideyoshi ends Warring States.
1598 C.E.	Tokugawa Ieyasu unifies, restores order.

GLOBAL CONNECTIONS

Europe

123 B.C.E.—Gracchi brothers in Rome

31 B.C.E.—Pax Romana

32 C.E.—Christianity begins

200 C.E.—Decline of the Roman Empire begins

481 C.E.—Clovis, King of the Franks

732 C.E.—Charles Martel defeats Muslims at Tours

800 C.E.—Charlemagne

1066 C.E.—William the Conqueror

1215 C.E.—Magna Carta

Africa

350 C.E.—Civilization of Axum

700 C.E.—Muslims move across North Africa

800 C.E.—Kingdom of Ghana

1250 C.E.—King Sundiata of Mali

1325 C.E.—Mansa Musa's Hajj

1480 C.E.—Portuguese trade with West Africa

Americas

100 B.C.E.—Nazca in South America

400 C.E.—Decline of Mayas

900 C.E.—Anasazi Cliff Dwellers in North America

1200 C.E.—Rise of the Aztecs

1450 C.E.—Machu Picchu built by Incas

1500 C.E.—Iroquois League in North America

Islam

610 C.E.—Muhammad's vision

632 C.E.—Start of the first five Caliphates

680 C.E.—Contact with Byzantine Empire

731 C.E.—Muslims create Moorish culture in Spain

859 C.E.—First madrasa opened

1099 C.E.—First Crusade

1174 C.E.—Saladin and the Third Crusade

1236 C.E.—Mongols in Russia

1299 C.E.—Formation of Ottoman Empire

1350 C.E.—Beginning of Delhi sultanate in India

1526 C.E.—Formation of Mughal Dynasty

Formation of the Islamic Religion, Culture, and Civilization

8

MECCA

The city of Mecca is located near the west coast of Saudi Arabia. The city itself was in the center of major caravan routes and other trading routes where goods from Africa, Europe, and Asia were traded. It was also the home to a famous sanctuary built for many of the pagan gods from the surrounding areas. Traders in the area, including Muhammad, had to understand and know each of these religions to entice customers and interact with them. Mecca was a highly competitive trading market between Bedouins, or nomadic trading Arabs, and settled nonnomadic Arabs. Mecca is where Islam began.

MUHAMMAD

Early Life

Muhammad was born circa 570 C.E. He was an orphan who was adopted into a lower-middle-class trading family. His adoption and low family status later impacted the development of the religion of Islam. Muhammad eventually married Khadija in 595 C.E., who was a widow and co-owner of a large, prosperous, and successful trading business. As he began to work at the forefront of the business, Muhammad grew troubled by the worldliness and paganism surrounding him. He learned that the same things were bothering traders from other faiths, so Muhammad studied with Jewish rabbis. He liked what he heard, but it did not answer all of his questions. Next, he studied with Christian priests and scholars. Again, he liked what he heard, but not all of his questions were answered. There seemed to be a piece of the puzzle missing.

> ### 🍽 DINNER TABLE TALK
>
> Did you know that Muhammad studied with Jewish and Christian scholars before he founded Islam? Did you know that he protected Jewish and Christian followers as people of the scripture because Allah (Islam), Yahweh (Judaism), and God (Christianity) are all the same God!

Muhammad's Vision

In 610 C.E., Muhammad went into the desert for solitude to think. Like Noah, Moses, and Jesus—prophets of the Old and New Testaments of the Christian Bible—Muhammad was in the desert for 40 days. While there, he had a visit from the archangel Gabriel (God's messenger). He told Muhammad that he had been chosen to rise and warn his fellow Arabs about their paganism and immorality, and he would teach them to worship their one true God, Allah. The message delivered by Gabriel became the Islamic Qur'an, or God's word. Muhammad was the very last in a line of prophets going back to the Hebrew's Abraham, chosen to bring God's will to the people. Moses brought the Ten Commandments to the Hebrew God's chosen people. Jesus had brought the Gentiles to know God. Now

Muhammad would bring the Arabs and complete what God had said, "All people of the Earth will come to me."

The Qur'an

One of the things that helped the spread of Islam was its simple, clear message. The prophet Muhammad was to rise and warn his people of the consequences of their immoral practices, their worshipping of false gods, and their abuses and injustices toward the weak, especially on the poor, orphans, and widows. Muhammad started life as an orphan in Mecca and grew up poor as well, which made him include their treatment into the religion of Islam.

The term *Islam* means "submissive to God's will." Because the nations and communities of earlier prophets had strayed from God's teachings, God was sending Muhammad one last interpretation of his message. Even other monotheistic believers—Jews and Christians—were supposed to hear and respond to the message of the Qur'an.

Becoming a Prophet

KHADIJA

Khadija was Muhammad's wife and a member of a rich and influential family. She was his first convert to Islam. Contrary to modern-day perceptions, early Muslim women had many rights, freedoms, and privileges. During her first marriage and after her first husband's death, Khadija was co-owner of a trading company, and she was a very successful businesswoman.

EARLY TROUBLES GAINING CONVERTS

Outside of Khadija, her uncle, and a few others, Muhammad's message fell mainly on deaf ears. Muhammad's message was upsetting the merchants. It threatened their polytheistic beliefs, but more importantly, Muhammad and his preaching began to drive people away from the shrines and trading companies. It hurt Mecca and its traders economically. As a result, Muhammad and many of his followers began to be persecuted. Khadija died in 620 C.E., and without her influence, Muhammad was forced to send followers from the city for their own safety.

Journey to Medina

Muhammad had a reputation of being a moral and holy man and was often used as an arbitrator or judge in solving disputes. Due to the increased persecution, Muhammad left Mecca in 622 C.E. He stayed with five tribes living near Medina, a city north of Mecca, to solve a dispute between the five tribes. This journey now signifies an important date. It became the starting point for the Islamic calendar, which is roughly 622 years younger than the Western calendar, so the year 2013 is year 1391 on the Islamic calendar.

Medina proved to be the opposite of Mecca as many people in Medina welcomed Muhammad and his message, and they became Muslim converts. Unfortunately, many Arabic Jews in Medina rejected his message. They plotted with his old enemies in Mecca to assassinate Muhammad. Their plot failed, and Muhammad's followers began to raid the trading caravans going into and out of Mecca, economically shutting down the trading business.

While the war with Mecca was being fought, Medina became known as the "city of the prophet." Muslims formulated the idea of a greater Muslim community, which became known as the Umma.

The Umma is the all-encompassing Islamic community to which all Muslims belong. Once a person is a Muslim, the person becomes part of the Umma, a distinctive Islamic community. The Umma was also where Islamic culture took shape and Muslim traditions were formed. With the creation of the Umma, Islam formalized its norms for society and began to spread the religion worldwide.

BASIC PARTS OF MUSLIM SOCIETY

1. Good Muslims needed to be honest in their personal and public affairs. Remember they were mostly merchants, so they could not act one way in public and another behind closed doors.
2. Good Muslims needed to practice modesty in all of their habits. Success was acceptable, but they could not flaunt it or be flashy as it was improper and against what Allah approved.
3. Consuming pork and drinking alcohol were strictly forbidden.
4. The role of and status of women needed to be improved. Muhammad's early life and his marriage to Khadija had important influences on Islam.
5. The property of an individual needed to be properly divided among his or her heirs.
6. A marriage was supposed to be a lifetime commitment and additional careful regulation needed to be implemented.
7. Once a person became a Muslim and professed allegiance to the Umma, his old tribal ties became secondary to the greater good of the Umma. Maintaining tribal ties was a centuries-old tradition and a way of life in Arabia. This new allegiance to the Umma would take time to change. Allegiance to the Umma caused problems after Muhammad's ascension.

Muhammad's Return to Mecca

A precedent was set in 632 C.E. as Muhammad returned to Mecca after the city surrendered to him. Following Allah's wishes, Muhammad forgave the people of Mecca for the assassination plot and the rejection of his message. Muhammad accepted the people of Mecca who wished to convert into the Umma. This precedent of peaceful conversion was important as it set a pattern for others to follow as Islam expanded across Africa, Asia, and Europe.

Tolerance of Other Faiths Under Muhammad

Under the leadership of Muhammad, accepting the authority or leadership of Islam brought tolerance and acceptance. Jews and Christians who accepted Muhammad's authority were left alone, except for paying a small head tax that all non-Muslims had to pay. This was an important practice, especially for people of the book or scripture (Jews and Christians) with whom Muhammad had studied.

The Death of Muhammad

In 632 C.E., Muhammad died/ascended into heaven. Muhammad had no son and did not designate a successor, so Islam faced its first big challenge. What to do without Muhammad? The new tribe, or Umma, had trouble immediately. Two sides began to argue, one group from Medina and another from Mecca. Each side believed that one of its members should be in charge. Another problem that arose was the Bedouin tradition of allegiances that lasted only while the two parties who made the agreement were both alive. After one of the two people died, the survivor's allegiance went back to his or her own individual tribe. After the death of Muhammad, many people who swore allegiance to Allah renounced their pledge to Muhammad.

THE FIVE PILLARS OF ISLAM

One of the factors that made the spread of Islam so fast was the ease of practicing the religion. Judaism had the Torah and the Ten Commandments. Christianity had the Ten Commandments and the teachings of Jesus, like the Sermon on the Mount. As Christianity was built on the foundation of Judaism, Islam was the third monotheistic religion, built on top of Judaism and Christianity. Muslims believed in the same prophets of the Old and New Testaments but saw Jesus as another prophet, like Muhammad. The daily practicing of the Islamic religion was somewhat straightforward.

These practices are still known as the five pillars of Islam, and every Muslim must do these daily or when applicable.

1. Every Muslim must ask forgiveness before worshipping. This includes reading or reciting the Qur'an.
2. Every Muslim must pray five times per day in the direction of Mecca, where the Kaaba (holy shrine) is located.
3. All Muslims who are able should make a tithe (a donation of money) to help the unfortunate, especially widows and orphans.
4. Every Muslim should participate in the Ramadan ritual fasting. This is similar to Christian Lent but on a deeper, more intense level. During the month of Ramadan, which changes every year, Muslims do not eat or drink during daylight hours. It is a time of prayer and reflection, and they try to do as Muhammad did in the desert before he had his visit from Gabriel.
5. Every Muslim who is able should travel to Mecca and take part in the celebration of the Hajj, or pilgrimage to Mecca. This is symbolic of Muhammad returning triumphantly to Mecca from Medina. Pilgrims march three times around the Kaaba stone. Today, this journey attracts millions of people every year.

THE EXPANSION OF ISLAM UNDER THE FIRST FIVE CALIPHS

The First Caliph (632–634 C.E.)

A man named Abu Bakr was eventually elected as the leader of Islam. He was Muhammad's uncle and oldest convert. Known as the caliph, he was able to establish leadership over the early followers from Medina. He was successful in getting the Arabic tribes that converted to Islam to accept being part of the Islamic Umma. Since they gave their pledge and faith to Allah, who was eternal, there was no revoking or ending to their word.

GLOBAL CONNECTIONS

As the Islamic culture grew, the people of Western Europe devolved into the so-called Dark Ages. The Islamic world preserved Greco-Roman learning and made advancements in arts, science, literature, and medical care, which the European people did not have access to for more than 400 years. The First Crusade reconnected Europe with the advancements made by the Islamic scholars during this period.

Expansion (632–732 C.E.)

During the next 100 years, Islam spread farther and faster than any other religion or idea in history. Islam even spread to some of the same territory as Alexander the Great's empire.

By 643 C.E., Islamic armies had spread Islam beyond the Arabian Peninsula into Mesopotamia. From there, they branched out east and west into Egypt and deeper into Asia, making it into Iran. This brought Islam into conflict with two other opponents, the Byzantine and Sassanid empires, which were fighting each other. Now, they turned their attention to the spreading Islamic armies. The Islamic armies were able to defeat the Sassanids by 651 C.E. and continued expanding into North Africa, following the shoreline of the Mediterranean Sea. They destroyed Byzantine sea power but fell short of capturing the Byzantine capital of Constantinople, which the Islamic leaders wanted due to its strategic location. From Arabia to Iran, people in this part of Asia were under Islamic control. By 710 C.E., Islamic armies had created an empire that reached the Indus River Valley where Alexander the Great stopped his expansion.

In North Africa, nomads known as Berbers were either conquered or converted to Islam. They helped spread the religion all the way to Morocco on the Atlantic coast.

By 711 C.E., Islamic soldiers were able to successfully raid into Spain. Spanish kingdoms were not united and easily defeated. Islamic armies also advanced northward from Turkey and had a solid foothold in Eastern Europe via the Oxus River in southern Russia. The Sassanid Empire was defeated, and the Byzantine Empire was cut in half before the Muslim armies of expansion were finally stopped. The army had advanced into northeastern France when they were stopped by the armies of Charles Martel at the Battle of Tours in 732 C.E.

In 100 years, Arabic armies conquered empires from the Loire River in France, across North Africa, all the way to the Indus River in modern-day Pakistan. This was a truly incredible feat that has never been equaled.

Reasons for Success

Conquering a territory of that size in record time was no easy task. The Islamic armies were able to do so for eight simple reasons.

Global Connections

Islamic culture successfully accomplished having land on multiple continents— Africa, Asia, and Europe.

1. The ease of practicing Islam made it easy to gain converts.
2. The Islamic armies had outstanding leadership from the first five caliphs, or successors of Muhammad, and the generals (amirs) that led the armies in battle.
3. Islamic society was open and peaceful and, as such, had the capacity to unite the Arabic tribes and entice non-Arabs to convert.
4. The religious commitment of the leaders to spread their religion was strong.
5. The two powers in the Middle East—the Byzantine and Sassanid empires—had been fighting each other and were somewhat weakened economically by warfare with each other.
6. Many of the citizens of the Byzantine and Sassanid empires were tired of the ongoing war, being caught between two armies. They welcomed Islam as a chance to escape not only the war, but also heavy taxes and other forms of persecution that they had endured under the two warring empires.
7. The Muslims were traders and had been for hundreds of years. Extending their trading network carried powerful motivation, especially in the early stages of conquest.
8. What cannot be overstated was the way the Islamic armies were careful to conduct their expansion with as little destruction to existing infrastructure as possible. Why destroy something that would have to be rebuilt? Since the empire was large and diverse, they kept many of the governing systems and governmental personnel in their jobs. Taxation was adjusted to Muslim terms, and in certain areas, forts were built. Other than that, life went on as it had before, with conquests featuring little bloodshed and little needless destruction. Plus, the Jews and Christians were allowed

to practice their faiths and culture, and they simply had to pay a non-Muslim tax and accept the Islamic government.

As a result of these techniques, the Islamic religion was able to undergo its record-breaking spread.

What to Do with Non-Muslims and Non-Arabs

After conquest, a new problem arose for the Muslim Umma. As most Arabs converted to Islam, breaking the centuries-old idea of family and tribal loyalty, it became customary that Muslims did not have to pay taxes. However, what about non-Arabs and non-Muslims (other than people of the scripture)? Did non-Arabs who converted have to pay taxes, or as Muslims were they equal to Arabic Muslims? These were questions the Umma was working on internally during the period of expansion. The Muslims brought a new culture into the lands they conquered and understood that it was going to take time to instill their culture in these new lands. They could not force it or do it rapidly, unlike the Ch'in Dynasty in China who chose rapid enforcement and failed (see Chapter 3).

Hierarchy

Leadership positions were created and necessary at this time. Muhammad was the prophet. After him, the next caliphs were named by the tribal leaders in agreement with the oldest Islamic converts of Muhammad. In order to be chosen as caliph, a person's religious and personal qualities were paramount, not only in the practice of Islam but also in their association with Muhammad.

Under the caliph, the next important position was the imam, or one who led Muslims in prayer (liken him to a Christian priest or Jewish rabbi).

After the imam came the amir, or general, who commanded the Islamic armies in battle. At first, these were the important hierarchical figures.

The first four caliphs were Abu Bakr (632–634), Umar (634–644), Uthman (644–656), and Ali (656–661). They had no problem commanding the respect of the faithful. They knew Muhammad personally, were with him daily when he was alive, and were among his oldest converts. During the reign of the fifth caliph, Mu'ayina (661–680), the connection with Muhammad was broken. Everyone who knew him personally was gone or too old to govern.

Civil War (746–750 C.E.)

Global Connections

Other nations that have had a civil war include England, France, the United States, Russia, Korea, and Vietnam, most of which occurred because of territorial, political, and religious disputes.

The Umayyads and the Abbasids were the first two dynasties. They built the foundation of the Islamic Empire that grew from the Atlantic Ocean to the Indus River Valley and India. The Umayyad Dynasty was the first dynasty that had to oversee the shift from a desert Bedouin lifestyle into one of an urban government, as they had their capital in Damascus, Syria. They governed a large multicultural and intercontinental empire, while ongoing conquests continued.

The first civil war occurred between the Umayyads and the Abbasid clan over differences in the treatment of non-Arabs. The caliphate of Mu'awiya of the Umayyad Dynasty fought against the Abbasid Dynasty, led by one of Muhammad's uncles. The Abbasids won the war and claimed that the Umayyads had become corrupted. The Umayyad Dynasty lasted until 750 C.E.

The Abbasid Dynasty followed in 750 C.E., and they lived and reigned in Baghdad. They controlled the caliphate until the time just before the Crusades in 1096 C.E. In the late 900s, the one single caliphate broke up and split into three different kingdoms, each with its own caliph. Even though there was no remaining single entity in Islam, the religion was still growing.

Ulama and the Creation of the Sharia

It was difficult for the caliphs to be political and religious leaders at the same time. The first four caliphs had this ability due to their relationship with Muhammad. However, a new generation had replaced them. Certain individuals, recognized for their piety and religious learning, became authority figures. They were concerned with preserving and applying the Qur'an and keeping the traditions as close as possible to those formed in Medina under Muhammad.

Ulama means "person of right knowledge." The first ulamas were able to set the standard of making Arabic the spoken and written language of the empire, which helped unify, or at least allow, people from the different parts of the empire to communicate. All education was done using a curriculum of study under the ulama's supervision. The discussions and interaction amongst the ulama ranged from education to how to deal with criminals and, most importantly, how to practice the religion. This turned into the Islamic divine law known as the sharia. The sharia set the standard for Islamic social and religious order in Muslim society. It became the center, the core, and governed Islamic social, legal, political, and commercial life. It governed not only what people did in public and in private but how they ran their businesses and interacted with others.

The ulama did not set out to create a formal Muslim clergy, but that was what happened. As they organized the religious and social order of Islam, they became a new class of people. The ulama were powerful enough to criticize caliphs who strayed too far from original Islamic practice. Many were advisors to caliphs, and the ulama are still an important part of Muslim society today.

Strength of the Qur'an

One of the primary strengths of Islam is that it is a universal religion that is open to everybody. Early on, this meant the loss of tax revenue as anyone who became a Muslim did not have to pay taxes. Ethnic and social background did not matter as all Muslims, even the caliph, were equal before Allah.

THE ISLAMIC SCHISM

Shiite vs. Sunni

The civil war between the Umayyads and the Abbasids also caused a schism, or split, in Islam.

Muhammad had no male heirs, but he did have a daughter, Fatima, who married one of Muhammad's cousins, Ali. Ali became not only Muhammad's son-in-law but also one of the first four caliphs based on his blood and family ties with Muhammad. Many people believed Ali to be the successor of Muhammad as Muhammad had appointed him to be the first imam. This group of Muslims, called Shia/Shiite Muslims, came to believe that the true leader of Islam must be descended from Muhammad as he passed his divine knowledge on through his blood. The descendants of Ali and Fatima had the prophet's blood, which was passed on in their children. For a Shia/Shiite, the true leader must be a direct descendent of Muhammad. This is the minority of Muslims in the world today.

Global Connections

India/Pakistan War and the Catholic/ Protestant War were also fought over differences of splitting faith.

Most Muslims today are Sunni Muslims. To a Sunni, the caliph was the best Muslim possible whose life and piety set him apart, and the caliph did not have to be from one single dynasty or family. For those chosen to be the caliph, personal character was paramount. It was the equivalent to being selected as the pope in the Roman Catholic church.

Becoming a caliph was not something easily done, and a person had to be selected. Sunnis acknowledged that the caliph governed a theocracy and a government controlled by a religious belief, and that the government was under divine authority. If a caliph had a problem or question when governing, he had several sources to help him govern:

1. The Qur'an—What does it say?
2. The precedents of Muhammad—for example: Muhammad forgave the people of Mecca and allowed Jews and Christians to keep their forms of faith, so forgiveness and acceptance are important.
3. The ruling of the ulama.

Sunni Muslims also believe that even though the caliph has great authority, he is also a temporary, earthly ruler whose job is to defend Islam and to administer its laws and government. He has no greater religious authority than any other Muslim as all Muslims are equal.

The Third Muslim Sect—Sufi

People of the third sect of the Muslim religion were known as Sufi Muslims. Sufi Muslims are missionary Muslims. They sought communion with all through meditation, fasting, and other rituals. They were respected for their piety, and through some of their miraculous powers (like Christian monks and nuns in Europe), Sufi Muslims helped spread Islam through missionary work. They carried the faith into remote areas. They were also more flexible and less rigid than either Shiites or Sunnis.

Shiite/Shia	Sunni	Sufi
Leader must be a direct descendant of Muhammad	Leader is elected and must be the best Muslim possible	Known as missionary Muslims and are much less rigid
Minority of Muslims in the world today	Majority of the Muslims in the world today	Their flexibility allows them to adapt and adopt other ideas more readily
Found primarily in Iran and Iraq		They bring local religions into Islam practies

Remember: All of these Muslim groups share the same beliefs based on the Qu'ran and Five Pillars.

GLOBAL CONNECTIONS

Many civilizations have experienced multiple periods of cultural growth. Some of these include the Han Dynasty, the Tang and Song Dynasties, the Ming Dynasty, Pax Romana, Athens during the reign of Pericles, the Nara-Heian period of Japan, the Italian Renaissance, and the Mayan, Aztec, and Incan civilizations in the Americas.

ISLAMIC ACHIEVEMENTS COMPARED TO WESTERN EUROPE: 600–1000 C.E.

Many Islamic accomplishments were made during a time when Western Europe was in the so-called Dark Ages. Learning regressed somewhat in Western Europe, and the Islamic world actually maintained and saved Greco-Roman learning. Islam was a cosmopolitan collection of ideas and learning that was vastly ahead of anywhere else in its sphere of influence.

ISLAMIC CULTURAL ACHIEVEMENTS: FROM MANUFACTURING TO ART TO SCIENCE

Manufacturing: Muslim artisans were excellent at producing fine goods, like steel swords from Damascus. They practiced acid etching using acid to blacken and make elaborate designs inside the metalwork. In Córdoba, Spain, Muslims taught the Europeans about advanced leatherwork techniques. Cotton was exported from Egypt along with other fine fabrics.

Agriculture: Muslim farmers cultivated everything from cotton to medicinal herbs to fruits and vegetables that were distributed throughout the Islamic Empire.

Art: Muslims do not believe in idol worship so worshipping or praying to a statue was strictly forbidden. The art form practiced by Muslims was mosaic patterns. They decorated their government and religious buildings with mosaic art by putting colored glass or tiles together, forming geometric patterns with very intricate designs.

Arabic Writing: Muslims turned flowing Arabic script writing into an art form, like Chinese calligraphy.

Architecture: As Muslim architects looked at the domes and arches from the Roman and Byzantine empires, they modified them somewhat by making the domes with a rounder edge. Along with building these domes on mosques, the Muslims also built thin tall towers called minarets where the call to prayer was made. Both the domes and the minarets became very ornate and very decorative with mosaic designs.

Literature and Poetry: Long before Muhammad was alive, the Arabic Bedouins, being a nomadic and oral people, had great stories and oral poetry that connected the many Arab tribes together. Coming out of this rich storytelling history were great books and tales that were written down by Islamic scholars and are still famous today. Stories such as *1001 Arabian Nights, Aladdin and the Magic Lamp, Ali Baba and the 40 Thieves,* and *The Tales of Sinbad the Sailor* all came out of the Arabic empire at this time.

Education: When it came to learning and education, Muslim scholars traveled to wherever they could from Europe to China to learn everything possible. This set the tone for the Muslim empire as eventually the city of Baghdad, Iraq, became home to a giant library where many scholars studied. This library and house of learning spread to other parts of the Islamic empire in West Africa. There was the city of Timbuktu with its school of learning, and in Europe, it was the University of Córdoba in Spain. Islamic education resulted in the creation of a madrasa, or a school of higher learning. Many things that were studied are comparable to what was studied at Alexander the Great's House of Muses at Alexandria.

Muslim scholars translated and copied the works of the Greek scientists and philosophers from Plato to Hippocrates. They copied and preserved Roman learning and law when most people were illiterate in Western Europe. The Islamic and Jewish scholars maintained their ideas before they were destroyed over the centuries. Muslim scholars looked at Hindu and Buddhist texts and translated early Christian writings. They also translated the writings of Aristotle from Latin into Arabic. They eventually were retranslated back to Latin after the Crusades.

Mathematics: Muslim scholars studied mathematics from India as well as Greece. A Muslim scholar named al-Khwarizmi pioneered the study of algebra. He wrote a textbook that became the standard mathematical textbook for Europe after the Crusades. Like scholars of the ancient world, the Muslims developed astronomical tables and built observatories from the Mediterranean Sea through central Asia. Muslims studied solar eclipses, measured the Earth's rotation, and were able to calculate the circumference of the earth to within a few thousand feet by using their astronomical observations. This occurred during the time when many Europeans thought the world was flat and greatly aided in advanced navigation.

Medical Advances: As early as the year 900 C.E., when Europeans were using leeches and bleeding as medicinal techniques, the Muslim physician Muhammad al-Razi was in the city of Baghdad, conducting research to determine where to build a hospital. As he moved around and studied the city, he put his hospital where he saw garbage decompose the most slowly as this indicated the cleanest part of the city with less bacteria and disease-carrying rodents. Muhammad al-Razi studied the effects of bacteria, and other Muslim scholars made remarkable advances in medicine.

The Muslim doctors had a chart of over several thousand prescriptions for different medicines to treat specific illnesses. They began to stress ideas of cleanliness, especially in wound care. By keeping the wound clean, disinfecting the wound, and using stitches, wounds healed faster and more permanently.

All of these Islamic cultural achievements, from manufacturing to art and science, were years ahead of what was going on in Europe at the same time. Only during the Crusades, starting in 1092 C.E., did many of the Europeans find out that what they were doing was the complete opposite of what was going on in the Islamic empire. While Europe was in what we call the Middle Ages or the "Dark Ages," the Islamic world made great advances in everything, including religion, art, science, and medicine. They preserved it and reeducated Europe.

One of the positive aspects of the Crusades for Europeans was a renewed access to learning. Not only had the Muslims kept Greco-Roman learning alive, but they also added to that body of knowledge.

TIMELINE REVIEW

570 C.E.	Muhammad is born.
595 C.E.	Muhammad marries Khadija.
610 C.E.	Muhammad has vision of Gabriel.
620 C.E.	Muhammad is troubled by paganism in Mecca.
622 C.E.	• Muhammad leaves Mecca for Medina.
	• Islamic calendar starts.
632 C.E.	• Muhammad's ascension into heaven
	• Start of the first five caliphates
632–634 C.E.	Abu Bakr, first caliph
634 C.E.	Umar, second caliph
644 C.E.	Islam expands beyond peninsula.
651 C.E.	Umayyad Dynasty
656 C.E.	First Civil War
656–661 C.E.	Ali, fourth caliph
661–690 C.E.	Mu'ayina, fifth caliph
680 C.E.	Conflict with Byzantine Empire

GLOBAL CONNECTIONS

Middle Ages Europe

500 C.E.—Kingdom of Franks established by Clovis

726 C.E.—Emperor Leo III of Byzantines and Pope Gregory VII fight over the use of religious icons

732 C.E.—Charles Martel halts advance of Muslim armies at Tours

800 C.E.—Charlemagne crowned Holy Roman emperor

843 C.E.—Treaty of Verdun: Holy Roman Empire divided between Charlemagne's grandsons

987 C.E.—Hugh Capet claims throne of France

China

581 C.E.—Sui Dynasty

605 C.E.—Grand Canal between Huang Ho and Yangtze Rivers completed

618 C.E.—Tang Dynasty begins: creates one of the most cosmopolitan civilizations in the world

868 C.E.—World's oldest known book is printed

907 C.E.—Tang collapse

960 C.E.—Song Dynasty: invent typography and the compass

Byzantine Empire

526 C.E.—Reign of Justinian: Byzantine Golden Age

610 C.E.—Heraclius is crowned emperor

693 C.E.—Constantinople is first attacked by Muslims

726 C.E.—Emperor Leo III bans the use of religious idols

924 C.E.—Constantinople attacked for the second time

Mesoamerica

500 C.E.—Maya empire city of Tikal is first great Mayan city

600 C.E.—City of Teotihuacan is mysteriously destroyed—Tikal has a population of over 500,000

899 C.E.—Tikal is abandoned

900 C.E.—Mayan civilization collapses

Japan

552 C.E.—Buddhism arrives from China

645 C.E.—Fujiwara family exerts influence over the Yamato court

710 C.E.—Nara becomes the first permanent capital of Japan

794 C.E.—Capital city is moved to Heian, which will become Kyoto

Africa

600 C.E.—Axum civilization revives in East Africa

800 C.E.—West African kingdom of Ghana begins

800-900 C.E.—Ethiopia becomes a Christian sanctuary

Middle Ages in Western Europe

9

FALL OF ROME AND BARBARIAN INVASIONS

Between 410 and 455 C.E., the city of Rome suffered three attacks by the barbarian tribes—the Visigoths, the Ostrogoths, and the Vandals—each of which overran the city. By 450 C.E., the ruling power was more in the hands of barbarian chieftains than in a Roman emperor. In 476 C.E., Romulus Augustulus was the last Western emperor of Rome, and he was deposed by an Italian soldier of German descent named Flavius Odoacer. The Byzantine emperor Zeno was the sole ruler of Eastern and Western Europe, but it was symbolic.

The once-mighty Roman empire was gone. From England all the way south to Africa, the land was ruled by barbarians. However, not all parts of Roman civilization were erased. The barbarian civilizations that controlled Roman territory learned much from those they conquered. In many places, Roman law and the Latin language were used by the barbarians. The Visigoths, the Ostrogoths, and the Vandals were already Christians, following Eastern Orthodox Christianity instead of Roman Catholicism, so this similarity made acceptance of Roman culture easier.

The barbarian clan of Franks settled in Gaul (what is today France) and converted the territory to Roman Catholicism, which was supported by the head bishop in Rome. The Franks played an important role in creating a new culture in Western Europe as they converted many barbarians to Christianity.

THE ROMAN CATHOLIC CHURCH

The single most important factor of the Middle Ages was the development and growth of the Roman Catholic Church. Throughout the High Middle Ages into the Renaissance, the one part of the Roman Empire that actually grew in Western Europe was the Catholic Church. This was because of its organization. It retained a hierarchy and central organized structure that modeled the government of the Roman Empire.

The head of this hierarchy was the bishop of Rome, who was eventually known as the pope. He was the head of the church, and then there were bishops subordinate to him who were placed in large cities. They looked to the bishop of Rome for spiritual and religious guidance. As many parts of the Roman Empire began to fall apart, especially in Western Europe, these bishops and their subordinate clergymen took the place of a legal government in the absence of power. In each town, village, or larger city, the local church or the big cathedral became the focal point. The local bishop or priest had almost complete authority. In

> ### 🌐 GLOBAL CONNECTIONS
>
> Remember the persecution of Christians in Rome that was reviewed in Chapter 5? In 313 C.E., Emperor Constantine issued the Edict of Milan, which gave Christians special status inside the Roman Empire. In 391 C.E., Emperor Theodosius made it the official religion. Christians had gone from being the most hated and persecuted people within the empire to the most favored.

Rome, the pope almost assumed the role of the emperor, and as political emperors faded in Western Europe, the Catholic Church was a successful model of Roman governmental administration.

The church survived the collapse of the Roman Empire and the successive waves of invasion by Germanic barbarians. The church was the one and only unifying element in the empire.

The Middle Ages are also called the Dark Ages. Life was very difficult during this time as it was full of famine, invasion, and disease. The message of Christianity—the worthiness of every person in the eyes of God—helped during the brutal life that people of the Middle Ages experienced.

The Catholic Church also offered sacraments that were the same for everyone, regardless of social class or gender. Baptism, confession, marriage, last rites, and communion were offered equally to everyone.

The church kept the governmental hierarchy in order. The most highly educated people in Western Europe worked for the church, and the ancient capital of Rome was its epicenter.

Doctrine of Papal Primacy

One other thing that helped the growth of the church was that bishops never allowed any royal intervention into church affairs. There was a strict separation of church and state. During the Middle Ages, there was no state government in Western Europe, which was different from the Eastern Europe/Byzantine Empire (see Chapter 10).

The bishop of Rome created the Doctrine of Papal Primacy in the 400s C.E. This simply made the bishop of Rome supreme within the church to define church doctrine. It allowed the pope to intervene in political affairs but prevented any governmental agent from interfering in church affairs.

During the Middle Ages, the Doctrine of Papal Primacy led to conflicts between popes and emperors. The pope claimed apostolic succession, meaning that all popes were direct successors of Jesus's head apostle Peter. They were God's representatives on Earth, and there was no higher authority than God, so the decisions of the Pope were off limits to royal intercession.

Role of Monasteries

The church also got help from a special group of people known as monks, who voluntarily served the church and were loyal to it for their entire adult life. Their lifestyle earned them a lot of respect from the people, and they were a source of strength during the difficult Middle Ages.

At first, monks isolated themselves, focusing only on worshipping God. However, a monk named Basil said monks should go out like Jesus and the apostles to care for the sick, the widows, and the orphans. Monasticism also received a large boost in popularity when, in 529 C.E., a monk named Benedict of Nursia wrote the Benedictine Order, a rulebook for monasteries. It broke down monastic life into periods of time to pray, to work, and to study. Along with that, Benedict set up a hierarchical structure inside the monastery, so monks would have as little downtime as possible. Having the monks focus on something all the time would promote the religion, their physical and educational well-being, and their discipline. Their hard work made monasteries almost self-sufficient, giving them economic and political power as they helped the surrounding towns and villages. Monks were able to take care of the sick, the poor, and the widowed, making them a spiritual force with whom regional rulers worked.

DIVISION OF CHRISTIANITY

With the two empires of Western Europe (centered around Rome) and Eastern Europe (centered around Constantinople), it seemed inevitable that Christianity would split as well. Some of this was due to differences in language: the Western Roman Empire spoke Latin and the Eastern half spoke Greek. Some of it was cultural.

The Eastern Empire always enjoyed a Hellenistic mix of Greek, Roman, Egyptian, and Asian culture, plus they interacted with a lot of polytheism. There were also some organizational differences in the religion.

The Eastern Empire also believed in what was called the Arian Creed. The Arian Creed stated the Father and Son are one being, and the Holy Spirit is a separate entity. The Western Empire believed in the Holy Trinity: the Father, the Son, and the Holy Spirit as three parts of one entity. This may seem like a small thing, but to early Christians, you had to choose one belief or the other. There was very little room for compromise.

Another major factor in the split of Christianity was the authority of the pope when it came to defining church doctrine in the East. In the Eastern Empire, priests liked to use the Bible and a council of bishops when they defined doctrine. In the Western Empire, the pope was supreme and defined all doctrine himself. This forced a split between the churches.

POLITICAL ORGANIZATION

As Rome was collapsing, a warrior king named Clovis converted to Christianity. During his reign from 466 C.E. to 511 C.E., he created what was known as the Merovingian Dynasty. This dynasty was created in the Frankish Empire, located in France and Germany in central Europe. However, King Clovis ran into a problem: in this difficult terrain, he didn't know how to govern so many people who wanted their independence. Clovis did this by creating a series of important titles and giving land (that he owned) to the newly titled people. They would govern the land for him in return for his protection. Eventually, this evolved into feudalism.

A new office in the Merovingian Dynasty was eventually created during the 600s. It was known as the Mayor of the Palace. The Mayor of the Palace was someone who talked to the different nobles and represented their interests to the king.

Eventually, the office of Mayor of the Palace was dominated by a noble family named the Carolingians. They eventually took over the kingdom and brought political organization to Western Europe. One of the more famous Carolingian rulers was Charles Martel. Charles Martel created a massive army by giving large plots of land—from a few acres to a couple of hundred square miles—to powerful noble Romans if they agreed to serve in his army. He was also known as Charles the Hammer as he defeated an incursion of Muslims at the Battle of Tours in 732 C.E., blocking Islamic expansion into Western Europe.

The Carolingians worked closely with the Roman Catholic Church in Rome. The church depended upon the Carolingians for protection from barbarians and attacks from the Eastern emperors, who were trying to rid themselves of the office of the pope. The church also played a large role in governing the Frankish Empire. The learned monks of the monasteries retained the remnants of Roman culture. Their religious teaching and their authority over the people gave them the ability to impose order on the surrounding population.

REIGN OF CHARLEMAGNE (768–814 c.e.)

Charlemagne, or Charles the Great, was the most famous of the Frankish kings. He and his family expanded the frontiers by brutally subjugating neighboring tribes and then converting them to Christianity. Charlemagne built a new palace in Aachen, Germany, modeled after Roman architecture.

Charlemagne allowed the church its independence, and he made sure it had everything that it needed as he used the church to promote stability within his empire. In return for supporting the church, Pope Leo III of Rome crowned Charlemagne as emperor on Christmas Day in the year 800 c.e. Charlemagne was the first emperor since the collapse of the Roman Empire. This created what became known as the Holy Roman Empire.

Organization of Charlemagne's Empire

Charlemagne ran his empire through the Office of Count and placed 250 branches throughout his empire. Their job was to maintain an army in case the king needed it to collect taxes for Charlemagne or to protect the people. The landowners, however, began to get greedy. When Charlemagne was not specifically in their province, they did whatever they wanted. Charlemagne tried everything to maintain control. He sent religious clergy to spy on them, he tried to appoint permanent governors, and he even tried to use the local bishops, who were forced to do their religious duty as well as political duty for Charlemagne. Nothing seemed to work.

Charlemagne's Accomplishments

Charlemagne achieved some significant accomplishments. He became the Holy Roman emperor, and he used the money from his conquering and unifying of the empire to hire the best scholars in Europe to revive culture and education. The scholars gathered at Charlemagne's palace at Aachen, with the most famous being Alcuin of York, who was supposedly the smartest man in Europe. The scholars created the Kings School, which combined classical Greco-Roman studies with Christian education. This was done because Charlemagne wanted to upgrade the administrative skills of his governing officials. He thought that by educating the sons of nobles to hold either a religious position or a job in his government, the kingdom would run much better. He tried to revive learning: the ability to read, write, and speak was necessary, all of which were taught in Latin, the official language in Charlemagne's empire.

FEUDALISM

Feudalism was a type of government where a king, who did not have enough currency to pay workers, gave the workers large plots of land instead to govern for him instead of paying them. This plot of land is known as a fief, and on it was the lord's manor.

Manoralism was the microeconomic system of feudalism. A lord would be given a fief to govern for a king. On that fief would be a large house, called the manor house; the fief would also include a nearby village or several villages. The lord would govern or manage the entire fief for the king. However, the peasants living on the lord's manor lived in their own microcosm of feudalism called manoralism. They grew the food and made the clothes directly for the lord of the manor in return for protection.

In feudalism, there were three basic social groups: the nobility, the clergy, and the peasants. The clergy would pray and give counsel to their lords, and the peasants who worked the land did everything that was required by their lords, caring for the manor and serving them.

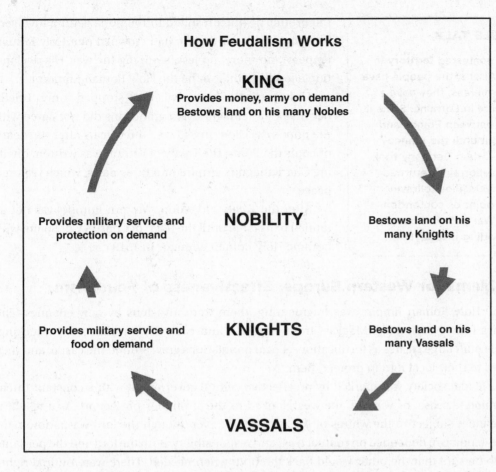

How Feudalism Works

KING
Provides money, army on demand
Bestows land on his many Nobles

NOBILITY

Provides military service and
protection on demand

Bestows land on his
many Knights

KNIGHTS

Provides military service and
food on demand

Bestows land on his
many Vassals

VASSALS

Among the nobility, there were great landed nobles who ruled over tiny kingdoms, but they were still vassals, who were servants of the king. In turn, these lords had lesser nobles, warriors, and knights, among whom they could further subdivide their land.

The Economics of Feudalism

The economy during the Middle Ages was almost exclusively agricultural as Western Europeans cut themselves off from the outside world. This was accomplished through tiny self-sufficient farming villages that existed on a lord's manor, where peasants labored in complete subordination to their lord. They were given land, a house, and protection, and in return, they had to give a portion of everything they grew or made to the lord of the land. The peasants provided the lord with everything, from the clothes he wore to the food he ate.

Treaty of Verdun—843 C.E.

Try as he might, even the great Charlemagne realized that his empire was too big to govern properly. Regional areas looked after themselves first, instead of understanding their role in a large empire. The more loyal the people were to their lord, the more removed they were from Emperor Charlemagne in Aachen.

When Charlemagne died in 814 C.E., his only surviving son, Louis the Pious, became emperor. Louis broke Frankish custom and did not equally divide the rule of his empire among his sons. He named his oldest son to be the sole emperor. His other sons received kingdoms, but his oldest son, Lothair, was going to be the emperor. This incited a war among

FUN FACT

I use a weird phrase to help my students remember the relationships in feudalism: All nobles are knights, and all knights are nobles, yet both are vassals to the king.

the brothers, which resulted in the pope getting involved. The pope declared that he had crowned one Holy Roman emperor, no more, no less, stopping the war. His declaration allowed Lothair to be the Holy Roman Emperor.

Unfortunately, the civil war stopped only briefly because Charlemagne's two grandsons did not agree with the pope's decision. In 843 c.e., three years after the death of Louis the Pious, the Treaty of Verdun was written, dividing Charlemagne's empire into three parts, which restored peace.

After the Treaty of Verdun, Western Europe was not as unified or as large until the reign of Charles V of Spain, who became Holy Roman emperor in 1519 c.e.

Problems for Western Europe: Effectiveness of Feudalism

As the Holy Roman Empire was fragmenting, there were invasions by new enemies. The Vikings from Norway, the Magyars from Hungary, and even the Muslims were attacking. People built large castles as fortifications. Local populations grew around the castle, and they looked to their local lord to protect them.

As feudal society was marked by no effective central government with a constant threat of famine, disease, or warfare, the weak looked to the strong for protection. As a result, it made them subject to the whims of the strong lord. Even though the lord was a dominant figure, feudalism depended on mutual trust and responsibility. Both the lord and the peasants had to be sure that the other would back them up when needed. There were mutual rights and responsibilities. The lord was responsible for protecting his people, the serfs provided him with food and clothing, and the knights needed to come to the lord's aid when called.

Feudalism was not perfect, but it provided a type of stability. Feudalism was also flexible. There was no rulebook, and depending on what circumstances arose, the feudal arrangement between lord, knights, and peasants could change as needed. Peasant life was not great, but the lord did understand that without the peasants, he could not exist either.

WESTERN EUROPE OWES A DEBT TO ISLAM

After the fall of Rome, Western Europe was a mess. The growing power of the church and no strong dominant political power made Western Europe very susceptible to invasion.

However, the spread of Islam in the 700s played an important role at this time. Arab invasions across northern Africa and the continuous battle between the Byzantine Empire and Muslims allowed Western Europe to have a semblance of peace. Western Europe could have been taken over by the Eastern Empire, but they were preoccupied with stopping the spread of Islam. This allowed Western Europe to have enough time to step back and survive on what they had available. They had time to find a way to combine the Germanic culture of the barbarians and the classical Roman culture to create a brand-new, separate, distinct culture. It also allowed the Frankish kingdom to consolidate its power.

TIMELINE REVIEW

400–700 C.E.	Barbarian tribes create kingdoms in Western Europe.
476 C.E.	Rome falls.
481 C.E.	Clovis, King of the Franks
526 C.E.	Benedict of Nursia monastery: Benedictine Order
732 C.E.	Charles Martel defeats Muslims at Tours.
800 C.E.	Charlemagne is crowned Holy Roman emperor.
814 C.E.	Charlemagne dies.
843 C.E.	Treaty of Verdun
896 C.E.	Magyars
900 C.E.	Vikings
950–1156 C.E.	Cluny Reforms begin.
1066 C.E.	William the Conqueror is crowned King of England.
1073 C.E.	• Pope Gregory VII • Cluny Reforms throughout church to prevent corruption
1092 C.E.	Pope Urban II launches the First Crusade.

GLOBAL CONNECTIONS

Japan

710 C.E.—Capital at Nara, Tang Chinese practices adopted

900 C.E.—Development of the Kana writing system

Middle East

570 C.E.—Muhammad is born

622 C.E.—Beginning of Islamic calendar

644 C.E.—Islamic expansion begins

Byzantine Empire

527 C.E.—Emperor Justinian

722 C.E.—Emperor Leo forbids worship of icons

1054 C.E.—The Great Schism

Mesoamerica

400 C.E.—Mayan civilization at peak in capital of Tikal

900 C.E.—Decline of the Mayans

900 C.E.—Anasazi Cliff Dwellers in North America

Africa

700 C.E.—Muslims move across North Africa

800 C.E.—Kingdom of Ghana

1050 C.E.—Almoravids conquer Ghana

China

618 C.E.—Tang Dynasty

960 C.E.—Song Dynasty

Quick Quiz: Chapters 7–9

1. Which Korean kingdom did the Yamato family of Japan use to unify the Japanese islands?

   A. Koguryo
   B. Fujiwara
   C. Silla
   D. Paekche

2. What is significant about the Yamato family in Japan?

   A. They are the only single dynasty in world history.
   B. They possessed Egyptian pharaoh-like power.
   C. They were able to manage their long empire without the use of nobles.
   D. They are the only rulers who claim to be descended from the sun god.

3. Japanese believe in Shintoism, which prompted powerful families to choose which of the following as their ancient ancestors?

   A. Large, powerful waves
   B. Powerful forces of nature
   C. Constellations and planets that could be seen moving throughout the heavens
   D. The different lakes and rivers that are prevalent in the Japanese archipelago

4. Who was the first shogun of Japan that helped create Japanese feudalism?

   A. Minamoto Yoritomo
   B. Ashikaga
   C. Paekche
   D. Shirakawa

5. What is the name for Islam's holy book that provides a simple, clear message and aided in the spread of the new monotheistic religion?

   A. Hajj
   B. Qanname
   C. Qu'ran
   D. Ulama

6. What is the term for the requirements of practicing Islam but also aided in the spread of the Islamic faith?

    A. The Umma

    B. The Five Pillars

    C. Ramadan

    D. Minarets

7. Under which caliph did the first civil war of Islam take place?

    A. Abu Bakr

    B. Umar

    C. Uthman

    D. Mu'awiya

8. Which sect of Islam believes the leader of the faith must be a direct descendent of the prophet Muhammad?

    A. The Sunni

    B. The Sufi

    C. The Shiite

    D. The Kharijites

9. Which one of the following institutions assumed the role of government during the Middle Ages in Western Europe?

    A. The manor

    B. The Byzantine emperor

    C. The Mayor of the Palace

    D. The Roman Catholic Church

10. When was Charlemagne crowned emperor, showing the first bit of unification in Western Europe since the fall of Rome?

    A. Summer solstice, 476 C.E.

    B. Christmas Day, 800 C.E.

    C. Christmas Day, 1066 C.E.

    D. Easter Sunday, 732 C.E.

11. Charlemagne tried to staff his government from this office whom he depended upon for loyalty.

    A. Counts

    B. Fiefs

    C. Abbots

    D. Bishops

12. What form of governmental structure was used in the Middle Ages of Western Europe and will also appear in other civilizations across the globe at different points in time?

    A. Aristocracy
    B. Feudalism
    C. Oligarchy
    D. Constitutional monarchies

Quick Quiz Answers

1. D; **2.** A; **3.** B; **4.** A; **5.** C; **6.** B; **7.** D; **8.** C; **9.** D; **10.** B; **11.** A; **12.** B

The Byzantine Empire and Russia

10

GEOGRAPHY

As the Western half of the Roman Empire fell in 476 C.E., the Eastern part of the empire, the Byzantine Empire, was flourishing. The Byzantine Empire was successful for three main reasons.

1. Many of the rich aristocrats and merchants left Rome with their wealth intact, heading to Constantinople.

2. Constantinople was located on the shores of the Bosphorus, a body of water that links the Black Sea and the Mediterranean Sea. Since the city was surrounded by mountains on three sides, it could only be attacked from the water, which was very heavily guarded and very safe.

3. The Byzantine Empire had access to the trade routes coming to Europe from Asia: The Silk Road from China, the Spice Route from India, wheat from Egypt, and even slaves and ironwork from Western Europe. Its geographical location allowed it to have access to money and trade that was not disrupted by the barbarian invasions in Western Europe.

The Byzantine Empire experienced a quick rise to a golden age as it continued the Hellenistic blending of Greek, Roman, Asian, and even Christian culture. Eventually, the empire entered a period of slow, steady decline ending in the 1400s.

EMPEROR JUSTINIAN

Justinian was the greatest Byzantine emperor. He reigned during its golden age from 527 C.E. to 565 C.E. Justinian tried to reconquer the Western half of the empire, but he was not successful. The attempt drained his treasury and nearly bankrupted him.

The power behind Justinian was his wife, Theodora, a former peasant. Theodora was not simply his wife. She was also a political advisor and backed him up during a revolt in the city of Constantinople. Justinian's advisors told him to flee, but it was Theodora who convinced her husband to stay. Her distain for the rebellion was obvious, and Justinian brutally subjugated the members of the rebellion, in large part due to his wife.

Theodora turned out to be quite a politician. She was strong enough at times to challenge her husband's authority, and she made her own decisions in an era when women did not have a lot of power. Theodora proved to be an excellent diplomat, negotiating with the Persian Empire. She was quick to give humanitarian aid to areas that needed help, and she helped build hospitals for the poor. Theodora advocated for the rights of women.

Corpus Juris Civilis

During his reign, Emperor Justinian decided to revise the confusing Roman legal code system. In 529 C.E., he created what is known as the body of civil law: the Corpus Juris Civilis. He put together a Byzantine assembly to study the laws of the Roman assembly to find out what worked and what did not, what was contradictory and what was redundant, and then he streamlined it. The Corpus Juris Civilis had a big impact on the church and Western European government. Medieval monarchs during the nation-building period of European history modeled their laws on its principles.

Justinian's Power

Emperor Justinian wanted to use the Corpus Juris Civilis as a tool to unite his empire. However, he was the sole ruler with complete authority, like the Roman emperors of old. He maintained a large bureaucracy to help carry out his government, and it was fairly efficient. Justinian even enjoyed one other facet of power that was not present in the West: he had power over the Eastern Orthodox Church. He was seen as the co-ruler with Christ on the Earth, so the Byzantine Empire had a deeply intertwined church and state, whereas church and state were staunchly and fiercely separated in the West. In the Byzantine Empire, there was one God and one religion.

EASTERN ORTHODOX CHRISTIANITY

The Eastern Orthodox Church differed from the Roman Catholic Church in many ways.

1. Church leadership. In the Byzantine Empire, the emperor was the head of the church. He oversaw and controlled church affairs. The emperor appointed a patriarch, who was the head official of the church, like a cardinal or an archbishop. The patriarch was subservient to the emperor, just as a cardinal or archbishop was subservient to the pope in the Roman Catholic Church.
2. Church control over lives of Christians. Roman Catholics believed that the pope controlled the lives of all Christians, which is opposite of Eastern Orthodox Christians.
3. Marriage of priests. Eastern Orthodox priests could marry and have families, but monks and bishops could not.
4. Bread for communion. Roman Catholics could not use leavened bread for communion, but Eastern Orthodox Christians could.
5. Religious icons. Perhaps the biggest difference was the dispute over the use of religious icons or holy images, statues, pictures, paintings, or stained-glass images of Jesus, Mary, Joseph, and other saints. Byzantine Emperor Leo III outlawed the practice of using religious icons. The pope in Rome excommunicated the Byzantine emperor for this decision, which meant that Leo III was kicked out of the church. This caused much anger on both sides and led to what is known as the Great Schism in 1054 C.E. The Great Schism was a permanent split between the two Christian churches, and both the pope and the patriarch of Constantinople excommunicated each other.

THE GREAT SCHISM

The Great Schism conflict in 1054 C.E. between the emperor and the pope started the collapse of the Byzantine Empire. The Byzantine Empire was struggling and had been led by some weak emperors. They were constantly fighting with Western Europe. They were battling the Sassanid Empire of Asia plus they were dealing with the growing Islamic expansion. The Byzantine Empire was constantly in battle.

This forced a drastic call for help in 1090 C.E. when Byzantine Emperor Comnenus had to ask the pope in Rome for assistance. In asking for help, the Byzantine emperor recognized the pope's authority. In return, Pope Urban II launched the First Crusade in 1092 C.E. with the hope of reunifying the church, and Pope Urban II was officially recognized by the Byzantine Empire.

However, the First Crusade had negative effects on the Byzantine Empire as well. It created a trade rivalry with Italian cities. Italy began to capitalize on merchant trade, further draining money from the Byzantine Empire. In 1453 C.E., the Ottoman Empire captured the city of Constantinople. The emperor was given a chance to leave, but he chose to continue the fight and was killed, leading to the collapse of the Byzantine Empire.

The Ottoman ruler, Mehmed II, entered Constantinople and renamed it Istanbul, which is the name of the city to this day.

FUN FACT

The emperor's famous phrase was, "I would be an emperor without an empire without Constantinople."

THE CONTRIBUTIONS OF THE BYZANTINE EMPIRE

The Byzantine Empire was built upon Hellenistic ideas. The empire made advancements in art, especially with mosaic work. They made further use of the Roman arch and the dome. Byzantine artwork made the Bible come to life in picture form. They began to use pillars and other types of architecture that blended the Greek, Roman, Persian, Arabic, and Egyptian building styles started by Alexander the Great. And most importantly, as the Western European world collapsed into the Dark Ages, Byzantine scholars preserved classical works of learning. They preserved everything from the current learning all the way back to ancient Greece.

Constantinople was a repository of culture and learning, and after the Ottoman Empire conquered the Byzantine Empire in 1453 C.E., many of the scholars and teachers in Constantinople traveled back to Western Europe. This began the reeducation and cultural flowering of the Western European people, ushering in what is now called the Renaissance (see Chapter 16).

FUN FACT

Mehmed II also converted the large Eastern Orthodox Church in Constantinople into an Islamic mosque, the Hagia Sophia. It is one of the icons of the city today showing the blending of architectural and religious styles.

FORMATION OF RUSSIA

The first Russian civilization developed in southern Russia in what is today the Ukraine. The Ukraine was located in what was known as the steppe, a flat, wide-open prairie with no natural barriers. It stretched from Europe all the way to Asia. Northern Russia had a lot of mountains and forests, and the south had many good rivers that the people used for transportation and farmland, but the wide-open space of the Ukraine was where the Russian civilization began.

Geography of Russia

Russia is the largest country in the world based on square miles, stretching from Europe to the Pacific Ocean in Asia. Russia gives validity to the word *Eurasia*, the combination of Europe and Asia, with the Ural Mountains as the dividing line.

West of the Ural Mountains, the people today still assume more Western European ethnicities. East of the Ural Mountains, the people have more Asian features, as their ancestors hailed from China, Japan, and Korea.

Russian People

The people of Russia were Slavic, meaning they spoke Indo-European Slavic languages. During Roman times, they did not have any wide-scale political organizations. Instead, they had tribal clans like the German barbarians. Between 700 C.E. and 800 C.E., a new group of people entered Russia: the Vikings. The Vikings traveled the good waterways of Russia, and the Russians and Vikings lived in peace, blending and assimilating to build the city of Kiev. The city of Kiev created a transportation link to the city of Constantinople for trading, and eventually the Vikings were absorbed into Russian society.

Influence of the Byzantine Empire

The Byzantine Empire sent missionaries to Russia to convert them to Christianity. In 860 C.E., these missionaries combined Greek and Cyrillic writing to write the Bible in a language that the Slavic people could understand. In 957 C.E., the princess of Kiev converted to Christianity. This enabled the religion to spread widely, especially under the rule of her grandson, who married a Byzantine princess.

The union between the Byzantine Empire and Russia fostered a written language, enabled the spread of Christianity, and helped create educated clergy. Russia also adopted styles of Byzantine art, music, and building techniques. The Russian rulers formed close ties with the church, and the Christian church became known as the Russian Orthodox Church.

Arrival of the Mongols

As Russian and Byzantine cultures were blending, a new influence arrived in Russia. In the 1200s C.E., Mongol war leader Genghis Khan united the central Mongolian tribes in Asia, and they had a large impact on Russia. One of Genghis Khan's grandsons arrived in Russia in 1236 C.E., and he brought the Golden Horde with him. The Golden Horde—named as such for the golden color of the army's tents—destroyed and burned the city of Kiev. They killed thousands of Russians, and they set up a new capital on the mighty Volga River, which ran north to south through Russia. The Mongols dominated Russia for about 250 years.

GLOBAL CONNECTIONS

The people had to treat the Mongols as the supreme lords, but remember that it was a long way from Mongolia to Russia. It goes back to the "proximity to authority." When you are a long way from your ruler, you can pretty much do what you want until your superior shows up!

MONGOL INFLUENCE

The Mongols were violent, tough conquerors, but they were also fair rulers. Even though Russian cities and territories had to pay heavy taxes in the form of tribute, the Russian princes did what they wanted as long as they recognized the Mongols' authority. The soldiers in the Golden Horde were Muslims, but they were tolerant of the Russian Orthodox Church.

However, paying heavy taxes was hard on many Russian peasants, who fled toward the West to escape the Mongols. Ironically, this was good for trading. The Mongols controlled enormous amounts of Russian land from Europe into Asia. Russian merchants benefited from the Mongol rule as they now had access to another trade route, which paralleled the Silk Road. This route was safe, and trade opened up further between Europe and Asia.

However, Russian rulers eventually used the Mongol concept of central control to create their own kingdoms. Eventually, because of the contact with the Mongols, Russia was cut off from Western Europe, and as great leaps of progress were made in Western Europe during the end of the High Middle Ages and into the Renaissance, Russia remained isolated and stuck with no progress.

CITY OF MOSCOW

The city of Moscow rose to the forefront during the Mongol rule. The noble princes in Moscow used Moscow's key location—in the middle of the western part of the country with its great river access—to help control trade routes. The Russian Orthodox Church made Moscow its capital, and the princes there were given jobs as Mongol tax collectors. They used this power and money to build a solid powerbase, and in 1380 C.E., the Russian princes in Moscow led a Russian revolt against the Golden Horde, which was weakening because of the distance from its homeland in Asia.

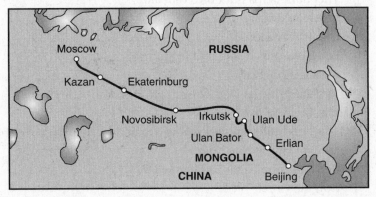

Ivan III or Ivan the Great

The Russian ruler Ivan III became known as Ivan the Great because he was one of the great driving forces behind Moscow's rise to power. Ruling from 1462 C.E. to 1505 C.E., Ivan the Great claimed much of northern Russia as his territory and began to build a solid foundation from which to work. Like the Mongol rulers, he wanted to limit the power of the Russian nobility, known as boyars. Ivan the Great wanted to control by himself.

Ivan the Great married the niece of the last Byzantine emperor and claimed the title of *czar/tsar*, meaning "Caesar," which harkened back to the ancient Roman Empire. He built the framework for absolute rule in Russia.

Ivan IV or Ivan the Terrible

Ivan IV is the grandson of Ivan III and ruled from 1533 C.E. to 1584 C.E. Like his grandfather, he further centralized the power of the new Russian monarchy. He accomplished this by completely cutting boyars out of his government. Ivan IV found loyal vassals and gave them land in exchange for their military service, which was the start of feudalism in Russia.

Russia kept up the practice of feudalism when it was declining elsewhere. While economic and social progress was being made in Western Europe, Russia stuck with what it knew. In 1560 C.E., Ivan suddenly became increasingly more violent, earning him the nickname of Ivan the Terrible. Ivan the Terrible killed his own son, and he had a hit squad of black-clad riders that attacked his enemies (whether they were real or imagined). Ivan the Terrible died suddenly in 1584 C.E., which was good for the Russian people as they were tired of his reign. They entered a period known as the Time of Troubles that lasted from 1604 C.E. to 1613 C.E. when a new dynasty came to power: the Romanov Dynasty.

The Romanov Dynasty will be covered in depth in Chapter 14. However, the foundation created by Ivan the Great and Ivan the Terrible allowed Russia to maintain autocratic, absolutist rule by various leaders throughout Russian history, including Peter the Great (see Chapter 18) up into the 20th century with Joseph Stalin.

TIMELINE REVIEW

330 C.E.	Byzantium and Constantinople
527 C.E.	Emperor Justinian
529 C.E.	Corpus Juris Civilis is created.
532 C.E.	Theodora helps put down rebellion.
565 C.E.	Justinian dies.
600s C.E.	Islamic invasions
722 C.E.	Leo III forbids worship of icons.
863 C.E.	Cyrillic alphabet
967 C.E.	Russian princess Olga converts to Byzantine Christianity.
1054 C.E.	The Great Schism
1090 C.E.	Emperor Comnenus asks Pope Urban II for help in driving back Muslims.
1236 C.E.	Mongol Horde/The Khans
1453 C.E.	Constantinople falls to Mehmed II.
1462–1505 C.E.	Ivan the Great
1560–1584 C.E.	Ivan the Terrible
1598–1613 C.E.	Time of Troubles

GLOBAL CONNECTIONS

India

1350 c.e.—Delhi sultanate

1360 c.e.—Tamerlane's conquests begin

Middle East

570 c.e.—Muhammad is born

644 c.e.—Islamic expansion begins

1299 c.e.—Ottoman Empire forms, one of three Gunpowder Empires

1500 c.e.—Safavid Empire forms, one of three Gunpowder Empires

1526 c.e.—Mughal Empire forms, one of three Gunpowder Empires

Mesoamerica

400 c.e.—Mayan civilization at peak in capital of Tikal

900 c.e.—Decline of the Mayans

1400 c.e.—Aztec civilization at peak, Tenochtitlan flourishing

1450 c.e.—Machu Picchu built by Incas

Africa

700 c.e.—Muslims move across North Africa

1050 c.e.—Almoravids conquer Ghana

1325 c.e.—Mansa Musa makes Hajj to Mecca

1450 c.e.—Kingdom of Songhai

China

618 c.e.—Tang Dynasty

960 c.e.—Song Dynasty

The High Middle Ages in Europe

11

PROCESS OF LAY INVESTITURE

Lay investiture forced a confrontation between popes and new emperors concerning who had the most authority in Europe: the church or the state. Beginning in the mid-1050s C.E., lay investiture was the creation of the designation of church offices. Under lay investiture, bishops and the heads of monasteries, called abbots, could be given those titles by kings and emperors, who were creating church offices to give themselves more political authority.

Many popes during the High Middle Ages wanted to end this practice. They said that only church officials had the authority to create bishops and abbots. For any layperson (a person who is not employed in a religious setting) to do this would cause the church to fall from its mission. However, as separate monarchies began to develop in modern nations, specifically in France, Great Britain, and parts of Germany, it was much easier to gain political authority if you worked with the church. Lay investiture caused the first confrontation in 1075 C.E. between Pope Gregory VII and Emperor Henry IV.

REVIVAL OF THE POWER OF THE EMPEROR

Since the Treaty of Verdun in 843 C.E., there was no single dominant emperor in Europe. This changed when a regional ruler, Otto the Great, inherited a strong position from his father. Otto the Great became king in 936 C.E., and he did not treat his feudal lords or dukes as rulers of their own tiny independent kingdoms, as many kings did. Instead, he treated them as subordinates in a hierarchical chain of a unified kingdom. As part of his government organization, he liked to use the church, specifically high-ranking bishops or prestigious monasteries in his larger cities. King Otto used them because the people listened to the bishops and monks as they had great authority. In turn, church officials liked the idea of a single empire. Otto the Great also liked to have clergy in his government because they would not create a competitive family that could dethrone him. Otto the Great named the clergy as royal administrators, acting as governmental agents of the king. In 962 C.E., Otto was crowned emperor. He quickly tried to assume full control of the church, causing a confrontation between him and the pope.

Cluny Reforms (950–1156 C.E.)

As the confrontation between the pope and Otto the Great escalated, a monastery in Cluny, France, was tired of the arguments. They believed the church was an open organization where, in theory, any believer could become the pope. More importantly, everyone was able to achieve salvation. The monks at Cluny were strict followers of the Benedictine Order, and they were determined to maintain a church that was spiritually focused. They rejected the idea that any member of the church clergy—from parish priest to the pope—should be subservient to an emperor. They claimed the pope was the sole ruler and controller over church offices.

POPE GREGORY VII VS. EMPEROR HENRY IV

The Cluny Reforms helped create one of the strong popes of the High Middle Ages. Pope Gregory VII was a strong advocate of church reforms, and he was willing to put the belief in the separation of church and state to the test. In the year 1075 C.E., Pope Gregory VII said that anyone who practiced the policy of lay investiture would be excommunicated from the church. *Excommunication* means "kicked out." An excommunicated person could not go to church and could not receive the sacraments. The belief at this time was that an excommunicated person could not get to heaven. Pope Gregory VII declared that to be acknowledged as a high-ranking clergyman, a person would need to receive a ring and a staff from the pope with church markings on them.

When Pope Gregory VII made this ruling, it was no longer possible for an emperor to give religious authority to a person. This was a shock to royal authority as many emperors had used lay investiture intentionally to make the church and religion part of their government. Emperor Henry IV considered Pope Gregory's ruling as an intentional challenge to his authority.

In 1077 C.E., Henry IV had to stand outside the pope's retreat in Italy, wearing peasant garb for three days before the pope forgave him. The pope emerged victorious, and the power of the church was deemed as supreme over political authority. The separation of church and state remained.

Germany's Interest in the Conflict

Germany was trying to maintain their independence from the Holy Roman emperor. There were 360 states or kingdoms inside Germany. They were watching this confrontation closely because they were hoping the church would win. If Emperor Henry IV was too busy focusing his attention on Pope Gregory, then this would allow their tiny kingdoms to retain some independence.

Concordat of Worms: End of Lay Investiture

In 1122 C.E., the controversy over lay investiture was settled at the Concordat of Worms. The new emperor, Henry V, formally renounced the power to create bishops. In exchange, the pope said the emperor could give grants of land, or fiefs, to a new bishop, but the church had the sole authority to give a title to a bishop. This showed that the church was more powerful than the emperor as they had the final authority over the naming of a bishop.

THE FIRST CRUSADE

The start of the First Crusade was one of the high points of the power and support of the pope. In 1090 C.E., the Byzantine Empire was under pressure from Muslims and Turks from the Middle East. The emperor needed help. He turned to one of the strongest popes in history: Pope Urban II. Pope Urban II launched the start of the First Crusade in 1092 C.E.

Before the First Crusade, there were many nobles in Europe who were constantly fighting among themselves for power. The Crusades offered a chance to get the nobles out of Europe to fight the invading Muslims and Turks. The Christian knights and nobles could focus together on an external enemy. The enemy looked different, spoke a different language, and practiced a different religion. The Christian knights and nobles were unified in fighting this common enemy, thus ending the fighting between themselves. Some nobles also realized that they could leave Europe and become wealthy, which especially attracted younger knights and nobles.

However, the primary inspiration for the First Crusade was religious devotion. It helped that the papacy was very strong, and Pope Urban promised what was called a "plenary indulgence." Plenary indulgence was total forgiveness of your sins should you die in battle on a Crusade. Thousands of crusaders left France, Germany, and Italy. They gathered in the city of Constantinople, and the crusaders were able to accomplish what no Byzantine army could: they defeated the Muslims in 1099 C.E. as they liberated Jerusalem.

Consequences of the Crusades

While the crusaders were able to end the Muslim siege of Constantinople as well as liberate Jerusalem, their behavior was shocking to the Eastern Empire. At the time, the Eastern Empire was more civilized than Western Europe. The knights were seen as barbarians, and it deepened the animosity between the two sects of European Christianity.

Even though Jerusalem was immediately reconquered by the Muslims when the crusaders left, the Crusades were very beneficial for Western Europe. For the first time in nearly 600 years, they had outside contact. They were awakened to see the advancements in medicine and technology that had occurred while they were in the Dark Ages. While in the Byzantine Empire and the Middle East, the Western European knights and nobles had access to trade goods, ideas, and technology. Cultural diffusion reemerged as Western Europe was reconnected to the global trading economy. This helped Western Europe develop during the High Middle Ages and eventually ushered in the Renaissance.

TOWN CHARTERS

During the Middle Ages in Western Europe, towns tried to maintain a small population of less than 1000 people, and feudal lords controlled and oversaw early townships. They began to create them by granting a charter, or giving permission for people to create a town if they agreed to live and work within it. The lord guaranteed their protection if they worked for him.

If a person was an artisan or had a useful skill, it gave the individual a small bit of independence. As long as the artisans and skilled laborers got their work done and made a profit, they could do it at any time. In contrast, farm laborers had to work from dawn to dusk. Wise lords began to acquire skilled workers who made items that other nobles valued. People who had a useful skill moved to these new towns because they realized that their skill could provide them with money and a small bit of freedom, which eventually led to a higher social status. This change did not go unnoticed by farming peasants who realized that people in towns got special privileges. In order to keep them from rebelling or complaining, the ruling lords had to give farming peasants more freedoms. This eventually brought down feudalism.

Role of Merchants

Just as in China, merchants were disliked at first. They were on the fringe of the established social network. Pretty soon, however, the nobility began to respect, and even need, the merchants. Early merchants were probably poor peasant serfs who decided to take a chance on being long-distance traders. They had to travel to the Middle East and bring back goods to sell. This provided them with the opportunity to make a lot of money, but they also assumed a great risk of being killed or captured during the arduous journey. More than likely, these poor serfs decided they had nothing to lose: if they got killed, it was better than being poor peasant farmers for the rest of their lives.

These merchants broke down the idea of the castle isolation system, where lords were self-sufficient within their castle walls. Merchants traveled the land and formed organizations, or guilds, which toppled the old way of doing things. Tax tariffs and charging to use roadways were abandoned to help the new business economy. It forced a battle between the old nobility and the new nobility who were creating towns.

Kings also began to form alliances with towns that wanted to become independent of their nobles. This led to the fall of the classic structure of feudalism.

New Forms of Government

Around 1100 C.E., the old nobility, who depended on the structure of feudalism, merged with a new ruling class of nobles, who ran newly developed towns. These two sets of nobles, as well as very wealthy merchants, formed the Berger class. This Berger class combined old-money people (who were rich by birth) and those who had become wealthy by becoming the first long-distance traders. They formed early city councils that ran each town. People who lived inside these towns began to think of themselves as free people who had a small bit of basic rights. For the first time in a long time, upward social mobility was possible. Merchants formed guilds to discourage imports, and only a certain number of people were licensed to trade in town. For example, if the town council said four blacksmiths were allowed in town, no other blacksmith could set up shop. These guilds set standards for the price of an item as well as the required quality of an item. This allowed all licensed artisans to make money because the quality of each item was equivalent, and no one could charge a cheaper price than anyone else.

Relationship Between Kings and Towns

The enterprising merchants created a new social class and new roles of government. In certain parts of Europe, these new towns were very attractive to the ruling king for multiple reasons.

1. There was a consolidation of educated workers and educated governmental ministers who understood ideas of Roman law.
2. The king now had access to a large source of cash reserves by charging taxes or chartering a town.
3. The king no longer had to give land to nobles in return for service.
4. In exchange for money, the king could hire and create his own army. He no longer needed a vassal to pledge his loyalty to him.

In England and France, plus areas in Germany, new towns began to thrive under royal recognition. The cooperation between new towns and the kings transformed classic feudalism into the growth of nation-states and national governments.

THE CREATION OF SCHOOLS AND UNIVERSITIES

During the depths of the Dark Ages in Europe, Jewish and Islamic scholars had saved Greco-Roman works of science and literature and ideas of Roman law. Some of it was also kept alive in the Byzantine Empire. After the Crusades, scholars in Western Europe used this knowledge to usher in a rebirth of learning. It led to the creation of schools and universities to recruit and educate young students.

The first university was created in 1158 C.E. in the Italian city of Bologna by Emperor Frederick Barbarossa. It was the first organization of teachers, called masters, and students who could earn a degree. Local bishops served as administrators of the early universities to make sure that the church approved of what was being taught. Thirsty for education, students helped form the curriculum and the credentials necessary for someone to be considered a master. The University of Bologna was the base model for universities that sprung up in Spain, Italy, and France. Some of these universities focused on the study of Roman law, and others focused on theology and religion. Every university required the old Greek liberal arts curriculum to be mastered before the student could advance.

Papal Decree of 1179 for Free Education

Also at this time, there was the creation of cathedral schools for nonreligious education. Cathedral schools were very similar to the Islamic madrasas (see Chapter 8). Before this time, all education had been done in cathedral or monastery schools strictly to train the religious clergy, and the material that was taught was strictly contained. Eventually, students seeking an education in nonreligious subjects in order to get a better job started coming to the cathedral schools. The Papal Decree of 1179 allowed that all nonreligious people who wanted to learn could come and be taught for free.

Interestingly enough, it was the access to education that caused the church to lose its grip on higher education. With the increased trading resulting from the Crusades, there was a demand for people who were literate. Due to the increased demand, towns began to create separate, nonreligious universities, and the towns grew into large urban areas. As towns grew in size, the church lost its grip on higher education.

By 1250, most universities became synonymous with their location. People knew the town by the university instead of the university being known by the town. In certain places, university students were given special rights and privileges by kings and princes. Royalty wanted to recruit scholars to work for the government, so university students received more privileges than a regular person.

University Requirements

The requirements for admission to a university during the High Middle Ages were fairly strict. Men began their studies in their early teens. They needed a good foundation of Latin and a well-rounded liberal arts education to earn a Bachelor's degree. It took three to four more years to earn a Master's degree. To become a high church official, a man needed a Master's degree in theology and then on-the-job training, all of which took about 20 years.

FRAMEWORK OF SOCIETY

Society continued to have three basic social classes throughout the High Middle Ages.

1. The nobles
2. The religious clergy
3. The peasants, which included the new long-distance traders and merchants

The nobility were the highest social class. Not all were wealthy men because they controlled differing and varied tracts of land. The higher nobility owned larger tracts of land, whereas the lower nobility were smaller landowners. Just like landowners in China and Japan, the nobility lived off the labor of other people, and everyone else was considered beneath them. For most nobles, the army was their profession, which gave them a chance to win glory. They could also add to their wealth as soldiers. If they were successful in conquering a civilization, then everything within the civilization was fair game.

Peacetime led to boredom for nobles, and too much time for self-reflection, so a code of behavior was drawn up. Nobles became knights, and their behavior was known as chivalry, which was similar to Japanese samurai's bushido. Depending on the knight's level of nobility, all knights were supposed to defend the church in some way. Becoming a knight was almost a religious sacrament, as priests or bishops were involved in the process. Because of the growing number of townspeople with new money and their increasing political power, knighthood was restricted to only men of old aristocratic birth. Knights had to be literate; they had to be able to sing, recite poetry, or play a musical instrument. Learning to be chivalrous occupied the nobles during peacetime.

The second social class was the religious clergy. This was a social class that was open to everyone: birth did not dictate place in this social class. It was based on training and behavior. However, many second and third sons of high-ranking nobles were not going to inherit the family lands or business, so they worked for the church.

Overall, all monks and secular clergy lived off the labor of others. They would receive money from revenue from church-imposed taxes, the collection plate at church services, and rent from church-owned land provided to farmers. Higher-order clergy—monks, cardinals, and bishops—were able to become extremely wealthy.

The wealth of some clergy was another reason for Pope Gregory to get involved in the lay investiture struggle. The church was vitally important, and clergy who took advantage of their position to gain personal wealth were frowned upon. Church property could not be taxed by an emperor, and if clergy committed a crime, they were tried under a church court. As corrupt church officials were placed in high-ranking positions by kings to secure political and monetary gain, the people got angry and resented the special treatment that the church received.

The third and largest social class was always the peasants. Though they did the work for virtually everyone else, and they lived on the estate manors of the nobility, most were considered the lord's property. They had to give a certain amount of what they made to the lord of the manor. Virtually the only freedom they had was that they were able to divide the labor as they saw fit, as long as the work got done.

There were two different types of manor houses.

1. The servant or servile manor mentioned earlier. These people had no skills, no privileges, and were subject to whatever the lord wanted as he held all political and judicial power. The lord also owned the artisan machines and could require a person to pay rent to use them.
2. The free manor. People owned small amounts of land and traded it for the lord's protection. They had a few more rights and privileges than the average everyday person because they chose to work *with* the lord.

While being a peasant was not very easy or enjoyable, it was wiser for the lord of the manor to keep his peasants somewhat happy, as he depended upon them for everything.

As the High Middle Ages moved toward the 1300s and the Renaissance, the manors changed. Populations increased, the land on manors shrunk, and new technology—like the horse collar, the mold board plow, and the three-field system—allowed more land to be cleared.

This caused a change in taxation. Up until now, each fief on a manor had to pay a certain amount of tax based on what was produced. Now, taxes were levied on individual people, and taxes were due only in money. With trade reborn due to the Crusades, some peasants were able to rent out their land, and they were able to overcome their low status. The only problem arose when times were tough on the manor. If there was a famine or a plague, the lord could ease your tax burden. Now, with rents and taxes being paid in cash, it was no longer possible to reduce the tax burden because of hardship.

WILLIAM THE CONQUEROR

Born in 1028, William the Conqueror was the illegitimate son of the duke of Normandy in France. Through William's maternal side of the family, he had a direct line to the English throne. After the duke died on a pilgrimage to the Holy Land, William should have inherited the land and title of his father in France. When the king of England died, the title should have also fallen to William the Conqueror. Instead, the English assembly chose a man named Harold Godwinson as their new king.

Angry at the way he grew up and for being overlooked by the assembly, William gathered his soldiers and sailed to England. William the Conqueror was only the second person to successfully invade the island nation of England. In 1066, he won the Battle of Hastings and was crowned king in Westminster Abbey, where all kings of England are crowned to this day.

He began to organize a new English government, one less dependent on ruling royalty and nobles around England, as these were the people who had tried to rub him out of his birthright. William went on a brutal 20-year campaign that forced every landowner in England to be his vassal, which was how he earned the nickname William the Conqueror.

William was smart. He assessed England's government and laws, keeping what worked for him. He liked the English taxation system so he kept it, and he liked to order court writs, or legal warnings, so he kept them. The process called parlaying was especially appealing to William, as he thought it would help him to govern his new kingdom. During the parlay process, he would periodically hold conferences with nobles or town councils to speak with them. They could also have a chance to ask questions or air their grievances. However, with a parlay, William did not have to act on anything they said; it was sufficient that William simply allowed them to speak. The process of parlay helped William gain control by making the nobles and town rulers feel respected and important.

William the Conqueror also started a county census, cataloging how many people lived in what town and village and what their production was in terms of goods and services. The information was written down in the Doomsday book. It was spelled "Domesday" but it was pronounced Doomsday. It was said that it was easier to escape death than it was to escape inclusion in William the Conqueror's Domesday book, which was completed in 1086. William the Conqueror was one of the first rulers to restart a strong, dominant monarchy and the building of nation-states.

ELEANOR OF AQUITAINE: ENGLISH AND FRENCH RIVALRY

Problems arose when William died without an heir. William was technically a vassal of the king of France as he was the duke of Normandy (region in northern France). However, he was also the king of England. In France, it was said that the king of England is a vassal to the French king. Clearly, this created a lot of animosity between the two countries. Some of this animosity surrounded a woman named Eleanor of Aquitaine of southwestern France. She

FUN FACT

In the Domesday book, William the Conqueror picked easy landmarks to name towns and locations as references within his book. For example, he mentions the "Ivybridge," which is now called the town of Ivybridge in southeastern England.

was married to the king of France but their marriage was annulled in 1152, and within a short time, she married King Henry II of England. Henry inherited a lot of territory in France as a gift from his new father-in-law, a French noble.

Eleanor became a very powerful woman. She was a positive example to women who wanted to work in business. When married to the king of France, she went on the Second Crusade with him in 1147. Eventually, her marriage to Henry II soured and ended with his death in 1189. She went back to France to live in the French city of Poitiers, where her court became famous for the literature they wrote, as they came up with the idea of courtly love and true love from afar. The most famous was the story of King Arthur and his Knights of the Round Table, which included the love triangle between Arthur, Guinevere, and Sir Lancelot.

It was the marriages of Eleanor of Aquitaine that created the growing animosity that eventually led to the Hundred Years War.

Global Connections

Eleanor of Aquitaine is often compared to Theodora of the Byzantine empire, who also played a large role in governmental affairs.

THE MAGNA CARTA (1215 C.E.)

As Henry II increased his territory outside of England, he became more oppressive at home. He tried to control the clergy, and he met with strong resistance from not only his nobles but also the pope in Rome. There was increasing resentment toward the English throne after the death of Henry II. King Richard the Lionheart assessed heavier taxes to pay for his involvement in the Third Crusade and a war with France.

FUN FACT

Prince John is the bumbling prince made famous in the Robin Hood stories. Robin Hood always manages to defeat the hapless Prince John!

When King Richard famously left England to go on the Third Crusade in 1189, he left his brother, Prince John, in charge. Prince John got into an argument with Pope Innocent III over naming the Archbishop of Canterbury the head church official in England. Prince John thought he could name one of his buddies to that post, and the pope said no. The pope was forced to place England under interdict in 1208. Interdict means the pope excommunicated the entire nation of England. There were no church sacrifices, no marriages, no baptisms, no last rights, and no burials. This was heavy ammunition. To apologize, Prince John had to publicly state that the king of England was a vassal to the pope. While he was stating this, he lost a battle with the French. Due to the heavy taxation of the people of England, coupled with his embarrassing military losses, the church clergy, his nobles, and the people forced Prince John to sign the Magna Carta in 1215, which means "the Great Charter." The Magna Carta became the foundation for English law forevermore. The Magna Carta stated that the king of England cannot act without the approval of Parliament and that the king of England is not above the law.

At this point in world history, the French had solidified their monarchical power, while the English king was now subject to the Magna Carta. However, it was the Holy Roman Empire—Charlemagne's old empire—that had politically fragmented again. Charlemagne's empire had been divided back in 843 C.E. at the Treaty of Verdun, and the different areas were now becoming a problem, primarily due to the 360 princes of Germany.

THE HOLY ROMAN EMPIRE

Emperor Frederick Barbarossa of Germany kicked off a brand-new phase in the pope–emperor conflict. It created an unparalleled level of anger. Frederick thought his feudal lords should obey only him, but the pope thought he was superior to all of them. Before Frederick could complete his job of trying to subjugate the pope, he formed an alliance with the Kingdom of Sicily in 1186, which boxed in the pope in Rome. With the pope hostile to the emperor, the princes in Germany once again achieved independence.

When Frederick Barbarossa's son Henry VI assumed the throne in 1190, the 360 German states were in total chaos. England and France backed two different families to be leaders of Germany. England backed an emperor named Otto, and France backed the Hohenstaufen family. To further complicate matters, Henry VI died in 1197, leaving a young son named Frederick II with a direct and legitimate claim to the throne of Holy Roman emperor. However, Frederick II was living with the pope, and he was crowned emperor. Frederick II never went to Germany as he liked living in Italy, but he clashed with different popes as he tried to increase his lands in northern Italy. While he did so, he lost his German powerbase. Because Frederick II tried to conquer parts of Italy, he was excommunicated many times.

The big victors in the Holy Roman Empire were the princes of Germany. Germany remained separated until the 1800s when it was unified under the Prussian leader Otto von Bismarck. Germany remained a bunch of different tiny princedoms with no monarchical power, so while England and France were on the way to nation building, Germany was left alone.

POPE INNOCENT III

Pope Innocent III reigned from 1198 to 1216 and was a firm believer in the Gregorian tradition of church independence. He made a statement that "the Pope is to the Emperors of Europe and the church is to the state like the sun is to the moon." This statement means that the church and the pope were superior to all political governments. Political governments were subject to church authority. This was a great statement, but Pope Innocent III did not have the power to enforce it. He confronted every German, French, and English emperor involved in the battle over the title of Holy Roman emperor.

As the High Middle Ages came to an end, the pope emerged victorious. Pope Innocent III took on all high-ranking members of European authority and subjugated them to his power. The church was at a high point, but it had not experienced its fiercest challenge yet as the Black Death was approaching.

THE BLACK DEATH

The Black Death arrived in Italy in 1347 on trading ships coming from the Black Sea. Soon after, the people began to fall sick, and within a few months, the epidemic, now known as the Black Death, was raging throughout Italy. The following year, it moved into Spain and France, and one in every three people in Western Europe died. The Black Death killed more people than all previous wars combined.

Ironically, the Black Death traveled quickly on the delivery system that brought increased trading, wealth, and technology to Europe: the Silk Road. The Black Death followed global epidemic models as it crossed from Asia and Russia on rats carrying tiny fleas that spread the disease. The fleas were so small that no one paid attention to them. The fleas spread to clothing of people traveling both east and west and then bit the human host. Not only was the European population decimated, but also the people in India, China, and the Middle East were hit with the plague as well.

The speed of the plague made it nearly impossible to stop. Known now as the bubonic plague, there would be a black bite mark, some swelling, and within two or three days, people were dying in horrible agony. The unsanitary conditions of the manors, the castles, and even the new towns helped spread the disease.

As fear gripped Europe, people at first turned to the church. When the church could not stop the disease, some people began to turn to magic and witchcraft. Some people blamed it on other ethnic groups, and the Jewish people began to be persecuted. Others thought it was God's punishment, leading to the end of the world. The plague killed in reoccurring waves over many years. The growing economy of Europe was plunged once again into darkness as many European workers were dead and dying. There was no more production of goods and services, which sent prices skyrocketing. It took 100 years before Europe began to recover.

Results of the Plague for the Church

The church suffered from the Black Death. Many priests and monks died fighting the plague, and the church did not have strong leadership at this time. The pope left Rome and moved to France. A strong antichurch sentiment grew among the people and from within the church. In England, the church corruption was attacked, saying that the Bible, and not the church, was the source of Christian teaching. The church needed to undergo some reforms heading into the Renaissance to regain the once-dominant power that it held under Pope Innocent III.

THE HUNDRED YEARS WAR

To compound the problems of the Black Death, economic decline, and the corruption of the church, England and France engaged in a series of battles between 1337 and 1453 known as the Hundred Years War. The Hundred Years War left England and France physically and financially drained. Going back to William the Conqueror and Eleanor of Aquitaine, English rulers wanted to hold onto their lands in France. Conversely, the French kings wanted the English out of France.

At a first glance, the Hundred Years War looked to be fought over royal title only. The Hundred Years War started in 1337 when King Edward III of England claimed to be king of France. However, it was also fought because of a growing economic trade rivalry and a new sense of what comes to be known as nationalism.

England had great national pride, and a string of victories early on bolstered the idea of nationalism. The English also had better weapons technology, namely the longbow, which could fire farther and faster than anything the French had.

Joan of Arc

Just as French morale was at a low point, a miracle happened involving a young 17-year-old peasant girl named Joan of Arc. Joan of Arc went before the uncrowned king of France in 1428 and said that God told her how to save France. To everyone's shock, young Joan inspired the battered French troops, and they began to win. Unfortunately, Joan was captured in 1430, was found guilty of being a witch, and was burned at the stake in 1431. However, her martyrdom inspired the French army.

The French developed a brand new weapon called the cannon. A cannon was much stronger than the English longbow, and with it, the French began to destroy old English castles in France. The English were driven out of France.

The Effects of the Hundred Years War

After the devastation of the Hundred Years War, England and France developed very differently from each other. The French kings greatly expanded their power, whereas the English kings had to constantly ask the nobles in Parliament for money.

However, it was not all bad news for the English. They gave up trying to form an empire in continental Europe. They began to look toward the ocean to acquire territory beyond the vast expanse of the sea.

Who won or lost the Hundred Years War was not important. The effects the war had were, however, very important. The idea that a mounted knight on horseback was necessary to win battles was proved wrong. England and France both realized that they needed large armies to fight their wars.

TIMELINE REVIEW

1066 C.E.	William the Conqueror
1076 C.E.	• Pope Gregory VII excommunicates Henry IV.
	• Lay investiture controversy begins.
1086 C.E.	William's Domesday book
1092 C.E.	First Crusade
1100 C.E.	Birth of Cathedral Schools
1122 C.E.	Concordat of Worms ends the lay investiture.
1180 C.E.	Philip II King of France
1187 C.E.	• Third Crusade
	• Richard the Lionheart vs. Saladin
1198 C.E.	• Pope Innocent III excommunicates Prince John of England.
	• Otto Wolf of the German States
	• Phillip II of France
	• Frederick II of Holy Roman Empire and Sicily
1215 C.E.	Prince John signs the Magna Carta.
1270 C.E.	Thomas Aquinas writes *Summa Theologica*.
1271 C.E.	Marco Polo sets off on his travels.
1302 C.E.	Estates General is created in France.
1337–1450 C.E.	Hundred Years War—England vs. France
1350 C.E.	Black Death plague
1429 C.E.	Joan of Arc rallies French troops.
1492 C.E.	• Spanish complete Reconquista.
	• Columbus begins his voyages.

GLOBAL CONNECTIONS

Russia

1462 C.E.—Ivan the Great

Japan

Circa 1000–1600 C.E.—Japanese feudalism

1192 C.E.—Minamoto Yoritomo becomes shogun

1274–1281 C.E.—Kublai Khan invasions fail

Africa

1480 C.E.—Portuguese begin to trade with West Africa

Mesoamerica

1200 C.E.—Apache in North America

1300 C.E.—Tenochtitlan built by Aztecs

1450 C.E.—Machu Picchu built by Incas

China

1279 C.E.—Song Dynasty ends

India

1350 C.E.—Delhi sultanate

1360 C.E.—Tamerlane's conquests begin

Middle East

1206 C.E.—Genghis Khan begins conquests

1258 C.E.—Hulagu Khan burns Baghdad

1299 C.E.—Ottoman Empire forms, one of three Gunpowder Empires

Quick Quiz: Chapters 10–11

1. Which emperor ruled during the Golden Age of the Byzantine Empire?

   A. Theodosis
   B. Constantine
   C. Justinian
   D. Comnenus

2. Which of the following describes the separation between the Roman Catholic Church and the Eastern Orthodox Church in 1054?

   A. Cluny Reforms
   B. Great Schism
   C. Benedictine Order
   D. Reformation

3. This is the group of Mongols that invaded Russia and eventually converted to Islam.

   A. Golden Horde
   B. Mamluks
   C. Khaninites
   D. Magyars

4. As the Mongol influence began to wane, Moscow rose to power under this emperor.

   A. Peter the Great
   B. Michael Romanov
   C. Nicholas II
   D. Ivan the Great

5. This was a movement that started in monasteries to reform the church to help maintain its spiritual focus.

   A. Benedictine Order
   B. Cluny Reforms
   C. Catholic Reformation
   D. Crusades

6. Which of the following is the controversy that led popes and emperors into great periods of conflict during the High Middle Ages?

   A. Crusades
   B. Wars between France and England
   C. The churches maintaining fertile farmland
   D. The practice of lay investiture

7. Which of the following powerful popes launched the Crusades in 1092?

   A. Pope Innocent III
   B. Pope Urban II
   C. Pope Gregory VII
   D. Pope Leo III

8. In the High Middle Ages, who did kings begin to turn to and ally themselves with to help them to defeat the nobles?

   A. The church
   B. Towns and townships
   C. Crusaders
   D. Monasteries and their powerful abbots

9. This important document written in 1215 was the first to place limits on the power of a king.

   A. Magna Carta
   B. English Bill of Rights
   C. Treaty of Verdun
   D. Edict of Milan

10. This influential queen of the Middle Ages was an advocate for women's rights, helped sponsor the Crusades, encouraged women to be merchants, and created wonderful works of literature at her court.

    A. Queen Guinevere
    B. Queen Elizabeth I
    C. Eleanor of Aquitaine
    D. Joan of Arc

Quick Quiz Answers

1. C; **2.** B; **3.** A; **4.** D; **5.** B; **6.** D; **7.** B; **8.** B; **9.** A; **10.** C

African States

12

GEOGRAPHY

The geography of Africa has always had a large impact on the people. Most of Africa consists of savanna grassland, starting south of the Sahara Desert and stretching all the way down to Zimbabwe. It is the largest climate zone in Africa. On this savanna, there is good soil and usually adequate rainfall, making it suitable for farming.

At the northern and southern ends of the savanna are two large deserts. The scorching Sahara Desert runs the width of Africa from the Atlantic Ocean to the Mediterranean Sea. Even though it became a major trade route, traveling through the Sahara Desert was very difficult to do.

Along the northern coast of Africa, the continent has a Mediterranean climate with fertile soil suitable for farming. Much of the land in the north also borders on the lush Nile Delta, another favorable environment for farming.

The fourth climate zone runs from the Atlantic Ocean through the widest part of Africa at a 45° angle. It covers the Great Rift Valley by Lake Victoria and continues along the massive Congo River. There are dense, thick rain forests.

Throughout Africa, there are many barriers to movement. It does not possess good harbors for sailing, even though it is surrounded by water. In the center of the continent, there is a giant plateau with rivers like the Zambezi, Limpopo, and Congo, but much like the Nile River, they have cataracts. Cataracts are waterfalls, and even though the rivers served as highways for goods, migration over the falls was very difficult.

There are a lot of natural resources in Africa, such as diamonds and emeralds, and lush mineral wealth like salt, iron, gold, and copper. Africa is also famous for its exotic animals: the lion, tiger, and gorilla. These resources will have an impact on African history.

MIGRATIONS OF PEOPLE

One of the most-often talked about migrations in world history was the great Bantu migrations that took place from 1500 B.C.E until 500 C.E. People often think of the Bantu migrations as one single migration, but it was instead a long series of migrations. The Bantu people migrated from their place of origin around the Gulf of Guinea and populated central and southern Africa. Today, about a third of the people speak a Bantu language. Language is very important in tracing the history of a people.

Throughout world history, the migration of people has contributed to massive diversity, which was experienced by people on the African continent. Migrations can be traced by studying root languages. The Bantu started on the Atlantic coast, then the Bantu herders migrated southward and eastward. Their herds grazed on the plentiful savannah grasses. There were times when the Bantu forced indigenous tribes to relocate due to a conflict

Global Connections

To connect the Bantu migrations globally, they began at the same time as the beginning of civilization in Greece and ended near the fall of Rome, a period of roughly two thousand years.

between the groups. Along the way, the Bantu spread their culture and their skills. Most notably, the Bantu contributed to cultural diffusion in farming and their work ethic.

Today, the African people speak many different languages but most of them are descended from a common root language: Bantu. As the Bantus migrated across Africa, they were able to adapt to the different climates and cultures they encountered. This further added to the diversity among cultures. Some Bantu settled down in these new areas, becoming cattle herders or farmers. In some of these regions, they built great empires. Other Bantu continued to migrate, living a nomadic lifestyle, which extended the Bantu people further across Africa.

The Paths of the Bantu Migrations

Different branches of Bantus migrated through Africa. One group moved along the west coast, southward to what is today Namibia and Botswana, just north of South Africa. Another branch traveled from the northwest coast, following the Niger River. This group made its way across the continent to Lake Victoria, Tanzania, and Uganda. One branch spread off into the interior, eventually following the Zambezi River into the Congo and Zambia. A fourth branch ran down the east coast of Africa on the Indian Ocean, landing on the eastern side of Zimbabwe. The entire lower third of the African continent experienced the great Bantu migrations.

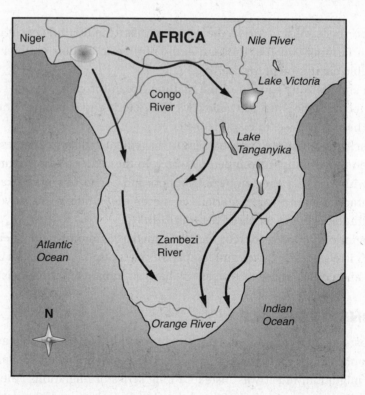

Swahili

The people who lived on the east coast of Africa did not use the same Bantu language, but instead used a different language called Swahili. Swahili has many different dialects, and Arab, Persian, and other migrants have added their own cultural infusion to the Swahili language. Swahili was used on the eastern coast, running up and down Africa from Tanzania through Ethiopia and Djibouti.

THE KINGDOM OF GHANA

The kingdom of Ghana was the trendsetter for all later West African empires. The kingdom of Ghana started to grow as an empire in 400 C.E., right as Rome was getting ready to collapse. By 800 C.E., Ghana had created a regional empire that lasted for hundreds of years. Ghana was in the middle of a major north-south and east-west trade network on the west coast of Africa. They had access to the Niger and Senegal rivers, making Ghana a perfect location to start an empire.

Royal Authority

Ghana was not a hereditary monarchy, meaning that it was not the son of the king who inherited the throne upon the death of the king. Kings were descended through the sister of the king. The son of the king's sister inherited the throne. This was a major difference between most of the other monarchies in world history.

The ruling and governance was done through a council of advisors, or elders, who were also ministers of the kingdom. They carried out the king's orders. Another big difference was that the king ruled as more of a head judge or supreme court leader. He actually spent a lot of his time in a court setting, hearing complaints or concerns of his people. Many other monarchs of this time in Europe and Asia were separated from their people, but the people of Ghana had direct access to their king. However, like many other kings, the king of Ghana was seen as blessed by the gods. The polytheistic believers of Ghana believed that the gods chose their king to be their leader.

Economic Power Base

Ghana was able to gain power in Africa because its economy was strong. The government controlled many things that people needed. It was able to gain tribute from many smaller regional tribes. It also earned money by renting or leasing royal lands, upon which grew very lush crops, like sugar cane and bananas. Ghana used the Senegal and Niger rivers to spread its power, influence, and trade goods.

Ghana taxed all exports and imports from other parts of Africa. Much like the Ch'in and Han Dynasties of China, Ghana imported salt, cloth, and copper, which it paid for in gold. However, the kings of Ghana had a monopoly on many necessary items, and in order to get them, other countries had to go through the king. The king was able to make money off of everything.

Eventually, gold was not exchanged for the imports of salt, cloth, and copper. Instead, Ghana started the slave trade to pay for their imports.

Impact of Islam on Ghana

As Islam spread across northern Africa starting in 600–700 C.E., it extended into the kingdom of Ghana. Although the kings of Ghana did not officially convert to Islam, they went to extravagant lengths to accommodate Islamic traders. Trading brought new goods and more money, so they tried to accommodate Muslim traders and their servants in any way possible. Many Islamic traders were welcomed at the king's court. Since many of the Muslims were literate, they eventually helped advise the king and became ministers in his government.

The Fall of Ghana

One of the reasons that Ghana stayed powerful for a long time was that it had a very large and well-trained military force. Eventually, in 1075, Ghana fell to a group of Islamic nomads: Bedouins, known as the Almoravids.

THE KINGDOM OF MALI

Located north of Ghana, the kingdom of Mali developed in the 1200s out of the chaos that followed the fall of the Ghanaian Empire. Much like many of the Chinese dynasties, Mali kept the parts of the Ghana Empire that worked. Most notably they continued to build on the same solid economic base as Ghana. The kingdom of Mali completely monopolized the gold trade. No gold moved in or out of Africa without going through the Malian government. Not only did Mali control the flow of gold in West Africa, but they also controlled the importation of copper and salt, just like the early Han Dynasty in China.

Sundiata

The empire of Mali was built by Sundiata. Under his reign from 1232 C.E. to 1255 C.E., there was a large population boom as a result of agricultural developments. With a large population and secure economic foundation, Sundiata wanted to extend his empire. He moved from the Atlantic coast to the interior of Africa, where he founded the city known as Timbuktu. Timbuktu became Mali's capital. It was built along the banks of the Niger River on seven small foothills, like a smaller version of Rome. Timbuktu was the African version of Athens, Rome, or Constantinople.

Timbuktu was a large, multicultural city with many different peoples, languages, and religious backgrounds. Sundiata's empire did not have a strong centralized government like early Rome or China; instead, Timbuktu was at the center of many small regions or provinces. The location of Timbuktu allowed the people of Mali to connect with their king. The provinces had some independence, but they paid taxes and acknowledged the leadership of Sundiata as their supreme sacred ruler.

Importance of the Malinke

The people of Mali had different clans, called keita, but it was a collection of the most powerful families that took over the leadership role. They were not the kings of Mali; instead, they were a group of people who were spread out in different Malian city-states. In the core of the kingdom were the Malinke people.

The Malinke lived in large, urban, walled cities, which were very similar to Greek city-states. Most communities had a population of up to 15,000 and were self-sufficient in their own little region. This confederation of Malinke city-states was an important key to ruling.

Farming and Slave Labor in Mali

The kingdom of Mali controlled all of the rich, fertile farmland along the Niger River as well as the trade. The rich Niger River delta gave the people of Mali a large surplus of food. To work this large area, the people of Mali began to use prisoners of war as slave labor. The slaves did all of the work for the people of Mali.

Global Connections

Using prisoners of war as slave labor in Mali was very similar to the Spartan helots and ancient Roman slaves. In Chapter 13, the Aztecs of Mesoamerica also used prisoners of war as slave labor.

Conversion to Islam

Around 1100 C.E., many of the Malinke converted to Islam, and several of their kings went on the Hajj to Mecca. This brought them into greater contact with other parts of Africa and the Middle East. After the conversion, there was a much greater Islamic influence in Mali, and it changed the political thinking and organization of the empire.

Mansa Musa

The greatest of the Malinke men was Mansa Musa. His pilgrimage to Mecca in 1324 was legendary. Mansa Musa was so wealthy that as he traveled across Africa through Cairo on his way to Mecca, he gave away so much gold that he deflated the value of Egyptian currency for a decade, causing years of inflation.

Mansa Musa came back from Mecca with many Islamic scholars, artists, and architects. A devout Muslim, he further aided the spread and acceptance of Islam in West Africa. Mansa Musa also helped Timbuktu become a leading cultural and trading city.

> **FUN FACT**
>
> There are multiple historical descriptions of the pilgrimage of Mansa Musa. Remember in Disney's *Aladdin*, when Aladdin, disguised as Prince Ali, entered the city with his huge entourage and parade to woo Princess Jasmine? That is eerily similar to what happened as Mansa Musa and his entourage crossed Africa!

The Fall of the Kingdom of Mali

Mali broke apart after the death of Mansa Musa in 1337. There was a large civil war to see who would replace him, and the fighting disrupted the trade and economic flow of the country, leading to the collapse of the great Malian Empire.

THE KINGDOM OF SONGHAI

Songhai picked up where the kingdom of Mali left off. Its rise to power happened between 1464 and 1492 under Sonni Ali. Under his leadership, the Songhai became a massive imperial power that dominated West Africa. Songhai was able to dominate all of West Africa because they controlled the lush agricultural and mineral base of Ghana and Mali. Songhai also had a riverboat navy and cavalry soldiers, giving them the ability to move throughout West Africa very quickly. They were easily able to increase and secure their empire.

Death of Sonni Ali

In 1492, as Christopher Columbus was discovering the West Indies, Sonni Ali died. His successor was Muhammad al-Turi. Muhammad al-Turi kept up the expansion of Songhai, moving up the Atlantic coast to the Sahara Desert and as far eastward as the middle of Sudan. Just like the empire of Ghana, Muhammad al-Turi nurtured and took control of the caravan routes that crossed Africa.

Muhammad al-Turi and Islam

Unlike Sonni Ali, who worshipped the traditional African gods, Muhammad al-Turi was a devout Muslim. He created a new Islamic dynasty and built his government to be a model of Islam. He recruited and hired Islamic scholars to come to his empire to help him govern. He used them as governmental ministers and judges throughout his empire. Muhammad al-Turi and his bureaucracy turned Timbuktu into a massive trading center for Muslims.

All of this came at a very high cost to the African continent. With so many Muslims arriving in western Africa, the native Africans were being displaced, which did not make them very happy with their king. Muhammad al-Turi tried his best to emulate the rule of Mansa Musa, but he was never satisfied with the level and depth of his empire. The great Songhai Empire collapsed in 1591 after a powerful, but short, reign. The Songhai were defeated by Moroccan warriors, who used a superior technology called gunpowder.

EFFECTS OF MANSA MUSA, SONNI ALI, AND MUHAMMAD AL-TURI

While Europe was in the Dark Ages, Africa was getting along perfectly fine. However, the empires of Mansa Musa, Sonni Ali, and Muhammad al-Turi brought a lot of attention to Africa. The amount of gold that was given away attracted the attention of Europeans, who were starting to go out into the world during the age of exploration, which started in the 1400s. They went to Africa for gold, but the slave trade quickly picked up as the Europeans began to change not only Africa's economy, but the global economy as well. This relationship eventually led to imperialism and colonialism of Africa as Europeans took the riches of Africa: gold, pepper, ivory, and slaves. All of this had a negative effect on Africa, which is still felt to this day.

PORTUGUESE ARRIVAL

There were some positive effects of Europeans arriving in Africa. The Portuguese were the first to explore West Africa in 1480, which reconnected Europe into the global economy. After Columbus's voyage to the New World in 1492, the Portuguese also introduced crops from the New World: corn, potatoes, and beans, all of which grew well in the West African climate.

The negative effect of the Portuguese arrival was that West Africa was divided into spheres of influence based on their main export. Regions like the Ivory Coast, Gold Coast, and Pepper Coast were formed based on the main export in that region.

Senegambia

Senegambia, the region between the Senegal and Gambia rivers that empty into the Atlantic, was the first area affected by European traders. This region was in close proximity to Portugal, which was a sailing kingdom. The Portuguese sailed the Atlantic and down the Mediterranean coast to easily arrive at this part of West Africa.

When the Portuguese arrived in 1480, they began to trade for gold, salt, cotton, and copper. The people of the African empires eventually brought slaves to the coast as well, selling them to the Europeans. About one-third of all slaves in the 1500s came from the Senegambia region of Africa. Eventually, the population decreased, which led to a decline in the slave trade in this region, and the slave trade shifted further southward.

By this time, other European countries were on their way to Africa. The English and the Portuguese tried to control the areas around the Gambia River while the French moved toward the Senegal River. The European sphere of influence increased dramatically at this time. Spain, the Netherlands, and Germany also came to Africa to colonize and trade, but the English and French ended up playing the largest role on the continent.

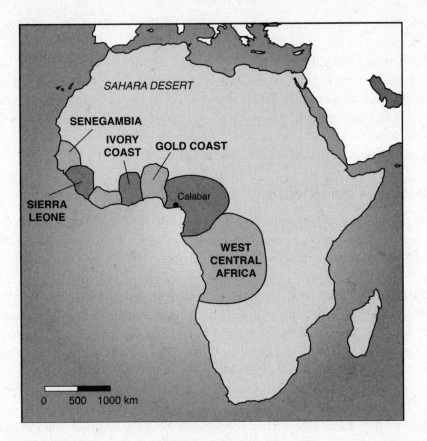

EUROPEAN EFFECTS ON THE GOLD COAST

The Gold Coast was named as such due to the importance of gold as the main export in the 1500s. The Portuguese built a fort in 1482 to protect their trade goods from rival nations, and the other European countries quickly followed suit.

The increased contact with Europeans and the spread of North American food crops resulted in a large population growth in Africa from 1500 to 1650. Because of the large amount of gold that the wealthy Africans gave to the Europeans, they were safe from the slave trade. They actually used poor Africans as slaves themselves. By the middle of the 1500s, slave trading was becoming a bigger business than the gold trade, and it began to disrupt the economy.

CENTRAL AFRICA

GEOGRAPHY

Central Africa had the most diversity in all of Africa. Central Africa runs in a large swath from the Atlantic, heading eastward to the Red Sea and the Indian Ocean. In the northern part of this area, there are thick, dense swamps. On the west coast, there are thick, beautiful rain forests. The south consists of desert lands, and in the east, there are African grasslands, including the highlands of the Serengeti Plain.

THE PORTUGUESE SLAVE TRADE

For much of world history, this rich geography provided natural barriers that protected the center land of Africa from the outside civilizations. However, by the 1500s, the Portuguese were able to finally make it through these natural barriers and into the protection of this interior isolation.

The Portuguese headed to the interior of Africa looking for mineral wealth. When they did not find any, they quickly turned their attention to ivory and then to the natural resource that fueled the transatlantic trade for hundreds of years: slaves. People from Central Africa were captured and doomed to be slaves. They were taken to work on Portuguese sugar plantations in the New World, and eventually they were taken to Brazil. The stereotypical plantation slave labor began with slaves from Central Africa.

THE KINGDOM OF KONGO

Kongo was the primary empire with whom the Portuguese dealt starting in 1483. It was a very wealthy kingdom in the middle of Africa. Kongo had a lot of fertile farmlands, access to salt mines, and very good metalwork and pottery. The wide Congo River ran through the empire.

The Portuguese brought Mediterranean items like wine and olive oil, plus luxury items from North Africa, which they presented to the king of Kongo as gifts. These gifts greatly increased his wealth. In exchange, the king of Kongo gave the Portuguese unlimited access to his empire and allowed them to take the resource of his people for the slave trade. The king exchanged his people for luxury consumable goods like tobacco and alcohol. Even though the Kongo had a large population, it was almost impossible to replace the number of slaves being carried out. To save their villages, regional chieftains in the Kongo captured their neighbors to give to the Portuguese so the Portuguese would leave their villages alone. This increased the warfare and unrest within the kingdom.

King Afonso I

King Afonso I was the king of Kongo from 1505 to 1543 as the slave trade epidemic began. King Afonso I was a Christian and had been educated by Portuguese missionaries. As a fellow royal, King Afonso wrote a letter to the king of Portugal, asking him to stop the slave trade. He explained that he wanted to build Kongo into a modern Christian state, and he welcomed Portuguese missionaries to help him build a Christian kingdom in Africa.

The Portuguese showed up in response to King Afonso's offer with the best of intentions. However, the lure of making a lot of money was too much for the Portuguese. Such high prices were being offered for slaves, King Afonso's efforts never worked. His actions were undercut by his own local officials. He continued to work against the slave trade because it was evil and against the teachings of the Christian Bible. He was able to restrict the Portuguese slave enterprises to just one port on his coastline. The Portuguese tried to assassinate King Afonso in 1540, but he survived. After the assassination attempt, the people rallied behind their king, and for a while, the people boycotted Portuguese goods.

Global Connections

King Afonso I was similar to the Yamato family in Japan because he sent his sons abroad to study other cultures.

Jaga Wars

After the reign of King Afonso I ended in 1543, there was a series of civil wars inside the Kongo known as the Jaga Wars. The Jaga Wars caused the empire to break apart and fracture in 1556. The Portuguese took advantage of the civil wars, helping to bring down the very prosperous, powerful Kongo Empire.

NUBIA

The ancient kingdom of Nubia was located south of Egypt. Nubia was sometimes called the Kush Empire. Nubia is located in what is today the Sudan. There were frequent interactions, and sometimes warfare, between Nubia and the ancient Egyptians. By 500 B.C.E., the kingdom of Nubia built a new capital called Meroë, and they controlled part of the Nile River and the savanna grasslands of the east coast. They began trading with people in the Middle East, and the Meroëic people were known for producing high-quality iron for tools and weapons. The Nubian Empire collapsed around 350 C.E. They were absorbed into a powerful kingdom of East Africa known as Axum.

AXUM

The kingdom of Axum conquered territory along the east coast starting in 350 C.E. in what is today Ethiopia. Axum was unique in its strategic location along the Red Sea. Axum facilitated a triangle trade route between Africa, the Middle East, and India. Products from the African interior came through Axum and then shipped across the Red Sea to the Middle East or to India via the Indian Ocean. Axum also controlled the north-south trade route along the east coast of Africa.

In the center of this international trade, there were Egyptian, Arabic, Jewish, Greek, and African people meshing in Axum. Christianity was introduced in 300 C.E., and it took root among the people. It strengthened ties between Axum and the empires of the Mediterranean. As Islam spread across North Africa, Axum remained a Christian stronghold.

Even though Axum declined over the course of world history, they had a string of commercial cities that were trading as far back as the days of ancient Phoenicia. The thousands of years of cultural diffusion found in Axum added to the rich diversity of this area, which can still be found in present-day Ethiopia.

Global Connections

Axum was an earlier version of Constantinople. It was a centrally located, large civilization where multiple ethnic groups were welcome to trade and share information.

THE PORTUGUESE MAKE IT TO EAST AFRICA

The Portuguese encountered the Swahili civilization on the east coast of Africa in the late 1490s, which brought about an abrupt end to the traditional Swahili civilization.

East African trade with the Middle East started to decline in the 1500s with the arrival of the Portuguese. The Portuguese realized that East Africa had a heavy Islamic influence with pockets of Christianity found in Ethiopia. They studied the massive international trade that went from Africa, the Middle East, and Indonesia. The Portuguese decided that they either wanted to control the East Africa trade monopoly or destroy the trade entirely along the Indian Ocean and Red Sea. They waged warfare against Islamic ocean trading, and they attacked and destroyed many of the Islamic city-states running along the East African coast.

Simultaneous with the Portuguese destruction, there was a long period of drought. Many Africans from the interior of the continent moved to the coast and attacked the Swahili civilization. The Swahili could not defend against the simultaneous attacks by their fellow Africans from the interior and the exterior attacks by the Portuguese.

Portuguese Economic Monopoly

The Portuguese simply wanted this territory for themselves. They fought to control not only the commerce but all the shipping ports as well. To convince the Portuguese government to provide military support, they told the government that it was a holy war and that they wanted to arrest control from the Islamic people. In reality, however, the Portuguese invaders made no effort to bring Christianity to the Islamic territory. The Portuguese simply conquered for economic gain.

The Portuguese attacks led to widespread destruction and massive economic decline on the east coast of Africa. What was once a powerful, rich trading empire was destroyed. Interestingly enough, the Africans from the interior refused to cooperate with the Portuguese. The Africans tried to blockade all the gold trade, and they actually reduced shipping from other parts of Asia to a trickle. In the 1600s, the Portuguese empire in East Africa finally began to decline.

Prazeros

The Portuguese left behind a destabilizing force in East Africa. Portuguese sailors who stayed behind became great landowners, and they married into the local African population. The mixed-blood Portuguese Africans became known as prazeros. Prazeros did not follow the Portuguese king or local African laws.

SOUTHEASTERN AFRICA

As the African east coast trading centers began to grow and flourish (before the arrival of the Portuguese), there was a completely different civilization in Southeast Africa that was reaching its zenith of power: Zimbabwe.

ZIMBABWE

The Civilization of Zimbabwe

The Zimbabwean civilization was located between the Zambezi River and the Limpopo River. The heart of the civilization was far enough inland that its geography was not coastal; instead, half was a large savanna, and the other half consisted of woodlands. As a result, Zimbabwe was fairly isolated from the Portuguese and the effects of Islamic trade. It was purely and solely an African civilization.

Around 800 C.E., a group of Bantu-speaking people known as the Shona built the large, prosperous state of Zimbabwe. Between 1200 and 1400, the civilization reached the height of its power. They lived in a collection of 150 city-states that were very similar to the city-states of ancient Greece that existed 1800 years before them. Some of the Shona people are still in Zimbabwe today.

The Great Zimbabwe: Stone Walls and Defenses

Of the 150 Zimbabwean city-states, the largest and most well known is the Great Zimbabwe. Similar to the Athenian Acropolis, it had a 60-acre acropolis/high city that overlooked other large structures. Defensive walls surrounded a large central tower, or silo. Just like in ancient

Athens, the Great Zimbabwe was mainly a shrine to the different polytheistic gods and also served as a fort.

Engineers and Artisans of Great Zimbabwe

The people of Great Zimbabwe were excellent stonemasons as the brick-like rocks that built the community and defensive walls were very intricately worked. The society had a great knowledge of engineering. The rocks fit together without mortar and are still intact today. Artists of Great Zimbabwe created elaborate stone carvings, which people in the area still create to this day. They were also excellent goldsmiths and coppersmiths.

Trading with Other Civilizations

As with many events throughout world history, historians are unable to explain how the people of Zimbabwe traded with other cultures. Artifacts ranging from Chinese glass and porcelain to Persian artifacts have been discovered in Zimbabwe. It is not known if the civilization traded directly with other cultures or if there was some type of external third party trading. Conversely, gold and ironwork from the Great Zimbabwe somehow made it out of the civilization as these artifacts and others have been discovered in other countries. However, it is known that there was a large portion of gold in the Zambezi River, and the rulers of Zimbabwe controlled the gold trade on it and its smaller tributaries.

Lifestyle in Zimbabwe

The Great Zimbabwe was the capital of the 150 city-states and consisted of ruling aristocrats. They controlled the city-states, where most people lived in tiny settlements. Many Zimbabweans depended upon agriculture and raising cattle for their survival, so they had a totally different way of life from their aristocratic rulers. This isolation and simple lifestyle allowed the people of Zimbabwe to flourish, and control of the gold trade allowed the aristocracy to flourish. The civilization developed uninterrupted while everyone else around them was being impacted by Europeans.

Unfortunately, the people of the Great Zimbabwe did not have a writing system. Everything was passed down by oral tradition as the civilization had not developed the need to write. Because of the lack of written artifacts, historians are not sure of what led to the downfall of this great civilization.

SOUTH AFRICA

South Africa is located at the southern tip of Africa. In 1652, the Dutch began a small settlement that they named the Cape Colony. Its original purpose was to serve as a supply station for the growing Dutch East India Trading Company. As Dutch ships began to make the run around Africa through the dangerous Cape of Good Hope to get to the east coast of Africa (and later India), they needed somewhere to resupply their water and fresh fruits for the long and dangerous ocean journey.

Over a period of 100 years, the Cape Colony grew substantially larger as many people began to stay in the colony instead of getting back on their ship. The Dutch who remained behind were called Afrikaners. The Dutch Afrikaners initially worked with the local native population known as the Khoikhoi. The Khoikhoi were mainly herders, and the Afrikaners traded Dutch items made of iron and copper, and then consumable tobacco. As the East India Trading Company grew bigger, more and more Dutch settled in South Africa. They decided to create large plantation-like farms, and they displaced the friendly Khoikhoi. When the Khoikhoi started to rebel in 1659, the Afrikaners used the conflicts as a reason to attack them openly. After the defeat of the Khoikhoi in 1677, the Dutch consolidated their power, and the Khoikhoi were eventually absorbed into the Dutch society. They were allowed to maintain their freedom, but instead of living their traditional life as they always had, they were stuck with becoming wage laborers. They worked on the large Dutch farms. They went from being native inhabitants, free to work the land, and then all of a sudden, they became subservient to the Dutch. This eventually led to the system of apartheid that plagued South Africa until the late 1900s.

CULTURAL AND ARTISTIC ACHIEVEMENTS OF THE AFRICAN CONTINENT

This is a vast topic as African diversity provided some amazing cultural and artistic achievements. From the pyramids of ancient Egypt, the stone fortresses of the Great Zimbabwe, and the Christian churches carved into Ethiopian mountains, these early civilizations had a lot of creative skill and technology. African artists worked with many natural resources: ivory, wood, bronze, and gold. They were able to make beautiful pottery and intricate jewelry that served both religious and social purposes. Carved African wooden masks and colored cloth influenced the development of art in other parts of the world.

Global Connections

African storytelling is similar to Confucius's proverbs, Aesop's fables, and the Japanese Noh play.

Unfortunately, there were not a lot of written records in Africa, so not much ancient African literature exists. In Egypt and some other areas, there are numerous pieces of literature, including written descriptions of Africa provided by the Arabic people. African literature was all in storytelling. A proverb or a parable was delivered in the oral tradition to express an idea. A good example of this was from West Africa. In their storytelling, West Africans said that an animal that is burnt once will leave fire embers be. In America, the saying is, "once bitten, twice shy." There were oral histories and folktales that traveled around Africa and eventually made their way to other civilizations. This old oral tradition helped form a sense of community during the long period of migrations throughout Africa.

5000 B.C.E.	Neolithic farmers Nile Delta
1500 B.C.E.–500 C.E.	Great Bantu migrations
900 B.C.E. –500 C.E.	Great Zimbabwe
750 B.C.E.	Kingdom of Nubia
500 B.C.E.	Nubian Empire has capital in Meroe.
350 B.C.E.	Kingdom of Axum
700 C.E.	Muslims move across North Africa.
800 C.E.	Kingdom of Ghana in West Africa
1000 C.E.	Mogadishu trading city in East Africa
1050 C.E.	Almoravids conquer Ghana.
1150 C.E.	Kingdom of Mali
1250 C.E.	King Sundiata of Mali
1325 C.E.	Mansa Musa Hajj to Mecca
1400 C.E.	Decline of Mali
1450 C.E.	Kingdom of Songhai
1464 C.E.	Sonni Ali begins conquest and expansion.
1480 C.E.	Portuguese trade with West Africa.
1500 C.E.	Kingdom of the Kongo

GLOBAL CONNECTIONS

Mesoamerica

1400 B.C.E.—Olmecs in Mexico

700 B.C.E.—Hopewell Mound Builders in North America

300 C.E.—Mayan civilization

1200 C.E.—Aztec civilization

Egypt

2700 B.C.E.—Old Kingdom with Egyptian pyramids

2050 B.C.E.—Middle Kingdom

1550 B.C.E.—New Kingdom

India

2500 B.C.E.—Twin cities in India: Harappa and Mohenjo-daro

500 B.C.E.—Vedas recorded

1350 C.E.—Delhi sultanate

China

1650 B.C.E.—Shang Dynasty

1027 B.C.E.—Zhou Dynasty

206 B.C.E.—Han Dynasty

618 C.E.—Tang Dynasty

960 C.E.—Song Dynasty

Middle East

622 C.E.—Islamic calendar starts

680 C.E.—Conflict with Byzantine Empire

900 C.E.—Abd al-Rahman III and Moorish culture

Mesoamerica, Spanish Conquest, and the Peoples of North America

13

MESOAMERICA AND NORTH AMERICA AFTER THE BERING STRAIT

About 25,000–30,000 years ago, Paleolithic nomads, called Paleo-Indians, migrated from Asia to North America, following food across the land bridge known as the Bering Strait. Today, the remnants of it are the Aleutian Islands.

Around 10,000 B.C.E., the Ice Age came to an end, and the Bering Strait melted. The Paleo-Indians still on the North American continent after the Bering Strait land bridge disappeared migrated south, deeper into North America and into South America. They were cut off from any worldwide cultural diffusion. These nomadic hunter-gatherers slowly moved south and eastward across the Americas.

At this point in world history, there was no Central America as it is known today. The area called Mesoamerica starts in central Mexico, continuing south through Central America, and includes the northern portion of South America.

Mesoamerica and North America were home to several early civilizations. However, there was not much cultural diffusion between these civilizations either. Even in North America, the civilizations did not interact often as the geographic barriers of North America made migration difficult and slow.

Geography of Mesoamerica

There was a lot of physical geographic diversity in Mesoamerica. This area contained dense rain forests, temperate farming land, grassy highlands, and low-lying river basins with fertile soil. These river basins were similar to the four river valley civilizations in Africa and Asia. Mesoamerica also contained many mineral resources and deposits that were viable as trade goods. Trade goods included such things as hardwood trees, decorative feathers from tropical rain forest birds, gold, and obsidian.

The Forming of Civilizations in Mesoamerica

Separate and distinct cultural traditions emerged in Mesoamerica, starting around 1500 B.C.E. and continuing until the Spanish arrived in 1500 C.E. In Mesoamerica, the people were ethnically and linguistically diverse. There were many ethnic populations in Mesoamerica, which was different from the civilizations of Egypt, India, and China. However, these different ethnic civilizations did not develop simultaneously as they did in Egypt, Mesopotamia, India, and China. Instead, they came one after the other.

The melting of the Bering Strait affected the Paleo-Indians in Mesoamerica because it cut off cultural diffusion with civilizations in Europe, Africa, and Asia. However, the Mesoamerican civilizations still did many of the same things as the other world empires, but these skills developed later.

One of the major differences was that Mesoamerica did not develop the wheel. As the Bering Strait melted, the hunter-gatherers continued hunting the same game as always. Mesoamerica did not have any large beasts of burden: horses, oxen, or donkeys. Without animals that could be domesticated to assist the people, there was no need for the idea of the wheel. All work was done on foot and by manpower.

Villages formed later in Mesoamerica as people continued living as hunter-gathers until 5000–2500 B.C.E., compared with Europe and Asia where villages began forming in 11,000–9000 B.C.E. Other parts of the world were developing civilizations just as villages got started in the Americas.

One of the things that make studying the Americas difficult is that in Mesoamerica, much of the written records were destroyed. Some writings were destroyed by time and natural disasters, but the main reason for their destruction was the conquest by the Spanish. They came in and destroyed everything, wiping away the ability to decipher the remaining Mesoamerican writings. Recently, historians have made progress in deciphering the language of the Mayans. Interestingly enough, the Incas in the Andes Mountains of South America never developed a writing system. Much of what historians know about the Incas came from European descriptions.

However, the long period of separation between Africa, Europe, and Asia and the Americas reaped havoc on historical documents. The documents simply did not survive, so much of the historical culture of the Americas will never be known.

The Olmec of Southern Mexico

The first civilization to develop in the Americas was the Olmec, who were located along the Gulf Coast of Mexico. The Olmec civilization came into prominence as the first Mesoamerican civilization, developing between 1500 and 400 B.C.E. During this time, the ancient Greek civilization was thriving in Europe. This part of Mexico was good for the Olmec as there was plentiful water and soil for the people to begin farming.

OLMEC CITIES

The Olmec did not have one capital, but instead they had a series of important cities. The two most prominent were San Lorenzo and La Venta. Neither was seen as a single capital. As San Lorenzo declined in importance, La Venta rose to prominence. However, due to the lack of written documentation, historians are not exactly sure how or why this shift occurred.

An elaborate system of drainage canals existed in the Olmec civilization. The canals stored water in reservoirs to make sure there was plentiful water for crops. Similar to other world civilizations, the Olmec built a 110-foot-tall Great Pyramid. It was only one-quarter the size of the Great Pyramid of Egypt, but it was a similar shape.

GLOBAL CONNECTIONS

An interesting fact about the Olmec pyramids was that they were made from large stones that were quarried from about 60 miles away. It was not the 600 miles that the Egyptian pyramid stones had to travel, but it was still difficult to move the stones a distance of 60 miles.

GOVERNMENT

The cities of the Olmec were run by priest-kings who had the authority to command the labor forces. The priest-kings and upper classes that lived in Olmec cities were supported by laborers, consisting of everyone else in the population. The raw materials found in Olmec cities were also located in other areas of Mesoamerica, which provides evidence of some type of early trade networks between the Olmec and other groups in Mesoamerica. Controlling these trade networks was necessary for the priest-kings to augment their authority.

From what historians can discern, the population of Olmec cities was not very large. Historians have also discovered that the Olmec worshipped a creature that was part jaguar and part human. This religious deity was also found in all other Mesoamerican civilizations, so it shows that there was some limited cultural diffusion, including a shared polytheistic religion.

The Olmec civilization began to fade around 400 B.C.E.

Global Connections

Does this sound familiar? It should! It is very similar to the other civilizations that practiced feudalism: Europe and Japan.

The City-State of Monte Albán

The city-state of Monte Albán in Mexico was another Mesoamerican civilization, which began circa 500 B.C.E. It was located near the Olmec civilization. The Monte Albán people were the first to capture prisoners of war. In Monte Albán, historians have found the first evidence of human sacrifice, which was prevalent throughout Mesoamerican civilizations. Historians are not sure of the purpose of some human sacrifices, but they do know that it started in Monte Albán. The Monte Albán civilization declined slowly from 200 to 800 C.E.

Early evidence of Mesoamerican writing and a calendar system have been found by historians in the city of Monte Albán. The Monte Albán calendar used an interlocking ring system, one for the sun and one for the moon. The Monte Albán calendar was used by the people of Mesoamerica until the Spanish arrived.

Global Connections

Teotihuacan was dominant during the height of power during Pax Romana and they continued to be powerful as Europe plunged into the depths of the Middle Ages.

The City-State of Teotihuacan

In the valley of Mexico, located in what is today Mexico City, there is a huge lake called Lake Texcoco. Found between the mountains on a high plateau of central Mexico, it formed the city of Teotihuacan. Teotihuacan dominated Mesoamerica from 100 to 750 C.E.

Teotihuacan was the first true city-state in Mesoamerica. It had many natural advantages due to its location. It was surrounded by the mountains, which had a vast network of caves for safety and storage. From these caves, the people of Teotihuacan were able to quarry obsidian, a decorative volcanic glass. The location of Teotihuacan was also on a perfect trade route between the Gulf Coast and southern Mesoamerica. It was a city-state of wealth and power, surrounded by large farming fields. The population was estimated at 150,000, making it one of the largest cities in the world at the time.

City Structure

Being a true city-state, Teotihuacan had a strong central governmental authority, which meant the government had the ability to organize large public works projects. The Teotihuacan authorities had knowledge of complex mathematics and geometry as the city was laid out in a grid plan.

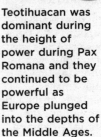 **GLOBAL CONNECTIONS**

When you think of monumental architecture from ancient civilizations, what do you think of? Most people think of the Egyptian Pyramids or perhaps the twin cities of Harappa and Mohenjo-daro. Despite being separated from Europe and Asia for many centuries, the empire of Teotihuacan added another great example of monumental architecture with the Avenue of the Dead.

All the roads led to the center of the city, which emptied out into a square where the main religious and administrative structures were housed.

At either end of the square, there were two pyramids. One of them was the Pyramid of the Sun, which was 210 feet tall (100 feet taller than that of the Olmec). The second pyramid was the Pyramid of the Moon, which was smaller. The two pyramids were situated precisely on the north-south, east-west axis.

People entered Teotihuacan on the three-mile long Avenue of the Dead. On either side of the road, there were large decorative faces of gods or spirits to guard against evil entering the city. Important priests or nobles of the city were buried inside the decorative faces. The Avenue of the Dead was an impressive piece of monumental architecture and city planning.

PEOPLE

The people in Teotihuacan lived in apartment-like structures located very close to the location of their job or trade. The people were skilled in pottery and in using the sharp volcanic glass called obsidian to make tools. Teotihuacan had a separate part of the city for foreign merchants. Foreigners could trade with other merchants, but they were segregated from the citizens of Teotihuacan.

As the city grew in power and prominence, Teotihuacan gobbled up the fertile fields surrounding it, displacing many local farmers. The farmers either had to become urbanized or move farther out from the city, and then clear more land for farming.

Global Connections

Building smaller versions of a large, powerful city was also done by Rome, as they built smaller versions of the city throughout the European empire.

The people of Teotihuacan also practiced human sacrifice. Instead of killing prisoners, the nobility of the city would draw their own blood and use it in religious ceremonies as their form of human sacrifice. In times of emergency, such as famine, floods, or warfare, an entire human would be sacrificed to appease the gods.

INFLUENCE

The city of Teotihuacan was copied throughout Mesoamerica. There were smaller cities around the Mexican highlands and south through Guatemala that were laid out like Teotihuacan. Many paintings made famous by the people of Teotihuacan showed polytheistic gods, as well as the first appearance of the winged feathered serpent known as Quetzalcoatl. Similar paintings have been found throughout Mesoamerica, showing the influence of Teotihuacan.

By 500 c.e., the influence of Teotihuacan began to wane. In the 700s, there was a massive fire that destroyed much of the religious centers and the houses of the ruling elites in Teotihuacan. While Teotihuacan was rebuilt, it never regained its powerful status.

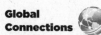

Global Connections

Starting during the height of Roman power through the end of the Middle Ages, it was the Mayans' turn to grow their rich civilization.

THE MAYAN CIVILIZATION

The Mayan civilization was dominant between 300 b.c.e. and 900 c.e. The Mayans were very good record keepers. They had an advanced writing system, and they wrote on not only paper, but also on stones and pottery. The majority of their writings recorded religious information. Historians are just now beginning to decipher Mayan writing, so there is much more to learn about them.

Tikal

The largest Mayan city was Tikal. Tikal had a population between 50,000 and 70,000. They developed terraced agriculture to control soil erosion by flattening and leveling off mountains. The Mayans in Tikal developed a grid irrigation system, and they used it to increase the amount of food that they could grow to support the growing population. Even though Tikal was the largest city, it was not the capital city. Mayan territory was governed through a series of smaller subcities that controlled their immediate region, very similar to the Greek city-states. Tikal was a little more powerful because it had access to a river system that led to the Gulf Coast and into the Caribbean Sea. Tikal was able to control the trade in those regions, and they formed a trading treaty with Teotihuacan.

The Mayan civilization was not run by a single ruling family, but instead, each smaller subcity had its own ruling family. There were frequent wars between Mayan cities and their royal rulers. They were also great practitioners of human sacrifice, which they needed to appease their gods. The Maya believed that sacrificing more people would greatly increase the power of the rulers.

Mayan Religion

The religion of the Maya was very intricate and complex. It deeply impacted political and social life. To the Maya, there was no real separation of the earthly world from the heavenly world. The Mayan leaders used religion to augment their political authority, so there was a complete and total integration of church and state. The Mayan rulers practiced very elaborate rituals and ceremonies. They would use Mayan temples to showcase their authority and justify their rule. Many of their ceremonies ended in mass sacrifice or some type of bloodletting. The Mayan civilization offered the first evidence of a ritualistic ballgame. Ruins of stadiums have been seen in such places as Chichén Itzá or the sacrificial temples of Tulum.

Global Connections

The ruling elites of the Mayan civilization were very similar to the Egyptian pharaohs and the emperors of Japan.

Technology

The Mayans developed a very complex mathematical system. They were among the first in the world to use the concept of a zero. With this, they developed a calendar known as the Long Count that was tied to a fixed point in the past. Using the Long Count calendar, Mayan astronomers created a calendar with months that were 29 1/2 days long, plus they incorporated a leap year. The Long Count calendar was helpful after Mesoamerican conquest because Europeans could match events that happened to the Mayans with the European calendars. Historians have been able to date Mayan monumental accomplishments and achievements with much more precision.

Global Connections

These cities were basically smaller versions of the Yamato family in Japan, with a single-family dynasty ruling.

Government

Individual Mayan cities were all ruled by their own dynasty. Each city was ruled by a single-line dynasty. One of the Mayan cities actually had two women become queen, and their rule was very similar to Hatshupset in Egypt (see Chapter 2).

Collapse of the Mayan Civilization

Between 800 and 900 C.E., the Mayan civilization collapsed. The dynasties came to a sudden halt, and they simply quit building their monumental architecture and stone carvings. They vanished very, very quickly, and the civilization was reclaimed by the jungles of Mesoamerica. Only in the last couple of decades have many Mayan artifacts been discovered, including the Long Count calendar. Historians do not know what caused the collapse—whether it was warfare, overpopulation, or some type of plague. However, the ending of the Mayan civilization gave rise to the most famous and powerful civilization in Mesoamerican history—the Aztecs.

THE WORLD OF THE AZTECS

The Aztecs came into central Mexico as nomads. They had a reputation of being fierce warriors, and they served as the military wing of a small empire known as the Toltecs. Slowly, the Aztec tribe began to consolidate its power. Between 1200 and 1400 C.E., the Aztecs created a massive empire. They reshaped religion and ritual practices of their local area, which they felt they were destined to control because they saw a vision from the gods.

The Aztec Army

The Aztec society was organized, but there was no standing army. All men took military training and practiced for combat all the time. The nobles went to an officer training school, and the commoners were the foot soldiers.

GLOBAL CONNECTIONS

The Aztec army was a blend of the Spartan warriors and the extractive Roman Empire. The entire Aztec society was very similar to ancient Rome and Sparta, having similar ideas about military service that was seen in the Roman legion and in the Spartan army.

The goals of the Aztec army were to capture new territory to enlarge their trading empire, secure natural resources, and capture and subdue prisoners for sacrifice. The Aztecs had the largest, most wide-scale use of human sacrifice in Mesoamerica. A man's combat status was measured by the number of captives he brought back. This was key as it was the only way to earn rewards and to socially advance. Failure in combat brought social disgrace and could leave him ostracized from Aztec society.

In some conquered territory, local leaders were left in place, but they had to acknowledge Aztec leadership. The Aztecs demanded a hefty tribute, not only in material goods but also in labor. Records show that people had to donate 7000 tons of corn or maize per year, two million cotton cloaks, other agricultural products, and pottery. Once the Aztecs conquered a territory, they began to economically deplete the civilization.

Global Connections

After conquering Carthage, Rome sucked the resources of the area dry and then destroyed the land with salt. In Sparta, after a civilization was conquered, they were absorbed into the Spartan Empire and made to work for them.

FUN FACT

Imagine Tenochtitlan as a Mesoamerican version of Venice!

Tenochtitlan

The Aztecs ran their empire from one of the greatest cities of Mesoamerica: Tenochtitlan. Tenochtitlan became the most populous city in Mesoamerica and dominated Aztec society from 1345 to 1521 C.E. It was built on islands in the center of a lake. There were bridges running to Tenochtitlan that could be knocked down or pulled out in times of warfare, making conquering Tenochtitlan very difficult. The Aztecs developed new technology called chinampa, which were floating garden beds filled with dirt that were anchored to the lake bed from which the Aztecs could grow food. The city had avenues for canoes where people brought trade goods to the market and tribute to the city. From descriptions written by Spanish conquistadors, historians know Aztec markets were enormous. They were well-organized and offered a large variety of goods from all over Mesoamerica. The market of Tenochtitlan often had 60,000 people a day go through it.

Tenochtitlan housed a population of 200,000 to 300,000 people. Many of the city buildings, palaces, and religious temples gleamed in the sun as they were decorated with gold. Much of what we know about the Aztecs comes from the diaries and descriptions of Spanish conquistadors, so even though it does maintain a Spanish bias, historians know a lot more about the Aztecs than any other Mesoamerican civilization.

Religion and Human Sacrifice

Along with extracting tribute from conquered people, the Aztecs were defined by the mammoth scale of their human sacrifices. It was the centerpiece to their religious beliefs. The Aztecs believed their main god, who was the sun, needed human blood to rise each morning. When the sun rose, it was going into battle against darkness, so the human blood was the fuel necessary to make the sunrise and fight the darkness. It was the main responsibility of the Aztec warriors to get enough sacrificial victims to power the sun. Aztec legend says that in times of massive drought, the Aztecs sacrificed 20,000 to 30,000 people per day, and in very bad times, the Aztecs not only sacrificed humans but also turned to cannibalism to absorb the power of the sun.

The Aztecs were very strategic when choosing their sacrificial victims. The Aztecs would not conquer everyone around them. They would conquer a village and only capture the warriors, leaving the women, children, and teenagers. They would wait 10 to 12 years, then come back to take the teens and children who were now old enough to become the new village warriors. This was intentional as they strategically reduced the number of fighting men. It also explained why so many of the surrounding villagers decided to help the Spanish, led by Hernando Cortés, when they arrived in Mesoamerica in 1519. They helped Cortés get rid of the hated Aztec domination.

Aztec Society and Government

Aztec society was very hierarchical, very authoritarian, and very militaristic. In many ways, it was the Mesoamerican version of Spartan society from ancient Greece. Everything was geared around the military and a strict hierarchy, like a military chain of command.

There were only two major social classes in Aztec civilization: nobles and commoners. There was a very tiny sliver of merchants and highly skilled artisans that formed a middle class, but mainly there were the two broad social categories.

Aztec nobles lived lives of great wealth and luxury. Status in society was very visually based. They wore very elaborate, extravagant uniforms or outfits that visually distinguished them from commoners. The more brilliant the colors, the higher the individual's social status was within the nobility. On the other hand, commoners wore rough, simple peasant garb. The color of the material (typically brown or white) signified the individual's job as a farmer or as a worker. Aztec society had many laws and structures in place that governed this practice. It was illegal to wear something other than a garment identifying rank in society.

Nobles had higher social standards set for them. They valued attributes typically found in the military: commands, obedience to commands, discipline, being respectful of superiors, and living a life in moderation. Nobles were expected to do things better than the commoners. Rules were enforced upon nobles more strictly, and even though they did live a life of wealth and luxury, there were limits on what they could or could not do. As in most militaristic societies, the punishments were swift and severe should a person break a law.

Commoners did all of the hard labor: farming, harvesting the crops, and working on building projects. Commoners lived in separate neighborhoods called calpulli. The neighborhood of a commoner was his whole world. It had its own temple and schools, where the children of the neighborhood received training in Aztec religious practices, ideology, and military training.

Global Connections

The ancient Roman patrician and plebeian designations are very similar to the class distinctions in Mesoamerica.

Global Connections

Nobles in the Aztec society were very much like Confucian scholars in China.

Each calpulli had elected officials, similar to a city council, and a neighborhood home-ownership that made sure taxes were paid, work was getting done, and workers arrived on time to important public works projects. The commoner neighborhoods were a simple way to organize society and have it structured to easily account for everything.

The tiny middle class consisted of professional traders and merchants. Since the Aztecs had an ever-expanding empire, traders and merchants were very important as they expanded. Merchants and traders were a driving force in the spreading of Aztec influence and ideology, similar to an Islamic trader in the Middle East. They organized their own guilds and had the freedom to establish their own regulatory customs. Some merchants amassed great wealth, but as part of Aztec society, they had to downplay it. They could not be more flashy or extravagant than the nobles above them. A good example was the very special gold-smiths. They had special status as gold was used for religious decorations and elaborate artistry, but they were also extremely wealthy because of their knowledge and possession of large quantities of gold.

> **GLOBAL CONNECTIONS**
>
> Think of the neighborhoods in America that settled during the time of massive immigration in the early 1900s. There was a Polish sector, an Italian sector, a Jewish sector, an Irish sector, plus many more.

The Role of Women

Aztec society was interesting in regard to the role of women. Aztec women could inherit and own property, they were allowed to conduct trading business in the market, and they could actually serve as small market officials. Women could enter the priesthood, but there was a limit—a glass ceiling, so to speak—to how high they could go. They could not assume the highest hierarchical positions, only the low-level and mid-level positions.

When it came to education, both boys and girls received an education, but the emphasis on warfare left women without much access to educational opportunities. As it was in most ancient societies, women held a secondary position to men. However, the number of children that a woman provided to her husband gained a woman higher status. In Aztec society, a woman going through childbirth was compared to men entering and fighting in combat.

The End of the Aztec Empire

In the mid-1400s, the Aztecs reached the zenith of their power. In 1500, the Aztec Empire had nearly 5,000,000 people, but in 1519, Hernando Cortés and the Spanish conquistadors arrived. Cortés was dumbstruck by the magnificence of Tenochtitlan, finding the city laden with gold.

The Spanish used the remaining enemies of the Aztecs as additional warriors to defeat them. With the use of superior Spanish technology, the end of the Aztec Empire was very quick and abrupt.

SOUTH AMERICAN CIVILIZATIONS

South America, especially the countries of Peru and Chile high in the Andes Mountains, was home to several early civilizations similar to Mexico.

The Chavín was the oldest culture in South America and provided the foundation for other cultures, specifically the Inca, which eventually developed on the west coast of South America.

Following the Chavín was the Moche people, who grew between 100 and 700 C.E. During the height of Rome, through the rule of the Byzantine Empire and into the Dark Ages in Europe, the Moche people built an empire along the north coast of Peru. They constructed roads to carry messages back and forth. This technology was later mastered by the Incas. Much of what historians know about the Moche comes from their incredible pottery works, decorated with frescoes of daily life. Historians can see what the lives of the Moche were like, from going into battle to the women making clothing. However, other than the pottery, there are not very many clues to piece together about these people. Historians know they existed, were formative, and helped the Incas to grow.

The Nasca people also helped in the development of the Incas. They were famous for the giant Nasca lines, which were figures of spiders and birds carved into Peruvian hills and mountains.

For thousands of years, different civilizations rose and fell in Peru, and they met their ruin at the same time the Aztecs were at the height of their power in the 1400s C.E. What remained of these early peoples merged into the great Incan Empire that stretched along the Pacific coast of South America.

The Incas

The Incan people were named for a series of ruins found high in the Andes Mountains. Around 850 C.E., these early people of South America constructed a large temple with many stone carvings or hieroglyphics, showing them worshipping their main god, who was part jaguar and part human.

GEOGRAPHY

In the early 1500s, the Incas had one of the largest empires in the world. It encompassed more than 2000 miles from the Pacific coast to the high, arid Andes Mountains, all the way to the Amazon River basin from northern Chile down to Ecuador.

It had a population in the millions, and a good comparison to it would be the empire that Rome controlled after conquering ancient Carthage. The Incas were very similar to the Romans as they both controlled a large and diverse empire.

THE CAPITAL OF CUZCO

The Incan people themselves called their land the land of the four quarters. They created a giant capital city named Cuzco that was located at the intersection of the north and south crossroads of the Incan Empire. Cuzco was home to the Incan king, and it was a great city of splendor and magnificence. There were two temples. One was made of gold and dedicated to the sun, and it was located at one end of the plaza. The other temple was made of silver, and it was dedicated to the moon.

RULING THE LARGE INCAN EMPIRE

As the Incas expanded their civilization throughout the world of the high Andes Mountains, they brilliantly enlarged their empire. They expanded through a combination of alliance, intimidation, and sheer conquest. The Incas would seek an alliance, asking a new territory to willingly join them. If that did not work, they would bring a warehouse of economic resources, so the territory could see the goods that the Incas controlled. The Incas hoped the military and monetary wealth would intimidate a territory into surrendering and joining the Incan Empire. If intimidation did not work, then the Incas just went in and destroyed them with their powerful army.

Global Connections

The god of the Incas was very similar to those of the Olmecs.

The Incas organized their realm into a strict hierarchy with a strong administrative structure. They placed ruling governors in conquered lands. To be part of the Incan Empire, the people had to speak the Incan language, which today is still spoken in parts of Peru. If part of the empire caused trouble or tried to rebel, the Incas would forcibly relocate people from one end of the empire to the other, removing them from their homelands and putting them in a geographic location completely opposite to which they were accustomed.

DEVELOPMENT OF THE MITA SYSTEM

The mita system was a form of tribute to the Inca government. Tribute was given in a variety of ways: labor, military service, and public works projects were a few examples.

The Incas demanded a series of different forms of labor taxation. All land was divided into categories. The local population was able to use some of the land for themselves to grow crops. Another part of the land was divided for state use and governmental use only. Some land went to the churches.

Locals in certain areas worked for the state on a regular basis, but everyone had to do a certain number of days of service per year for the state. Some people participated as athletes in state-sponsored games for entertainment. Men were required to serve a certain amount of time in the army. Others worked on large public works projects for the good of the empire.

The Incas developed incredible technology, and the invention of the mita system was a way to organize and control the large Incan Empire. Using this system of service, they built cities high in the mountains. They built an amazing series of roads, using what the Moche had started and making them even bigger. They were able to carve flat tables out of the steep hillsides, called terracing agriculture, so that as the water ran down the mountain it would not wash away the plants and soil. The Incas performed one of the greatest building feats in world history with the construction of Machu Picchu circa 1450. This colossal city structure was built in a very low oxygen environment in the Andes Mountains at 10,000 feet above sea level.

COLONIZATION

Colonization was another strong suit of the Incas as they were able to colonize and control multiple ecologically diverse regions. As previously mentioned, they sometimes moved entire communities great distances to keep down rebellions, but they also moved people to take advantage of plentiful natural resources. Incan colonization required a lot of work and organization, but it was a relatively peaceful way to maintain discipline and unity throughout the empire.

Global Connections

The mamaconas were very similar to the vestal virgins in ancient Rome.

MAKUNA (MAMACONAS)

Through the mita system, everyone served the Incan government. However, the most famous of this group is known as the mamaconas. They were women of wealth and privilege who served the Incan government for life. They lived a very regimented lifestyle and were mainly celibate, but at times they could be given as wives to cement alliances with new groups.

However, their main role was economic and religious. The mamaconas were weavers and clothing makers. They made clothing for the elite Incans to be used at religious festivals, during wartime, or for state ceremonies. Clothing was a symbol of wealth for the Incas. The various insignias and animals on the clothing or woven materials showed a person's rank in society.

INCAN TECHNOLOGY

The technology of the Incas was incredible. Throughout the empire, they built a chain of storehouses for food, clothing, and crafts. The storehouses were linked by an elaborate series of roads with relay stations and depots, so everybody in the empire had what they needed. The warehouses also fed those people doing state-sponsored labor services and were symbols of the power that the Incas had.

The Incan road network was just as incredible. The Incas built 14,000 miles of roads. Some roads were massive, wide major interstate-like highways for trade and travel, whereas other roads were built on tiny narrow trails on steep mountain cliffs. When a road intersected with a river or a cliff, Incan engineers created elaborate suspension bridges made of rope. On some very steep slopes, they carved steps up one side and down the other. Along the road system, they had relay stations with runners to help with transportation. Mesoamerica had no large beasts of burden, so there was nothing equivalent to "The Pony Express." Instead, it was relay runners that spread information or goods and connected the empire together.

Although the Incas did not have a writing system, they were able to record information on what was called a quipu, which was a series of leather bands tied to a circle or a hoop. Like a Native American dreamcatcher, they had different colored leather beads representing different words.

THE FALL OF THE INCAN EMPIRE

The trade and technology of the Incas allowed them to adapt to the various environments of their empire, from the oxygen-deprived Andes Mountains to the hot and humid Brazilian rain forest. The Incas thrived and prospered.

However, everything that made the Incas great and powerful was also very attractive to conquerors. In 1532, Francisco Pizarro entered the Incan Empire in search of gold, and he found that the Incas had a large vein of silver running through their empire. Just like the destruction of the Aztecs, the Incas were at the zenith of their power when they were destroyed by the Europeans. After just 100 years, the Incan Empire came to an end when Francisco Pizarro and his Spanish conquistadors defeated the Incas with superior weapons technology and gunpowder.

Global Connections

The importance of Incan clothing and the symbolism behind it was similar to the Aztecs or the powerful symbols of nature used in ancient Japan.

SIMILARITIES OF THE MESOAMERICAN AND SOUTH AMERICAN EMPIRES

The empires of Mesoamerica and South America had striking similarities.
- They had accurate calendars.
- They practiced polytheism, worshipping the gods of nature.
- They practiced a ritualistic soccer/basketball game.
- They had large urban centers arranged along center squares or plazas that housed the religious and government buildings.
- They were linked by trade and the development of gold and silver for ceremonial objects.
- They used other implements for weapons and tools, like obsidian, flint, or stone.
- They used monumental architecture in temples to the gods, especially the sun and the moon.
- All (except the Incas) had an elaborate writing system.

Global Connections

The urban centers of Mesoamerica and South America were very similar to the ancient Greek and Roman forums.

THE NORTH AMERICAN CONTINENT

The North American continent is big and rich in its native diversity. Its major contribution to the world was the development of maize, or corn, and beans. These plants, which are rich in protein, are native to North America, along with tomatoes and chili peppers. Beans, squash, and corn were planted well over 1000 years ago, giving the early inhabitants of North America a dependable source of food that could be prepared in a variety of ways.

The Native Americans in the Southwest

In present-day Arizona and Colorado, near the Four Corners region, there was a group of people called the Anasazi. They formed their civilizations between 900 and 1300 C.E. The Anasazi built large villages in difficult-to-settle locations and developed irrigation for their crops. They built their houses in large apartment-like complexes in the sides of canyon walls, where they lived high off the ground. They climbed a series of ladders to reach their homes. The ladders could be pulled up to give them protection from other raiding tribes. Their farming fields were located on the canyon floor below their homes. This type of dwelling also kept them cool in the blistering heat of the summer and warm in the chilly cold nights of the desert.

The Anasazi are better known today as the Pueblos. They were renamed by the Spanish, and Pueblo ruins can still be seen in New Mexico and Colorado. The American Southwest was also home to the Hopi Indians, the warlike Navajo, and the Apache.

The Native Americans in the Pacific Northwest

Living on the plateau of the Pacific Northwest were the Nez Perce. The Nez Perce were a peaceful group of people who survived using game from the woodlands and catching salmon in the great Columbia River. The Nez Perce lived as hunter-gatherers in small family groups. They used kayaks to live off the wealth of the sea and the surrounding forests.

The Native Americans in the Plains

The Blackfeet were a large group of Plains Indians, along with the tribes of Crow, Lakota, Apache, and Comanche. The Plains Indians lived in stereotypical tipis seen in movies about the American West. They hunted animals, most notably buffalo and elk. The animals provided everything they needed to meet their basic needs: food, skins for shelters, bones for weapons, and skins for clothing. Several large, rich, diverse Native American civilizations developed on the Great Plains of the United States.

The Native Americans in the Mississippi and Ohio River Valleys

Along the Mississippi and Ohio River Valleys, a Native American farming culture began to emerge. From what historians can tell, the famous Hopewell Indian Mound Builders were thriving as early as 700 B.C.E. These people left behind great earthen mounds in the shape of animals, the most famous being the great serpent mound in southern Ohio. It stretches, twists, and winds in the shape of a giant serpent for almost a quarter of a mile. This mound is significant because it shows historians that there were plenty of resources available for building, and it provides evidence of strong central authority to organize the labor necessary to create this large piece of monumental architecture. The Hopewell Indian mounds also show that the Hopewells were great traders, as the mounds contain shells, shark teeth, and copper. To get these, the Hopewell would have needed to travel through the wilderness to the Gulf of Mexico in the south and the Great Lakes in the north.

The Native Americans in the Eastern United States

In the eastern United States lived the great Iroquois League. They dominated the eastern woodlands from the Great Lakes over to the Atlantic Ocean.

In the late 1500s, as the Spanish were conquering the Aztecs and Incas, the Iroquois League formed an alliance of five nations with the Huron, Chippewa, and Mohawk nations. They spoke the same language and shared similar traditions, and the Iroquois hoped to bring peace to the member nations. Although it did not always succeed in keeping the peace, it was the most organized political group in North America. The alliance was run by a council of men, who were elders set forth by every nation. Just as the Iroquois League and alliance of five nations was forming, the Native Americans encountered the Europeans. When the Europeans began to clear land and build villages in the forests, many people came into contact with the Iroquois.

The Native Americans in the Southeast

In the Southeast, the great Cherokee nation developed in the mountains of North Carolina, Virginia, and Tennessee. The Natchez Indians also lived in the Southeast. The Natchez grew corn, squash, beans, and other crops, and they had a very important corn ceremony each year to celebrate the corn harvest. Corn was so important to the Native American culture that it was considered a sacred plant. Tribes from the southwestern deserts all the way to the Iroquois League gave thanks to corn. Corn was the symbol of fertility and provided much of the sustenance to the Native American tribes throughout the Americas.

GLOBAL CONNECTIONS WITH THE AMERICAS

- The great empires of Mexico, the Incas, and the Iroquois League developed at the same time as western and central Sudan.
- Just as Mesoamerica, Ghana, Songhai, and Mali achieved the height of their power, they all experienced detrimental contact with Europeans, though each experienced it at different points in world history.
- The city-states of Zimbabwe were at their high point simultaneously with the Aztecs and Incas.
- While King Solomon was ruling Jerusalem, the giant monumental architecture of the Olmecs was being built.
- While the city of Rome was growing to its greatest heights and then beginning its long and steady decline, the city of Teotihuacan was forming to create the first city-state in the Americas.
- As the new religion of Islam burst forth from the Middle Eastern heartlands, the Mayan rulers of Tikal brought the city to its greatest height of power before its abrupt collapse.
- The Mayan accomplishments in math and astronomy, with their accurate astronomical clock, rivaled anything that was occurring in Africa, Asia, and Europe at the same point in world history.
- As Europe was struggling to break free of feudalism and the Dark Ages before their emergence into the Renaissance and Age of Exploration, the Aztecs and Incas were creating and consolidating their empires.

28,000 B.C.E.	Paleolithic hunters cross the Bering Strait.
10,000 B.C.E.	Bering Strait melts.
8000 B.C.E.	Indigenous crops: corn, tomatoes, peppers, sweet potatoes
1400 B.C.E.	Olmecs in Mexico
850 B.C.E.	Chavín in South America
700 B.C.E.	Hopewell Mound Builders in North America
500 B.C.E.	City-state of Monte Albán
200 B.C.E.	Pyramid of the Sun in Teotihuacan
100 B.C.E.	Nazca in South America
50 C.E.	Natchez Native Americans in North America
100 C.E.	Moche in South America
300 C.E.	Mayan civilization
400 C.E.	Tikal at high point (Mayans)
900 C.E.	• Decline of Mayans • Anasazi Cliff Dwellers in North America
1000 C.E.	Indigenous crops flourishing
1200 C.E.	• Rise of the Aztecs • Apache in North America
1400 C.E.	• High point of Aztec power • Incan civilization emerges in South America.
1450 C.E.	Building of Machu Picchu by Incas
1500 C.E.	Iroquois League
1519 C.E.	Arrival of Cortés into Aztec civilization
1532 C.E.	Defeat of Incas by Pizarro
1700 C.E.	Contact with the Nez Perce in NW North America

Tang and Song Dynasties: The Golden Ages of China

14

CHINA AFTER THE HAN DYNASTY

After the collapse of the great Han Dynasty, China was once again plagued with 350 years of internal civil war. The Sui Dynasty was the final dynasty during this era of violence from 589 C.E. to 618 C.E. The Sui rulers were influential in the spread of Buddhism throughout China. In the end, China was able to escape the complete and total collapse that plagued its fellow empire: Rome.

UNIFICATION DURING THE TANG AND SONG DYNASTIES

Unification happened under two great dynasties: the Tang Dynasty and the Song Dynasty. The Tang Dynasty lasted from 618 C.E. to 907 C.E., and the Song Dynasty lasted from 960 C.E. to 1279 C.E. Under both of these dynasties, China achieved a well-ordered society where the emperor presided over the court system and a large governing bureaucracy, which was needed to control the vastness of the Chinese empire.

In China, agriculture began to expand and diversify. The growing silk trade brought in necessary income on the Silk Road. Buddhism continued to spread widely and became more accepted by all Chinese people. Unlike the Germanic barbarians that invaded Rome, barbarians that invaded China were absorbed into Chinese culture. Instead of destroying and laying waste to Chinese cities, they followed and practiced Chinese culture. As a result, China was able to achieve a level of unity and thrived under the old Confucian ideas once again.

TANG DYNASTY

Tang Taizong

Tang Taizong was a 16-year-old who was already a famous war hero. He followed in his father's footsteps, and in 626, Tang became the second emperor of the Tang Dynasty (which was named after him).

After becoming emperor, he changed his name to Tang Taizong, which means "great general." In addition to being a military man, Tang was also an educator. He was committed to governmental reform and became one of China's greatest emperors in their long, vast history.

Expansion

Tang decided to keep the Han policy of empire building. The strength of a Chinese emperor was based on how much he expanded the empire, so he moved westward into what is today Afghanistan. He also moved eastward, farther into the Korean Peninsula, and southward into Southeast Asia into what is today Vietnam.

Tang decided to let the power and the wealth of China impress the new peoples that he conquered. Tang allowed them to keep their local governments, but they had to send taxes, or tribute, to him as a conquered people.

Empress Wu Zetian

In 690, the Tang Dynasty featured an empress named Wu Zetian (also called Wu Zhao). Having a ruling empress was strange for the patriarchal societies of the time, like China. However, Wu helped to rebuild the Han Dynasty's functional governmental structure in China. The idea was for people of ability to eventually govern the empire, so schools were opened in villages and towns to teach the Confucian classics. The civil service exam was once again used to help improve the function of government. As a result, the Tang government ran smoothly.

Tang Government and Economy

Under the Tang, land was redistributed to needy peasants. This helped the people become more devoted to the emperor while it weakened large, wealthy landowners. Before the rule of the Tang, China had operated under a land ownership system similar to feudalism in Europe. The wealthy landowners were shamelessly expanding their empires while the people labored for them. With the people having their own land, the creation of towns and townships began. Chinese peasants started to make money by becoming merchants or traders. All of these changes allowed the emperor to collect additional taxes, and with the added source of revenue, the emperor gained even more power.

> **DINNER TABLE TALK**
>
> A good example of this is oranges and maple syrup! Oranges grow well in Florida, and maple syrup is readily available in Vermont. You can't make either product in the opposite location. Using this example, the Grand Canal would have allowed the Tang to ship oranges to Vermont and maple syrup to Florida!

To help facilitate the growth of the economy, the Tang expanded what was known as the Grand Canal. The Grand Canal linked the Huang Ho and Yangtze Rivers, allowing easy access between the northern and southern halves of China. This was an important trade highway. Different goods and services were available in the south that could not be attained in the north and vice versa. The Grand Canal was also the largest canal dug with purely human labor in world history.

The Fall of the Tang Empire

As was seen time and again in Chinese history, some emperors were not as effective as others. Arriving at the bottom of the Chinese dynastic cycle, these emperors, once again, forgot the hard work that made their successful empire. They became increasingly greedy for new money. Not able to control their spending habits, they imposed a series of increased taxation on their own people. Near the end of the Tang Dynasty in 907, some emperors imposed heavy taxes throughout China, causing them to slowly lose territory in the west. In the northern provinces of China, invading Islamic armies arrived from the east. To make the meltdown of the Tang complete, there was a series of severe famines and droughts. The Chinese people saw these natural disasters as signs that it was time for them to rebel. The great Tang Dynasty was overthrown in 907 C.E. Fortunately for China, the period between the Tang and Song Dynasties was extremely short.

SONG DYNASTY

Birth of the Song Dynasty

The Song Dynasty began in 960 C.E. and lasted about 320 years. The Song Empire was smaller in size and scale than the large territory controlled by the Tang. This was the result of a renewed threat from the traditional Chinese enemy from the north: the Mongols (who make an appearance in many subsequent chapters).

Song Agriculture

The Song became powerful due to a change in farming and agriculture. The Song increased the number of rice paddies throughout southern China. Rice began to replace wheat as the main source of food. Increased irrigation techniques and the ability to grow two crops a year led to a food surplus, which, once again, led to a massive population boom. The food surplus also gave the Chinese people free time. They developed new ideas in commerce, art, and other cultural achievements that symbolized the Song Dynasty.

Merchants and Trading

The Song became a vast trading empire as merchants arrived via the Silk Road on land and on ships by sea, coming from India and as far away as the Middle East. Previous Chinese technology, coupled with the development of the compass and the stern post rudder, encouraged this sea trade. Porcelain from the Song era has been found in eastern Africa, meaning there was trade, either directly or indirectly, between the Song in China and people in Africa. During this time, a wealth of cultural diffusion took place between China and outside traders. China had several cities with populations that exceeded one million people. They were the only country in the world at this time to have this ability, which showed the wealth and power of ancient China.

Song Society

The Song society kept true to its basic social structure. They had three tiers of people in society: the nobles, the peasants, and the merchants, who still struggled with being accepted in Chinese society.

Large, wealthy noble landowners still dominated much of Chinese society. They could afford the time necessary to study to be Confucian scholars so they could serve as government officials. Still, only a few nobles achieved the high test scores on the rigorous civil service test that were needed to work for the government directly. Many of these aristocrats worked in a supportive role as secretaries and servants of the powerful, governing officials.

The secondary societal level was the peasants. As seen throughout world history, the peasants worked the land as agricultural laborers. With the introduction of new crops and land, most peasants lived in small, self-sufficient villages. With the sheer size and scope of China, the emperor did not have time to check on most remote villages or provide them with their every need. These villages looked after each other and helped each other out. Only in dire straits would a peasant involve the Tang or Song government. However, different from most societies at the time, peasants could gain higher status if they had time to study for the civil service exam. If they were naturally bright and passed the civil service examination, both the boy who passed and his family rose in status. No matter what social class a person was during the Song Dynasty, gaining an education was extremely important.

The merchants were on the bottom level of Chinese society. This was strange because they were extremely wealthy and prosperous. However, because they made their money off of other people's labor, they had to accept their lowly status. Even though trade thrived under the Song Dynasty, merchants were always looked down upon, regardless of their increasing importance and wealth.

Role of Women

The status of women in the Tang and Song Dynasties did not improve much from previous dynasties. Due to the growing population, once a woman was married, she was expected to cut off ties with her family and be completely absorbed into her husband's extended family.

It was also at this time that the painful process of foot binding became fashionable. A young girl would have her feet wrapped, basically taking a girl's toes and bending them over to the bottom of her feet. The feet and toes were wrapped in tight bandages, and as the girl grew, the bones of the toes bent under the feet. Feet wrapping was said to make a woman's foot look like a beautiful flower. As this was very painful, it was mainly for upper-class women as peasant women still had to be able to work the farm. Feet wrapping kept the upper-class women homebound as it was painful to walk.

Global Connections

The status of Chinese merchants was completely opposite of what was going on in Europe at the same time. After the Crusades, European merchants steadily rose in society.

TANG AND SONG ACHIEVEMENTS IN ART AND LITERATURE

During the Tang and Song Dynasties, many stories were written. Included were stories about religion, philosophy, magic, and the always-popular romance and adventure stories. However, the Chinese loved poetry. Poet Li Bo was a famous poet during the Tang Dynasty. His poetry spoke about the deep connection that the Chinese have with nature. The Chinese believed in living in balance and harmony with nature. This was reflected in the poetry but also in the art. The Chinese began the practice of landscape painting, showing their love of the natural world. Landscapes included mountains and trees, coupled with an image of the sea or a river, bringing all the elements of the natural world together.

TECHNOLOGICAL ADVANCEMENTS

Technology under the Tang and Song Dynasties was just as important as it had been since China's development as an early river valley civilization. The Chinese developed a very intricate and elaborate mechanical water clock that ran by a series of interconnecting cogwheels powered by water so it was always steady and rotating. To weave their silk and fine thread, the Chinese invented the spinning wheel. They developed a foot pedal that would be pumped to turn the spokes of the spinning wheel, turning the raw silk into thread.

The Chinese had invented gunpowder centuries before, but it had only been used for fireworks or decorations. During the Song Dynasty, the Chinese adapted gunpowder for use in weapons and explosive cannons. It made the Song army even more formidable.

One of the biggest, most impressive accomplishments was the development of the world's first movable block printing press in 1040. Chinese characters were carved onto wooden blocks, and the characters could be shifted around and mounted in different combinations. An entire sheet of paper could be printed at one time with the ability to create many copies very easily, instead of repeatedly copying a document line by line onto multiple sheets of paper.

The Chinese were always on the cutting edge of medicine development. They developed different techniques and medicines using different herbs to cure sickness and pain. They developed active acupuncture. They observed symptoms of illnesses and what would cure them, which they wrote down and printed on the new printing press to be distributed throughout China.

The Song Dynasty was vast and powerful, but unfortunately, by the 1200s, a new threat emerged on the horizon. There was a resurgence of the traditional Chinese enemy: the Mongols. Coming out of Mongolia, they were led by the great Genghis Khan. The Mongols brought an end to the golden ages of the Tang and Song Dynasties. Genghis Khan created a massive empire of his own, which is discussed in Chapter 20.

TIMELINE REVIEW

220 C.E.	Collapse of Han Dynasty
350 C.E.	Warring States Era
618 C.E.	Beginning of Tang Dynasty
626 C.E.	Emperor Tang Taizong
649 C.E.	Period of Tang expansion
690 C.E.	Empress Wu Zetian
700 C.E.	Poet Li Bo
700s C.E.	Mechanical clock and block printing
850 C.E.	Gunpowder
907 C.E.	Tang Dynasty near collapse
960 C.E.	Beginning of Song Dynasty
1000 C.E.	Spinning wheel
1040 C.E.	Movable type
1100 C.E.	Song merchants and foreign trade flourishing
1125 C.E.	Foot binding becomes widespread.

GLOBAL CONNECTIONS

The Tang and Song Dynasties were brilliant ages in ancient China. They developed simultaneously with

- the Middle Ages to the High Middle Ages of Europe
- the birth and the spread of Islam
- the kingdoms of trading states of West Africa
- the height of the Mayan Empire and then rapid decline

Quick Quiz: Chapters 12–14

1. Which of the following is one of the great misconceptions concerning migrations in world history?

   A. The Swahili dialect is spoken throughout much of sub-Saharan Africa due to their displacement by the ancient Egyptians.
   B. There was very little migrating in and around the continent of Africa.
   C. The Bantu migration was one singular migration instead of a prolonged series of migrations lasting nearly 2000 years.
   D. There was mass migration throughout Africa as the geography made moving easy throughout the vast continent.

2. How were the kings of Ghana different from many of the other kings or rulers of their era?

   A. They had access to their people, and the heir to the throne was determined matrilineally.
   B. The kings never saw their people because they were worshipped as gods and lived in isolation.
   C. The kings were voted into office by both men and women in the Ghanaian civilization.
   D. Each individual village in Ghana had its own king.

3. Which king of the Songhai Empire followed Islam only to increase trade when Islamic merchants were nearby instead of solely following the preferred worship of the traditional African polytheistic gods?

   A. Mansa Musa
   B. Muhammed al-Turi
   C. Afonso I
   D. Sundiata

4. Which of the following would be an example of how Europeans named port cities in West Africa as a result of Portuguese exploration and renewing trade with Africa?

   A. Point Noir
   B. Gold Coast
   C. Cape of Good Hope
   D. Senegambia

5. Which kingdom in Africa most often dealt with the Portuguese and dealt with them for the longest period of time?

   A. Mali
   B. South Africa
   C. Kingdom of Axum
   D. Kingdom of Kongo

6. Which Christian kingdom in eastern Africa endured a long period of trade, largely with the Middle East?

   A. Kingdom of Nubia
   B. Portuguese kingdom of the Congo
   C. The Great Zimbabwe
   D. Kingdom of Axum

7. Which large civilization in southern Africa was able to remain free of European influence during the period of Portuguese expansion?

   A. Cape Colony
   B. Kingdom of Nubia
   C. The Great Zimbabwe
   D. Senegambia

8. Why were the civilizations of Mesoamerica behind the rest of the world when it came to technology?

   A. They never had use for the wheel or most simple machines.
   B. They tried to remain isolationists and not participate in the sharing of ideas.
   C. The landscape was too diverse to make large-scale interaction possible.
   D. Once the Bering Strait melted at the end of the Ice Age, the Americas were cut off from cultural diffusion and the ideas being shared in Africa, Asia, and Europe.

9. Which is the oldest civilization in the Americas, meaning it was the original founder?

   A. Aztecs
   B. Olmecs
   C. Incas
   D. Nazca

10. Which Mesoamerican civilization created an intricate calendar consisting of an interlocking solar and lunar calendar?

   A. Chavín
   B. Monte Albán
   C. Teotihuacan
   D. Olmec

11. Which civilization used the Long Count, which allowed Europeans to match events in the Americas with known events in Europe?

    A. The Maya
    B. Aztecs
    C. Incans
    D. Hopewell mound builders

12. Which Mesoamerican empire was an extractive empire in terms of resources from the surrounding lands?

    A. Incas
    B. Aztecs
    C. Olmecs
    D. Monte Albán

13. What is the process that the Incas used to complete large public works projects?

    A. They forced conquered peoples to complete the work.
    B. They required everyone in the empire to work on them during the growing season.
    C. They used the mita system where every male was required to work a certain number of days per year on the public works projects.
    D. They used large-scale slave labor intermixed with skilled Incan engineers.

14. What is the commonality that exists between all civilizations of Mesoamerica and South America?

    A. Monumental architecture and great works of engineering
    B. The writing system, which was easy to read and decode
    C. Universally worshipping the same gods and following the same practices
    D. Collective resistance to European conquest

15. As the Tang Dynasty of China grew to its height of power, in which era of history was Western Europe engaged?

    A. Dark Ages of Europe
    B. Renaissance
    C. Roman Empire in the West was collapsing
    D. Age of Absolutism

16. What significant accomplishment created by the Tang helped the economy of China?

    A. Taxes were redistributed and lowered on the peasant class.
    B. Merchants were recognized as essential members of society and had their status increased.
    C. The emperor encouraged exports to Japan and the Koreas.
    D. The Grand Canal was dug, linking northern and southern China so goods could be transported and shared throughout the empire.

17. Choose the painful process that aristocratic women went through during the Song Dynasty as it was thought to make them look more beautiful.

    A. They had to wear elaborate headdresses.
    B. They had to wear many multicolored layers of silk.
    C. The practice of foot binding became widespread.
    D. They were forced to endure heavy layers of makeup.

18. Which of the following was the most impressive technological accomplishment of the Song Dynasty?

    A. Linking of the entire Great Wall together
    B. Inventing a simple-to-follow crop rotation method
    C. Gunpowder
    D. The first instance of movable type with wooden block printing

Quick Quiz Answers

1. C; **2.** A; **3.** D; **4.** B; **5.** D; **6.** D; **7.** C; **8.** D; **9.** B; **10.** B; **11.** A; **12.** B; **13.** C; **14.** C; **15.** A; **16.** D; **17.** C; **18.** D

731 C.E.–1526 C.E.

Middle Eastern Expansion: Islamic Empires, Mongols, Turks, and the Gunpowder Empires

15

THE EFFECTS OF ISLAMIC EXPANSION ON RELIGION

In the mid-600s, as Islam broke from the heartlands of the Middle East and spread westward into Africa, northward into Europe, and eastward deeper into Asia, there was a fracturing of the religion. By 850–900, there developed between Shiite and Sunni followers a schism that broke down the power of the central caliph, and there was no longer one ruler or governor of Islam. Coupled with this was the empire of the great Genghis Khan, which was spreading westward from China during the Islamic expansion. The result was a breakdown of the power of the caliphate and the creation of several regional Islamic kingdoms.

Orthopraxy vs. Orthodoxy

Despite all of their disagreements over leadership, Muslims were in agreement in the way that they tried to define Islam by their practice or what they did, known as orthopraxy. This was in contrast to Christianity, which was defined by its orthodoxy, or what the people believed. Whether they were Shiite, Sunni, or Sufi, all were Muslims. The religious and legal scholars agreed that they were all Muslim because they followed the same, clearly defined Muslim practices. So in other words, they worshipped the same way. Their only difference was leadership.

The Domination of the Sunni

After the control of one central caliph broke down between 850 C.E. and 900 C.E., it was the ulama who became the religious and political elite of the Islamic community. They intertwined with the different local businesses and landowning bureaucracies, which helped the higher classes to identify more deeply with Islam. From 1000 C.E. onward, the ulama became a separate kind of social class of their own. While all Muslims were equal, the ulama's word and rulings carried more weight.

Creation of the Madrasa

The madrasa was an Islamic university, and it started in 859 when the ulama began to teach Muslims at local mosques. Eventually, teaching became a permanent job for the ulama. Regional rulers, through patronage and physically building schools, recruited the best teachers to help spread the religion. The teachers also helped the regional rulers run their governmental territories. In contrast to universities in Europe, where there was a set curriculum, in Islam, it was the teachers who personally certified when their students had attained a mastery of their material. There was not a set four-, six-, or eight-year curriculum. Those who mastered the material could advance much quicker. The decision was all up to the teacher. After receiving their certification, the students could become teachers themselves, so the teachers and the madrasa became one more unifying element of Islam.

Creation of Moorish Culture in Spain

Different regional developments in the Islamic world began to develop. Traveler Ibn Batutta used the term *Dar al-Islam* meaning "the abode of Islam." When the Islamic religion and culture finished its worldwide spread, it stretched from the Atlantic Ocean in Spain throughout Southeast Asia.

In the western half of the Islamic world, which was considered Spain, Morocco, and most of North Africa, there was a western caliphate, or leader of Islam. There was a blending of Islamic and Spanish/European culture known as Moorish. Today, the Moorish culture is still visible in the Spanish city of Cordoba, where there is the Alhambra Mosque and madrasa near the Alhambra Castle.

This area of Spain and Africa was a creative and cultural center for 200 years while most of Europe was locked in the Dark Ages. The cultural explosion was due to a grandfather and his grandson: Abd al-Rahman I and Abd al-Rahman III. They opened the madrasa in Spain and Africa in the late 800s, attracting not only Islamic students but European and Christian students as well. Together, the different groups made advances in medicine and science, as well as excellent works of literature. They developed an elegant, courtly lifestyle not seen in many other places.

However, attending school together did not foster religious understanding between the groups. There was still a strict barrier of separation between both Islamic and Christian students, even though they interacted with each other on a daily basis.

After the death of Abd al-Rahman III in 961 C.E., Islamic power in Europe began to decline. This led to the Reconquista of Spain by the Christian nobles, led by the great warrior El Cid. El Cid worked to push the Muslims out of Spain in the mid-1050s.

Harun al-Rashid

During the height of the Middle Ages of Europe, Islam had one regional caliph, Harun al-Rashid, from 786 C.E. to 809 C.E. Harun al-Rashid ruled over an empire larger than any European king at the time. He was seen as a role model ruler. He welcomed educators and education, and his territory was known to be very wealthy and visibly beautiful. The reason for the splendor of his empire was that he liked the ideas of universities, which were still formative at this point. He was a great patron of the arts. He was to the Islamic world what the Medicis were to the city of Florence during the Renaissance.

Shift in Islamic Leadership

Despite the teaching by the madrasa and the leadership of Harun al-Rashid, at this point in Islamic history, there was a vast splintering of the different Islamic territories. Islam shifted from being an Arabic-dominated religion and empire to more of a Turkish one. As leadership changed frequently, the Arabic-led Abbasid Dynasty (who were Sunni Muslims) fought the Egyptian-led Fatimid Dynasty (who were Shiite Muslims).

THE SELJUK DYNASTY

The Seljuks formed the first major Turkish dynasty in 1037. They were a warrior clan and devout Sunnis. They liberated the city of Baghdad in 1055 and were seen as the savior of the Sunni people from the Shiites. The Seljuks were the first to take on the new title of *sultan*, which means "temporary authority."

Seljuk Architecture and Art

It was the Seljuk who pushed Islamic rule deep into the heartlands of Turkey between 1037 and 1200. They also liberated the cities of Mecca and Medina from the Shiite dynasty, the Fatimid. The Seljuk Dynasty built a lot of new roads, complete with rest stops and inns, which increased trade and allowed the completion of the Hajj to be easier. They brought mosaic art, acid-etched metalwork, and architecture to a higher level by putting their Turkish flair on it.

SALADIN AND THE CRUSADES

During this period, there was the great Islamic warrior, Saladin. Saladin was a Sunni who conquered much of Mesopotamia, Syria, and Palestine. He was the founder of a new dynasty in 1171: the Ayyubid Dynasty.

Saladin was able to completely wipe out Shiite philosophy from the Tigris and Euphrates river valleys, all the way to Egypt when he defeated the Fatimid Dynasty in 1173. He was, however, most well known for fighting in the Third Crusade in 1174 against King Richard the Lionheart of England. Saladin was able to unite the Islamic tribes in 1187, defeating the crusading armies and pushing them out of Jerusalem. Saladin not only conquered and defeated the Crusaders but he also slowed the breakup of Islam.

Decline of the Fatimid Dynasty

There was a Shiite dynasty in Cairo, Egypt, known as the Fatimids. Named after Muhammad's daughter, their influence lasted only a couple of hundred years. The Fatimids managed to exist because of the remaining male descendant of Fatima. The Shiites believed that the true leader of Islam must have Muhammad's blood in his veins, and the Fatimids were the only Shiite tribe with this connection. However, 400 years had passed since Muhammad had died, and that belief was fading as Sunnis became the dominant sect of Islam.

THE MAMLUK DYNASTY AND BAYBARS

The new Turkish-led Sunni dynasty, the Mamluk, came to power in 1260. Their most famous king, Baybars, led the Mamluk Dynasty from 1260 to 1277. During his reign, Baybars worked to create peace and open new trade routes with the Byzantine Empire. As a result, the Mamluks were the only Islamic dynasty able to withstand Mongol invasion.

MONGOL EXPANSION

To complicate matters further, a new invasion came from China that had an impact on Islam: the Mongols. The Mongol Empire moved from China like a boomerang. They came from the east into central Asia, the Islamic heartlands, and Europe. Then they boomeranged back across Europe and the Middle East in a southern line, going through what is today Iran, Afghanistan, and India.

As they expanded and came into contact with Muslims, some Mongols converted to Islam, which had an impact on the leadership and the spread of the religion.

Genghis Khan

At 20 years old, a Mongol man named Temujin became a war leader in 1182 as Mongol nomads in northern China conquered the Chinese people all the way to the steppes of Central Asia. Temujin took the name Genghis Khan, which means "great from birth."

Between 1182 and 1227, Genghis Khan united the Mongol clans and enforced a strict disciplinary code of absolute obedience and loyalty from his people. The Mongols were already excellent riders who had the ability to remain on their ponies for days on end. With Genghis Khan's leadership and discipline, the highly trained Mongol warriors had unprecedented mobility. They overwhelmed opponents, starting in China and heading westward. Genghis Khan quickly developed a ferocious reputation. However, he had a saying, "You must always keep people off balance. One minute display violence and cruelty, and the next minute, be generous." For towns and villages that fought bravely, Genghis Khan would pardon the people and sometimes give them positions within his army.

After many years on the outskirts of China, the Mongols invaded the main body of the country. To topple China's many cities, they used Turkish and Chinese technology. They mastered the use of cannons and other weapons. In 1227, Genghis Khan died, not living to witness the Mongol conquest of China. However, he created the biggest empire the world had seen.

Extent of the Mongol Empire

Genghis Khan's descendants kept up the Mongol expansion over the next 150 years. In 1236, they traveled all the way to Russia, becoming known as the Golden Horde.

From 1200 to 1300, Genghis Khan's grandsons enlarged the empire and encouraged trade, linking the Silk Road with Europe. They also unknowingly helped to spread the Black Death as they boomeranged through Europe and Asia.

Mongol and Muslim Encounter

During this period of conquest, the Mongols encountered Muslims in the Middle East. When the Mongols conquered a territory, they allowed the people to retain their local government and customs as long as the people acknowledged Mongol leadership and paid tribute. If they paid tribute, the empire was completely safe and tolerant of diversity.

In 1255, one of Genghis Khan's grandsons, Hulagu Khan, led a massive army into Turkey, assimilating some of the Seljuk Turks into his army. In 1258, he burned the Islamic capital of Baghdad to the ground, killing the Abbasid caliph and his four sons. Hulagu claimed to be religiously tolerant, so he spared all of the Christians. Hulagu was later defeated by another Mongol cousin, Berke Khan, who had converted to Islam. This defeat signaled the total breakup of Genghis Khan's single Mongol Empire. Separate Mongol spheres began to form.

Yuan, the Mongol Dynasty

It took the Mongols until 1279 to finally defeat China. Genghis Khan's grandson, Kublai Khan, established the Yuan, or foreign, Dynasty. Kublai Khan tried to keep the Mongols separated so they would not be absorbed into Chinese culture. In the Yuan Dynasty, only Mongols were allowed in the military and could attain high government positions. Kublai Khan, however, welcomed many foreigners to his court, including Marco Polo and the famous Islamic traveler Ibn Battuta.

The Mongol legacy expanded human contact across continents. The pope even sent priests and bishops to visit the Mongol Empire, and Muslims moved and set up their own communities within the empire in China. All of this furthered trade and cultural diffusion.

Tamerlane

Tamerlane led a half-Turkish, half-Mongol army across central Asia in the late 1300s. Tamerlane was not interested in creating an empire but in sheer conquest. He led his army into Mesopotamia, Persia, and India. Tamerlane was an ambitious ruler. Different from his predecessors, he left a wake of ruin, death, disease, and political chaos across the eastern Islamic world. He tried to spread the Islamic religion, but the destruction made it difficult for this area to recover. When Tamerlane died in 1405, there were three caliphs: one who ruled Spain and North Africa, one who ruled the Middle East, and one who ruled India.

CREATION OF THE DELHI SULTANATE

Between 1306 and 1350, Islamic rule was spread to northern India. This brought about a clash between the traditional Hindu people and the new Islamic society. Initially, not only had there been trade between the two peoples, but Islamic scholars also came eastward to India. As they spread, they brought ideas and classical learning from Greece and Persia. The ideas of the Hellenistic world were flourishing in the Indian civilization. However, Tamerlane destroyed much of the peace that existed between the two groups when he invaded India in 1398. This caused a fracture in India as Hindu and Islamic peoples were forced to merge into one society.

There were several difficulties when it came to merging the Indian and Islamic societies.

1. Hinduism was an old religion. It was thousands of years old, going back to the ancient river valleys, whereas Islam was a relative newcomer.
2. Hinduism had many gods and representations of these gods. Islam was monotheistic with no artistic representation of God or Allah allowed.
3. Hinduism had a strict hierarchy, known as the caste system, as an integral part of its beliefs. Islam had a basic belief that everyone was equal.

It took a long time before the two religious groups found a way to work together. In northern China, indigenous Hindus had to pay a head tax and were actually seen as second-class citizens. Many Hindus converted to Islam to take advantage of better business opportunities in trading. Many lower caste members adopted Islam as a way of throwing off the caste system.

FUN FACT

These empires are known as the Gunpowder Empires because they had cannons and rifles.

THE OTTOMANS, SAFAVIDS, AND MUGHALS

The Mamluk and Seljuk Turks merged in 1299 to become the great Ottoman Empire, one of the Gunpowder Empires. The Ottomans became known for their great absolute monarchs.

The Ottoman Empire

The Ottoman Empire lasted from 1299 to 1918, finally collapsing at the end of World War I. It was one of the longest lasting dynastic empires in the world. The Ottomans were Turks from

Central Asia and northern Turkey, and they conquered territory from Turkey all the way to southern Europe. The Byzantine Empire had been fighting Islamic advances for almost 800 years, and the Ottomans were finally able to defeat them and capture the city of Constantinople in 1453. The city of Constantinople was renamed Istanbul, which it remains today.

The Ottomans expanded for a period of 200 years, eventually controlling territory from modern-day Hungary into the Arabian Peninsula. Until their collapse in 1918, they had one of the largest and most powerful Islamic empires to rule since the first Muslims left the Islamic heartlands.

Safavids

From 1500 to 1736, the Safavid Empire grew in what is today Iran in the old Persian Empire. The Safavids were Turks as well, and they were caught between the great Ottoman and Mughal empires. The Safavids were always at war, either with the Ottomans or Mughals, because the Safavids were the minority sect of Islam. They were Shiites, who believed the leader of Islam must be directly descended from Muhammad. Today, Iran has a large Shiite population.

The Safavids were strict in imposing their beliefs on those they conquered, which put them nearly always at odds with the Ottomans as their territory bordered on each other. The Safavid king, Abbas the Great, shared a similarity with two of his contemporaries in the Ottoman and Mughal empires. He was a strong central monarch, and the Safavid Empire revolved around him. He was a hands-on emperor who directed the empire. He was also able to force diplomacy with the Ottoman Empire at times, due to their control of many key trading routes through the Safavid Empire. Abbas the Great was tolerant of non-Muslims, which helped facilitate and create economic activity.

The Mughal Dynasty

The Turkish/Mongol armies, previously led by Tamerlane in the early 1400s, made it back to India in 1526 C.E. They destroyed the Delhi sultanate, the Indian leader in the city of Delhi. The new rulers were known as the Mughal Dynasty. The Mughals were most known for their famous king, Akbar the Great. He was a devout Muslim, which was different from many monarchs of his day. He worked alongside the Hindus in his empire, and he welcomed them. Akbar the Great decided to work with India's vast diversity rather than against it. This allowed him to form a strong power base across the vastness of India, a large and diverse empire. Akbar the Great was able to find a way to rule a country that was full of different ethnic, cultural, and religious traditions.

SUFI MUSLIMS

Sufis were a third sect or tradition of Islam. They favored a life of more godly worship, instead of just following the five pillars of Islam. Sufis tried to bridge the separation between themselves and God, blending in meditation, fasting, and lives of self-denial.

Sufis were also great missionaries. They went out to remote villages, and they were flexible enough to adopt local traditions. When they found a shrine or temple built by the indigenous people, the Sufis would find a way to make the indigenous shrine work within the rules and customs of Islam. The Sufis became the chief spreaders of Islam as they were able to attract many people.

Islam was a lasting religion and culture. It spread from the Middle East, up into Greece and the Balkans, into Russia, over through India, then into southeastern Asia to Malaysia,

Global Connections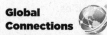

Sufi Muslims led lives of poverty and chastity, similar to the European monks.

Indonesia, and the Pacific. Both coasts of Africa also became important centers of Islamic political and commercial power.

Islam was able to spread for three main reasons.

1. The Sufis. They went out amongst the people and helped them convert to Islam. They were able to gain a lot of ground as they helped repair the damage caused by the spread of the Mongol Empire.
2. The merchants. They migrated and settled in the eastern cities of the Islamic empire to gain access to trade with India and China.
3. Conquest. Whether by Arabic armies spreading Islam, Turks and Central Asians converting to Islam then enlarging the territory, or the boomerang effect of the large Mongol invasion, Islam spread efficiently and effectively. Islam was dominant from the Pacific Ocean to the Atlantic Ocean.

By combining all of this territory, rich religion, and ethnic diversity, many artistic and technological achievements were created.

ISLAMIC ACHIEVEMENTS

Starting during the life of the prophet Muhammad, merchants and trading were important in Arabic society. Islamic traders crossed the Sahara Desert into West Africa. Islamic merchants traveled the Silk Road into China. Arabic merchant ships traveled to East Africa and India, spreading ideas, technology, and their religion. Islamic artisans produced many different trade goods, including high-strength steel decorated with acid etching, leather goods from North Africa and Spain, and cotton from Egypt. Persian carpets were woven with a very high thread count, making it very tough, vibrant, and brilliant. Items that were highly sought by many cultures were created by Muslims.

Artistic Achievement

Muslims decorated their buildings with geometric artwork or patterns that were also shown in their Persian carpets. Because artists were forbidden to make human figures, elaborate geometric patterns, like giant puzzle pieces, were created so that people could artistically express themselves.

Architecture

Muslims specialized in the adapted use of the dome and arch. In Jerusalem, there was the famous Dome of the Rock, a shrine capped with a great dome, which used the arches from the Byzantine Empire. Very tall towers called minarets, which borrowed some architecture from Rome and the Byzantine Empire, were created so the Islamic leaders could issue the call to prayer. Minarets dotted the landscape, giving Islamic cities a look of beauty and splendor. Muslims were able to convert Christian churches, such as the Hagia Sofia, from Greek and Byzantine architecture to that of Islamic architecture.

Medicine and Science

The ideas of Islamic medicine were transferred to the Western world through the trade network, which also helped spread ideas about different ways to use writing and Arabic numerals. Islamic doctors were highly skilled and had to pass a test before they were able to practice medicine. The medical world of the Muslims was far ahead of anything that had been seen in Europe. They helped get medical practices moving forward again after the Dark Ages.

TIMELINE REVIEW

731 C.E.	Abd al-Rahman I Moorish culture
809 C.E.	Harun al-Rashid
850–900 C.E.	Breakup of central caliph
900 C.E.	Abd al-Rahman III Moorish culture
910 C.E.	Muhammad al-Razi
987 C.E.	Great Mosque of Cordoba
1099 C.E.	• First Crusade • El Cid and the Reconquista
1171 C.E.	End of the Fatimid Caliphate
1174 C.E.	Saladin and the Third Crusade
1206 C.E.	Genghis Khan conquests begin.
1221 C.E.	Growth of Sufism
1236 C.E.	Mongols make it to Russia—Golden Horde.
1250 C.E.	Mamluk Turks
1258 C.E.	Hulaga Khan burns Baghdad.
1260 C.E.	Hulaga Khan vs. Berke Khan
1279 C.E.	Kublai Khan establishes the Yuan Dynasty.
1299 C.E.	Ottoman Dynasty, one of the three Gunpowder Empires
1350 C.E.	Delhi sultanate in India
1360 C.E.	Tamerlane's conquests begin.
1429 C.E.	*1001 Arabian Nights*
1500 C.E.	Safavid Empire, one of the three Gunpowder Empires
1526 C.E.	Mughal Dynasty, one of the three Gunpowder Empires

GLOBAL CONNECTIONS

Europe

1300 C.E.—Renaissance begins in Italy

1456 C.E.—Gutenberg's movable type

1500s C.E.—Michelangelo, Raphael, and Leonardo da Vinci

1517 C.E.—Martin Luther's *95 Theses*

Russia

1462 C.E.—Ivan the Great

Japan

Circa 1000–1600 C.E.—Japanese feudalism

1192 C.E.—Minamoto Yoritomo becomes shogun

1274–1281 C.E.—Kublai Khan invasions fail

Africa

1480 C.E.—Portuguese begin to trade with West Africa

1500 C.E.—Kingdom of the Kongo

Mesoamerica

1300 C.E.—Tenochtitlan built by Aztecs

1450 C.E.—Machu Picchu built by Incas

1519 C.E.—Arrival of Cortés into Aztec civilization

China

907 C.E.—Tang Dynasty ends

960 C.E.—Song Dynasty begins

1279 C.E.—Song Dynasty ends

The Renaissance and Reformation

16

REBIRTH: THE STARTING POINT—ITALY

Between 1300 c.e. and 1600 c.e., the Renaissance was born in Western Europe. *Renaissance* means "rebirth." During this time, there was a renewal of interest in the classics and the liberal arts curriculum. It was a time of vast creativity that brought changes to every facet of life: political, cultural, social, and economic. It was simply a rebirth that was needed to create order from the unending chaos of the Middle Ages. The Renaissance placed a renewed emphasis on human achievement and what a single individual could accomplish. When a person is called a "Renaissance man," it implies that he or she is a person with many talents, and he or she is doing perfect work with those talents.

The Renaissance started in Italy in the 1300s and spread northward, reaching its peak in the mid-1500s. With the renewed interest in classical learning, which was developed in ancient Rome, it made perfect sense that Italy was the starting point for the Renaissance.

Many of Italy's cities were able to survive the Middle Ages because of their close proximity to Rome and their distance from the invading Germanic barbarians. Some cities, like Venice and Florence, became large centers of manufacturing and trade. In these cities, there were wealthy and powerful merchants as a result of the Crusades. Using the influence of their money and power, they stressed the importance of education and learning. Along with their economic and political leadership roles, the powerful merchants had the ability to push the Renaissance forward and finance many of its projects and achievements.

The Medici Family

No family in the Renaissance was more famous than the Medici family. In the 1300–1400s, the Medici family ran a prosperous banking business headquartered in the Italian city of Florence. Florence was a city that visibly symbolized what the Renaissance stood for—art, beauty, and learning. With their wealth and influence, the Medici family became the unofficial rulers of Florence for years. The most famous was Lorenzo de Medici, who became a great patron and financial supporter of the arts and artistic achievement.

Petrarch and Humanism

Francisco Petrarch was a citizen of Florence during the Medici's unofficial reign. He believed in the concept of humanism. Humanism was the study of classical culture, which today is known as the humanities. Humanism focused on worldly subjects, rather than transfixing on religion and the afterlife, both of which were the main foci of the Middle Ages. Petrarch felt that people needed a broad educational background. This broadened background would heighten and stimulate a person's creativity. To aid this process, Petrarch became a teacher and built a large library, which included every copy or original manuscript of Greek and

Roman history, plus the ideas, thoughts, and philosophies of the ancient scholars. The study of humanities helped stimulate the Renaissance.

Renaissance Art, Sculpture, and Architecture

The Renaissance was most famous for its works of art, which were supported by the rich patrons, like the Medicis, and religious clergy, including multiple Roman Catholic popes. Renaissance artists painted with new techniques and were fond of painting famous religious figures in a Greek or Roman forum. Some artists even put themselves in their paintings.

Before the Renaissance, the Greek sculpture and painting style was idealistic, whereas the Roman style was realistic. The Renaissance painters created a new style called perspective. In a perspective painting, the artist created lifelike images in the background, which they painted smaller. As a person moved closer to the front of the painting, the images looked bigger, giving the illusion of depth in their painting.

The most famous artists of the Renaissance period are Donatello, Leonardo da Vinci, Michelangelo, and Rafael.

FUN FACT

An easy way to remember these four men is to call them the Ninja Turtle artists. The Ninja Turtle cartoon characters were actually named after these four Renaissance artists!

- Donatello (1386–1466) created the first life-size sculptures seen since the Roman Empire. He made them life-sized and as real as possible.
- Leonardo da Vinci (1452–1519) was the most versatile of the artists, most famous for painting the *Mona Lisa*, which today hangs in the Louvre in Paris. However, da Vinci was more than just an artist. He was a scientist who studied human anatomy. By studying the human body, he could create more accurate lifelike portrayals in his art. He kept notes of his dissection of human bodies that were later used by doctors studying anatomy.
- Michelangelo (1475–1564) was a painter, sculptor, and architect. He created many fine masterpieces that today are seen by millions of people. The statue of the *David* in Florence, which was Michelangelo's home city, was one of his most famous sculptures. The statue of the *David* symbolized David before he fought Goliath. Michelangelo designed the head and the hands of the David larger than the rest of the body. They were out of proportion entirely, but in Michelangelo's mind, it symbolized a human's ability to think and then to act on that thought.
- Rafael (1483–1520) studied the works of Leonardo da Vinci and Michelangelo. He created a famous painting from the school of Athens, which showed the utopian gathering of great scholars of the past. He made it to honor them and painted himself and his role models—Michelangelo and da Vinci—into the painting as well. He also painted another famous painting called *The Marriage of the Virgin*. This showed great use of the idea of perspective as the lines narrow like a train track going in the background, giving the painting depth and looking more lifelike.

Women in the Renaissance

Sofonisba Anguissola was a woman who became famous with her art during the very patriarchal, male-dominated Renaissance. In the 1500s, she was invited to be the court painter of King Philip of Spain. Anguissola made significant strides for women's rights because she was an excellent painter. Christine de Pisan was a French poet in the early 1400s whose diverse writings include poems of courtly love. She was an outspoken artist who championed the rights of women.

Renaissance Architecture

Filippo Brunelleschi led the way in Renaissance architecture. He broke away from the large building style of the Middle Ages and returned to a more classical style, like the idea of using the Roman arch to construct a dome. Using these techniques, he covered the cathedral in Florence with a dome in 1446. The Duomo in downtown Florence is considered today to be one of the most beautiful cathedrals in the world. The inside of the dome of the Duomo was covered with a very intricate painting using the technique of perspective. Brunelleschi's Duomo inspired Michelangelo to create the dome over St. Peter's Basilica in Rome.

DINNER TABLE TALK

What other famous dome was inspired by Michelangelo? The dome over the U.S. Capitol! It was completed during the 1860s during the U.S. Civil War.

Renaissance Literature

The Renaissance included more than just art. There were also classic works of literature. Baldassare Castiglione (1478–1529) wrote a how-to manual of sorts, which explained how to be a perfect or ideal member of a royal court.

Another famous piece of Renaissance literature was a book written by Niccolò Machiavelli entitled *The Prince*. Machiavelli was a diplomat and advisor to many kings, princes, and foreign governments. He wrote *The Prince* in 1513 for the Prince of Florence. It was a manual on how to achieve and keep power. The big question asked in the book was, "Is it better to be feared or loved by your people?" To Machiavelli, it was better to be feared. He said it was acceptable to use any means possible to accomplish a task. To him, the end result always justified the means.

RENAISSANCE IN NORTHERN EUROPE

While the Renaissance was flourishing in southern Europe, it slowly moved northward. It took much longer to gain traction as Northern Europe was still recovering from the effects of the Black Death. In 1450, the Northern Renaissance started in what is today Belgium and the Netherlands.

Northern European Artists

Jan and Hubert van Eyck from Belgium were brothers who were famous for painting lifelike scenes of townspeople doing real, everyday activities. In the early 1400s, the van Eyck's also created a new style of paint that was more oil-based. It allowed them to create more vibrant colors. The oil paints took longer to dry in the damp climates of the north, but once it dried, it lasted much longer. Today most paints are still oil-based.

Northern European Literature

Northern humanists liked classical learning, but they also clung to the religious ideas of the Middle Ages. They used these ideas to bring about a moral reform.

The best examples of these were the ideas of Erasmus. In 1516, Erasmus wrote a revised edition of the New Testament of the Christian Bible, and he translated it into the vernacular of the people of the day. This way, more people could read and understand the Bible. Erasmus also held the church accountable for their wrongdoings as the church had been unassailable when deviating from its spiritual mission.

Sir Thomas More—known more famously as Saint Thomas More—wrote a book called *Utopia* in 1516. The book included his version of the perfect world while very subtly criticizing his king and the church. Saint Thomas More pressed for reforms in society, and in his perfect world, everyone worked, everyone learned, and everyone experienced peace and harmony. There would be no social class separation, and the world would run beautifully and smoothly.

William Shakespeare

The most famous writer of Renaissance literature was William Shakespeare (1564–1616). Shakespeare wrote 37 plays, many of which are still performed to this day. He was also credited with creating 1500–1700 words in the English language. His plays showed a range of emotion: love, jealousy, acquisition of power, and how the powerful can be brought down by their weaknesses. In Shakespeare's plays, the emotions of the characters were what made them so endearing to audiences. He showed that the powerful were very much like normal people.

Another famous writer was Miguel de Cervantes (1547–1616), who hailed from Spain. According to some historians, Cervantes wrote the most-read book in the world: *Don Quixote*. *Don Quixote* was a satire, summing up the changing world from the Middle Ages to the Renaissance. Don Quixote was a medieval knight who longed for the days of old, when he used to be powerful. Instead, it was his squire, Sancho Panza, who became the new model of society. Sancho Panza was a Renaissance man—a leader who was practical and logical and possessed many talents.

The Effect of Johannes Gutenberg's Printing Press

What cannot be understated was the importance of getting the written word to a mass population. In 1456, Johannes Gutenberg's printing press became one of the biggest breakthroughs in world history.

China was a leader in the printing process, creating paper centuries earlier and having woodblock printing during the Tang and Song Dynasties. (See Chapter 14.) However, in 1456, a German named Johannes Gutenberg created a movable type printing press that used paper, not parchment, to print the Christian Bible. Within a short time, printing presses were popping up all over.

The material that was published led to widespread changes in European society. Printing became cheap and easy. Access to written material encouraged more and more people to learn to read. With the ability to read and knowledge available to more people, the effects cannot be understated. Knowledge led people to question the world around them, which facilitated one of the biggest changes in European history—the Protestant Reformation.

THE PROTESTANT REFORMATION (1517–1648 C.E.)

During the great changes during the Renaissance, the powerful Roman Catholic Church began to lose power for the very first time. Much of the church hierarchy had become corrupt, and the visible wealth and worldliness of the religious clergy was drawing the attention of the people. No longer were the clergy focused on the spiritual mission of getting people into heaven, which led to a call for change known as the Protestant Reformation.

Popes and Bishops

Popes in Rome and high-ranking bishops began to live with wealth like kings. Many of them were seeking power to control everything. There were still some good religious clergy, and some of them were patrons of great works of art, but, overall, they behaved horribly.

One of the ways the clergy acquired such wealth was by selling indulgences. An indulgence allowed people to literally pay for their sins. To be forgiven, they could make a monetary donation to the church, not an honest confession. People could also prepay for their sins. Many people did not like this practice as the church had become too secular and worldly. These abuses brought about the downfall of the church.

FUN FACT

Think of an indulgence as a debit card for sinning!

Martin Luther

Martin Luther was a German monk who unintentionally launched a revolt against the church. Luther had become upset at the corruption of the church. When he saw that indulgences were being sold in his hometown, it was the proverbial last straw. People were giving money for themselves or for their dead relatives, and the clergy promised them entry into heaven. As was customary of the time, Martin Luther wrote out his grievances in 1517 and nailed them to the front door of his local cathedral. This document became known as Martin Luther's *95 Theses*.

Gutenberg's printing press played a large role in spreading Luther's ideas. Printers quickly copied the *95 Theses* and spread them throughout the area. The church tried to force Luther to retract his word. Instead, he urged others to speak out about what they saw as wrong as well. As a result, Martin Luther was excommunicated in 1521 by the Roman Catholic Church and declared a criminal by Charles V, the Holy Roman emperor.

However, Luther had touched on something that resonated with the people: that salvation could be achieved through faith in God alone and that the Bible was the sole source of truth. Luther also said that church officials did not have special powers, meaning that bishops and popes were men (and sinners) like everyone else. Luther called for a cleaning up of the church.

Peace of Augsburg

Though Martin Luther unknowingly created instability, many German princes agreed with him. There were 360 princes in Germany, and they sought a way to get more power for themselves, as well as to resist Charles V. They did not want to pay as much money to the church because they wanted more money and power for themselves. When the commoners in Germany began to riot for a change in their lifestyle and that of the church, Charles V invited several German princes for peace talks. Many German princes had already started following a new religion called Lutheranism. In 1555, the Holy Roman emperor and the rulers of Germany signed the Peace of Augsburg. This treaty allowed each territorial ruler to decide the religion of his territory, whether it was Catholic or Lutheran, as a way to bring about peace.

John Calvin (1509–1564)

A French monk named John Calvin built upon Luther's foundation. Calvin said the Bible was the only source of truth, God was all-powerful, and man was a sinful creature by nature. Calvin pioneered the belief in Christian predestination. Predestination said that God decided who made it to heaven, even before a person was born. Calvin set up communities in Geneva, Switzerland, that followed the ideals of the old Benedictine Order: hard work, discipline, honesty, and focus on religion. This applied for both men and women.

This type of community attracted attention, and people tried to transplant what Calvin had done all over Europe. The effect was that it kickstarted battles over religion all over Europe as the Roman Catholic Church tried to reassert itself. The most violent battles happened in France between Catholics and French Protestants, known as Huguenots.

England Creates a New Church Under Henry VIII

King Henry VIII of England led a different type of separation, as it was more political. Henry VIII had been a good Catholic and had been rewarded by the pope for his stand against combating Lutheranism. However, Henry VIII wanted an annulment of his marriage, meaning he wanted it erased as if it had never happened. In 1527, he wanted to annul the marriage to his wife, Catherine of Aragon, who had not produced any male heirs. Henry wanted a male heir to ensure the stability of his throne. However, the pope refused because he thought that, as the king, Henry VIII should be a role model for his people. In addition, the pope did not want to upset Catherine's nephew, who was Charles V, the Holy Roman emperor.

Henry VIII decided to take a stand, break with the pope, and form his own church. To that end, Henry VIII passed laws proclaiming himself, not the pope, to be head of the Church of England. He then had a loyal archbishop annul his marriage so that he could remarry in 1533. Henry VIII closed monasteries and convents, and he seized Catholic Church lands and money. He gave most of it to powerful nobles and friends, which helped them agree to his split with the Roman Catholic Church. The differences between a Roman Catholic church service and a Church of England service are few, but the split continued to spark fighting over religion during the Reformation.

FUN FACT

By the time Henry VIII dies, he will have gone through four marriages! Of the four marriages, only one son was produced.

THE CATHOLIC REFORMATION (1545–1648 c.e.)

After seeing the religious fractures in Germany, France, and England, the new Pope, Paul III, made the decision to end this reformation and put the church back on track for its original mission: saving souls. He pushed back the Protestant movement, and he started cleaning up the papacy itself. Paul III got rid of bad and corrupt officials, and he formed the Council of Trent.

The Council of Trent met from 1545 to 1563, figuring out how to reestablish Roman Catholic doctrine and the best way to go about it. They instituted harsh punishments for anyone who was corrupt. The Council of Trent was a good idea, in theory, but it led to even more problems.

The Inquisition

As a result of the Council of Trent, a church court was established. Its purpose was to find nonbelievers and other heretics who did not believe in God. They also searched for Protestants using any means possible. They destroyed any book that questioned the Catholic Church, like the books written by Luther and Calvin. A new order of monks was created to spread Catholic doctrine.

Role of the Jesuits

This new order of monks was led by Ignatius of Loyola, a former knight who was determined to spread Catholicism. Tapping into his military training, Ignatius wanted his monks to practice a strict moral and religious discipline. The idea of the Jesuits was to be missionaries to spread the Word throughout the world. Since European exploration had begun, the Jesuits did not stay in Europe but traveled to Protestant-held territories across the world: the Americas, Africa, and Asia.

Religious Persecution

In Europe, Catholics and Protestants were competing for spiritual dominance, which flared up into violence. In this frenzy of religious reform, someone had to be blamed for the violence. There were witch hunts, and those found guilty were drowned or burned at the stake. Normally, it was people on the fringe of society, the social outsiders, who were blamed.

SCIENTIFIC ACHIEVEMENT DURING THE REFORMATION

During the Reformation, there was also creativity and advancement, mainly in the area of science. One side effect of the reformation of the church and the collapse of its power was that its stranglehold on education was lessened. People sought to be educated, and they began to study the physical world. As the church could no longer force its own thoughts on people, the stifled creativity of scientists began to expand.

Nicolaus Copernicus (1473–1543)

Nicolaus Copernicus restated the heliocentric theory of the universe. Copernicus said the Earth and the other planets revolved around the sun, not the other way around. Copernicus was a big problem for the church because his scientific findings were opposite to what the church taught. If Copernicus proved the church was wrong about this, it could lead to a lot of unwanted questions.

Tycho Brahe (1546–1601)

Tycho Brahe followed Copernicus. He created an observatory with a telescope. He was able to chart the heavens, the movements of the planets, and after a period of years, he proved that Copernicus was correct.

Johannes Kepler (1571–1630) and Galileo (1564–1642)

Johannes Kepler was inspired by Brahe and Copernicus. He, and fellow scientist Galileo, charted the orbits of planets and moons with powerful telescopes. They said that the planets moved and rotated. They also said that the Earth rotated once every 24 hours. Galileo was persecuted and condemned by the church. During the Inquisition, a religious panel condemned him until he publicly stated that he was incorrect. In a famous bit of history, Galileo publicly said, "Yes, I am wrong." However, as he turned and left the Inquisition, he whispered under his breath, "Yes, it does move. We are correct." Galileo's work inspired Isaac Newton.

Isaac Newton (1643–1727)

Isaac Newton was studying at the University of Cambridge, pondering deep thoughts when an apple from a tree landed on his head. This incident inspired Newton to use mathematics to prove his theory of gravity. Newton proved that planets do move and that it was mathematical principles, not natural philosophy, that governed the laws of gravity. Newton showed that all motion could be studied and measured with mathematics.

Francis Bacon (1561–1626) and the Scientific Method

The great philosopher Aristotle was wrong in his thoughts about the governance of the physical world. He said the answer to questions could only be arrived at following the end of a long period of study. Francis Bacon favored the Scientific Method. The Scientific Method involved forming a hypothesis, running an experiment, recording thoughts and observations, and running the experiment again. If the same conclusion was found after several experiments, then the answer was found.

René Descartes (1596–1650)

René Descartes emphasized that it was the ability of humanity to reason and solve problems that provided the basic truths of learning. Descartes believed in looking at a problem and finding different ways to tackle it. Descartes also made the great statement, "I think, therefore, I am."

TIMELINE REVIEW

1300 C.E.	Renaissance begins in Italy.
1330 C.E.	Francisco Petrarch creates humanism.
1400 C.E.	Medici family begins to dominate Florentine government.
1446 C.E.	Filippo Brunelleschi's Duomo in Florence
1455 C.E.	Donatello creates *Penitent Magdalene*.
1456 C.E.	Gutenberg's movable type
1492 C.E.	Lorenzo de Medici as patron
1500 C.E.	Sofonisba Anguissola
1504 C.E.	Raphael's *The Marriage of the Virgin*
1509 C.E.	Erasmus's *The Praise of Folly*
1512 C.E.	Michelangelo paints the Sistine Chapel.
1513 C.E.	Niccolò Machiavelli's *The Prince*
1516 C.E.	Renewed Jewish persecution
1517 C.E.	• Leonardo da Vinci's *Mona Lisa*
	• Martin Luther's *95 Theses*
1528 C.E.	Baldassare Castiglione's *Book of the Courtier*
1534 C.E.	King Henry VIII creates the Church of England.
1540 C.E.	Ignatius of Loyola creates Jesuits.
1541 C.E.	John Calvin's colony in Geneva, Switzerland
1543 C.E.	Nicolaus Copernicus publishes heliocentric theory.
1545 C.E.	Catholic Reformation begins under Pope Paul III.
1555 C.E.	Peace of Augsburg
1590 C.E.	Shakespeare begins to write.
1605 C.E.	Cervantes publishes *Don Quixote*.
1620s C.E.	• Bacon: Experiment and observation
	• Descartes: human reason
1633 C.E.	Galileo's trial on movement of planets
1687 C.E.	Newton's law of gravity

GLOBAL CONNECTIONS

Russia

1462 c.e.—Ivan the Great

1560 c.e.—Ivan the Terrible

1600s—Time of Troubles

Africa

1480 c.e.—Portuguese begin to trade with West Africa

1500 c.e.—Kingdom of the Kongo

Mesoamerica

1300 c.e.—Tenochtitlan built by Aztecs

1450 c.e.—Machu Picchu built by Incas

1532 c.e.—Defeat of Incas by Pizarro

Middle East

1299 c.e.—Ottoman Empire

1500 c.e.—Safavid Empire

1526 c.e.—Mughal Empire

17

European Exploration

In the early 1500s, just as the Islamic Gunpowder Empires were reaching their height, Europeans in Western Europe began reaching out into the oceans. Like the ancient Phoenicians, who were the first long-distance sailors, the Portuguese began to test the waters beyond Europe. The Portuguese developed a new ship called a caravel. It combined elements of the best sailing technology in the world at the time:

- The stern post rudder, which was technology of the old Chinese junks
- The triangular sail, known as the lateen sail, of the Islamic merchant vessels
- Viking shipbuilding technology
- Shipbuilding ideas from ancient Phoenicia

The Portuguese attached the stern post rudder and the lateen sail on the caravel, giving them the ability to handle all types of winds and ocean currents. They could actually sail when there was very little wind, and sometimes even into the wind.

PORTUGUESE ROLE

The Portuguese were trying to find a shortcut to Asia to take advantage of Asian trading. This was a dangerous journey, but with the money that could be made with spices from India and Southeast Asia, it was worth the risk. These Portuguese sailors began to explore the oceans in tiny ships. Overland trade along the Silk Road had previously been the only way to take advantage of trading. However, with the breakup of the Mongol Empire and the three different Islamic Gunpowder Empires now in place, it was more dangerous and difficult. The Portuguese, aided by shipbuilding technology, began to incorporate other scientific technology that allowed them to travel across the Atlantic Ocean.

Scientific Technology

The first instrument that aided the Portuguese was the magnetic compass. It employed a needle that floated on a liquid, like mercury, and it pointed toward magnetic north. By using it, sailors could tell the direction they were traveling. However, it was not very accurate.

In the 1400s, the Portuguese began to use the astrolabe. This device allowed people to measure the angle of the sun and certain stars, such as the North Star and Venus, in relation to their distance from the horizon. As a result, people could track their route and keep their bearings.

Because the Portuguese used the astrolabe, they adapted the use of the Mercator projection in 1569. This was exactly like a modern-day map with lines running east and west (latitude) and north and south (longitude). The straight lines cut a globe into sections or squares to aid in navigation.

The sextant, which combined the astrolabe and the Mercator projection, helped measure the sun's altitude. It was developed in 1731. By comparing the altitude of the sun with a ship's current latitude and longitude, the Portuguese could accurately place the location of their ship.

Combining these new technologies allowed cartographers, or mapmakers, to map the known world with greater accuracy. With the Portuguese maps, people were able to travel farther and safer than it was ever thought possible.

Prince Henry of Portugal

In 1415, Prince Henry, also known as Henry the Navigator, kicked off a new era in the exploration of the world. He wanted to meet a very wealthy Christian African king known as Prester John. Prince Henry wanted to help Prester John combat the spread of Islam, but he also wanted to find a way to tap into the African gold trade. To help the success of his venture, Prince Henry assembled a large team of scientists, cartographers, and brave successful sea captains. All three groups practiced together so they could make increasingly longer voyages from Portugal. Eventually, they began a series of leapfrogging voyages down the coast of Africa, going farther and farther south during each voyage.

However, Prince Henry died in 1460 on the voyages going farther south. After his death, the Portuguese team kept up the mission and discovered the dangerous Horn of Africa at the tip of southern Africa. Now known as the Cape of Good Hope, it separated the Atlantic Ocean and Indian Ocean. It is called the Cape of Good Hope for two reasons.

- Voyagers hoped that they made it successfully around the Horn.
- Voyagers hoped that it led to a quicker route to Asia.

SPANISH COMPETITION

At this time, Western Europe featured many competitive kingdoms. The rulers of Spain did not want to lose ground to their Portuguese neighbors, so they decided to break into the long-distance trade exploration. They hired Italian sailor Christopher Columbus, who had a different and daring plan to find riches. He wanted to sail west to find a shortcut to Asia, bypassing the dangerous trip around Africa's southern tip.

King Ferdinand and Queen Isabella

The king and queen of Spain, Ferdinand and Isabella, financed Columbus's trip in 1492. They were looking for new sources of revenue, but they also wanted to spread Catholicism. Their main goal was to cut out the middleman, like Islamic merchants, so they could dominate the trade routes. Their decision to allow Columbus to sail west changed much of the known world.

Christopher Columbus Discovers the New World

On August 3, 1492, Christopher Columbus sailed with three ships—the *Nina*, the *Pinta*, and the *Santa Maria*. After a rough voyage nearly two months long, Columbus's fleet found land on October 12, 1492, in what is today the Caribbean Sea. He was still looking for China as he sailed around the Caribbean. He thought he had reached the East Indies in the Pacific Islands. Since he thought he had reached the East Indies, he called the people "Indians" and returned to Spain, a conquering hero. Columbus returned three more times, still always thinking he was in Asia. However, shortly after his death in 1506, Europeans realized that this was a new world. Lines of influence were drawn up, dividing the territory between Spain and Portugal. Dividing the territory did not go smoothly, causing Pope Alexander to get involved to prevent a war between Spain and Portugal.

Vasco de Gama

In 1497, another Portuguese sailor, Vasco da Gama, traveled around the Cape of Good Hope in Africa and made it all the way to India. On this dangerous journey, he lost many ships. He also lost many sailors to thirst, to hunger, and to what is now known as scurvy, a vitamin C deficiency. Even with the loss of men and ships, this fleet made enormous sums of money when it returned to Portugal. Da Gama made so much money that he immediately outfitted a new fleet and sent them right back out. This time, da Gama left behind willing Portuguese merchants in India to cheaply store valuables and spices until the next fleet of his ships returned to pick them up. By the year 1502, Portugal had become so wealthy that other European nations also built outposts in foreign lands to support the international trade. This helped many of them create vast trading empires.

Ferdinand Magellan

A Spanish sailor, Ferdinand Magellan, undertook what was arguably one of the most fantastic and dangerous voyages of exploration in human history. Magellan had been influenced by the voyages of da Gama, so King Charles of Spain financed Magellan's quest for an all-water route through the New World—now known as the Americas—to Asia. Magellan interviewed and recruited soldiers for a two-year voyage. During the interviews, he did not tell the applicants where they were heading or the overall plan. Magellan was able to sign a multicultural crew for the voyage.

Magellan and five ships headed out on September 20, 1519. On the way across the Atlantic, Magellan handled difficult storms and a few mutinies until finally spotting the coast of South America. After exploring the coast of South America, Magellan rounded the Cape of South America off the coast of Argentina in November 1520, which is now known as the Straits of Magellan. Despite the very turbulent and stormy weather, Magellan and his crew were able to head into the vast Pacific Ocean and into the unknown.

Unfortunately for Magellan and his crew, they did not know how vast the Pacific Ocean was, and after four months of sailing with little food, the starving soldiers landed in the Pacific island nation of the Philippines. Magellan had initial success in the Philippines and was able to spread Christianity. Unfortunately, he was killed during fighting between two different Filipino tribes in 1521.

Even with their leader gone, Magellan's fleet sailed onward. On September 8, 1522, after being gone for just over three years, they made it back to Spain after circumnavigating the entire globe!

The interconnectedness of Africa, Europe, and Asia migrated outward and incorporated the Americas into a world economy. This had an impact on the entire world, but its effect was felt especially in Europe and by the Native Americans. It vaulted Europe from the Dark Ages to the most powerful continent as they controlled more money, resources, and land than ever before.

THE NETHERLANDS: UNLIKELY RIVALS FOR SEA POWER

The kingdom of Portugal was dominant at sea because of their large head start in exploration. However, it was a small country on the North Sea in northern Europe that rose and challenged the dominance of the Portuguese at sea: the Netherlands. The Netherlands had been connected to the Spanish Habsburg Empire, and in 1599, a Dutch fleet returned to the Netherlands after a long absence while traveling to Asia. When the fleet returned to port, all of the investors in the fleet made astounding sums of money from the profits. Seeing the amount of money that was made, everyone in the Netherlands wanted in. This was the best get-rich-quick scheme ever!

The Dutch East India Company

Dutch men who had become wealthy from this trade with Asia created the Dutch East India Company in 1602. It fought Portugal in a quest to be ranked among the power elites in Europe. They wanted to be like Spain and Portugal, so they traded with China and were able to monopolize trade with Southeast Asia. Part of their success was because the Dutch were able to form better relations and alliances with the native populations. Some Dutch assimilated into native culture and married natives. Unlike the Spanish and the Portuguese, who were bent on religious conversion as well as trade, there was no large religious push for conversion on the part of the Dutch. They only wanted access to trade goods. As a result, the country of the Netherlands became dreamily wealthy.

Global Connections

Themistocles of ancient Athens also built a dual-purpose fleet to trade throughout the Mediterranean and defend Athens from Persia.

The Dutch equipped a dual-purpose fleet. This fleet was for trade, but it was also equipped for battle. The Dutch wanted to set up colonial outposts like those that da Gama started for the Portuguese. Not wanting to draw attention to themselves, the Dutch stayed away from the mighty Spanish fleets, and they started a settlement in 1652 in what is now Cape Town, South Africa. (See Chapter 12.) This settlement was designed to resupply and repair ships for the dangerous trip around the Cape of Good Hope.

TIMELINE REVIEW

1000s C.E.	Magnetic compass
1400s C.E.	• Europeans begin to explore.
	• Astrolabe
1415 C.E.	Prince Henry of Portugal begins the School of Navigation.
1460 C.E.	Prince Henry dies.
1492 C.E.	Columbus's voyage of discovery
1497 C.E.	Vasco da Gama rounds the Cape of Good Hope.
1519 C.E.	• Ferdinand Magellan
	• Cortés conquers the Aztecs.
1569 C.E.	Mercator projection
1602 C.E.	Dutch East India Company
1731 C.E.	Sextant

GLOBAL CONNECTIONS

Americas

1450 C.E.—Machu Picchu built by the Incas

1500 C.E.—Iroquois League

1519 C.E.—Arrival of Cortés in Mexico

1532 C.E.—Pizarro defeats the Incas

Africa

1400 C.E.—Decline of the Malian Empire

1450 C.E.—Empire of Songhai begins

1480 C.E.—Portuguese make contact with West Africa

Asia

1299 C.E.—Ottoman Empire

1500 C.E.—Safavid Empire

China

1405 C.E.—Zheng He's voyages during Ming Dynasty

1406 C.E.—Forbidden City

India

1568 C.E.—Akbar the Great of Mughal Empire expands

Quick Quiz: Chapters 15–17

1. Which family was influential in the rebuilding or beautifying of the city of Florence, Italy?

   A. The Medici family
   B. The Habsburg family
   C. The da Vinci family
   D. The van Eyck family

2. During the Renaissance, Miguel de Cervantes wrote this work of literature, which is reportedly one of the most-read books in the entire world.

   A. *Moby Dick*
   B. *The Legend of King Arthur and the Knights of the Round Table*
   C. *Don Quixote*
   D. *The Count of Monte Cristo*

3. Who started the Protestant Reformation after getting angry at the selling of indulgences?

   A. John Calvin
   B. Oliver Cromwell
   C. King Henry II
   D. Martin Luther

4. Which English king created the new Church of England and broke relations with the pope because his marriage would not be annulled?

   A. King Henry VIII
   B. King Charles II
   C. King George I
   D. Richard the Lionheart

5. Who charted planetary movements and was almost excommunicated for his explanation of the concept of planetary rotation around the sun?

   A. Isaac Newton
   B. Prince Henry
   C. Nicolaus Copernicus
   D. Galileo

6. As the power of the caliphate broke down, who united the practitioners of Islam?

   A. Madrasas
   B. Ulama
   C. Sharia
   D. Imam

7. During this time, the main caliph of Islam switched from being led by Arabs to this new group of Muslims.

   A. Moors
   B. Mongols
   C. Turks
   D. Sufis

8. Moorish culture is a blending of which of the following two cultures?

   A. Islamic and Spanish
   B. Spanish and Malian
   C. Egyptian and Turkish
   D. Byzantine and Islamic

9. Who is the famous Islamic traveler who coined the term "Dar al-Islam"?

   A. Marco Polo
   B. Zheng He
   C. Ibn Batutta
   D. Mansa Musa

10. Of the three Gunpowder Empires, which of the following were practitioners of Shiite Islam?

    A. Ottomans
    B. Mughals
    C. Fatimids
    D. Safavids

11. Which European country took the lead during the Age of Exploration?

    A. Spain
    B. Portugal
    C. Italy
    D. England

12. Which famous monarchy financed the voyages of Christopher Columbus to the New World?

    A. Ferdinand and Isabella of Spain
    B. Louis XIV of France
    C. Queen Elizabeth I of England
    D. Prince Henry of Portugal

13. This Portuguese explorer was the first to round Africa's Cape of Good Hope and make the voyage to India.

    A. Vasco de Gama
    B. Ferdinand Magellan
    C. Henry the Navigator
    D. John Cabot

14. What is the name of the shipping and trading company that set up an outpost, and later a colony, in South Africa?

    A. The British East India Company
    B. The House of Trade
    C. The Dutch East India Company
    D. The Prazeros

Quick Quiz Answers

1. A; **2.** C; **3.** D; **4.** A; **5.** D; **6.** B; **7.** C; **8.** A; **9.** C; **10.** D; **11.** B; **12.** A; **13.** A; **14.** C

The Age of Absolutism

18

CHANGES IN WORLD POWER

After the Age of Exploration, northwestern Europe completely dominated the world until 1950. Due to changes in military technology and the cost of fighting a war, which increased dramatically, it was the overseas colonies of North America that gave European monarchs access to money. This allowed the monarchs to become dominant. The monarchies that were able to secure a solid financial base, as well as achieve independence from nobles or legislative assemblies, achieved absolutism. They were the absolute, total, and sole rulers of their countries. Some nations and their monarchs will succeed while other monarchies will fail. This period in world history is known as the Age of Absolutism.

THE TUDOR DYNASTY IN ENGLAND (1485–1603 C.E.)

From 1485 to 1603, it was the Tudor Dynasty that ruled England. The most famous Tudor ruler was King Henry VIII, who took over the Church of England, renaming it the Anglican Church. The English Parliament legally passed the Act of Supremacy stating that Henry VIII was the new head of the church. Even though Henry was a dominant ruler, he did work with the English Parliament on a regular basis. When new taxes were needed, Parliament had to agree to implement them. As they nearly always voted the king's wishes into law, Parliament grew accustomed to being part of the process. Henry's daughter, Queen Elizabeth I, had the same arrangement when working with Parliament. She was known for being kind to Parliament, guiding them with firmness and toughness. When Elizabeth died in 1603, a branch of the royal family that ruled in Scotland came to power in England.

THE STUART DYNASTY IN ENGLAND (1603–1714 C.E.)

In 1603, James I of Scotland became King James of England. As king, he inherited a large royal debt and a troubled nation. The church was fiercely divided between English Anglican Protestants and traditional Roman Catholics. When James I assumed the throne, he claimed that he was ready to rule by English law. Since Parliament only met when summoned, James rarely did so. He developed new sources of revenue, such as a new customs tax. This angered Parliament as they were the keepers of the royal purse. King James I angered Parliament even more when he went against the Church of England. The Puritans, who wanted to purify the English Church from any remnants of Catholicism, expected the king to further their goals. King James did not.

The biggest problem created by King James I was his foreign policy. He sought peace with Spain, which was a Catholic country. He then tried to have his son, Charles, marry either a Spanish or French princess. As Spain and France were both dominant Catholic countries, he aroused suspicion among Parliament and the people, and he was quickly seen as pro-Catholic. This led to trouble for his descendants and the English crown.

Charles I

King Charles I was the son of King James I, ruling from 1625 to 1649. King Charles picked up where his father left off. He was a firm believer that being king was a divine right, meaning that God placed him on the throne because he was chosen above all others to be the king. Thus, Charles I began to behave like an absolute monarch. He imprisoned political opponents and bled his countrymen dry of money to further his plans.

Nonetheless, Charles I quickly ran out of options to make money. He was forced to call Parliament to a session. As the members of Parliament arrived, they said Charles needed to sign a document called the Petition of Right. The Petition of Right said that there could be no new taxes or political imprisonments without the consent of Parliament. Badly needing money, Charles signed the agreement. His next act as king was to immediately dissolve Parliament. This was known as the Short Parliament.

In 1637, the religious practices of King Charles I started a war in Protestant Scotland. The king needed money to quell the rebellion, and by 1640, he was forced to call Parliament to a meeting. This was known as the Long Parliament because they met over a period of 13 years, eventually igniting a civil war in England. Struggling with the king for power, Parliament executed some of the king's chief ministers, and they said they would no longer be dissolved without their consent. King Charles I responded by leading troops into the House of Parliament to arrest the leaders. This action resulted in civil war as the leaders escaped and created their own army.

English Civil War

The English Civil War lasted from 1642 to 1649. The king led a force known as the Cavaliers, named for their dashing helmets and long hair. The Cavaliers were made up of rich nobles and friends of the king. Their opponents were known as Roundheads. They were mostly plain, ordinary countrymen with bowl haircuts. Since the Cavaliers were trained military men, they were supposed to win an easy victory. However, the Roundheads picked a Puritan leader named Oliver Cromwell, who was a military, organizational, and strategic genius. He led the Roundheads to victory. In January 1649, King Charles I became the first and only English king to be executed. The British Parliament dissolved the monarchy, which shocked the royals across Europe. If this could happen to a king in England, what might happen to their thrones? For the next 10 years, there was no monarchy. England declared itself a Commonwealth, and Oliver Cromwell was the leader of the country.

Cromwell's Leadership

Since Oliver Cromwell was a Puritan, his reign was seen as very stodgy and boring. Cromwell's priority was to purify the Church of England, so theaters were closed, dancing was forbidden, and many types of music were off limits. Pubs and taverns were closed. Cromwell said there was freedom of worship, but it was only for Protestants. Catholics were not allowed to publicly practice their religion.

During the reign of Oliver Cromwell, there were many problems in England. Supporters of Charles II, the son of King Charles I and the heir to the throne, began to attack England from Ireland, forcing Cromwell back into battle. In 1658, Cromwell died. With him gone from leadership, the people were able to admit that they were tired of the overbearing Puritan laws. In 1660, Parliament voted to bring Charles II back to England and return him to the English throne.

King Charles II

After negotiations with Parliament, King Charles II returned from Ireland to England. He was a handsome, charming man who was a great speaker with a great deal of political skill. He brought England back to the hereditary monarchy government, and he agreed to let Parliament meet. Charles II retracted all of Cromwell's boring laws. Music, dancing, and taverns were back in action. King Charles II wanted to unite the people with religious tolerance. He allowed freedom of worship to Catholics and Protestants, stating that people were free to worship as they wished. Even though Charles II did have Catholic sympathies and worked with the very powerful Catholic French king, Louis XIV, Charles II also wanted to be an absolute monarch. To achieve this, he avoided many of the confrontations with Parliament that plagued his father and grandfather. He would do things more subtly.

King James II

The brother of King Charles II, King James II, took the throne in 1685. Once again, he fanned the flames and fears of Protestants by being pro-Catholic. James II flaunted his Catholic faith, and he angered Parliament by making and abolishing laws at will without consulting them. He replaced members of Parliament who disagreed with him. He would then appoint known Catholics to these high governmental positions.

In the end, King James II imprisoned seven Anglican bishops. This attack on the church was too much for the people, who felt religious clergy were entitled to legal privileges. King James II was trying to act under a guise of religious toleration, but what he was trying to do was slowly make all institutions in England subject to his monarchical power. However, Parliament could not stand by and allow King James II to reinstitute absolutism (and Catholicism) in England. So, in 1688, Parliament invited new monarchs to take the throne.

THE GLORIOUS REVOLUTION

In 1688, Parliament invited King James II's own daughter, Mary Stuart, and her Protestant husband, William of Orange from the Netherlands, to take the throne. The overthrow of King James II was peaceful.

In order to assume the throne in 1689, William and Mary had to sign a very important document: the English Bill of Rights. The English Bill of Rights was written to limit the power of the monarchy. It gave basic civil liberties to only the noble, aristocratic classes, meaning only the wealthy in England were guaranteed civil liberties. However, it was a start to greater participation by the people in government. From this point on in world history, all English monarchs were subject to law. Parliament would be supreme over the monarchy. It was also written into law that other royals could assume the throne if there was no English heir. King George I, a German prince from the kingdom of Hanover, became the King of England in 1714. However, the English Bill of Rights did not strip away all authority from the ruling monarch, and the king still had a lot of power.

Global Connections

Prohibition in the United States in the early 20th century followed many of the ideas of Cromwell.

Global Connections

This document eventually served as the model for the United States Bill of Rights.

King George I

King George I inherited a difficult situation in England, so he enlisted the aid of a man named Robert Walpole. Walpole took over the government and became the first prime minister of England from 1721 to 1742. He set up a cabinet of advisors to help the king, and he required that all ministers publicly agree on policy. They could disagree in private, but in public, they all supported the king.

The English king was no longer an absolute monarch, and the English Parliament was not necessarily a democratic or representative institution. It was still made up of large, wealthy landowners, so they did things to benefit themselves. Nonetheless, the English Parliament created a political unity that did not exist anywhere else in Europe.

The people of England had a little bit more freedom in politics than people on the European continent. The power held by King George I and Robert Walpole had definitive limits. The government could not ignore the wishes of the greater population, and the people were allowed public debate and free speech, two things that did not happen on the European continent.

Not achieving absolutism in England was very positive. The new system that Robert Walpole put into place brought a peace and stability that England had not seen for nearly a century. This allowed the English to focus on trading from North America to India. The resulting prosperity allowed England, a small island nation, to become the dominant major world power. They formed "the Empire on which the sun never sets." England did not achieve absolutism, but they came out stronger in the long run.

ABSOLUTISM IN FRANCE

Nobody in all of Europe was as successful as the French in ruling with an absolute monarchy, especially with the most dominant and powerful absolute monarch in European history: King Louis XIV, the Sun King.

Cardinal Richelieu and Chief Minister Mazarin

Louis XIV took the throne of the French monarchy in 1643 when he was four years old. Richelieu and Mazarin were advisors to the father of Louis XIV. Their heavy handedness set off rebellions among the French nobles. When he began to rule, Louis XIV realized that policies such as these would endanger his monarchy. If he was going to concentrate on gaining unprecedented authority, he decided to be much more subtle about it. Achieving absolutism would give Louis XIV the ability to make the monarchy the most powerful and important institution in France. Instead of destroying the nobles, Louis XIV worked with them, allowing the nobles to keep their social standing and political influence at the local level in their small, remote areas.

The Sun King

Louis had three councils: foreign affairs, the military, and domestic policy. He was able to spend hours each day with the head ministers of each of these offices. The ministers and their staff were chosen from either trusted families that were long in royal service or trusted families that were just starting their ascent to power. Whereas the second group of people was in good standing with the royal family, they had no ancestral powerbase, so they depended upon the king for their standing in society as well as their job in the government.

Louis made sure that the nobles and other wealthy groups benefited from the increase in his authority. Although he controlled things on the national level and limited the nobles' influence on his monarchy, he allowed them to be powerful at the local level, controlling things for which he did not have time.

The Palace of Versailles

Louis XIV was a master of propaganda. In 1682, he built a palace and village known as Versailles, outside the city limits of Paris, to showcase his power. The structure and the grounds were all designed to augment the power and glory of Louis XIV. However, it took half of France's annual tax revenue to construct and pay for Versailles.

To get anything from the French government, a person had to go through the patronage system, designed by Louis XIV. In the patronage system, if the king favored a person, then he would allow him to get a job or complete his assigned task. A person's social standing was dependent upon Louis. Louis XIV organized his court at Versailles around his daily rules and routine of patronage. The rules of patronage did not make sense as a way to run a government as they included a long list of etiquette and special rules that had to be followed in and around the king. Since an audience with the king was highly sought after, a person had to do things the way the king wanted. Whatever Louis wanted, everyone did.

Louis also made many of the nobles build châteaus and residences around Versailles. This was not just to keep an eye on them. It cost a lot of money to "hang out" with Louis. He was financially weakening the nobles, which prevented them from being a threat to his power.

King by Divine Right

It was Louis's tutor, Catholic bishop Jacques-Bénigne Bossuet, who gave Louis the idea of his royal authority. Bossuet said that only God could judge a pope, so therefore it was only God that could judge a king. He also said that God's divine king should not be subject to the whims of nobles. Bossuet came up with the phrase *L'État, c'est moi*, meaning "I am the state." This phrase meant that Louis XIV embodied France, and France existed solely because of him.

Even though Louis had achieved mastery and absolutism, he did not oppress the daily lives of his people. Primarily, he used his absolute power to

1. decide which countries France would make peace with and against which countries France would go to war
2. regulate religion and make France predominantly Catholic
3. oversee the economy of France

The Effects of Louis XIV's Leadership

By the mid- to late 1660s, France was far and away stronger than any other European nation in terms of national unification, military power, and governmental efficiency. Louis XIV had the ability to maintain a large and powerful army, and many other monarchs were trying to copy what he had done. The culture of France became the model for all of Europe. Everything was copied: the style of painting, the music, and the architecture. French culture replaced that of the Renaissance.

Just as Louis reached the height of his power, he had to spend the rest of his long reign trying to combat the two traditional enemies of France: England and the Habsburgs of Spain. Louis XIV governed France until 1715, for a total of 72 years, outliving his sons. He ruled longer than any monarch in all of French history. However, Louis started making a series of mistakes that led to the end of French dominance.

The Mistakes of Louis XIV

1. In 1685, Louis revoked a policy for the freedom of worship called the Edict of Nantes. Louis was determined to unify France along religious lines and to get rid of the 10 percent of Protestants in France. Louis banned Protestants from governmental offices and important professions, and he closed Protestant schools. This caused about 250,000 Protestants to leave France, many of whom were wealthy merchants and artisans. A great deal of tax money went with them.

2. Louis had a large and powerful army, and he decided to explore outside of his borders. He began to fight wars overseas against England and Sweden in 1668 and on the European continent against Spain from 1701 to 1714 in the War of Spanish Succession. The major German states, called the League of Augsburg, were terrified that Louis was going to dominate all of Europe. Germany went to war against France from 1689 to 1697. France made initial gains on all fronts; however, taking on most of Europe while also fighting England for the right to North America was just too much. Even with Louis's powerful army and his money, France could not succeed.

War of Spanish Succession

When the king of Spain died in 1700, the other European powers partitioned Spanish territory in a way to preserve the balance of power, not letting any one country get too much. However, the kingdom that was left to one of Louis's grandsons included all of the Spanish territory in America. The rich trading profits were funneled to France, giving Louis more money and power than he already had.

Because of this, the Holy Roman Empire, the Netherlands, and England went to war against Louis XIV and France from 1701 to 1714. For the first time during his long reign, Louis went to war without enough money, even with his vast riches from North America. The British used newer military technology that they had developed specifically to combat Louis XIV, and England won.

The Collapse of the Monarchy of Louis XIV

When Louis XIV died in 1715, his dominant monarchy collapsed. France was nearly economically ruined. What had once been the strongest nation in Europe was affected greatly by years of warfare, coupled with heavy taxes and bad harvests. Louis's descendants did not have his dominance or his genius. Louis had been a hands-on ruler, but his descendants were spoiled rich kids who did not pay attention to the throne. The most dominant monarchy in Europe never again attained the heights of power created by the Sun King, Louis XIV.

ABSOLUTISM IN SPAIN: THE REIGN OF THE HABSBURG DYNASTY

The country of Spain reached its Golden Age under the Habsburg Dynasty. Spain conquered and controlled a vast territory throughout the world. In Europe, the Habsburgs ruled from Portugal to Sicily/Naples. In the New World, they ruled from Mexico to Peru, and their dynasty even reached the Philippines.

Habsburg Emperor Charles V ruled Spain from 1500 to 1558, when the empire was at its greatest size and the biggest empire in Europe. Charles V acquired all of this land from his grandparents. One set of grandparents were the famous Ferdinand and Isabella of Spain, through which he gained the empire in the Americas. From his other grandparents, he gained Austria, the Netherlands, and the Holy Roman Empire.

However, Charles found it very difficult to rule so many lands in Europe and across the globe. His absolutism was affected by the Protestant Reformation and the Peace of Augsburg, which allowed the German princes to determine their own religion. However, in Spain, Charles V was beloved by his Spanish subjects. They respected him, even though he spent Spain's almost inexhaustible supply of riches fighting many wars against the French and the Turks.

In 1556, Charles did something radical. He divided his empire between his brother and his son. Charles believed it was just too big for one person to govern. He gave the Austrian part of his empire to his brother, Ferdinand. To his son, Philip II, he gave the Holy Roman Empire, the Spanish empire of the Americas, the Netherlands, and the Italian port of Naples.

The Reign of Philip II: The Second Golden Age of Spain

Under King Philip II, Spain experienced the second Golden Age from 1556 to 1598. Spain became the most powerful nation in Europe. The Spanish fleets brought treasure back to Spain from all over the empire, including gold from Mexico and silver from Peru. With this wealth, the Spanish army, the great Spanish navy, priests, and missionaries fanned out across Europe and the Americas. Philip also devoted himself to running the empire, which was the hallmark of dominant absolute monarchs. Successful absolute monarchs had a small number of ministers that they spent time with every single day. He devoted himself not only to running the empire but also to ridding the empire of heretics in order to restore unity to the Roman Catholic Church. His passion to reunify Europe under Catholicism led him to send missionaries out across European lands. Unfortunately, this drew Spain into many wars.

Revolt in the Netherlands

Philip II was even wealthier than Louis XIV in France. It was Philip's efforts to completely centralize Spain that led him into a struggle with the people in the Netherlands, which was part of his empire.

For a long time, the Netherlands was a center of trading. However, the people of the Netherlands did not like the fact that Philip II always seemed to put the interests of Spain above those of the Netherlands. Religious differences finally set off the revolt. Philip II learned the hard way about the problems his father, Charles V, encountered while trying to rule an extremely large empire. Seven northern provinces of the Netherlands declared their independence from Spain in 1581, and the Spanish army killed more than 18,000 Protestants. This angered not only the people in the Netherlands but also those in England.

Queen Elizabeth I of England

Queen Elizabeth I of England was concerned about Spain. She did not support the attack on the Netherlands as she was a Protestant. She was afraid that once Spain finished with the Netherlands, Spain would come and attack England next since Philip wanted to get rid of

Protestantism. Therefore, Queen Elizabeth allowed English sea captains to wage an unofficial war against Spanish vessels. One of her captains, the sea dog Sir Francis Drake, was very adept at attacking Spanish ports in America and then seizing their ships and treasure. Philip II sent a letter to Queen Elizabeth, saying that he wanted Drake punished, and if she did not stop Drake, he would. Queen Elizabeth promised she would do so, but when Sir Francis Drake met with the Queen, she knighted him. This was the final insult to King Philip II, and he decided to take action.

The Spanish Armada

In 1588, Philip sent his pride and joy to England—68 enormous ships of the Spanish Armada. On board were 60,000 Spanish soldiers. They sailed into the treacherous English Channel to put down the rebellion and deal with England and the Netherlands. There was a combination of bad weather, Spanish overconfidence in their navy, and bad decisions by their admiral, causing Spain to meet its destruction. Sir Francis Drake commanded the smaller, more maneuverable English ships that were familiar with the intricacies of the English Channel. They destroyed much of the mighty Spanish Armada. They saved not only the Netherlands, but England, from invasion. The English gained a feeling of invincibility on the high seas.

The Century of Spanish Cultural Flowering

Despite the setback against England, under the leadership of Philip II, Spanish culture blossomed. Philip's reign was called the Century of Gold as great masterpieces of art and literature were created and written. For example, Cervantes's famous novel *Don Quixote* was completed in 1605.

Economic Problems

Even with the Century of Gold, Spain began to encounter severe economic problems. Spain lost its power in Europe, but retained a large empire in the Americas. The Spanish had grown accustomed to what they felt was an endless supply of gold and silver coming from the Americas, so they spent money in the expectation of getting the treasury renewed. Soon though, the Americas ran out of riches. The royal treasury was empty, and Spain could not pay for the many wars in which they were involved. Spain also began to have problems governing its territory in the New World.

Philip II and his descendants had to borrow money from bankers in Germany and Italy, so the treasure that did make it back to Spain went right into the hands of these bankers. There was a period of massive inflation inside Spain, and foreign imported goods were cheaper than those manufactured in Spain.

The reign of Philip II ended in 1598, and within 100 years, the amount of troubles inside Spain were too much for the Habsburg monarchs to deal with. Religious persecution caused many to flee the country. Agricultural and industrial production fell off. There were rivalries between regions of Spain. The Spanish Habsburgs, once the richest and most powerful monarchy in Europe, fell to a second-tier power and were no longer able to dominate or determine events on the continent. However, the Habsburg family in Austria and the Holy Roman Empire continued to play a role in European affairs through the end of World War I.

ABSOLUTISM IN RUSSIA

Absolutism in Russia was a little different. Geographically, it was far away from the other European capitals, and it was only a courtesy that European leaders considered Russia as part of Europe. Russia was different politically as well. It also had no access to a warm water port to help with trade and communication.

The Romanov Family

As the reign of Ivan the Terrible ended in 1584, there was a period of Russian history known as the Time of Troubles from 1604 to 1613 where Russia was in chaos. At the end of the Time of Troubles, a group of Russian nobles, called boyars, elected a member of their group as their leader. He was a 17-year-old boy named Michael Romanov. He formed the Romanov Dynasty, which lasted until 1917. Michael Romanov and his next two successors brought stability and centralized control to Russia. However, the country was still recovering and impoverished from the Time of Troubles. The boyars were difficult to work with, and at times, the Russian secret police force, called the streltsy, caused great instability.

Peter the Great

In 1682, a pair of 10-year-old twin boys became the rulers. Peter and his weaker twin brother Ivan clung to a fragile throne based on the power of the streltsy. Peter and Ivan's claim to the throne was surrounded by bloodshed and violence. In 1689, Peter took over the throne when his brother Ivan was murdered. Peter exiled his older sister because the dangers of his childhood were enough to convince Peter that the power of the Russian king, or czar, must be kept safe. The jealousy of the Russian boyars and the instability of his streltsy led Peter the Great to create a powerful Russian military.

Peter's Travels to Western Europe

Peter the Great was convinced that the answers to building his powerful army could be found within the resources and technology in Western Europe. Peter was determined to try and copy what they had done. In 1697, he visited Western Europe in disguise, where he studied the shipyards, manufacturing, and military hardware. Unfortunately, Peter stood out among the crowd. He was given permission to talk with the powerful nobles and monarchs of Europe. However, Peter did not understand the etiquette created by Louis XIV of France, and so the powerful European leaders thought that he was a barbarian. Peter returned from Western Europe with engineers that were going to help him copy what he had seen.

Peter the Great's Plan

When Peter returned to Russia, the engineers from Europe saw that he had no factories or mines, and many of them returned to Europe. Peter was forced to do everything himself. He had four main problems to handle:

1. Tame his boyars and the streltsy
2. Achieve control of the Russian Orthodox Church
3. Streamline and organize central control of his government
4. Develop an industrial economy in Russia

Taming the Nobles and Streltsy

Upon his return from Western Europe, Peter had a meeting with his boyars where he removed the symbols of noble power from them. He cut off their long beards and tore the sleeves off their coats, which were decorated with brilliant, elaborate symbols. The long beards and elaborate coat sleeves were both symbols of their noble authority, and Peter removed them, demanding that they serve him. In 1722, he instituted a policy known as the Table of Ranks. This indicated a man's standing in the army and the social and political privileges that came with that rank. A man's position in the nobility no longer mattered. It was a man's military rank that was important.

Peter's bodyguards and secret police, the streltsy, were treated even more harshly. When Peter was in Western Europe in 1697, he heard there was a rebellion within the streltsy, so Peter had 1200 of his secret police force executed. He left their corpses on display as a sign of what happened when people crossed Peter the Great.

Achieving Control of the Russian Orthodox Church

Peter treated the Russian Orthodox Church with the same aggressiveness as the nobles. Peter wanted to avoid trouble with the Russian Orthodox Church by preventing their clergy from opposing his plans toward modernization and adopting Western philosophies. To do so, Peter replaced the patriarch of the Russian Orthodox Church in 1721 with a synod. The synod was a layperson, or nonreligious person, who was appointed by Peter. This made the church part of the governmental bureaucracy headed by Peter. With this in place, Peter controlled the church, which willingly went along with his reforms.

Streamlining and Organizing Central Control of His Government

Peter adopted a Swedish style of governmental administration. The system was made up of several officials of equal rank and power, rather than through ministries headed by a single minister. Much like Louis XIV, Peter kept the number of officials small. They dealt with taxes, foreign affairs, war, and the Russian economy. With only four groups to meet with, Peter could stay hands-on. Peter's idea behind this was that people were freer to express their opinion when there was not a department head, but a series of people. No one person was inferior or superior. Peter hoped that this would rejuvenate his bureaucracy, which again was geared toward making money to support his large army.

Developing an Industrial Economy in Russia

Peter sought to control the economy, and he geared it toward the manufacture of iron. The iron industry was closely related to what the military needed for weapons and machinery, and there were many iron ore deposits in the Ural Mountains.

Mistakes of Peter the Great

Though his methods were ruthless, Peter the Great achieved absolutism in Russia. However, in the end, it was his own ambition that came back to haunt him. Peter was determined to gain access to a warm-water, all-weather port so he could trade openly with the West and take part in European affairs. This led to a war with Sweden in 1700, which Peter lost. Peter again attacked Sweden in 1703 and was able to gain enough territory to build a city that still bears his name—St. Petersburg. In St. Petersburg, he built a smaller model of Versailles. He made the nobles build houses close to him, very much like Louis XIV. To gain more territory and liberate some areas of Russia from the rule of the Ottoman Empire, Peter went to war with them from 1722 to 1723 and lost.

Unfortunately, Peter was so focused on securing his monarchy and expanding Russian economic and military power that he did not train a successor, even though he reigned for 43 years. While he was able to make the modernization of Russia a possibility, there was no one with Peter's power and charisma that could manage a stable Russian government. After Peter the Great's death in 1725, Russia once again moved backward as the boyars reasserted their control.

ABSOLUTISM IN ASIA: THE MUGHAL DYNASTY IN INDIA

The Mughal Dynasty ruled India as descendants of the conqueror Tamerlane. The founder of the Mughal Dynasty was Babur in 1526. The Mughals were able to end a lot of the fragmentation and divisiveness of northern India.

The greatest ruler of India and the Mughal Dynasty was Akbar the Great. Akbar was the grandson of Babur, and he ruled for a long time (1556–1605). Akbar created a strong absolute monarchical government in India, earning him the name Akbar the Great. At this time in world history, Akbar was as great as any of the European powers, from Elizabeth I in England to Charles V of Spain. Many historians believe Akbar the Great may have been a more powerful ruler than any of the European absolute monarchs.

Reforms of Akbar the Great

Akbar was a conqueror, but he is more renowned for how he ran his government. He made great governmental reforms and was a sponsor of cultural patronage. What set him apart from many of his contemporaries—the Stuarts in England, Louis XIV in France, and Philip II in Spain—was Akbar's religious toleration. He wanted to provide an honest government that worked for the good of the vast diversity of his empire.

Akbar's Government

Akbar the Great recreated his central governmental administration as well as the provincial governmental systems of India. At first, he took over dominant control by reorganizing the tax system of India. Like other rulers before him, Akbar ordered a census and a survey of the agricultural yield in each region. The regions that grew more food or consumed more resources had to pay more in taxes than areas with a lower population and lower food production.

Role of Religion

Akbar removed a special tax on nonbelievers and on non-Muslims even though he was a devout Muslim. To help further unify his people, Akbar married a native princess, and he appointed Hindus to high governmental positions. This reduced the palpable tension between Muslims and Hindus. Akbar the Great was known to gather representatives from different religions—Muslim, Hindu, Buddhist, Christian, Confucian—to discuss religion and find out what they had in common. Under Akbar's reign, India flourished. Unfortunately, his ideas of unification and toleration died with him in 1605.

End of the Mughal Dynasty

Akbar's reign was the Golden Age of the Mughal Empire. His successors were able to make some small achievements, but none were able to sustain what Akbar had started. Sustaining an empire as large and diverse as India had its problems. Many of the cultural achievements and excessive building projects required vast sums of money. Continuing wars also eroded the empire's firm power base. Emperors after Akbar withdrew his tax reforms, and this had a negative effect on the Mughal economy.

Costly Mistakes

Emperor Jahangir allowed the British to build trading posts on the coasts of India in 1614 to get into the spice trade, which was unfortunate. He did not know that once the British set up a colony, it would be very hard to get rid of them. Slowly but surely, the British increased their power in India. Another emperor, Shah Jahan, ruled from 1628 to 1658. He was an unsuccessful conqueror as he tried unsuccessfully to expand the empire and replenish the economy. His policies, unfortunately, had the adverse effect on India. Not only did his military adventures cost a lot of money, but he also built the famous Taj Mahal in 1648 as a burial monument for his princess, which also cost a lot of money. He was building an identical one across the river but never finished it because he went broke. Shah Jahan also ended his ancestor's policy of religious tolerance.

ABSOLUTISM IN ASIA: THE OTTOMAN EMPIRE

Islamic culture and government reached its high point between 1450 and 1650 with the simultaneous spreading of the three Gunpowder Empires—the Safavids, the Mughals, and the Ottomans.

> ### 🍽 DINNER TABLE TALK
>
> The Safavids, Mughals, and Ottomans are named the Gunpowder Empires because they owed much of their success to the ability to use gunpowder in the forms of cannons and muskets. Gunpowder enabled their foot soldiers to defeat the more-powerful horse cavalries of many of their opponents.

The Ottomans had two absolute monarchs that helped define absolutism in the long-lasting Ottoman Empire. The Ottoman Order was formed during the rule of Sultan Mehmed II from 1451 to 1481. Also known as Mehmed the Conqueror, he was able to break the power of the old tribal chieftains. Mehmed II was finally able to break the Byzantine stronghold of Constantinople in 1453. This allowed the Ottomans to secure southeastern Europe, along with increasing their ability to trade with the Italian trading states. The great city of Constantinople was renamed Istanbul. He also started a new form of governmental legislation that he called the kanunname, or law book. This law book placed the ulama under the control of one single sultan. It governed all aspects of Ottoman life, including social class, rank, and privileges.

SULEIMAN THE MAGNIFICENT

By the early 1500s, the Ottoman Empire was flourishing. Ottoman power was secure from Turkey all the way northward to the Ukraine. Absolute monarch Suleiman I, or Suleiman the Magnificent, expanded this territory even further during his reign from 1520 to 1566, making the Ottomans a major Asian absolute monarchy as well as a European empire with which to be reckoned. At this point in world history, Ottoman military power was second to none. Building upon what Mehmed had started, Suleiman organized the Ottoman state under one massive military umbrella. Status in society during the Ottoman Empire equated to the individual's job and rank in the military. The Ottomans had a standing military that was under the leadership of Suleiman the Magnificent. The higher the rank in the army, the greater the privileges. However, with a higher rank also came additional responsibilities to the Ottoman Empire. The Ottomans ruled a large, diverse empire including Muslims and non-Muslims. Everyone was expected to have allegiance to the emperor.

Global Connections

This is very similar to what Peter the Great did in Russia.

SULEIMAN I AND HIS GOVERNMENT

Suleiman's governmental organization was similar to that of the other absolute monarchs. He had four basic governmental bureaucracies, making government small and functional so the emperor could stay hands-on.

- His palace and his court. Suleiman's court lived within the palace, and their job was to advise Suleiman.
- The administrative branch, made up of Suleiman's main advisor, his small cabinet, and his treasury secretary. This allowed Suleiman to control and govern his empire directly. All facets of the day-to-day running of the empire were run through this administrative branch.
- The military wing. This was headed by a general but led by the sultan.
- The religious institutions. Suleiman controlled the mosques (and the ulama) and the educational institutions (the madrasas), so he could control what the people were taught in the schools, as well as keep an eye on what the ulama were doing.

RELIGION IN THE OTTOMAN EMPIRE

Suleiman began to dominate and conform the religious institutions of his empire. Under the new laws, religious clergy became servants of his state under a theocracy. The ulama became an extension of the government, and they followed the religious authority in the Ottoman Empire, which was Suleiman. This allowed him to control everything from local village schools up to the giant madrasas in his empire. With the ulama working for him, the Ottoman Empire became committed to maintaining the Islamic sharia. This was a benefit to the law as it unofficially elevated the status of Muslims in society.

Although Suleiman sounded domineering, the Ottoman laws were meant to be something good and different for the people. They were meant to be preventative and functional in nature. Suleiman defined what was legal and illegal in society, and he published them so everyone would know them. Using the ulama and the sharia to help govern his empire, Suleiman the Magnificent created a comprehensive, legalistic code of laws meant to curb and prevent problems, which was one of the reasons for the success of his absolute monarchy.

REPLACING THE SULTAN

To be the ruler of the Ottoman Empire was a difficult undertaking. Unlike most absolute monarchs, who did not train their successor because they were so busy running the empire, the Ottomans focused on leadership training from a very young age. The sons of the emperor were taken out into the provinces, learning how to govern small villages. They would move up to medium-sized towns and then to larger cities to gain leadership, command, and control experience. However, since the Ottoman Empire was a theocracy, it was up to Allah

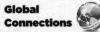

to decide who became king. To prevent the law of succession, the Ottoman Empire used the policy of fratricide. When the sons of the sultan had all reached ruling age, each brother had to form his own plan to execute his brothers and stay alive. The last man standing would be the emperor. It was a tough system, but it worked.

MILITARY POWER

To maintain a powerful army, the military needed to be loyal to the empire. The Ottomans used a form of provincial conscription where a certain number of boys from each district would be selected for the army. In the Ottoman's case, they selected young Christian boys from peasant families. The boys were taken from their parents and raised as Muslims. They were trained to serve the emperor as well as his governing bureaucracy. Every soldier was fed, clothed, trained, and cared for by the emperor, so they were extremely loyal to him. The most famous subgroup will be the janissaries, which were the special forces soldiers of their day. They were a dominant, ferocious presence in battle with allegiance devoutly pledged toward the emperor.

EMPERORS AFTER SULEIMAN

After Suleiman died in 1566, his son and future emperors after him allowed the empire to become plagued with corruption throughout the military and governmental institutions. There were agricultural failures as well, plus the rise of the power of Europe. Even though the Ottoman Empire lasted until 1918, it slowly lost territory to European influence.

During the height of the Ottoman Empire, this multiethnic, religious empire was run by a powerful and dominant absolute monarchy, which was equal or superior to any in the world at the time.

ABSOLUTISM IN JAPAN (1600–1868 C.E.)

Tokugawa Ieyasu emerged as the leader of the unified Japan in 1600. He set up a capital in the city of Edo, which is modern-day Tokyo, and he took the title of shogun. He used his vast military power to recreate and reorganize Japan.

National Policy of Seclusion

In 1630, Tokugawa instituted a national policy of seclusion, cutting Japan off from most of the world. Small cultural happenings came from Korea and China, but except for a few restricted ports for Chinese and Dutch traders, no foreigners were allowed to enter Japan. A foreigner who entered Japan would be put to death. In addition, no Japanese were allowed to go abroad. This was much different from China where they encouraged Chinese young men to study and learn in Japan. Japan was cut off from the entire world. This was similar to Western Europe during the Dark Ages, except that Japan is an archipelago (a collection of islands), which made isolation easier to enforce. Throughout world history, Japan had always been isolated, but during the time of absolutism, it truly focused only upon itself.

Redrawing the Japanese Domains

After defeating internal warring factions, Tokugawa Ieyasu confiscated the lands of his defeated enemies. He rewarded his daimyo and samurai with lands taken from his enemies.

Tokugawa relocated inhabitants from 229 enemy daimyos, moving them from one domain, or fief, to another. This broke the link between the enemy daimyo and his loyal supporters.

Tokugawa had a three-step method to redraw the Japanese domains.

STEP 1 He controlled the largest domain, the Tokugawa domain. To help him govern, he used many long-trusted daimyo and as many as 17,000 lower ranking samurai who had demonstrated their loyalty to him, even before he became the shogun. These were his most trusted and loyal supporters, forming an inner core ring of defense.

STEP 2 Tokugawa used his nephews to form a second line of defense and a middle perimeter of daimyo. The nephews were second and third sons of family members who had a bloodline that linked directly with that of Tokugawa Ieyasu.

STEP 3 The outside daimyo were people who fought against Tokugawa Ieyasu in the wars of unification. They were removed from their traditional homelands and put on the outer edges of Japan. By doing this Tokugawa Ieyasu had taken his enemies and moved them away from the shogun. In order to attack Tokugawa, his enemies on the outer edges would have to fight through the second ring of defense, consisting of members of Tokugawa's family. After that, they would have to fight Tokugawa's trusted supporters in the interior perimeter. However, the enemies on the outer edges had problems of their own. They were the first to be attacked during any foreign invasion, so most of their resources had to be allocated to defense.

Tokugawa Government and Controlling the Daimyo

After building these three rings of defense, Tokugawa drew up new legal codes that regulated his governmental bureaucracy. To help him, Tokugawa wanted men of ability and men who had leadership experience in running their samurai warriors and controlling their separate domains. As chosen daimyo by the shogun, his men were held to a higher standard. They had to live their lives frugally, excessive drinking was forbidden, gambling was forbidden, and they had to ask Tokugawa for permission to even get married. Tokugawa's reasoning for this was that because these men were chosen members of his government, they had to be role models for the people.

Tokugawa also created the hostage system. The daimyo from his outer ring of defense (his former enemies) had to come and live for one year within Tokugawa's palace. The following year, they would leave to govern their territory that he had given them in the outer ring. However, the daimyo's family was required to stay behind in Tokugawa's palace. Tokugawa used the daimyos' families as insurance they would not lead a rebellion. Officially, this was called the Alternate Year Attendance Plan.

Tokugawa's Economy

From the early 1600s, through the reign of Tokugawa and his immediate successors, Japan experienced a period of incredible economic growth. Tokugawa encouraged the growth of agriculture by providing better tools, better seeds, and the use of fertilizer. Tokugawa had gained access to many resources geared for war during the civil wars that put him in power. He applied those resources to improve agriculture and farming. Tokugawa was determined to control Japan, so he held onto exclusive access to resources. The entire country was beholden to him. The result of increased agricultural output was an immediate population boom that doubled Japan's population.

Global Connections

Confucian scholars and ministers in China were also held to the same high standards of moral and social conduct.

Global Connections

Tokugawa's Alternate Year Attendance Plan was similar to the actions of Louis XIV and Peter the Great, who also forced their nobles to live near them.

Furthering this economic growth were merchants, who once again were permitted to travel throughout the archipelago. Merchants were not able to trade with Japan during the warring states era of the country. Merchants revived trade and turned it into a Japanese national economy. Japan's economy was unified under one shogun, Tokugawa.

The Benefit of the Alternate Year Attendance Plan

Surprisingly, the Alternate Year Attendance Plan, which started in 1635, was an economic success. After spending a year with the shogun in Edo, the daimyo unintentionally encouraged overland trading as they headed back to their homelands to rule for the following year. This broke down barriers and allowed a national economy to grow. A diverse offering of goods was spread throughout the entire nation.

By the end of the 1600s, the political reorganization of Tokugawa Ieyasu was finished. At this point, Tokugawa believed there were no changes necessary and no new ideas to implement. Thus, Japan had implemented a national policy of seclusion.

Tokugawa Government

Tokugawa was brilliant in the way he set up the bureaucracy of his empire. He was able to maintain a balance of dominant, central control as the shogun. Technically, Tokugawa worked for the emperor, and Japan was unique in that no daimyo tried to overthrow the shogun or the emperor. Tokugawa was similar to Louis XIV in that he was smart enough to know he could not micromanage everything. He allowed some of the daimyo to run their own separate domains, or fiefs. Tokugawa took care of national problems, but tiny, local problems were left to the daimyo.

Only samurai could attain governmental posts, and there was rigid control of the Japanese government. Again, Tokugawa and his successors knew they could not do everything. So they made sure that only high-level samurai, noted for their skill and leadership, attained governmental posts where they had decision-making power and authority.

The Tokugawa Legacy

Following the foundation set by Tokugawa, Japan had achieved its limit of growth by 1700. The country was as large as they could hope to achieve while staying isolated. The population was stable, taxes were stable, food supply was steady, and families regulated their size. Japan, who had studied discipline and structure for centuries, believed that they had achieved the best government possible.

ABSOLUTISM IN CHINA: THE MING DYNASTY

The Ming Dynasty replaced the Yuan Dynasty of Kublai Khan in 1368. The Ming Dynasty was the last true Chinese dynasty.

The Ming Dynasty was one of the Golden Ages of Chinese history, lasting from 1368 to 1644. The population doubled, growing to more than 120 million people. As the population grew, it kick-started the growth of commerce and merchants. The scholarly class rose to prominence, forming a national economy. Food supply increased as new crops from the Americas, such as white corn, arrived in China. The Ming Dynasty started six centuries of growth in China where technology increased and the death rate declined. It was the longest continuous period of sustained growth in Chinese history, even more so than the Han Dynasty. The Ming Dynasty was China's version of Pax Romana.

Emperors and the Chinese Economy

Throughout world history, the emperor of China was seen as a living god. The man who started the Ming Dynasty is Emperor Zhu Yuanzhang in 1368. He and the other early Ming emperors were isolationists, keeping themselves separate from the outside world. Believing in China's own resources, they tightly controlled the use of foreign products. They also maintained the governmental monopolies of China's economy as had been the custom of Chinese emperors. This curtailed trading outside of China and innovation within China. However, by 1550 as the Ming Dynasty continued, the Chinese economy started to grow to keep up with a growing population. The economic growth forced the Chinese emperors to be more laissez-faire toward the economy.

Shensi Banks

When the Chinese emperors began to relax restrictions in the economy, one of the main reasons for the growth in commercial enterprise was the amount of silver being imported. Silver was coming from Europeans via colonization and conquest in Mexico and Peru. This allowed the creation of shensi banks. Shensi were private banks that operated branches in cities throughout China. This allowed a merchant not only to transfer money but also to carry monetary records and use credit, like the Islamic traders. They would deposit money in one bank, get a letter of credit from the bank, then travel to a different province and get the money out of the bank.

Global Connections

An example here in the United States would be Philadelphia (the large metropolis), Pittsburgh (the mid-sized intermediary city), and Youngstown, Ohio (the small province).

This led to a commercial boom as new cities were formed linking the tiny village provinces to mid-level trading cities. These mid-sized cities linked to the large metropolises on the east coast of China. Goods and resources were traded back and forth between the small, medium, and large cities. The growth of these new cities led to inflation of products and forced a change in tax collection. Instead of paying taxes with goods, taxes could only be paid in Chinese money or silver.

The Forbidden City

King Louis XIV built Versailles and Peter the Great built St. Petersburg, but no absolute monarch had built an actual city to showcase his power—until the Ming Dynasty! The Ming emperors built the Forbidden City between 1406 and 1420. An icon of majestic power, the Ming emperors wanted an entire city to handle the business of China and their enormous kingdom.

The focus of the Forbidden City was on the awesome power of the Chinese emperor. As a person entered to meet the emperor, the walls slowly got narrower and narrower. Then, they stepped into a vast chamber, and looking up, they would see the emperor sitting on a high throne chair. The purpose was to showcase the awesome power of the emperor of China plus humble and belittle his people.

Like the other absolute monarchs, the Chinese emperor maintained a small bureaucracy. It included very few people, but he would talk to them every day to maintain a hands-on presence. The bureaucracy revolved around the military, the administrative branch, and what was known as the censorate, which kept track of the people, the products, and the money. The emperor controlled the Chinese treasury, working in much the same way as a head auditor.

Confucian Officials

The Confucian teachers and scholars were very good at providing solid government workers. It allowed China to achieve a time of prosperity up into the 1800s. To create a successful absolute monarchy in a country as large as China, the all-powerful emperor needed excellent governmental workers. Chinese governmental Confucian scholars had a lot of prestige and power, and the competition to become one was cutthroat and fierce.

There were three different examinations that were taken after years of study. When scholars made it past the first examination, they governed one of the small villages or towns. After years of proving their skills, another evaluation was given. When scholars passed the second round, they were assigned to help govern one of the mid-sized trading cities. The mid-sized cities served as the intermediary between agricultural villages and the large east coast urban cities, which provided products coming from all over China as well as imports. After more years of service, a third evaluation was given. This evaluation was extremely difficult to pass. Only one in 100 people was even chosen to take the test, and it was so difficult that after it was over, many scholars were mentally and physically broken. A scholar only received one chance to take the test, and the failure rate was enormous. However, those who passed became excellent bureaucrats.

Confucianism became more necessary and widespread than ever before. Confucian schools were built in every tiny village and town to look for these men of ability.

The Ming Dynasty: Stronger Than Ever

As a result of the Ming Dynasty government, there was an unbroken chain stretching from the emperor's palace in the Forbidden City, to the district officials, to the Confucian scholars, to the oldest male in every family in China. The emperor's reach stretched from the largest city to the tiniest village in China. China was like a large family, with everyone assuming rights and responsibilities that were ironclad at every level. The country was unified, making the emperor stronger than ever before. The government officials who ran the day-to-day affairs of China were incredible. However, the emperor still made all the important decisions. Throughout the Ming Dynasty, the emperor had direct personal control over everything in China. His scholarly officials were good, but it was still the emperor that set everything in motion, giving him incredible, dominant power inside of China.

Ming Expansion

The Ming Dynasty started as isolationists, but they eventually began to act like every other Chinese dynasty: they wanted to expand their empire. Between 1405 and 1433, they were aggressive in their expansion, reaching what is today Vietnam all the way to Central Asia. The people conquered were instituted in a tribute system where the conquered people had to send an ambassador to China who would be forced to recognize the absolute power of the emperor. The ambassador had to provide the emperor with a gift, which had to be the very best of what the people had to offer. If it was seen as a worthy gift, the conquered people would be peacefully absorbed into the Chinese empire, and they could take part in the rich trade economy of China. If the gift was not worthy, then the people would be quickly conquered.

To showcase China's power, nothing worked better than the expeditions of Chinese admiral Zheng He, also known as Cheng Ho. From 1405 to 1433, Zheng He's fleet of 62 massive ships sailed from China through the Indian Ocean to as far away as eastern Africa. His large, powerful ships were designed to open up trade with China and make China's power known throughout the world.

Some historians believe that Zheng He sailed across the Pacific and landed on the coast of Chile just barely 50 years before the Portuguese began to expand around Africa. However, after seeing the arid land of Chile, Zheng He turned around and went back to China.

Zheng He's fleets paid huge dividends in the expansion of China. Unfortunately, the mighty Ming Dynasty, as rich as it was, experienced a period of financial trouble. Building the Forbidden City was expensive, and Zheng He's fleet was scrapped.

Contact with Europe

The Ming Dynasty had contact with Europe and the West in the late 1550s when Jesuit missionaries began to arrive. The missionaries used their knowledge of geography and firearms to get positions at the emperor's court. However, when the missionaries told the emperor that the pope forbade the age-old practice of ancestor worship, the emperor kicked out the missionaries and banned Christianity in his empire.

While missionaries were kicked out, a small number of trading partners were allowed in. Portuguese sailors, who had been cooped up on their ships for many months during the voyage, horrified the Chinese with their appalling behavior. As a result, the Portuguese were removed from China, and all other foreigners were isolated to a strict port in Canton. This started the Cantonese System, which lasted from 1760 to 1842. Foreigners could trade in China, but they were separated from the Chinese people. They could get off their ships on a peninsula of Canton land, but they could not come into China proper. They were also subject to Chinese laws and business systems. This was the price of doing business with China and how China operated until the age of European imperialism (when Europeans decided to bully their way in to China).

TIMELINE REVIEW

1368 C.E.	Zhu Yuanzhang founds the Ming Dynasty.
1405 C.E.	Voyages of Zheng He
1405–1433 C.E.	Ming Dynasty expansion
1406 C.E.	Building of the Forbidden City
1451–1481 C.E.	Mehmed II Ottoman Empire
1453 C.E.	Mehmed II captures Constantinople and renames it Istanbul.
1519–1556 C.E.	King Charles V of Spain
1520–1566 C.E.	• Suleiman the Magnificent
	• Ottoman Empire Golden Age
1526 C.E.	Mughal Empire India
1550–1560 C.E.	Spain's Golden Century
1556 C.E.	Reign of Akbar the Great Mughal Empire
1556–1598 C.E.	• Habsburg Dynasty in Spain
	• King Philip begins his reign.
1588 C.E.	Sinking of the Spanish Armada by England
1598 C.E.	Tokugawa Ieyasu
1603 C.E.	King James I starts the Tudor Dynasty in England.

1605 C.E.	• Death of Akbar the Great
	• Mughal Empire
1625 C.E.	King Charles I starts the Stuart Dynasty in England.
1627–1658 C.E.	Shah Jahan
1629–1640 C.E.	England's Years of Personal Rule
1631 C.E.	Building of Taj Mahal in India
1603 C.E.	Edo becomes capital of Japan.
1630 C.E.	Japan's national policy of seclusion
1635 C.E.	Japan's Alternate Year Attendance Plan becomes law.
1642 C.E.	English Civil War
1643 C.E.	Louis XIV begins his reign in France.
1649 C.E.	Charles I is executed.
1649–1658 C.E.	Puritan Oliver Cromwell rules England.
1650 C.E.	Spain's Habsburg Dynasty begins to decline.
1658 C.E.	Charles II is named king of England.
1661 C.E.	Louis XIV takes over all rule of France by himself.
1664 C.E.	Building of Versailles
1685 C.E.	England's King James II
1685 C.E.	Revoking of Edict of Nantes
1688 C.E.	Glorious Revolution
1689 C.E.	English Bill of Rights
1689 C.E.	Peter the Great of Russia becomes czar.
1697 C.E.	Peter the Great begins his journey to the West.
1700s C.E.	Russia goes to war with Sweden and the building of St. Petersburg.
1722 C.E.	Table of Ranks
1725 C.E.	Peter the Great dies.

GLOBAL CONNECTIONS

Americas

1492 C.E.—Voyage of Christopher Columbus

1552 C.E.—Bartolomé de Las Casas writes *The Black Legend*

1620 C.E.—*Mayflower* lands at Plymouth

1763 C.E.—Seven Years War/French and Indian War

Africa

1450 C.E.—Kingdom of Songhai

1500 C.E.—Kingdom of Kongo

Mercantilism: The Creation of the Transatlantic Economy and Its Effects on the World

19

LINKING EUROPE, THE AMERICAS, AND AFRICA

By the late 1700s, Europe, Africa, North America, and South America had become tied together in a vast transatlantic economy. For Europe, this economy existed to remove or extract raw materials and agricultural products from the Americas for shipment to Europe. This was done for the sole profit of the mother country and was made possible initially by Native American slave labor and, later, African slaves.

Ever since Portugal's Prince Henry the Navigator had started the Age of Exploration in the 1400s, the interaction between Europeans and the rest of the world was dictated by exploration. Three distinct periods emerged as Europe dominated the world.

1. Discovering and exploring the New World from 1400s to 1500s.
2. Conquest and settling territory in the Americas from 1500s to 1700s. This led to an intense rivalry among England, Spain, and France for trade dominance in the colonies.
3. European interaction with non-European inhabitants of the empires they created in Africa and the Americas from 1700s to 1800s.

MERCANTILISM AS AN ECONOMIC THEORY

The economic theory behind the rise of the European empires in England, France, and Spain was mercantilism. This was an economic system in which governments would closely guard trading due to a desire to increase their national wealth at home. The best way to gain advantage over competitors was to have a large supply of currency. In Europe at this time, there was a great deal of gold and silver. A nation was truly wealthy when it had a lot more gold and silver than its primary competitors.

The first country to dominate the Atlantic Ocean trade routes was Spain with the Spanish Armada. Since the Spanish were the first into the New World, they got a head start in setting up specific political and commercial institutions geared to create a maximum level of exploitation of natural resources and governance of their new territory.

To do most of the heavy labor for the extraction of gold, silver, and other raw materials, Europeans used slave labor to maximize profits. Countries were trying to create monopolies in the New World, which required their overseas colonies to trade only with the mother country and no one else. However, since these colonies were thousands of miles away, true monopolies never formed. This created tension between European powers, leading to military conflicts around the world during this period.

SPANISH EMPIRE IN THE AMERICAS

Less than 20 years after Columbus discovered the New World for the Spanish empire, Spanish explorers searching for gold occupied the major islands in the Caribbean Sea. The Spanish used them for staging areas for further exploration and conquest.

The Brutality of Spanish Conquest

With their superior military, technology, horses, gunpowder, and disease, the Europeans were able to very quickly overtake these numerically superior opponents in Mesoamerica. Technology was the difference and had an effect on the Americas almost immediately.

The Spanish conquests of the Aztecs and Incas were perhaps the most savage and brutal in the entire span of world history. They were distinctive because at this point in their history, the native peoples in the Americas had created great civilizations, despite being cut off from cultural diffusion. Thousands of years of Mesoamerican history—great architectural, artistic, and technological achievements—were completely wiped out and destroyed by European countries looking to exploit them to make money. Mesoamerican writing systems, languages, religions, art, and architecture were destroyed simply because it was not Spanish.

Role of the Roman Catholic Church

The Catholic Church and religion also played a small role in the conquest and exploitation of the New World. Catholic monarchs were competing for souls against Protestants in Europe. Mexico, South America, and the Caribbean islands were brand-new territories. They provided key areas for priests and missionaries to spread Catholic doctrine. Similar to the Crusades 500 years before, the Spanish monarchy asked permission from the church to militarily conquer these areas so the people could be easily converted to Catholicism. By getting rid of the pagan native practices, the rulers of Spain argued that military conquest was justified as it became a Christian crusade. The goal of the crusade was to convert these pagan souls and expand the power of the Spanish monarchy. When Spain received religious sanction, the conquerors had almost free reign.

The pope recognized that this vast missionary undertaking would be expensive and difficult, so he gave authority and power to the Spanish monarchical government to bring Catholicism to this area. Thus, the Spanish would not only have a monetary and natural resource monopoly, but a religious monopoly as well.

Missionary Movements

Catholic missionary sects consisting of the Franciscans, the Dominicans, and the Jesuits were the primary agents of conversion. Early on, they were able to make great gains. The indigenous people of the Americas converted to Catholicism so they would not be wiped out. The Catholic missionaries wanted to remove all traces of indigenous, polytheistic practices, especially human sacrifice, which bothered the Europeans. Catholic conversion was another way that Europeans destroyed an important part of indigenous culture. When the Native Americans converted, it did not mean they were on equal footing with their Spanish conquerors. They were still considered slaves.

Bartolomé de Las Casas

Bartolomé de Las Casas was a missionary who began to speak out against Spanish practices. He said that conquest was not necessary for conversion, and that the people would convert on their own. He wrote a book known as *The Black Legend.* When it was published in Spain, people were horrified at the inhumane treatment of the Native American peoples by the Spanish government. The Spanish government and the church each made minor concessions, but in the end, it made little difference. There was too much money to be made and too much land to be gained, so there was only a minimal attempt at protecting the Native Americans.

Spanish Methods of Control

Gold brought early conquerors to Mexico, but when it ran out, silver was just as good. The Spanish crown had a large interest in mining because 20 percent of all revenue coming back to Spain went directly to the Spanish crown. The Spanish government also monopolized the use of mercury. Mercury acted as a magnetic agent, attracting the gold and silver, leaving behind the rock, sand, and useless matter. The use of mercury was a great example of the extractive economy of Spain. Mining was tough and dirty, and the Spanish were not going to do it; thus, they forced Native Americans to do it. In doing so, their skin came in contact with mercury. The Spanish also threw mercury in their lakes and streams where the indigenous people caught fish and hunted game. The Native American inhabitants all quickly began to die due to mercury poisoning. The wealthy Spanish conquistadors and nobles wanted their precious metals, so they began to look for another group of people who would do the dirty, hard work. The Spanish sought out people who could survive the hard work in an equatorial climate. They also needed slaves who were resistant to malaria. Remembering the plantations of the kingdoms of Ghana and Mali, the Spanish started the African slave trade.

Spanish Methods of Controlling the Labor Population

The Spanish used three basic types of labor supervision to get the work done.

1. Use of the encomienda. The encomienda was a series of institutions geared to maximize the exploitation of Native American labor. The Spanish government gave the authority to conquistadors or Spanish nobles to use a set number of Native Americans for labor for a set amount of days. For example, a noble would be given the use of 30 Native Americans for 60 days to accomplish the labor task. Then the noble had to get another grant from the crown to continue. This was inefficient, and the Spanish turned to a new idea.

2. The new idea known as repartimento. Repartimento was an idea borrowed from the Inca mita system. The Spanish government required all male Native Americans to work a certain number of days per year for the Spanish government. Under this method, many Native Americans were literally worked to death.

3. The hacienda. A hacienda was where the agricultural projects were handled, like the growing of food and raising of cattle. Large plantation-like farms were given to a group of people known as peninsulares. They were Spanish-born nobles living in the New

> **GLOBAL CONNECTIONS**
>
> The hacienda was like the old company store idea: Workers got paid in company dollars, with which they paid their rent, bought groceries, and paid their electric bill. All of these were owned by the company! They had no access to any money except company money, which went right back to the company! The workers were trapped.

World. Farming was not as difficult as mining, but the natives were still slaves. They had to stay on the hacienda to survive. The slaves were given no money of their own and the only supplies to which they had access were the ones provided by the hacienda.

Death of Native Americans Led to African Slavery

When Columbus arrived in the West Indies in 1492, the Native American population was somewhere near 50 million people. Mexico itself had 25 million people. By 1600, a little over 100 years after Columbus landed, there were barely two million Native Americans left. Most had been killed by Spanish armies, in the Spanish mines or other economic enterprises, and disease. Thus, there was no longer a pool of exploitable labor in the New World. This forced European countries to form the Triangle Trade during the 1500s to early 1800s. There was the trade from the mother country in Europe heading to the Americas, and the route from Europe to Africa as European countries went to Africa to purchase slaves to fill the needs of this large labor pool.

Slavery was a key component of the transatlantic trade, or the Triangle Trade. It was where Europe, Africa, and the European colonies in North and South America intertwined. Africa supplied slaves to be the cheap labor, and slaves were Africa's main export. Slaves were then taken to the Americas, who supplied raw materials in return: lumber, copper, gold, silver, cotton, tobacco, and sugar (which was extremely labor intensive to make). Raw materials were loaded onto European ships, which took them to Europe where they were used to supply factories to make finished products—manufactured goods and textiles. The process was repeated over and over.

The Spanish House of Trade (Casa de Contratación)

At this time, the power of the Spanish monarchy was nearly unlimited. Spain governed its territory in the Americas through an institution known as the Council of the Indies. Spanish governors formed a network that created and carried out Spanish law in the colonies. The goal of these governors was, once again, to further maximize the economic goals of Spain. This resulted in the House of Trade, or the Casa de Contratación, in Seville, Spain, in 1503.

The House of Trade managed all trade with the New World. One port city, Cadiz, was used primarily for trade in the Americas. Groups of ships would journey to the New World, pick up cargo such as gold, silver, or other raw materials; then they would spend the winter under the protection of the Spanish lords in the West Indies. Come springtime, they would travel back to Spain while another half of the fleet was on its way over to the Americas.

ENGLISH COLONIES

While Spain was dominating Mexico and South America, the English were settling the mid-point of the North American East Coast. The English had enormously complex interactions with the Native American populations in what is today the United States. Unlike the Spanish, the English cared very little for missionary work. However, just like the Spanish, the diseases brought over from England took a toll on the Native American population.

The Native American populations in North America were different from South America. In South America, the Indian populations lived in large urban cities like Tenochtitlan. In North America, there were smaller villages, spread out over a much larger area. There was a lot of intertribal warfare and anger with which the English had to deal. Early on during the

British conquest, the different Native American tribes quit fighting each other to focus on the English. However, the English became master manipulators, learning how to pit one tribe against another to gain advantage. This advantage was not only for British economic gain but to help the British defeat their main rival in the Americas: France.

Victory for the English in North America

Almost as soon as the English colonies were settled, Native Americans quickly became involved in the struggle between the English and French. The English and the French were fighting not only in Europe but in the Americas. Starting with the French and Indian War, natives were involved in the struggle for the Americas.

The Seven Years War, commonly known as the French and Indian War, was fought from 1756 to 1763. The English defeated the French. England, France, and Spain signed the Treaty of Paris, which gave England the rights to resources in North America. England's alliances with the natives helped them win the French and Indian War, which started over a trade monopoly. With the English now having unlimited access to North America, they looked to agricultural products and lumber (not so much gold and silver) to make money to grow the power of the English empire.

England's Involvement in the Triangle Trade

For both the Spanish and the English, the key to extracting raw materials to turn into monetary wealth was cheap labor. At this point, European countries were nearly totally dependent upon slave labor for their resources.

Slavery had been around since the beginning of world history. Normally when people became prisoners of war, they became slaves. The triangle slave trade was something completely and totally new. The triangle slave trade was based on racial differences. It impacted areas from Africa to Europe to North and South America, and it lasted all the way into the end of the 19th century.

African Side of the Slave Trade

The slave trade did not start as a result of racism. Instead, it was created because the European powers needed to find a way to maximize profit. The competition for profit and the need to defeat each other allowed the Europeans to exploit a technologically weaker group of people. It was visions of gold that brought the first Europeans to Africa, but it was the slave trade that kept them coming back for nearly 400 years. The demand was great in the growing colonies for this new transatlantic slave trade. The money that was made helped propel Europe to world dominance.

Many Africans were willing participants in the transatlantic slave trade. European slave traders bought slaves from other Africans, who would travel inland to capture slaves and then bring them to the European ports on the East Coast of America. There were several reasons for their participation.

1. Africans wanted to control part of the trade. Europeans were not able to venture inland into Africa because they were highly susceptible to malaria and other types of tropical diseases. Africans would capture the slaves inland and then bring them out.

2. Europeans bought slaves using consumable addictive products that Africans wanted, like alcohol and tobacco. Africa lost a nonrenewable resource—people—in exchange for consumable luxury items. Early on in the slave trade, the most sought-after slave was a young male to do much of the hard labor, causing Africa to lose generations of people.

3. The sugar consumption skyrocketed in the African kingdoms of Mali and Songhai, plus the Portuguese needed more slaves to grow sugarcane in the West Indies and Brazil.

4. The tobacco crop in North America and the ability of cotton to be grown in the American South (which was much closer than India's cotton) increased the need for slavery, bringing more money to Africans who provided slaves.

Slavery allowed the plantation economy to grow. Plantations existed to produce cash crops—sugar, tobacco, and cotton—to sell as an export. Plantation owners could also buy finished or manufactured products from the mother colony with their income, thus increasing the money for the mother country. Remember, the goal of mercantilism was to make money for the mother country!

Slavery was the last ingredient of the extractive economy of the New World. Slavery existed from territories in South America to New England in what is today the United States. As the number of Native Americans declined, Europeans turned to imported African slaves. The life of a slave was difficult, and the death rate was high. Their sole job was to produce goods for the European mother country.

FRENCH INTERACTION

The French were the last mercantilism society of Europe to thrive in North America. The French were different from the Spanish and the British in that they believed in good treatment of the Native Americans and would not use African slaves.

As the French explorers moved down the St. Lawrence River during the 1600s looking for the passage to Asia, French fur traders followed shortly thereafter. After the fur traders came French Catholic missionaries, who were supported by the French crown. By the end of the 15th century, there was a small, but powerful, French outpost in what is today Canada. The French settlement of Québec began in 1608 and grew steadily thereafter. The French got along better with the Native Americans because they did not try to set a claim on Native American land or territory. There was less violent interaction between them.

The French were after the fur trade—beaver, rabbit, sable, deer, and bear—to be turned into high-priced luxury items in Europe. Trading defined the French colonies and their participation in the transatlantic trade. Even though it was peaceful, there was ecological damage done due to the large number of native species that the French hunted and trapped.

1440 C.E.	Portugal explores West Africa.
1450–1750 C.E.	Triangle Trade
1492–1650 C.E.	Columbian Exchange
1503 C.E.	• Casa de Contratación
	• House of Trade in Seville
1519 C.E.	• Cortés conquers the Aztecs.
	• Franciscans and Dominicans in the New World
1529 C.E.	Haciendas
1532 C.E.	Pizarro conquers the Incas.
1542 C.E.	Use of the encomienda
1543 C.E.	Repartimento
1552 C.E.	Bartolomé de Las Casas *The Black Legend*
Late 1500s–1800s C.E.	Transatlantic slave trade
1607 C.E.	English at Jamestown, Virgina
1608 C.E.	French establish Quebec in Canada.
1619 C.E.	Transatlantic slave trade grows as result of deaths of Native Americans.
1620 C.E.	*Mayflower* lands at Plymouth, Massachusetts.
1756–1763 C.E.	Seven Years War (known as the French and Indian War)
1763 C.E.	Treaty of Paris ends French and Indian War.

GLOBAL CONNECTIONS

Asia

1526 C.E.—Mughal Dynasty

1631 C.E.—Building of the Taj Mahal

Japan

1598 C.E.—Tokugawa Ieyasu

1630 C.E.—Japan begins policy of isolation

Africa

1500–1800 C.E.—Slave trade

The Enlightenment

20

NATURAL LAWS

The political ideas of the Enlightenment stemmed directly from the Scientific Revolution. The ideas of men like Copernicus brought about a new way of looking at the physical world. If reason could be used to govern the physical world, then reason could also be applied to understanding natural laws. Natural laws are the laws that govern the basics of human nature, and thereby it stood to reason that if natural laws were applied to society, they could solve the social, economic, and political turmoil of the day.

During the reign of the Stuart Dynasty in England (1603–1714), John Locke and Thomas Hobbes were two Englishmen who lived through the English Civil War. They had differing thoughts on natural laws.

John Locke

John Locke, a philosopher, believed that people were basically good and moral. In his 1689 book, *Two Treatises of Government,* he stated that people were entitled to natural rights, which were things that everyone has from the time they are born. Locke's beliefs were that everyone had the right to life, to liberty, and to property. Locke also believed that governments should be formed specifically to protect these natural rights. The best form of government had to be one of limited power, not like the absolute monarchs of his time. According to Locke, the government had an obligation to its citizens. If a government failed to live up to its obligations or did not respect a person's basic rights, then it was the people's right to overthrow that government and create a new one.

Global Connections

Locke's ideas foreshadowed the coming American Revolution.

Thomas Hobbes

Fellow English philosopher Thomas Hobbes had an opposite, darker view of human nature. In his 1651 book, *Leviathan,* Hobbes said people were greedy and selfish; therefore, they needed the government to control them. According to Hobbes, people existed in what he called a state of nature. In this state, people were uncontrolled, and life would be, as he famously stated, "poor, nasty, brutish, and short." Therefore, what must be created was a social contract where people would willingly give up their state of nature to create an organized society. The best way to create this society was to have a powerful government that could make its people do what was necessary for the good of the society. For Hobbes, an absolute monarchy was the best form of government.

Baron de Montesquieu

In France in the 1700s, the Baron de Montesquieu had studied all forms of government, from ancient to modern. Much like John Locke, Montesquieu did not like the idea of absolute monarchy. In his 1748 essay, *The Spirit of the Laws*, Montesquieu credited the British and their idea of a limited monarchy. He liked how the British implemented what he considered to be three separate branches of government—the executive, legislative, and judicial branches. To Montesquieu, a separation of powers was the best way to maintain liberty.

Montesquieu's system is used in America today. It is called the "checks and balances" system, where no one branch can be more powerful than the others.

Francois Marie Arouet, Better Known as Voltaire

Voltaire famously said that he lived to say what he thought. He was a very controversial figure in France and used a combination of clever comedy and fiction to express his opinions on the problems of his time. In his famous work *Candide*, published in 1759, Voltaire specifically denounced governmental corruption, the practice of the slave trade, and religious exclusivism. His ideas angered not only the Roman Catholic Church but French government officials as well. Voltaire was exiled, and many of his books were burned, but he kept going. He believed in free speech so much that he defended it no matter how he was punished. One of Voltaire's famous quotes was, "I may disagree with what you say, but I will defend to the death your right to say it."

Denis Diderot

Diderot published a 28-volume set of encyclopedias between 1751 and 1772. In these encyclopedias, he printed the works of all the political philosophers, like Voltaire, Montesquieu, Locke, and Hobbes. Diderot said his goal was to change the way people thought about government. Diderot's encyclopedias challenged the theory of divine right of absolute monarchy. The French government accused Diderot of eroding the morals of the people of France. The pope threatened to excommunicate anybody caught reading Diderot's encyclopedias. However, despite efforts to stop people from reading Diderot's encyclopedias, over 20,000 were printed. People read about the ideas of the Enlightenment not only in Europe but across the sea in America as well.

Jean-Jacques Rousseau

French philosopher Rousseau also felt, as John Locke did, that people were good. However, people were constantly being corrupted by society. In 1762, Rousseau wrote *The Social Contract*. He said that men were born free, and it was society that constantly made people change from good to bad. Rousseau felt that society controlled the way people were shaped and behaved. However, to Rousseau, some social controls were necessary. A consenting form of government that the people themselves chose was necessary for the common good. Otherwise, people would surrender their rights. When governed in a system that was based on their consent, they retained their freedoms because the government was chosen based on the will of the majority. Common good should win, so unlike John Locke, Rousseau believed that one should aim for the good of the community rather than the good of the individual.

Natural Rights for Women

To many people, the free and equal ideas of the Enlightenment did not apply to women. Many people felt that women did not have natural rights, or that if they did, they were much more limited in scope than they were for men. In the 1750s, a small number of women began to argue against this idea. The most famous was Mary Wollstonecraft from England. She protested that women had been left out of the social contract. She felt that a woman should, first and foremost, be a good mother to her children. However, a woman should also be able to think for herself and not be solely dependent upon her husband as a breadwinner. In 1792, she wrote *A Vindication of the Rights of Woman* in which she claimed that the same education that was given to a boy should also be given to a girl because education was a path to freedom and independence.

A NEW FORM OF ECONOMIC THOUGHT: LAISSEZ-FAIRE

As scientific thought gave rise to the idea of a person's natural political rights and the best form of government, new forms of economic thought were also developed.

One new idea of economic thought that gained attention in the 1750s was laissez-faire, meaning that business and economic enterprise should be allowed to operate without any governmental interference. This new idea was the complete opposite of the ideas of mercantilism on which the European economies were running at the time. In mercantilism, nations measured their wealth against each other by the acquisition of precious metals. The new economic philosophers of the Enlightenment said the new wealth was going to come in different forms from gold and silver. Enlightenment philosophers said one should make land as productive as possible, and new wealth would be determined by farming and logging. They said there should be free trade in these areas, not the restricted isolation that defined mercantilism, where colonies could only trade with the mother country. Philosophers of the Enlightenment wanted to open up the colonies to share resources in order to make money.

Adam Smith

In 1776, Adam Smith wrote *The Wealth of Nations* in which he described what he called the free market system. In a free market system, a national economy would be subjected to the forces of supply and demand, which would naturally regulate business activity. According to Smith, in business, everything was tied together. From the manufacturing of products to the amount of money an employee was being paid to the level of profit an owner made, all were part of the supply and demand process. If there was a demand for a product, the demand would be met better in an economy run with no government interference. To Smith, the government's job was to focus on ensuring justice and protecting its people, not interfering with the economy. As the Industrial Revolution grew and spread, Smith's ideas shaped the world all the way to the 20th century.

TIMELINE REVIEW

1651 C.E.	Thomas Hobbes: *Leviathan*
1689 C.E.	John Locke: *Two Treatises of Government*
1748 C.E.	Baron de Montesquieu: *The Spirit of the Laws*
1751 C.E.	Denis Diderot's encyclopedia
1759 C.E.	Voltaire: *Candide*
1762 C.E.	Jean-Jacques Rousseau: *The Social Contract*
1776 C.E.	Adam Smith: *The Wealth of Nations*
1792 C.E.	Mary Wollstonecraft: *A Vindication of the Rights of Woman*

Quick Quiz: Chapters 18–20

1. This dynasty tried unsuccessfully to bring forms of religious toleration and absolute rule to England.

   A. Tudor Dynasty
   B. Cromwellian Dynasty
   C. Stuart Dynasty
   D. Flavian Dynasty

2. Which Puritan leader of England led the Roundheads during the English Civil War?

   A. Richard the Lionheart
   B. Prince John
   C. William of Orange
   D. Oliver Cromwell

3. What mistake did King Louis XIV make, resulting in the departure of many Protestants from the kingdom of France?

   A. Revoking the idea of plenary indulgences
   B. Forbidding the practice of lay investiture
   C. Revoking the Edict of Nantes
   D. Signing the Treaty of Dover with England

4. This event spelled the end of Spain as a dominant power in Europe.

   A. The Spanish Armada was sunk.
   B. King Charles V divided the empire.
   C. The Aztec civilization began to run out of gold.
   D. The Protestants in the Netherlands revolted.

5. This absolute monarch traveled to Western Europe to learn industrial techniques in order to help him solidify his power in his own country.

   A. Ivan the Terrible
   B. Emperor Leo III
   C. Czar Alexander II
   D. Peter the Great

6. This absolute ruler wisely ruled through a sense of toleration, something that separated him from many of his contemporaries.

   A. Tokugawa Ieyasu
   B. Suleiman the Magnificent
   C. Akbar the Great
   D. Ashoka

7. Mehmed II created this document to have a preventative legal code to help govern his empire.

   A. Code of Suleiman
   B. The kanunname
   C. The sharia
   D. The Domesday Book

8. This Japanese shogun began the national policy of seclusion as he felt Japan had reached near perfection in society.

   A. Minamoto Yoritomo
   B. Tokugawa Ieyasu
   C. Emperor Shirakawa
   D. Hideki Tojo

9. This Chinese era or dynasty can be compared to the Roman Pax Romana.

   A. Song
   B. Tang
   C. Manchu
   D. Ming

10. To symbolize and showcase their power, several monarchs (Louis XIV, Peter the Great, the Ming Dynasty, and Indian emperor Shah Jahan) followed this same practice or technique.

    A. They all built walled, large palaces.
    B. They all enforced strict legal codes.
    C. They were all worshipped as the sun.
    D. They forced their nobles to live close to them to prevent any rebellions.

11. What was the goal of mercantilism, which to some the best example of which would be the transatlantic economy or the Columbian Exchange?

    A. To establish the transatlantic slave trade
    B. To create territories for religious freedom
    C. To make money to increase the wealth of the mother country
    D. To subjugate and dominate natives of conquered lands and convert them to Christianity

12. Which Spanish subject wrote *The Black Legend*, chronicling the treatment of Native Americans at the hands of the Spanish conquistadors?

    A. Simón Bolívar
    B. Bartolomé de Las Casas
    C. Hernando Cortés
    D. Christopher Columbus

13. The death of millions of Native Americans in the New World had this result.

    A. Gave rise to the transatlantic slave trade
    B. Ended the Spanish monarchy as a dominant monarchy in Europe
    C. Forced the scrapping of the famous Spanish Armada
    D. Allowed England to become the dominant power on the seas

14. Which European country had the most complex relations with the native populations to further their own interests more than any other colonial empire?

    A. The French
    B. The Dutch
    C. The British
    D. The Spanish

15. Which European country was least invasive or disruptive to native cultures in the Americas?

    A. The Spanish
    B. The French
    C. The Portuguese
    D. The English

16. Which event gave rise to the ideas known as the Enlightenment?

    A. Renaissance
    B. Reformation
    C. Scientific Revolution
    D. Industrial Revolution

17. This Enlightenment thinker wrote *Leviathan*, saying that, at their core, people are bad and selfish and that favored absolutism is the best form of government to control their nasty, short, and brutish lives.

    A. John Locke
    B. Thomas Hobbes
    C. Voltaire
    D. Jean-Jacques Rousseau

18. This enlightenment thinker wrote *The Wealth of Nations* and described his thoughts on the free market as a laissez-faire economic system.

    A. Karl Marx
    B. Denis Diderot
    C. Thomas Hobbes
    D. Adam Smith

19. This major proponent of free speech and Enlightenment thinker wrote *Candide* to express his thoughts on society and government and said, "I may disagree with what you say, but I will defend to the death your right to say it."

A. Voltaire
B. John Locke
C. Baron de Montesquieu
D. Denis Diderot

Quick Quiz Answers

1. C; **2.** D; **3.** C; **4.** A; **5.** D; **6.** C; **7.** B; **8.** B; **9.** D; **10.** A; **11.** C; **12.** B; **13.** A; **14.** C; **15.** B; **16.** C; **17.** B; **18.** D; **19.** A

Revolutions Across the World

21

AMERICAN REVOLUTION

Inspiration for the American Revolution

During the 1700s and 1800s, European monarchs went on a quest to find new avenues of money for many reasons. One reason was that a large amount of money was spent fighting the French and Indian War (also called the Seven Years War) from 1756 to 1763. Another reason was the desire for European rulers to become absolute monarchs in their own countries. In pursuing this desire, they destabilized not only their countries, but also their colonies in the Americas. Between 1775 and 1825, several revolutions occurred throughout European colonies overseas. As a result, North America and South America reshaped the political landscape of the world.

"No Taxation Without Representation," Boston Massacre, and Boston Tea Party

When the French and Indian War ended in 1763, tensions between the colonies in America and England became visible. The war drained the treasury of the English monarch, King George III. His Parliament felt that the colonies should pay for the war since, after all, it was fought to protect them. Thus, Parliament and the king began to enforce long-forgotten trade laws, and Parliament raised taxes on the colonists.

In North America, the 13 colonies were angry. They had worked hard to become self-sufficient, and they thought the king did not do much to help them. If their taxes were going to be raised, they wanted representation in Parliament. This belief started the famous quote, "No taxation without representation."

In 1770, after hurling snowballs at frightened British soldiers, some of the soldiers fired on civilians in the crowd, killing several including the runaway slave named Crispus Attucks. This became known as the Boston Massacre. In 1773, the Boston Tea Party involved colonists sneaking aboard British ships, disguised as Mohawk Indians, and throwing British tea into Boston Harbor.

The First Continental Congress

Leaders from the colonies met at the First Continental Congress in 1774 to determine the next steps of the colonies. At the First Continental Congress, men like John Adams, Benjamin Franklin, and Thomas Jefferson became known as the Founding Fathers. They discussed the relationship of the colonies with England and created the Continental Army. The Congress appointed George Washington as general of the army.

The Second Continental Congress and the Declaration of Independence

By June 1775, the fighting against England had begun, and the Second Continental Congress was held in Philadelphia. Early on, the war went badly as the Continental Congress had few funds and even fewer military supplies or abilities. They were going against one of the largest and most professional armies in the entire world: the British.

In July 1776, the Congress voted on the approval of the Declaration of Independence. The document articulated many of the ideas written down by John Locke. Locke's philosophies were interwoven with American reasons for declaring independence from England. The Declaration of Independence is considered one of the greatest documents written in human history.

The United States Revolutionary War

Heading into the revolution, England had many advantages.

- Large professional army
- Vast resources to draw from
- Many American colonists who remained loyal to England

The 13 colonies of the new United States had volunteer citizen soldiers, no navy to speak of, and no money or other resources on which to fall back. The only advantage was that they were fighting on home ground. When large cities like Boston, New York, and Philadelphia were occupied, the fighting moved into the countryside.

During the early years, victory looked hopeless. Then, on Christmas night 1776, General George Washington crossed the Delaware River with the U.S. Army and won the Battle of Trenton. Morale was growing. And then, the U.S. Army spent the terrible winter of 1777–1778 at Valley Forge. Despite the terrible winter, the Army trained throughout the encampment period. In the spring, when the Continental Army went up against the British, they had the training to stand up to the English military veterans.

American victories emboldened the French to recognize the colonies and join in an alliance against their old enemy, Great Britain. With the French alliance came money, supplies, veteran French soldiers, and, most importantly, the French Navy. In 1781, the French fleet blockaded Chesapeake Bay as General George Washington boxed in British Lord Cornwallis in the Virginia city of Yorktown. The surrender at Yorktown signaled the collapse of the British war effort in the New World.

Two years later in 1783, the Treaty of Paris was signed by England, recognizing the existence of the United States of America. The American Revolutionary War ended with the United States becoming an independent country.

The United States Constitution

In the hot summer of 1787, the current United States Constitution was being written at the Constitutional Convention in Philadelphia. The Constitution framed out a strong federal government that had the ability to grow, flex, and change with time. The legislature under this new system would have two houses:

- An upper house called the Senate. In the Senate, every state received two votes.
- A lower house called the House of Representatives. In the House of Representatives, representation was proportional to each state's population.

The leader of the United States would be a president, who would lead a federal republic (taking the ideas from ancient Greece and Rome). There would also be a nine-member Supreme Court.

In total, there would be three branches of government—executive, legislative, and judicial—to check and balance each other so no one group could take over.

The document was strong and adaptable. It became a living document that could change and grow with the times. It was inspired by the work of men from the Enlightenment, like John Locke and Baron de Montesquieu.

The United States became a federal republic in 1789. The new government was a representative government and was run by an elected legislature. To vote, a person had to be a free white man. African Americans, Native Americans, and women were not able to vote. However, at this point, it was the freest government the world had seen since Rome.

Also written at the same time as the Constitution was the Bill of Rights. The Bill of Rights contained the first ten amendments of the Constitution. It spelled out the basic rights of people, such as freedom of religion, freedom of the press, freedom of speech, and many other ideas that can be traced back to John Locke and the Enlightenment.

FRENCH REVOLUTION

The Beginning of the French Revolution

When the U.S. Constitution was ratified in 1789, the most republican government of the day was born. The United States and its new government were a beacon that shone across the Atlantic to Europe and then boomeranged back to Latin America. In 1789, revolution for liberty began in France, becoming one of the most storied revolutions in history.

Collapse of the Estates General System

The French Revolution was one of the most complicated, yet important, historical events in world history. It was not one revolution, but a series of them, which continued internally in France as they wrote several constitutions.

France was divided into three political divisions called the Estates General. The most important Estate was the high-ranking religious clergy. Second was the nobility, and third was everyone else in the kingdom. More than 90 percent of the people were in the Third Estate. The problem with this was that when it came to making decisions, France voted by the Estate as a whole, not counting how many people were part of each Estate. Even though they had the majority of the people, the Third Estate was always outvoted two to one in every vote, getting beaten by the wealthier classes. The Third Estate wanted to vote by individual head so they would have a chance. However, King Louis XVI wanted the Third Estate to meet separately so they would not sit with the clergy or the nobles, thus having no power to influence French policy.

Discontent and Louis XVI's Economic Troubles

Along with political discontent among the Estates General, King Louis XVI was beaten in the French and Indian War in North America. He was deeply in debt as financing the war overseas cost a lot of money. The assistance he provided to the American revolutionaries deepened the financial stress on his kingdom.

Even worse was that, at this time, France actually was economically prosperous, whereas France's opposition in Europe was in debt. France should have been financially solid, but the big problem was the king's inability to fairly collect the taxes that could pay off his debts. During the mid-1780s, Louis XVI appointed several economic ministers to correct this problem. Every one of them failed as they were not able to get the church and the nobles to pay new taxes. The result was that the taxes were simply lumped onto the Third Estate.

The Estates General had not met in well over 100 years as Louis XIV was an absolute monarch, making all of the decisions for France himself. However, Louis XVI agreed to call the Estates General to help him find a way out of France's financial crisis. This was where the problems began.

Some members of the Third Estate were fairly educated, hardworking French citizens, and they refused to meet separately from the other two Estates. In June 1789, they invited sympathetic members of the clergy and the nobles to join them in creating a new legislative assembly that would be called the National Constituent Assembly.

As the members of the National Constituent Assembly arrived at their normal meeting location, the door was locked. Believing that the king did this on purpose, they marched to his palace and met on his tennis court. They refused to leave until France had a new constitution, making this incident known as the Tennis Court Oath. King Louis finally gave in and told the first two Estates to join the new legislature. The National Constituent Assembly was going to institute voting by individual person. This, in theory, ended the French government that was run by those of wealth and privilege.

Storming of the Bastille

King Louis tried to reassert himself by having troops maneuver near his Palace of Versailles, outside of Paris. This set off a domino effect of events, which led directly to the French Revolution and the overthrow of the monarchy.

Most members of the National Constituent Assembly wanted a constitutional monarchy, similar to the one in England. However, King Louis refused to hear this.

The other problem was that the poor, starving people of Paris were very wary of the French military. Since they began maneuvering just outside the city, there had been several bread riots in the city. Citizens began to collect weapons in case the military was sent in. On July 14, 1789, 800 people—from artisans to shopkeepers—marched to the prison fortress of the Bastille, trying to get weapons. The troops were safe inside, but just like the British troops during the Boston Massacre, they grew afraid and fired on the crowd, killing 98 people. This enraged the people of Paris, who then stormed the Bastille, releasing all the prisoners inside. However, they did not find the huge cache of weapons they hoped to find in order to defend themselves.

The storming of the Bastille was very important, and it is still celebrated in France today. It is known as the first of many Journées—or journeys—where the people of Paris changed the course of the French Revolution.

Similar problems were showing up around smaller cities throughout France. King Louis tried to make some concessions by instituting a new city government of Paris. He tried to pacify the French people.

A New Constitution

On August 27, 1789, the National Constituent Assembly combined the ideas of Thomas Jefferson's Declaration of Independence with the ideas of Locke and Montesquieu in the

Enlightenment. They came up with their own constitution, which they called *The Declaration of the Rights of Man and of the Citizen*. The National Constituent Assembly said that all men were born (and remained) free. They were equal in basic rights, liberty, property, and security; therefore, it was the government's responsibility to protect these rights. The rest was very similar to the United States Constitution, but King Louis XVI delayed the ratification of it. This caused many people to speculate that he might send in the army to disrupt or destroy the work of the National Constituent Assembly.

Women in the Revolution

In October 1789, several thousand women marched from Paris to Versailles, demanding more bread to feed their starving families. This was the first of several occasions when women played a significant role in the French Revolution.

War at Home and Abroad

When the Constitution was ratified, the National Constituent Assembly tried to reconstruct France. Unfortunately, the Assembly returned to the ideas of protecting as much wealth and property as they could and severely limiting the national role of the peasant class. Civic equality was great in theory, but the old, monarchical social class system just would not go away. Social equality was not a goal of this new Constitution.

At this time, the National Constituent Assembly began to suppress guilds. They forbade the organization of urban workers trying to get better labor practices. They made a huge mistake when they captured and sold lands held by the Roman Catholic Church and then tried to force the Roman Catholic Church into being a wing of the state government. This caused tremendous opposition as the pope was not consulted. As a result, the pope condemned the new French Constitution and the people of France became divided internally: those who supported the new Constitution and those who supported the church.

Marie Antoinette, the French queen, and many nobles had already fled France for other European capitals. They finally convinced King Louis that he should leave France as well because the situation was getting out of control.

Before Louis could get out of the country, he was discovered. On August 27, 1791, as Louis was brought back into the city, Holy Roman Emperor Leopold II of Austria and Emperor Frederick William II of Prussia (who were family members of Marie Antoinette) said they would militarily intervene to protect the royal family. Many other European monarchs agreed, and the revolutionaries in France who were trying to change the government felt they were surrounded by monarchies that did not like them.

The French Revolution had not been overly violent, and up to this point, people had organized themselves into political parties. The largest and most successful were a group of people known as the Jacobins. They assumed leadership in the Assembly, and with France reeling from internal and financial turmoil, the Jacobins declared war on Austria.

This war changed the revolution and its goals. It led to what is called the Second Revolution, where, in 1792, the constitutional monarchy was disbanded and a republic was established. When the war with powerful Austria took a turn for the worse, the government of Paris changed from elected individuals to representatives from the different neighborhoods or wards of Paris. This new government invaded the Royal Palace, and they forced the king and queen to seek refuge in the new legislative assembly building and live under house arrest.

The Convention and Downfall of the Monarchy

The first week of September 1792 is known as the September Massacre. French citizens killed more than 1200 people—all in city jails—who were thought to be working against the revolution. This was led by a subsect of the Jacobins known as the sans-culottes. The sans-culottes were working class wage laborers who felt completely ignored by all other governments. They wanted relief from food shortages and inflation. They hated social class distinction, and they wanted a government that would enforce universal male suffrage.

They forced the National Constituent Assembly to write another democratic constitution. This convention declared France to be a republic. Since the sans-culottes were numerous and powerful, the Jacobins in the Assembly worked with the sans-culottes to overthrow the monarchy. In December 1792, King Louis XVI was put on trial, and he was beheaded in early 1793. The new government went out of control after beheading Louis, and Queen Marie Antoinette was also beheaded in October 1793. Then, they declared war on England, the Netherlands, and Spain. France, who was already fighting Austria, was now taking on much of Europe. While fighting the whole of Europe, a French civil war soon followed, causing further unrest and destabilization at home.

Maximilien Robespierre: The Reign of Terror

In April 1793 (between the beheadings of King Louis and Queen Marie Antoinette), the government of France established two committees:

- The Committee of General Security, which protected them from external threats
- The Committee of Public Safety, which took care of internal threats

To carry out the executive office functions of the government, these committees had almost unlimited power as they were supposed to protect the revolution from enemies at home and across Europe. They passed a fully democratic Constitution on June 24, 1793, but immediately suspended the rights and privileges provided by the Constitution. Because of the national crisis of the civil war at home and the external wars with all of Europe, there was a military draft to put all available males into the army.

Historically, it has always been easier to get rid of democratic practices during a crisis and in times of war. The new French government believed they had established a republic in which the civic virtue of the people would thrive instead of corruption. The leader of the Committee of Public Safety was a man named Maximilien Robespierre. Early on, Robespierre did not like the wars, but he felt that everyone should buy into this new republican government. He also believed that politicians working for selfish gains should be eradicated. A series of tribunals were set up to publicly interrogate people who were said to be enemies of the new government. Robespierre presided over many of these tribunals. There was no defined enemy of the state other than being a member of the royal family or other wealthy aristocrats.

These tribunals started in Paris in 1793, and they moved to other parts of France. Thousands of people were executed. By mid-1794, Robespierre even turned his Reign of Terror on political figures that agreed with him. He executed the leaders of the sans-culottes; then he executed anybody who he thought could threaten his new position. He pushed through the Assembly laws that allowed him to convict suspects without any evidence, and then he gave a speech to the Assembly that they were antirevolutionaries. He wanted to execute them. However, since Robespierre was speaking to the very people he was going to execute, the Assembly had him arrested in July 1794 and guillotined the next day.

Aftermath of the Reign of Terror

From 1793 to 1794, the Reign of Terror led to the death of 40,000 French citizens. Due to the tremendous horrors inflicted by Robespierre, the Civil War ended, and the war with Europe was stalemated. The French created another new government, which created the Constitution of 1795. France was run by a five-man government known as the Directory. It had a two-house legislature governed by males who owned property. They severed ties with the sans-culottes, and they sought peace with France's European enemies.

The Directory

The Directory governed France from 1795 to 1799. It was a weak government, and there was still growing discontent among the starving, poor people as members of the Directory became rich. As members of the sans-culottes started food riots once again, the Directory brought in a military hero, hoping to use his name to form a better government. The Directory brought in Napoleon Bonaparte. Napoleon had his own ideas and wanted to unite France under the ideas of nationalism, where the people of France would be the most important, not the symbolic king and queen.

The Rise of Napoleon

From 1799 to 1815, Napoleon Bonaparte was a force to be reckoned with in Europe. He was a 20-year-old lieutenant in the army during the French Revolution. In 1793, he defeated the British, driving them out of key ports in France. In 1799, he defeated powerful Austria in a series of battles. After he was named as General of the French army, he overthrew the Directory and had a new constitution written. The new constitution declared him as the consul of France for life, harkening back to ancient Rome. In 1804, he was declared the emperor of France. Trying to mend ties with the Catholic Church, Napoleon invited the pope to come to Notre Dame to crown him as emperor. However, as Napoleon was being crowned, he seized the crown from the pope and placed it on his own head, showing that he was in charge and no one else.

On his rise to power, Napoleon had the French citizenry voting for him, and in return, he informed them about what he was doing every step of the way. He did do some good things. He modernized France, demanded an educated and trustworthy government, and appointed excellent military officials. He promoted the idea of public schools and achieved peace with the Catholic Church.

Le Grande Armée

Napoleon commanded what he called Le Grande Armée. He took on the combined powers of Europe, defeating many of them. Napoleon transformed France into an empire of its greatest size in history.

In June 1812, Napoleon led a disastrous attack on Russia. With 600,000 soldiers, he headed into Russia. When the Russian soldiers retreated deeper into Russia, Napoleon's army froze to death in the cold Russian winter. Only 100,000 soldiers survived the trek into Russia.

In 1813, Napoleon was forced to step down from the throne of France and was exiled on the island of Elba. King Louis XVIII was inserted as the king of France, but as an economic depression again hit France, Napoleon was able to escape exile and return to France. In March 1815, Napoleon reentered Paris as emperor once again. However, on June 18, 1815, after being back for barely 100 days, Napoleon lost the famous battle of Waterloo. He was exiled once again to a small island called St. Helena in the Atlantic Ocean, where he died in 1821.

Congress of Vienna

With France putting a military scare into Europe several times, European heads of state met for 10 months from September 1814 to June 1815, coming up with what was known as the Congress of Vienna. The goal was to create peace on the continent in order to protect European monarchies. They had witnessed the fall of the French king as well as the formation of a new country: the United States.

Austrian Prime Minister Clemens von Metternich was determined to revive and keep the European monarchical system in power, so they worked out an outline for peace that affected Europe until World War I. They created a balance of power called the Concert of Europe. It was a peacekeeping force that all the major European states agreed to maintain. The balance of power was achieved by not letting any single country grow to be more powerful than another. If they witnessed a monarchy getting into trouble (the way the French had), they would militarily intervene to preserve the monarchy. France returned to a monarchy as Louis XVIII was put back on the throne, and other monarchs were returned to power in Spain, Portugal, and the different Italian states.

WARS OF LATIN AMERICAN INDEPENDENCE

The success of the American Revolution, as well as the wars of the French Revolution, instigated multiple revolutions and ignited independence movements throughout Latin America.

Between 1804 and 1824, the European powers of France, Portugal, and Spain all had to withdraw from their American colonies. Part of the problem stemmed from the hierarchical system that existed in some of the colonies. Portuguese-born and Spanish-born nobles in the Americas were known as peninsulares. By moving to the New World, peninsulares could claim the top jobs in the government and in the church.

The Creoles

Creoles were seen as secondary nobles and could have their jobs preempted by any peninsular who arrived in the Americas. They wanted to gain independence from the stranglehold of the mother countries in Europe.

The Creoles felt that while achieving independence from Spain and Portugal was necessary, they did not want to lose their social position in Europe. They also wanted to keep their slaves, which was a crucial element in keeping their economic and social status. Basically, they wanted independence for themselves but not for their workers.

Creoles, along with other merchants in Latin America, also wanted to trade freely within their own regions for their own benefit, rather than doing everything for the good of the motherland.

Haiti: The First Movement of Independence

The revolution in Haiti happened because France could not control its colonies during its own revolution. The large uprising of a repressed social class is a recurrent theme in most revolutions, and Haiti was no different. Also called Hispaniola, Haiti achieved independence from France in 1804 following a slave revolt that started in 1791.

Haiti was one of the most valuable colonies of France in the late 1700s. French nobles owned large sugar plantations that were very profitable due to the high demand of sugar in Europe. These plantations were run by hundreds of thousands of slaves. Also in Haiti were free French people, but they were half-French and half-native, and they were treated very badly by the French.

TOUSSAINT L'OUVERTURE

The Haitian independence movement was led by Toussaint L'Ouverture. Toussaint was born a slave, but his father was part of a noble West African family. He taught Toussaint to take pride in his African heritage, and Toussaint learned the language of his West African ancestors. He also learned to read and speak French, so as he read French philosophies during the Enlightenment era, ideas began to stick with him. A slave revolt broke out in 1791 when Toussaint was 48 years old. His intelligence and skill as a military leader earned him the position of general. Toussaint's army of slaves fought trained armies of Spain and England, each of which had sent armies to Haiti. It was one of the bloodiest revolutions in the Americas, but by 1798, Toussaint achieved his goal. The enslaved Haitians had been freed, and although technically still a French colony, Toussaint controlled much of the island. Toussaint started to rebuild his country, which had been devastated by long years of war. He worked with the French nobles on the Haitian island to expand trade, create a Haitian constitution, and even open a government where whites, mixed-race Haitians, and even Africans could work together.

STRUGGLE AGAINST FRANCE

During the slave revolt in Haiti, Napoleon Bonaparte had risen to power in France. He tried to recapture Haiti in 1802 so he could use it as a staging depot in order to hang on to his North American colonies. Toussaint once again led Haiti as its military leader.

However, the French troops started falling victim to yellow fever and could not fight, so during this time, Toussaint was invited to a house for peace talks. French soldiers seized him and took him aboard a French warship, where he was taken to France and died. However, in 1804, Haitian leaders declared their independence, and Napoleon had to abandon Haiti.

Over the next 16 years, different Haitian leaders fought for power, but in 1820, Haiti became a new republic. It was the only nonslave working nation in the Americas.

REVOLUTIONS IN THE SPANISH COLONIES

By the late 1790s, Spain had suffered losses in wars with Napoleon, and they were experiencing financial problems. The Spanish crown was looking for new avenues of wealth, and the easiest solution was to increase taxes on colonists in the Americas, which is exactly what England did. This angered Spanish colonists who did not want to lose their wealth or their status. Being keenly aware of how the American colonies had defeated the British, Spanish citizens in the New World began to rebel against Spain as they believed Spain was finally vulnerable.

Argentina

The first region to fight for independence from Spain was Argentina. In 1806, the Argentinian colonists fought off the British in the city of Buenos Aires. The colonists had been paying the

Spanish crown for protection, but after defeating the British, they quickly decided that they did not need Spain to be their military. Believing they could defend themselves, Argentina declared independence from Spain in 1810.

JOSÉ DE SAN MARTÍN

With Argentinian independence secured from Spain, José de San Martín led military forces into Paraguay and Uruguay to liberate them from Spain. Even though San Martín lost some battles, Spain knew it had clearly lost control of these colonies. Paraguay declared its independence, and San Martín decided to liberate Peru. With its mountainous terrain, Peru was seen as the greatest fortress of power on the South American continent. In 1817, General San Martín led his army over the Andes Mountains to Santiago, Chile. For three years, San Martín stayed in Chile, building a navy to transport his army to Peru. When San Martín arrived in Peru, he drove out the Spanish. Spain had controlled Peru since 1532 when Pizarro conquered the Incas, and now Spain was pushed out. Two-thirds of South America was now free from Spanish control.

Venezuela and Simón Bolívar

While San Martín was liberating the southern part of South America, Simón Bolívar was doing the same thing in Venezuela to the north. In 1810, Bolívar helped organize the Venezuelan liberation.

Bolívar tried to implement a military takeover of the Venezuelan capital of Caracas, but he was unsuccessful on multiple occasions. Civil war broke out, and royalists challenged the republican government that Bolívar wanted to set up. Eventually, Bolívar was forced into exile on one of the Caribbean islands. However, in 1816, Bolívar returned to Venezuela and launched another invasion against the Spanish government. By the summer of 1821, his forces finally captured Caracas. Bolívar was named the president of Venezuela.

BOLÍVAR AND SAN MARTÍN

In 1822, Bolívar and San Martín joined forces to liberate Ecuador. After Ecuador's liberation, they met in the city of Quito to discuss the future of Latin America. Unbelievably, San Martín wanted to set up monarchies. Bolívar wanted to set up independent, democratic republics. San Martín left South America and lived the rest of his life in Spain.

By 1824, Simon Bolívar had driven out the last of the Spanish forces, completely liberating South America and ending the longest-lasting European empire in South America. As a result of his success in instituting democratic republics, Simon Bolívar is known as the George Washington of South America.

Mexico

In 1810, there was a Creole priest named Miguel Hidalgo. Father Hidalgo called for the Mexican natives in his parish to rebel, protest their treatment, and ask for land reforms. The Mexican people began to march toward Mexico City, gathering more and more followers along the way. By the time they arrived in Mexico City, Father Hidalgo was leading 80,000 followers to fight for independence. During the journey, Spanish military forces captured some of the protesters and executed them as a deterrent to the others. In response, the Mexican rebels captured Spanish soldiers and did the same thing.

In 1811, Father Hidalgo was captured and executed. The royalist soldiers and the rebels continued to commit horrible acts of violence on each other. Father Hidalgo was succeeded by José Pavón, a Mestizo priest. José Pavón was even more radical, calling not only for land reform but also for an end to slave labor in the New World. In 1815, Pavón was captured and executed, ending the peasant uprising.

SPANISH ARE DRIVEN FROM MEXICO

By 1820, a revolution was going on in Spain, which forced King Ferdinand VII to accept a new Spanish Constitution. In Mexico, the peninsulares feared the loss of their title and position with the new Constitution. A royalist named Agustín de Iturbide took charge, and in 1821, Iturbide declared Mexico to be free and independent of Spain.

Mexico was no longer governed by Spain, but it was governed by people who did not want social reform and who wanted to remain plantation owners. This delighted not only British trade ships but also the United States. In 1823, U.S. President James Monroe issued the Monroe Doctrine, which prohibited further European colonization in the Americas, keeping the Americas under the United States' sphere of influence. Even though Iturbide gained independence for Mexico from Spain, the poor people of Mexico did not benefit. With the Monroe Doctrine, the United States became a greater presence in the region.

GLOBAL CONNECTIONS

This same thought occurred in the southern United States. Yes, America was free from England, but the southern plantation owners wanted to keep their way of life, which included keeping the institution of slavery. The decision to keep slavery when they achieved independence led to the American Civil War.

Brazil

Unlike many of the Latin American revolutions, Brazilian independence was granted easily and peacefully. When Napoleon conquered Spain and Portugal and gave Napoleon's brother the Portuguese crown, the Portuguese royal family fled to the New World. In 1807, they landed in Rio de Janeiro. Realizing that Brazil was bigger than Portugal and had even more resources, the royal family set up their new government and new court to make Brazil its new kingdom. Brazil was no longer a colony but the new seat of the Portuguese government. It was bigger and more prosperous than Portugal, and the European Portuguese government tried to reclaim it but could not. Eventually, the royal family existed in a state of luxury, so it made Brazil an independent republic. The process of peace leading to the new Brazilian democracy was fairly easy and was well accepted in the Americas.

TIMELINE REVIEW

1754–1763 C.E.	French and Indian War
1763 C.E.	U.S. colonists are required to pay more taxes.
1765 C.E.	The Stamp Act in American colonies
1770 C.E.	Boston Massacre in American colonies
1773 C.E.	Boston Tea Party in American colonies
1774 C.E.	First Continental Congress is held in U.S.
1775 C.E.	Lexington and Concord battle in U.S. Revolution
1776 C.E.	Declaration of Independence is written in United States.
1777–1778 C.E.	France assists American colonists in Revolutionary War.
1781 C.E.	• Treaty of Paris ends U.S. Revolutionary War.
	• Articles of Confederation are written to govern the U.S.
1787 C.E.	U.S. Constitution and the Bill of Rights are written.
1791 C.E.	French Constitution creates new legislature.
1792 C.E.	• French Legislative Assembly declares war on Austria and Prussia.
	• August–September Massacre in France
1793 C.E.	King Louis XVI is executed.
1793–1794 C.E.	Reign of Terror in France by Robespierre
1795 C.E.	New French government called the Directory is formed.
1798 C.E.	Napoleon's Egyptian campaign
1799 C.E.	Napoleon becomes political leader of France and overthrows the Directory.
1801 C.E.	Toussaint L'Ouverture takes Santo Domingo.
1802 C.E.	• Napoleon takes title consul for life.
	• French troops land in Haiti.
	• Haitians will end revolution if French agree to end slavery.
1803 C.E.	Toussaint L'Ouverture dies in jail in France.
1804 C.E.	• Napoleon is crowned emperor of France.
	• General Dessalines renews Haitian Revolution and declares independence.
1807 C.E.	Portuguese royal family leaves Lisbon during Napoleon's invasion.
1808 C.E.	Peninsular War: French invasion of Portugal and Spain

1810 C.E.	• Simón Bolivar's first attempt at independence in Venezuela
	• Father Miguel Hidalgo of Mexico begins to call for independence.
1811 C.E.	• Father Hidalgo is executed in Mexico.
	• José Pavón takes over movement in Mexico.
1812 C.E.	Disastrous French invasion of Russia for Napoleon's Grande Armée
1814 C.E.	• Napoleon gives up French throne and is exiled to Elba.
	• Bolívar is exiled to Jamaica.
1814–1815 C.E.	Congress of Vienna
1815 C.E.	Napoleon returns to France.
1816 C.E.	• José de San Martín helps Argentina win independence from Spain.
	• Bolívar's second attempt at independence in Venezuela
1817 C.E.	San Martín leads Argentina's army through Andes Mountains to Chile.
1820 C.E.	Haiti becomes a republic.
1821 C.E.	Napoleon dies on St. Helena.
1822 C.E.	Bolívar and de San Martín join forces but have different points of view on government.
1824 C.E.	Peru is liberated by San Martín.

The Industrial Revolution Across the Globe

22

ENGLAND LEADS THE INDUSTRIAL REVOLUTION

Around 1750, the northwestern European economy began to industrialize. It was this event that set Europe apart from the rest of the entire world, followed shortly thereafter by North America.

Industrialization gave Europeans a large quantity of new goods to sell. In turn, this created an international market where Western industrialized countries provided finished products in exchange for raw materials extracted from other nations across the globe. The result of this was that countries across the world became dependent on European and American products. The vast income generated from this lopsided balance of trade allowed European countries to dominate the globe.

England was the leader of the Industrial Revolution until the late 1800s when they were finally overtaken by the United States. There were several reasons for British dominance.

1. England was separated from continental Europe. As a result, they did not experience many of the continent's problems.
2. England was the largest free trade area in all of Europe. Merchants and businesses could move freely through England's very good infrastructure without paying any polls or taxes.
3. England had a large supply of natural resources needed for industrialization, namely large deposits of iron ore and coal.
4. At this time, England's banking system was one of the best in the world.
5. Taxes were approved by Parliament, and they were collected fairly.
6. At the start of industrialization, there was a lot of consumer demand for England's finished products in the American colonies, providing England with a steady source of revenue from overseas.

New Methods of Production

The Industrial Revolution started when modern industry became deeply connected to the countryside. During the spring, summer, and fall, the peasants worked the land as their main occupation. In the darkness and cold of winter, they did jobs inside the warmth of their houses, like spinning wool into thread. Then, in the spring, large textile manufacturers would make a finished product out of the thread. In this way, industrial development took place because of the work being done in the countryside.

However, this rural system of industrialization created bottlenecks in the system. The demand for textiles began to grow faster than the older, rural ways of production. England's population was growing, and North America was growing. People started developing machines to save time and labor to meet this demand. In 1769, British inventor Richard Arkwright developed the water-powered spinning frame to speed up the process of making raw cotton into fabric.

The Invention of the Steam Engine

Mill machines were originally powered by water and wind. This dependence on the weather led to the most important invention of the Industrial Revolution—the steam engine. Originally created in the 1600s, British engineer James Watt vastly improved the design of the steam engine. The steam engine was originally used to pump water out of coal mines. Enlisting the help of two partners, Watt modified the engine design to work on transportation systems. By the early 1800s, steam engines were put on ships and railroad cars, which very quickly became the main movers of heavy industry.

The Production of Iron

High-quality iron was much in demand to make railroad lines, railroad cars, steamships, and, of course, more steam engines. However, the problem was that the current system of smelting iron was extremely inefficient. James Watt's steam engine greatly improved the process. The steam engine was applied to the blast furnaces used to smelt iron, increasing the intensity of the heat and the speed of the smelting. It created stronger iron, it provided a much greater supply, and it did so very quickly. People learned how to shape it to make it even stronger and easier to use. Iron was now able to be shipped everywhere. This helped fuel the Industrial Revolution.

GROWTH OF CITIES

Rural to Urban Migration

Industrialization and the steam engine caused changes in society as well. Cities began to grow much larger. During the Middle Ages, most cities stayed very small. However, by the early 1800s, cities had doubled in size. More than 350 cities in Europe and the United States had populations of more than 10,000. Seventeen cities across Europe had populations of more than 100,000. Massive growth in new urban populations was due to industrialization as it created jobs and attracted people from the countryside for employment.

These new cities were no longer located on the old, medieval trading paths. Instead, they were mainly on the coastline, where cities like Plymouth, Portsmouth, Hampton, and Liverpool took advantage of trading along the Atlantic Ocean. Inland cities that were important in medieval times did not grow as rapidly.

Inland Cities

Even though inland cities did not grow as rapidly, they remained vital to growth during the Industrial Revolution. Labor was cheaper outside the urban cities, and it was cheaper to build a factory in the countryside.

Factories formed a link between the large urban centers and the countryside. As factories were built, towns grew around them to serve the factory workers. They needed houses, grocery stores, and entertainment. An entire service economy developed around the factory since there was a large concentration of workers.

SOCIAL STRUCTURE DURING THE INDUSTRIAL REVOLUTION

New cities and towns built by industrialization caused changes in the social structure. On the top of the social hierarchy were "the nobles," who now were bankers, large business owners, and high-ranking clergy. These men formed oligarchies that ran the economic structure of each town.

However, with industrialization, a new force came into play: the middle class or "the bourgeoisie." Members of the bourgeoisie were successful but not extremely wealthy. By themselves they could not match the wealth of the upper classes; however, it was their strength in numbers that gave them power. For years, they had been trying to become upwardly mobile in society, but they were thwarted at every turn by the aristocratic class, which wanted to hang onto its power. Eventually, the middle class began to acquire more power in society.

One of the largest criticisms of the middle class during the Industrial Revolution was that once they began to acquire power, they quickly tried to hold down the lower classes, which they saw as a drain on their resources. This is ironic, considering that even though they did not like being suppressed by the upper classes, they quickly did the same to the lower classes beneath them.

Artisans suffered the most in industrialization. For a long time, skilled laborers—carpenters, blacksmiths, printers—had maintained their guild practices. Within the guild, they were able to guarantee that each skilled laborer who worked inside their city would be able to fetch a specific price for a specific quality of an item. With the Industrial Revolution, their economic position was threatened because industrialization made it possible to produce the same products quicker, faster, and cheaper.

Changes in the Structure of the Family

Family structures were also changed by the Industrial Revolution. Typically throughout world history, families worked together. Mothers and fathers would teach their children the skills they needed to do their job. Home life and their economic life were interwoven. However, with the Industrial Revolution, fathers began to work in factories, becoming separated from the home for many hours each day. By the mid-1830s, most textile production was done in a factory run by machinery. These machines required workers with little or no skill, just laborers.

With fathers gone at the factory for up to 12 hours a day, children were no longer receiving education at home, as mothers had to do the work of both parents to tend to the home. Children were sent to work in the factories as well. The plight of child labor has been well documented in the Industrial Revolution. However, because children were no longer being taught by their parents (and discipline and education were thus transferred to the workplace), England passed the English Factory Act in 1835. It mandated that children could not work more than eight hours in one day, and that they had to attend two hours of education paid for by the factory.

It should be noted that not all children had to work full-time in the factories. With fathers making more money as factory workers, many children no longer had to work at such a young age. In some cases, they were able to go to school.

Women also experienced positives and negatives during the Industrial Revolution. In some cases, families could live on only the wages of the factory-worker father. This allowed for stereotypical gender roles to develop as mothers became linked with being housewives.

For middle-class and upper-class women, it was their job to support the family and create a welcoming home environment. Often, the mother was in charge of the finances, as well as running the household, which gave her a sense of empowerment never before experienced in world history.

For younger women, the beginning of a wage economy and growth of cities allowed them to have more choices than ever before. For the first time, a woman had the option of deciding whom she was going to marry. A girl born in the countryside could go into a city and earn enough money for her own dowry, which gave her a greater sense of choice. On the negative side, women who worked in low-skilled factory jobs were often exploited. People knew that many of these women had nowhere else to go, so women in sweatshops were subjected to extremely low pay, terrible working conditions, and constant harassment because they had no protections whatsoever.

ADAM SMITH

As a result of industrialization, some people began to reject the ideas of mercantilism in the transatlantic trade, which required governmental regulation to keep trading balanced.

The new term *laissez-faire* was developed. Laissez-faire was an economic environment in which businesses were allowed to operate with little to no government interference. In 1776, Adam Smith wrote *The Wealth of Nations* in which he said he wanted a free market economy. In a free market economy, the natural occurring forces of supply and demand, not a government, should regulate how business operates. According to Smith, when the people (consumers) in a free market demanded goods and services, businesses would seek to meet that demand, allowing more things to be created and sold at a lower price so that everyone could afford them. A free market, laissez-faire economy would thereby be beneficial for everyone. During the Industrial Revolution and through the 1900s, Smith's ideas gained a lot of support as businesses were heavily influenced by *The Wealth of Nations*.

KARL MARX

Contrary to Adam Smith, German philosopher Karl Marx wanted to combat the gulf that he said was created by capitalism and a laissez-faire free market. He believed in socialism, where everything was publicly owned and each person was paid according to his or her abilities and needs. With Marxism, people would own the means of production.

In 1848, Karl Marx and Friedrich Engels wrote *The Communist Manifesto*. The Manifesto described communism, which is an extreme form of socialism. According to Marx, the bourgeoisie, middle-class business owners were locked in battle with the proletariat, or common everyday wage workers. The Manifesto said the workers would eventually win this struggle and then set up a classless, communist society. In communism, everything is shared. People would get what they needed based on what their abilities required them to receive.

Marx hated capitalism as he said it created poverty. He wanted all working people of all countries to unite against the bourgeoisie that was exploiting them. Marx's thoughts had little immediate effect. However, they would later influence the world when, in the late 1800s, some Russians welcomed the ideas of socialism, fueling the Russian Revolution of 1917. Marxist theories were neither scientifically based or proven, and many areas of Western Europe did not believe in it because the standard of living had improved so much already. In Western Europe, industrialization was seen as a good, not as an evil.

PROLETARIANIZATION

Karl Marx made a valid point when stating that the bourgeoisie would exploit the lower classes, as this did happen to some factory workers and urban artisans. In northern Europe, certain artisans and factory workers did go through a process known as proletarianization. Proletarianization occurred when workers lost control of ownership of the means of production. During the Industrial Revolution, workers simply supplied labor for a salary. They were subordinate to the will of the factory. The tools and equipment they used, as well as the way their trade was practiced, was now dictated to them. Of utmost importance were highly efficient machines. Humans did not matter as the machines did everything. As a result, workers lost control over the quality and the price of an item.

As less skill was needed to operate the factories, workers became less valuable. A machine that could run for 24 hours did not need to go home and did not need sleep; thus, skilled artisans and workers began to lose control of the means of production.

WORLD REACTION TO INDUSTRIALIZATION

The Industrial Revolution forced nearly everyone else in the world to react. The continents of Africa and South America became almost completely dependent upon the West. In Asia, Japan tried to imitate Western Europe and the United States, whereas China, with her vast size and resources, was exploited. Southeast Asia and the Middle East were colonized simply to supply resources to Western countries that were geared for industrial development.

Industrialization was one of the most rapid quantum leaps forward in world history since the Neolithic Revolution. Although the Industrial Revolution was a great leap forward, it came at a cost for much of the planet. Industrialization gave Europeans vast amounts of new goods to sell. The first true global market was created as Western Europe and the United States extracted raw materials from Africa, South America, Asia, and even North America. In return, they supplied finished products. As a result, much of the nonindustrialized world became dependent on Europe and the United States, and Western Europe dominated the globe for the next 100 years.

TIMELINE REVIEW

1764 C.E.	James Hargreaves invents the spinning jenny.
1765 C.E.	James Watt improves the steam engine.
1769 C.E.	Richard Arkwright invents the water-powered spinning frame.
1793 C.E.	Eli Whitney invents the cotton gin.
1807 C.E.	Robert Fulton adapts the use of the steam engine for a ship.
1820 C.E.	Steam locomotives are used in England.
1833 C.E.	English Factory Act is adopted.
1848 C.E.	*The Communist Manifesto* is published.
1850 C.E.	The number of cities of 100,000 people increases from 22 to 47.
1856 C.E.	Bessemer process of steel production is invented.
1866 C.E.	Alfred Nobel invents dynamite.

Quick Quiz: Chapters 21-22

1. What was the origin of the conflict that grew between King George of Great Britain and the 13 American colonies?

   A. The colonies decided to increase their level of trade with France.
   B. Great Britain increased taxes on the colonists to pay for the French and Indian War.
   C. Religious disputes erupted between Catholics and members of the Church of England.
   D. The Crown forbade colonists to travel over the Appalachian Mountains.

2. What was the name of the French legislature up to the beginning of the French Revolution?

   A. Estates General
   B. Directory
   C. Senate
   D. National French Assembly

3. During the beginning of the French Revolution, which specific event led the French people into action?

   A. The calling of the Estates General
   B. The election of King Louis XVI and his marriage to Marie Antoinette
   C. The taking of the Tennis Court Oath
   D. The storming of the Bastille

4. Which leader of the French Revolution was the architect of the Reign of Terror?

   A. Olympe de Gouges
   B. Maximilien Robespierre
   C. Baron de Montesquieu
   D. Marquis de Lafayette

5. In which revolution in Latin America did the slaves and peasants not receive any benefits after gaining independence?

   A. Argentina
   B. Uruguay
   C. Cuba
   D. Haiti

6. Which country had its independence movement led by priests?

   A. Mexico
   B. Brazil
   C. Venezuela
   D. Paraguay

7. Which country was home to the Industrial Revolution?

   A. United States
   B. Germany
   C. Great Britain
   D. France

8. In what region/area did the Industrial Revolution have its beginnings?

   A. Urban cities
   B. Medieval trading centers
   C. Towns located along the routes used by crusaders
   D. Out in the countryside

9. The success of the Industrial Revolution quickly sponsored the growth of which of the following?

   A. Conversion from agriculture to textiles
   B. New waterways and better infrastructure
   C. The growth of new cities
   D. End of feudalism

10. Which of the following problems in society was associated with the Industrial Revolution?

    A. The increased separation of families and child labor
    B. The breakdown of traditional values
    C. The increased isolation of women
    D. The further exclusion of industrial working peasants from political representation

Quick Quiz Answers

1. B; **2.** A; **3.** D; **4.** B; **5.** D; **6.** A; **7.** C; **8.** D; **9.** C; **10.** A

Nationalism in Europe and Russia

23

WHAT IS NATIONALISM?

Nationalism is the patriotic feeling that people have when they are loyal and proud of their country. Nationalism became one of the most powerful political vehicles and forces of the late 19th century into the early 20th century. One of the main principles of nationalism is the idea that one's country is better than all those around them. This was particularly powerful in Western Europe and to a slightly lesser extent in Asia.

Along with pride in one's country, nationalism is the idea that a state or nation is made up of people who are linked together by several factors.

1. They speak a common language.
2. They share the same culture: they dress the same, they practice the same religion, they eat the same type of foods, etc.
3. They have the same type of customs, including holidays or similar rituals.
4. They have a long and shared history that goes back significantly over time.
5. They share the same governments, and historically in Europe, the governments had been monarchies.

Global Connections

The fears raised by the American and French Revolutions led Clemens von Metternich to ask others to suppress revolutions at home to keep the monarchies in power and to assist monarchial neighbors abroad, if necessary.

THE CRIMEAN WAR

In 1856, the Concert of Europe faced its first immediate challenge. The Crimean War broke out after Russia attacked and tried to seize Ottoman lands along the Black Sea and the Danube River in the Crimean Peninsula.

Many Christians went on pilgrimages to the Holy Land and Christian shrines, which took them inside the territory of the Ottoman Empire. To defend their Christian countrymen from Russia while they traveled through the Ottoman Empire, France and Great Britain entered the Crimean War on the side of the Ottoman Empire.

Thus, the Crimean War was Russia against the Ottoman Empire, Great Britain, and France. Russia was defeated, which shattered the idea that Russia was unbeatable (this idea came about when Napoleon failed to defeat them). These three allies—the Ottoman Empire, France, and Great Britain—worked together toward a speedy resolution.

However, the Crimean War demonstrated that the Concert of Europe was unable to solve conflict, igniting the flame of nationalism and allowing other people to form nation-states.

NATIONALISM IN ITALY

The concept of nationalism was something that had existed in Italy for quite some time. They had all five factors needed for nationalism, especially their long history going back to the Roman Empire. Geographically unifying the Italian states into one country should have been easily completed: they shared the same language and traditions. These factors should have linked Italy, giving them the ability to modernize, but everyone who had tried this had failed.

Giuseppe Mazzini and Giuseppe Garibaldi

The northern part of Italy was controlled by the powerful Austria-Habsburg Empire. There were two men, Giuseppe Mazzini and Giuseppe Garibaldi, who wanted a modern republican-democratic government. They advocated using force to drive out the Austrian empire, but most people thought this was way too difficult.

Victor Emmanuel and Count Camillo Cavour

In 1852, the king of the small states of Sardinia and the Piedmont appointed Count Camillo Cavour to be his prime minister. Cavour was a noble, but he also saw the benefits of modernization. As prime minister, Cavour knew that when his king gained power, he would gain power as well. As such, Cavour was willing to do whatever it took to accomplish his goals. Cavour believed that if Italy was unified and demonstrated their modern and industrious economy, then some of the established European powers would help them gain independence from the Austrian-Habsburg Empire.

Cavour had to get rid of Austrian domination of Italy, and he felt the only one that could help him was France and Emperor Napoleon III. Due to Sardinia and the Piedmont's contribution (though minimal) against Russia in the Crimean War, they received a seat at the peace conference ending the war. During the conference, Cavour formed a friendship with Emperor Napoleon III. Napoleon III privately agreed to help Sardinia and the Piedmont in a war against the Austrian-Habsburg Empire.

Cavour Provokes a War

Count Camillo Cavour now had to start a war with the Austrian-Habsburg Empire but he had to make it look like Italy was attacked by the Austrian-Habsburg Empire. The war started in April 1859, becoming known as the Summer War as it occurred between spring planting and fall harvesting. The Austrian-Habsburg Empire was attacked not only by France and Sardinia and the Piedmont but also by the state of Prussia from Germany. The Austrian-Habsburg Empire lost, and, as a result, they had to give up some of their territory in northern Italy.

Encouraged by the victory of Italy over the Austrian-Habsburg Empire, other Italian states joined the kingdom of Sardinia and the Piedmont, and they acknowledged Victor Emmanuel as king of Sardinia and the Piedmont as well as their king.

Total Unification of Italy

With the upset victory over the Austrian-Habsburg Empire, Garibaldi and Mazzini forced the Italian king to work with Prime Minister Cavour to plan for total unification of Italy. Heading to southern Italy and Sicily, Garibaldi landed with 1000 soldiers called the Red Shirts. Cavour provided Garibaldi with weapons and other support. Garibaldi attacked the kingdom of Sicily to bring it into a unified Italy.

However, Garibaldi wanted to unify Italy under a republican government, not a monarchy as Cavour had planned. By the time Garibaldi reached the city of Naples, Cavour had to send out trained troops in order to stop him because Cavour wanted to prevent the formation of a republican Italian government.

At this point, Garibaldi knew he could not win against Cavour. He accepted the rule of King Victor Emmanuel from Sardinia and the Piedmont. In 1861, King Victor Emmanuel was proclaimed king of a unified Italy. It was the first time Italy had been unified since the fall of the Roman Empire.

There were problems for this new, unified Italy. They lacked many natural resources, and for thousands of years, local areas had thought more about themselves than being part of one nation. Try as they might, Italy was never able to achieve the economic and political levels of strength to contest the great European powers. However, Italy was unified, and a new nation was born—or reborn for the first time since the fall of the Roman Empire—in Western Europe.

THE UNIFICATION OF GERMANY

Unifying the 360 German states into one empire and one country was the single most important event in Europe between 1850 and 1930. This act directed events for the continent, and the world, until the end of World War II.

Kingdom of Prussia

In 1862, King Wilhelm I of Prussia turned to a Prussian noble named Otto von Bismarck to help unify Germany. Bismarck believed in traditional, noble ideals that made his country strong: the monarchy, the nobility, and a strong military. Otto von Bismarck accomplished what no one had been able to do since Charlemagne: unify the 360 German states into one modern, powerful nation.

Bismarck had sharpened and honed his political skills while serving as an ambassador to France and Russia. He studied the people in the government, gauged their reaction to decisions, and learned their languages. He also had an amazingly strong will. When he wanted to see something happen, he could make it happen. He often used his uncanny ability to make people do things that he wanted them to do, while making them believe it was their idea in the first place.

Realpolitik

Perhaps what set Bismarck apart from his contemporaries was his mastery of the concept of realpolitik. Realpolitik was realistic goals and policies based not on what the state wanted but solely on what the state needed. Bismarck believed that, no matter what, the end justified the means. He was a master of large-scale planning, and his goal was not total unification but to gain power for his king, thus giving himself more power. This allowed Bismarck to have a free hand in running Prussia. He made decisions that seemed harsh and horrible, but to Bismarck, they were absolutely necessary.

The Prussian Parliament

Otto von Bismarck wanted to strengthen the Prussian army and raise taxes, but he was blocked by the Prussian Parliament, who was trying to gain more power over the monarchy. Bismarck found provisions in the Prussian Constitution that allowed him to collect old, overdue taxes. With this provision, he could collect and spend money without having to go through Parliament. The Prussian Parliament fought him on this issue, and in the 1863 elections, Bismarck's political party lost many seats. However, he was already building a massive new army. To deal with the losses in Parliament, he decided to redirect the country's attention from the political situation at home and focus the people on something different. The easiest way to do that was to start a war, but just like Italy, he decided to make it look like it was somebody else's fault.

War with Denmark

In 1864, Bismarck sought to liberate the German-speaking states of the kingdom of Denmark, located just due north of what is today Germany. Bismarck formed an alliance with the Austrian-Habsburg Empire to solidify their chances of winning. After Denmark's defeat, Bismarck fairly split the newly liberated states between Austria-Habsburg and Prussia. Austria-Habsburg received the southern state of Holstein, while Prussia got the northern state of Schleswig.

War with the Austrian-Habsburg Empire

Now that he had used Austria-Habsburg to win the war with Denmark, Bismarck was ready to form a more formidable alliance with France. In 1866, Bismarck declared war on the Austrian-Habsburg Empire, joining in a new alliance with France. Then, France and Sardinia and the Piedmont attacked Austria-Habsburg on behalf of their new ally, Prussia. The war lasted only seven weeks, and the Austrian-Habsburg Empire was defeated. Bismarck annexed some territory from Austria-Habsburg, saying it was now part of Prussia. Always the master politician, Bismarck let Austria-Habsburg keep four southern states, allowing the country to "save face" and also to avoid another war with the empire in case they wanted their territory back.

The outcome of the wars with Denmark and the Austrian-Habsburg Empire was that Bismarck had added territory to Prussia, increasing the power of King Wilhelm.

Franco-Prussian War

France was not pleased with the outcome of their alliance with Prussia. The ease with which the new army of Prussia defeated the Austrian-Habsburg Empire worried French Emperor Napoleon III. A growing rivalry developed between France and Prussia, exploding into war in 1870.

The Franco-Prussian War started over the vacated Spanish throne. The next in line to the throne of Spain was a cousin of King Wilhelm I. France immediately protested. They felt threatened as they did not want to be boxed in between King Wilhelm of Prussia and a family member in Spain.

Otto von Bismarck gave a key speech in Prussia, bringing up memories of the threat of the "specter of Napoleon." Reminding the people what Napoleon did to Europe earlier in the century, Bismarck said the French were just hiding behind the border, waiting to attack them again. Bismarck spoke of German nationalism and superiority. He said countries are not made stronger by speeches and majority votes but by blood and iron. That was what separated Germany from everybody else, Bismarck said. Germany was a strong unified nation and did not need idle talk to decide its fate.

Meanwhile, France's Napoleon III was having his own political and economic troubles at home. There were negotiations between Napoleon III and King Wilhelm as they tried to work out a peaceful settlement. When Bismarck intercepted a message going from King Wilhelm to Napoleon—now called the Ems Dispatch—Bismarck edited it. He changed the tone and reply from Wilhelm to one that insulted France. When French honor was insulted, Napoleon III declared war. Once again, Bismarck made it look like it was somebody else's fault.

The vastly superior Prussian army hammered the French, and they were forced to surrender. As a final insult to the French, the surrender was signed in the Hall of Mirrors at Versailles. Versailles was seen as the home of French monarchical power, and in the same room as the throne of Louis XIV, Napoleon III signed the surrender to Germany. The country of Germany/Prussia became an empire.

King Wilhelm I took the title of kaiser, meaning "Caesar." German nationalists began to call Wilhelm's reign the Second Reich, after King Otto's Holy Roman Empire in the year 900. In just a matter of years, Bismarck had dealt devastating and damaging blows to two major European empires: Austria-Habsburg (the oldest monarchy in Europe) and France. Before Bismarck, Germany and Prussia were barely in the top 10 of major powers in Europe. Now, Germany vaulted itself into a leading role as the number two superpower, just behind Great Britain (who held onto power for the simple fact that Great Britain had already industrialized). Unified Germany was now a power to be reckoned with.

Prussian Constitution

Bismarck wrote a constitution where there was a bicameral legislature, allowing all men to vote. Bismarck also included that all power still flowed through the king and his second in command, the chancellor. Bismarck was the chancellor! Bismarck affected international politics up through the year 1900. One of the key items that Bismarck put into the constitution was Article 48. Article 48 harkened back to ancient Rome, stating that in times of crisis, a dictator could come to power to solve the crisis. Unfortunately, Article 48 was used by Adolf Hitler in 1933 to gain power over Germany and was a major factor in starting World War II.

NATIONALISM IN THE AUSTRIAN-HABSBURG EMPIRE

Nationalism was able to unite the people in Italy and in Germany. However, the old world empires of Austria-Habsburg and the Ottomans began to fade. The Austrian-Habsburg Empire and the Ottoman Empire both ruled large, multiethnic peoples. The many ethnic groups began to each have nationalist feelings and wanted a country of their own. It caused these peoples to break free of their old world masters.

The Makeup of Austria-Habsburg

By the year 1800, the Austrian-Habsburg Empire was the oldest ruling dynasty in Europe. They had territory throughout much of Eastern Europe from the Ukraine and Poland into what is today the Czech Republic and Slovakia. Their empire was large, multiethnic, and diverse. A large part of their empire was the country of Hungary.

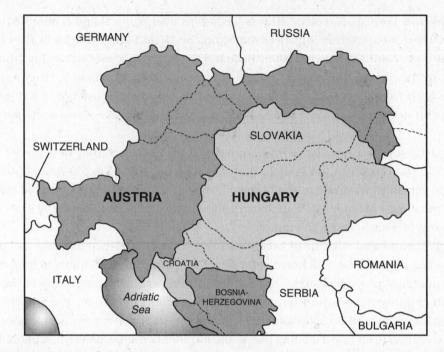

Since the conclusion of the Congress of Vienna in 1815, Emperor Francis I and his Prime Minister Clemens von Metternich worked hard to reassert absolutism throughout the empire. Any writings or speeches containing the word *constitution* were outlawed. While everyone else around them was rapidly industrializing due to the Industrial Revolution, the Austrian-Habsburg Empire tried to stay traditional. They limited the amount of industrialization inside the empire, which spread discontent among the workers. The Austria-Habsburg Empire was governing nearly 50 million people. German-speaking Austrians made up approximately 25 percent of the country, and they had nationalist feelings and demands. Instead of talking to the people, the rulers of the Austria-Habsburg Empire ignored their pleas. There were a few revolts in 1848, and they were quickly and brutally crushed. However, the rest of Europe was keeping an eye on Austria-Habsburg. They controlled a large part of Eastern Europe, and the stability of Europe was at stake.

When the Austrian-Habsburg Empire was defeated by France, Sardinia and the Piedmont, and Prussia, Emperor Francis I realized that in order to strengthen his grip on his empire, reforms were needed. His answer was to create a constitution that set up a parliamentary legislature. However, this was just a smoke screen. The legislature was dominated by German-speaking noble Austrians. It accomplished absolutely nothing except upsetting many of the citizens of the empire, especially the Hungarians.

The Dual Monarchy

Because of the outcries of the Hungarians, Emperor Francis I reached a compromise by supporting Hungarian nationalism. The Austrian-Habsburg Empire became a dual monarchy. In 1867, Emperor Franz Joseph was the emperor of the Austrian Empire, and at the same time, Franz Joseph was also the king of an independent Hungary. The two countries shared finances, foreign affairs, and defense ministries but were separated in all other areas. The Hungarians welcomed this as a compromise.

However, most other minority groups, especially Czechs, were angry at being left out. They called for all other Slavic people of Russian descent to unite by claiming, "only through liberty, equality and fraternal solidarity" could Slavic peoples fulfill their "great mission in the history of mankind." Many of these minority nationalities thought that they deserved to be independent states or part of the Russian empire, whom they depended upon for protection. Also, while the greater German population in Austria stayed loyal to Emperor Franz Joseph, there were some who would not have minded being assimilated into Bismarck's growing, young, and vital Germany.

Foreshadowing

There were three big empires—Austria-Habsburg, Germany, and Russia. All three were home to large numbers of ethnic Poles, plus a minimum of two other ethnic groups, all of whom had nationalistic tendencies. Also, each ethnic group focused on its own local interests and did not really worry about the empire as a whole. These populations had a major effect on each of the three empires from 1867 through World War I. Nationalism was the first spark that ignited the flame of World War I.

NATIONALISM IN RUSSIA

By the year 1800, Russia was the largest and most densely populated country in Europe. Russia was also blessed with tremendous natural resources, perfect for industrialization. The sheer size of the country—running from the Baltic Sea to the Black Sea all the way to the Pacific Ocean—gave it global capacity and influence.

However, Russia was nearly always rejected by the West, which did not like their old world style of government. Some czars, such as Peter and Catherine, tried to bring westernization to Russia, but it was the boyars (Russian nobles) and weak czars that constantly held it back. They were afraid that westernization and modernization would threaten their absolute position of rule.

In the West, the Enlightenment and the French Revolution had influenced reforms, but these reforms had no effect on the Russian czars. In 1800, Czar Alexander I thought about making reforms, but Napoleon's invasion of Russia in 1812 changed his mind. At the Congress of Vienna, Czar Alexander I agreed with Metternich when it came to suppressing any thought or action that could threaten his monarchy.

In 1825, Alexander I died. A group of his army officers, who had learned of Western ideas while fighting Napoleon, led what is known as the Decembrist Revolt, demanding democratic reforms. The new czar, Nicholas I, brutally put down those rebellions. He outlawed Western books, jailed intellectuals, and used secret police to root out people who opposed his regime.

Czar Nicholas I built Russia on three pillars to reassert his absolutism.

1. He stressed orthodoxy—strong ties between the church and his government.
2. He believed in autocracy—the absolute, unquestioned power of his government.
3. The idea of nationalism—a respect for Russian traditions and ideals.

Any group that disagreed with Czar Nicholas was eliminated. However, Nicholas saw that there was a need to modernize his country and make necessary economic reforms to compete with the West. He could not think of a way to do it without upsetting the boyars. Then, Russia got involved in the Crimean War in 1853, and Czar Nicholas I died in 1855. On his deathbed, he told his son, Alexander II, "I wanted to take everything difficult, everything serious, upon my shoulders and to leave you a peaceful, well-ordered, and happy realm. Providence decreed otherwise. Now I go to pray for Russia and for you all."

Reforms of Alexander II and Attempts at Modernization

Seeing the debacle of the Crimean War, Czar Alexander II knew that reforms were not only necessary but at long last possible as many of his people were demanding reform. In 1861, he announced an end to the centuries-old policy of serfdom in Russia, much to the dismay of the Russian boyars.

It was not an easy process. There was little immediate effect or benefit for the people who were freed from serfdom. The serfs were given some land, but it was too small to support their families. They had to pay for their new land with mortgages lasting almost 50 years. This increased the resentment felt toward the government.

Getting rid of serfdom also meant that the Russian government had to reorganize itself. Instead of boyars collecting taxes, providing education, and maintaining infrastructure, it was local village officials known as zemstvos who oversaw everything. A new judicial system was also created.

Even though new industry was embraced, and young men and women were encouraged to head West to bring back ideas that would help modernize Russia (like Peter the Great), none of the reforms worked out.

Problems with Reform

When Czar Alexander II's reforms did not work, the high hopes of his people, especially among students and other intellectuals, quickly came to a halt. They formed a movement in the 1870s that became known as populism. Populism was a grassroots movement that believed that all people should be equal. The Populist movement in Russia was called "Land and Freedom." Coming on the heels of Karl Marx's *Communist Manifesto*, the Land and Freedom movement staged a revolution founded on communal life.

The idea of the Land and Freedom movement was that students would educate the Russian peasants, who made up the bulk of the society, to gain their trust and prepare them for the upcoming revolution. However, the peasants did not trust the students and turned them over to the Russian police. Czar Alexander II was lenient, and the penalties were very light. However, he let it be known that if this happened again, heavy penalties would be handed down.

After the crackdown, the Land and Freedom movement split apart. A more radical group formed in 1879, known as the People's Will. They were dedicated to completely overthrowing the czar. They decided the only way to do this was to assassinate him, and in March 1881, Czar Alexander II was assassinated. Czar Alexander II's reign is now known for two things: his attempt at reform and the major opposition against him.

Alexander III

Alexander III ruled more like his grandfather, and he responded to his father's assassination swiftly and brutally. After quickly killing his father's assassins, he repealed reforms and decided to increase the power of the czar by recentralizing the government. Alexander III strengthened the secret police and unleashed them on the people. His goal was to suppress the cultures of all non-Russian people, and he deemed Russia would have one language, one church, and one government. These actions confirmed in the minds of the revolutionaries that Russia should no longer have an absolute government with direct control over the Russian people. Czar Alexander III sowed the seeds of doom for his family. The Romanov Dynasty ended with their murders in 1918.

1800 C.E.	Habsburgs of Austria are the oldest ruling house in Europe.
1814–1815 C.E.	Congress of Vienna
1815 C.E.	• Russia is the largest and most populated country in Europe.
	• Czar Alexander I of Russia sees the need to modernize, but boyars will not back him.
1840s C.E.	• Austria-Habsburg Empire is industrialized.
	• Majority of people in Austria-Habsburg are Slavic, and begin to ask for independence.
1848 C.E.	Austrian government violently puts down attempts at nationalism.
1852 C.E.	Victor Emmanuel of Italy names Count Camillo Cavour as Prime Minister of Sardinia and the Piedmont.
1853–1856 C.E.	Crimean War
1855 C.E.	• Cavour of Italy gives support to England and France during Crimean War.
	• Czar Alexander II of Russia comes to throne during Crimean War.
1856 C.E.	After loss in Crimean War, Czar Alexander II now knows reforms are necessary in Russia.
1858 C.E.	Cavour of Italy achieves secret alliance with France.
1859 C.E.	• Cavour of Italy provokes a war with Austria-Habsburg.
	• Defeat by Prussia and Sardinia forces Franz Joseph of Austria to focus on his empire at home.
1860 C.E.	Cavour supplies Italian nationalist Giuseppe Garibaldi with weapons to attack separate kingdoms in the south of Italy.
1861 C.E.	• Victor Emmanuel II is crowned king of Italy.
	• Russia emancipates surfs.
1862 C.E.	• Otto von Bismarck is made Prime Minister of Prussia.
	• Russia begins further reforms on Three Pillar system—many do not work.
1864 C.E.	• Bismarck makes alliance with Austria-Habsburg.
	• Prussia defeats Denmark and acquires duchies of Schleswig and Holstein.
1866 C.E.	• Bismarck attacks Austria-Habsburg.
	• Austria-Prussian War: Austria loses the war to Prussia.
1867 C.E.	Dual monarchy is created with Austrian emperor and king of Hungary.
1870 C.E.	Franco-Prussian War begins.
1871 C.E.	• Prussia defeats France.
	• William I of Prussia becomes Kaiser Wilhelm I of a united Germany.
	• Germany's unification makes it an industrial power.
1878 C.E.	People's Will Movement begins in Russia.
1878–1880 C.E.	Czar Alexander II of Russia cracks down on protestors and movements.
1879 C.E.	Land and Freedom revolutionary group forms in Russia.
1881 C.E.	• Czar Alexander II is assassinated.
	• Czar Alexander III repeals reforms, brutally represses dissent.

Nationalism in Asia

24

China and Japan experienced nationalism a little later than Western Europe. The nationalist movements in China and Japan are intertwined, which can get confusing. In this chapter, many of the same historical events will be shown from the perspective of China and Japan during their nationalist movements.

NATIONALISM IN CHINA

In 1912, the last Chinese emperor, Puyi, left the throne, after it was given to him in 1908 when he was two years old. The Chinese system of monarchies was thousands of years old, going back to the Shang Dynasty, and the system ended in 1912 with the Qing Dynasty.

China entered a new era, and they were not sure what to do. The leading statesman of China, Sun Yat-sen, was named the first president of the Chinese republic. Sun Yat-sen faced an uphill battle as China had known nothing but dynastic emperors for 4000 years. On top of that, for nearly the next four decades, China was either fighting an internal civil war or defending itself from different foreign invasions, both economic and physical.

In 1912, Sun Yat-sen turned his power over to a military leader named Yuan Shikai. Being a military man, Yuan was accustomed to having things be in order. To that end, he created a strong centralized government that was streamlined along military beliefs. However, Yuan wanted to institute himself as an emperor, while the borderland warlords disagreed and reasserted their own control. As a result, the Chinese peasants were trapped in the middle of warring leaders and had to pay the price.

Foreign Domination

Foreigners began to dominate Chinese ports and exert their influence over China. In 1915, the growing Asian power of Japan issued a list of 21 demands to the Chinese government. The demands would have made the Chinese empire part of the Japanese state. This was insulting to China as more than one thousand years earlier, China had given ideas and technology to Japan, allowing them to become a nation. And after the Treaty of Versailles, China was further infuriated when the victorious powers gave German colonies in China to Japan.

The May Fourth Movement

On May 4, 1919, Chinese students began to protest the actions of Japan in the city of Beijing. The May Fourth Movement to strengthen China quickly spread. Their slogan was "China's territory may be conquered, but it cannot be given away. The Chinese people may be massacred, but they will not surrender." The students began to organize boycotts of Japanese goods. Ironically, the students hoped that Western science, technology, and political ideas (like democracy) would solve China's problems and end foreign domination. Initially, they rejected what had always been there to help them, like the ideas of Confucianism.

Return of Sun Yat-sen

Sun Yat-sen was seen as the father of Chinese nationalism. He had studied and traveled extensively in the West. Before the last emperor died in the early 1900s, he helped organize the idea of Chinese nationalism, which, like Russia, was built on three pillars.

1. Nationalism would provide a way for China to break free from foreign domination.
2. China would form some type of Republican representative democracy.
3. Chinese resources would be used to provide economic security for the people of China.

In 1921, Sun Yat-sen created his nationalist party, known as the Kuomintang (KMT). However, after forming the party, Sun Yat-sen was not able to make much progress. He turned to the democratic West to get help. Unfortunately, the Western powers in Europe were trying to recover from the devastation of World War I. The United States was still bristling from the treatment they received at the hands of the European powers and had entered isolation. No one listened to China, which was a big mistake. When the West would not help Sun Yat-sen, he had to choose a different option. He went to the Soviet Union, and he would later claim that they were the only real friends of China.

Chiang Kai-shek and the Crucial Year of 1925

Sun Yat-sen sent his most trusted aide, Lieutenant Chiang Kai-shek, to the Soviet Union to study. He was supposed to be gone for a couple of years but returned a few short months later with an entourage of Soviet advisers. Upon returning, Chiang Kai-shek created a Chinese military academy to form an army for the KMT nationalist party.

In 1925, university students began to protest the treatment of Chinese workers and the presence of foreign-owned factories in the large port city of Shanghai. Police fired on the demonstrators, hoping to drive them off, but instead it only fueled the anger of the people. The nationalist movement really began to grow.

Also in 1925, Sun Yat-sen died, which was unfortunate as this was a very crucial time for China. The Army had about 100,000 soldiers, and the KMT political party had about 200,000 members. They were clearly the largest political force in the country, but their leadership rarely agreed. Further complicating the problem were the changes that were taking place in Chinese society. As a result of the new government, industry grew and so did cities. The workers began to form unions, and a middle class was created that wanted broader political representation. China was experiencing the growing pains that Europe had gone through 150 years earlier.

Creation of the Chinese Communist Party

One major side effect of the students being fired upon in Shanghai was the creation of the Chinese Communist Party known as the CCP. This party was popular with students and labor unions. Before his death, Sun Yat-sen let some communists join the KMT. He felt that together, they could work in cooperation with the upper middle class in the national struggle against foreign imperialism.

Chiang Kai-shek Responds: The KMT vs. the CCP

In 1926, Chiang Kai-shek went into the northwestern part of China with his army to quell the unruly warlords that were ravaging the countryside. Suddenly and inexplicably, he stopped to attack the Chinese communists as he believed they were going to undermine his authority. After this, Chiang Kai-shek enjoyed the support of wealthy business owners and large land-owners who did not like communist ideas interfering with their workforce.

In 1927, Chiang Kai-shek ordered a Stalin-like purge of the leadership of the CCP, plus he killed many urban industrial workers that supported them. The public outcry and anger over the killing of the Chinese workers caused problems for Chiang for the next 20 years. When the CCP realized they could not entice large numbers of the KMT to join them, they were forced to flee into the mountains.

Chiang was now the central figure in the new government in the capital of Nanking. Chiang was a strict military leader who liked to be feared, and he was also seen as incorrupt-ible. His power rested on the strength of the army and the dominance of the Nationalist Party running the government. Chiang also created a secret police to ferret out Chinese commu-nists. Chiang became the official president of the KMT.

Mao Tse-tung

Chiang had a rival in the CCP named Mao Tse-tung. Mao had escaped Chiang's purge, and he felt that the way for China to gain power was through the support of the overwhelming number of Chinese peasants. Though he was constantly hunted by Chiang Kai-shek's forces, Mao gave a great quote, "A single spark can start a prairie fire."

Japanese Invasion

To make matters worse for China, the Japanese invaded the Chinese province of Manchuria in 1931. Japan wanted to add Manchuria's natural resources to their growing empire. Chiang's generals were waiting for Chiang to mobilize and hunt down the Japanese. Instead, he squan-dered his resources and said that the Chinese army stood no chance against the power of the Japanese. Chiang was forced to bury the hatchet with the CCP and form a united front against the Japanese. China was successful for the next five or six years. By 1937, the KMT and Chiang Kai-shek once again controlled most of China. The KMT also won recognition from Western powers as the official government.

The Long March

Even though the KMT and CCP fought together against Japan, Mao Tse-tung was being hunted by Chiang Kai-shek's forces. From 1934 to 1935, Mao led 90,000 Chinese commu-nists on a journey of 6000 miles across difficult terrain in the interior of China. Only 20,000 survived, but during the Long March, Mao told his followers, "Be nice to the peasants. If you need something, offer to pay for it. If you can't pay, offer to work for it. Do not steal or destroy property." Following these rules, Mao was able to gain acceptance by the Chinese peasants. Russian populists tried this with their Land and Freedom movement and failed; however, it actually worked in China. Mao Tse-tung began to set up a government inside of China.

The Japanese Return

In 1937, the Japanese renewed their attacks, this time in the heartland of China. The Japanese were going for all-out defeat. Chiang was forced to flee into the center of China, and he was joined by thousands of urban workers and students. Chiang's resistance was admirable but pointless as the CCP had already taken over inside China, including areas that the KMT had controlled. Chiang was separated from his people. The United States sent equipment to assist him against the Japanese, but Chiang wanted to save it to use on the communists and not on the Japanese.

Japanese Invasion Assists Mao

Oddly enough, it was the invasion of the Japanese that provided a ripe opportunity for Mao Tse-tung to seize power. With Chiang on the run himself, Mao now had a break from being hunted. He consolidated his power, and his people began to educate the peasants and promote literacy in the villages. He had the peasants form village councils and taught them how to self-govern. The kind way that he treated them gained Mao widespread support.

1937–1945

By the end of World War II in 1945, the Chinese Communist Party had gained 1.2 million members, which was larger than the KMT. Mao Tse-tung now reigned supreme. He gave himself to the people as the true heir and successor to Sun Yat-sen, even though he believed in Lenin-style communism. Even though Chiang and the KMT ruled China through government-appointed officials and aristocratic landlords, Mao had created a grassroots bureaucracy and an army of nearly one million soldiers. His charisma and leadership linked the people of China together with him as their leader in a manner that Chiang never could understand.

End of World War II

Global Connections

It was very similar to the way the rich people of Rome fled Rome for Byzantium centuries earlier.

When World War II ended in 1945, the United States forced Japan to surrender to Chiang Kai-shek and the KMT since they were still the official government of China. Shortly after, a Chinese civil war broke out. In 1947, just two short years later, Mao and his communist army went on the offensive, and in 1949, Mao Tse-tung achieved control of China. He was now known as Chairman Mao. Many intellectuals and big businessmen fled mainland China to the islands of Hong Kong and Taiwan.

Overall, the people of China saw Chairman Mao as a liberator. For the first time in hundreds of years, China was controlled and ruled by Chinese, and their future rested upon them, not imperial powers.

NATIONALISM IN JAPAN: 1850–1945 C.E.

In 1853, the isolated Japanese islands were shocked when Commodore Perry of the United States sailed into Tokyo Bay, demonstrating the advanced technology of the U.S. Commodore Perry forced Japan to sign a Treaty of Friendship, which began a new era for Japan.

The Japanese were forced to take an introspective look at themselves. They realized that their perfect society had fallen behind the rest of the world. The Japanese saw themselves as perfectly civilized Confucian believers, but the world saw the Japanese as mindless barbarians. After seeing Perry's technology, they could no longer afford to believe in Japanese superiority.

Fukuzawa Yukichi

As in the past, the Japanese sent out aristocratic, educated young men to figure out how to help Japan. When a young man named Fukuzawa Yukichi went abroad across the Pacific Ocean, he spent all his time in the engine room of the steamship, talking to the mechanics and operators. Fukuzawa Yukichi invented a more efficient steam engine.

Fukuzawa Yukichi also brought Western ideas about science, government, economics, and legal systems back to Japan. He explained to the Japanese that the Western way of life was intertwined with their freedom. He said that freedom must exist because it was the independent spirit that drove them to better themselves. In the West, people put their hearts into their jobs, and they made more money because they worked for it. People who put forth the minimum effort had no chance to advance.

The Japanese Constitution

At the end of the 19th century, Japan realized all of its efforts by becoming the first non-Western country to build a modern nation-state. It had progressed toward its goal: to rival the wealth and power of the industrialized West. Political parties had formed, drawing on Western ideas. The right to hold elections was written into the Constitution to inspire the people to work their hardest. The national assembly was created to unite the emperor to his people, getting rid of the old traditional ways.

The Japanese Constitution was written based on Otto von Bismarck's model from Prussia. They adapted it and made it fit for Japan, giving the emperor great power and limiting the power of the Japanese legislature, known as the Diet. The emperor was still seen as sacred and incorruptible. When the Diet was not in session, he commanded the military, was able to appoint the prime minister, and issued imperial decrees. The Constitution was presented as a gift to the Japanese people from the emperor. Japan had industrialized and was now going to show the world what it could do.

War with China

From 1894 through 1895, Japan went to war with China over interests in Asia. Japan gained territory, and they also forced China to sign an agreement saying that if any Japanese businesses or factories in China were threatened, the Japanese military could intervene. When the Chinese rebelled, Japan sent in their troops. This incident is known as the Boxer Rebellion, and Japan achieved victory.

With the signing of the business agreement and success of putting down the Boxer Rebellion, the Japanese were looking for a bigger target to showcase their power. They secured an alliance with the United States and England that said if Japan went to war with Russia, the other Western powers would not intercede.

War with Russia

The Japanese declared war on Russia in 1906. They destroyed the Russian fleet, but it quickly turned into a stalemate. United States President Teddy Roosevelt wrote a peace treaty to end the conflict that heavily favored Japan. However, even with this, Japan felt they were still on the receiving end of treaties that more heavily favored the West instead of them. They decided to enter the imperialism race to grab colonies in order to compete with the West.

The Empire of the Rising Sun Is Created

Emperor Hirohito reigned from 1926 to 1989. During the 1920s, Japan started to move toward democracy as their political party system. All males in Japan were allowed to vote. During World War I, the Japanese industrial economy achieved incredible growth since much of the West was embroiled in fighting. Other countries sought goods made by the Japanese, and it gave them a free hand to expand into Asia.

Internal Struggles

Unfortunately, problems arose toward the close of the 1920s. Urban workers were enjoying a newfound prosperity, which caused problems in society. Young people had begun to emulate the West in their dress and entertainment. They had forgotten the age-old, traditional Japanese values of discipline and respect. There was also a growing rivalry between the military and the civilian government. Military officers said the Western influence had corrupted the Japanese governments, and Japan needed to return to the old way of doing things.

Effects of the Great Depression

The Great Depression was one of the final blows. As Japan was recovering from an earthquake, the Great Depression hit it hard. Japanese items were of such good quality that foreign buyers could no longer afford to buy Japanese products. With a backlog of goods in warehouses, companies were forced to lay off many workers. This unemployment fed the discontent of the extreme nationalists and military leaders, who said this was the government's fault for giving into Western demands. Western powers had taken over across the globe. Their question was, "Why couldn't Japan do the same thing?"

Global Connections

The exact same situation with unemployment occurred in Germany during the Great Depression, and it gave rise to the Nazi Party and Adolf Hitler.

Japanese Nationalists Angry at World Status

Another thing that made the nationalist movement grow in Japan was that Western countries—like the United States, Canada, and Australia—had closed their borders to Japanese immigrants. Japan was proud of their industrial achievements, and banning Japanese from Western countries was an insult. The Japanese military felt that, once again, Japan needed to expand into new colonies to force the West to recognize them.

During the invasion of Manchuria in 1931, the Japanese military intentionally blew up a section of the Japanese railroad and then said the Chinese did it. They needed an excuse to enact the rules of the treaty, which allowed their army to intervene and take over. Overwhelmingly, the Japanese population stood behind the army, so they began to expand their military at home and in Asia.

Revival of the Samurai

By the early 1930s, Japanese nationalists enjoyed overwhelming support for foreign conquest and finally stood up to the Western powers. By 1937, the government was dominated by military men. They ended democratic reform and tried to get rid of socialists and communists.

To promote their platform, they revived the ancient samurai warrior values. School children were taught absolute obedience to the emperor, and that the greatest thing they could do is lay down their lives for the emperor when it came to total war.

Japan also took advantage of the ongoing conflict in China between Chiang Kai-shek and Mao Tse-tung to grab more territory in China. When Japan invaded China in 1937, they wanted a quick victory, which did not happen. When World War II broke out and spread to Asia, Japan joined the Rome to Berlin axis.

In order to secure resources for their growing empire, they made a grave mistake. On December 7, 1941, they attacked their one-time ally, the United States. Japan's Admiral Yamamoto said, "I fear we have awoken the sleeping giant."

TIMELINE REVIEW

1600–1853 C.E.	Japan is isolated from the world.
1853 C.E.	U.S. Admiral Perry signs Treaty of Friendship with Japan.
1859 C.E.	Fukuzawa Yukichi of Japan makes first trip to the U.S.
1867 C.E.	Bakufu government system collapses in Japan.
1868–1912 C.E.	Meiji Restoration in Japan
1889 C.E.	New Japanese Constitution gives power to emperor.
1894–1895 C.E.	War between Japan and China
1899 C.E.	Boxer Rebellion in China
1901 C.E.	Sun Yat-sen in China: Three Principles of the People
1904–1905 C.E.	Russo-Japanese War
1908 C.E.	Empress Cixi of China dies—2-year-old inherits the throne.
1910 C.E.	Japan annexes Korea as a colony.
1911 C.E.	• Qing Dynasty falls in China. • Sun Yat-sen is named president of Chinese Republic.
1912 C.E.	Sun Yat-sen steps down as leader of China and appoints Yuan Shikai as replacement.
1918 C.E.	Japan is invited to Paris Peace Conference (Treaty of Versailles).
1919 C.E.	May Fourth Movement in China
1921 C.E.	• Sun Yat-sen forms Kuomintang Chinese Nationalist Party (KMT). • Chiang Kai-shek of China is sent to study in the Soviet Union.
1923 C.E.	Major earthquake hits Tokyo.
1925 C.E.	• Chiang Kai-shek of China assumes power of KMT after the death of Sun Yat-sen. • Communist Party of China is formed.
1926 C.E.	Chiang Kai-shek and KMT attack warlords in northern China.
1926–1986 C.E.	Reign of Emperor Hirohito in Japan
1927–1949 C.E.	China Civil War
1929 C.E.	Great Depression hits Japan.
1931 C.E.	Japan invades Manchuria.
1932 C.E.	Ultranationalists rise to power in Japan.
1934–1935 C.E.	Mao Tse-tung leads Chinese communists on "Long March."

1937 C.E.	• Japan invades China.
	• Chiang Kai-shek is recognized by international community as leader of China.
1940 C.E.	Japan, Germany, and Italy become the Axis Powers.
1941 C.E.	Japan attacks the U.S. at Pearl Harbor.
1945 C.E.	• Japan signs WWII surrender.
	• U.S. makes Japan surrender to Chinese leader Chiang Kai-shek.
1947–1949 C.E.	• Chiang Kai-shek fights Mao Tse-tung for leadership of China.
	• Mao Tse-tung achieves victory and becomes supreme leader of China.

Quick Quiz: Chapters 23–24

1. Which event or meeting was held to sort out Europe's problems after the French Revolution?

    A. The Treaty of Paris
    B. The Berlin Conference
    C. The Dual Monarchy
    D. The Congress of Vienna

2. In which European country did the concept of nationalism as a way to encourage unification make the most sense?

    A. Germany
    B. Austria
    C. Italy
    D. Russia

3. Which country/empire was attacked by three countries in one summer and, as a result, suffered a loss in territory?

    A. Russia
    B. Austria
    C. Germany
    D. France

4. Which event signaled to Czar Nicholas I of Russia that reforms were finally necessary?

    A. The Crimean War
    B. The Congress of Vienna
    C. The creation of the dual monarchy
    D. The Franco-Prussian War

5. Who was the father of Chinese nationalism?

    A. Chiang Kai-shek
    B. Mao Tse-tung
    C. Sun Yat-sen
    D. Yuan Shikai

6. Which action was taken by students in China to protest abuses by foreign countries?

    A. The Great Leap Forward
    B. The May Fourth Movement
    C. The movement of Chinese people to Hong Kong
    D. Tiananmen Square protests

7. Who did Sun Yat-sen consider to be the one true friend of the Chinese people?

    A. The United States

    B. The Soviet Union

    C. Emperor Hirohito of Japan

    D. Mao Tse-tung

8. During the Chinese civil war, which country inadvertently aided Mao Tse-tung by giving him time to build support for the Communist Party?

    A. The U.S. giving aid to Chiang Kai-shek

    B. The Japanese invasion of China

    C. The success of the Russian Revolution

    D. The separation of India and Pakistan

9. Who opened Japan after centuries of self-imposed isolation?

    A. Commodore Perry

    B. Fukuzawa Yukichi

    C. Ferdinand Magellan

    D. Chester Nimitz

10. What grave mistake was made by the government of Japan as a result of the success of their nationalism?

    A. They did not implement the constitution they had written.

    B. They attacked the U.S. Naval base at Pearl Harbor.

    C. The government did not reward the people after accomplishing so many long-term goals.

    D. Many zaibatsu failed to renew economic trading treaties with Western countries.

Quick Quiz Answers

1. D; **2.** C; **3.** B; **4.** A; **5.** C; **6.** B; **7.** B; **8.** B; **9.** A; **10.** B

Imperialism and New Imperialism

25

Dinner Table Talk

In my classroom, I named this the Big Box Effect. When a larger chain store moves into a small town, it puts all the mom-and-pop businesses out of business. The Big Box chain dominates that region.

Imperialism is when one country is able to exert their power and influence over a weaker country either through diplomatic means or, when that fails, military power. The stronger country uses its influence to take over and exploit a weaker one. Combined with nationalism, imperialism fueled the Western world and was a driving force behind World War I.

MOTIVES AND REASONS FOR IMPERIALISM

One of the motives for imperialism was that the Europeans believed that their way of life and their civilization was clearly better and superior to all those around the world. The Europeans believed that it was their mission and responsibility to help the people in what they saw as backward, or inferior, territories. Coupled with this was a religious drive and competition to convert the natives to Christianity.

Perhaps the biggest motivation for European imperialism was economic. In Western societies, powerful industrial businesses needed either raw materials or extra space to grow. A natural extension was for them to move to the so-called inferior countries where there were no industrial economies.

The third motive was military. Europeans were always competitive. If France gobbled up a country, then England wanted three countries, and then Germany would want to keep up with everyone else. The belief in imperialism meant Europeans continued to increase the number of imperial colonies. European countries also sought to have colonies that bordered their opponents to maintain the balance of power. Eventually, European countries would colonize anywhere. It did not matter if it was useful or not because if they had it, then their competitors would not have it!

> **FUN FACT**
>
> A good modern example is the New York Yankees baseball team. They will put a player on the Yankees roster and pay him a large sum of money just so they don't have to compete against him! They may not need him, but at least their competitors wouldn't have him.

Western Advantages

It was industrialization, the ability to mass-produce items, strong militaries, and the invention of the steam engine that gave Europe the ability to impose its will on other people. The Europeans opened up Africa as they never could before. For example, with the steam engine, they could sail up to a waterfall, whereas before they could not. With their technology, they could build a railroad around the waterfall, whereas before they could not.

They also had the mindset that while imperialization was about making money, they were also doing a good thing by helping to industrialize inferior countries. The industrialized world did not care what was happening to native populations because it did not impact them. All they knew was they were making money, and they were getting the natural resources they needed.

KING LEOPOLD II OF BELGIUM MOVES INTO AFRICA

Going back to the late 1400s, Europeans moved around the coast of Africa. By the 1800s, European countries began to explore the interior of Africa. They followed rivers to their source in order to map the interior. They discovered Mount Kilimanjaro and Lake Victoria. Since Africa is such a large continent, several times larger than Europe, the people, culture, and languages are very diverse. People had existed in Africa for millennia, and now European governments were hiring explorers to learn about Africa.

In 1870, King Leopold II of Belgium kicked off what is known as the Great Scramble. He hired American explorer Henry Stanley to chart and explore the Congo River and, if possible, arrange trade agreements with different kings or chieftains. Back home in Belgium, King Leopold told his public that it was his Christian mission to help civilize people in the interior of Africa. However, this was to garner their support. His goal was conquest. He wanted territory, and he wanted resources to rival the main industrial powers of Europe.

Once King Leopold II started the Great Scramble, England, France, and Germany fell over themselves trying to get territory in and around the Congo River.

THE BERLIN CONFERENCE

The Berlin Conference was an attempt to avoid wars stemming from imperialism, which could erase much of the monetary growth achieved in Europe. In 1884, major European powers met at an international conference in Berlin. However, not one single African king or tribal chieftain was invited. The European powers literally sat around a table with the map of Africa and divided it up.

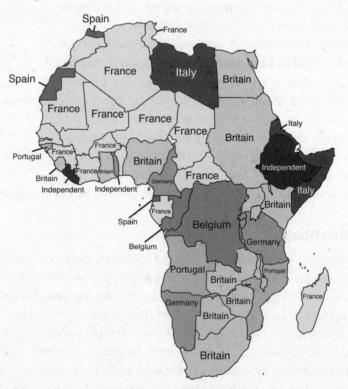

England, France, and the Netherlands recognized Belgium's claim to the land in the Congo, but they demanded that there be open access for free trade along the major rivers. The Conference also stated that to control a territory, a country had to have some type of governmental presence. A country could not just say, "This is ours" and not do anything else. This gave England an advantage as they immediately said that every person working for the British East India Company was now a worker for the Crown.

Initial Impact on Africa

After the Berlin Conference, European powers began to extend their power over local tribes and villages in an all-out sprint to colonize Africa. However, Europeans did this without understanding the local geography or the traditional way that Africans had existed. Europeans broke down Africa based on physical boundaries: lakes, rivers, forests, grasslands, and mountains. Because no Africans were invited to the Berlin Conference, the Europeans did not understand that they were interfering with migration routes of numerous African peoples and their flocks. Europeans cut off land from animals and peoples that had used the land for centuries. By the time the Europeans were done, only the territory of Liberia, which had been purchased by the United States, and the country of Ethiopia, which fought to defend itself, remained independent and untouched by European hands.

European Support for Imperialism Back Home

In Europe, there was a growing interest in Africa among the people and businesses. They saw Africa as an outlet to either gain necessary natural resources or a market for their finished products. England gobbled up the most territory as they used indirect administration to govern their territories. On the other hand, the French used a different system known as direct control. They built governmental outposts and sent soldiers to run them. The famous French Legionnaires in the African deserts are a great example of the French direct control in Africa.

Further Impact on Africa

Even though world history is full of violence, exploitation, and conquest, the imperialist takeover of Africa is one of the darkest and most violent parts of world history. Coupled with the Spanish conquest of the New World, this is one of the most outright exploitations of people and resources in world history.

One positive effect was that a segment of the African population was educated in the West, and new intellectual movements arose. However, the African people were divided. Some said Africans must learn from the West and copy some of what they were doing in order to move forward. On the other hand, many more Africans did not like the West and did not want to abandon the traditional ways that had been followed for thousands of years.

Eventually, an African nationalist movement was created, and the world is still seeing the repercussions of it to this very day. However, during the imperialistic conquest of Africa, the educated African population used any means necessary to broker trade agreements, create diplomatic envoys, and even declare war.

IMPERIALISM IN INDIA

By the 1600s, it was the British East India Company who controlled trade coming out of India. Investors in the company had ships bring back raw materials to be bought or sold, and they expected a great deal of profit. They were able to gain access to two trading ports on the coasts of India.

British East India Company and the Mughal Empire

The British East India Company was also smart. As the Mughal Dynasty began to weaken in India, the company slowly, almost imperceptibly, increased their power over the land, its people, and its resources. The British East India Company controlled almost the entire northern section of the Mughal Empire. By exploiting the diversity among the people of India—religion, language, ethnicity—they were able to often instigate conflicts between groups.

Goal of the British East India Company: Positives for India?

The main goal of the British East India Company was simply to make money for its investors. However, some things that were done to aid the East India Company had a positive effect on India. Because of India's large size, it did not have a lot of infrastructure, so in order to sell goods and acquire resources, the British developed a new road system. They also built a large railroad network throughout India. The British presence also kept the crime rate low and reduced conflict between opposing groups.

The British also thought their way of life was better so they wanted to bring social change as well. They wanted to get rid of the caste system, especially the practice of the sati, where when a Hindu woman's husband dies, she is supposed to throw herself on his funeral pyre. Christianity was a new religion that was introduced more deeply to compete with that of the traditional Hindu and Islam. Since Hindu was a polytheistic religion, Christians felt they were pagans and must be converted.

Sepoy Rebellion

England's lack of cultural understanding led to conflict. The British reserved the top positions in business and the military for Englishmen. Even Western-educated Indians were not allowed to serve in these positions. England dominated all the businesses and industrial growth, and they would not let any Indians benefit from this.

The most egregious of these errors was British treatment of Indian soldiers, known as Sepoys, in the British army. The army made two huge mistakes.

1. Because of the large size of the British empire, England needed soldiers. They took some Hindu soldiers and said they were going to ship them to other parts of the British empire. The problem with this is that Sepoys were forbidden to travel outside of India. It was an offense to their religion.
2. In 1857, the British came up with a technological advancement to speed the process of loading and firing a rifle. Instead of using a powderhorn, the British premeasured gunpowder in a paper tube, using the paper tube as their wadding over the top of the barrel and the mini ball. The paper cartridges would get wet during the ocean journey from England to India. The British used beef tallow or pork fat as a wax to keep shipping containers watertight. The problem was that cows are sacred to Hindus, and Muslims are forbidden to touch pork as it is unclean. When they complained about this, the British discharged the Indian soldiers from the army.

Both British decisions were seen as an insult to the Sepoys' honor, and support rose up for them against the British officers. The Sepoy Rebellion kicked off in 1857 in the northern part of India, and, in response, the British massacred Indian settlements and villages.

British Government Response

As a result of the Sepoy Rebellion, Parliament ended the reign of the British East India Company and indirect control of India in 1858. Instead, India was placed under the direct authority of the English crown. To make sure that violence stopped, more soldiers were sent to India. Just as they had done to the American colonies, the Indian citizens had to pay the British taxes.

When India became a direct colony ruled by the Queen, she sent a governor to rule in her name. India continued to play a large role in the British economy. The British government said that by working with the high-caste Indians, India would become the crown jewel of the British empire. The governmental and economic policy of India revolved around making it fit into the comprehensive British economy. However, the main goal continued to be making money. The British government justified its actions by saying it was helping India to modernize. They enforced ideas of Western technology and culture to maximize the raw material resources to make British manufactured goods. The road system and the railroad network allowed greater movement and communication within India.

The Indians vs. the British

They had differing viewpoints on most things and were divided. Indians who had been Western educated were evenly split: some thought that British industrial power and technology were necessary for progress. However, other Indians thought that since they were a culture that had roots as an ancient river valley civilization, their traditional Hindu and Islamic cultures should not be radically changed by emulating the West.

Ram Mohun Roy

In the 1820s, the great Indian scholar Ram Mohun Roy also had divided beliefs. Roy believed that India should learn what it could from the West and then modify it to invigorate and reshape traditional Indian culture for the modern world. He said that the caste system was a bad idea and kept India from progressing. He also believed that the divisiveness between India's religions did not help either. His movement kick-started the movement for which Mahatma Gandhi is famous: Indian nationalism.

The British Viewpoint

As for the British, they were also divided in their opinions of India. Some intellectuals were fascinated by ancient Indian philosophy and Hinduism. They had learned of India's ancient river valley heritage and respected it. Unfortunately, most of the people in England knew very little about India or its achievements, so they looked down on the people as inferior.

The Indian National Congress

In 1885, the people of India created the Indian National Congress. It was made up of educated people, mostly professionals, who thought that diplomacy and peaceful protest would earn them their independence. They also supported modernization and industrialization.

However, England did not want to let India go. Eventually, the leader of the Indian National Congress movement became Mahatma Gandhi. Gandhi led India's independence movements after World War II as England was trying to recover. In 1947, India achieved independence from the British, but then it turned into a struggle between Indian Hindus and Indian Muslims. This led to the creation of the new nation of Pakistan in 1948, another byproduct of imperialism (see Chapter 32).

AUSTRALIA

Australia and Captain Cook

In 1770, Captain James Cook, a British explorer, stopped just south of the modern-day city of Sydney, Australia, on the east coast of the continent. Cook named the land Botany Bay as he discovered new plant and animal life that had never been seen before. Cook claimed the entire continent for King George III.

Botany Bay

In 1786, the British cabinet approved the establishment of a new colony for prisoners near Botany Bay. Great Britain was having a difficult time dealing with its many criminals so Botany Bay became a permanent island prison for criminals. In 1787, 11 ships set sail for Australia with 1,000 felons, jailers, and other officers of the British government. They landed in Botany Bay in January 1788. The new British governor of Botany Bay, Arthur Phillip, moved the colony to the site of present-day Sydney. Governor Phillip put the criminals to work, stating that if they did not work, they would not eat. However, many of the prisoners knew nothing about agriculture.

Australian Society Forms

The settling of the island by the British was done by pure human labor. The prison guards and military soldiers did not believe that they should have to participate in the back-breaking work, so they left it for the criminals to do. Both men and women were sent as convicts, and both were subjected to harsh discipline, such as beatings and lashings. Many of the prison guards and military officers were from the low to middle class in England, and they began to create a new Australian colonial gentry class. They tried to become an aristocracy and separate themselves from the criminals. When, and if, the Botany Bay prisoners served their sentences and were released, they were still subjected to being the "lower-class citizens" of the continent.

With the imperialization of Australia, Great Britain gained a large continent and a brand-new colony. It grew not just as an outlet for British criminals. Those seeking fortune and land in a faraway overseas colony also traveled to Australia.

THE OTTOMAN EMPIRE

In 1798, Napoleon invaded Egypt to emulate his heroes Alexander the Great and Julius Caesar, and renewed contact between Europe and the Islamic empires. The Ottoman Empire was beginning to lose its grip of power because it was not industrially on par with the West. This opened up the possibility of European nations gaining access to either the Ottoman Empire or other Muslim territories.

Extent of the Muslim World

By 1800, the Muslim world extended from Morocco and North Africa, across the Middle East into India, and throughout Southeast Asia. Quite simply, Muslims controlled an enormous swath of territory involving three continents.

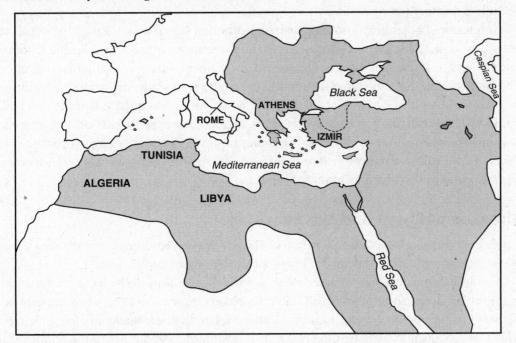

For the last 300 years, it had been controlled by the three Gunpowder Empires:

1. The Mughal Empire in India
2. The Safavid Empire in Iran
3. The Ottoman Empire in Turkey and in the Middle East

In the early 1800s, all three empires were in decline. The once-dominant absolute monarchs were not strong enough to control their societies. While combating internal disorder and governing large, diverse empires, a new problem arose in the form of Western European imperialism.

The Slow Collapse of the Ottoman Empire

At its all-time height of power, the Ottoman Empire spanned from North Africa and Eastern Europe into the Middle East. By the early 1800s, it was facing many internal obstacles. Small provincial rulers, far away from the seat of power, began to look after their own interests, almost returning to feudalism. The Ottoman sultan was fully opposed to the nationalist movement growing in Western Europe.

As the Austrian-Habsburg Empire lost territory, Italy formed itself into a nation. The Ottoman Empire was similar to the Austrian-Habsburg Empire in that they both had a large multiethnic, multireligious empire with small populations, but they controlled a wide swath of territory. However, the Romanians, Greeks, and Serbians wanted independence. The people began to rebel in Saudi Arabia, Lebanon, and even Egypt. As the Ottoman army went to put down protests and rebellions, a new protest would erupt elsewhere in the Ottoman Empire. All of these rebellions were suppressed, but in doing so, the Ottomans lost one of their most precious territories: Egypt.

The Crimean War

As Russia and the Ottoman Empire engaged in the Crimean War from 1853 to 1856, England and France joined with the Ottomans to defeat Russia. They did so because they hoped to benefit from the imminent collapse of the weakened Ottoman Empire because they would gain more territory to imperialize.

As a result of accepting European help, the Ottoman sultan realized they had fallen far behind, and he wanted to modernize. He wanted European officers to train the Ottoman army as well as implement Western models of government, taxation, and industrialization. The Ottoman Empire sent young men to Western colleges to study, but when they returned to bring back Western ideas, they talked about democracy and equality, both of which did not fit with a monarchical sultan. By the 1890s, a group of young Turkish citizens formed a movement known as the Young Turks. The Young Turks were bent on trying to overthrow the sultan. They instigated many rebellions and protests, allowing European countries to sneak their way into controlling the Ottoman Empire.

The Loss of Egypt and the Suez Canal

A perfect example of imperialism was the way England achieved control over the Suez Canal. It also represented one of the biggest losses for the Ottoman Empire.

The Suez Canal links the Mediterranean Sea with the Persian Gulf, giving greater access to the Indian Ocean and Pacific Ocean. After Napoleon's invasion in 1798, many in Egypt saw the need for economic reform. Egyptian leader Muhammad Ali made sweeping changes, which poised Egypt to be one of the first fully industrialized economies in the Middle East. Taxation laws were rewritten, irrigation canals were updated, and the cotton industry was revived, all of which gave Egypt more access to world trade. However, Muhammad Ali died in 1849, right as Europe was in the heyday of imperialism. Europe quickly pounced on Egypt.

Because of Napoleon, the French already had a large influence in Egypt. A French engineer came up with the idea to build a 100-mile canal to speed trading with East Asia. It was named the Suez Canal. Realizing that money could be made with the completion of the Suez Canal, the Egyptian government seized the opportunity to build it. However, by the late 1870s, Egypt had run out of money to build the canal. The Egyptian prime minister decided to sell shares of the canal, as if it were a corporation, in order to get the necessary money to complete the building. The British government became sinister in their acquisition of the canal. British Prime Minister Disraeli very quietly used money from Parliament to buy the majority of shares in the Suez Canal, but he did it through several different sources and companies. When all was said and done, the Egyptian people realized that England controlled the only water access between the Mediterranean and the Indian Ocean. To control the canal, the English made the country of Egypt a protectorate of Great Britain. While technically the government of Egypt was the Ottoman sultan, it was now under British rule. The Ottoman Empire lost Egypt, and the British gained territory, money, and, most importantly, control of a major trade route.

CHINA AND NEW IMPERIALISM

New Imperialism, also called Neoimperialism, is a little different from traditional imperialism. In New Imperialism, a larger country acquired new territory or politically controlled others by controlling the smaller country's economy.

Industrialized Western European countries would invest industrial capital in a smaller nonindustrialized country, where they would build a powerful corporation. The multinational corporation was doing the imperializing, rather than just the government. The country and its companies would build a factory and transportation facilities: ports and railroads. They would hire local natives to do the work, and while they gave the people jobs, the Europeans would insist on trade agreements that made them money and always favored them. By military threat or bribery, local governmental officials would become wealthy. One of the best examples of New Imperialism happened in China.

Problems with Trade Agreements

For centuries, China had controlled its own trade. However, after industrialization in the 1800s, the Western powers slowly began to impose their will and influence on China. Previous to this, with the Cantonese system, Western countries had been restricted to small ports in the south of China. Being an ancient river valley civilization, China had always been able to balance what it exported with what it imported. China was always able to export more than it took in. Europeans had to deal with Chinese trading laws until the Industrial Revolution. When the British asked for greater trade rights in China, the Qing Dynasty Emperor Qianlong told the British absolutely not, saying England had nothing that China needed. Unfortunately, industrialization changed that.

The Opium War

In the late 1700s, the British realized they could trade opium, grown in India, for tea grown in China for enormous profit. Since opium is a consumable addictive narcotic, the Chinese became addicted to it and wanted more in exchange for tea or silver. For Great Britain, it was a win-win situation as they made 100 percent profit. When China wanted the opium trade stopped, the English government declined. So in 1839, Chinese ships attacked British merchant vessels, starting what is known as the Opium War. In this war, England showed off its industrial power when the power of their new, modern navy destroyed China's military efforts.

Series of Unequal Treaties and Extraterritoriality

The Treaty of Nanking was the first in a series of treaties where China lost control of its trading. In 1842, Great Britain made China accept the Treaty of Nanking, which gave Great Britain control over trading with China. As soon as this happened, other industrial powers like France and the United States quickly followed. As a result of the treaty, Great Britain received the island of Hong Kong and payment for the losses to property, which is called an indemnity. The British also got to use more ports throughout China.

To add insult to injury, Great Britain also demanded extraterritoriality. Under extraterritoriality, British citizens in China followed only English law, not Chinese laws. The Chinese government had no power over them.

The final blow to China was when Great Britain demanded what is known as the "most-favored nation" clause. This is a big deal, even today. It is where a country gets the same, or better rights, than all of its competitors.

Global Connections

President Clinton went up against China in 1995 over the "most-favored nation" clause.

The Taiping Rebellion

As a result of these treaties, problems began to grow for the Qing Dynasty as its power was beginning to fade. China had experienced a population boom, which made it more difficult to feed the people, plus the river valleys had flooded out of control. So many people were living in poverty while, as usual, the Chinese emperor lived a life of lavish luxury.

At this time across the world, major advances were being made. The transatlantic cable had been laid, linking Europe to America. Karl Marx had written *The Communist Manifesto*. All the world was developing, and China was suffering. A former teacher named Hong Xiuquan began to speak out against the Qing Dynasty. His efforts culminated in the Taiping Rebellion.

In this rebellion, at least 20 million Chinese people were killed between 1850 and 1854. Hong wanted land reform for the peasants, better education for young people, better treatment of women, and, most of all, an end to the dynasties that had governed China for thousands of years. It almost worked. The Qing Dynasty was pushed to the breaking point and was forced to rely on nobles in the provinces. While China was dealing with its own internal disorder, European powers from Russia, Great Britain, France, and Germany began to encroach.

War with Japan

From 1894 to 1895, China went to war with Japan. Japan won, showing off their Western industrial techniques and capacity. For its victory, Japan took the Korean Peninsula, the island of Taiwan, and other coastal territories for natural resources. The signing of the peace treaty showed the great disparity between the two nations. The Chinese showed up wearing traditional robes, and the Japanese showed up wearing Western business suits. China was no longer as powerful as it once had been.

Great Britain took the Yangtze River Valley, and the French took much of Southeast Asia. As the relative newcomer to the imperialistic game, in 1899, the United States forced everyone to agree to what is known as the open door policy. It meant that everyone should be a trade partner with China, and no one could be excluded.

Reform Movements

The Chinese saw the need for reform but were divided in their approach. Some in China wanted to adopt Western ways in order to compete, but most scholarly officials were adamantly against it. Even though growing the economy was necessary, merchants were still not seen as important. Scholars also did not like Christian missionaries, who were condemning the traditional Chinese way of life, even though Confucianism had worked just fine for 4,000 years.

Officials in China said the country needed to be cautious as Western technology was dangerous because once it was in place, they would never be able to get rid of it. Some Western ideas were tried, but since the public was mainly against it, the government did not give the reforms their full support.

The Boxer Rebellion

The result of China's loss to Japan was a growing anger toward all foreigners, which kicked off the next rebellion in China. The Boxer Rebellion took place in 1899, led by a martial arts group known as the Righteous and Harmonious Fists. The Europeans dubbed the group as "Boxers" after watching them train.

Anger in China spilled over in 1900 as the Boxers began to attack foreign companies and settlements. Since China was required to allow other nations to send in their militaries if their businesses were threatened, the newly industrial Japan headed an international force that brutally put down the Boxer Rebellion. This made the Chinese angry, but the failure of the Boxer Rebellion required China to make even more concessions toward the industrialized powers.

However, China eventually began to industrialize. In 1911, China experienced the collapse of the 4000-year-old dynastic cycle system when the last Chinese dynasty, the Qing, collapsed. Sun Yat-sen founded the Republic of China.

TIMELINE REVIEW

1500–1700 C.E.	Gunpowder Empires rule from North Africa to Southeast Asia.
1500–1800 C.E.	Europe dominates much of the globe through industrial growth.
1600s C.E.	British East India Company obtains trading rights at the edge of the Mughal Empire.
1773 C.E.	Great Britain demands greater trading rights with China.
1798 C.E.	Napoleon invades the Ottoman Empire in Egypt.
1805 C.E.	Muhammad Ali is appointed governor of Egypt.
1820s C.E.	British introduce Western education to India.
1830s C.E.	Ram Mohan Roy: Father of Indian Nationalism
1839 C.E.	Start of Opium War between China and Britain
1842 C.E.	British force China to sign Treaty of Nanking.
1849 C.E.	Muhammad Ali of Egypt dies.
1850 C.E.	England controls most of India.
1850–1864 C.E.	Taiping Rebellion in China
1853–1856 C.E.	Crimean War: Ottoman Empire (with Britain and France) vs. Russia
1856 C.E.	British East India Company requires Sepoys in India to serve overseas.
1856–1858 C.E.	China is forced to sign treaties with France and Russia.
1857 C.E.	Sepoy Rebellion in India
1858 C.E.	British Parliament takes direct control of India from BEIC.
1859 C.E.	Suez Canal construction begins in Egypt.
1870 C.E.	• Henry Stanley explores the Congo River on behalf of King Leopold II of Belgium. • Great Scramble for Africa begins.
1875 C.E.	Great Britain controls the Suez Canal.
1882 C.E.	• Egyptian nationalists rebel against the Ottoman Empire. • Britain makes Egypt a protectorate.
1884 C.E.	Berlin Conference divides up Africa with no Africans present.
1885 C.E.	Indian National Congress is formed to gain independence from Britain.
1890 C.E.	Young Turks begin reforms in the Ottoman Empire.
1894–1895 C.E.	China is at war with Japan.
1899 C.E.	U.S. calls for Open Door Policy when trading with China.
1899–1902 C.E.	Boer Wars in South Africa between England and Dutch settlers.
1900 C.E.	Boxer Rebellion in China

1908 C.E.	Young Turks overthrow the Ottoman Empire sultan.
1911 C.E.	End of the last Chinese dynasty, the Qing.
1914 C.E.	Egypt enters World War I.
1918 C.E.	Ottoman Empire ends.
1930 C.E.	Mahatma Gandhi leads Salt March in India against British taxation.
1947 C.E.	India achieves independence from Great Britain.

Japan Modernizes

26

NATIONAL SECLUSION

From the start of the reign of Tokugawa Ieyasu in 1603 well into the 1800s, the Japanese practiced their policy of national seclusion. However, during this time, much of the world had undergone a great transformation during the Industrial Revolution. By the late Tokugawa era, the Japanese economy was completely different from that of the Western world.

The Japanese economy was stuck in the past and was well behind the rest of the industrialized world. Believing they had formed the best society possible, the Japanese had a system where nearly 80 precent of its people lived as farmers in the countryside, living merely hand-to-mouth. The rice farming techniques were the same that were used in medieval times. They required a lot of labor as there was no fertilizer or mechanized machines to help them. Coupled with that, to support the aristocracy and the samurai class, taxes were very high and were paid in foodstuffs. The Japanese farmers still did not use a lot of cash currency.

Japan in the mid-1800s was very similar to Japan in the 1300s during feudalism. There was no factory machinery, no steam engine, no mechanized production, and as such, there were no large pools of monetary capital. Things were going on the way they always had.

UNITED STATES COMMODORE PERRY

Japan started to change in 1853 when U.S. Naval Admiral Commodore Perry sailed into Tokyo Bay with a steamship, showing the power of the cannon and pistol. The Japanese believed they were symbols of a dragon, which was a very powerful figure in Japanese mythology. Admiral Perry forced the Japanese to sign what is known as the Treaty of Friendship. The United States was entering the imperial game, and the Treaty of Friendship was designed to give the United States a favorable trading agreement with Japan.

This completely revolutionized Japan. Within 15 years, the feudal system collapsed, and modernization and industrialization began almost overnight. Japan, who saw itself as a highly civilized country, had to make a radical shift that will be known as the Meiji Restoration.

THE MEIJI RESTORATION (1868–1912 C.E.)

As Japan began to look at itself differently, they sent young men to Western countries to study their technology, government, legal systems, science, and industry. When these young men returned, the primary goal of the government became the formation of a modern Japanese economy. This was during the age of imperialism, so Japan saw military strength and military power as a way to get what it wanted or needed. They wanted modern implements, like a telegraph system, the steam engine, railroads, and factories for industrial goods. The Japanese imperial government was in charge of industrial development, and things started slowly. Production was barely measurable, and it was going to take time to train the new workforce.

One of the first things that was created was the Japanese corporation known as a zai-batsu. The hardest part of industrial growth was getting enough cash and capital to grow Japanese corporations. A former samurai named Iwasaki Yataro solved this problem in a unique way. He managed a small shipping fleet as a samurai. Drawing on this experience, he bought old outdated ships from the government and slowly began a shipping business. As his business grew, he bought better ships until he had the makings of a large fleet. With the money he made in shipping, Yataro created a bank known as Mitsubishi. It became the foundation of the modern Mitsubishi Corporation that still exists in Japan. Other zaibatsu corporations followed suit.

What really helped Japan was a new railroad system. It was difficult and expensive to ship things internally on the Japanese archipelago due to the mountainous terrain. However, the railroads solved this problem, and areas that had once been untapped and isolated were now connected. This opened up a new source of labor and new resources.

Because the Japanese people were united under this effort, it created a stable environment. The Japanese people took on a very interesting mindset where they were able to sacrifice short-term tangible gain for a long-term result. The Japanese knew they might not live long enough to see all the fruits of their labor, but their children and grandchildren would. In a short span of 30 years, Japan moved from a feudal economy to a modern industrial economy, practically overnight.

JAPAN AFTER 1900

By the early 20th century, Japan had made incredible gains, and the people sought acknowledgment for what they had done. Believing that acquisition of colonies and imperial conquest by the military was the way to get Europe's attention, the Japanese went to war with a European opponent.

From 1905 to 1906, Japan entered into a war with Russia, where Japan defeated the Russian fleet in the Pacific. Unfortunately, Russia had never been given any respect or credence by the other European countries, so no one acknowledged it, angering the Japanese. Then, the Japanese drove the Russians out of part of mainland Asia and Manchuria. Japan gained this territory in a peace treaty written by Theodore Roosevelt of the United States. It heavily favored Japan.

By the outset of World War I, the Japanese were acquiring raw materials that helped their industry grow, especially iron production, coal mining, and chemical manufacturing. During World War I, Japan was one of only two functioning industrial economies in the world (the United States was the other). As a result, Japan was given a seat at the Paris Peace Conference at the Treaty of Versailles. Japan was very proud of its achievements, but by the 1920s, the Europeans were angry that Japanese manufactured goods were competitive in quality and price. Western Europe and the United States underwent growing pains to industrialize, experiencing the trial and error of industrialization, but Japan fully industrialized in record time, between 1868 and 1912. In barely 40 years, they were ready and industrialized.

Japan in the 1920s

By the 1920s, Japan had a completely modern look. The cities were looking more Western, the standard of living had been raised, and boys and girls went to school at a high rate. The people in the workforce still worked long hours, but Japan was catching up.

Unfortunately for Japan, just before the Great Depression hit the Western world, a massive earthquake struck the country, erasing all the economic gains that were made. Because Japan tried to do all the rebuilding internally, there was massive inflation for Japanese products as it was hard to get raw materials, and the manufacturing centers were heavily damaged. Most imported items were now cheaper.

Japan and the Great Depression

While rebuilding from the earthquake, Japan received another setback in 1929 as the Great Depression reverberated worldwide. There was massive unemployment in Japan. As a result of this, there was a switch in the government from civilian-minded to more militaristic. Japan not only industrialized quicker and faster than anyone in world history, but it also recovered faster from the Great Depression. By 1934, the Japanese had recovered.

The reason for this recovery was that the industry was geared toward the military manufacturing of weapons and goods for war, mainly iron and steel production. They built electrical power plants and chemical factories, focusing on new technology and better science. By the mid-1930s, in the heart of the Great Depression, Western countries were being outdone by the upstart Japan.

Japan was still craving recognition from the great Western imperial powers, so around young Emperor Hirohito, ancient samurai values were revived. His militaristic group of advisors believed that if the West could conquer foreign lands, then so could Japan. Emperor Hirohito became revered as the head of the government.

While China was fighting its own war of nationalism between Chiang Kai-shek and Mao Tse-tung, the Japanese went after territory rich in natural resources, such as oil and rubber. This threatened not only the Western European powers but also the United States. The Japanese government joined Italy and Germany, forming the Axis Powers.

TIMELINE REVIEW

1800 C.E.	Shogun system and Policy of Isolation are not working in Japan—widespread corruption and unrest
1853 C.E.	Arrival of U.S. Admiral Perry in Tokyo Harbor, Japan
1854 C.E.	Treaty of Friendship with U.S. and Japan
1859 C.E.	Fukuzawa Yukichi of Japan travels to U.S. for the first time.
1868 C.E.	Meiji Restoration begins.
1870 C.E.	Iwasaki Yataro creates first zaibatsu.
1876 C.E.	Japan forces Korea to open ports to Japan.
1894–1895 C.E.	Japan is at war with China.
1906 C.E.	Russo-Japanese War
1912 C.E.	Meiji Restoration is complete.
1914–1918 C.E.	Tremendous economic growth in Japan during World War I

Quick Quiz: Chapters 25–26

1. Which movement was unintentionally started by Belgium's King Leopold II?

   A. Great Scramble
   B. Slave trade
   C. Military rearmament
   D. Building of complicated alliances

2. Which conference was held by the European Powers to avoid conflict by redrawing the map of Africa?

   A. Concordat of Worms
   B. Treaty of Versailles
   C. Berlin Conference
   D. Treaty of Paris

3. How did European imperialism have a positive effect on the continent of Africa?

   A. Infrastructure was built, linking the vastness of the continent.
   B. An educated African elite grew, which helped spurn African nationalism.
   C. French was adopted as the unifying language for trade within the country.
   D. Many African leaders learned of the concept and importance of democracy.

4. Which of the following is one of the largest and most damaging errors by the British government in India?

   A. Forcing an ending to the caste system
   B. Moving the capital to Mumbai
   C. Relegating the Mughal emperor to a figurehead ruler only
   D. Dismissing of the Indian soldiers, known as Sepoys, after they complained about their treatment and the violation of their religion

5. Which of the following events in the mid-1800s provided a signal to the Ottoman sultans that reforms were necessary?

   A. Assassination attempt on Franz Ferdinand
   B. Creation of the Young Turk political movement
   C. Creation of the Dual Monarchy
   D. Crimean War

6. Which conflict raised the alarm in China as they realized they had lost the upper hand in writing their own trade treaties?

   A. Russo-Japanese War
   B. Opium War
   C. Chinese Civil War
   D. Taiping Rebellion

7. What is the name given to the Japanese industrial movement?

   A. Meiji Restoration
   B. Zaibatsu
   C. Rapid urbanization
   D. Utilitarianism

8. Which of the following was the biggest help to Japan during their industrialization period?

   A. The increase in shipping ports and facilities
   B. The adoption of the steam engine to aid Japanese farming techniques
   C. The building of a railroad to link the remote parts of Japan with the urban areas
   D. The creation of new cities where none had existed before

9. What did Japan accomplish before any other industrialized country during the 1930s?

   A. They began to mobilize for World War II.
   B. Japan was able to recover from the Great Depression.
   C. Japan created a policy to resist the spread of communism.
   D. Japan formed large multinational corporations while gaining raw materials from new sources in different countries.

Quick Quiz Answers

1. A; **2.** C; **3.** B; **4.** D; **5.** D; **6.** B; **7.** A; **8.** C; **9.** B

World War I to the Treaty of Versailles

27

MOTIVES

There were several motives for World War I. Much of it was economic, fueled by the imperial expansion phase and capitalistic practices that Europe experienced during the 1800s. As large, powerful industrial countries gobbled up smaller countries that were rich in natural resources, it was difficult to maintain the balance of power. Another motive was to gain military superiority through imperialism. Each European country believed that the more colonies they had, the more power and importance they commanded on the world stage. Unfortunately, this led to a domino effect as each country constantly strived to be larger and more powerful than everyone else.

NATIONALISM TO MILITARISM

Nationalism is the binding of a country together through national pride. When nationalism was a strong force in Europe at the turn of the century, it led to a growing rivalry between France and Germany, especially over the disputed territory of Alsace and Lorraine. Germany felt extremely proud of its unification, and it had beaten France in the Franco-Prussian War. France, on the other hand, was angry at their embarrassing defeat and the loss of this territory. They wanted nothing more than to seek revenge on Germany.

Militarism is the glorification of war. At this point, Europe had enjoyed about 100 years of peace. Except for the Crimean War and the smaller wars of Bismarck (like the Franco-Prussian War), not since Napoleon had there been a large-scale war. Nobody in Europe really remembered the horrific side of warfare. So by the late 1800s, there was a feeling of militarism throughout Europe. Flags were unfurled, the powers of Europe greatly expanded the armies and weapons of war, and everyone thought it would be a grand adventure.

Due to their geographic position in central Europe, Germany led the way. Being surrounded by other countries, they felt the need to enlarge their army. England, the leader in the Industrial Revolution, had the largest navy to rule the British empire. However, many of its industrial facilities, as well as its navy, were close to being outdated. On the other hand, the newly industrialized Germany had modern, efficient industrial facilities and was building a brand-new, faster, more powerful navy. England felt economically and militarily at odds with Germany.

Nationalism in Eastern Europe

Nationalism was playing a role in Eastern Europe as well. Many of the Eastern European countries were Slavic, meaning they were descended from Russians. There was a stirring of nationalism among the smaller Slavic countries that were part of either the Austrian-Habsburg

Empire or the Ottoman Empire. Nationalistic movements were further complicated when Russia proclaimed that it felt duty-bound to defend all Slavic nations against threats from larger empires. A small conflict in a portion of Eastern Europe known as the Balkans led to a much larger problem for the world.

TRIPLE ALLIANCE & CENTRAL POWERS VS. TRIPLE ENTENTE

The alliance systems in Europe were some of the most complicated in world history. The balance of power created by Clemens von Metternich at the Congress of Vienna was changed forever by Germany. Austria had lost territory, and French power and honor were lost during the Franco-Prussian War. German Chancellor Otto von Bismarck knew that Germany's position was precarious. He wanted to avoid a war that could upset the newfound peace. However, he was also determined to make sure France and any other power (especially Austria or Russia) would not become allies; otherwise, Germany would be surrounded. Bismarck said several times that Germany could not afford to fight a war on two fronts: in the West and in the East.

In 1873, Bismarck established the Three Emperors League. The League was an agreement between Germany, Austria, and Russia. It aligned the Central and Eastern European powers into an alliance.

However, with the Ottoman Empire showing signs of decay, Russia broke the League agreement by supporting Slavs in Bosnia during a rebellion against the Ottoman Empire. Russia hoped to obtain territorial expansion and gain the coveted city of Constantinople if the Ottoman Empire collapsed. The Ottoman Empire, faced with the threat of Russian intervention, asked for a peace agreement. In 1878, the Treaty of Sans Stefano was signed, giving some Ottoman territories their freedom as independent states.

This action scared Austria and England. England wanted to protect its balance of power in the Mediterranean Sea by blocking Russian access, and Austria simply did not like Russian intervention. At an international conference in Berlin, Austria-Hungary annexed the Slavic states that were just freed from the Ottomans, and tensions were running high. Russia did not like being forced into accepting a smaller territory, and it was clear that some Western countries would not help them.

Otto von Bismarck capitalized on this when he realized the anger of Russia. He formed a secret alliance with Austria—a Dual Alliance—in which both countries agreed that if either country was attacked by Russia, the other country would either help or stay neutral. Russia, who always felt isolated, was isolated even further. Bismarck was fully aware of all of this, so he worked to get Russia to rejoin the Three Emperors League.

In 1882, Bismarck formed the Triple Alliance with Italy. Under the leadership of King Victor Emmanuel, Italy wanted to gain colonies like the other European powers had done. Italy was also angry at France for claiming territory in North Africa. To Bismarck, nothing could be better. He now had Austria-Hungary and Italy as allies in the Triple Alliance. Both Italy and Austria-Hungary were friendly with Great Britain, meaning France was now further isolated.

When Kaiser Wilhelm I of Germany died in 1888, things began to unravel. His son, Wilhelm II, fired Bismarck as he was determined not to be a puppet for the German chancellor. However underhanded Bismarck was, he had Germany on a path to becoming the most dominant power in the world. When Bismarck was relieved, all of his secret alliances and maneuvering fell apart. When this happened, none of the treaties were renewed. The two countries that Bismarck alienated—France and Russia—formed their own alliance. When Wilhelm II could not persuade Britain to join the Triple Alliance, the two became quick rivals.

The British response was to form the Entente Cordiale, or friendly agreement. As Germany, Austria-Hungary, and Italy became known as the Central Powers, distrust and animosity led the great Western powers to form their own counteralliances. France and Russia had begun an alliance in 1894. During this time, Great Britain had been seeking alliances as well, first with Japan to have extra support against Russia in the Pacific. Trouble started in North Africa when Germany overstepped its bounds by trying to drive a wedge between Great Britain and France through two crises in Morocco. Germany wanted to demonstrate that this new friendship between Great Britain and France was not going to last. And Kaiser Wilhelm II supported independence for the kingdom of Morocco, which the French wanted as a territory. By doing this, Kaiser Wilhelm II was too aggressive, and he forced the two old enemies—Great Britain and France—together.

In 1904, the Triple Entente formed between Great Britain, France, and Russia. Bismarck had always said that Germany could not afford to fight a war on two fronts, but due to the lack of understanding of the new German kaiser, there was a distinct possibility of having to do just that.

ROLE OF BOSNIA AND SERBIA

Bosnia and Serbia were small Slavic nations who wanted their independence in the Balkans. The more radical, nationalistic elements saw Serbia as the centerpiece for a brand-new nation. Serbia wanted to unite all the Slavs to break away from the Austria-Hungary Empire.

Other nations tried to act before things got out of hand. At an international peace conference, Russia and Austria supported each other's demands. Austria wanted to annex Bosnia and Herzegovina, and Russia wanted access to the Dardanelles between the Black Sea and the Aegean Sea, which would serve as their long-sought-after warm water port. The British, being concerned about the Mediterranean, rejected Russia's request. This strained the new relationship. The Slavic nationalists did not like Bosnia being gobbled up by Austria. Nationalism came back into play as Russia felt betrayed and too weak to do anything. Germany did not like how their relations with Russia had become strained but stood more in line with Austria than anybody else. The failure of Great Britain and France to support their new Russian ally also strained their alliance.

The second problem in the Balkans arose in 1911 when Italy, angered that the French were controlling Morocco, attacked the Ottoman Empire to acquire the country of Libya. This started a series of revolts by Ottoman-controlled Balkan states to try to gain their independence. Austria's imperial government was upset by this as it threatened Austria-Hungary. In 1913, Great Britain led a peace conference that would restore peace and included terms that were in Austria's favor. Serbia did not like this, and its response forced Austria to talk about open warfare to put down the Serbian threat. Russia's Czar Nicholas II had spoken about protecting the Slavs, but when push came to shove, Russia let Austria win the day.

From the Balkan Wars (which Bismarck correctly labeled as a problem) a few major issues came to light.

1. Russia was angered by its own lack of action.
2. Austria was embarrassed that tiny Serbia stood up to the empire at the peace conference.
3. Many countries said open warfare would have gotten quicker and easier results.

 GLOBAL CONNECTIONS

Going back into history, on June 28, 1389, Serbia had been conquered by the Ottoman Empire. On June 28, 1912, Serbia thought it had gained independence from the Ottoman Empire only to find out they had been annexed by Austria-Hungary.

THE ASSASSINATION OF ARCHDUKE FRANZ FERDINAND

The fear and mistrust between the great European powers and the movement of nationalism in the Balkans spilled over on June 28, 1914. On this date, the heir to the throne of Austria, Archduke Franz Ferdinand, visited the city of Sarajevo. When Franz Ferdinand's wife exclaimed, "I cannot wait to see my people," the people of Serbia and Bosnia were infuriated. This started in motion eleven steps that led to World War I.

1. On the morning of June 28, 1914, five members of the nationalist organization Black Hand tried to assassinate the archduke. The attempt was unsuccessful, and four of the five assailants were arrested. The fifth, 19-year-old Gavrilo Princip, did not know what to do. When the archduke left Sarajevo that afternoon, he wanted to visit his wounded bodyguards. However, his driver was not made aware of the detour and had to turn the car around. When he began to turn around, they stopped right in front of Princip. He took this as a sign, stuck a pistol into the window of the car, and shot Archduke Franz Ferdinand and his wife, killing both of them. The assassination of the archduke enraged not only Austrian Emperor Franz Joseph but other European royals as well.
2. Austria and many others thought that only a swift, severe punishment would do.
3. Austria-Hungary gave Serbia several harsh ultimatums: capture everyone involved, try them, convict them, and execute them, and Serbia would allow Austria to help.
4. Serbia agreed to all of the ultimatums except the last one, saying Serbia could handle this itself.
5. All of Europe had condemned the assassination. When Austria wanted to attack Serbia, everyone was in support of this. They assumed the powerful Austria-Hungary

Empire would handle Serbia quickly, putting an end to some of the problems with the Eastern European countries.

6. There was the threat of Russian interference if powerful Austria attacked smaller Serbia, so Kaiser Wilhelm II supported Austria, encouraging Austria to attack. He announced a "blank check of support" for Austria and offered anything it might need.

7. Tiny Serbia knew that it was no match for Austria and Germany, so Serbia asked Russia for help, based on its prior promise to protect the Slavs. Not wanting to appear passive, Czar Nicholas II told Austria to back off and began to mobilize for war. This was a mistake because it signaled to everyone that Russia was ready for war. If they had not mobilized, the outcome might have changed. However, now all European nations were getting ready for war. German support of Austria was supposed to keep Russia at bay, but Archduke Franz Joseph of Austria had now been waiting nearly a month for revenge. On July 24, Austria made the final ultimatum to Serbia. When they did not back down, Austria declared war on July 28.

8. Russian mobilization scared Germany because Germany knew it would be practically impossible to fight a war on two fronts. So Germany responded by declaring war on Russia with the hope that Germany could defeat Russia before Russia's army was fully mobilized.

9. Russia appealed to its ally in France, who saw a chance for revenge against Germany. The British were trying to avoid war and called a peace conference, but most of the warring powers did not attend the conference.

10. The French had their doubts about victory, so France gave Russia a "blank check of support" as well. Kaiser Wilhelm II demanded the French stay neutral. France retorted that its national honor and pride were at stake, so Germany could not tell France what to do. So Germany declared war on France.

11. The Germans executed their plan of attack known as the Schlieffen Plan. They invaded Luxembourg on August 1, with the goal of defeating France quickly so they could focus on Russia. Next, Germany invaded Belgium on August 3, which was in violation of a treaty signed years earlier between the British, the French, and the German states, which guaranteed the neutrality of Belgium. With the invasion of Belgium, the British had to attack. Germany invaded France on August 4, and Great Britain officially declared war on Germany.

THE SCHLIEFFEN PLAN IN THE WESTERN FRONT

Otto von Bismarck had feared a two-front war for Germany. General Alfred von Schlieffen had come up with a plan to avoid this. He reasoned that it would take Russia so long to get their military mobilized that Germany could quickly defeat France by marching through Belgium.

As war broke out, Europe was actually excited as there had not been a large war for many years. The Triple Entente believed they had more men, and the British navy believed it would win easily. As the Germans began to execute the Schlieffen Plan, the general in charge was too slow and stopped the attack just when success was within his grasp. The French dug in and put their trust in a large offensive (which ended up failing). The war zone ranged from the disputed region of Alsace and Lorraine, to Switzerland, and all the way to the North Sea. Stereotypical trench warfare began as both sides hunkered down. The nasty stalemate of World War I began.

In Eastern Europe, Russia finally mobilized. Long supply lines and poor communication, coupled with Russian mistakes, spelled disaster for the Russian army. In the small German town of Tannenberg, the Russian army was forced to retreat. Russia quickly found itself ill-equipped to fight what would be the first modern war.

NEW TECHNOLOGIES AND THEIR IMPACT

World War I featured five new inventions and pieces of technology.

1. The automatic machine gun allowed for just a few gunners to attack and destroy a much larger force.
2. The newly invented airplane was used for observation, reconnaissance, and bombing.
3. The creation of the tank replaced the horse-drawn cavalry to go through obstacles, take out machine guns, and fire on soldiers, but they were slow and unreliable.
4. Different poison gases—mustard gas and chlorine gas—were used to blind, choke, or severely burn opponents. Gas masks were available, but they were unreliable. Poison gas was also difficult as it depended upon the weather.
5. The creation of the submarine, or U-boat, launched underwater missiles and torpedoes to fight on the seas. It was the use of U-boats that further escalated World War I.

SINKING OF THE *LUSITANIA*

As Great Britain employed a blockade of German ports, Germany responded with submarine warfare around the British Isles. It was a war zone where not even neutral countries were safe. When the British ship *Lusitania* was sunk with American passengers on board in May 1915, President Woodrow Wilson warned Kaiser Wilhelm II that the United States would be forced to intervene on behalf of the Allies if the sinkings did not stop.

1916 was a crucial year as the British, French, and Russian allies and the Germans launched major offenses. The Germans and French fought the great Battle of Verdun causing more than one million casualties on each side. The British attacked in Belgium along the Somme River, where in one single day at Passchendaele, 60,000 British soldiers were killed. Over the five-month battle, millions were lost with neither side gaining an advantage. In December 1916, President Wilson tried to bring about peace, but neither side wanted to back down.

In 1917, after making no progress on the land battle, the Germans renewed their submarine warfare on any ship viewed as a threat. President Wilson wanted to remain neutral; however, with Germany once again practicing unrestricted submarine warfare, President Wilson declared that America must make the world safe for democracy. On April 6, 1917, the United States declared war on Germany.

END OF THE FIGHTING

America's entry was key for the Allied Powers as the Russian Revolution had begun in March 1917 as the people tried to overthrow the Romanov Dynasty and the monarchical rule of the czar. Because of the Russian Revolution, Russia had to essentially withdraw from the conflict. This was the high watermark for the German army as now they could focus only on the Western Front. However, Great Britain and France, along with Germany, were near their manpower limits. Each thought one last massive assault would win the war. In Germany,

General Paul von Hindenburg launched one final attack. However, the U.S. forces, commanded by General John Pershing, had arrived in France. In the fall of 1918, a huge counteroffensive took place. The United States fought around Verdun on the Meuse-Argonne battlefield, the largest battle that the United States had ever been in. The American troops shattered the German defense known as the Hindenburg Line. After that, the allies were nearly unstoppable. As a result, German Prime Minister Ludendorff decided to make peace before Germany was thoroughly beaten and destroyed. No foreign soldier had ever entered German territory on the Western Front, and Ludendorff wanted to protect German citizens by seeking immediate peace.

The Fourteen Points Plan

The German government asked for peace on the lines of President Wilson's proposed Fourteen Points plan of peace. The Fourteen Points plan was a utopian view of the world where every nationality had independence, there would be free shipping and trading on the seas, diplomacy would solve international problems, and the world would be governed by a League of Nations designed to make sure a war like the Great War would never break out again. King Wilhelm II of Germany abdicated the throne, leaving the Social Democrat Party in charge. Germany was made a republic called the Weimer Republic to prevent any influence from the growing movement of communism.

Hostilities ceased on November 11, 1918, at 11:00 A.M. as the Social Democrat Party of the Weimar Republic signed an armistice. This was a key factor as an armistice is not a surrender. It is a cease-fire. There was no winner or loser. Everybody just agreed to stop fighting.

More than 13 million people were killed or wounded in World War I. Many people were homeless, and fields, crops, and livestock were destroyed in France and Belgium. When the Germans were promised only mild reparations for the war, the German people felt betrayed. The German army had not been defeated, it was never pushed back, and invaders had never crossed their border; yet, they were punished by the peace settlement. The new German government—the Weimar Republic—had allowed the Allies to claim victory.

THE COST OF THE WAR

The cost of the war was high, not only in terms of the 13 million dead, but financially and politically as well. Most of Western Europe was in financial ruin. Since the 1500s, Western Europe had dominated the globe with colonization, transatlantic trade, the Industrial Revolution, and imperialism. Because of World War I, Great Britain, France, and Germany had lost an entire generation of young men. Power shifted westward, and as Europe was in tremendous financial debt, the United States became the new industrial and financial capital of the world. The centuries-old international order of monarchies was gone.

The Austrian-Habsburg Empire was gone as their colonies were looking for independence. The new Germany was in chaos. The Romanov Dynasty in Russia was gone, with anticapitalist communists trying to establish a government. The 600-year-old Ottoman Empire of Asia and Europe finally collapsed, adding to the chaos. Europe's imperial colonies were looking to escape from underneath the heel of their European masters. Europe was forced to deal with the idea that they were no longer the epicenter of the world. The failure to adjust to this fact when they signed the Treaty of Versailles was a factor that led to the start of World War II.

THE TREATY OF VERSAILLES

The French palace of Versailles was chosen to be the site of the treaty negotiations. Long had it been the symbol of French power, and it's where Bismarck had forced France to sign the treaty at the end of the Franco-Prussian War. Led by U.S. President Woodrow Wilson in January 1919, those invited to the Paris Peace Conference included Prime Minister David Lloyd-George of Great Britain, Prime Minister Clemenceau of France, King Victor Emmanuel, and Prince Konoye from Japan.

President Wilson hoped to form the League of Nations, an international government that 40 nations had already agreed to join. The destruction caused by World War I was so shocking that countries agreed to mediate or negotiate disputes rather than, once again, risk a disastrous war. The League would agree to work collectively to take action against anybody who threatened the peace. Even though the League of Nations was formed, the United States never joined. Plus, it quickly became a reality that Wilson's utopian outlook would be hampered by secret treaties made between Great Britain and France during the war and their quest to recoup money for the damages they incurred. Shockingly, neither Germany nor Russia was invited to the Paris Peace Conference. The people of Britain and France were told that Germany would pay for the war. France wanted to make sure Germany could never threaten them again.

The Peace Settlement

The peace settlement at the Treaty of Versailles is actually five separate treaties. Since Germany and the new Soviet Union were not present at the peace conference, Germany was forced to accept a treaty that they later claimed was dictated to them. The Soviet Union was engaged in its own civil war so the focus was on Germany. In Germany, the biggest problems were that France got Alsace and Lorraine back, and a demilitarized zone was created that went 30 miles deep into Germany. Germany was also to be permanently disarmed. They were able to maintain a small National Guard, but no offensive weapons were allowed. Ships, planes, tanks, and poison gas were eliminated.

The nations of Poland and Czechoslovakia were created as modern republics to box in Germany to hopefully remove its threat. Colonies of the old Ottoman Empire, the Austrian-Habsburg Empire, and Germany were divided up by the so-called victors (even though it was an armistice, not a surrender, that was signed).

Reparations

Reparations are payments made for damages done during conflict. Before the armistice was signed, Germany had agreed to pay for all damage done to the civilian populations and their property. An astronomical price between 15 billion and 25 billion German marks was thought to be correct. However, Britain and France had to pay their lend lease debts to the United States for money and supplies loaned to them during the war. When they looked at their loss of manpower in industry, Britain and France decided to tack their lend lease debt onto Germany to make them pay for the full cost of the war. This was written into the treaty without German input. There was no way Germany could pay this amount, so Germany was told to pay $5 billion a year. By 1921, a fixed amount would be set, and Germany would then get 30 years to pay it off.

The Germans were outraged at this amount. They had also lost important industrial territory and keen minds that could have been used to get raw materials to pay off the debt.

Plus, they were told that they lost the war when they signed an armistice! They were also forced to accept this treaty with no input whatsoever. This spelled doom for the new German government, the Weimar Republic, as they were never able to gain widespread acceptance due to the signing of the treaty. France was excited because if Germany failed to pay, it could be militarily invaded. The Germans would either bankrupt themselves or be attacked if they failed to pay.

Evaluation of the Peace Treaty

Shortly after the Treaty of Versailles was written, it endured some harsh criticism. France did not think it was harsh enough, whereas the United States and some English leaders thought it violated the democratic goals that Western society tried to promote.

British economist John Maynard Keynes wrote an essay called "The Economic Consequences of Peace." Keynes compared the Treaty of Versailles to what the Romans had done to the city of Carthage when they salted the earth to ruin Carthage forever. Keynes also harshly criticized President Wilson, who was being hailed as a conquering Caesar by coming to Europe with his Fourteen Points plan. President Wilson was drawn in a political cartoon as a court jester, getting kicked in the rear back to the United States.

In the United States, the criticism of the president caused the United States to wall itself off from world affairs and pursue a policy of isolation. The U.S. banks and industry were sought after to rebuild Western Europe, but the U.S. government decided to let the Europeans handle their own mess. The American isolation, along with Keynes's criticism of the treaty, caused Great Britain to back out of the treaty.

Consequences

As a result, France was now left to defend itself against an angry Germany. Germany lost territory and a good portion of its male population and was under tremendous debt. However, as the reparation payments were scaled down in the 1920s, Germany was back on the road to success and was about to be reintegrated into the European fraternity until the Great Depression hit.

However, the biggest failure was leaving out Russia and Germany from the peace process. Their location, their size, and their industrial capability meant that they should have been included in the affairs of Europe. Anger was festering in Germany. Without military support, the League of Nations could not enforce the peace.

TIMELINE REVIEW

1879 C.E.	Germany's Bismarck forms Dual Alliance with Austria-Hungary.
1882 C.E.	Italy joins Germany and Austria-Hungary, forming the Triple Alliance.
1887 C.E.	Bismarck in Germany achieves new treaty with Russia.
1890 C.E.	• German Kaiser Wilhelm II forces Bismarck to resign.
	• Germany's treaty with Russia ends.
1892 C.E.	Russia forms treaty with France.
1904 C.E.	Great Britain forms entente (alliance) with France.
1907 C.E.	• Triple Entente forms as Russia joins Great Britain and France.
	• Triple Alliance vs. Triple Entente

1908 C.E.	Austria annexes Bosnia-Herzegovina from Ottoman Empire.
1914 C.E.	• Austria's Archduke Ferdinand is assassinated in Sarajevo, Bosnia-Herzegovina.
	• Austria issues ultimatums to Serbian government.
	• Russia mobilizes army.
	• Germany declares war on Russia.
	• Germany wins the Battle of Tannenberg—a major defeat for Russia.
	• Germany enters Belgium, drawing Great Britain into World War I.
1915 C.E.	• Stalemate on the Western Front
	• British passenger ship *Lusitania* is sunk by Germany.
1916 C.E.	• Battle of the Somme in France
	• Russia's war effort is near collapse with 2 million dead.
1917 C.E.	United States enters World War I.
1918 C.E.	• United States begins Meuse-Argonne offensive, shattering German hopes of winning the war.
	• Armistice is declared on November 11, ending World War I.
1919 C.E.	• Opening of the Paris Peace Conference
	• Signing of the Treaty of Versailles
1919–1921 C.E.	Germany tries to pay $5 billion annually in reparations.

The Russian Revolution

28

BACKGROUND

The Russian Revolution was not planned or led by any one single faction. Rather, it was the complete and total failure of the czarist government to run the vast country of Russia. Poor leadership, military failures, enormous casualties, starving people, and industrial workers going on strike fed into the unrest.

In 1905, a revolution occurred in Russia with the hope that Czar Nicholas II would change the Russian government from an autocracy into a republic. Diverse groups protested throughout the country, which included economic strikes, student-led riots, and terrorist attacks. The groups were also pushing for the adoption of a Russian constitution.

As a result of the Russian Revolution in 1905, one of the most peculiar reforms made was the creation of the Duma. The Duma was a legislature with no real power.

At the onset of World War I, Russia and its empire was massive, stretching from Eastern Europe all the way to the Pacific Ocean. It was a large country with many natural resources but also a large and diverse population. However, to the increasingly industrialized Western Europe, Russia was seen as caught in slow motion. They were still a country where the government was based on feudalism. Most of the population was poor peasants. There was a tiny middle class emerging as Russia was just starting to industrialize. Some czars had made reforms up to this point, but not enough to improve the lives of Russian citizens. The current czar, Nicholas II of the Romanov family, did not like to make any changes that could undermine his power and authority. While clinging to this belief, his country had become corrupt and had not changed the way it had done things in hundreds of years.

When World War I broke out, it reignited Russian patriotism and nationalism for a small time, bringing the Russians together. However, after a small number of initial gains, the Russian army suffered a tragedy in the small city of Tannenberg, Germany. Hundreds of thousands of Russians were killed and wounded. Coupled with this loss, the fledgling Russian industry could not keep up with demand for war products. They simply did not have enough resources. By 1915, the Russian soldiers were badly equipped and even more poorly led.

In early 1915, people in St. Petersburg, the seat of the Romanov Dynasty's power, began to strike. Army troops were sent out to stop them, but they did not fire on the crowds. Some even joined the protest.

By 1917, the Russians had endured almost two million casualties. The war was going poorly, and there was continued bad leadership.

THE FEBRUARY REVOLUTION: 1917

The difficulties on the battlefield were even more glaring when the czar went to personally take charge, and things did not get better. On the homefront, there was not enough food and not enough fuel, and it brought about the collapse of the monarchy. In St. Petersburg, workers went on strike, shouting for food. When the troops refused to fire on the protesters, the government was helpless. With his Council of Advisors advising him, Czar Nicholas II abdicated the throne on March 15, 1917. The Duma was dissolved, and the government fell into the hands of the separate governments that ran the Russian provinces. They called themselves Social Democrats.

The problem was that instead of focusing on their internal problems, these provincial governments thought it best to uphold their duty to the alliance and keep fighting Germany. At home, the majority of Russians had had enough of war. The problems at the front caused many Russian soldiers to abandon their military units and return home. In the urban areas, people wanted relief from the food shortages that occurred because of the need to supply the army.

Some provincial governments stuck with the Allied alliance and continued to fight Germany. However, when a massive offensive launched in July 1917 was a complete and total failure, the continued problems of hunger and land reform undermined those provincial governments.

CREATION OF THE SOVIETS

Working against these provisional governments were a group of people who believed in Karl Marx's ideas of socialism, and they wanted a different path for Russia. They went out among the common people, whom they called the proletariat—factory workers, iron ore miners, and urban workers—and tried to prime the proletariat to lead a revolution. They called these people Soviets.

Vladimir Lenin

Lenin was born to a wealthy middle-class family, and when his brother was executed by the czarist government, he began to look for a way to overthrow the czarist regime. He was heavily influenced by Karl Marx's *Communist Manifesto*. He worked tirelessly, mostly among students and urban workers, to spread Marxist ideas and promote the idea of socialism. What made Lenin so powerful was that he was able to change Marxist thoughts to meet the needs of what was happening in Russia. Marx had said that working classes would unite and overthrow the corrupt and greedy capitalists. The difference for Russia was that Russia did not have a large number of workers who believed in this, as of yet. So Lenin wanted a small selection of the Soviets to lead a revolution. Then, he would create a mechanism of leadership to govern the proletariat. Lenin intentionally picked the name *Bolshevik* for his party because *Bolshevik* means "majority." Lenin made it seem as if all the people wanted this! As a result of his agitation of the people, the Russian government arrested and exiled Lenin to Switzerland in 1907.

Lenin's Return and the Bolshevik Revolution

By April 1917, the Bolsheviks had organized themselves, and they were working against the democratic provincial governments. To help in the war effort against Russia, Germany orchestrated Vladimir Lenin's return to Russia from exile, hoping that he would cause further problems for the provincial governments. When Lenin got off the train in St. Petersburg, he was met by his supporters. Lenin immediately made a statement saying that all government power should go to the Soviets, the common workers. Lenin launched a failed coup, and he and his right-hand man, Leon Trotsky, were exiled and put into jail.

This exile did not last long. Vladimir Lenin returned in the fall of 1917, and this time, many people backed his ideas. On November 6, 1917, Lenin led the Bolshevik Revolution as they destroyed an attempt at common elections. At this point, Lenin demanded that land be turned over to the peasants and factories turned over to the workers. Churches were closed, and the Soviets controlled all the banks. Lenin was supported by Germany, thus he was forced to sign the World War I armistice with them. The armistice was costly for Russia as they had to give up territory to Germany and pay large war damages. It was difficult for Lenin, but he needed time to consolidate power as a civil war was about to break out in Russia. The revolution would be between the Red Russians, who supported the Lenin revolution, and the White Russians, who opposed the Bolsheviks and Vladimir Lenin.

The November Revolution

Vladimir Lenin focused on expanding the revolution. He worked with Leon Trotsky, a firm believer in Marxist ideas, to promise the people three things: peace, land, and bread. This sounded great to the starving Russian people who were tired of war. When, in the summer of 1917, the provincial governments had tried the last-gasp offensive against Germany and failed, the troops refused to keep fighting and went home as another cold Russian winter was on the horizon. Lenin and his Bolsheviks used this pervasive sense of despair as a vehicle to launch them into power.

Bolsheviks in Control

As Lenin's ideas grew, factory workers began to arm themselves and call themselves the Red Guard. Their numbers swelled as sailors from the former Russian fleet joined up. They were able to openly attack the provincial governments. While in a meeting at the Winter Palace in St. Petersburg in late 1917, the provincial governments surrendered as it was clear they no longer had any support or power whatsoever. Unfortunately, this was the end of the last period of peace in Russia for some time. The Bolsheviks moved the capital to Moscow, and they made the Kremlin, a walled fortress, their new headquarters.

It was at the Kremlin that Lenin declared that the Russians were going to set up a proletarian socialist state. There would be no more private ownership. Large industrial factories and land were turned over to the peasants. All of this sounded good to the Russian peasants, who for the first time thought they were finally going to be in charge. The new government took the name *Communist*, but unfortunately for the peasants, the Communists were soon going to dominate them, just as the former autocratic government had.

RUSSIAN CIVIL WAR: RED ARMY VS. WHITE ARMY

A civil war began raging in Russia. The war lasted from 1918 to 1921, ravaging the countryside. The Red Army, or Army of the Communists, battled the White Army, or Russian people who did not like the Communist revolution. Some of the White Army remained loyal to the czar, yet other White Army members did not like the czarist regime but also did not like Lenin's Communist leadership either. Some White Russians felt Russia should also continue the war against Germany.

During the civil war, newly industrialized Japan captured some Russian territory in 1918. This prompted England, France, and the United States to actually send supplies and soldiers to help the White Russians combat the Communist Army. However, the cost was high on both sides as each group demonstrated it would go to great lengths to win the war.

The White Army tried to assassinate Lenin and began a policy of executing prisoners. To counter this, the Red Army went on a French Revolution–like reign of terror where they executed Russian peasants, even if there was just a rumor that the peasants were non-Communists. The most famous tale of this was when Czar Nicholas II and the entire Romanov royal family were executed in 1918. During the fighting, the Red Army took over all industrial mines and factories and sought to control the new railroads. The peasants shouldered the brunt of this as they were forced to give anything extra that they had to the army, who were giving the food to people in the large urban cities, who supported the Communists. The peasants were not happy about this, but there was little they could do. Leon Trotsky had been training the peasant Communist Army into a reliable fighting force, and his main weapon was elaborate speeches of patriotism, giving the soldiers reason to fight. As a result of brutal tactics and Trotsky's passionate speeches, the Communist Red Army defeated the White Army in 1921.

Even though the Red Army was victorious, there were still a lot of problems facing Russia. Millions had died in the combination of World War I and the civil war, Russian industry was inefficient, and the land was ravaged. Lenin had put himself in place to solve these problems and build a new Russia. Now, he was poised to do just that.

Lenin's Communist State

Lenin worked tirelessly to reshape Russia. His ultimate goal was to develop a perfect society where there were no social classes. The society was going to be governed by the people, who for the first time were in control of the capital. The proletariat would determine the means of industrial production, land usage, and rebuilding of Russia. While Lenin worked hard to complete this goal, he was never able to fully realize it. In 1922, his government created a constitution where all political power and resources for production belonged to the workers, and anyone over the age of 18 could vote. However, it was all an illusion as it was Lenin's Communist Party who ran the show. On December 30, 1922, Russia became known as the Union of Soviet Socialist Republics or the U.S.S.R.

New Economic Policies: 1922

As Lenin began to build his utopian society, he had to focus on the economy, which was near total failure. His earlier policies were not working at all as some peasant farmers had stopped farming, knowing that anything they produced would be confiscated by the government. Lenin implemented some New Economic Policies (NEPs), and he took a lot of criticism for this as it was a small shift from his utopian Marxist views. Under the NEPs, most things essential to the government would be under Communist state control; however, nonessential businesses could sell things for a profit. This included small, local, private businesses. To appease the farmers, they were allowed to sell any surplus food or grain that they had for personal profit. Although he took criticism early on, by the end of the 1920s, the economy was on the rise again. Lenin thought the NEPs would only be a temporary solution, but it looked as if they were going to stay.

DEATH OF VLADIMIR LENIN AND THE RISE OF JOSEPH STALIN

Vladimir Lenin died in 1924 before his plans could be totally realized. Unfortunately for the people of Russia, his death created a power vacuum between his longtime friend Leon Trotsky and the head of the Communist Party, Joseph Stalin. Trotsky was an accomplished motivational speaker and firm believer in Marxism. He had helped Lenin orchestrate the successful Communist Revolution.

His opponent, Joseph Stalin, was none of this. Lenin believed Stalin was easily confused and did not quite know how to use the power that he had. Lenin knew Russia had to be careful if Stalin came to power. However, Stalin was a good organizer and manipulator within the Communist Party. After the death of Lenin, Trotsky and Stalin were each maneuvering to become the new leader of the country.

The two men also had different ideas on communism. Trotsky wanted to return to its roots and start a worldwide revolution against capitalism. Wisely, Stalin manipulated the minds and hearts of the Russian people. Stalin wanted to focus on the problems at home before Russia exported ideas to others. He reminded the people of the problems that were created when Russia got involved in world affairs during World War I. Stalin very deftly maneuvered his backers into the top positions within the Communist Party and the Communist Army. Slowly but surely, Trotsky was being maneuvered out of power, and while in exile in Mexico, Trotsky was assassinated by Joseph Stalin's secret police.

TIMELINE REVIEW

1905 C.E.	Russian Revolution leads to the creation of the Duma.
1917 C.E.	• Russia withdraws from World War I.
	• Vladimir Lenin seizes power in Russia.
1918 C.E.	Brest-Litovsk Treaty between Russia and the Central Powers
1920 C.E.	Russian Civil War: Red Army vs. White Army
1921 C.E.	• Red Army Communists win.
	• Lenin creates New Economic Policies (NEPs) to revive economy.
1922 C.E.	Russia becomes Union of Soviet Socialist Republics: U.S.S.R.
1924 C.E.	Lenin dies and is succeeded by Joseph Stalin.

The Great Depression and the Road to World War II

29

THE ROARING 20s

In the first seven to eight years of the 1920s, the United States achieved great prosperity. American banks and companies provided the capital and equipment to rebuild Europe. Coupled with many new inventions of the 20th century, this led to unseen levels of wealth and prosperity. It gave rise to the advertising industry as products were coming out so fast that everyone needed a competitive edge. As a result of the new levels of money, industrial workers saw their wages climb as industrialism boomed even further. One of the leading contributors was Henry Ford. His invention of the assembly line during the creation of the Model T automobile allowed every common person to afford a car.

The economic skyrocketing in America was in complete and total contrast to what was happening in Europe. Even though the war had ended, Europe had many problems. France and Belgium experienced total destruction of infrastructure and had lost an entire generation of young men. The Old World order had died in Europe, but there were still sharp divisions within European society as the few wealthy people that existed in Europe were from old, traditional families.

Nonetheless, the United States was riding high. More workers were hired, more products were manufactured, and products were being churned out at an incredible rate. Things were so good that few thought to stop and think what would happen if something were to change.

ECONOMIC COLLAPSE IN THE UNITED STATES

During the 1920s, large manufacturing corporations did not invest much in the maintenance of their factories. They were looking for profits. Sudden drought conditions led to an agricultural crisis. When the U.S. agriculture began to suffer, there were already economic difficulties and depression in Europe plus instability in Latin America. Unexpectedly, outlets for American products dried up. With no need for new products, everything that was stockpiled in U.S. warehouses stayed there. A backlash was heading toward U.S. industries.

After many years of hiring by U.S companies, workers were no longer needed, and a rise in unemployment began. Everybody from small shops to large industrial plants witnessed layoffs. Cities had grown, becoming large urban centers, and now many of these people were unemployed. Agricultural prices dropped so low that it cost farmers more to harvest their crops than to leave them in the field. Banks began to fail and close up as they loaned out more money than they had.

The presidential administrations of Warren G. Harding, Calvin Coolidge, and Herbert Hoover had not implemented any new laws or programs that could deal with a crisis of this magnitude.

FRANKLIN DELANO ROOSEVELT

When the U.S. stock market collapsed in October 1929, the first three years were desperate for most Americans. Then in 1932, presidential hopeful Franklin D. Roosevelt created a campaign slogan called "The New Deal." Roosevelt's primary goal was to change the people's opinion about the government. He wanted to offer a new deal for the American people.

Herbert Hoover campaigned using the mantra of "You are responsible. You have to pick yourself up and dig yourself out of this hole." Roosevelt wanted to show the people that he cared, and so did the government. When Roosevelt won the election in 1932, he worked tirelessly for the first 100 days to curb many problems plaguing the United States. The first 100 days of Roosevelt's administration are still to this day a nearly legendary event in presidential history.

As the banking crisis was reaching its zenith, President Roosevelt ordered all banks to be closed. After an evaluation, the banks that were financially solid and stable could reopen. The president also passed several acts aimed at helping the farm workers, including the Farm Credit Act to give loans to farmers to harvest their crops. One of the most well-known projects created by President Roosevelt was the Civilian Conservation Corps or the CCC. The CCC was created to build roads and parks, providing jobs to people who wanted to work hard. President Roosevelt was also famous for his "Fireside Chats." He would speak to the people over the radio with such calmness and caring that it helped the people get through the Great Depression.

Global Connections

This is similar to the strategy of Pisistratus in Greece and Julius Caesar in Rome. The idea is that when the workers get paid, they will put that money back into circulation by spending it.

Economic Changes Led by President Roosevelt

The president and the government played a greater role than it had ever before in the American economy. President Roosevelt was directly involved in regenerating the economy in cities located on the Tennessee River. The Tennessee Valley Authority was formed as hydroelectric power plants were created to provide and sell electricity.

To make sure the economic collapse never happened again, the Social Security Agency was created to ensure everyone had economic security. Organized labor was encouraged. The automotive, steel, and mining industries became unionized to help negotiate wages, monitor working conditions, and also sponsor competition.

Roosevelt's New Deal sounded good, but it never completely solved the unemployment problems. Even into the late 1930s, the economy was not back to pre-Depression levels. However, the U.S. economy was in much better shape compared to Europe, whose economic situation was dire. America was still seen as somewhat of an experiment, but it showed that a nation with vast industrial and natural resources, as well as a diverse labor force, could take on a major economic crisis and work through it, proving that democracy works.

PROBLEMS FOR THE BRITISH EMPIRE

England encountered many problems before, during, and after the Great Depression. Although Great Britain was on the side of the victors in World War I, it suffered a major blow to its overseas trading network. The German submarine fleet had destroyed many British shipping vessels.

England was the first to fully industrialize, but many of its factories had not been updated and, therefore, were woefully out of date and in need of modernization. As the 1920s wore on, Great Britain fully realized the dramatic loss it had suffered. Faced with tremendous debt, wages for industrial workers remained very low and unemployment was very high. This caused the British citizens to go on strike in 1926. Several necessary industries went on strike at the same time, involving as many as 3 million workers. The Liberal Party, the ruling political party during this time, quickly began to lose position to the Labour Party, which began to promote ideas such as socialism. However, England's middle class "movers and shakers" backed a third party during this time known as the Conservative Party. The Conservative Party spoke out against ideas such as socialism and communism, and they retained a lot of power during this period. When the economy did not get better, the leaders of all three parties—Labour, Liberal, and Conservative—began to work together to find a way to alleviate some of the more severe problems.

National Movements Within the British Empire

Just before World War I, a major crisis facing England was independence for some of its colonies, a byproduct of nationalism. By 1916, Irish nationalists were tired of waiting for independence, so on Easter Sunday 1916, they began a series of small revolts against the British rule. The uprisings were quickly quelled with the execution of many leaders, but a flicker of unrest remained alive.

By 1919, when World War I ended, a British civil war broke out as some militant members created what was known as the Irish Republican Army, or the IRA. The IRA ravaged Ireland and Great Britain, using hit-and-run guerrilla tactics that often trapped innocent civilians, who became casualties of the conflict. Finally, in 1922, an agreement was reached. A large portion of Ireland became the independent Irish Free State, while the Protestant northern sector of Ireland remained under British rule. This was never fully accepted, and there were difficulties between the British and the IRA up into the 1990s.

Along with Ireland's quest for independence, Great Britain also had to deal with demands from other parts of the empire: Australia, Canada, South Africa, and New Zealand. In 1931, they became self-governing countries known as the British Commonwealth of Nations. Each member of the Commonwealth could look after its own interests but would still be economically linked to Great Britain.

In addition, England never really believed in the Treaty of Versailles. They feared that an overly weakened Germany would be susceptible to communism from the Soviet Union, allowing the French once again to dominate the continent. Thus, there was a total lack of cooperation between the victorious English and French, which was necessary to prevent World War II from breaking out.

THE FRENCH POSITION

Even though France emerged from World War I as a victor, it too suffered enormous losses in manpower, industry, and agriculture. The French, however, got back the agricultural territories of Alsace and Lorraine. They also received more German war reparations than most countries.

However, the onset of the Great Depression caused France to be politically unstable. Many political parties—Communists, Isolationists, and Conservatives—were battling for power while forming coalition governments. France underwent a series of political crises and what was clearly demonstrated was the need for a strong, dominant leader to take care of the people of France as well as the tense international political situation.

THE GREAT DEPRESSION HITS EUROPE

The severity of the Great Depression in Europe was due to multiple simultaneous events.

1. The financial collapse in England, France, and Germany coming out of World War I
2. The reparation mandates of the Treaty of Versailles
3. The lack of strong leadership and visionary leaders from England, France, and the newly isolationist United States
4. The determination of the French to make Germany pay them billions of dollars in war reparations
5. The determination of the United States to collect on loans made to European countries after World War I

All of these challenges led directly to World War II.

France Determined to Make Germany Pay

In 1923, France declared that Germany defaulted on its reparation payments. According to the Treaty of Versailles, France could now use military power against Germany, so the French army occupied the Ruhr River industrial sector. In protest of this, the German government ordered its citizens to passively resist by going on strike. As the German coal and iron ore miners and industrial iron workers went on strike, the French shipped in their own unemployed citizens. The French took over the German's jobs while the Germans were essentially put out into the street.

Things were going well until the October 29, 1929, stock market crash in the United States. American money had poured into Europe since World War I, but with the crash, there was no money left to invest. In 1931, a major German bank collapsed. The only thing done to alleviate the crash was a one-year grace period until Germany was required to pay off their debts. Along with the stock market crash, agricultural prices reached a record low. Even though more European farmers were receiving no money, industrial workers had seen a rise in their salaries. This made things more expensive for the farmers who could not pay their mortgages and farming loans. As prices plummeted worldwide on agricultural goods, the financial turmoil caused by the stock market collapse and the growing unemployment magnified the crisis. Governments were afraid of spending money, and their financially conservative actions actually made the problem worse.

All of this came back to haunt Europe as many farmers who were unemployed and angry turned away from the democratic government. They listened to parties such as the new growing National Socialist Workers' Party, which became known as the Nazi Party.

Coming out of World War I, the Allies no longer worked together. Nobody knew how to confront these new problems, and, historically, when people are angry and scared, they sometimes become irrational. They listen to any voice, especially when the voice says who is to blame for their problems. In Germany, there were many unemployed industrial and agricultural workers who had served as soldiers. They had fought for their country and had been treated poorly. Believing that they were owed a job and security, they listened to any voice who gave them an option.

The Weimar Republic: Article 48

Germany would never be able to overcome the problem of trying to pay the reparation payments required by the Treaty of Versailles. Germany's new form of democratic government was called the Weimar Republic. The Weimar Republic was a constant target for military leaders who blamed Germany's financial problems on them.

The problem with the German political process was the Weimar legislature, known as the Reichstag. The Reichstag allowed every political party to have seats in the legislature, even if the party had only a few members. There were no dominant parties, and there was constant turmoil when trying to get anything accomplished. It led to instability. While the Reichstag was in place, the president and chancellor of Germany had the power. Harkening back to the days of Rome and the dictator Cincinnatus, the Germans wrote an article into their Constitution known as Article 48. Article 48 stated that in a dire emergency, a dictator could be elected to solve the country's problems.

GLOBAL CONNECTIONS

Similar turmoil has been seen in other countries that have multiple political parties. Even the United States, with the Democrats and the Republicans, and England, with the Labour Party and the Liberal Conservative Party, have experienced their fair share of instability.

Germany Before the Great Depression

During the 1920s, the German government had to put down several rebellions. There were strikes among the workers, and the reparation payments constantly weighed down the effectiveness of the German government. The other problem for Germany was their idea of unemployment insurance. The German government would pay wages for unemployed workers until they got a new job. All of this caused massive inflation in Germany. To pay off their debts, the German government kept printing German dollars called marks. When the French invaded the Ruhr mining area, the government could not pay all of the unemployed German workers. There was just too much for them to handle.

Adolf Hitler Appears

During this unstable period of German history, Adolf Hitler made his first appearance. Adolf Hitler fought in Flanders in World War I and received the Iron Cross, Second Class. In his mind, he was a bona fide German war hero who fought for the kaiser. He also believed that Germany did not lose World War I.

After World War I, Hitler settled in the German city of Munich. While there, he heard a speech by a member of the Christian Socialist Party, who fed on the fears of German workers by promoting German nationalism and condemning Marxism and Judaism. Hitler believed deeply in these ideals and decided to join the Nazi Party.

The Nazi Party had a platform called the 25 Points. The Nazi Party said that the 25 Points program, if followed, would restore Germany. Some provisions included canceling the Treaty of Versailles, excluding Jews from citizenship, and getting the people back to work. The Nazis believed they would unite the German people together as one nation.

The leaders of the Nazi Party saw that their message struck a chord with the poorest classes and the lower middle class, so they created a civic group to teach these groups about leadership. In reality, it was a way to teach military ideals and build an army without breaking the Treaty of Versailles. The boys in the group became known as stormtroopers. The Nazi Party billed the group as providing military discipline and training, but the stormtroopers were used as thugs.

When the French took over the Ruhr district in September 1923, they played right into the plans of the Nazi Party. They said the French were to blame for Germany's problems and the Weimar Republic was powerless, but the Nazi Party would take care of the people.

In the meantime, Hitler had become a rock star in the Nazi Party. He discovered that one of the few skills he had was public speaking. He knew how to use his voice, when to speak softly, when to scream and shout, and how to use inflection and tone to attract others to the party. On November 8–9, 1923, Hitler led a coup in Munich known as the Beer Hall Putsch. It failed miserably, and Hitler was arrested. Hitler used his trial as a vehicle to make himself a household name inside of Germany. While on trial, his statements were printed in the newspapers and broadcasted over the radio. Hitler spelled out his plan for getting rid of the Treaty of Versailles to restore Germany. He also spelled out how he would kick the Jews out of Germany.

Hitler was sentenced to five years in prison, and during his imprisonment, he wrote a book called *Mein Kampf* (*My Struggle*).

Gustav Stresemann

In 1923, Gustav Stresemann stepped in as chancellor and began to return Germany to respectability. After just a few months serving as chancellor and implementing positive changes in the government, Stresemann resigned as chancellor to serve as the foreign minister so he could lobby for Germany on an international scene. Stresemann thought he could help Germany more as foreign minister. He reached out to the Western powers in 1924 and helped reconstruct the reparation payments with an American plan called the Dawes Plan. The Dawes Plan allowed Germany's payments to be flexible based on how the economy was performing. The better the economy, the more Germany would pay, and when the economy was doing poorly, they would pay a smaller amount.

Aging World War I hero Paul von Hindenburg supported Stresemann's policies and was elected as the German president in 1925. As foreign minister, Stresemann gave concessions to the Western powers in an effort to maintain Germany's part of the Treaty of Versailles.

All of this effort allowed the German economy to slowly grow. Foreign investors infused capital into German industry, and Germany looked as if it was going to get back on track. However, Stresemann had other plans as well. He wanted to get back some of the territory in Eastern Europe that had been carved out of German territory, specifically in the new countries of Poland and Czechoslovakia. There were Germans living as minorities in those countries, and the countries were created to box in Germany, which did not sit well with Stresemann.

Locarno Accords

In 1925, Stresemann negotiated the signing of the Locarno Accords. Stresemann was a good ambassador, and Great Britain and France were leaning toward accepting Germany with a clean slate. With Great Britain and Italy serving as mediators, the Locarno Accords gave Germany a guarantee that the French would never again come into Germany's manufacturing district and possibly allow for a revision of the location of the eastern border of Germany with Poland. Germany had achieved respectability and was back in the fold with the Western European powers.

However, while this was going on in the West, Germany was looking for a strong ally for themselves, and they began a secret military alliance with the new Soviet Union. Politicians and powerbrokers were enjoying the new relationship with the West, but many people in Germany were still bitter over the Treaty of Versailles and the treatment Germany had received. They did not trust the Locarno Accords, believing that it was just another trick by the Western powers to make Germany pay.

With U.S. loans and building materials coming into the continent, Europe was on the edge of returning to prosperity. Even the bitterness at the Weimar Republic was starting to ebb. Then, the Great Depression hit in October 1929. It changed all the work that Germany and Stresemann had done.

Effects of the Great Depression on Germany

As the Great Depression hit, a stalemate occurred in the German Reichstag. The issue was over reducing or eliminating the unemployment insurance. Some parties believed that to balance the German budget, they could not continue paying it. They pointed to the rampant inflation that hit them in the early 1920s as an example. By March 1930, there was no solution to the stalemate so President von Hindenburg used Article 48 to appoint a man named Heinrich Bruning to solve the problem. Bruning was known as a financial wizard, but unfortunately for him, no matter what he tried, things just got worse, and unemployment doubled in two years.

Capitalizing on the effects of the Great Depression, the Nazi Party was able to gain support from big business leaders and military men. They were able to sway huge numbers toward their cause. Much of this was due to Hitler, who got out of prison in 1928. The Great Depression thrust Hitler back into the limelight. Using his oral mastery to get people to support the Nazis, the party grew rapidly. While Hitler was in prison, the Nazi Party had only 12 seats in Parliament, but by 1930 the number had grown to 107 seats.

HITLER'S ASCENT TO POWER

By 1932, the economic situation of Germany was not improving. President Hindenburg was up for reelection, and one of his many opponents was Adolf Hitler. Since Hindenburg was a war hero, no one thought the election would be close, but it took a runoff election for Hindenburg to win. Hindenburg chose a new chancellor and invited Hitler to be part of the cabinet as he wanted to draw on his overwhelming popular support. Hitler declined this invitation.

During the next Reichstag election in 1932, the Nazi Party won an amazing 230 seats. Hitler announced that he would enter the president's cabinet if he was made chancellor. His offer was turned down. However, when the situation in Germany continued to deteriorate, Paul von Hindenburg appointed Adolf Hitler as the chancellor of Germany on January 30, 1933.

Hitler had been legally handed the power over Germany. All governmental services in Germany had to listen to Hitler, though some in Germany were not happy. Roman Catholics in the south spoke out, but it was quickly squelched. Lutherans protested in the north, and the same thing happened. Drawing on his experience as a soldier, Hitler was able to tap into the anger felt by unemployed young men or farmers. He told them he was going to keep them safe from the Communists in Russia and make the enemies of Germany pay (namely France and the Jews). Hitler restored and revived pride in German culture and built a sense of ultra-nationalism inside of Germany.

Hitler Has Complete Control

Shortly after Hitler became chancellor, a fire was set in the German Reichstag. A card-carrying member of the Dutch Communist Party, who happened to be a one-legged old man, was arrested for the crime. Hitler used this event to state that Germany was under a threat and named himself as dictator based on the rules of Article 48. He passed an immediate decree that stopped all civil liberties until the crisis was past. The decree was not overturned until Hitler's death in 1945.

By March 1933, just two months after Hitler came to power, the Reichstag passed a law that allowed Hitler to rule by verbal decree, and he had no limits whatsoever on his power. Any leader or institution—economic, legal, or religious—that stood in his way was arrested, and the business was seized.

By July 14, 1933, the Nazi Party was the only political party in Germany. The stormtroopers had over one million members, and under their leader Ernst Rohm, they were ready to do Hitler's bidding. However, wary of the power held by Rohm, Hitler had him eliminated and many of the stormtrooper officers were killed in a purge. Hitler took over the leadership of the stormtroopers. In 1934, German President Paul von Hindenburg died. After his death, there was no one to question or stop Adolf Hitler.

Germany Becomes a Police State

Hitler appointed his second-in-command, Heinrich Himmler, with the job of creating a bodyguard unit called the SS, or the Secret Police. The SS eliminated Hitler's opponents in the Nazi Party, and they began to practice widespread anti-Semitism. Heinrich Himmler was the creator of anti-Jewish propaganda and instituted many restrictions for Jews.

- In 1933, all Jews were excluded from civil services.
- Starting in 1934, all Jewish businesses were boycotted.
- In 1935, Hitler passed the Nuremberg Laws, stripping Jews of their German citizenship.

By 1938, the Nazis began to promote the idea that the Aryan race was the master race. Heinrich Himmler was the architect behind all of this.

Hitler also sponsored a cultural program that taught young children to love German culture, German fairytales, German food, and German dancing. He began a massive effort to rebuild the military, blatantly breaking provisions of the Treaty of Versailles. However, nothing was done to stop Hitler, leading the world down the road toward World War II.

RUSSIA DURING THE 1920s

Coming out of World War I and the Russian Revolution, things were going poorly. Vladimir Lenin instituted New Economic Policies (NEPs) allowing farmers to sell surplus crops for profit; nonessential businesses were also permitted to sell things for profit. The new policies angered many Russians, claiming they deviated from true socialism. When Lenin died in 1924 without naming a successor, problems arose. Lenin's two henchmen—Leon Trotsky and Joseph Stalin, the head of the Communist Party—both wanted control over Russia.

Rapid Industrialization

The rivalry between Trotsky and Stalin was over a difference in opinion about Russia becoming fully industrialized. Leon Trotsky wanted rapid industrialization. He wanted the farmers to collectivize their land and materials, and he wanted Russia to export the Communist revolution to other parts of the globe. By spreading communism, Russia could get friends and allies and use their skills to get them industrially up to speed.

Stalin aligned himself with old-school Communists, and Stalin spoke out on the position that Russia could accomplish socialism alone. They did not need help from anybody else as they could do it themselves. Eventually, Trotsky was exiled to Mexico where he was murdered by a Stalin henchman.

Stalin's Plan for Industrialization

Stalin's policy of self-sufficiency killed millions of his own people. By 1929, there were massive food shortages. Stalin blamed the food shortages on the farmers, claiming they were not loyal to Russia. He took control over all privately owned land. When the farmers began to resist by destroying their crops and killing their livestock, Stalin rounded them up. Between eight million and ten million farmers were either executed or worked to death in Siberia. Those who remained brought their farms together into what were called collectives.

> ### DINNER TABLE TALK
>
> I call this the Star Trek Borg strategy! The Borg Collective does everything as one unit ruled by a Borg Queen. The Soviet government saw the country's farms in the same way. Since the government gave the Soviet farmers equipment and machinery, they controlled everything and dictated what the farmers would get and how much food they were supposed to grow.

Stalin decided that Russia needed to industrialize rapidly to gain equal footing with the West. This was actually Leon Trotsky's plan, but Stalin took credit for it.

The Gosplan—Soviet State Planning Committee

As the United States, Great Britain, Germany, and France fell victim to the Great Depression, Russia took advantage of it. During the Great Depression, Russia made more rapid advancements in their economic system than any other country during the same time period. Russia's industrial output increased several hundred percent, but they started from so far behind that they still struggled to catch up to other industrialized countries.

The Five-Year Plans were created in 1928 to collectivize agriculture and to provide a constant supply of food to the workers during the rapid industrialization. Collective farming and the Five-Year Plans were set up by an organization known as the Gosplan. The Gosplan was every bit the face of the Soviet Union, and their main goal was to achieve the objectives of their Five-Year Plans.

The Soviet Union was a complicated organizational network that required everything to work on time as planned. Any delay caused a domino effect, so to prevent that, the entire Soviet society was disciplined and regimented to make sure nothing went wrong.

By the 1930s, with the Great Depression still in full effect, three Five-Year Plans had been accomplished. For the first time ever, Russian manufacturing was able to overtake Western countries. However, even though Russia was growing, the working conditions of the workers were horrible. Millions of people died of starvation or overwork. Entire villages were relocated to provide labor. None of that mattered as long as Stalin's goals were met.

STALIN'S PURGES

Stalin began to fear for his position. He was constantly criticized for moving too far away from Vladimir Lenin's vision, so Stalin began to imagine there were enemies everywhere. He began to eliminate everyone who could stand in his way. Members of the Politburo, the leading nine-member group of men who led the Soviet Union, were arrested. Throughout the Soviet Union, people were put in prison or executed. The only people that were not bothered were old World War I veterans and the heroes of the Russian Revolution.

The Communists in Russia formed an authoritarian government that lasted until the last decade of the 20th century. They believed that combining everything in a regimented, collective lifestyle could sustain the people. The Soviet Union helped shape and determine many events from the Great Depression through the end of the 20th century.

ITALY DURING THE GREAT DEPRESSION: THE RISE OF FASCISM WITH BENITO MUSSOLINI

Many Italians became upset and disenfranchised by the outcome of the Treaty of Versailles. Italy expected to be rewarded as a victor and get new territory as a result. However, parts of Italy were taken away to form the new country of Yugoslavia, which became a homeland for many small ethnicities from the defeated and collapsed Austrian-Hungarian empire. Seeing the peasants revolt in Russia, many Italian workers went on strike and tried to seize land. An exciting orator named Benito Mussolini, a passionate and fanatical Italian nationalist who was angry at the outcome of World War I, helped create the Fascist Party in Italy in 1919.

Very similar to the economic situation in Germany, many Italian war veterans could not find work. It was at this point that Benito Mussolini experienced a dramatic change of heart. At one time a socialist, Mussolini became more and more passionate and nationalistic. Mussolini began to speak to fellow veterans who felt just the way he did. And as he spoke, not only did former soldiers listen to his message but other lower- and middle-class people listened as well. Mussolini created the Fascist Party in 1919, named for an ancient Roman symbol that meant authority. Mussolini was a great speaker, very similar to Adolf Hitler. Mussolini said Italy needed to end governmental corruption and the complete ineptitude of its politicians. Italy needed to return to Roman greatness.

Fascism

The political ideology of fascism is hard to define. Fascism is total authoritarian government. It is different from communism and existed in several different countries, from Spain to Italy to Germany, but it looked a little different in each country. One commonality that all three versions had was passionate nationalism. Swift action and violence could be used if necessary. Unwavering obedience to the state was required. To Mussolini and the other fascists, a democracy only had one end to it: greed and corruption. Those two things weakened a country. In those systems, individuals were put above the goals of the country. In fascism, the country comes first.

Fascism vs. Communism

Fascists believed they were the archrivals of socialists and communists. As communists wanted to export their ideology, fascists wanted to focus on their own nation and achieve national goals. Instead of getting rid of big business leaders and other wealthy groups, fascists sought to work with them, as well as work with the middle-class people who made money. Communists targeted the lower peasantry or the lower classes, which did not happen in a fascist state.

However, even though there were significant differences, there were also some striking similarities between fascists and communists.

- Both were able to gain a foothold during the hard economic times brought about by the Great Depression.

- Each ideology used the situation to invoke social change by harkening to the "good old days" of the past.
- They both put the blame squarely on outside countries, saying that the problems were not their fault, but that someone else had done this to them.

Mussolini was the first in this era to run a totalitarian government, but Hitler, Stalin, and Franco of Spain also used many qualities of a totalitarian regime. The appeal of fascism was that the people were promised that the government would be stable. They were told that democracy had led them into the abyss, that the people's choices were strong, and that the fascist leaders knew how to return the country to its former glory.

Mussolini Seizes Power

In 1922, Mussolini began to organize his followers in a militaristic fashion, calling them combat squads. They all dressed in the same uniform ("Blackshirts"), and they were opposed to any form of democracy. Instead, they favored very quick, decisive, and sometimes violent action. If there were any other political rallies—Socialist, Democratic—they would be broken up. Newspapers that supported parties other than the fascists were destroyed. Any attempt at unionization of workers was stopped. Very similar to the stormtroopers in Germany, the Blackshirts intimidated and terrified everyone, especially democratically elected officials in Italy.

In 1922, the fascists made a grab for power in Naples. They announced they were going to march on Rome to demand the ineffective government make changes. Hearing of their approach, King Victor Emmanuel III caved in and asked Mussolini to serve as his prime minister to help him reform the government. Without a lot of violence, Mussolini obtained a legal position from the king, and from that point began to take over.

At first, the Fascist Party only had control over a few important governmental posts, but by 1925, that began to change. Mussolini took the title *Il Duce* which means "the Leader." Like Stalin and Hitler, Mussolini removed rival parties, controlled what was said in the press, and restricted voting rights. While Italy maintained the illusion that it was a parliamentary monarchy like Great Britain, it was a total dictatorship. Any disagreement was met with violence. Anyone who spoke out against Mussolini was sent to prison, or at best was exiled. Many were executed as a secret police force carried out Mussolini's wishes.

Global Connections

Sound familiar? Yes, Adolf Hitler did the same thing!

Mussolini's Economic Policies

To bring stabilization to Italy, Mussolini sought to find a way to get the economy to grow. He wanted business owners and workers to cooperate. Since he felt they could not do that on their own, Mussolini put the economy under his direct governmental control. However, he did preserve capitalism. He was not a communist. Mussolini called Italy a corporate state where different members from the government, business leadership, and workers met to control Italian business. In the short term, this helped as production increased, but the workers did not benefit from it. They were paid poor wages, were not allowed to form any union whatsoever, and were forbidden from striking.

Mussolini's Ideals

To Mussolini, people were supposed to subordinate themselves to the will of the state, similar to the ideals of the ancient Greek philosopher Plato. He used propaganda that encouraged a return to the glory of ancient Rome and stated that one minute in combat was worth a lifetime of peace. Since women were not allowed on the battlefield, special awards were given to women who had large families as the woman's place was in the home. To Mussolini, it was women in the workplace and industrial machines that caused unemployment.

Such was life under a totalitarian regime. Italian children were brought up with fascist goals in mind, again similar to the Hitler Youth, as schools were designed to strengthen the children. They were taught to have strict military discipline, and tales were told of Roman heroes and the Roman Empire. Italian children were taught in school that Mussolini's ideals were correct.

Global Connections

Education under Mussolini was almost like being educated in ancient Sparta.

TIMELINE REVIEW

1919 C.E.	Fascism begins to rise when Italy does not receive territory as part of the Treaty of Versailles.
1920s C.E.	Key to world economy is U.S. economic prosperity.
1920–1929 C.E.	U.S. isolation and the Roaring 20s
1921 C.E.	• Weimer Republic signs Treaty of Versailles, leading to massive inflation in Germany.
	• Lenin begins New Economic Policies (NEPs) in Russia.
1922 C.E.	• Russia renamed Union of Soviet Socialist Republics.
	• Benito Mussolini founds the Fascist Party and is named Prime Minister of Italy.
1923 C.E.	• French invade Rhur River valley in Germany.
	• Hitler attends Christian Socialist Party rally in Munich, Germany.
	• Hitler leads Beer Hall Putsch.
	• Hitler is arrested and writes *Mein Kampf* while in prison.
1924 C.E.	• Dawes Plan: U.S. loans money to Germany to pay reparations.
	• Lenin dies—power struggle for leadership of U.S.S.R. between Joseph Stalin and Leon Trotsky
1925 C.E.	Locarno Accords: England and France give Germany a fresh start.
1928 C.E.	• Stalin exiles Trotsky and is in sole command of U.S.S.R.
	• Stalin begins Five-Year Economic Plans and collective farming in the Soviet Union.
1929 C.E.	• U.S. stock market crashes.
	• Young Plan reduces reparations based on German economy.
	• Great Depression hits Germany as Hitler is released from jail.
1930 C.E.	• Massive inflation worldwide
	• High German unemployment sends thousands to join the Nazi Party.
1931 C.E.	• England imposes high protective tariffs and raises taxes.
	• Japanese economy struggles.
1932 C.E.	• Hitler runs for president of Germany and barely loses to World War I hero Hindenburg.
	• U.S. elects Franklin D. Roosevelt as president.
	• New Deal programs are designed to get Americans working again.

1933 C.E.	• One million French workers are unemployed.
	• Hindenburg legally names Hitler as chancellor of Germany.
	• Stalin turns on Soviet Communist leadership and "purges" his rivals.
	• Millions of Soviets die because of Stalin's agricultural plans.
1934 C.E.	Hindenburg dies, leaving Hitler as the sole ruler of Germany.
1935 C.E.	Mussolini attacks Ethiopia.
1936 C.E.	• The French Coalition government—the Popular Front—leads reform.
	• Italy forms Rome–Berlin Axis with Adolf Hitler.

Quick Quiz: Chapters 27–29

1. Which European statesman created a series of alliances to try to prevent further wars in Europe?

   A. Otto von Bismarck
   B. Clemens von Metternich
   C. Camillo Cavour
   D. Henri Petain

2. Which growing movement/factor heavily influenced the people of the Balkans in the late 1800s and early 1900s?

   A. Militarism
   B. Imperialism
   C. Nationalism
   D. Industrialism

3. The invasion of which country was the final straw that drew Great Britain into World War I?

   A. France
   B. Belgium
   C. Netherlands
   D. Luxembourg

4. Which event caused Russia to have to withdraw from fighting during World War I?

   A. Decembrist Revolt
   B. Defeat of the Russian offensive at Tannenberg
   C. Beginning of the Russian Revolution
   D. Revealing of Lenin's New Economic Plans

5. What was the main cause of the massive number of casualties in World War I?

   A. The number of empires involved in the conflict
   B. The large number of soldiers who were professionals and not conscripted citizens
   C. The fighting in areas that were densely populated with civilians
   D. The number of new technologies involved in the conflict

6. What was the name given to the common people who were expected to lead the Russian Revolution?

   A. Streltsy
   B. Populists
   C. Proletariat
   D. Bolsheviks

7. Which country heavily involved in the fighting of World War I aided Vladimir Lenin's return to power?

   A. Germany
   B. France
   C. United States
   D. Great Britain

8. What did Lenin name his plans that became controversial as he tried to revive the failing Russian economy?

   A. Five-Year Plans
   B. Collectives
   C. New Economic Plans
   D. College System

9. Which country chose a policy of isolation after World War I?

   A. Japan
   B. United States
   C. Germany
   D. Great Britain

10. Which of the following actions was taken by France in 1923 when they claimed Germany defaulted on its reparation payments?

    A. Increased the amount of reparations
    B. Sent the matter to the League of Nations for a ruling
    C. Invaded the Ruhr River mining district
    D. Annexed the mineral-rich areas of Alsace and Lorraine

11. Why was Adolf Hitler sent to prison in post–World War I Germany?

    A. He was a leading speaker for the Nazi Party.
    B. He led an attempted coup in Munich called the Beer Hall Putsch.
    C. He went public with the Nazi 25 Points program.
    D. He was a vocal and open critic of the Weimar Republic and encouraged members of the Nazi Party to attack members of the current government.

12. As Joseph Stalin succeeded Vladimir Lenin as leader of the Soviet Union, which of the following did Stalin use to organize the agriculture and industry in the Soviet Union?

    A. Collectives
    B. Gulags
    C. Five-Year Plans
    D. Go Plans

13. From 1918 to 1939, which other leader most closely resembled Germany's Adolf Hitler?

    A. Benito Mussolini of Italy
    B. Joseph Stalin of the Soviet Union
    C. Francisco Franco of Spain
    D. Neville Chamberlain of Great Britain

Quick Quiz Answers

1. A; **2.** C; **3.** B; **4.** C; **5.** D; **6.** C; **7.** A; **8.** C; **9.** B; **10.** C; **11.** B; **12.** C; **13.** A

World War II Through the Creation of Israel

30

The world had high hopes after the signing of the Locarno Accords in 1925, but the Great Depression in 1929 changed the world. The world peace that everyone had hoped would last was quickly challenged, first by the Japanese.

Japanese military leadership had revived a spirit of ultranationalism after the success of the Meiji Restoration. Their goal was to be equal to the Western powers in Europe and the United States, but one thing Japan lacked was natural resources. In 1931, the Japanese occupied the Chinese province of Manchuria to gain land and resources. China immediately appealed to the League of Nations for help. The League condemned Japan's action, but no one really wanted to impose sanctions on them as many countries were working economically with Japan.

In Germany, Adolf Hitler watched this unfold and saw the pacifism of Great Britain, France, and other Western European countries as a sign of weakness. Their pacifism further encouraged Hitler and other dictators to see how far they could expand before they were stopped.

MUSSOLINI INVADES ETHIOPIA

In October 1935, Benito Mussolini of Italy took his brand-new army and his new imperialist goals and attacked Ethiopia. Forty years earlier, the Ethiopians had defeated Italy, and it was still a source of embarrassment for Mussolini. He had promised to restore Italy to the heights of Roman glory.

The League of Nations immediately opposed Mussolini's action and imposed some economic sanctions on Italy. However, the sanctions stopped short of doing the one thing that could have slowed down and hurt Italy: restricting the sale of oil to Italy. The British and French did not want to upset the new leader of Italy by imposing harsh sanctions. With the League of Nations clearly lacking the ability to enforce its will, Mussolini turned to fellow dictator Adolf Hitler to form an alliance. On November 1, 1936, they announced the Rome-Berlin Axis. Mussolini and Hitler declared that central Europe would "turn on the axis" of their two great empires: Italy and Germany.

ADOLF HITLER IN GERMANY

Hitler had always said the Treaty of Versailles was the source of Germany's problems. His goal was to bring all German people together into one unified nation, including parts of the old Austrian-Hapsburg Empire. Hitler felt his new German nation would need room for the people to grow, and since the Treaty of Versailles did not protect any territory in Eastern Europe, Hitler figured he would use that as an area for his new German nation. The native peoples would be forced to work for the greater German people, and he wanted to purify the territory from Jews, especially in Poland and the Ukraine.

Hitler knew that sooner or later, his objectives would probably lead to war. What set Hitler apart was that he did not mind war. He actually wanted war. Hitler also knew that people would go to great lengths to avoid war, so he could be as aggressive as he wanted until finally someone stood up to him.

Shortly after coming to power in 1933, Hitler withdrew from the International Disarmament Conference, which was part of the League of Nations. Hitler also stated he was going to rebuild the German army, which was illegal according to the Treaty of Versailles. In 1934, Hitler formed a nonaggression pact with the country of Poland. A nonaggression pact meant that if either country got involved in a war, the other one would not interfere. Poland was specifically created by France to border Germany in the East as a French "security blanket." The nonaggression pact removed France's protection.

When Mussolini invaded Ethiopia, Hitler began to form a new German air force, the Luftwaffe, and started to draft soldiers into his army. The League of Nations renounced Hitler's plans at rearming; however, Great Britain and France could not complain too loudly because they did not disarm themselves to the levels they had promised.

The Rhineland

Hitler decided he was going to test the strength of the Western powers. On March 7, 1936, he further violated the Treaty of Versailles by sending a small military force into the Rhineland. The Rhineland was an area between the border with France and the Rhine River. It was supposed to be a demilitarized zone to provide a buffer between France and Germany. When Hitler entered the Rhineland, Great Britain and France launched a strongly worded letter in the League of Nations, instead of dealing directly with Hitler to stop his aggression.

Global Connections

The current demilitarized zone between North and South Korea is still active, providing a buffer zone between communist North Korea and democratic South Korea.

POLICY OF APPEASEMENT

Great Britain was still recovering from World War I, trying to recapture its imperial empire. France was going through its own internal problems as the old guard was being challenged by young, forward-thinking military officers and politicians. Because of their own internal problems, coupled with problems of the Great Depression, both Great Britain and France followed a policy of appeasement toward Germany. Great Britain and France both hoped that by pacifying Hitler with a letter of admonishment, he would eventually go away.

So as Hitler was rapidly rearming a new modern army in Germany, British Prime Minister Neville Chamberlain put forth the policy of appeasement. Many in Europe agreed that Germany had legitimate arguments that they were wronged by the Treaty of Versailles, so Chamberlain stated that Hitler's rearming of Germany was limited and acceptable. Chamberlain was determined to prevent another war.

EFFECTS OF THE SPANISH CIVIL WAR

During the 1920s, Spain was ruled by a monarchy, and the government was dominated by wealthy landowners who were directed by the Roman Catholic Church. Most Spaniards were poor peasants. Beginning in 1931, the anger of the young people forced the king to leave, and a new Spanish Republic was born. Using a new constitution, the government passed a series of reforms that divided the country. Much of the church land was taken, and some of it was redistributed to the peasants. Spanish women were also given the right to vote.

In response to the new Republic, General Francisco Franco started the ultranationalistic Fascist Party in 1936. Franco led the army against the Republican government and started the Spanish Civil War. The three-year civil war killed more than one million people. Russia sided with the Spanish people, known as loyalists, who supported the new Constitution, whereas Italy and Germany sided with Franco and sent him a great deal of support.

The Spanish Civil War accomplished two things.

- It brought the fascist dictators of Hitler and Mussolini closer together.
- It allowed Hitler's new modern weapons of war to be used in combat.

The Spanish Civil War is often referred to as a scrimmage match for World War II. When the power of the German army was displayed, nationalist Japan notified Hitler that it wanted to form an alliance with them. The Rome-Berlin-Tokyo Axis was created between Italy, Germany, and Japan.

HITLER CONTINUES HIS AGGRESSION

Austria

Adolf Hitler wanted to bring all German-speaking people into his new government, the Third Reich. As Germany began to promote the idea of the Aryan, or master, race, Hitler felt Germany needed room to grow. According to Hitler, the Slavic people to the east were inferior and, therefore, could be removed from their land. Hitler also wanted to annex Austria, and many of the Austrian people supported Hitler and the Nazi Party. Hitler was born in Austria, and the nostalgia of Europe's oldest monarchy would give some prestige to Germany. After a failed meeting between Hitler and Austrian Chancellor Kurt von Schuschnigg in February 1938, Schuschnigg caved to the will of the people, saying he would let Austria vote to see if they wanted to unify with Germany. Hitler was wary of democracy because if he lost, it would look bad, so Hitler invaded Austria on March 12, 1938.

Hitler's Next Goal: Czechoslovakia

After easily annexing Austria, Hitler next went after Czechoslovakia. Czechoslovakia was created by the Treaty of Versailles to box in Germany. It was democratic and pro-Western, and two of its allies were enemies of Hitler: France and the Soviet Union. Plus, a section of the newly formed Czechoslovakia, the Sudetenland, was originally part of Germany. It was rich in natural resources and housed 3.5 million Germans who did not like being part of Czechoslovakia.

Still committed to the policy of appeasement, British Prime Minister Neville Chamberlain told the Czech representatives in September 1938 to surrender the Sudetenland without a fight. Chamberlain returned to Great Britain, saying he had bought peace with honor and achieved peace for our time. However, British Parliament member Winston Churchill fired back, stating that Chamberlain had done nothing but promote war. In March 1939, Hitler captured the rest of Czechoslovakia, hoping that someone would stand up to him. At this point, the Western European powers began to realize that appeasement was not going to work. They began to prepare for war.

With the failure of the policy of appeasement, most people in Great Britain believed it was worth a war to stop Hitler. Prime Minister Chamberlain did not agree, but he felt he must respect the will of the British people. However, he went too far when Chamberlain announced a joint British and French statement guaranteeing Poland would not be touched by Germany. They guaranteed Polish independence. Hitler knew the Western countries were not ready for war, and he also knew that Great Britain and France could not get to Poland directly to provide any assistance.

The Nazi-Soviet Pact

Hitler was afraid of another two-front war, so Hitler and Stalin made an agreement not to fight each other and to divide up parts of Eastern Europe between the two countries. With his eastern border secured in August 1939, Hitler focused all of his efforts on Western Europe, specifically France.

The world was shocked to hear of the Nazi-Soviet pact. No one had thought this was possible because Hitler and Joseph Stalin did not like each other. Their political ideologies simply did not line up. However, after Stalin's purge of his military officers, Great Britain and France had shied away from the Soviet Union, and the Soviets were angry that they had been left out of many of the political happenings of the 1920s and 1930s. They did not like playing "second fiddle" to the West. When Hitler approached Stalin with the agreement not to fight each other, Stalin jumped at the chance to get territorial gain. If Germany won the war, Poland would be divided. Russia would get Latvia, Lithuania, and Estonia. They would then negotiate the division of the rest of Eastern Europe. Stalin did not trust Hitler, but he knew that they needed each other.

The Invasion of Poland and World War II Begins

Poland was now sitting in Eastern Europe all alone. On September 1, 1939, barely a week after the Nazi-Soviet Pact, Hitler launched his invasion of Poland. Using lessons learned during the Spanish Civil War, the Nazi army overwhelmed Poland with surprising speed, using a policy now known as Blitzkrieg. On September 3, 1939, France declared war on Germany.

Blitzkrieg and Modern Technology

With the lightning warfare of Blitzkrieg, Germany's new modern army was able to roll across the plains of Poland with surprising speed. The Polish army fought back with everything they had, but they could not stop the modern, motorized troops of Nazi Germany. While Poland was trying to mobilize to fight Germany, the Soviets attacked from the east. Within three weeks, Poland was forced to surrender. Hitler divided Poland, claiming territory to the east as far as Warsaw. Stalin received a smaller share of Poland, but he did capture the three Baltic states of Latvia, Lithuania, and Estonia.

The Defeat of France

As France began to prepare for war, they relied on a defensive strategy that depended upon the Maginot Line. The Maginot Line defense network ran from Switzerland to Belgium. However, in the spring of 1940, the Germans crashed out of the Ardennes Forest on the French border, which was thought to be impenetrable. They also annexed parts of Denmark and Norway, and then they quickly moved into Belgium and the Netherlands.

As Great Britain arrived in France, the British navy imposed a blockade of Germany on the North Sea. The French forces fought bravely, but they were undersupplied and the leadership was divided between old military officers from World War I and younger modern officers. The German army pushed the British and French expeditionary forces back to the small French port of Dunkirk. More than 300,000 English soldiers and 60,000 French soldiers escaped to England, but they left behind all of their supplies. Although Great Britain celebrated the return of its army, Winston Churchill, the new British prime minister, addressed the nation on the radio, saying, "Wars are not won by evacuation."

The German Blitzkrieg accomplished in barely six weeks what four years of combat in World War I could not achieve: the Germans occupied over half of France, including land along the English Channel and the Atlantic Coast.

By June 1940, the French government, under the leadership of World War I General Henri-Philippe Pétain, was forced to ask for an armistice. France was divided into the southern section, which was run by what was known as Vichy, a government led by Pétain in collaboration with the Germans. The Germans left southern France unoccupied. The northern section of France was occupied by the German army.

Battle of Britain and the London Blitz (1940–1941)

With France out of the war, Great Britain was the last democracy Hitler had left to fight. However, new Prime Minister Winston Churchill, who replaced the pacifistic Neville Chamberlain, had long been a warning voice against Hitler's aggression. In a speech to the British Parliament on June 4, 1940, Churchill gave a famous oration known as the "We shall fight them on the beaches" speech. Churchill told the British, "We shall fight with growing confidence and growing strength in the air, we shall defend our Island, whatever the cost may be, we shall fight on the beaches, we shall fight on the landing grounds, we shall fight in the fields and in the streets, we shall fight in the hills; we shall never surrender." Churchill had no idea that the fight to save Great Britain was going to be something new, never seen before in warfare. It became known as the Battle of Britain.

Hitler hoped to achieve an agreement with the British because he respected them for their empire. Hitler also thought the Brits would quit quickly. Hitler was going to let them keep their empire if they left him alone on the continent. When Great Britain would not surrender, Hitler ordered Operation Sea Lion, an invasion of Great Britain. Hitler's advisors told him that first he must weaken British airpower.

The Battle of Britain turned into a fight fought solely by air. It began on August 13, 1940, when the Germans began flying over England and dropping bombs. However, using the new technology of radar, and by breaking the German code, the British were able to send their fighters exactly where the Germans were showing up. The Royal Air Force fought constantly, slowing down the Germans. Then, Hitler decided not to send the German Luftwaffe after British fighters; instead, he attacked the city of London and other large cities. He wanted to bomb the cities into annihilation, and during the London Blitz, Hitler bombed the cities continuously until the summer of 1941.

As the weather began to turn cold, Hitler realized he would not be able to capture England. He stopped the Battle of Britain and looked for a new target. When the battle was over, Churchill got back on BBC Radio. He gave another inspirational speech, saying how Britain owed so much to the Royal Air Force pilots and volunteers from other countries. They handed Hitler his first defeat.

THE WAR ON OTHER FRONTS

As the Luftwaffe was fighting the Royal Air Force, the military forces of Benito Mussolini headed into North Africa and Libya. Their objective was to reach Egypt and the important shipping lanes of the Suez Canal. When Mussolini was stalled by British forces, Hitler sent in a young, brilliant leader who had demonstrated great leadership in Poland, Erwin Rommel. Rommel led his Afrika Korps to a series of victories across North Africa, earning him the nickname of the Desert Fox. Mussolini also sent forces into Greece and Yugoslavia, spreading the armies of the Axis Powers across Eastern Europe, Southern Europe, and North Africa.

OPERATION BARBAROSSA

Hitler, stinging from the first defeat at the hands of Royal Air Force, attacked his next opponent. In June 1941, Hitler launched Operation Barbarossa against the Soviet Union, turning on Stalin, his ally. Hitler made a crucial mistake that even his modern army could not handle: fighting a war in the Soviet Union during the cruel Russian winter.

Global Connections

Hitler attacked the Soviet Union on the same date that Napoleon launched his invasion of Russia.

Hitler wanted the rich resources of the Soviet Union: raw materials like iron ore, coal, and lumber, as well as agricultural resources. In addition, Hitler wanted to get rid of the hated communism. Hitler sent three million soldiers into the Soviet Union; Stalin was not prepared but told his troops not to withdraw. The Soviet army was not ready because many of the officers who could have led the men had been killed by Stalin in his purges. The Soviets quickly used an age-old tactic of war. They slowly withdrew into the interior of their country, and on the way, they burned the crops, killed the livestock, poisoned the wells, and drained the gasoline from their equipment to keep everything from falling into German hands. The Germans quickly rolled across the Russian plains, and by late fall 1941, they were closing in on two major Soviet cities: Leningrad, formerly St. Petersburg, and Moscow.

Hitler's hubris came back to haunt him. Hitler's drive into the Soviet Union stalled in the winter of 1941 in the same area where Napoleon's drive stalled in 1812. Hitler felt that the German army was about to achieve victory over the Soviet Union, so winter weather gear was not sent forward to the troops. As the weather turned brutally cold, the army began asking for supplies. Hitler's staff lied to the troops, telling them that supplies were on the way. The German forces were condemned to freeze to death in the Russian winter.

Global Connections

Remember the Greek and Roman warnings about hubris in their theatre performances in Chapters 4 and 5? According to the ancient Greeks and Romans, hubris would be the downfall of humanity.

The Russians, especially in Leningrad, suffered hardships of their own as food was rationed. People had to eat industrial cellulose, pine needles, even their own leather boots. As a result, millions of Russian soldiers and civilians were lost.

THE JAPANESE ATTACK PEARL HARBOR

Japan had joined the Rome-Berlin-Tokyo Axis by signing the Tripartite Pact in 1940. However, when Hitler attacked the Soviet Union without consulting his Japanese allies, the Japanese decided to follow their own strategy. As a result, they made the decision that proved to be fatal to their imperial interests: they decided to go to war with the United States.

In June 1941, as Hitler was conquering France, the Japanese occupied the Southeastern Asian country of Indochina/Vietnam. The United States responded by limiting exports to Japan, who had long been a friend of the United States. One month later, when Japan continued conquering more of Southeast Asia, the United States stopped all exports of oil to Japan.

Japanese military leaders had assumed control of the government, and they wanted to go after the oil-rich islands of the Dutch East Indies. Some believed that this was too dangerous since the United States had a presence in the Philippines. The Japanese called upon Admiral Yamamoto to try to take out the United States with one massive blow. Admiral Yamamoto had spent years perfecting a plan to knock out the United States in one quick, fatal blow so Japan would have time to secure their empire in Asia.

General Hideki Tojo ordered that Japan attack the United States naval fleet in Pearl Harbor, Hawaii. On December 7, 1941, the Japanese attacked the American fleet at Pearl Harbor. All eight of the large U.S. battleships, the offensive power of the navy, were damaged or sunk. Eleven other ships were damaged as were hundreds of planes on the ground. Nearly 2500 people were killed in the attack.

Admiral Yamamoto of Japan issued a prophetic statement, "I fear all we have done is awakened a sleeping giant." Also, the Japanese had missed two primary targets.

1. The three American aircraft carriers, which were out at sea
2. The U.S. fuel oil reserves in Honolulu

While Japan was attacking Pearl Harbor, they simultaneously attacked the island of Guam, the American territory in the Philippines, the British stronghold in Singapore, and Hong Kong. Burma, in French Indochina, was also completely taken over by Japan. As 1942 began, Germany and her Axis allies had an amazing record of success.

The U.S. Congress declared war on Japan on December 8, 1941, as did Great Britain. Several days later, Germany and Italy declared war on the United States. The United States was the only country upon which Hitler actually declared war. These actions made World War II truly a world war.

TOTAL WAR

Both sides—both Axis and Allied—began a policy known as total war. Total war meant all governmental resources were geared toward the war effort. To that end, all economic and industrial resources were converted to work for the war. In the United States, automotive manufacturers like Ford and General Motors stopped making cars. They began to make jeeps and tanks. Airplane manufacturers made fighter planes and bombers. The government rationed things necessary for the war effort, like rubber, sugar, tin, and aluminum. Wages and prices were fixed. As men signed up for the army and navy, someone had to replace them in the industrial jobs to make munitions and weapons. Women replaced them, becoming welders, riveters, pipefitters, shipbuilders, truck drivers, and even test pilots. In the jobs that used to be reserved for men, women replaced them.

In the United States, there was even some censorship of the press. Japanese–American citizens also lost their freedom after Pearl Harbor when they were put into internment camps. The government wanted to monitor them to make sure that they were not going to attack the United States. Although there was loss of freedoms and wrongful internment, the war effort created jobs overnight. World War II gave governments around the world the ability to overcome the Great Depression.

GENOCIDE IN EUROPE

After Germany conquered Eastern Europe, Hitler ordered all resources—economic and natural—to be gathered for Germany's war effort. Hitler also ordered other countries to be robbed of their great works of art, their industrial equipment, and other resources. The people would be used as slave laborers for the Nazi war effort. Central to Hitler's mindset were his racist theories. He saw Slavic people as subhuman, more beast than human. He believed it was their job to work for Germany. Heinrich Himmler, head of the elite SS Guard, gathered 30 million Slavs and removed them to make room for Germans.

Even more central to Hitler's mindset was his hatred of the Jewish people. On Hitler's orders, Himmler came up with a special plan for Jews known as the Final Solution. Himmler ran extermination camps, mainly for the Jews. This was genocide, or an intentional murdering of Jews in Europe. The concentration camps were also used for Slavs, gypsies, homosexuals, and anybody that Hitler did not like. Special camps were built in far Eastern Germany and in Poland. The most famous are Poland's Auschwitz and Bergen-Belsen, where Anne Frank died, and Dachau, located near Munich, Germany. Six million Jews were sent to their deaths.

The Jewish people in Poland were first sent to ghettos (small isolated communities), and then they were sent on trains to the concentration camps. At the camps, they were stripped of their valuables, their hair was cut, and they were worked hard until they were no longer useful. They were then sent into gas chambers. Nazi doctors also used living human beings as test subjects for horrible medical experiments. All of it was an attempt to rid Europe of Jews, whom Hitler blamed for all of Germany's problems.

THE TIDE TURNS: NORTH AFRICA AND THE EUROPEAN THEATER

Hitler had gone from victory to victory except for the Battle of Britain. However, starting in 1942, the tide slowly began to turn.

- In 1942, British General Bernard Law Montgomery won the Battle of El Alamein in western Egypt and began to push the German army across North Africa to Tunisia.
- From August 1942 to February 1943, the Battle of Stalingrad was taking place in the Soviet Union. The battle was one of the most brutal in the entire war. During the freezing winter, the Germans ran out of supplies. They surrendered after the death of 300,000 German soldiers.
- In November 1942, the Allies opened the second battlefront in North Africa. The United States, led by General Dwight D. Eisenhower, began Operation Torch. The invasion of North Africa pinned German soldiers between British forces driving west and U.S. forces driving east.
- In early 1943, the Americans and the British invaded the island of Sicily. Upon their landing, the Italian peasants overthrew Mussolini's government and joined the Allies.
- Rome was liberated on June 5, 1944.
- June 6, 1944 is known as D-Day. The Allied troops successfully landed the largest invasion force in European history on the beaches of Normandy in northern France.
- The Battle of the Bulge occurred from December 16, 1944 to January 25, 1945, ending with the German troops retreating back into Germany ahead of the Allied advance on their borders.
- On March 23, 1945, U.S. troops crossed the Rhine River into Germany.

The Pacific Theater

- On June 7, 1942, the United States won a dramatic victory on the Pacific island of Midway, just seven short months after the attack on Pearl Harbor. Admiral Yamamoto had been ordered to destroy the U.S. Navy, and U.S. Admiral Nimitz planned a deceptive counterattack that completely destroyed the Japanese fleet. The Battle of Midway turned the tide of the war in the Pacific.
- On August 7, 1942, the United States successfully invaded the island of Guadalcanal but suffered a horrible loss of life. After the battle, the United States began a policy of island-hopping as it was too costly to attack the Japanese simultaneously on all of the Pacific Islands. The United States conquered the Pacific island strongholds in strategic order. They leapfrogged from one island to the next, but the strategy was still difficult due to fanatic Japanese resistance. While the United States was victorious on Tarawa, Saipan, and Okinawa, unimaginable losses occurred on both sides on the conflicts.

- The battle of Iwo Jima took place in February 1945. Iwo Jima is a tiny island 660 miles from Tokyo and was designated as a necessary landing site for the new B-29 bombers. The battle raged for 72 days, racking up tens of thousands of casualties on both sides. Soon after the U.S. victory, the first B-29 superfortress planes took off from the secured airstrips, and the heavy bombing of Japanese cities began.

DEFEAT OF NAZI GERMANY

In March 1945, the Allies crossed the Rhine River into Germany, and the German war machine began to crumble. The Soviets closed in from the east, and when they were within reach of Berlin, Adolf Hitler committed suicide on May 1, 1945. His reign lasted only 12 terrible years. Germany unconditionally surrendered on May 8, 1945. After achieving victory in Europe (V-E Day), the United States turned its full military focus toward Japan.

DEFEAT OF JAPAN: DROPPING OF THE ATOMIC BOMB

Japan realized the mistake of attacking the United States. The longer the war lasted, the greater the industrial capacity of the United States became. Japan was being slowly strangled to death as American forces closed in on the home islands.

The U.S. military estimated that an invasion of the home island of Japan would cause between two million and five million casualties in American soldiers and Japanese civilians. The cost was unacceptable. New, innovative technology played a key role as the United States was given a secret alternative to invading the Japanese home islands. Called the Manhattan Project, it was a secret initiative led by scientists across the United States to split an atom and then harness the atomic energy into a bomb.

Two atomic bombs were delivered to the island of Tinian. On August 6, 1945, the new U.S. President Harry Truman ordered the bomber plane *Enola Gay* to drop the first atomic bomb on the Japanese city of Hiroshima. More than 70,000 people were killed instantly, and 200,000 died in the weeks and months that followed. No one could believe the destruction they saw. When the United States asked Japan to surrender, the Japanese leaders refused. The Soviet Union declared war on Japan on August 8. On August 9, President Truman ordered the second atomic bomb to be dropped on the city of Nagasaki, which killed more than 40,000 people.

After the second atomic bomb, Japanese Emperor Hirohito overruled his military, and on August 10, he did something unheard of in Japan: he surrendered. On September 2, 1945, the Japanese signed the surrender on the American battleship U.S.S. *Missouri* in Tokyo Harbor. With the victory in Japan (V-J Day), World War II was over.

AFTERMATH OF WORLD WAR II

World War II lasted 6 1/2 years and claimed 69 million lives. Major sections of Europe were destroyed for the second time. Unlike in World War I, Germany also felt the pain and destruction of war as a large part of Germany was destroyed. Mass genocide was committed, and parts of Japan were annihilated from the atomic bombs. Major damage was also found in the Koreas, China, and other Southeast Asian nations from bombing by the Japanese Imperial Army.

However, with the ushering in of the atomic age, people felt that another such war could destroy the human race. There were several friendly agreements between the Allies going as far back as 1943, but by 1945 when the war had ended, the Allies began to split. Joseph Stalin had used the war to capture more territory for the Soviet Union and had effectively increased and centralized his power. The Soviet Union declared itself the epicenter of the world, and they were dedicated to exporting their communist ideology throughout the world.

The United States and Western Europe believed they had to contain the growing spread of communism. The world split into two camps:

1. Capitalists, led by the United States
2. A Soviet sphere, led by the Soviet Union and the ideals of communism

As old territories that had been governed by imperialist European powers for centuries became free, the United States and the Soviet Union tried to woo these small countries to their side. The Cold War had begun. However, before U.S. President Franklin Roosevelt died, he had strongly urged the creation and adoption of the United Nations organization to avoid these tensions. The United Nations was to be a group of countries that would enforce peace, not requiring any one country to shoulder all the burden of peacekeeping.

CREATION OF THE UNITED NATIONS ORGANIZATION

In April 1945, 51 nations met outside San Francisco in the redwood forest of Muir Woods to create the United Nations charter. Since its inception, the UN has played a large role in world affairs. In the UN, every member country has a seat in the General Assembly, where each vote is equal. The countries meet to discuss and debate pressing issues and concerns facing the world.

Global Connections

Think of the member countries of the United Nations as members of the U.S. House of Representatives: no single representative has more power than anyone else. They are all equal.

Separate from this is the smaller, more prestigious Security Council. The Security Council has 15 member nations. Five nations have permanent seats: the United States, Great Britain, and France (the three victorious powers from World War II), the Soviet Union, and, due to its size, China. The other ten member nations rotate. The UN Security Council focuses on issues of world security with the goal of keeping and enforcing peace. The five permanent members, however, have veto power over any sanction or international law being passed. If one of them does not like a resolution, they can veto it. All five have to agree to achieve consensus.

However, with the growing Cold War in the 1950s, the ideological differences between the powerful rival nations—particularly the United States and Soviet Union—prevented the United Nations from taking concrete action on some of the more controversial issues. Fortunately, most of the early work of the United Nations did get done. They worked on preventing or eradicating disease, improving education, providing economic aid and assistance to Third World countries who were trying to rebuild, and protecting refugees during natural disasters and war. Security, however, was an issue for the remainder of the 20th century.

ISRAEL IS FORMED

Global Connections

Think of the Security Council of the United Nations as the U.S. Senate. It is a smaller governing body with longer term limits.

After World War II, many Jews wanted to leave Europe. As the British were governing the territory of Palestine, the British government mandated an area in Palestine be set aside as a state for the Jewish people to return to their homeland. The Jews had religious ties to the land as it was where Judaism and the religion began thousands of years ago. (See Chapter 3.) All of the victorious Allies felt the need to act in response to the genocide of the Jews at the hands of Hitler and the Holocaust. In 1947, the brand-new United Nations passed an international resolution to divide the territory into a state that was one-half Jewish and one-half Arab. The Arab states in the region staunchly refused to accept this resolution. To them, it did not exist. In addition, the Palestinians were never asked for permission and were angry that they were being displaced because of European persecution of the Jews.

In May 1948, Jews in Palestine proclaimed the formation of the new, independent state of Israel. The United States was the first country to recognize the existence of an independent nation of Israel, so the United States and Israel became allies.

War in 1948

The Israeli proclamation in 1948 set off a war between Israel and its Arabic neighbors: Syria, Lebanon, Jordan, Egypt, and Saudi Arabia. They all attacked Israel; not only were they all defeated by Israel, but they also all lost territory to Israel. Since this time, there has been a state of either truce or open warfare between Arabic nations, including the Palestinians, and the country of Israel. Israel and its ally, the United States, have been aggressive in ensuring that Israel is able to survive.

Attacks on Israel in the 20th Century

In 1956, Israel went to war with Egypt and took the Sinai Peninsula. In 1967, there was the June War with Syria, during which Israel took what is known as the Golan Heights. From the kingdom of Jordan, Israel claimed Jerusalem and the West Bank of the Jordan River to serve as a buffer zone between them and those bent on Israel's destruction. In 1973, there was another attack by Egypt, which wanted its occupied lands back, but Egypt was again defeated. Israel refused to negotiate the return of any land until their existence was recognized by the Arabic nations. To this end, the Israeli government began to put settlers in these occupied territories, displacing even more Arabs. Even when there was not war, the displaced Arab citizens were made to feel inferior to the Israelis, and began to rebel. In Palestine, the Palestinian Liberation Organization (PLO) was created by Yasir Arafat to wage guerrilla war against Israel. However, in 1979, at the risk of their own credibility, Egypt recognized the existence of Israel when Egyptian president Anwar Sadat signed the Camp David Peace Accords in the United States under U.S. President Jimmy Carter. During this time, the United States backed Israel, and the Soviet Union aided Arabic powers, and the two superpowers armed their allies vying for control of the region.

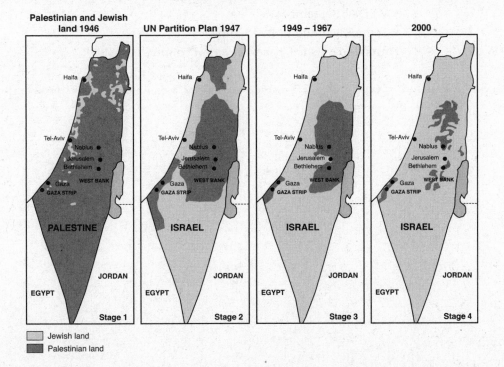

1931 C.E.	Japan invades Manchuria.
1935 C.E.	• Mussolini invades Ethiopia.
	• Hitler renounces disarmament provisions of Treaty of Versailles.
	• Hitler begins to build German Armed Forces.
1936 C.E.	• Spanish Civil War begins.
	• Germans march into Rhineland demilitarized zone.
	• Great Britain urges appeasement toward Germany.
	• Rome–Berlin Axis forms between Italy and Germany.
1938 C.E.	Hitler annexes Austria and then Czechoslovakia.
1939 C.E.	• Nazi-Soviet Pact is formed between Hitler and Stalin.
	• Germany invades Poland.
1940 C.E.	• Germany attacks France, leading to evacuation of French and British troops at Dunkirk.
	• Mussolini attacks North Africa with German allies.
1940–1941 C.E.	The Battle of Britain
1941 C.E.	• Germany invades U.S.S.R.
	• Japan attacks Pearl Harbor—U.S. enters World War II.
1942 C.E.	Battle of Midway in Pacific Theater
1942–1943 C.E.	Battle of Stalingrad in Russia
1943 C.E.	Allied invasion of Italy
1944 C.E.	• D-Day invasion in France
	• Battle of the Bulge in Ardennes Forest in Europe
1945 C.E.	• Battle of Iwo Jima in Pacific Theater
	• V-E Day: May 8
	• The U.S. drops atomic bomb on Hiroshima: August 6.
	• The U.S. drops atomic bomb on Nagasaki: August 9.
	• V-J Day: September 2
	• Founding of the United Nations
1948 C.E.	Formation of Israel, becomes a new country

Origins of the Cold War; Creation of NATO and the Warsaw Pact Alliances; Conflicts in Europe, Korea, and Vietnam

31

ORIGINS OF THE COLD WAR: THE IRON CURTAIN

The United States and the Soviet Union were the only two major powers left standing after victory was achieved in World War II. Furthermore, both had vast economic resources and mobilized military power to dominate the globe. However, these one-time allies had become bitter rivals as their opposing political and economic ideologies did not go well together. Each had a deep distrust of the other.

After World War II, a new struggle quickly grew that shaped events for the rest of the 20th century. This would become known as the Cold War, which was simply a constant era of tension and hostility among different nations without direct armed conflict. The United States and the Soviet Union fought each other, but it would not be directly. They used other smaller countries, and the United States and the Soviet Union never squared off.

Iron Curtain Descends

In its early stages, the main focus of the Cold War centered over Eastern Europe. Stalin had two goals in mind for Eastern Europe.

1. He wanted friendly neighbors so he could spread communism into all of the Eastern European regions.
2. He wanted a safety net, or buffer zone, of like-minded governments to give him protection against Germany, should it decide to attack Russia for the third time in the century.

So as the Red Army shattered Nazi forces and pushed them out of Eastern Europe, Stalin left behind parts of his army to occupy this territory. Stalin wanted to heavily influence this territory and impose his own social system. As the United States and Great Britain began to complain bitterly, Stalin responded by saying that the United States did not consult the Soviet Union when they concluded their own individual peace with Japan. The Western powers disagreed, saying that concluding peace was completely different than leaving an occupying force behind. Stalin eventually promised so-called democratic elections, but he quickly went back on this promise. The Red Army and local communists in Eastern Europe, especially in Czechoslovakia, Hungary, and Poland, came out in support of Stalin and were able to beat down any opposing political thoughts, especially those that were democratic.

On March 5, 1946, at Westminster College in Missouri, British Prime Minister Winston Churchill gave his now-famous speech, which included the quote, "From Stettin in the Baltic to Trieste in the Adriatic, an iron curtain has descended across the continent. Behind that line lie all the capitals of the ancient states of central and eastern Europe." The term *Iron Curtain*, coined by Winston Churchill, came to symbolize the Cold War. It was used by the West to show the spector of communism, the Soviet sphere of influence, and the West's growing fear of it.

THE MARSHALL PLAN

Immediately after the war, several factors made communist ideals appealing for Western Europe, which was heavily damaged by conflict. The two biggest factors were poverty and hunger. To prevent democratic governments from failing and turning to communism, U.S. Secretary of State George C. Marshall created and offered a massive aid package to governments of Europe. The Marshall Plan was designed for the United States to send tons of food and billions of dollars in economic assistance to help European countries rebuild from the destruction of World War II. This money helped the destroyed areas of Central and Western Europe to recover more quickly than was thought possible. The United States earned the goodwill of these countries, and they willingly followed the lead of the democratic United States. President Truman also approved the offer of Marshall Plan aid to areas in Eastern Europe. However, Joseph Stalin did not allow any Eastern European government or country to accept this aid, promising it was his responsibility, and the Soviet Union would help them.

FATE OF GERMANY AND THE BERLIN AIRLIFT

Germany was another focal point of the Cold War. The Soviet Union destroyed factories in the German zones that it occupied as they feared a newly restored Germany. The zones monitored by the United States, England, and France helped Germany to rebuild their industry, infrastructure, and economy.

At this time, Germany divided into two nations:

- West Germany was a democratic Germany that wrote a democratic constitution. It was allowed to govern itself and received Western economic aid to become an industrial power.
- East Germany was governed by a communist government, which was heavily controlled by Moscow.

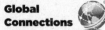

Global Connections

Germany was divided into two halves, much like Rome was divided into an East (Byzantium) and West (Rome) before it fell.

The capital city of Berlin, which lay in the Soviet sphere, was also divided into four zones. The three Western Allied zones were surrounded by communist territory. The first flashpoint of the Cold War came in the form of a crisis over Berlin.

In 1948, Stalin tried to push the Allies out of Berlin by sealing off all the access points to the city: roads, railroads, and bridges. Now called the Berlin Airlift, the United States responded by dropping parachutes of food, medicine, and supplies around the clock. Stalin backed down, but the embarrassment led to a deepening of the hostilities between the former allies. The Cold War had begun.

THE TRUMAN DOCTRINE AND CONTAINMENT POLICY

President Harry Truman saw the ideology of communism as an evil force that was trying to slowly spread across the world. Unlike the isolationist U.S. presidents after World War I,

Truman took a leading role in global affairs to combat the threat of communism. On March 12, 1947, he came up with the Truman Doctrine and Containment Policy. It stated that the United States must support any free people of the world who were resisting attempted subjugation by armed minorities or by outside pressures. The countries of Greece and Turkey were among the first to receive aid so they could withstand the growing specter of communism. Truman also stated that the free people of the world looked to the United States for leadership. The Truman Doctrine was the main factor that led the United States foreign policy for the next 50 years. At its essence, the Truman Doctrine was designed to resist the expansion of communism, no matter where it was in the world.

The Containment Policy was designed to limit communism to areas where it already existed and to make sure it was not going to spread. American economist George Kennan was one of the architects of the Containment Policy. He said that communism simply could not exist long term and eventually would collapse upon itself. Kennan stated that the United States would be able to prevent expansion from where communism currently existed. However, Joseph Stalin viewed the Containment Policy as an attack because it meant the Soviet Union, and its communist countries, were surrounded by the ideals of Western capitalism.

THE NORTH ATLANTIC TREATY ORGANIZATION

Shortly after the Truman Doctrine was written and the crisis over Berlin ended, the North Atlantic Treaty Organization (NATO) was created in 1949. NATO was developed by the United States, Canada, and other Western European countries that decided to form a military defensive alliance. The eleven members of NATO promised immediate help to one another if any of them were attacked by the Soviet Union, or by a country under Soviet domination.

CREATION OF THE WARSAW PACT

To counter the formation of NATO, the Soviet Union developed its own military alliance in 1955 known as the Warsaw Pact. Seven Eastern European countries, called Soviet satellite states, pledged that if anyone were attacked by a Western capitalist country, the rest would come to that country's aid. In the eyes of many, the big difference between NATO and the Warsaw Pact was that the NATO alliance members volunteered to join and were openly democratic countries. The Warsaw Pact countries were dominated by the Soviet Union, who used the Warsaw Pact as a tool to control their countries and force them to follow the commands coming from the Soviet Politburo in Moscow.

THE COLD WAR ARMS RACE

As NATO and the Warsaw Pact countries were at odds, tensions ran high. Both believed that a deterrent would prevent an attack, so both sides—Western capitalist and Soviet communist—built bigger, faster, and more powerful weapons. The United States felt secure early on because of the success of the atomic program, demonstrated in the bombing of Hiroshima and Nagasaki. However, the Soviet Union was able to successfully steal some atomic plans, and by 1949, as NATO was being created, the Soviet Union also had a successful atomic program.

Most of the second half of the 20th century was defined by the United States and the Soviet Union, both becoming known as the superpowers. They spent exorbitant sums of money developing not only conventional military weapons, like planes and tanks, but also nuclear arsenals. The intercontinental ballistic missile and nuclear missile could be fired to a point anywhere in the world. By countering each other over and over again, the balance of world power was maintained. Eventually, they had achieved mutual assured destruction. Neither country could fire its nuclear missiles without a retaliatory response from the other because there were enough nuclear missiles to blow up the entire planet. The balance of power became a balance of both terror and fear.

DEVELOPMENT OF THE PROPAGANDA WAR

During this Cold War era, the Soviet Union and the United States did not directly attack each other, but the hostility between the two spilled over into tertiary battles and wars in faraway places like Korea and Vietnam, both of which siphoned off resources from the two superpowers. However, the United States had an economy that was able to spend while replenishing its treasury. The Soviet Union had a much more difficult time supporting their economy, eventually leading to its collapse.

COLD WAR CONFLICTS

Korea

The Korean War was another conflict during the Cold War. The United States, the Soviet Union, North and South Korea, and communist China were involved.

The Korean Peninsula was occupied by a homogeneous people who had the same culture. They spoke the same language, and they had the same heritage, but they quickly became a divided nation, something that lasts to this day. After World War II in 1945, the United States and the Soviet Union agreed to temporarily split the country of Korea along the 38th Parallel. At this split, the United States and its forces occupied the southern half of the Korean Peninsula, whereas the Soviet Union occupied the northern half. The division became permanent after North Korean dictator Kim Il Sung became an ally of the Soviet Union.

This situation was exactly what the Truman Doctrine was created to prevent. The United States backed South Korean leader Syngman Rhee. There was an era of tension and hostility until 1950 when northern communist forces invaded South Korea. The goal of North Korea was to occupy and unify the entire country. The Allied forces were fleeing toward the Port of Pusan when the United Nations organized a defense of South Korea. The United States was put in charge, and World War II hero General Douglas MacArthur was given the task of commanding the international troops. MacArthur coordinated a risky landing at the Port of Inchon behind the communist troops, which quickly destabilized North Korea's attack. Slowly, the United Nations forces pushed the North Korean army back to the 38th Parallel and into North Korea. However, MacArthur was ordered by President Eisenhower not to aggressively push too far into North Korea so as not to anger or upset communist China and Chairman Mao Tse-tung.

When MacArthur went ahead and attacked near the Yalu River on the North Korean/Chinese border in October 1950, communist Chinese forces entered the battle. The United Nations troops were pushed back to the original starting point of the 38th Parallel. As a result, MacArthur was relieved of command in April 1951. An armistice was created in 1953, and after the three years of war ended, the dividing lines of Korea were drawn in the same location where they began.

Currently, this area is the largest demilitarized zone in the world. Millions of landmines and North Korean troops are on the north side and thousands of troops from the Republic of Korea and the United States are on the southern side. It remains the longest state of warfare in modern history, lasting from 1953 to the present day.

Cuba

Another Cold War flashpoint happened on the island of Cuba. Located just 90 miles from the tip of Florida, Cuba had existed as an independent country, dominated by United States influence. The Cuban government enjoyed having the United States so close, but Cuba was not very well run. The leaders of Cuba were either corrupt or incapable of looking after their citizens. By the early 1940s, many student groups were angry about the lack of progress and ineffective government in Cuba. They began to protest governmental leadership and actions. By the 1950s, Cuba was led by United States-backed leader Fulgencio Batista. Batista's leadership was not only ineffective but widely corrupt as well. On July 26, 1953, university students began an attack on Batista's government. One of these student leaders was Fidel Castro, who led the Cuban revolutionary movement, aptly named the July 26 Movement. In 1956, Castro and his followers openly attacked Batista's government, and on New Year's Eve 1958, Batista fled the country. In January 1959, Fidel Castro arrived in the Cuban capital of Havana as a victorious revolutionary leader, as well as the new president of Cuba.

CUBAN REVOLUTION AND CASTRO'S REFORMS

Now that he was in power, Castro began to take a communist slant in his ideology. He began the most widespread overhaul ever experienced by an entire country. Castro wanted to rebuild Cuba from the ground up—politically, socially, and economically. Castro opposed any form of democracy, believing it was better for him to rule in an authoritative manner in order to get things done.

In 1970, Castro created an executive cabinet of advisors, but he was the unquestioned head of the government. At this time, Castro started a large land redistribution program as he wanted to improve Cuba's agricultural output, especially its crop of sugar, which was a main export.

However, Castro experienced the same problem that Peter the Great experienced back in the 1600s in Russia. Everything was done as fast as possible, and speed was more important than output. The results were disappointing as no one in the country, not even the governmental leaders or farmers, had any training on a project this large and extensive. Fearing a collapse, the Soviet Union stepped in and provided large cash subsidies to keep Castro in power. The Soviet Union used Cuba as a propaganda tool for communism, as well as a way to keep an eye on the United States. The Soviet Union and other Warsaw Pact countries promised to be trading partners for exports of Cuban products.

THE BAY OF PIGS INVASION AND THE CUBAN MISSILE CRISIS

As a result of Castro's aligning Cuba with the Soviet Union, the U.S. government viewed Castro as a communist threat. In 1961, the United States enlisted exiled Cubans to carry out an invasion whose goal was to topple Fidel Castro and install a pro-American democratic regime. The invasion was known as the Bay of Pigs, and it was a poorly executed attack that failed miserably. It was an embarrassment for the U.S. government but also increased the hostility and tension between the United States, Cuba, and the Soviet Union.

One year later in 1962, the Cuban Missile Crisis brought the world closer to mutually assured destruction and nuclear war than any other time in world history. When the Bay of Pigs invasion solidified Castro's relationship with the Soviet Union, Cuba agreed to allow the Soviet Union to construct nuclear missile batteries in Cuba, just 90 miles from the United States. The U.S. government and President John F. Kennedy were angered and terrified.

Acting on the threat, President Kennedy set up a blockade around Cuba, stopping any ship leaving or coming into Cuba. The United States demanded that the Soviet Union admit to having nuclear weapons in Cuba and immediately remove them. During 13 days in October 1962, the world readied itself for nuclear war, which seemed not only possible but probable. In the end, Soviet Premier Nikita Khrushchev backed down and agreed to remove the missiles from Cuba in exchange for the removal of U.S. missiles from Turkey. The United States also agreed not to overthrow Castro's leadership or invade Cuba.

The crisis passed, and the Soviet communist ideology had a foothold in the Americas. Castro had promised the Soviet Union that he would send troops to different parts of Latin America to help spread communist ideology. However, with the collapse of the Soviet Union in 1991, Castro found himself without resources from the Soviet Union. They still have major economic problems today; however, recent negotiations between the United States and Cuba have called for an easing of the trade embargo. The negotiations look positive for U.S./Cuba relations.

Vietnam

During World War II, Ho Chi Minh, a Vietnamese communist, helped organize defenses against Japanese invasion using guerrilla war tactics. By the end of World War II, Ho Chi Minh controlled much of North Vietnam and was a well-known figure among the people. In 1946, the government of France wanted to regain its empire in Vietnam, which was called French Indochina. However, the nationalist movement in Vietnam did not want to be ruled by France. They began to resist European efforts to recapture their once-colonial empires that stretched across Southeast Asia. One of the leading Vietnamese nationalists was Ho Chi Minh himself. He enjoyed the massive support of the peasant people, using the same tactics to defeat the French that he used against the Japanese. The French were forced to leave Vietnam in 1954.

HO CHI MINH AND VIETNAM: SOURCES OF CONFLICT FROM WORLD WAR II TO THE PRESENT

Unfortunately, the Cold War between the United States and Soviet Union interfered with Vietnam's quest for independence. The Truman Doctrine and the Containment Policy of the United States wanted to stop the spread of communism. The United States did not mind new countries becoming independent as long as they were not communist. All across Southeast Asia, countries wanted to modernize—including Vietnam, Laos, and Cambodia—but they lacked the experience necessary to govern themselves. They found themselves as unwilling participants in the Cold War.

After Vietnam won its independence from France in 1954, it found itself caught between two superpowers: the United States and the Soviet Union. At a conference in Switzerland, the Soviet Union and Western leaders agreed on a temporary division of Vietnam, similar to the division they had agreed upon in Korea. The United States backed South Vietnamese leader Ngo Dinh Diem, whereas in North Vietnam, Ho Chi Minh had become the leader of the communist government. Other Southeast Asian nations, such as Cambodia and Laos, became fully independent. The agreement also called for Vietnam to hold free elections in 1956 to reunite the country. Based on the outcome of the vote, Vietnam would be run by either communist leadership or Western democratic leadership. The Western leaders were concerned about the domino theory. The theory was that if one country fell to communism, it would have a dominant effect throughout the rest of the region. South Vietnamese President Diem and the United States were concerned that the communists might win the election in Vietnam.

THE VIETNAM WAR BEGINS

Vietnam was involved in multiple phases of war that lasted from 1959 to 1975. Ho Chi Minh wanted Vietnam to be reunited as a single country, so he began to support communist citizens in South Vietnam known as the Vietcong. The Vietcong were rebels trying to overthrow the democratic government. To make sure Diem's government did not flounder, the United States sent massive aid packages of supplies, and then sent military advisers. In the 1960s, President Kennedy expanded the U.S. involvement in Vietnam throughout his term in office, and President Lyndon Johnson continued to expand U.S. involvement.

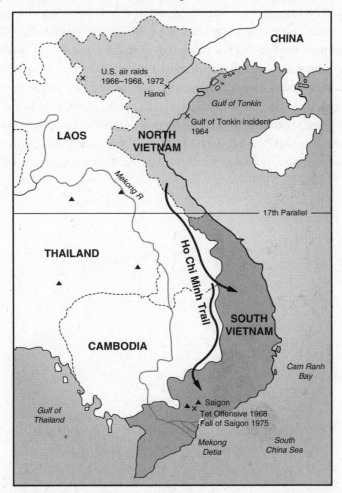

The local struggle for Vietnam quickly turned into a major conflict. More and more soldiers from the United States were sent to battle the communists, and in 1964, there was a major campaign to bomb northern Vietnamese cities and to deforest the jungles of Vietnam.

However, the massive armament of the United States was not enough to stop Ho Chi Minh and his rebel forces. By the mid-1960s, nearly 500,000 American soldiers had been sent to Vietnam. Ho Chi Minh received help from the Soviet Union in terms of weapons and supplies, but no Soviet Union troops were sent. No matter what the United States sent to South Vietnam, Ho Chi Minh and his communist forces proved difficult to defeat.

By the early 1970s, the number of Americans killed in Vietnam had swung the opinion of Americans against the war. President Richard Nixon arranged a cease-fire and negotiated a treaty in 1973. The South Vietnamese capital of Saigon fell in April 1975 and was renamed Ho Chi Minh City.

Ho Chi Minh's success was very similar to that which brought Mao Tse-tung to power in China. Ho Chi Minh was popular and had led guerrilla victories against the powerful Japanese and U.S. invasions. Ho Chi Minh's new government began to rebuild Vietnam in the hopes of recovering from the destruction caused by almost 30 years of constant warfare.

CAMBODIAN REVOLUTION AND THE COLD WAR

As the Vietnam War wore on, Cambodia was affected as the North Vietnamese communists were shuttling men and supplies through Cambodia to the Vietcong in South Vietnam. When the war ended in 1975, Cambodians who believed in the communist ideology overthrew the government and set up a new government called the Khmer Rouge. The Khmer Rouge was led by a dictator named Pol Pot. Pol Pot wanted to erase all remnants of Western ideology and culture from his country. He saw urbanization as a form of Western influence and corruption, so he forced his own citizens from the cities and relocated them to the countryside to work in agriculture. Thousands starved to death, and those who complained or did not work hard enough were executed. Some estimates place the deaths in Cambodia at more than one million. By 1979, things had become so bad in Cambodia that Vietnam invaded to save the citizens. Vietnam remained in charge until the United Nations sent in peacekeepers in the early 1990s.

1945 C.E.	Yalta Conference
1946–1954 C.E.	Ho Chi Minh in Vietnam resists French.
1947 C.E.	• Marshall Plan begins.
	• Truman Doctrine is adopted.
1948 C.E.	Berlin Airlift
1949 C.E.	Formation of NATO
1950 C.E.	North Korea invades South Korea.
1953 C.E.	Korean Conflict, formation of Demilitarized Zone (DMZ) at 38th Parallel
1955 C.E.	U.S.S.R. creates Warsaw Pact.
1959 C.E.	• Fulgencio Batista flees Cuba.
	• Fidel Castro assumes control of Cuba.
	• U.S. begins Vietnam War.
1961 C.E.	• Berlin Wall is built.
	• Failed Bay of Pigs invasion in Cuba by U.S.
1961–1962 C.E.	Presidents Kennedy and Johnson send advisors to Vietnam.
1962 C.E.	Cuban Missile Crisis
1964 C.E.	U.S. bombing campaign of North Vietnam
1968 C.E.	Tet Offensive led by Vietcong against South Vietnam and the U.S.
1973 C.E.	• South Vietnam capital of Saigon falls.
	• Ho Chi Minh wins control over Vietnam.
1975 C.E.	Pol Pot overthrows Cambodian government.
1976 C.E.	Saigon is renamed Ho Chi Minh City.
1979 C.E.	After Pol Pot slaughters millions in Cambodia, Vietnam invades.
1993 C.E.	U.N. peacekeepers supervise elections in Cambodia.

Quick Quiz: Chapters 30–31

1. Between World War I and World War II, which leader came up with the appeasement policy?

   A. Winston Churchill
   B. Franklin Roosevelt
   C. Francisco Franco
   D. Neville Chamberlain

2. Where did Hitler test out and put on display his newly built military weaponry?

   A. During the invasion of Poland
   B. During the Spanish civil war
   C. During the annexation of Austria
   D. During the Nuremberg parade

3. Why was the Battle of Britain unique in world history?

   A. It took place with live media coverage.
   B. It was the first successful attack on Great Britain since William the Conqueror.
   C. It directly involved English civilians who were called upon to save their soldiers.
   D. It was the first battle fought entirely in the air.

4. Which battle in the Pacific Theater of World War II was the turning point of the conflict in the Pacific?

   A. MacArthur's return to the Philippines
   B. Battle of Midway
   C. Marine landing at Iwo Jima
   D. Japanese attack on Pearl Harbor

5. Post–World War II, what became the biggest threat to Western Europe and the United States that leaders in those countries felt they had to contain?

   A. Communism
   B. Decolonization
   C. Genocide
   D. Refugee migration

6. What was the first large-scale action of the new international organization named the United Nations?

   A. Splitting of Germany into two countries
   B. Creating the DMZ in Korea
   C. Creating the country of Israel
   D. Presiding over the Nuremberg trials in Germany

7. Which European statesman coined the phrase *Iron Curtain*?

   A. Neville Chamberlain
   B. Leon Trotsky
   C. Winston Churchill
   D. Charles de Gaulle

8. Which of the following was President Harry Truman's policy on communism following World War II?

   A. Marshall Plan
   B. Containment Policy
   C. Dawes Plan
   D. Big Stick Policy

9. Where was the first flashpoint of the Cold War between U.S. capitalism and communism that is still visible today?

   A. creation of the Berlin Wall
   B. DMZ in Korea
   C. renaming of Saigon to Ho Chi Minh City
   D. Hindenburg Line

10. Which event brought the world the closest it would ever come to nuclear war?

    A. Cuban Missile Crisis
    B. Gary Powers U-2 crash
    C. Berlin Airlift
    D. Bay of Pigs invasion

11. Which Cold War event involved genocide as the self-imposed leader of a country worked and starved to death millions of his own people?

    A. Vietnam War
    B. Korea War
    C. Cuban Revolution
    D. Cambodian Revolution

Quick Quiz Answers

1. D; **2.** B; **3.** D; **4.** B; **5.** A; **6.** C; **7.** C; **8.** B; **9.** B; **10.** A; **11.** D

Decolonization in Africa and Asia

32

Decolonization was the unraveling of colonialism. It occurred when a nation separated from its colonial ruler, and it established and maintained its own territory. Decolonization was a major "door hinge of history," meaning that history changed drastically and quickly. As the door hinge of history swings, it closes on one important period of history and opens onto another. Decolonization ended the old European empires, some of which went back to the Spanish conquistadors in the 1500s. Europeans had created enormous empires across Africa, Asia, and Latin America. People in these European colonies thirsted for, and eventually won, their freedom.

THE CHALLENGE OF DEMOCRACY

The Cold War played an enormous role in decolonization as the United States reinforced the right of people everywhere to create their own government, as long as it was not communist. In turn, the Soviet Union spoke out against Western imperialism and its evils. Both superpowers competed for new allies, which aided independence movements. Many factors influenced this competition, but one major factor was that Europe was no longer a major superpower. European countries were worn out from not one, but two world wars in 50 years, and did not want more conflict.

New nations in Africa and Asia became known as the developing world. While they were in different parts of the globe, they all had commonalities:

- They had a stable government.
- They found a way to modernize.
- They developed some sort of economy.

Around the world, different nations pursued different paths to accomplish their goals toward decolonization. The United States and Soviet Union offered a wide range of military and economic assistance to these nations in order to woo them to pursue their brand of government and economy.

Decolonization was not easy to accomplish. There were many problems, especially in Africa, which had been chopped up by Europeans even before the Berlin Conference. There were hastily drawn borders that combined people who spoke different languages and had different ethnic identities. This had been done on purpose by the Europeans to fracture the people to make them easier to control.

The challenge of democracy arose as these new nations created and wrote constitutions modeled on those of the United States, Great Britain, and France. The new nations did not have the existing European infrastructure needed to implement a new government, and they simply did not comprehend how much the European colonial powers had done for them. Democratic rule was difficult to maintain as many of these new nations were not prepared to govern themselves.

When things did not get better quickly, there were civil wars, revolutions, or greedy leaders who controlled the government and the economy at the expense of the people. To keep order, a military dictator or some type of authoritarian regime would simply take over. They banned other political parties and rallied the people around ideas of nationalism. However, as long as the country was an ally in the Cold War, the United States and the Soviet Union supported whichever government was in charge and turned a blind eye to the internal problems.

THE TRANSFER OF POWER FROM GREAT BRITAIN AND FRANCE

Great Britain and France were the two largest imperial powers throughout the world, especially in Africa. Each of them adopted a slow-approach policy designed so their African colonies could eventually attain independence. However, England and France were accustomed to being colonial powers. As they began to enact their reforms, they discovered they could not maintain the slow, steady approach that they had set down for their former colonies to follow. When the British and French methods were not quick enough, different types of protests forced Europeans to speed up their timetable for independence. All over Africa, new leaders, many of which were educated in Western universities, organized different political parties. In larger cities, newspapers began to be published, enforcing the concepts of freedom of speech and democracy. Large nationalistic rallies were held to get the common people to buy into the ideas of independence.

GHANA AND KENYA: DIFFERENT ROUTES TO INDEPENDENCE

West Africa, once home of the great kingdoms of Ghana, Songhai, and Mali, became the starting point for African independence. This area, rich in African history, was named the Gold Coast by the Europeans as it was a large exportation area for gold out of Africa. It was also a British colony. In East Africa, Kenya was also a British colony. Both Ghana and Kenya achieved independence but took very different routes toward achieving their goals.

Ghana and Kwame Nkrumah

After World War II, a young citizen of the Gold Coast named Kwame Nkrumah grew frustrated with Great Britain's slow but steady approach for independence. As a student, Nkrumah had spent time studying in the United States and also learned about the independence methods of Indian leader Mahatma Gandhi. When he returned to Africa, Nkrumah started an independence movement in 1949 by quickly organizing a radical political party. He asked for concessions from the British government, and when Great Britain did not comply, his party organized strikes and boycotts of European goods to get recognition and attain the concessions for which they asked. Unfortunately, these protests quickly got out of hand and many citizens of the Gold Coast rioted. As a result of the destabilization, Nkrumah was arrested in 1950 and served a one-year sentence.

In 1957, the former colony of the Gold Coast won independence from Great Britain. At this time, Nkrumah was elected as the prime minister of a newly independent nation.

Nkrumah's first act was to change the name of his new country. Harkening back to the Golden Age of the West African empires, he called it Ghana. Nkrumah did this intentionally as he wanted to remind Africa of its great past. He wanted to throw off the yoke of colonialism, encourage nationalism, and have his people take pride in the new nation of Ghana.

Ghana became the first country in sub-Saharan Africa to attain its freedom from a former colonial superpower. In the following years, Nkrumah and his government became corrupt, and the country fell into massive debt. In 1966, Nkrumah was overthrown in a military coup.

In 1981, a young officer named Jerry Rawlings became the leader of Ghana. Rawlings took quick measures to stabilize and strengthen Ghana's economy, which by this time depended mostly on the sale of cocoa and gold in overseas trading. However, Rawlings is most known for bringing democracy back to Ghana. Under his leadership, political stability returned to the country. In 1992, he won the first real election in Ghana, and after governing for 10 years, he stepped down when he lost an election to a new opponent. As the first country to achieve independence, Ghana was a model for decolonization.

Kenya and Jomo Kenyatta

Kenya's path to freedom was more violent than that of Ghana. Jomo Kenyatta, a young man educated in an English mission school in Kenya, became a Kenyan nationalist leader in 1946. Kenyatta went to a university in England, and while there, he began to work in an organization whose goal was to return the land of Kenya to the traditional tribesmen called the Kikuyu. The Kikuyu were displaced by English settlers more than 100 years earlier. Kenyatta returned to Kenya in 1946 and helped lead the movement for independence.

As a new leader in the movement, Kenyatta emphasized the need to peacefully coexist with the white settlers who had been living in Kenya. Unfortunately, this did not happen. Years before, when white settlers came to Africa, they created large farms on the fertile plains of Kenya. When they did so, the local tribesmen were pushed out. Over time, the white settlers had created laws not only to keep themselves in power but also to maximize their profit. Kenyatta stated that the land belonged to Kenyans, not the Europeans, who, after a century in the country, viewed themselves as Kenyans. Kenyatta wanted the native people to get their land back.

When Kenyatta's efforts did not immediately gain ground, radical leaders in Kenyatta's movement turned to guerrilla warfare. They began to raid the farms of white settlers, killed livestock, and destroyed crops, all in the hopes of forcing the white European settlers to leave. When guerrilla warfare did not work, they began to openly attack Africans who were working for the large white settlers' farms. By the 1950s, the British government sent in troops to fight the guerrilla threat, whom they called the Mau Mau. As the visible leader of the independence movement, Kenyatta found himself arrested in 1952, even though he wanted to curb the violence. He and other Kenyans were forced into camps guarded by the British. The British brought in the Royal Air Force and used bombers to break up Mau Mau resistance, who had no access to modern weapons. Fighting with only traditional East African weapons, the Mau Mau were destroyed by 1956.

When the imprisoned Kenyatta was released in 1959, the freedom movement continued to grow. His time in prison made Kenyatta a national hero, and he was elected as the first prime minister of the new nation of Kenya in 1963. Under Kenyatta, the new government jailed its political opponents and outlawed rival political parties, something that Kenyatta originally fought against.

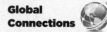
Large, violent protests sprung up around Kenyatta's regime during the mid-1990s, and Kenyatta and the ruling party held off truly free elections until foreign investors forced the country to move toward greater democracy. In 2002, the people of Kenya enjoyed the first free election, and Kenyatta and his party lost control of the government. The new Kenyan government remained corrupt, and ethnic conflicts have led to thousands being killed or left homeless.

NIGERIA

After World War II, the British government slowly acknowledged the growing demand for independence in their colony of Nigeria. When Nigeria won independence in 1960, there was hope that it could develop very rapidly due to their large quantity of natural resources: cocoa, palm oil, and crude oil, which was discovered on the Niger River in 1961. However, during the age of imperialism, Nigeria housed a combination of more than 250 different ethnic groups, many of which wanted power. The three largest groups dominated the country: the Igbo people and the Yoruba people, who were Christians in the south of Nigeria, and the Hausa-Fulani people, who were Muslims in the north.

Civil War

Nigeria created a constitution, but it sought mainly to protect the different regional areas. By 1966, the first military coup was led by a group of Hausa officers. When the Hausa took over Nigeria, 20,000 Igbos were massacred. This severely angered the Igbo people, who declared the creation of a new country, the independent state of Biafra in 1967. The civil war that commenced between the Hausa-Fulani and Igbo lasted nearly three years. It ended when Biafra had its ports blockaded and the people of southern Nigeria were starving. They had to surrender.

Oil and Its Effects on Nigeria

The oil industry, once again, was the road that Nigeria could take to bring in money from abroad. It allowed the government to set up many large industrial projects. In order to pay for these industries, Nigeria borrowed money from Western governments and was expected to pay it back. The lure of jobs in industry led to a massive rural-to-urban migration, and by the late 1990s, the capital city of Nigeria had nearly 6 million people.

When oil prices collapsed in the 1990s, the wildly corrupt Nigerian government could not pay back its large debt. Nigeria had continued to be run by several military governments, each who had promised to end corruption and give the people freedom and an honest government. In 1999, free elections were finally held, and democracy returned to Nigeria. However, the many different religions and ethnicities made it difficult to fully unify Nigeria.

ZAIRE/CONGO

In central Africa, no territory was more exploited than Congo, starting with the decision at the Berlin Conference in 1884 to give control over Congo to Belgium.

Congo was rich in resources, such as copper and rubber. It was in a great location on the Congo River, and its many tributaries and offshoots made it easy to get goods to the coasts. After World War II, Belgium, which had been ravaged during the fighting, wanted to hang on to its prized colony. However, after watching other colonial conflicts unfold throughout Africa, Belgium suddenly reversed its position in 1960. Belgium granted the nation of Congo its independence, but Belgium did nothing to help Congo prepare to become a modern country. Just as in Nigeria, there were nearly 200 different ethnic groups in Congo. It seemed that each one had its own need for a political party. The nation quickly began to fall apart.

Patrice Lumumba became the first prime minister of Congo in 1960, and he quickly learned that he ruled over a divided country. The southeastern part of the country, the Katanga province, had a large vein of copper. One of the local leaders, Moise Tshombe, declared in July 1960 that the Katanga province and all of its copper would be its own independent country. Tshombe quickly gained the support of the Belgian mining owners, who wanted to keep hold of their copper mines. Hearing this, Lumumba went to the United Nations for aid but became embroiled in the Cold War as Congo received help from the Soviet Union.

During this turmoil, the Congo military led a coup. They placed Colonel Joseph Mobutu in power. He became known as Mobutu Sese Seko. Mobutu captured Lumumba and handed him over to Tshombe, who had Lumumba executed. Tshombe assumed the leadership role of Congo until 1965 when he was overthrown by Mobutu. Mobutu quickly changed the name from Congo to Zaire, and for the next 32 years he ruled over his country.

Using brutal tactics and bribery, Mobutu stole billions of dollars from the country of Zaire and worked many of its people to death. With the amount of resources in Zaire, it could have become one of the continent's richest countries. Under Mobutu's leadership, the people were some of the poorest in the world as the infrastructure collapsed, agriculture failed, and the copper and precious gem mines were all closed. Mobutu was aided in power because of his anticommunist sentiments. Even though Western countries did not like him, they needed his cooperation during the Cold War.

However, in 1997, Mobutu was finally ousted by Laurent Kabila. The people of Zaire were looking for a change, but Kabila, while promising democracy was going to return, bribed all other political parties so he could stay in power. In 2000, with another civil war looming, several different groups of Zaire rebels tried unsuccessfully to overthrow Kabila's regime with one of their own.

DECOLONIZATION OF SOUTHERN AFRICA

Rhodesia/Zimbabwe

In southern Africa, the British colony of Rhodesia enjoyed an excellent location and climate for farming. For more than 300 years, white settlers had come to southern Africa and created large, very prosperous farms and plantations. They grew everything from necessary food crops to cash crops, such as tea and cotton. Rhodesia also had a lot of precious metal mines: gold, copper, and even coal. It had plentiful natural resources, making it a rich, thriving nation.

White settlers, however, made up a tiny portion of the Rhodesian population, but their large farms took up more than half the landmass. The rich property landowners also controlled the government. After World War II, as independence and nationalism came to Africa, the white settlers were pressured to give up their land and share power with the black majority. The predominantly white Rhodesian government rejected this idea. Even when Great Britain supported a new majority, the whites of Rhodesia refused. Led by a prominent member of the government, Ian Smith, Rhodesia declared its independence in 1965.

MAJORITY RESISTANCE

The minority government began to encounter active resistance from Rhodesian guerrilla forces led by Robert Mugabe, who led a resistance movement that lasted over 15 years. Unfortunately, the guerrilla campaign led by Mugabe spilled over into other neighboring countries, leading to a lot of poverty and disaster for the southern African region. By 1979, Mugabe's forces controlled much of Rhodesia, and many of the rich white settlers fled the country. To halt the suffering and violence, the United Nations had to impose economic sanctions, which hurt the prosperous Rhodesian economy. Mugabe and white minority leader Ian Smith accepted a negotiated treaty in 1979 that would allow a new black majority government in Rhodesia.

CREATION OF ZIMBABWE

In 1980, Rhodesia was renamed Zimbabwe and faced the challenge of recreating itself. The problems were many as 15 years of civil war had ravaged the country. They also needed to recover from the economic sanctions imposed by outside countries. On top of those calamities, there were several years of severe drought. Those factors, combined with a struggle for power in the political realm, kept Zimbabwe from growing.

Mugabe became the first elected president of Zimbabwe in 1980. Because of the differences between the Shona people, who were the majority, and the minority people, the Ndebele, Mugabe claimed it was better to have a one-party system behind which people could rally. He said it would unify the new nation of Zimbabwe. Once in power, Mugabe did not like opposition to his authority. He tried to rebuild the industry and agricultural potential that Zimbabwe possessed, but this was done at the price of freedom.

Mugabe encouraged some of the white plantation owners to stay and help their new country to recover and reach its potential. However, Mugabe began to redistribute land, giving much more to the black majority, but they had difficulty overcoming the drought as many of the irrigation systems were destroyed in the civil war.

South Africa

The country of South Africa had been controlled by colonial rulers for nearly 350 years. It was a racially divided country where a small white minority controlled the much larger black majority. By 1910, South Africa was able to gain self-rule from the British empire, and in 1931, it became part of the British Commonwealth. South Africa did have a Constitution, but the government heavily favored the white minority.

INTRODUCTION OF APARTHEID

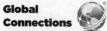

Global Connections

A good comparison to this would be the "Indian Reservations" that Native Americans were placed upon during America's westward expansion.

In 1948, the Afrikaner National Party came to power and instituted a policy known as apartheid. Apartheid means the complete separation of the races. Under apartheid, all South African citizens were required to register by their race: white, black, mixed ancestry, and Asian. The Afrikaner government said apartheid would allow each race to develop its own separate, unique culture within the country. In reality, it was a way for the white minority to dominate the government of South Africa. Everything became segregated. From schools to hospitals to where you could live, the best, premier areas always went to the white minority.

In 1959, the South African government set up reserves called homelands for the country's black majority. The policy of creating homelands was clearly unbalanced since the black majority made up more than 75 percent of the population. On the homelands, they received the smallest and least productive parts of the land.

AFRICAN NATIONAL CONGRESS

In 1912, shortly after independence from Great Britain, black South Africans created the African National Conference (ANC) as a way to fight for rights. In the 1950s, the ANC began to organize strikes, marches, and boycotts to protest their treatment and the racist policies of the government. In one of these protests in 1960, 69 men, women, and children were killed in a black township in what is known as the Sharpeville Massacre. The Sharpeville Massacre pushed many who were pursuing a nonviolent policy to one of a more armed struggle as they saw what was happening throughout South Africa.

One of these people was Nelson Mandela. Mandela was famous for being able to recruit young South Africans to peacefully resist apartheid laws, but after the Sharpeville Massacre, Mandela joined the militants. In 1961, the ANC was banned, and Mandela was arrested in 1962. Mandela was sentenced to life in prison for treason against apartheid. While he was in prison, he became the symbol of freedom for the black majority in South Africa.

THE END OF APARTHEID

By the mid-1980s, the South African apartheid government was under increasing international pressure to change. A black South African bishop, Desmond Tutu, spoke out against apartheid, receiving the 1984 Nobel Peace Prize, and encouraged international countries to impose sanctions on South Africa until Mandela was freed and apartheid abolished. Many nations agreed with Tutu, and South African athletes were banned from the 1984 Olympic Games in Los Angeles. Due to his efforts in bringing down apartheid, Nelson Mandela also won the Nobel Peace Prize in 1993.

APARTHEID COLLAPSES

In 1989, newly elected South African President F. W. de Klerk declared that his primary goal was to end the economic isolation of South Africa. By early 1990, the ANC was restored, and Nelson Mandela was released from prison. Over much of the next two years, many apartheid laws were repealed, and South Africa began to be transformed.

One of the largest obstacles was forming a new multiracial government of both blacks and whites. In April 1994, South Africa held its first open election for all races. President de Klerk and Nelson Mandela were the main candidates for president. Fot the first time, voters from every race could participate, and Nelson Mandela was elected president of the truly democratic South Africa. Mandela coined a phrase, "Let us build together," as he hoped to heal the country. He asked old political foes to work with him and his government, saying that only together could South Africa succeed. In 1996, South Africa passed a new, more democratic constitution. It included a Bill of Rights, modeled on the United States. It guaranteed equal rights for all of its citizens.

BUILDING BRIDGES IN SOUTH AFRICA

Many South Africans looked for success overnight. The country had many natural resources, but there was a need for education in every area: housing, industrial development, farming, and job training. Not every problem could be handled at one time. In 1999, Nelson Mandela stepped down as president but continued to be a major governmental influence. Mandela stood out as an example as he worked with one-time political enemies. However, the gap in common education remained large between blacks and whites. Under Mandela's leadership, the country was able to build bridges between ethnic groups, helping South Africa move forward. The changes that took place in South Africa were an example for the rest of the continent as democracy and hope were able to succeed.

Continued Struggles for Africa

Africa today still faces many changes and challenges. Their independence from colonial rule created new nations, but many experienced civil war, corrupt dictators, and fledgling economies. During the Cold War era, countries that were anticommunist were able to receive support from Western governments, while countries that did not like democracy and turned more toward socialism were isolated by the Western powers. Africans also have a strong sense of loyalty to their own tribe or region, not to a large, national government created by European rulers, making the creation of a central African government difficult.

Another difficulty to overcome was the rapid population growth. Smaller plots of land were depleted, making it difficult to grow enough food. In the late 20th century, massive drought and famine destroyed much of Africa's agriculture and killed African livestock. Disease also ravaged Africa. Malaria, river blindness, the AIDS epidemic, and the modern-day Ebola disaster emphasize that there is a lack of adequate health care throughout the continent.

Many military men, like Idi Amin in Uganda, tried to use their military might to curb problems and restore civilian rule. However, they often used it as a way to gain power and not give it back. There has been genocide in Uganda and Rwanda and a continued drought in Somalia, where the Somalis have resorted to piracy. There are many challenges that still face a decolonized, independent Africa.

Obstacles to peace in Africa continue to be:

- Racism
- Regional genocide
- Implementation of an even distribution of technology
- Wealth distribution throughout the continent

Another problem is how to bridge the new urban movement with African customs and tradition. When Africans move from the villages to a city to look for work, they become urbanized and forget many of the village customs and traditions with which they grew up. The United Nations continues to work in Africa to bring peace, stability, and education in areas where it is needed.

DECOLONIZATION OF ASIA

Japan

After World War II, Japan was forced to accept foreign occupation for the first time in its history. Throughout its long history, Japan had successfully learned from cultures. They were very selective in what they borrowed from other cultures, and they adapted it to fit a specific Japanese need. The Japanese did this once again, borrowing Western ideas of technology and industry as it recovered from World War II. Japan was devastated after World War II. The

Allied firebombing campaign across the entire country, along with the atomic bombs of Hiroshima and Nagasaki, left large urban areas in ruins.

UNITED STATES AND GENERAL DOUGLAS MACARTHUR

To curb Japanese homelessness and provide direction for the Japanese people, General Douglas MacArthur was named the military governor of Japan in 1945. He had two primary goals:

- Destroy Japan's military
- Ensure a democratic government

In 1946, a new Japanese constitution was written, stating that Japan would never use its military forces except for defense. It also said that the emperor would no longer have power, but Japan would instead be governed by a legislature known as the Diet. The Japanese constitution also included the same basic rights found in the American Bill of Rights: freedom of speech, freedom of thought, and freedom of the press.

As the Cold War began, the United States wanted to end its occupation of Japan and help its former enemy become an ally against communism. When the Korean War erupted in 1952, the United States and Japan signed a peace treaty, ending the formal American occupation of Japan. However, the United States maintained large naval, marine, and army bases throughout the Japanese archipelago. The Japanese were happy to live under the protection of the American military so they could invest their money in industry, not defense. This led to Japan's post–World War II success.

JAPANESE INDUSTRY GROWS

After World War II, the Japanese manufactured mainly textiles. Not wanting to compete with other Asian countries that made textiles, Japan moved toward the automotive and electronics industries. In the 1950s, Canon and Sony began to manufacture electronics, such as cameras and televisions, and Honda began to sell Japanese cars to the United States in 1970. Japan sold its products inexpensively all over the world. Although Japan still had to import many of its raw materials, its products were of good quality. The Japanese were able to export more than they imported. When the oil crisis of the mid-1970s hit, Americans began buying even larger quantities of fuel-efficient Japanese cars. Not having to spend money on defense, Japan was able to purchase property around the world to get its necessary raw materials.

By the 1980s, Japan was an economic superpower, rivaling its former occupier, the United States. The Japanese factories were newer and more inventory-efficient compared to the old worn-out factories of its competitors, including the United States.

The Japanese also had other reasons for their success.

1. People in Japan were highly educated with a technically skilled workforce.
2. Before World War II, Japan was already highly industrialized, going through the Industrial Revolution faster than anyone else during the Meiji Restoration, so they already had a base of industry.
3. The Japanese people were unified as it was a very homogeneous country.

Everyone got behind the new industrial efforts, and just as they did during the Meiji Restoration, Japan completely transformed. Factory owners and the laborers worked well together based on their Japanese unity, and Japan surged forward. When the United States began to feel vulnerable, it threatened to impose tariffs on Japanese goods, which kept the countries engaged in economic talks for years.

One thing Japan could not do without was oil, and when the oil crisis hit in the mid-1970s, it caused a shockwave throughout Japan. As a result, Japan had to form new relationships with the oil-producing countries of the Middle East. It also led the Japanese to build more fuel-efficient cars than its American competitors.

Japan's economic success, as well as their actions during World War II, created some bitter feelings, especially in the Koreas and China. However, Japan is acknowledging its role in World War II. Japan's strong support of the United States during the Cold War and its anticommunist government throughout the late 20th century gave Japan a greater role in world affairs.

South Korea

After the Korean War ended in 1953, the United States stayed in South Korea along the Demilitarized Zone to help guarantee the peace. Just like Japan, South Korea became an economic powerhouse as South Korea grew by leaps and bounds. South Korea began to export textiles and other clothing, and starting with the Hyundai Corporation, South Korea began to export automobiles. They created large, transoceanic shipping ports and invested in shipbuilding and steelmaking. Many international investors invested in South Korea.

During the early years of economic growth, the Korean workers were paid a relatively low wage. However, as industry grew rapidly, prosperity increased as did the South Korean standard of living. By the late 1990s, corporations such as Hyundai and Samsung were producing high-quality products that were innovative and fairly inexpensive.

South Korea's government did remain somewhat dictatorial, but when Seoul hosted the Summer Olympics in 1988, it was the so-called coming-out party of South Korea. They showcased their prosperity and achievement, becoming a major economic player on the world market.

India

INDEPENDENCE IN INDIA

After World War II, the citizens of India once again demanded their independence from Great Britain, just as they had been doing for the last 70 years. A new issue arose as to how the Hindu majority and the Islamic minority could get along in an independent country of India. A Muslim leader, Muhammad Ali Jinnah, advocated for a separate Muslim state that would be called Pakistan. Violence broke out between the Hindu majority and the Muslim minority, which quickly forced Great Britain to divide the subcontinent of India. In 1947, during the midst of this violence, British governmental officials quickly drew up borders that created a new nation. There was the majority Hindu nation of India and the Muslim country of Pakistan.

DIFFICULTIES OF THIS DIVISION

The hastily drawn border between India and Pakistan further complicated the separation. Now, Hindus and Muslims lived right next to each other, and in many cases, they were stuck on the wrong side of the border. There was not a Demilitarized Zone, as is seen between North and South Korea. India and Pakistan were intertwined on the subcontinent, right next door to each other. In 1947, there was a massive migration between east and west as millions of Hindus moved into what was now India, and Muslims moved into what was now Pakistan. During this massive shift in population, the animosity and mistrust between Hindus and Muslims, which the British had used for years to exploit the population, erupted into violence. When Hindu and Sikh Indians massacred Muslims traveling to Pakistan, Muslims retaliated, killing Hindus and causing millions to flee their homes.

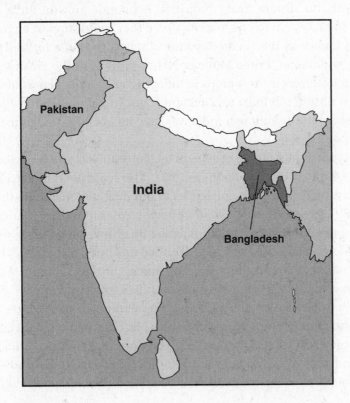

MAHATMA GANDHI

Upset not only at the partition of his country, but the graphic violence being displayed, Mahatma Gandhi, leader of the Indian independence movement, stepped up and asked for an end to the violence. On January 30, 1948, Gandhi was assassinated. Indian Prime Minister Jawaharlal Nehru issued his famous quote, "The light has gone out of our lives and there is darkness everywhere." The assassination of Gandhi was the trigger that ended the violence as it discredited the violent extremists. People began to listen to reason, even though Hindu and Muslim tensions remained high.

INDIA'S DIVERSITY

The people of India have always had diversity in language and religion. They were finally able to unify in their efforts to gain independence and drive out the British. However, after independence was achieved, those deep religious and ethnic divisions remained. The people of India were not just Hindus. They were Christians, Buddhists, and Sikhs. There was also a large number of ethnic and language difference.

To handle this, India used the U.S. Constitution as a model. They divided up the powers between a strong central government and smaller state governments. The Constitution, enacted in 1950, recognized more than 15 official languages of India.

Starting with Prime Minister Jawaharlal Nehru, the Nehru family sat atop the Indian government for nearly 40 years. Nehru tried to build a modern state set upon the ideas of social justice set forth by Gandhi. After Jawaharlal Nehru died in 1964, Indira Gandhi, Nehru's only child, served as the next successful prime minister. After her assassination in 1984, her son Rajiv Gandhi served as prime minister, only to be assassinated in 1991.

The main goal of India was to achieve industrial growth. India lacked a lot of the natural resources it needed to sustain heavy industrial economic growth. India also needed to retool its educational system to create a workforce that could support a growing economy.

A movement known as the Green Revolution started in India in the 1960s to feed its rapidly growing population. Prime Minister Nehru advocated the creation of new hybrid seeds in different fertilizers to grow crops in India because India then would be able to feed itself. The biggest obstacle in India was its rapidly growing population, which was growing faster than its food output. Although India was now independent, 33 percent of its people lived below the poverty level.

Perhaps the biggest threat India faced was religious unrest, which started after two Sikh bodyguards assassinated Indira Gandhi in 1984. The religious differences and struggles within the caste system were major obstacles in building national unity throughout all of India. By the mid-1980s, there were two dominant parties in Indian politics: the Congress Party and a Hindu nationalist party known as the Bharatiya Janata Party, or BJP. The main goal of the BJP was to create a government founded on Hindu principles. This required the closing or elimination of many other religious centers throughout India. Although controversial, the BJP has made vast improvements to India's infrastructure.

Today, India has the world's second largest population and the world's largest democracy. India has also gone a long way toward modernization. With its large labor force, India has become a major industrial power and a telecommunications giant and has a booming entertainment industry known as Bollywood. India has also focused on advancing medical technology. Through its diversity, India has become a positive postcolonial example in South Asia.

Pakistan

When Pakistan achieved its independence from India in 1947, it quickly became a divided country of its own. Western Pakistan was located near the northwestern corner of India. Eastern Pakistan, across the subcontinent, eventually became known as Bangladesh. The western half quickly dominated the new Pakistani government, even though it was more sparsely populated than the eastern half. The economic development was focused mainly in the west, whereas the east remained heavily populated and in deep poverty.

THE GOVERNMENT OF PAKISTAN

From 1947 until today, Pakistan never achieved a long period of political stability. Along with the regional and ethnic differences in eastern and western Pakistan, the new influence of Islamic fundamentalism also played a large role in the unrest. Islamic fundamentalists wanted to build a government that would create a very strict society dedicated to following Islamic principles. Other Pakistanis opposed the Islamic fundamentalists because they wanted a strong separation between the church and the state. Most of Pakistan's leaders have been military men backed by military power.

At the end of the Cold War in the 1980s, the Soviet Union invaded Pakistan's neighbor, Afghanistan. Many Afghan refugees crossed the border into Pakistan and were welcomed by Islamic fundamentalists. They took advantage of the refugees' anger and turned them into freedom fighters called the mujahideen. The mujahideen fought the Soviet invaders in Afghanistan, and after driving the Soviets out of Afghanistan, the group focused their anger on the United States.

The United States had a large influence and presence in the Middle East, and the Islamic fundamentalists wanted them to leave. During the 1990s, the Islamic fundamentalist group known as the Taliban took over Pakistan and openly gave their support to a terrorist group known as al-Qaeda. However, after the September 11 attacks on the United States, and the subsequent retaliation by the United States against al-Qaeda, Pakistan has been an ally of the United States in the war on terror. However, when al-Qaeda leader Osama bin Laden was discovered and killed by the United States in Pakistan in May 2011, the relationship became strained. The two countries have remained allies, but Pakistan continues to face government instability to this day.

Bangladesh

In 1971, the eastern section of Pakistan declared its independence under the new name Bangladesh. The ethnic group that lived there were the Bengali people, and *Bangladesh* means "land of the Bengalis." The western Pakistani government sent in the army to put down this independence movement; however, the country of India was supporting the Bengali rebels, and the Pakistani army was defeated. As a result of this defeat, Pakistan was forced to recognize the independence of the new nation of Bangladesh. Bangladesh was run mainly by military men who controlled much of the fledgling economy. Beginning in the 1990s, Bangladesh opted for a more democratic government.

Bangladesh has had many obstacles to overcome. It is one of the three most populated countries on the planet and is also one of the poorest. Nearly 150 million people live in a small area next to the Ganges River, which is highly susceptible to flooding. In December 2004, a tsunami struck multiple countries on the Indian Ocean, including Bangladesh. Thousands were killed, and millions were left homeless without basic human necessities and sanitation. Bangladesh is still mired in poverty and Third World status. Many countries of the subcontinent, including Bangladesh, India, Pakistan, and Sri Lanka, are facing the problem of child labor. Children are exploited for a very low salary as their products are taken and sold in industrialized countries at a high profit.

The Island Nation of Sri Lanka

During the 1970s, ethnic conflict led to war in Sri Lanka, which is located just off the southern coast of India. The majority of the people of Sri Lanka were Buddhists. However, there was a tiny Hindu minority who spoke a dialect of Tamil. The Tamil accused the Sri Lankan government of discrimination. When their complaints went unheard, they formed a rebel movement known as the Tamil Tigers, which wanted to have its own separate independent nation. Since the 1980s, thousands of people have been killed in this quest for independence. Indian Prime Minister Rajiv Gandhi tried to reach a peace agreement in 1983 and sent in Indian troops to disarm the Tamil Tigers. Gandhi's actions led to his assassination. The Indian troops left in 1990, and tensions remain high to this day.

Burma/Myanmar

Another country to gain independence from Great Britain during the Cold War was Burma. Burmese nationalist leader Aung San helped British forces drive the Japanese out of Burma in 1945. Ethnic tensions then became an obstacle to Burmese independence from Great Britain. Burmans made up the largest portion of the population and dominated the country and its government. As a result, many military dictatorships arose.

In 1962, General Ne Win set up an oppressive regime as he tried to make Burma a socialist state modeled after what Mao Tse-tung was doing in China. As Japan had done under Tokugawa Ieyasu, Burma decided to isolate itself from the world and strictly limit foreign investment and trade.

In 1988, young students were pressing for governmental reform when the daughter of Burmese nationalist hero Aung San returned from abroad. Her name was Aung San Suu Kyi and she took part in the new National League for Democracy. She was arrested and placed under house arrest. In 1989, Burma was renamed Myanmar. In 1990, the National League for Democracy overwhelmingly won the majority of seats in the government, but the military rule did not recognize the election. Aung San Suu Kyi won the Nobel Peace Prize in 1991 while under house arrest. She was eventually released in 1995, and although she still lives in Myanmar, she is under heavy surveillance.

The Philippines

On July 4, 1946, the Philippines achieved its independence from the United States after nearly 50 years of American control. The new Constitution was set up to favor a democratic government, but the wealthy elite of the Philippines still controlled most of the government and the economy.

Even though the Philippines had won its independence, the United States still played a large role in Filipino politics. The United States wanted to maintain its military presence in Asia, especially with the growing threat of communism and the Cold War. With the Soviet Union and communist China close by, the United States wanted to protect its supply of raw materials. When the Philippines achieved its independence in 1946, the United States insisted on a 99-year lease that allowed U.S. military bases to remain in the Philippines. The Philippines had been devastated during World War II, and the government was dependent upon American aid, so they agreed to the lease.

In 1965, Ferdinand Marcos was elected president on the platform of land reform. However, he quickly made himself a dictator and pillaged millions of dollars from the Filipino people. Marcos exiled opponents, strictly controlled free speech, and had his chief opponent, Benigno Aquino, assassinated in 1983. In the 1986 election, Marcos ran against Corazon Aquino, the widow of his main rival. Aquino won decisively, but Marcos refused to accept his loss. As he declared himself the winner, the public backlash in the Philippines was tremendous. Ferdinand Marcos was forced into exile, and the United States allowed him to live in Hawaii until his death in 1989.

During that time, the new Filipino government tried to recapture millions of dollars in wealth from Marcos's bank accounts across the world. As President Aquino came to power, a new constitution was ratified. The United States agreed to end their lease for military bases much earlier than 99 years. President Aquino wanted to set the precedent of a single six-year term for the president as a way to curb the dictatorship and abuses in power that kept

Ferdinand Marcos in power for more than 20 years, so in 1992, a new president of the Philippines was elected: Fidel Ramos.

The Dutch East Indies Becomes Indonesia

During World War II, the Japanese set their sights on the Dutch East Indies as their source of industrial materials, such as oil and rubber. When the Japanese surrendered in 1945, an Indonesian named Sukarno quickly proclaimed that Indonesia was independent of the Netherlands. The Netherlands, however, wanted to maintain their grip of power over Indonesia. Unlike other colonial powers whose citizens returned home, many of the Dutch people living in Indonesia wanted to remain. They tried to block the attempts of native Indonesians to gain access to government positions and higher education. As a result, the Indonesians waged a guerrilla war. When the United States and the United Nations pulled their support from the Netherlands, Indonesia was granted their independence in late 1945.

Indonesia is made up of over 13,000 islands that have several hundred ethnic groups, speaking as many as 250 languages. It is also home to the world's largest Islamic population, with more than 90 percent of the people being followers of Islam. Sukarno declared that it was his job to lead this nation. Indonesia was to have a parliamentary democracy representing its vast diversity, but Sukarno declared himself president for a lifetime. In 1965, some military officers tried to overthrow his regime in a coup. However, in 1967, a military general named Suharto put down the rebellion and then put himself in power instead of Sukarno. As a result of the unrest, as many as one million Indonesians were killed as Suharto turned Indonesia into a police state and declared martial law.

Over Suharto's reign of 32 years, there was persecution of religious and ethnic groups and rampant corruption. A massive economic crisis hit Asia in 1997, and because of his repressive tactics at home, Suharto was forced to step down in 1998. A new leader was elected in the first-ever democratic election in Indonesia, President Abdurrahman Wahid. President Wahid sought to end the religious and ethnic persecution. He also wanted to rebuild his country, especially after the devastation of the Christmas Day tsunami of 2004. However, with all of its ethnic conflicts and religious diversity, Indonesia is still troubled by violence to this day.

China

POST–WORLD WAR II

After World War II, Mao Tse-tung's communist forces continued to fight the Chinese Nationalist Party. In 1949, Mao ushered in the formation of the People's Republic of China, and after decades of fighting, China was finally united under communist leadership. Chairman Mao had emerged victorious because of the support he had garnered from the enormous peasant population. The Chinese peasants had been abused by Chiang Kai-shek, Chinese landlords, and heavy taxes. Chairman Mao had promised to redistribute land to the poor and get rid of the dominating landlords. Women also supported Chairman Mao as he said he rejected the old Confucian models of society where women were inferior, saying that women are equally important as men. Many others were drawn to Chairman Mao's Communist Party because they wanted a new China, one that would not be dependent upon foreigners who had abused China for the last several hundred years. When support for Chairman Mao continued to grow, the Chinese nationalist population began to leave China.

Global Connections

The first American president, George Washington, did the same thing during the birth of the United States. He set the term limit for the presidency at two four-year terms.

After achieving victory, Mao wanted to turn a poor, agricultural China into a modern, industrial giant. He quickly nationalized all Chinese businesses, and following Joseph Stalin's Five-Year Plan, Mao created plans to increase coal and steel production, which would then be used to help develop other industries. Mao invited Soviet engineers to build electric plants, railroads, and other types of infrastructure. Land was redistributed to Chinese peasants, who rose up and killed their former aristocratic landlords. Mao's government asked the peasants to form collective, or cooperative, farm communes to pool their labor and land resources to be more beneficial.

Chairman Mao ruled with a one-party totalitarian regime, and as such, the old Confucian standards of traditional China were gone. Chinese characters were simplified, making it easier for people to learn how to read and write. New schools were opened to promote Chairman Mao's new political educational system. Doctors were sent into the rural areas to help teach hygiene. Chairman Mao was actively trying to make the life of the Chinese people better, as far as the people could see.

THE GREAT LEAP FORWARD

In 1958, Mao Tse-tung promoted the idea of the Great Leap Forward. This was a plan to achieve maximum efficiency when it came to agriculture. Giant communes were created with several villages surrounding the land. Each commune was tied together with its own school, factories, and houses. Each individual commune was given a quota, and they had to organize their labor resources not only to grow the food but to build necessary infrastructure, like irrigation systems and flood controls. They were also expected to set up and maintain factories. In the end, the Great Leap Forward was a disaster for China. The rural industries never developed, the commune system was inefficient as food production actually decreased, and then a famine hit China. Within three years, up to 30 million people in China starved to death.

In response to the failure of the Great Leap Forward, Mao instituted what he called the Great Proletarian Cultural Revolution in 1966. It was geared to get rid of all noncommunist revolutionary tendencies. Many teenagers formed groups called the Red Guards, and they openly attacked anybody who was not procommunist. Any figure who had authority—factory managers, professors, artists—could be arrested, beaten, or killed, even if the individual was a member of the Communist Party. As a result, many of the new schools and universities were closed. Thousands were left jobless and homeless, and as the economy began to fall apart, civil war threatened once again. Mao used the Chinese army to restore order, and then many of the soldiers were sent to work in agricultural or industrial jobs to keep things going.

CHINA AND THE COLD WAR

As a result of its communist relationship with the Soviet Union, tensions between China and the United States deepened visibly during this period, especially with General Douglas MacArthur's attack near the Yalu River in 1951. However, in 1971, China was admitted to the United Nations, and in 1972, President Richard Nixon traveled to Beijing to improve relations with Chairman Mao Tse-tung, touting the new open-door policy.

Even though China was a communist country, it had different ideas about communism than the Soviet Union. Joseph Stalin had sent economic assistance and aid to help China modernize, but Stalin and Mao fundamentally disagreed on many issues. Mao said that he had taken the idea of Marxism and molded it to fit Chinese needs. As there was no large industrial class, Mao shifted the rise in power to the peasants. During the Cold War, China and the Soviet Union also competed for influence in Third World countries to export their own brand of communism.

DEATH OF MAO TSE-TUNG

Chairman Mao Tse-tung died in 1976. Throughout the disasters of the Great Leap Forward and the Cultural Revolution, he was admired by all of China for his ability to rid China of the foreigners who had taken advantage of them for centuries. In 1978, a reform organizer, Deng Xiaoping, was named the leader of China. Deng was focused on economic output and promoted his idea called the Four Modernizations. The Four Modernizations focused on

1. Agriculture
2. Industry
3. Science and technology
4. A strong defense

Deng was a moderate reformer who allowed some small private ownership of property. He got rid of the communes and replaced them with farmland given to each peasant family, where they received a quota from the government. When that quota was met, the family could sell the rest on the free market for money. Some entrepreneurs were permitted to create their own businesses, and managers of factories were given the freedom to expand and try new things, as long as it ended with greater output and efficiency. Deng's reforms brought foreign investment into China, and the standard of living for some in China was raised.

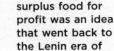

Global Connections

The selling of surplus food for profit was an idea that went back to the Lenin era of the Soviet Union.

CHINA'S POPULATION GROWTH

As the 1980s approached, China's population had surged to more than 1.2 billion. It was seen as a strain on the economy, so China instituted the One Child Law in 1979. Chinese families were allowed to have only one child and received rewards for doing so. Families who had more than one child had to pay a fine, though many rural families still had multiple children to help them on the farm. Unfortunately, because boys were highly sought after, there was a large, widespread practice of infanticide as baby girls were killed, or girls were sent to orphanages so they could have the option of trying for another child.

TIANANMEN SQUARE

In the 1980s, there was also a quest for political reform. As the standard of living improved for some, the gap between rich and poor also increased. Many believed that the ruling government officials were taking advantage of the people and stealing from the country. China was also experiencing an influx of Western tourists, and Chinese students began to study abroad and learn about Western democratic ideals. Upon returning to China, the students wanted more political freedom. This culminated in April 1989 when 100,000 students occupied the main square of Tiananmen Square in Beijing. The students protested for democracy, and the students enjoyed large support from across the country and the world. During the protest, as many as one million people came to Tiananmen Square.

DENG'S RESPONSE

In response to the Tiananmen Square protest, Prime Minister Deng declared martial law. He sent 250,000 soldiers to surround Beijing, and on June 4, 1989, the standoff at Tiananmen Square came to an end. Thousands of armed soldiers crashed into the crowd, and tanks drove through barricades. Hundreds were killed, and thousands were wounded.

After the brutal putdown of the Tiananmen Square protest, Prime Minister Deng instituted more economic reforms, which led to a booming economy and the acquisition of the 2008 Olympics in Beijing. Following the death of Prime Minister Deng in 1997, China was forced to deal with its poor human rights record and repair their relations with the United States. The United States pressured China to release political prisoners and increase basic rights for political opponents.

China is transitioning economically, but politically it is still under a tight grip, and many Chinese people desire greater freedoms. However, the increased economic power of China, its industrial might, and the amount of money that it has loaned across the world shows that China is slowly becoming more capitalistic. Many hope that soon political freedoms will grow as well. In 2000, the United States voted to normalize trade relations with China. Supporters of the idea believed that the best way to prompt improved human rights and political change in China was to increase economic engagement instead of imposing isolation and economic sanctions.

1945 C.E.	Indonesia declares independence from the Netherlands.
1946 C.E.	• Japanese Constitution
	• U.S. grants independence to the Philippines.
1947 C.E.	Great Britain creates Pakistan.
1947–1964 C.E.	India is governed by Jawaharlal Nehru.
1948 C.E.	• Mahatma Gandhi is assassinated.
	• Sri Lanka and Burma achieve independence from Great Britain.
1949 C.E.	Mao Tse-tung begins rule in China.
1952 C.E.	U.S. occupation of Japan ends.
1953 C.E.	North Korea establishes collectives and isolates itself.
1958–1961 C.E.	China's "Great Leap Forward"
1960 C.E.	South Korea begins to develop industry with U.S. aid.
1963 C.E.	Ferdinand Marcos is elected president of the Philippines.
1964 C.E.	Indira Gandhi takes over India.
1965 C.E.	Military governments begin to reign in Indonesia.
1966–1976 C.E.	Cultural Revolution in China
1970 C.E.	• Japanese cars and electronics are in high demand around the world.
	• Zhou Enlai replaces Mao Tse-tung as leader of China.
1971 C.E.	• Bengali Rebellion leads to a new nation of Bangladesh.
	• China receives membership into the United Nations.
1973 C.E.	Last U.S. forces leave Vietnam.
1975 C.E.	• North Vietnam begins reeducation of South Vietnam.
	• U.S. imposes trade restrictions on Vietnam.
1976 C.E.	• Indonesia annexes East Timpor.
	• China's current leader (Zhou Enlai) and former leader (Mao Tse-tung) die.
1980 C.E.	Deng Xiaoping is new premier of China and implements Four Modernizations.
1981 C.E.	Civil war in Sri Lanka
1986 C.E.	Corazon Aquino becomes president of the Philippines.
1987 C.E.	South Korea adopts democratic Constitution.
1988 C.E.	Seoul, South Korea hosts the Summer Olympics.
1989 C.E.	• Burma is renamed Myanmar—internal struggles continue.
	• Tiananmen Square protests in China
1990 C.E.	• South Korea achieves one of the world's fastest growing economies.
	• Bangladesh achieves democratic rule.
1994 C.E.	Foreign investment into Vietnam begins as U.S. lifts trade embargo.
1997 C.E.	Hong Kong is returned to China.
1999 C.E.	Indonesia has first democratic elections.
2000 C.E.	U.S. and China expand trade relations.
2008 C.E.	Beijing Olympics

The Decolonization of the Americas

33

SOUTH AMERICA

Argentina

In the early 1900s, Argentina was one of the wealthiest nations in all of Latin America. They enjoyed a relatively stable government that was dominated by wealthy landowners. Unfortunately, the Great Depression hit Argentina especially hard and led to a military government that lasted for the next 50 years.

JUAN PERÓN

In 1946, Argentinian army colonel Juan Perón became the elected president of Argentina. Using a platform of limiting multinational corporations, he was going to increase wages and allow the organization of labor. As a result, he was a favorite of the working classes in Argentina. Very similar to Byzantine Emperor Justinian, Perón enjoyed the popularity that his wife, Eva Perón, helped him gain. Eva Perón worked tirelessly in medical clinics and schools to help the poor and unemployed.

As Perón was governing, however, he slowly began to suppress any opposition. As a result of his tactics, many of the scholars and educated elite left Argentina for other countries. Perón also took over many heavy industries that Argentina could not support, leading the country into an economic tailspin as they had enormous debt. As Perón's power began to fade in the 1950s, Argentina was beginning to suffer the effects of high inflation. They were also reeling from the death of Eva Perón in 1952, who was beloved by the people of Argentina. Perón was kicked out of Argentina by the military and exiled in 1955.

ARGENTINA (1950–1970)

For the next 20 years, different military factions came in and out of power in Argentina. During this time, there were many supporters of Perón who were clamoring for his return. In 1973, when things were not getting better, Perón was brought back from exile and elected president. However, he died in 1974 before the first year of his new regime was over. His new wife, Isabel, was elected to be the first woman president in Latin America. Unfortunately, Isabel Perón was unable to handle the economic tailspin as rebels and other terrorists were beginning to attack various parts of the country. By 1976, Isabel Perón was kicked out of power by the military.

MILITARY RULE FOR ARGENTINA

To fight their opponents, the Argentinian army waged a war on its own citizens (the Dirty War), terrorizing anyone who was an enemy of the state. Some estimates said that more than 20,000 Argentinians disappeared or were killed. In 1982, the Argentinian military hoped to distract the people from their economic troubles by capturing the British-controlled Falkland Islands off the coast of Argentina. The Argentinian army miscalculated the British response and were overwhelmingly defeated, damaging the military's honor and authority.

Global Connections

The actions of the Argentinian army were very similar to the actions of Robespierre during the French Revolution.

DEMOCRACY RETURNS TO ARGENTINA

As a result of the defeat in the Falkland Islands, the military government held free elections, and by 1983, a new democratic government was established in Argentina. The Argentinian people wanted the new government to conduct an investigation into the military's role in the war on its own people, feeling that only after the facts were revealed (and leaders punished) could the nation begin to move forward.

Despite the troubling economy and constant corruption, democracy survived. Throughout the 1990s, Argentina's economy grew and thrived. They had a high literacy rate and enjoyed many natural resources. After 50 years of trouble and corruption, Argentina is still climbing toward its goal of being a completely developed First World country that is on the path toward success.

Cuba

CASTRO BEGINS TO EXPORT THE COMMUNIST REVOLUTION

After the embarrassment of the Bay of Pigs in 1961 and the terror of the Cuban Missile Crisis in 1962, Fidel Castro used subsidies provided by the Soviet Union to bring his version of the Communist Revolution to other Latin American countries. He also sent his troops to the continent of Africa in 1975 to help the fledgling socialist government in the country of Angola. As a result, the United States continued to economically isolate Cuba with sanctions. The United States aided anticommunist, anti-Castro regimes and rebels throughout Latin America.

AFTER THE COLLAPSE OF THE SOVIET UNION

When the Soviet Union collapsed in 1991, Castro wanted to preserve communism. He adapted by encouraging the country to use some ideas of a capitalist economy, including allowing foreign investment in Cuba. Castro wore his military uniform as a symbol of the success of the Communist Revolution. Castro also pointed to Cuba's high literacy rate, access to basic health care for all citizens, and equality for women as examples of the success of the Communist Revolution. Today, other countries, including the United States, are easing back their sanctions against Cuba.

Brazil

Unlike many of its neighbors, Brazil won its independence peacefully. Brazil has many rich natural resources—from oil to minerals to agriculture—as well as the mighty Amazon River. Brazil is also home to a much more diverse population than many of its neighbors. Even though Brazil had a series of dictators and military governments, the country has tried to be progressive.

From 1930 to 1945, Brazil was ruled by a dictator named Getúlio Vargas, who worked closely with Juan Perón in Argentina. Vargas made some reforms that aided his country, but he was eventually thrown out in a military coup. The military did allow elections, and a series of presidents ruled Brazil over the next 20 years. The growing threat of communism led the military to take control once again. They heavily regulated the country as many civil rights and freedoms were repressed, and critics could be jailed or killed.

BRAZILIAN ECONOMY

Despite the military dictatorships in Brazil, the country had rapid economic growth, unlike many of its neighbors. With its large population, rich natural resources, ample financing, and growth in technology, Brazil rapidly became an economic superpower. By the late 1990s, the Brazilian government was able to pay off the international debts that they accrued while industrializing. Not only has Brazil become a major economic superpower, but it has also become a mecca for tourism, enjoying the international stage as the host of the 2014 World Cup and the Summer Olympic Games in 2016.

CENTRAL AMERICA

Nicaragua

In Central America after World War II, there was a constant threat of conflict as the longtime rulers—the landowning aristocracy and the military—ran the governments and controlled the economies. Many poor people grew angry, and the spread of communism was always a threat. In many countries, the United States intervened in some capacity.

From 1936 to 1979, the Somoza family ruled over a dynasty in Nicaragua. The family was able to stay in power because they were anticommunist and enjoyed the funding and aid sent to them by the United States. However, by the early 1970s, different groups began to oppose and fight against the current ruler, Anastasio Somoza.

GROWTH OF THE SANDINISTAS

The rebels who wanted to throw out the Somoza family called themselves Sandinistas after a Nicaraguan revolutionary leader from the 1930s named Augusto Sandino. The Sandinistas were a nationalist group who wanted to reform the government of Nicaragua to give more power to the poor and to women. The Sandinistas had support from young, educated students, who realized the stranglehold of power that the Somoza family had over Nicaragua.

In 1979, the Sandinistas were successful at throwing Anastasio Somoza out of power. After that was achieved, they wanted to reform Nicaragua. They elected Daniel Ortega as the president of Nicaragua. Ortega's reform policies included land redistribution to the people, which bore the characteristics of socialism. Terrified that Nicaragua would follow Fidel Castro's path, U.S. President Ronald Reagan began to secretly fund another Nicaraguan group in 1981 who opposed the revolution, known as the Contras. As a result of the Sandinista/Contra civil war, Nicaragua's economy suffered, and the people were trapped in the middle of the struggle. The Sandinistas were able to remain in power, and in 1990, a truce was reached. Free elections were held in Nicaragua in 1990, and the new president was Violeta Chamorro. The Sandinista government honored the election but still retained control of the army.

Since then, Nicaragua has set about trying to repair the economy and the damage that had been done, not only from its own civil war but from the era of colonization and imperialism as well.

Mexico

In the mid-1870s, Mexico had a new ruler, Porfirio Diaz. Diaz had come to power as he rose through the army and became a general, and in 1876, he ousted the president with the support of the military. Diaz promised land reform to Mexican Indians and small farmers, so they supported him as well. However, Diaz was very corrupt, as he offered no land or governmental jobs to anyone who did not support him. He quickly became an authoritarian leader, and his motto was "Order and Progress." Diaz remained in power for nearly 40 years until 1911.

1900s IN MEXICO

After 30 years of Diaz's rule, many Mexicans began to speak out against Diaz and his harsh policies. Some groups wanted more freedoms, and farm workers wanted more land. As a result, a wide variety of political factions began to form.

One of Diaz's main opponents was a man named Francisco Madero. Madero was a member of a very old and wealthy family of Mexico. Madero had been educated in the United States, where he learned of the ideas of democracy. In 1910, he offered himself as a candidate for the president of Mexico. Diaz had him arrested and then exiled. Some of Madero's followers began to call for an open, armed revolution to oust Diaz. The Mexican revolutionaries came from all walks of life. There was Pancho Villa from the wilds of northern Mexico, and in the south, there was Emiliano Zapata. Both men led armies that fought against Diaz. They campaigned for the rights of the poor in Mexico, and by 1911, they forced Diaz to step down.

 GLOBAL CONNECTIONS

Francisco Madero bears a strong resemblance to Tiberius and Gaius Gracchus of ancient Rome in that he used his wealth and influence to positively influence the government of his country. Also similar to the Gracchus brothers, Madero's own countrymen had him assassinated.

THE RETURN OF MADERO AND CONTROL BY CARRANZA

Francisco Madero was elected president in 1911, but he was very quickly swallowed up by the tremendous job he had to do and was assassinated in 1913. Replacing him was a Mexican general, Victoriano Huerta. Unfortunately for Huerta, he was wildly unpopular with most people in Mexico, including the two revolutionary leaders Villa and Zapata. Venustiano Carranza was elected as the new Mexican president in 1914. When Carranza took control of the government, he unleashed his army on his former allies, Villa and Zapata, bringing the Mexican civil war to an end.

Carranza then began to reform and rewrite the Mexican Constitution, which was adopted in 1917. The Constitution promoted land reform and education. However, it took until 1920 for this Constitution to be formally ratified. The new Constitution had three primary goals.

1. It wanted to break up and redistribute the large estates of the aristocracy and give the land to the people of Mexico.
2. It wanted to allow the government to have main control of Mexico's natural resources.
3. It wanted to limit the amount of foreign control and businesses inside Mexico.

ROLE OF THE UNITED STATES

During the Mexican Revolution, the United States had provided financial support to leaders they thought could help further American interests. In 1916, the United States sent General John Pershing into Mexico to capture Pancho Villa because of raids he organized within the United States. Unfortunately, the United States and its intervention were very unpopular in Mexico.

When U.S. President Franklin Roosevelt was elected in 1932, he decided on a new tactic toward Latin American countries. He called this the Good Neighbor Policy and did not intervene in Mexico. The United States also brought home troops that had been stationed in outposts in Haiti and Nicaragua because of the Good Neighbor Policy.

THE INSTITUTIONAL REVOLUTIONARY PARTY OR PIR

In 1929, leaders of the Mexican government organized the party known as the Institutional Revolutionary Party, or PIR. The PIR dominated the Mexican government for decades. The PIR was able to find a way to work with all groups in Mexican society, from military leaders to industrial leaders to peasant farmers. The PIR allowed small political parties that did not threaten them. For decades, the PIR clung to power by combating the problems within its society: increasing education and providing better health care. Even though there was still poverty and anger inside of Mexico, some of the PIR initiatives were working, and Mexico was relatively peaceful.

However, in 1968, students used the worldwide stage of the Summer Olympics in Mexico City as a forum for their protests against the PIR. The Mexican police and army worked together to quickly and forcefully suppress the riots. While the world witnessed the drama unfold, the PRI regained control of the country.

MODERN MEXICO

In the 1970s, the discovery of oil helped Mexico have a quick economic spurt, but a recession hit Mexico hard, and up through the 1980s, Mexico became a society of haves and have-nots.

Starting in the late-1980s through today, industry arrived in Mexico as the United States and Japan sought Mexico's cheap labor for manufacturing and parts assembly. Everything from automobiles to electronics are manufactured in Mexico, which are then shipped back to the United States and Japan and sold at a much higher cost. As a result, many Mexicans remain very poor.

In 1994, Canada, Mexico, and the United States implemented the North American Free Trade Agreement (NAFTA). People who supported it felt that it would boost Mexico's economy by lowering trade barriers and opening up a North American market. Initially, the NAFTA agreement brought some business to Mexico. However, a lot of Mexican businesses were not able to compete with the onslaught of finished products coming from the United States and Canada, which were higher in quality and as cheap in price.

CURRENT SITUATION

Mexico has long lived under the shadow of its powerful economic neighbor, the United States. Through the modern day, Mexico has continued to rely on investment from the United States to bail it out of economic crisis. Recently, there has been added tension with the growth of illegal immigration and drug importation coming from Mexico across the southern border of the United States.

In 2000, the PRI saw the 75-year reign as leaders of the Mexican government come to an end. A new candidate, Vicente Fox, was elected as president of Mexico. Fox promised to end corruption and reduce poverty, things that modern Mexico is struggling with to this day. In 2012, the PRI returned to power.

Caribbean Nation of Haiti

During the Age of Revolution, the Caribbean nation of Haiti was the first to win its independence in 1804. But since that time, Haiti has been beset by difficult times. Haiti was governed by a string of dictators who were quickly overthrown by other rebellions.

DICTATORS REIGN IN HAITI

During the Cold War from 1957 to 1971, Haiti was governed by a man named Dr. Francois Duvalier, who was known by the nickname Papa Doc. Duvalier quickly created a secret police force that ended any and all opposition to his reign.

After his 15-year reign ended, Duvalier's son, Jean-Claude Duvalier, who was known as Baby Doc, took over in 1971. Jean-Claude continued to brutally run the country until he was thrown out of power in 1986. It was not until 1990 that Haiti, under close watch from human rights groups, held its free elections and Jean-Bertrand Aristide, a Haitian priest, was elected. Aristide was seen as a folk hero to the poor, economically repressed people of Haiti. Aristide said his main goal was to move toward dignified poverty.

Haiti was beset with many problems, and a military takeover forced Aristide into exile in 1991 as the conservative forces of Haiti wanted to maintain power. The military went after many of his supporters. As a result, the United States and the United Nations were forced into action to quell the killings by the Haitian military. When Aristide returned to power in 1994, he promised to build a functioning democracy. Aristide was ousted again from power in 2004.

THE ECONOMY OF HAITI

Haiti is one of the poorest Third World countries in the Western Hemisphere. It lacks education, health care, and industry. In 2010, Haiti's problems were exacerbated by an earthquake that ravaged the country. Many children were left homeless and orphaned, as the country desperately tried to survive. Rather than trying to find the next living relative, many of the children were sold on the open market and "adopted."

ORGANIZATION OF AMERICAN STATES

Latin America has existed under a sphere of American influence. Many Latin Americans admire the technology, the freedom, and the quality of life in the United States. Many are often frustrated and angry at the influence the United States has on the political and economic situation in their own respective Latin American countries.

To aid Latin American countries, the United States formed the Organization of American States, known as the OAS. The OAS was created in 1948 to help promote democracy, prevent communism, and forge economic ties between the United States and Latin American countries. Throughout most of the Cold War, the United States was able to exert tremendous influence over the OAS. From 1960 to the modern day, the United States has invested or loaned millions of dollars to Latin America, trying to promote education and land reform, fight poverty, and improve health care. The United States supported anticommunist leaders and was involved in regional conflicts, such as the invasion of Grenada in 1983. They also sent troops to Panama in 1989 to overthrow military dictator Manuel Noriega and stem drug trafficking into the United States.

Some countries that found natural resources, like Venezuela, were able to break away from American dependence. Others exported their food and natural resources to the growing Asian countries of Japan and Korea. As a result, the Japanese heavily invested in Latin American countries, especially Brazil.

STRUGGLES CONTINUE TODAY IN LATIN AMERICA

Many areas of Latin America remain underdeveloped and exploited. During the 1980s, illegal drug trade grew as Central and South American countries—including Peru, Panama, Colombia, and Bolivia—began to export cocaine to the United States. As the illegal drug trade expanded, U.S. President Ronald Reagan declared what he called "a war on drugs" in 1982. He pressured South American countries to move against the large drug lords, such as Pablo Escobar in Colombia. Many Latin American countries had a difficult time with this as the drug czars, as they were known, were able to influence the government and the military. Latin American countries complained that it was the demand for illegal drugs coming from the United States, and not their supply, that was the problem. The illegal drug trade remains a source of contention to this day.

Poverty and civil war has forced many people to leave their homelands, and a flood of illegal immigration began in the 1990s from Latin American countries to the United States. By the spring and summer of 2014, large numbers of illegals—including immigrant children—were crossing from Latin America and Mexico into the United States seeking a better life. Red Cross shelters and border patrol agents were unable to keep up with the tide of people, causing the illegal immigration problem to flare up once again. Many want to return the illegal people to their home countries, whereas others say that because their countries lack education and health care, the United States must provide for them.

1889 C.E.	Brazil becomes a republic.
1917 C.E.	Mexican revolution ends with the creation of the Mexican Constitution.
1920–1934 C.E.	Series of generals serve as president of Mexico.
1930 C.E.	Getúlio Vargas becomes dictator of Brazil.
1933 C.E.	Anastasio Somoza becomes dictator of Nicaragua.
1934–1940 C.E.	President Lázaro Cárdenas of Mexico improves lives of peasants.
1946 C.E.	• NRP changes its name to Institutional Revolutionary Party (PRI) in Mexico. • Juan Perón is elected president of Argentina and becomes a dictator.
1950s C.E.	Cuba is led by Fulgencio Batista, who is a U.S. backed dictator.
1952 C.E.	Death of Eva Perón in Argentina
1953 C.E.	Fidel Castro leads attempted coup in Cuba.
1955 C.E.	Argentinian military throws Perón from power.
1955–1973 C.E.	Argentina's military is in power and economy crumbles.
1959 C.E.	Batista flees Cuba—Castro is in power.
1961 C.E.	Failed Bay of Pigs invasion by U.S. in Cuba
1962 C.E.	Cuban Missile Crisis between U.S. and U.S.S.R.
1964 C.E.	Military takeover of Brazilian government
1968 C.E.	Students are massacred in Mexico City while protesting for economic change.
1970s C.E.	Castro creates Executive Council in Cuba to help govern and reconstruct Cuba.
1973 C.E.	Perón is back in power in Argentina.
1974 C.E.	Perón dies in Argentina.
1976 C.E.	Military assumes power in Argentina and issues Reign of Terror on citizens.
1979 C.E.	• Communists in Nicaragua overthrow Somoza family rule. • Daniel Ortega is the new leader in Nicaragua.
1980 C.E.	• Brazilian recession • Argentina is at war with Falkland Islands.
1983 C.E.	Raúl Alfonsin is elected president of Argentina.
1987 C.E.	U.S. aids anti-Sandinista rebels who are called Contras in Nicaragua.
1988 C.E.	PRI rule is challenged in Mexico by new parties.
1989 C.E.	End of Soviet subsidies to Cuba
1990 C.E.	• Democracy is reestablished in Argentina. • Civil war ravages Nicaragua—Ortega promises free elections.
1994 C.E.	NAFTA (North American Free Trade Agreement) is signed by Canada, United States, and Mexico.
1996 C.E.	New Nicaraguan President Arnoldo Alemán is elected.
1998 C.E.	Fernando Cardoso of Brazil creates better economy and growth of democracy.
2000 C.E.	First time the PRI no longer majority in Mexican Congress

Quick Quiz: Chapters 32–33

1. What was the first sub-Saharan country to gain independence from its European ruler?

   A. Kenya

   B. Ghana

   C. Zaire

   D. South Africa

2. Which African leader stole billions of dollars from his own people after Zaire achieved independence?

   A. Mobutu Sese Seko

   B. Jomo Kenyatta

   C. Nelson Mandela

   D. Ferdinand Marcos

3. Which African nation had a great climate for farming where white farmers created large farms and plantations?

   A. South Africa

   B. Nigeria

   C. Congo

   D. Rhodesia

4. Which Asian country was the first to become an economic superpower in Asia?

   A. Korea

   B. India

   C. Japan

   D. Myanmar

5. During decolonization, which country had to be divided over a religious dispute that threatened to turn violent?

   A. Burma

   B. Israel

   C. Afghanistan

   D. India

6. Which U.S. colony/territory was the first to gain its independence?

   A. Guam
   B. Puerto Rico
   C. Philippines
   D. Japan

7. In post–World War II China, which idea by Mao Tse-tung turned out to be a disaster for the people of China?

   A. The Great Leap Forward
   B. The Cultural Revolution
   C. The annexation of Hong Kong
   D. The May 4th Movement

8. What effect did the Great Depression have on Argentina?

   A. It finally enabled Juan Perón to become elected as president.
   B. It allowed a military government to come into power.
   C. Many scholars and educated business owners left Argentina.
   D. Large multinational corporations swept in and bought up Argentinian corporations.

9. Which communist leader wanted to export the Communist Revolution?

   A. Fidel Castro
   B. Juan Perón
   C. Getúlio Vargas
   D. Francisco Madero

10. Why was the Somoza family able to remain in power in Nicaragua?

    A. They received massive amounts of Soviet subsidies.
    B. They controlled the powerful drug cartels.
    C. They were close allies with Fidel Castro.
    D. They were supported by the United States as they were anticommunist.

11. Which agreement was signed by North American countries to specifically lower trade tariffs?

    A. North American Free Trade Agreement (NAFTA)
    B. Monroe Doctrine
    C. Organization of American States
    D. Good Neighbor Policy

Quick Quiz Answers

1. B; **2.** A; **3.** D; **4.** C; **5.** D; **6.** C; **7.** A; **8.** B; **9.** A; **10.** D; **11.** A

Collapse of the Soviet Union 34

SOVIET UNION

Stalin

When the Soviet Union emerged among the victorious Allies in World War II, the Soviet people were not able to enjoy their newfound power or the fruits of victory. Joseph Stalin quickly reverted to the ruthless tactics he employed before the outbreak of World War II. Enemies of the state, or anyone who might be an enemy of the state, were sent to labor camps. Stalin, afraid of losing his power, began a purge of his military and political rivals.

Nikita Khrushchev

When Stalin died in 1953, Nikita Khrushchev, one of Stalin's right-hand men, became the new Soviet leader. In 1956, Khrushchev began to criticize the abuse of power employed by Joseph Stalin. Khrushchev led a movement that he called De-Stalinization. There were not many changes overall; however, Khrushchev did seek to scale back the effects of the Cold War. He wanted to have a peaceful existence with the United States and Western powers. Khrushchev did not want to change the overall goals of the Soviet Union, and he wanted to maintain the Iron Curtain countries. In 1956, when the starving Soviet people began to rebel against communist rule, Khrushchev was aggressive. He sent in soldiers and tanks to crush the rebellion. While he was in the process of De-Stalinizing the Soviet Union on a worldwide scale, any harsh criticism at home was quickly and forcibly put down.

Leonid Brezhnev

Based on the lack of growth of the Soviet economy and the growing Cold War, Nikita Khrushchev was forced to resign his post in 1964. Succeeding Nikita Khrushchev was Leonid Brezhnev, who remained in power until 1982. To secure his grip on power, Brezhnev quickly clamped down on any dissension, action, or verbal criticism of his government. Soviet citizens could be arrested, sent to prison, or even sent to asylums if they were seen as enemies of the state.

Soviet Accomplishments Under Stalin, Khrushchev, and Brezhnev

After World War II, Soviet factories were rebuilt, and industries began to grow as equipment was taken from Germany and brought to the Soviet Union. The Soviet Union also spent much of the country's monetary resources on the development of technology and science, mainly geared toward weaponry. The Soviet Union received a giant boost in morale in 1957 when the Soviet Union, under Nikita Khrushchev, launched the space satellite, *Sputnik*. *Sputnik* became the first man-made craft to orbit the Earth. It was a major political and propaganda victory against the Western powers. Using this as a political platform, Khrushchev touted that the Soviet Union had a system of free health care and that virtually everyone was employed.

Problems for Khrushchev and Brezhnev

While enjoying the Soviet Union's propaganda success, neither Khrushchev nor Brezhnev could solve the fundamental problems with the Soviet economy. The Soviets depended upon a state-planned economy, and over the short term, it produced results. These results were mainly centered around Cold War weaponry and things necessary for *Sputnik* in the space race.

However, Stalin's idea of having collectivized farms and farmer collectives did not work. The Soviet Union could not feed itself. It was normally forced to purchase grain to feed its citizens. Compared to the capitalist economies of the West, who had not only agricultural goods but plentiful products for consumers to buy, the Soviet Union could not adequately compete. For example, the appliances and clothing the Soviet Union produced were unreliable and of a lower quality than those produced in the West. Western countries enjoyed things like television sets, washers and dryers, and plentiful food in the grocery stores, whereas Soviet citizens had to wait in food lines for hours to get basic necessities. They certainly did not have access to luxury items like a washer and dryer, or even a vehicle.

The cause of this was the Soviet method of central planning. Central planning was a group of Soviet advisers far removed from the people and from the factory floor. They worked as part of an enormous governmental bureaucracy, a labyrinth that decided what was going to be produced and how much of it was going to be produced, all within the time frame that they set. None of these decision makers had an adequate knowledge of factory production, supply of raw materials, or possible output of goods. To them, it was just their job to put the schedules down on paper.

Soviet central planners were guaranteed a job for life, so their decisions rippled through the economy for decades. Soviet workers would come to work without raw materials, and if the only thing they had to do was meet a quota and not go beyond that quota, they did not. They were not obligated to work hard because they gained no extra money or extra benefits by working longer or harder. Making a better product was not an incentive either. However, through the Cold War, the manufacturing of weapons chugged slowly along.

When Brezhnev took over the reins of power, he instituted what became known as the Brezhnev Doctrine in 1968. Premier Brezhnev said that the Soviet Union had a right and a responsibility to militarily intervene if there was a problem in any Warsaw Pact nation.

EASTERN EUROPEAN NATIONALIST AND INDEPENDENCE MOVEMENTS DURING THE COLD WAR

Throughout the Cold War and after the Warsaw Pact, the Soviet Union closely watched over its satellite states and its own Soviet districts. In some of these satellites, there was unhappiness that they were under direct communist control from Moscow. With a growing number of people experiencing nationalist feelings, they began to grow angry at Moscow's domination.

Hungary

The first of these independence movements took place in Hungary. In 1956, a Hungarian nationalist named Imre Nagy ended the one-party control within his country. Nagy told the Soviet troops they were no longer welcome and sent a message to the Soviet leadership in Moscow that he wanted to withdraw Hungary from the Warsaw Pact agreement. Immediately, President Khrushchev sent in Soviet troops with heavy tanks to forcibly put down the independence movement. Hungary asked for support from the Western countries; however, reinforcements and aid never came. As a result, Nagy was executed in 1958, and many of the Hungarian rebels were killed.

Poland

Picking up where Hungary left off, the country of Poland quickly became the biggest thorn in the side of Soviet communist domination. Going back to the Stalin era, Poland had been dealt with very harshly. Soviet persecution of the Roman Catholic Church was predominant inside of Poland. It was the church that became the quiet and subtle voice that helped bring down communism in Poland.

Coinciding with the rebellion in Hungary, Poland was experiencing economic turmoil. When things under communist control did not get better, there were a series of strikes by Polish workers, which ended in riots. To keep the Soviet Union from directly interfering, the Polish government made some concessions to the workers. However, it was not enough to end the anger and the unsettled feelings that existed toward communism.

POPE JOHN PAUL II

In 1978, Karol Wojtyla, the Roman Catholic cardinal of the Polish city of Krakow, was elected as Pope of the Roman Catholic Church. Taking the name Pope John Paul II, he was the first non-Italian Pope in nearly 500 years. From his influential office in the Vatican, Pope John Paul II very subtly supported the anticommunist feelings that were growing throughout Eastern Europe. On a return trip to his home country in 1979, Pope John Paul II was able to criticize the communist leadership of his country without fear of direct retribution.

LECH WALESA

The Pope's encouragement inspired other leaders within Poland. In 1980, a group of dockyard workers were organized and led by Lech Walesa. Walesa was able to create a union that was independent of communism, which became known as the Solidarity Movement. Soviet leadership in Moscow forced the Polish government to immediately suppress the Solidarity Movement. As a result, Solidarity was outlawed as a union within Poland, and the leadership of its nearly eight million members, including Lech Walesa, was arrested in 1981. However, Walesa's arrest made him a national hero throughout Poland. Walesa's arrest, combined with another visit by Pope John Paul in 1983 where he spoke out against communism, brought worldwide attention to the situation.

THE EFFECTS OF DÉTENTE

At several points during the Cold War, especially during the Brezhnev era, there were times when countries called for the easing of tension or hostility toward each other. This policy became known as détente.

The détente talks between the United States and the Soviet Union were centered around disarmament and the reduction of nuclear missiles, but when the Soviet Union invaded Afghanistan in 1979, the détente talks ceased. However, the invasion of Afghanistan brought about a change in the Soviet Union as the war was one more weight that the Soviet economy could not support. It began to cause unrest in the people at home.

SOVIET UNION COLLAPSE

By 1985, with the war in Afghanistan nowhere near ending, a new leader emerged in the Soviet Union: Mikhail Gorbachev. Gorbachev was younger, possessed more energy, and saw things differently than his older predecessors. Gorbachev wanted to correct the inefficient operation of the Soviet government and boost the economy.

Reign of Mikhail Gorbachev

The first priority of Premier Gorbachev was to end the Cold War that was sapping the economy of the Soviet Union. He got rid of the Brezhnev Doctrine in 1989 and began to negotiate and sign a series of arms control treaties with the United States. He also removed the Soviet troops from Afghanistan in 1989.

Gorbachev also declared that he would not interfere with Eastern European reform or independence movements. So in 1989, the Solidarity Movement was able to grow and became a legal political party in Poland. The country of Poland was allowed to have its first free election in over 50 years. As the votes were counted, members of the Solidarity Party overwhelmingly defeated their Communist Party opposition. Solidarity leader Lech Walesa was the newly elected president of a democratic Poland. For the first time since Hitler invaded Poland in September 1939, Poland was in control of its own government and destiny. It faced a long road to transition the government and the economy, but Poland had achieved its freedom.

Glasnost and Perestroika

Inside the Soviet Union, Gorbachev presented a new reform movement in 1985 that was comprised of two different parts.

1. Glasnost, or openness. He encouraged people to speak out and describe the problems from which they were suffering. Gorbachev wanted to stop the censorship and fear of reprisal. He was able to hear what the people wanted and needed, and then he could try to provide it for them.
2. Perestroika, meaning an overhaul of the government and the economy to make it vastly more efficient. Perestroika would downsize the elaborate Soviet bureaucracy, thereby increasing the economic output of the country.

Gorbachev also allowed and introduced some capitalist, free-market policies, making sure that they worked with the communist plan of the government overall. Corrupt or ineffective government officials were fired, and Gorbachev advocated that factory managers at the local level should have a greater say in the planning of their production and output, not a central planner. Factory owners and managers were granted this privilege as long as output was increased. Better land, farm equipment, and fertilizer were granted to farmers, and after the government got its share to feed the people, the farmers were able to sell the surplus food for profit.

Global Connections

The selling of surplus food for profit was an idea that went back to the Lenin era of the Soviet Union.

Effects of Gorbachev's Changes

Unfortunately for the Soviet Union, just like the reforms that Peter the Great tried, things spiraled out of control. Instead of following a plan from conception to implementation, the Soviet Union tried overhauling the whole process at one time. As a result, economic turmoil ensued. There were shortages of food and raw materials, which resulted in inflation. Factories did not know how to operate without government help or subsidies, so they began to close. People were jobless, and they did not like the reforms, saying the reforms were anticommunist.

Gorbachev had the best of intention with perestroika and glasnost, but while the Soviet Union was focused on itself, other Soviet districts began to cry for their independence. Areas that were captured by the Red Army's westward advance in World War II wanted to be independent countries.

In 1991, when the Baltic states of Latvia, Lithuania, and Estonia were granted independence, other Soviet republics began to rebel. East Germany wanted to reunify with West Germany. By 1991, the once wildly popular Mikhail Gorbachev found himself threatened. There was a coup attempt by the Soviet military to lock him in his estate, but the coup was thwarted when another popular Russian reformer, Boris Yeltsin, went out to the people and asked them not to listen to the old hard-line military.

The coup forced Gorbachev, the man who began Soviet reforms, to resign in 1991. Even though things did not go as he planned, Gorbachev helped bring about an end to the Soviet Union and communism, which had been in place since the end of the Russian Revolution in 1921.

Boris Yeltsin and Democracy for the Russian Republic

When Mikhail Gorbachev lost power in 1991, Boris Yeltsin, the mayor of Moscow and a member of the Russian legislature, was voted in as president. Yeltsin became the first president of the new Russian Republic. It was Yeltsin, not Gorbachev, who witnessed the breakup of the Soviet Union into many independent republics, including the re-formation of the country of Russia, formerly the largest Soviet state.

After the Soviet Union began to break up, Yeltsin had several problems to face. The new Russian Federation wanted to write a new constitution. However, being separate from the West for so long, democracy was a difficult thing to implement overnight. As democracy was trying to grow, there were the economic setbacks that happened during the conversion from the communist to the capitalist economy. Many people did not want to wait for the conversion to be completed. They wanted immediate gratification. Yeltsin began to have difficulties with the newly elected parliament, which was made up of old communist officials. When things did not immediately get better, parliament wanted to return to communism. Unemployment and inflation continued to grow, and the Soviet Union had no one to depend on for help.

Other problems arose when religious and ethnic minorities in the former Soviet states began to want freedom from the satellite republics. In 1994, the region known as Chechnya revolted, causing Yeltsin once again to use the Soviet military to put things down, further straining the country's resources. While the new Russian Republic was reducing its nuclear weapons, it did not like that Eastern European countries were looking to join NATO.

Democracy is still trying to grow inside Russia to this day. Former Soviet republics, like the Ukraine, the state of Kazakhstan, and Belarus (or Belorussia), got rid of their nuclear weapons under the terms that they could begin trading with Western European countries. The Soviet Union, once a world power, saw its power and influence dwindle as Soviet satellite states declared their independence.

THE BERLIN WALL FINALLY COLLAPSES

As Poland was achieving its independence, in East Germany, the long-standing symbol of the Iron Curtain came down. The Berlin Wall, separating East and West Berlin, was completed on August 13, 1961, and came down on the night of November 9, 1989. The long-standing symbol of the Cold War and Eastern Europe, the collapse of the Berlin Wall reunified the two Germanys. The reunification was officially ratified on October 3, 1990, which signaled the immediate breakup of the Soviet Union.

Soviet Satellite Nations

After October 3, 1990, many other former Soviet satellites declared their independence:

- Latvia
- Lithuania
- Estonia
- Belarus
- Moldova
- Georgia
- Ukraine
- Yugoslavia
- Czechoslovakia

- Armenia
- Azerbaijan
- Turkmenistan
- Uzbekistan
- Kazakhstan
- Kyrgyzstan

Czechoslovakia

Some of these Soviet states further subdivided into separate countries because of the large combination of ethnic groups within the country. Shortly after independence, the former country of Czechoslovakia was one of the few countries to peaceably split apart into Slovakia and the Czech Republic.

Yugoslavia

The former Yugoslavia had a lot of trouble as it split into several different countries, divided up among a series of ethnic groups. It became the new countries of Slovenia, Croatia, Bosnia and Herzegovina, Serbia, Montenegro, and Macedonia.

The three main ethnic groups were Roman Catholics, Serbians who were Eastern Orthodox Christians, and a large population of Muslims. After communism fell, the ethnic groups began fighting. Serbian leader Slobodan Milosevic began to "ethnically cleanse" the Muslims from Bosnia from 1992 to 1995, which became a very bloody civil war.

Chechnya

Coinciding with the problems in the former Yugoslavia were problems in a southwestern Russian Republic known as Chechnya. Chechnya also had a large Muslim population. Since 1991, Boris Yeltsin had denied Chechnya from becoming an independent country, and in 1994, he sent in Russian troops to control the situation. During bloody fighting, Yeltsin won reelection, but as the war continued into 1999, Boris Yeltsin resigned as president of the Russian Republic. Yeltsin called upon Russian Prime Minister Vladimir Putin to take over as president.

VLADIMIR PUTIN

New president Putin quickly and forcibly suppressed the rebellion in Chechnya. Putin was going to guide the new era of Russia, free from independence movements and nationalist movements in new countries. Putin was going to help grow democracy and the Russian economy. In 2008, Vladimir Putin, who had served his term as Russian president, became the prime minister once again. In 2012, Putin was reelected as the president of Russia. He still controls much of the Russian Federation and helped Russia win the bid to host the 2014 Winter Olympic Games in Sochi.

However, shortly after the Sochi games, some people around the world began to look at him as a dictator as he tried to reclaim territory when he annexed the Crimean peninsula of the Ukraine into Russia in the spring of 2014.

1978 C.E.	John Paul II from Poland is elected Pope.
1980 C.E.	Lech Walesa heads Solidarity Movement.
1981 C.E.	Solidarity is outlawed in Poland.
1982 C.E.	Mikhail Gorbachev is named general secretary of U.S.S.R.
1985 C.E.	Glasnost and perestroika policies are enforced in the Soviet Union.
1987 C.E.	Gorbachev announces Democratization in U.S.S.R.
1988 C.E.	Solidarity is legalized in Poland.
1989 C.E.	• Hungary dissolves Communist Party. • Anticommunist protests in East Germany • Berlin Wall comes down—Berlin is opened to East Germany and West Germany.
1990 C.E.	• Lech Walesa is elected president of Poland. • Germany is reunited into one country. • Lithuania declares independence from U.S.S.R.
1991 C.E.	Boris Yeltsin becomes first elected president of Russia.
1992 C.E.	Bosnia-Herzegovina civil war
1993 C.E.	Czechoslovakia splits into two countries.
1994 C.E.	• Declaration of Independence of Soviet Republics • Yugoslavia breaks apart further into six countries.
1998 C.E.	Rebellion in Kosovo
2000–2008 C.E.	Vladimir Putin serves as president of Russia.
2012 C.E.	Putin is reelected as president of Russia.

The Middle East Through Persian Gulf Wars

35

Since the end of World War I, Arabic nations in the Middle East, sometimes called Western Asia, have been trying to become independent from imperialist Western European powers. During the 1950s and 1960s, many of the countries wanted to unite the Arab populations through a program known as Pan-Arabism where Arabic heritage could be shared. Member countries could work collectively on building sound economies.

However, independence became difficult as Arabic countries still had the bulk of their economic systems tied to Western countries due to the age of imperialism. The banks and industries were owned and managed by Westerners. It was the Western countries that provided the technology, innovation, and industrial capital in the Middle East.

PROBLEMS WITH THE BORDERS

The most visible problem left over in the Middle East after independence was the borders that were created during the age of imperialism (mainly the borders created by Great Britain and France). Just as they had done in Africa, the Europeans had created borders without regard or knowledge of the way of life of the local inhabitants. The borders forced different Middle Eastern groups of people to live in a certain location. The prime example is the British creation of Iraq in 1948, which combined one large ethnic group and several smaller ones in one area, which is still causing problems to this very day.

OIL VS. ARABIC NATIONALISM

The main export from the Middle East is oil. The Middle East is home to one of the largest oil reserves in the entire world. After World War II, the United States, the Soviet Union, and other Western countries looked for ways to gain allies in the Middle East, using political and economic inroads, and if needed, their militaries.

The nations of Saudi Arabia and Kuwait have a great deal of oil, and they worked well with Western countries. This created tension when it came to Pan-Arabism as other Middle Eastern countries were focused more on unifying Arab countries, not on making money selling oil.

Organization of Petroleum Exporting Countries (OPEC)

In 1960, the organization known as OPEC—Organization of Petroleum Exporting Countries—was created. Inaugural OPEC member countries were Iran, Iraq, Kuwait, Saudi Arabia, and Venezuela. These countries were able to use their profits from oil to build infrastructure and create better schools. Due to their success, other countries in the region became angry, leading to conflicts that affected the stability of the region.

SAUDI ARABIA

Saudi Arabia is in a unique position with one of the world's largest oil reserves underneath it. Since the 1920s when World War I ended, Saudi Arabia has been ruled by the Saud family dynasty. Saudi Arabia is also home to the birthplace of Islam, one of the great monotheistic religions. The Saud family maintains adherence to strict Sunni Islam.

After World War II, Saudi Arabia became wealthy by sending their oil exports to the United States and other Western industrialized countries. In 1973, the OPEC countries stopped oil shipments to the United States because the United States was a close ally of Israel, an enemy of the OPEC countries. This caused a worldwide economic depression as industrialized countries depended upon this flow of oil. The depression reverberated across the world, affecting even the OPEC countries. Since then, OPEC agreed to control the price rather than stop selling oil altogether.

Due to the adherence to the Sunni sect of Islam by the royal family of Saudi Arabia, they supported some fundamentalist Islamic leaders throughout their country. This created a problem in that some of these Islamic leaders were critical of the Saudi government, saying they were becoming corrupted by the West. The kingdom of Saudi Arabia has worked to maintain stability and modernization to keep the flow of oil going, bringing income to Saudi Arabia, its government, and its people.

OTHER PERSIAN GULF COUNTRIES

Most of the governments in the Middle East follow some sort of autocratic or monarchical control. Others are run by military leaders, so it is either a dictatorship or a family-run dynasty. Some of the countries with a vast amount of oil stretch along the Persian Gulf, including Saudi Arabia. Smaller countries include Kuwait, Bahrain, Qatar, and the United Arab Emirates. While having a diverse population within their borders, these countries get along peacefully and also depend upon exporting their oil to the Western powers.

It is difficult for Pan-Arabism to exist between countries and within countries because of religious tensions between the different sects of Islam. There is also a large dichotomy between economies as there are wealthy Middle Eastern countries and poor Middle Eastern countries. Incidences of violence and tension occasionally flare up.

EGYPT

Egypt Becomes a Leader in the Arab World

Egypt is an African country that borders on the Middle East and the Suez Canal. For thousands of years, Egypt has been closely linked with the Middle East. Egypt also has the largest population of any Arabic country.

In 1952, General Gamal Abdel Nasser seized power in Egypt and became a powerful figure throughout the region. Nasser was determined to get rid of the foreign domination of his country. He was also focused upon turning Egypt into a modern country. With these two primary goals in mind, Nasser took over and nationalized the Suez Canal, putting an end to the British domination of the canal. His move against the Western power heightened his reputation and standing throughout the Middle East.

The Nationalization of Egypt

Nasser began to nationalize Egyptian businesses and the banking industry. He became more socialist as he began to redistribute land from large plantations to the peasant farmers. As a result, he was attracted to the Soviet Union, and they were likewise attracted to him. Slowly, Nasser and Egypt became more communist-like. Egypt played a large role in the Middle Eastern battles of the Cold War and depended upon Soviet aid.

Nasser and Israel

Nasser was a loud critic and opponent of Israel. He led several unsuccessful attacks against the country. He attacked Israel in both 1956 and 1967 and was defeated both times. After the failed Six-Day War in 1967, Israel claimed territory previously belonging to Egypt, including the Sinai Peninsula and the land that became known as the Gaza Strip. Israel claimed this as a buffer zone of security between itself and Egypt.

Coupled with the losses against Israel, his economic plans only met with partial success. Nasser was unable to fully see his vision for Egypt carried out when he died in 1970.

Egypt Under Anwar Sadat

Anwar Sadat succeeded Nasser as the president of Egypt, and in 1973, he also attacked Israel. Initially, the Egyptian armies were able to regain some of the land that was taken from them in 1967, but after the Israelis began to counterattack, the Israelis reclaimed much of the territory. By the end of October 1973, a truce was signed.

At this time, Sadat decided on a new direction for Egypt. He broke ties with the Soviet Union and called for an Opening of Egypt. Sadat was trying to lure foreign aid and investment into his country as well as expand private business ownership. To achieve this, Sadat moved closer to the United States and away from the Soviet Union.

Egypt Recognizes the State of Israel

After the Yom Kippur War in October 1973, people in the Middle East were still very tense, waiting for another war to start with Israel. President Anwar Sadat then boldly did something that no other Arab country had done: he recognized the existence of the state of Israel.

In 1978, U.S. President Jimmy Carter invited Anwar Sadat and his Israeli counterpart, Prime Minister Menachem Begin, to come to the presidential retreat at Camp David in Maryland. They were protected from reporters and press agents for two weeks while they discussed the issues. In September 1978, the Camp David Peace Accords were written, which was the first agreement between an Arab country and Israel. Several provisions were attached to this recognition by Egypt, including recognition of rights for Palestinian citizens and the removal of Israeli soldiers from territory that Israel had captured in 1967.

Unfortunately, many Arabic countries and their leaders were angry at the Camp David Peace Accords, and in 1981, Anwar Sadat was assassinated. Egypt's new leader, Hosni Mubarak, kept the peace treaty with Israel while working to fix the relations with his Arabic neighbors.

Egypt faced four main problems:

- Rapidly expanding population
- Lack of farm production
- Expansion of urban slums
- A call for Islamic fundamentalism

Organizations began to spring up, saying they could fix the problems that the government could not. The government brutally suppressed and put down these growing movements but succeeded in only increasing support for the growing radical Islamists in Egypt.

IRAN

The discovery of oil in the Middle East and the wealth generated by selling it to the West caused more of a conflict with traditional values in Iran than in any other country.

In 1941, Iran was led by a young shah, or leader, named Mohammad Reza Pahlavi. The Shah was a young man, happy to work with Western governments and take money from Western oil companies. However, some within Iran were angry at this because they wanted to nationalize the Iranian oil industry. When a leader of the Nationalist Party, Mohammad Mosaddeq, was elected prime minister of Iran in 1951, he took over the Iranian oil companies from the British, forcing the Shah to leave Iran. The United States grew afraid that Iran might turn toward the Soviet Union, so in 1953, the United States removed Prime Minister Mosaddeq from power and reinserted the Shah.

Iran Under Shah Pahlavi

To strengthen his grip on power, the Shah began a modernization program in 1953. He took the money made by selling oil to the West and built industry inside Iran. He developed a growing economic infrastructure, he granted more rights to women, and he instituted a major land redistribution policy where he took land from religious institutions and gave it to the peasants.

He also tried to separate the Iranian Shiite Islamic sect of religion from his government. The Shah greatly reduced the power of the religious teachers, the ulama, and their grip on power in his government. Many of these ulamas, or ayatollahs, began to speak out against what the Shah was doing. The ayatollahs said the Shah was becoming morally corrupted by the West and that Iran should return to strict adherence to Islamic law, the sharia.

Ayatollah Khomeini

The most outspoken leader was the Ayatollah Khomeini. He was exiled from Iran in 1964 but was leading the opposition from his home in exile. By 1978, riots were erupting throughout the major cities in Iran. The Shah was forced to flee in January 1979 after being in power for nearly 25 years.

The Ayatollah Khomeini Returns

Ayatollah Khomeini returned from exile in February 1979 and became the head of a strict Islamic state, or theocracy, over Iran. His first move was to rid Iran of all Western influences that the Shah had allowed. He reinstated strict Islamic values and overturned all of the government laws favoring the rights for women. Once in power, the Ayatollah squashed all opposition as forcibly and brutally as the Shah had during his reign.

The United States Hostage Crisis

At the center of the Ayatollah Khomeini's foreign policy was his distain for the United States. He believed the United States had influenced his country for way too long. As the Shah was flying to the United States for cancer surgery in November 1979, the Ayatollah influenced a group of young Islamic revolutionaries to attack the U.S. Embassy in the capital city of Tehran. Fifty-three American hostages were captured and held prisoner for 444 days. Iran demanded that the Shah be turned over to them to stand trial for crimes against Iran, but the United States would not return him. The hostage crisis kicked off heightened tensions between the United States and Iran and it has been sour ever since. The Iranian hostages were released during the early days of Ronald Reagan's presidency on January 20, 1981, after being held as prisoners for more than 14 months.

Iran and Iraq

The Ayatollah Khomeini wanted his Islamic fundamentalists to travel to other countries to overthrow their nonreligious leaders or dictators in order to export his revolution. Instead of unifying the Muslims, it increased the tension with Iran's neighbor to the west: Iraq. The Iranians were Shiite Muslims, and Iraq was ruled by a dictator, Saddam Hussein, who was a Sunni Muslim. Making the situation more difficult was that Saddam Hussein ruled a secular, or nonreligious, government.

While the Iran hostage crisis was going on, Iraq attacked Iran. War broke out between the two countries lasting from 1980 to 1988. Millions of Iranians and Iraqi citizens were killed during the eight years of war. The United States was selling weapons and providing aid to both sides during the war. Iraqis were given weapons to hopefully overthrow the Iranian government. The Iranians were given weapons to defend themselves in exchange for the release of our hostages. In 1988, the United Nations stepped in and successfully negotiated a cease-fire, but the populations of both countries were devastated with the heavy loss of life.

As the 1990s progressed, Iran became more of a theocracy. Currently, there are high tensions in the world as many Western countries and Middle Eastern countries are afraid that Iran is developing a nuclear program that could destabilize the region.

ISRAEL

As conflict grew in the Middle East over oil and imperialism, a regional conflict that had been raging for many years continued between the people of Israel and Arabs in Palestine.

When the country of Israel was created in 1948, many Arabs living in the territory of Palestine (where Israel was created) protested the creation of Israel. There have been persistent conflicts in the area, resulting in wars in 1948, 1956, 1967, and 1973.

During the Yom Kippur War in October 1973 (named as such because the attacks occurred on the high holy days on the Jewish calendar), several Arab nations attacked Israel all at once. Again, the Arab nations met with defeat. The area claimed by Israel is now called occupied territory by the Arabs as the Israeli government allowed Jewish settlers to build houses in the area that had once belonged to Palestine.

The Palestinian Liberation Organization

During the 1960s, many Palestinians began to resist what they saw as Israeli domination. The Palestinian Liberation Organization (PLO) was headed by Yasser Arafat. The PLO enjoyed widespread support from Palestinians who wanted Israel destroyed. In the 1960s and 1970s, there were a series of attacks on the Israeli homeland and on Israelis abroad, the most famous being the hijacking of an Israeli plane in 1968 and the killing of Israeli athletes at the 1972 Olympic Games in Munich, Germany. As the military portion of the PLO continued to fight against Israel, the Israelis began attacking bases in Palestinian towns. The Israelis also went over the border in Lebanon to destroy PLO strongholds.

In the late 1980s, a new wing of the PLO was created known as the Intifada, or uprising. The movement was led mainly by young teenage Palestinians, and their disobedience took the form of protests and demonstrations. They disobeyed curfews, verbally yelled at Israeli soldiers, and threw rocks at them. The Israelis quickly cracked down on the actions of the Intifada, but they had captured the attention of the world. All of a sudden, Israel was accused of being too heavy-handed against the Palestinian teens.

Oslo Accords

In Oslo, Norway, in 1993, secret talks produced a sudden agreement between Israel and Palestine. Israel, under the leadership of their new prime minister, Yitzhak Rabin, agreed to give Palestine territory in the Gaza Strip and the West Bank, along with the ancient town of Jericho. Rabin and Yasser Arafat signed the Oslo Accords on September 13, 1993.

In 1994, King Hussein of Jordan made peace with Israel, but King Hussein and Yitzhak Rabin knew that peace would not come quickly as there had been war for a very long time. When Golda Meir, the prime minister of Israel, was assassinated in 1995 by a fellow Israeli, it further complicated the peace process. Some Israelis thought that Rabin was being too soft on Palestine.

In 1996, the new Israeli prime minister was a man named Benjamin Netanyahu. Netanyahu had originally not liked the Oslo Accords, but he made a concentrated effort to uphold the agreement. In 1997, the Israelis met with Arafat again, planning to withdraw their forces from the West Bank. However, in 2001, Israel's new prime minister, Ariel Sharon, said he would only uphold the agreement if Yasser Arafat was no longer the head of the PLO. Sharon asked for this because there were repeated terrorist attacks, suicide bombings, and other acts of violence in the occupied territories.

The peace process further intensified with the death of Yasser Arafat in 2004. The new leader of Palestine, Mahmoud Abbas, would try to earn the trust of Israel. However, violence is still occurring in the region today with conflicts between Israel and a new group known as Hamas. Several U.S. presidents, including George W. Bush and Barack Obama, have laid out what they call a roadmap to peace where they hope that Palestinians can govern themselves in their own country. It continues to be a long and difficult process.

AFGHANISTAN

The Soviet Invasion of Afghanistan

Afghanistan became an independent country in 1919 just after World War I, and the governmental system chosen at the time was a monarchy. The Afghan government tried different efforts to modernize the country. By the end of World War II, the country was moving forward. In 1964, Afghanistan developed a constitution and was going to transition to a more democratic form of government. However, most people seemed happy with the monarchial system, so democracy never developed. Even while remaining a monarchy, Afghanistan had formed relationships with many Western countries and was able to interact globally.

Effects of the Cold War

As the Cold War between the United States and the Soviet Union intensified, Afghanistan was caught up in the middle. Trying to remain a monarchy while located at the southern border of the communist Soviet Union was difficult. Afghanistan was heavily subjected to Soviet influence. By 1970, a group of close-knit former military men were in charge of Afghanistan. In 1973, the Afghan government, loyal to communism, held all influence over the military leaders, who then overthrew the monarch. Most of the common people of Afghanistan did not like this because communism conflicted directly with the religion of Islam, which was practiced by almost everyone in Afghanistan.

The Mujahideen

The common people, opposed to communism, began to cobble together a resistance force known as the mujahideen, or holy warriors, to combat the Soviet-backed Afghan government.

The success of the mujahideen forced the Soviet Union to directly intervene. The Soviet army entered Afghanistan in 1979. This action was condemned by many in the world, mainly by the United States as it claimed the Soviet Union was trying to expand its communist empire. President Jimmy Carter boycotted the 1980 Summer Olympic Games in Moscow in protest.

The Soviet Union had advanced weaponry and an enormous firepower advantage. They expected a quick victory. However, the mujahideen had a much better knowledge of the land. In the mountainous terrain of Afghanistan, they used guerrilla fighting techniques to wear down the Soviet Union. After ten years, the Soviet Union withdrew its troops in 1989 and departed Afghanistan after what is called by many the Soviet Union's Vietnam.

Global Connections

Similar to when the United States had to withdraw from Vietnam, a smaller, understrength force had defeated a superpower.

The Taliban

When the Soviet Union retreated from Afghanistan, the common enemy that bound the mujahideen fighters together was gone. Once again, the many different ethnic groups within Afghanistan began to fight each other to try to dominate the country.

An ultraconservative group of Islamic fundamentalists known as the Taliban eventually won victory. By 1997, they controlled the majority of Afghanistan. Only a tiny section of the northwestern part of Afghanistan was held by a competing group, known as the Northern Alliance. The Taliban raised hopes of ending corruption and binding together Afghanistan after a decade of war. However, the Taliban followed a very fundamentalist, extreme interpretation of the sharia, or Islamic law. The Taliban thought that the sharia should be applied to every part of society in their country. Any form of Western influence was gotten rid of— books, music, television, and movies. Everything was heavily censored. Women, and their status in society, regressed as they were told to wear a head-to-toe covering known as a burqa. Women were not allowed to hold jobs or even receive an education.

The punishment for breaking the Taliban's interpretation of the sharia was immediate imprisonment, public beating, and even execution. Starting in 2001, major military action was implemented by coalition forces to fight the Taliban. In 2004, Afghan officials developed a new government headed by a new president named Hamid Karzai. The government headed by Karzai had to find a way, once again, to unify and rebuild the country after the oppressive regime of the Taliban.

Afghanistan remains in flux to this day. Many different ethnic groups live in the country, making unification difficult. In 2013, the Taliban began making a resurgence when the leadership of Karzai ended.

WAR IN LEBANON

To the north of Israel is the country of Lebanon. As the fighting between Israel and the PLO intensified, it affected the stability of Lebanon. The Lebanese government depended on a balancing act between Christians and both sects of Islam: Sunni and Shiite. As the war between Israel and Palestine raged on, refugees from the fighting began to flood over the border into Lebanon. The influx of refugees began to upset this delicate balance of power as the Muslim population was quickly increasing. The PLO also began to operate and recruit soldiers in different refugee camps. As a result, the country of Lebanon sunk into a bloody civil war in 1975.

As both Muslims and Christians began to battle for Lebanese turf, the fighting was fierce in the capital city of Beirut. As the fighting intensified in 1978, Israel attacked from the south, and then Syria invaded from the north. All sense of order and stability vanished from Lebanon. The United Nations, seeking to bring peace, sent in troops from France and the United States, but they were unable to bring an end to the fighting. When the UN forces began to suffer attacks, they were forced to withdraw. By 1990, the civil war was over as the PLO was forced out of Lebanon. Lebanon began the painful process of rebuilding its infrastructure. They also tried to find a way to get the country to work together and bury the antagonisms that still existed between the different religious groups.

PERSIAN GULF WAR I

At the conclusion of the Iran-Iraq War in 1988, Saddam Hussein of Iraq began to expand in a different area. In 1990, Hussein invaded the neighboring country of Kuwait. Kuwait not only had a vast amount of oil resources, it was also on the Persian Gulf, a vital waterway necessary to get oil to foreign countries.

Hussein claimed that Kuwait was not a real country. He said it was just a region of land that Great Britain claimed was separate but that was actually part of Iraq. Neighboring Middle Eastern countries, such as Saudi Arabia, saw Saddam Hussein's action as a threat, so the United States was asked to lead an international coalition to destroy and remove Saddam Hussein's forces from Kuwait. U.S. President George H. W. Bush was able to put together a coalition of 39 nations, including European allies and Arabic nations. The coalition declared war on Iraq in 1991 after economic sanctions had no effect. Using superior technology, especially airpower, the Iraqi forces were quickly destroyed, and Kuwait was freed.

Saddam Hussein was allowed to remain in power, but the United Nations placed economic sanctions in Iraq, which prevented it from selling its oil abroad.

PERSIAN GULF WAR II

After the first Persian Gulf War, it was reported that Saddam Hussein was developing weapons of mass destruction and then using them on the Kurdish population of his country in northern Iraq. As part of the treaty and cease-fire that ended the first Persian Gulf offensive, United Nations inspectors were allowed to periodically inspect Iraqi weapon manufacturing facilities. They were to make sure all of the weapons of mass destruction had been destroyed and that no more were being produced.

This happened regularly under U.S. President Bill Clinton, but in 1998, the United Nations inspectors were suddenly blocked or rerouted, not able to complete their inspections. After the September 11 terrorist attacks against the United States in 2001, President George W. Bush felt that Saddam Hussein might be, once again, building weapons of mass destruction that could be used against the United States.

The United States began its war on terror in March 2003 when the U.S. Army was ordered to invade Iraq, along with Allied troops from England. Within a month, Saddam Hussein's government fell, and Saddam Hussein himself was captured hiding in a small spider hole in the desert. He was sent to stand trial in his own country where he was executed in 2006.

The United States and its allies hoped to bring democracy to Iraq; however, the different ethnic factions in Iraq quickly fell into violence as they competed for territory. The Iraqis did not like the foreign intrusion of the United States, and when no weapons of mass destruction were found in Iraq, the United States implemented a plan to slowly scale back and withdraw troops from Iraq to allow them to eventually self-govern.

ROLE OF THE UNITED STATES

The United States has long been an ally of Israel, leading to hostility against America in the region. There is also the need for oil in the United States, so the U.S. Navy has a large presence not only in and around the Persian Gulf but in the Indian Ocean and Mediterranean Sea as well. As a result of the terrorist attacks on September 11, 2001, Afghanistan was identified as one of several countries helping the terrorist network called al-Qaeda and possibly harboring the head of al-Qaeda, Osama bin Laden. Afghanistan was home to many of bin Laden's reported training grounds. The United States demanded that if bin Laden was in Afghanistan, the Taliban leadership needed to turn him over to the United States. When that did not happen, the U.S. military took action, beginning a bombing campaign against Taliban forces and the leadership. The United States also gave support and weapons to the Northern Alliance, who eventually helped drive the Taliban from power. In 2011, American troops led a raid to capture al-Qaeda leader Osama bin Laden, which ended with bin Laden's death.

Coupled with the continued unrest in Syria and the evolution of the terrorist group ISIS, the United States is still a military presence in the region.

1953 C.E.	Shah Pahlavi is U.S. backed dictator of Iran.
1956 C.E.	• Egypt is at war with Israel.
	• Suez Canal crisis
	• General Abdul Nasser seizes power in Egypt.
1964 C.E.	Yasir Arafat founds Palestinian Liberation Organization (PLO).
1967 C.E.	Egypt is in Six-Day War with Israel.
1970s C.E.	PLO begins fighting against Israel.
1973 C.E.	Egypt attacks Israel again (Yom Kippur War).
1975 C.E.	Israel invades Lebanon.
1977 C.E.	Anwar Sadat of Egypt offers peace to Israel.
1978 C.E.	Riots break out in Iranian cities.
1979 C.E.	• Camp David Peace Accords with U.S., Egypt, and Israel
	• Shah flees Iran—Ayatollah Khomeini takes over Iran.
	• U.S. hostages are captured in Iran.
	• U.S.S.R. invades Afghanistan.
1981 C.E.	• Hosni Mubarak of Egypt maintains peace with Israel.
	• U.S. hostages released in Iran—strict fundamentalist government continues today.
1982 C.E.	Israel invades Lebanon again.
1987 C.E.	• Intifada begins Palestinian disobedience.
	• Hamas terrorist group is created in Lebanon.
1988 C.E.	Cease-fire between Iran and Iraq
1989 C.E.	Soviets withdraw from Afghanistan.
1990 C.E.	Iraq invades Kuwait.
1990–1991 C.E.	Persian Gulf War with U.S. led military coalition
1991 C.E.	First peace talks between PLO and Israel
1993 C.E.	Secret Oslo Peace Talks between PLO and Israel
1996 C.E.	Taliban fundamentalist government begins in Afghanistan.
1997 C.E.	• Netanyahu of Israel meets with PLO's Arafat to talk about withdrawal from the West Bank.
	• Hezbollah terrorist group is created in Lebanon.
1998 C.E.	End of Soviet subsidies in Cuba
2001 C.E.	Ariel Sharon is military leader of Israel.
2003 C.E.	Operation Iraqi Freedom begins—American occupation of Iraq.
2004 C.E.	Yasir Arafat dies.

Millennial Unrest: Era of Terrorism and Technology

36

CHINA: TIANANMEN SQUARE TO THE BEIJING OLYMPICS

When the new president of China, Deng Xiaoping, took control of China in 1978, he began to support new, more moderate economic policies known as the Four Modernizations.

The policies of President Deng brought about many changes in Chinese society. Foreign investment and technology were introduced into China, bringing about new products like televisions and other Western-style appliances. With the economic opening of China, it also became a new, exotic tourist destination for people around the world, especially the West. People came to see ancient Chinese culture, the Forbidden City, the Great Wall of China, and the terra-cotta warriors.

Some of President Deng's policies began to have unforeseen complications. As living conditions improved, more people could seek an education, especially among the middle class. The gap between haves and have-nots began to widen almost as much as was seen during the Shang Dynasty in 1600 B.C.E. Many Chinese people, especially poor people, began to believe that the government was profiting from their positions of power.

Another problem was that the increasing amount of Western investment and tourists began to bring Western ideas of politics and democracy with them. Many students in China began to study and travel overseas. As these students learned about democracy, a prodemocracy movement began to form when they came back to China. The students began to question their lack of individual freedoms and governmental censorship.

Tiananmen Square

In April 1989, some of these students kicked off a popular uprising that shocked the leadership of China to the core. A hundred thousand students occupied one of the main squares in the capital city of Beijing: Tiananmen Square.

Instead of listening to the students, President Deng took aggressive measures to stop this movement. He declared martial law in China, and Chinese soldiers were ordered to surround the capital of Beijing. These aggressive retaliatory measures caused many of the students and the people to go home, but around 5000 determined protesters stayed in Tiananmen Square. They built a statue called the Goddess of Democracy. On June 4, 1989, heavily armed troops entered Tiananmen Square on orders from President Deng. Tanks crushed the hastily erected barricades, the soldiers began to fire into the crowds, and the Goddess of Democracy was crushed. The assault shocked the world as many were killed and thousands were wounded. In turn, the Chinese government sent a message to the world: they would not tolerate this kind of protest. Many Chinese people were imprisoned, and the Chinese government heavily censored the media to make the protest seem much smaller than it was. However, the events in Tiananmen Square attracted the attention of the world.

Global Connections

The Goddess of Democracy stood for many of the same principles as the Statue of Liberty in France and the United States: freedom, justice, and liberty.

New Leadership in China

President Deng remained in control of China until his retirement in 1992. He was replaced by the general secretary of the Communist Party, Jiang Zemin. President Zemin had a lot of leadership experience as he was the former mayor of Shanghai, the largest city in China. However, he did face some opposition from old hard-core communist officials who wanted to return to more traditional Chinese policies.

Internationally, President Zemin had to deal with the human rights records of China, especially after Tiananmen Square. Another problem that was left for Zemin to deal with was the 1950 Chinese annexation of Tibet and the continued disagreements between the Chinese government and the Dalai Lama.

During his eight years in office (1992–2000), U.S. President Bill Clinton and his administration pressured China to ensure basic rights for its citizens, especially those of differing political views. He also demanded the release of some of the political prisoners that had been arrested at Tiananmen Square. However, this did not happen, and even though China was growing economically, prodemocracy movements were still stymied within China. In 1995, a major trade dispute began between the United States and China over the pirating of computer software, movies, and music. President Clinton had to threaten to revoke China's "most favored nation" clause in order to see the piracy stopped. In a state visit to the United States in 1997, President Zemin was met with protesters who were calling for more freedoms inside of China. While acknowledging the protestors, the Chinese president said that while China has done some things wrong, China was not going to change anytime soon.

Hong Kong Returns to China

On July 1, 1997, Great Britain returned the province of Hong Kong to China after over 150 years of colonial rule. During the communist takeover of China in 1949, many wealthy business owners and educators fled mainland China for Hong Kong. Hong Kong became a powerful capitalist business center as part of the British empire. As Hong Kong prepared to return to China, the Chinese government promised to leave Hong Kong's powerful economic system in place, as well as the political freedoms that they enjoyed. China wanted to absorb Hong Kong's economic power, but some of the residents of Hong Kong were mistrustful and worried about losing their way of life. However, many thought it was great to have all parts of China brought back together so China could once again be unified.

A New President Helped Earn the Beijing Olympics

In 2002, the new president of China, Hu Jintao, began to further promote China's movement toward a free-market economy. With the new leadership that started in 1978, China did see a massive reduction in poverty at most levels. China said the reason for this success was their slow, but steady method of ending the era of inefficient, state-owned industries to more of private ownership.

With the improved economy, the middle class expanded. Middle-class children received education, and social conditions improved as well. With global interdependence and access to new technology, Chinese ideas traveled quicker and faster than ever before. China left its era of isolation, and to showcase to the world how far they had come, China won the right to host the 2008 Olympic Games in Beijing. The opening ceremony was a celebration of Chinese culture, starting thousands of years ago during the River Valley Age, showing how China had transformed to become a modern economic giant in the world today.

GLOBAL COMMUNICATIONS

The competition during the Cold War greatly aided the growth of global communications. As the United States and the Soviet Union were competing against each other for dominance, they began an era of cooperation with other countries, especially when it came to launching satellites into space.

As far back as the 1960s, satellites were used as part of a global communications network. Over time, they became stronger and more reliable so today, an event happening in one area of the world can be transmitted immediately to everywhere else.

TECHNOLOGY CHANGES THE WORLD

Few inventions have been more impactful or changed the human world more than the computer. During World War II, the world witnessed its invention, leading to the Age of Information.

The Age of Information

In the late 1970s and early 1980s, companies like IBM and Apple began to introduce the personal computer, or PC. These were relatively big machines, but for the first time, people could use them at home. Using floppy disks, they could run programs on their computers to perform such tasks as word processing and calculations. Over time, computers have become faster and smaller. Today, most people in developed countries have at least one computer inside their home.

Computers have become an essential part of the global economy. Computers are used in industry to operate factories, replacing some of the assembly line workers. They control satellites, students use computers in the classroom, and they are used to track the delivery of packages. When you think of what computers do for the world, the list seems almost endless.

Development and Effects of the Internet

The main communication network used by computers was developed in the 1960s, but it did not spread rapidly until the 1990s. It was known as the World Wide Web, or simply, the Internet.

The Internet was revolutionary, allowing for the instant sharing of information. The Internet linked computer networks anywhere in the world to exchange information. Today, most people access the Internet via satellite, and the number of people using the Internet is close to 750 million. It revolutionized the way the world conducts business.

The youngest generations of people around the globe do not remember life without the Internet. Pictures and documents can be broken down digitally and then instantly transferred across the world. It has changed how people work, making things happen faster than anything ever before.

As faster communications have grown, there has been a dramatic increase in the information and integrated technology industries. Companies that operate in the financial markets, conduct worldwide research, or deal in global communication need for workers to develop and fix the Internet. The integrated technologies workforce has grown tremendously. First World countries are seeing an economic switch in industry as they are no longer looking for industrial or trade workers. They are looking for information workers: people whose jobs require them to work exclusively with information, from stock trading to communication to computer network engineers.

A Truly Global Economy

There has been international trade since the days of the Phoenicians. Through the days of colonization and imperialism, goods and services were shared between Europe and its colonies in the transatlantic economy. However, international borders are crossed faster than ever with the invention of the computer and the satellite network. Financial transactions are quick and easy with the push of a button. Giant cargo ships and air freight goods can be transferred quickly across the world as shipping is controlled and monitored through computer networks.

The Internet and technology have ushered in the development of the multinational corporation. A multinational corporation is a company that will have different parts of itself existing in different countries. One part of the corporation may be the home headquarters that deals with financing, another part can be involved in research and product development in a different country, and still another part can be manufacturing and assembling the parts somewhere else. When the product is completed, it can be shipped and sold to another area of the world. Multinational companies range from gas and oil companies, automotive companies, electronics companies, and even shoe companies. These companies are able to find places where raw materials and labor are cheap, and then the product can be shipped all over the world.

It is a truly global economy because different countries and areas of the world are linked. With different companies that only work via the Internet—like Amazon—the entire globe is truly a possible marketplace for goods. Territorial boundaries, as it comes to the buying and selling of goods, are rapidly disappearing. However, some critics say that it is the First World countries, or developed countries, that are benefiting from the global economy. Critics are worried that the emerging nations are being taken advantage of in the quest to make more money. Trade agreements are exploiting native people, even though many will say that technology has improved the standard of living for people across the world. Multinational corporations give back and help the infrastructure and industry of an emerging nation, combating poverty in areas where they do business.

THE GREEN REVOLUTION

One result of the new global economy was the idea of helping to increase food production in areas where that had been difficult. In the late 1950s, scientists focusing on agriculture began the idea that became known as the Green Revolution. The Green Revolution was developed to help increase food production as the population of the world began to increase rapidly.

In the 1950s and 1960s, the revolution focused on the growing use of chemical fertilizers and different pesticides to allow crops to grow rapidly and protect them from insects. Although famines were temporarily stopped and food began to grow in areas of the world where it had once been difficult, the Green Revolution began to have setbacks as well. Increased use of fertilizer and pesticides caused chemical damage. In some areas, there was an increase in cancer as well as destruction to different waterways and wildlife from chemical runoff.

New seed strains and fertilizer were also developed. Hybrid plant strains were created that would be unattractive to predators and/or resistant to agricultural pests. Genetically modified plants that could grow in different soil conditions like rocky soil and drought-ridden soil were developed.

Multinational corporations also began to research how to increase the spread of crops. The Green Revolution continues to bring about increased food production to meet the needs of the growing global population, especially in China and India, the world's two most populous countries, and in other large population centers in South and Southeast Asia.

THE UNITED NATIONS AS PEACEKEEPER

As the Cold War ended, new ethnic groups around the globe wanted to proclaim their independence. The question of the security of different people across the world began to gain worldwide attention. Upon its inception in 1945, the United Nations began to use its resources to help offer security for as many people as possible.

Nations that were part of NATO and the Warsaw Pact began to give their support for military and economic aid where it was needed around the world. The key to using these resources was to make sure they prevented war or the threat of war altogether. Thus, the United Nations began to take part in peacekeeping roles and peace negotiations across the world.

At certain times, the United Nations also employs a small number of peacekeeping forces. The United Nations peacekeeping force is comprised of soldiers from different UN member nations. The job of the peacekeeping force is to enforce peace agreements, instill cease-fires, and quell fighting so peace negotiations or agreements can take root. This force is made up of around 50,000 soldiers and military policemen that work around the world.

Mogadishu, Somalia

A United Nations peacekeeping force was in Mogadishu, Somalia when in 1991, a civil war broke out between new president Ali Mahdi Muhammad and his opponent General Mohammed Farah Aidid. The civil war spilled over to affect many people in the impoverished nation of Somalia. In January 1992, the United Nations imposed economic sanctions on Somalia to end the fighting. When that did not work, in November 1992, the United States volunteered to lead 24 different countries in a UN mission named UNOSOM, or the United Nations Operations in Somalia. The goal of this coalition was to create a safe environment so that humanitarian aid, in the form of foodstuffs and medicine, could be given to the people while the different warring factions could be disarmed and peace returned to Somalia.

Twenty-two thousand United Nations peacekeepers entered Somalia in March 1993. The situation was difficult to control as the UN force was not large enough to spread out over the entire country. More United States forces entered Somalia to assist, leading to the famous Battle of Mogadishu on October 3–4, 1993.

The embarrassment of the failed mission to capture General Aidid caused President Clinton to withdraw some of the U.S. fighting force. The United Nations kept trying to bring about peace, but when several cease-fire agreements were violated, the United Nations withdrew its support, and UNOSOM ended in March 1995. The events in Somalia are one example of how the United Nations may try, but may not be successful in every area.

United Nations and Human Rights

Human rights have been an issue for thousands of years. However, the new era of interconnectedness and communication has brought human rights issues and awareness to the world in a way that has never before been seen. With instantaneous pictures available via the Internet, many abuses of human rights are seen throughout the modern world. Many times, there is no government able to enforce or put a stop to human rights violations.

In 1948, the United Nations approved the Universal Declaration of Human Rights. The declaration states that all humans are born free and equal in their dignity and rights. Therefore, all humans have the right to life, liberty, and personal security. In 1975, the United Nations made a further commitment to human rights with the Helsinki Accords. The Helsinki Accords addressed the idea of freedom of information between people. The United Nations specifically stated that they would ensure the basic rights of human beings with the hope that humanity was respected across the world. To this day, the United Nations and other subsidiaries are encouraging people to work toward peace.

Slovenia and Croatia

The United Nations mission for peace was demonstrated after the fall of the Soviet Union with the breakup of Yugoslavia. In 1991, Slovenia and Croatia were able to gain independence, but new Serbian leader Slobodan Milosevic sent his army into Slovenia and Croatia as well as the territory of Bosnia and Herzegovina, which also wanted independence.

Even though Slovenia and Croatia successfully defended their independence, Bosnia and Herzegovina had such a diverse population that the people were divided. The Muslims and Croatians living in Bosnia and Herzegovina were supportive of independence, but the ethnic group of Serbians did not want Bosnia and Herzegovina to undergo a further splintering of their country. In March 1992, a war broke out. Milosevic and his Serbian army used execution, murder, and other types of brutal violence to try to kill the Muslim population living in Serbian-held lands in Bosnia and Herzegovina.

In 1995, the United Nations brought together the Serbian, Croatian, and Muslim leaders to enforce a peace treaty. This is an example of where direct United Nations intervention to protect human rights and prevent genocide was successful.

Rwanda

In 1994, the president of Rwanda was killed in a plane crash. The president was a member of the Hutu tribe, which controlled the government of Rwanda. However, a minority of the people of Rwanda belonged to the Tutsi tribe. The two tribes have long had distrust and dislike for one another. After the death of the president, radical Hutu leaders encouraged the execution and slaughtering of their Tutsi neighbors. The resulting violence killed nearly one million Rwandans, and another three million lost their homes and livelihood due to destruction caused by the civil war.

The United Nations quickly intervened and eventually began a war crimes investigation to internationally punish those guilty of war crimes and genocide. This is an ongoing process, and even though the United Nations is helping Rwanda recover from the civil war, there is still a lot of tension, hostility, and poverty in East Africa today.

THE FORMATION OF THE EUROPEAN UNION

The European Union is part of a continuing effort in Europe to organize itself. As far back as 1952, France, West Germany, Belgium, Netherlands, Italy, and Luxembourg tried to work together to eliminate quotas and tariffs within the coal and steel industries. The same nations formed the European Economic Community (EEC) in 1957 to try to create a free trade zone in Europe. There was additional unification in 1967 as multiple economic communities joined together to form the European Community (EC).

In 1993, a treaty that allowed for the formation of the European Union (EU) was created. The EU had 12 original members:

- Belgium
- Denmark
- France
- Germany
- Greece
- Ireland
- Italy
- Luxembourg
- Netherlands
- Portugal
- Spain
- United Kingdom

The inaugural members of the EU worked to integrate and combine the European economic community. The goal of the EU was to form policies that would create a flow of labor, industrial capital, and manufactured goods among European nations. Along with forming economic policies, EU nations adopted the use of a common currency known as the euro. The euro would replace the age-old system of different European currencies. Only Great Britain remained tied to the British pound. In 2016, Great Britain chose to leave the EU with the historic Brexit vote.

By 2000, the European Union had doubled in size, including many countries from Eastern Europe and some former Soviet satellites. Turkey tried to enter the EU but was not accepted. Borders were opened, making it easier to drive through Europe. The practice of having passport checkpoints going into and out of EU countries was disbanded. Combining their economic power and resources, the European Union was able to compete with the reigning economic superpower, the United States, as well as powerful Japan.

The formation of the EU has brought fear to some nations, especially in Eastern Europe, who worry about being gobbled up by the EU after decades of being controlled by the Soviets. Currently, there is a call for slower and stable growth in order to integrate, if requested, the many different countries not currently in the EU. There are many different social and religious systems throughout Europe, and the European Union aims for a peaceful inclusion into the EU of all peoples who desire membership.

TERRORISM AROUND THE WORLD

Perhaps the biggest threat to modern global security is the new threat of terrorism. Terrorism is the use of violence against a civilian population by a group or groups of extremists trying to achieve their own political, religious, or social goals. Most terrorists today are spurned by extreme radical religious and/or cultural ideals against what they see as evil.

Terrorism in Africa

Poverty, the effects of imperialism, and civil war are responsible for most of the terrorist activities on the continent of Africa. Africa is also a recruiting ground for the dominant terrorist group operating in the early 21st century, known as al-Qaeda. Al-Qaeda has camps, or cells, throughout the world. They have led multiple attacks against foreign people, especially the United States:

- The attack on U.S. soldiers in Somalia that killed 18 in 1993
- The bombing of the United States Embassy in Kenya in 1998
- The attack on the American CIA station in Benghazi, Libya, on September 11, 2012

Al-Qaeda leader Osama bin Laden built many recruitment facilities and training camps in the country of Sudan while he was living there during the mid- to late 1990s.

Terrorism in Eastern and South Asia

South Asia has also seen a rise in terrorist activity. In 2008, there was a terrorist attack in Mumbai, India, where Islamic terrorists of the group Lashkar-e-Taiba attacked a hotel frequented by foreigners. Over four days, they killed many innocent civilians and held out against police until all but one were killed.

In East Asia, the effects of terrorism were felt in Japan in 1995 when members of a radical religious cult, Aum Shinrikyo ("Supreme Truth"), released deadly saran nerve gas in a subway station in Tokyo. Twelve people died and nearly 6000 were injured.

Modern Terrorism in Europe and the United States

- **APRIL 15, 2013:** Two brothers placed explosive devices near the finish line of the Boston Marathon, killing 3 and wounding 260 spectators.
- **NOVEMBER 13, 2015:** Paris suffered a series of terrorist attacks, beginning with bombings at a soccer game. Then, a series of terrorist shootings and suicide bombings occurred at various restaurants, followed by a mass attack at a concert hall. The attacks killed 130 victims, and ISIL (also known as ISIS) claimed responsibility for the attacks.
- **DECEMBER 2, 2015:** In San Bernardino, California, a married couple attacked a holiday party, killing 14 people and wounding 22 others. The two claimed to be motivated by ISIL.
- **MARCH 22, 2016:** Three suicide bombers attacked Brussels. Two of the attackers were at the Brussels airport and one attacked a Metro station. The blasts killed 32 people from around the world, halted airport traffic in Europe, and closed the city of Brussels for days. ISIL also claimed responsibility.
- **JUNE 12, 2016:** In Orlando, Florida, a shooter opened fire at a night club, killing 49 people and wounding 53 others before being killed by police. It was the worst terrorist attack in the United States since 9/11. The shooter claimed to be a member of ISIL.
- **JULY 14, 2016:** In Nice, France, a member of ISIL attacked a Bastille Day celebration by driving a heavy truck into crowds of people, killing 86 people and injuring 434 people.
- **DECEMBER 19, 2016:** Inspired by the Nice attack, a member of ISIL drove a heavy truck into a crowded Berlin Christmas market. The attack killed 12 people and injured 48. The attacker was tracked to Italy where Italian police shot him while he was trying to flee.

Terrorism in the Middle East

Many terrorist groups were founded in the Middle East to fight land conflicts in the area, ranging from fighting over the formation of Israel to clashes between ethnic and religious groups.

The Middle East has also become a training ground for terrorists due to the influence of Osama bin Laden. The remoteness of Afghanistan and Pakistan has made them a safe harbor for international terrorist organizations, such as the Taliban and al-Qaeda. The mountainous terrain makes it difficult to track terrorists and find their training camps. From Afghanistan, Osama bin Laden encouraged al-Qaeda to attack the United States or any U.S. ally.

The ongoing wars in Iraq and Afghanistan only further fueled terrorists and their attacks, especially toward the United States. After nearly ten years of hunting Osama bin Laden, the United States killed bin Laden during a raid in Pakistan on May 2, 2011. The world hoped his death would be the fatal blow to the al-Qaeda terrorist network and other terrorist groups.

Many of these groups are sponsored by Islamic fundamentalism, which is a belief that all society should be governed by theocracy strictly adhering to Islamic sharia law. Fundamentalist Islamic groups have used violence to try to take over many countries throughout the world. In recent history, there has been an upsurge in terrorist recruitment and violence. The terrorist group ISIL beheaded at least four journalists and unleashed attacks in Syria and Iraq in the fall of 2014.

Weapons of Mass Destruction

Another factor that worries many people is weapons of mass destruction (WMD). Saddam Hussein in Iraq used WMDs against his own people. Biological weapons were used in the terrorist attack in the Tokyo subway station in 1995. World leaders are concerned that WMDs once held by Hussein in Syria will possibly fall into the hands of ISIL.

Terrorism in Latin America

Terrorism in Latin America takes on a different shape. Latin American terrorist attacks are not given a lot of attention worldwide, but they still take place. Colombia, where the powerful cocaine cartels support Pablo Escobar, has witnessed terrorist attacks because of the influence of the cartels on the country. There is a group known as the Revolutionary Armed Forces of Colombia (FARC), a guerrilla group that has hijacked and bombed various targets to capture wealthy foreigners for ransom. Recently, Colombia has been a recruitment center for Islamic extremists.

Terrorism in the United States Before September 11, 2001

The United States had seen instances of terror from two homegrown terrorists: Timothy McVeigh, who bombed the Oklahoma City federal building in 1995, and Ted Kaczynski, the Unabomber who sent bombs through the mail from 1978 through 1995.

In 1993, the United States experienced radical Islamic fundamentalist terror for the first time when Khalid Sheikh Mohammed orchestrated the underground bombing of the World Trade Center in February 1993.

September 11, 2001, and the Response of the United States

What happened in the United States on September 11, 2001 shocked and changed the world forever. On the morning of September 11, 19 Arabic terrorists hijacked four planes from New York, Boston, and Washington, D.C. Two planes crashed into the upper floors of the north and south towers of the World Trade Center in New York City. Shortly after, one of the planes crashed into the Pentagon, just outside of Washington, D.C., and one plane was downed in a field in Pennsylvania when the passengers fought back to retake the plane from the terrorists.

Four large planes flying across the United States, fully loaded with fuel, became high-speed missiles for the hijackers. The resulting damage caused by the collapse of the World Trade Center towers, symbols of American power and finance, effectively shut down New York City. In the end, the terrorist attacks claimed nearly 3000 lives.

U.S. President George W. Bush immediately took action. The U.S. government began an exhaustive effort to identify those responsible. It was determined that Osama bin Laden of al-Qaeda helped plan the activity from Afghanistan, where he was protected by the regime of the Taliban. President Bush said in a famous quote, "Whether we bring our enemies to justice or bring justice to our enemies, justice will be done."

When President Bush called the attacks an act of war, it was a new type of war. It was not a clearly defined war against an enemy in a clearly defined boundary. Terrorists could be anybody, anywhere in the world. President Bush waged war on global terrorism and pursued any nation that provided aid or safe haven to a terrorist group. The United States identified several nations as centers for possible terrorist activity:

- Iran
- Iraq
- North Korea
- Sudan
- Afghanistan
- Lebanon

The country of Pakistan offered its cooperation and assistance to help the United States track down the people responsible for the attacks. While the United States government was conducting their worldwide war on terror, they also built an international coalition to help. Member nations included Canada, China, Great Britain, and Pakistan. Other nations offered to share intelligence and to arrest terrorists found within their borders.

The World After September 11

People saw the world change before their eyes as they experienced the events of September 11. People who once felt safe were afraid. The Office of Homeland Security was created to connect all the intelligence bureaus. Airport security changed forever as new screening methods were implemented. Airline prices went up immediately, and there was an extensive searching process of persons and luggage.

The Patriot Act was also adopted by the U.S. government after the September 11 bombings. The Patriot Act is an antiterrorist law that gives increased powers to the government, allowing them to arrest foreigners suspected of terrorism and holding them for a week before charging them with a crime. The law also allows telephones to be tapped, email and Internet usage to be monitored, and new search warrants that cross state boundaries to be issued. The Patriot Act also states that there is no statute of limitations on any terrorist crimes.

As a result of the war on terror, the United States and President Bush underwent severe criticism as some of the areas that the U.S military went into—especially Iraq—were not seen as part of the attack on the United States. However, the possibility that WMDs might fall into the hands of terrorists was enough reason for President Bush. He believed that the best deterrent against terrorism was the spread of democracy, and he was going to spread democracy anywhere he could, regardless of the criticism against him.

Cyberterrorism and the Internet

With the growing global interconnectedness via the Internet, another threat is intentional attacks on financial records or computer systems, known as cyberterrorism. Cyberterrorism can be hacking into a competitor's computer systems, stealing government secrets from online data, downloading a virus to ruin operations, or stealing secrets, military or financial. Because of the growing use and spread of computers, cyberterrorism is most likely going to increase. More effort and technology will be developed to combat against it. Recently, there have been allegations that Russian groups have hacked into U.S. banking records and influenced the 2016 Presidential election. China has allegedly been trying to hack into U.S. military systems. With data being shared worldwide and the interconnectedness of computers and multinational corporations, it makes them prime targets for cyberterrorism.

SOCIAL MEDIA AND ITS EFFECT ON THE WORLD

A new revolution of the global age is the effect of mass media. Images, music, television shows, and radio stations can be broadcast anywhere now because of satellite capabilities. Popular culture ebbs and flows quickly as movies, music, clothing and fashion, sports, and more are available worldwide. The Western media dominates what is seen and heard, as the most-watched news station across the world is CNN, based in Atlanta, Georgia. As a result, the influence that the West has on many different cultures today can be seen around the world.

The invention of Facebook in 2004 gave people greater access to social media through their smartphones, iPads, or tablets. Many hope that social media can help positively influence thinking around the world to spread ideas of peace, democracy, and individual freedom.

In many Third World and emerging countries, having access to these devices is seen as something mainly for the wealthy. However, social media can be a way to share art, music, and pictures from any culture, anywhere in the world. Different architectural designs or music and pictures from an isolated region can be spread across the world via social media. Works of art and poetry can be shared with the public.

Social media is not only for the Western world. It gives all nationalities a way to promote their nationalism, their works of art, and their culture to a much broader audience.

SCIENCE AND MEDICINE

One positive effect of an interconnected world is the increased research when it comes to science and medicine. Medical treatment has improved dramatically in First World countries, but there are still many people throughout the world where poor health or lack of health care is a way of life.

In the 1980s, a global disease drew worldwide attention: Acquired Immune Deficiency Syndrome, otherwise known as AIDS. AIDS attacks the immune system so an infected patient has little resistance to infection. The AIDS virus, called HIV, spread to people around the world. In Africa, AIDS has become an epidemic. As a result, the United Nations began to work on combating this epidemic. The groundwork was laid for cooperation between international researchers to combat AIDS.

While public health crises can hurt economies, the work to develop advances in medicine and technology to prevent disease and illness has created a booming industry. The Internet and global communication networks allow doctors and researchers from around the world to share information and work together on a problem, instead of just being isolated in their individual laboratories.

A new industry has grown that is known as biological technology. Biotech companies specialize in the technology of medicine. They make the medicines or vaccinations to combat the spread and severity of illness. They even develop products that can clean up environmental disasters that could affect humanity. For example, a new bacteria was introduced in the Gulf of Mexico to combat the BP oil spill of 2010.

There has also been an increase in the study of genetics. Understanding how a person's DNA and his or her heredity could affect health has led to new preventive treatments. Knowing if an individual has a greater risk of getting certain diseases affects fertility and family planning as well. Genetic research is also being used to create different plant and animal species that are resistant to disease, allowing them to grow and thrive in an area without a lot of natural resources.

The Human Genome Project

The Human Genome Project (HGP) was the largest, worldwide biological research program to map all the genes of human beings. The combination of human genes in the body is known as a person's genome.

The HGP discovered that there are about 20,500 human genes and mapped their locations in the cells of the body. The HGP provided detailed information about the structure, organization, and function of human genes. The genome can be thought of as instructions for the development and function of a human being.

The Human Genome Project started in earnest in the mid-1980s but had its origins dating back to 1911 when the first gene map of a fruit fly was made. The U.S. government became involved in the project in 1986 because it needed information on how to protect people from radiation that could alter or destroy their genes. In February 2001, the HGP had a 90 percent complete sequence of all three billion base pairs in the human genome, and the full sequence was complete in April 2003.

Understanding the building blocks of human life has enabled researchers to progress even more rapidly in their discovery and creation of new medicines that could help humanity.

CULTURAL DIFFUSION: FASTER THAN EVER BEFORE

Since the days of the ancient river valley civilizations, cultural diffusion—the sharing of ideas and technology between cultures—has always been a part of human society. Today, cultural diffusion is spreading more quickly than ever before because of mass transportation, the Internet, social media (Facebook, Instagram, Twitter, etc.), and the greater use of smart devices (laptops, cell phones, tablets, etc.).

HOPE FOR THE FUTURE

Technology, medicines, and the defeat of terrorism will hopefully lead to a better quality of life for people around the world. Treating disease and providing medical care will increase the life expectancy of many people. The world continues to struggle to find ways to adequately feed the world's growing population. Humanity is also working to combat the effects of global warming, depletion of the ozone layer, and deforestation.

TIMELINE REVIEW

1950s C.E.	Green Revolution
1976 C.E.	Genetic testing is invented using DNA.
1982 C.E.	Personal computers are available for household use.
1990 C.E.	Creation of the Internet
1992 C.E.	Cell phones begin to be used by the consumer market.
1993 C.E.	• Battle of Mogadishu between Somali rulers and the U.S.
	• World Trade Center in United States is bombed by al-Qaeda.
1994 C.E.	Rwandan genocide
2001 C.E.	September 11 attacks against United States by al-Qaeda
2003 C.E.	Darfur genocide in Sudan
2004 C.E.	Facebook is founded by Mark Zuckerberg.
2011 C.E.	U.S. military finds and kills Osama bin Laden, the leader of al-Qaeda.

Quick Quiz: Chapters 34–36

1. Who succeeded Joseph Stalin as leader of the Soviet Union?

   A. Leon Trotsky
   B. Vladimir Putin
   C. Boris Yeltsin
   D. Nikita Khrushchev

2. Which was the first Warsaw Pact country to try to gain independence from the Soviet Union?

   A. Poland
   B. Hungary
   C. Czechoslovakia
   D. Romania

3. Which event brought an end to détente between the United States and Soviet Union?

   A. The Soviet Union's refusal to attend the 1984 Olympics
   B. The closing off of the city of Berlin
   C. The Soviet invasion of Afghanistan
   D. The Hungarian Rebellion

4. Which former Soviet republic split into several different countries after the fall of the Soviet Union due to the many different ethnicities that lived there?

   A. Czechoslovakia
   B. Yugoslavia
   C. Ukraine
   D. Poland

5. During decolonization, what was the most visible problem for Middle Eastern independence?

   A. The many different ethnic groups inhabiting the country
   B. The unequal distribution of oil deposits
   C. The borders that were redrawn by European countries
   D. The inability of Arab states to unify

6. Which event caused worldwide economic depression?

   A. OPEC stopping shipments of oil to the United States
   B. The Iranian Revolution
   C. The creation of Israel
   D. The U.S. invasion of Iraq

7. Which country's revolution involved the capture of 53 American prisoners, who were held for 444 days?

   A. Iraqi Revolution
   B. Egyptian Uprising
   C. The Lebanese War
   D. Iranian Revolution

8. Which group became the main opponent of Israel?

   A. OPEC
   B. PLO
   C. Pan-Arab League
   D. The Shah

9. Which ultraconservative group assumed control of Afghanistan?

   A. Infantata
   B. Palestinian Liberation Organization
   C. Taliban
   D. Hamas

10. Which modern invention has brought the world closer together and allowed information to be used and stored quicker and faster than ever?

    A. Personal computer
    B. Satellite links
    C. Cell phones
    D. Globalization

11. Which issue is the biggest problem confronting Africa in the present day?

    A. Genocide
    B. Terrorism
    C. Health and medical issues
    D. Corrupt and inefficient governments

12. Which modern invention/creation enables the West to influence cultures and trends worldwide?

    A. Cable television
    B. Social media
    C. Personal computers
    D. Digital photography

13. Which collaboration is the largest biological research project to date?

    A. The Green Revolution
    B. The development of the Internet
    C. The U.N. infectious disease response center
    D. The Human Genome Project

Quick Quiz Answers

1. D; **2.** B; **3.** C; **4.** B; **5.** C; **6.** A; **7.** D; **8.** B; **9.** C; **10.** A; **11.** C; **12.** B; **13.** D

ANSWER SHEET
Practice Test 1

1. (A) (B) (C) (D) (E)
2. (A) (B) (C) (D) (E)
3. (A) (B) (C) (D) (E)
4. (A) (B) (C) (D) (E)
5. (A) (B) (C) (D) (E)
6. (A) (B) (C) (D) (E)
7. (A) (B) (C) (D) (E)
8. (A) (B) (C) (D) (E)
9. (A) (B) (C) (D) (E)
10. (A) (B) (C) (D) (E)
11. (A) (B) (C) (D) (E)
12. (A) (B) (C) (D) (E)
13. (A) (B) (C) (D) (E)
14. (A) (B) (C) (D) (E)
15. (A) (B) (C) (D) (E)
16. (A) (B) (C) (D) (E)
17. (A) (B) (C) (D) (E)
18. (A) (B) (C) (D) (E)
19. (A) (B) (C) (D) (E)
20. (A) (B) (C) (D) (E)
21. (A) (B) (C) (D) (E)
22. (A) (B) (C) (D) (E)
23. (A) (B) (C) (D) (E)
24. (A) (B) (C) (D) (E)

25. (A) (B) (C) (D) (E)
26. (A) (B) (C) (D) (E)
27. (A) (B) (C) (D) (E)
28. (A) (B) (C) (D) (E)
29. (A) (B) (C) (D) (E)
30. (A) (B) (C) (D) (E)
31. (A) (B) (C) (D) (E)
32. (A) (B) (C) (D) (E)
33. (A) (B) (C) (D) (E)
34. (A) (B) (C) (D) (E)
35. (A) (B) (C) (D) (E)
36. (A) (B) (C) (D) (E)
37. (A) (B) (C) (D) (E)
38. (A) (B) (C) (D) (E)
39. (A) (B) (C) (D) (E)
40. (A) (B) (C) (D) (E)
41. (A) (B) (C) (D) (E)
42. (A) (B) (C) (D) (E)
43. (A) (B) (C) (D) (E)
44. (A) (B) (C) (D) (E)
45. (A) (B) (C) (D) (E)
46. (A) (B) (C) (D) (E)
47. (A) (B) (C) (D) (E)
48. (A) (B) (C) (D) (E)

49. (A) (B) (C) (D) (E)
50. (A) (B) (C) (D) (E)
51. (A) (B) (C) (D) (E)
52. (A) (B) (C) (D) (E)
53. (A) (B) (C) (D) (E)
54. (A) (B) (C) (D) (E)
55. (A) (B) (C) (D) (E)
56. (A) (B) (C) (D) (E)
57. (A) (B) (C) (D) (E)
58. (A) (B) (C) (D) (E)
59. (A) (B) (C) (D) (E)
60. (A) (B) (C) (D) (E)
61. (A) (B) (C) (D) (E)
62. (A) (B) (C) (D) (E)
63. (A) (B) (C) (D) (E)
64. (A) (B) (C) (D) (E)
65. (A) (B) (C) (D) (E)
66. (A) (B) (C) (D) (E)
67. (A) (B) (C) (D) (E)
68. (A) (B) (C) (D) (E)
69. (A) (B) (C) (D) (E)
70. (A) (B) (C) (D) (E)
71. (A) (B) (C) (D) (E)
72. (A) (B) (C) (D) (E)

73. (A) (B) (C) (D) (E)
74. (A) (B) (C) (D) (E)
75. (A) (B) (C) (D) (E)
76. (A) (B) (C) (D) (E)
77. (A) (B) (C) (D) (E)
78. (A) (B) (C) (D) (E)
79. (A) (B) (C) (D) (E)
80. (A) (B) (C) (D) (E)
81. (A) (B) (C) (D) (E)
82. (A) (B) (C) (D) (E)
83. (A) (B) (C) (D) (E)
84. (A) (B) (C) (D) (E)
85. (A) (B) (C) (D) (E)
86. (A) (B) (C) (D) (E)
87. (A) (B) (C) (D) (E)
88. (A) (B) (C) (D) (E)
89. (A) (B) (C) (D) (E)
90. (A) (B) (C) (D) (E)
91. (A) (B) (C) (D) (E)
92. (A) (B) (C) (D) (E)
93. (A) (B) (C) (D) (E)
94. (A) (B) (C) (D) (E)
95. (A) (B) (C) (D) (E)

Practice Test 1

1. Two philosophers who did not see themselves as innovators were
   A. Aristotle and Plato.
   B. Confucius and Socrates.
   C. Buddha and Mahavria.
   D. Thales and Mencius.
   E. Lao Tsu and Zoroaster.

2. The historic development of Japan demonstrates striking similarities with what other area of the world?
   A. Northwestern Europe
   B. South America
   C. Southern China
   D. Northwestern Africa
   E. Upper India

3. After World War II, Latin America was forced to adhere to which of the following policies?
   A. They had to stand on their own and depend less on the United States.
   B. They had to remain dominated by the economic policies of Europe.
   C. They had to exist in the shadows of the United States and the Soviet Union.
   D. They began to end the massive political corruption.
   E. They were able to finally exert their independence and begin self-rule with no outside interference.

4. If Tutankhamen was a minor pharaoh, why is he/she important in our study of Egypt?
   A. She was the first female pharaoh; she ruled for 22 years and traded with the interior of Africa.
   B. He tried to convert to monotheism.
   C. His is the only intact tomb ever found.
   D. He was a military pharaoh who expanded Egypt's borders to its greatest size.
   E. He had the names of other pharaohs chiseled off monuments and had his name written on his own.

5. The single most important political development in Europe between 1848 and 1914 was which of the following?

    A. Unification of Italy

    B. Unification of Germany

    C. End of the Crimean War

    D. Prussian defeat of Austria

    E. Speed of German victory in the Franco-Prussian War

6. When comparing the above photo to what historians know about Mesopotamian ziggurats and the cities of Harappa and Mohenjo-daro in India, what can we tell about these ancient societies?

    A. They understood complex mathematics.

    B. They had great and plentiful building materials.

    C. They had well-organized and strong central governments to make sure these structures were completed.

    D. They all shared building ideas.

    E. Both A and C

7. What change took place between the late Tokugawa and early Meiji periods in Japan?

    A. The Meiji economy was backward, while the Tokugawa became modern and industrial.

    B. The Tokugawa economy was backward, while the Meiji was modern and progressive.

    C. The Meiji encouraged learning Western methods of technology and society, then developing them to fit Japan.

    D. The Tokugawas encouraged learning Western methods of technology and society, then duplicating them in Japan with few modifications.

    E. Both B and C

8. The leading intellectual center of sub-Saharan Islamic religion and culture was

    A. Mali.

    B. Timbuktu.

    C. Cairo.

    D. Changamire.

    E. Zanzibar.

9. The concept of the polis is most closely associated with which of the following civilizations?

    A. Athens

    B. Sparta

    C. Babylonia

    D. Persian Empire

    E. Indus River civilizations

10. What did the subcontinent of India depend on for survival that was different from all other river valley civilizations?

    A. A flooding river

    B. Snow melt from the mountains of Turkey

    C. Trade winds blowing from eastern Asia

    D. Monsoons

    E. The spring thaw of the Himalayas

11. The conquest of the Americas by Spain during the 15th through 19th centuries resulted in which of the following?

    A. Spanish dominance as the longest-lasting of the European mercantile trading nations

    B. The decimation of Native American civilizations

    C. Temporary dominance of Spain as a major power in Europe

    D. A conscious effort to establish more port cities

    E. Both A and B

12. The initial goal of the American occupation of Japan following World War II was

    A. To return Japan to prewar economic revitalization.

    B. The immediate demilitarization and democratization of Japan.

    C. The institution of a provisional government.

    D. To prevent communism from taking over the Japanese Diet.

    E. The renunciation of war and the use of force for Japan.

13. The layout and construction of the Great Zimbabwe in southern Africa closely resembles which other civilizations/empires throughout history?

    A. Mali and Ghana

    B. The Roman and Byzantine Empires

    C. Centralized governments of Pharonic Egypt and Zhou Dynasty China

    D. The city-states of ancient Greece and cities of the Mayan Empire

    E. Civilizations of Sumeria and Axum

14. Compared to a Chinese nobleman, a peasant in China would be different in all of the following EXCEPT

    A. an equal rate of literacy due to Confucian schools.

    B. a lower level of wealth.

    C. a greater belief in the polytheistic gods of nature.

    D. a greater dependence on land as the basic economic resource.

    E. a lack of belief in the Dynastic Cycle.

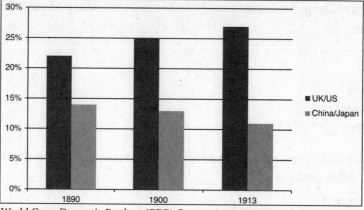

World Gross Domestic Product (GDP) Comparison: UK/US and China/Japan

15. Using the data from the chart, when viewed from the perspective of late 19th/early 20th century Europeans, East Asia appears

A. dynamic and innovative.

B. unknown for the most part due to a period of isolation.

C. to be moving at a rate of slow motion.

D. a mirror image of what Europe was doing.

E. to be still stuck in a feudal past.

16. Which best describes a *madrasa?*

A. A new and more radical Islamic sect

B. A college of higher learning created by Islamic mosques that taught students who were willing to learn

C. The intellectual scholars of Islam who interpreted the Qur'an

D. The merchant class of Islam that traveled the length of the Silk Road

E. The peasant class of Islam whose daily life changed little from the formation of Islam

17. The people of the Americas never developed the wheel because they

A. were inferior engineers.

B. had no large draft animals.

C. had no ready access to wood and iron.

D. were nomadic hunter-gatherers.

E. had no need for it.

18. How did Egypt differ from Mesopotamian civilization?

A. Well-organized, stable empire

B. Extensive trade

C. Firm religious beliefs

D. Greater social equality

E. More modest building projects

19. In an 1823 letter to the British Governor General Lord Amherst about the opening of a British-sponsored school to teach Sanskrit and Hindu literature, why did important Nationalist leader Ram Mohan Roy state the school should "promote a more… enlightened system of instruction, embracing mathematics, natural philosophy, chemistry, anatomy, with other useful sciences…"?

    A. He was an advocate of the reform of British colonial policy.
    B. He wanted to mesh concepts from Christianity and Hinduism to unite his people.
    C. He alienated his Hindu supporters.
    D. He encouraged Indians to learn industrial and technological techniques from the British and use that knowledge to end imperial rule.
    E. He adopted a U.S.-style constitution for the new India.

20. As the White Russians and Red Russians began to fight, the war in Russia developed into what type of conflict?

    A. World war
    B. Civil war
    C. War against communism
    D. Guerilla war
    E. A summer war.

21. Where did the great scientists and thinkers like Euclid, Pythagoras, and Archimedes do most of their work and study near the end of the Greek era of dominance?

    A. Athens
    B. Persepolis
    C. House of Muses
    D. Delos
    E. Delphi

22. The different civilizations of the Americas—Olmec, Maya, Aztec, and Inca—all shared which of the following commonalities?

    A. All had some type of monumental architecture.
    B. All were polytheistic, worshipping the gods of nature.
    C. All practiced human sacrifice at some level.
    D. All had a variation of a ritualistic ball game.
    E. All of the above

23. As the Soviet Union and its communist ideology began to weaken in the late 1980s, it triggered what two world-changing events?

    A. The Solidarity Movement of Poland and the Hungarian Revolution
    B. The tearing down of the Berlin Wall and the Tiananmen Square protest in China
    C. Polish Cardinal Karol Wojtyla becoming the first non-Italian pope and the Soviet invasion of Afghanistan
    D. The nationalist war between Iran and Iraq
    E. Cuba becoming further isolated and a war of ethnic cleansing in Yugoslavia

24. What Byzantine emperor was responsible for attempting to recreate the Roman Empire after 533 C.E.?

A. Constantine
B. Justinian
C. Diocletian
D. Theodosius
E. Michael II

25. By studying the map of the great Bantu migrations between 2000 B.C.E. and 500 C.E., which of the following are possible results from this long period of migration?

A. A language pattern was spread across much of eastern and western southern Africa.
B. Cultural diffusion took place as the West African farmers spread their technology and ideas.
C. The migrations contributed to the rich diversity of the African continent.
D. The Bantu migration forced a displacement of many earlier groups of settlers.
E. All of the above

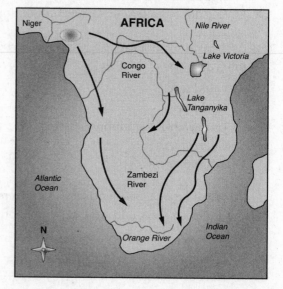

26. Which emperor was behind the idea of reorganizing the tremendous amount of legal codes that governed his empire, and he had his scholars create the Corpus Juris Civilis?

A. Constantine
B. Marcus Aurelius
C. Justinian
D. Trajan
E. Augustus

27. The Great Depression of 1929 had what effect on Japan?

A. It polarized both political parties in the Japanese Diet.
B. Although it did have a strong effect, Japan was affected less than other countries because they had "gone off" the gold standard and, instead, focused internally on creating an industry to pull them out of depression.
C. It destroyed all the industrial gains that Japan had worked so hard to accomplish.
D. It allowed the Japanese to inherit Southeast Asian colonies from Germany, who defaulted on its reparation payments.
E. It allowed the Imperial War Council to take power from the civilian government as Western methods were seen as invalid.

28. What debt does Western Europe owe to the Byzantine and Muslim empires, who were at war with each other?

   A. They learned many new technological and medical ideas.
   B. It forced Western Europe to fall back on its own resources and create its own separate and distinct culture.
   C. They were taught new farming techniques.
   D. It forced Europe to adopt a functional governmental structure for the first time since the fall of Rome.
   E. It was a model of governmental bureaucracy that intertwined church and state.

29. Upon returning from his visit to Western Europe, what was Peter the Great's main goal for Russia?

   A. To resist Western ideas and culture because they were too corrupt
   B. To control the Russian Orthodox Church
   C. To cut off the beards of the boyars and make them subject to his will so he could be an absolute monarch like Louis XIV
   D. To copy the technology and manufacturing methods of the West to increase the size and strength of his military
   E. To secure political recognition for Russia as a Western European power

30. Which of the following provides the best example of the many difficulties being experienced by emerging African states?

   A. A lack of unity and direction indicates their basic need for maintaining colonial ties.
   B. The difficulties being experienced create a clear picture as to how little the former colonial powers cared or did for their colonists in Africa.
   C. The difficulties are the result of basic Apartheid laws and institutions.
   D. The difficulties can be traced back to the trade agreements the West African empires made with the Portuguese.
   E. They lacked monetary or natural resources to overcome the obstacles that were being faced.

31. The religion that was nearly erased under Muslim control in India was

   A. Christianity.
   B. Hinduism.
   C. Buddhism.
   D. Jainism.
   E. Coptic Christianity.

32. What happened to the cultures of North and South America after the Bering Strait melted at the end of the Paleolithic Age?

   A. Even though they were cut off from cultural diffusion, they accomplished what other civilizations did, but they were between 1,000 and 3,000 years behind in technology.
   B. They established their own separate and distinct cultures.
   C. They followed a path through the eight factors of civilization.
   D. They evolved along the same lines as the other four river valley civilizations, nearly simultaneously.
   E. They were not colonized during Paleolithic or Neolithic times.

"The people of the Middle East yearn for peace so that the vast human and natural resources of the region can be turned to the pursuits of peace and so that this area can become a model for coexistence and cooperation among nations."

—Preamble, The Camp David Accords, 1978

33. What was the outcome of this event?

   A. Finally established the legitimacy of the Palestinian Liberation Organization
   B. Created a permanent border between Syria and Egypt
   C. Broke down quickly as Lebanon refused to uphold its end of the agreement
   D. Established peaceful relations between Egypt and Israel
   E. Concluded a successful end to the Yom Kippur War

34. In creating their absolute systems of government, all of the absolute monarchies shared this common theme?

   A. Created a system to use trained bureaucratic officials
   B. Changed their respective societies too quickly and lost power in the end
   C. Caused massive splits inside their empires over religion
   D. Created and then worked within small, efficient, and easily controlled bureaucracies
   E. Controlled the "hearts and minds" of the people by tying religion to the central government

"All mankind...being all equal and independent, no one ought to harm another in his life, health, liberty, or possessions."

35. Which Enlightenment thinker wrote this?

   A. John Locke
   B. Baron de Montesquieu
   C. Voltaire
   D. Thomas Hobbes
   E. Jean Jacques Rousseau

36. The two major rivers on the Indian subcontinent that gave life to India are the

   A. Tigris and Euphrates.
   B. White and Blue Nile.
   C. Volga and Danube.
   D. Indus and Ganges.
   E. Ganges and Yangtze.

37. After Charlemagne's empire collapsed, what happened or changed in the political structuring in Western Europe, if anything?

   A. Government was dominated by the strong empire that Charlemagne's sons and their heirs inherited.
   B. Government was modeled on the success of the Byzantine Empire.
   C. Once again, government returned to small clans and tribes with regional or local loyalties.
   D. A new emphasis was focused on religious control of states and politics.
   E. They returned to a government run by regional monarchies with strong aristocracies.

"Its objective [is] to contribute effectively to the prevention of the proliferation of nuclear weapons in all its aspects, to the process of nuclear disarmament and therefore to the enhancement of international peace and security…"

—Nuclear Test Ban Treaty, 1963

38. Which event was in conflict with this document, as well as the idea of détente, thus leading to a renewed feeling of mistrust between the United States and the U.S.S.R.?

A. Fall of the Berlin Wall
B. Iranian hostage crisis
C. Election of Mikhail Gorbachev as premier
D. Soviet invasion of Afghanistan
E. Idea of a European Union

39. The effect of European imperialism and colonialism on the continent of Africa

A. resulted in a positive period of innovation.
B. was encouraged by the native population.
C. proved to be destructive for the native population.
D. was positive as Western ideas of government and justice were copied across the continent.
E. built a foundation of opposition to European governing styles.

40. Aztec civilization was centered at

A. Teotihuacan.
B. Tenochtitlan.
C. Cuzco.
D. Chavin.
E. Pochteca.

41. Compared to river valley cultures in Egypt and Mesopotamia, Chinese civilization

A. probably developed after civilizations in the Nile valley and southwest Asia.
B. predates the rise of civilization in both Egypt and Mesopotamia.
C. developed simultaneously with Egypt and Mesopotamia.
D. did not rely on heavy irrigation as year-round water was plentiful.
E. has no verifiable historic origins and left no written record.

42. Which three European powers had significant Polish populations and had their governmental structures overturned by the end of World War I?

A. Russia, Germany, England
B. Austria, Hungary, Germany
C. France, Germany, Austria
D. Russia, Germany, Austria
E. Germany, England, Austria

43. The Crimean War was a war between which of the following empires?

    A. Britain, France, and Russia against the Ottoman Empire and Austria
    B. Britain, France, and the Ottoman Empire against Russia
    C. Prussia and Russia against the Ottoman Empire and Britain
    D. Russia and the Ottoman Empire against Prussia and Austria
    E. Austria, Hungry, and Germany against the Ottoman Empire and Russia

44. In which of the following periods of Japanese history was Chinese cultural influence NOT significant?

    A. Taika
    B. Nara
    C. Heian
    D. Yoritomo/Kamukura
    E. Warlord

45. How did the government officials of Ieyasu resemble the Ming Confucian scholar officials?

    A. They were men of ability who were expected to lead by example.
    B. They undertook a rigorous exam system.
    C. They received their jobs based on *what* they knew instead of *who* they knew.
    D. They had to refrain from gambling, drinking, and looking opulent in public.
    E. They saw themselves as members of a family, forming an unbroken chain from the emperor to the peasants, and from the village to the trading towns to urban centers.

46. Which best describes the coronation of Charlemagne by Pope Leo III?

    A. It was an effort by the pope to enhance the church's stature and gain leverage over the king.
    B. It was a critical triumph for the papacy in securing church over state policy.
    C. It greatly enhanced the reputation of Charlemagne.
    D. Both A and C
    E. It put an end once and for all to the power struggle between the pope and the emperor.

47. Following the aftermath of the Vietnam War in the 1980s and early 1990s, what was the pattern that some East Asian governments began to follow?

    A. China turned increasingly to a market economy.
    B. China maintained its communist dictatorship.
    C. North Korea accepted the move to a market economy.
    D. Parliamentary democracy was the preferred system of government.
    E. Both A and B.

48. Which civilization developed the first form of writing called cuneiform?

    A. Assyrians
    B. Egyptians
    C. Babylonians
    D. Sumerians
    E. Phoenicians

"Let a ruler base his government upon virtuous principles, and he will be like the pole-star, which remains steadfast in its place, while all the host of stars turn towards it."

"By nature, men are nearly alike; by practice, they get to be wide apart."

"If I am walking with two people, both will be my teachers"

—Confucius, The Analects

49. What do these quotes tell us about the purpose of Confucian social relationships?

A. Established a hierarchy and insisted upon reciprocal duties between different people
B. Taught its parishioners to seek inner harmony by meditation
C. Used lavish rewards and severe punishments for transgressions to modify behavior
D. Were based on love and forgiveness
E. Stressed the welfare and the interests of the state over those of the individual

50. As William of Orange and Mary assumed the English throne, what did they, as royals, recognize that tied the throne to Parliament, changing monarchical power for England ever since?

A. Magna Carta
B. English Bill of Rights
C. Declaration of Indulgence
D. Petition of Right
E. Grand Remonstrance

51. Until the First Crusade, how long had Western Europe been out of contact with the rest of the world and unable to experience cultural diffusion?

A. 300 years
B. 400 years
C. 600 years
D. 1000 years
E. 180 years

52. Which of the following best allows modern-day scholars and historians to study Roman culture and civilization with relative ease?

A. The large number of physical Roman remains across Europe, Africa, and Asia—roads, bridges, aqueducts, and buildings
B. Written descriptions of Roman civilization by ancient historians
C. Frescos and other works of art that depicted daily life
D. Accounts written by citizens whose civilizations were conquered by Rome, which provided a realistic point of view
E. The many ideas of Roman law government and technology that we still use today

53. The following quote given in a speech by Sir Winston Churchill is regarded as the start of which conflict? "From Stettin in the Baltic to Trieste in the Adriatic, an iron curtain has descended across the Continent."

    A. Hitler's invasion of the Soviet Union

    B. Cold War

    C. World War II

    D. Franco-Prussian War

    E. Mussolini's quest to conquer Ethiopia

54. Both Confucians and Hindus place value on which of the following?

    A. Being solely focused on the conditions of the afterlife

    B. The justification of social inequality in both societies

    C. Placing increased stress on the importance of political activity

    D. Trying to prevent the expanding of the empire

    E. The building of magnificent palaces and temples

55. Identify the Straits of Magellan on the following map:

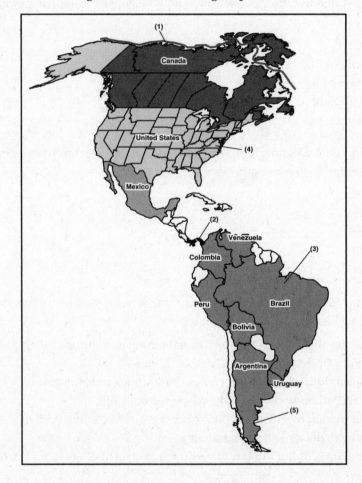

    A. (1)

    B. (2)

    C. (3)

    D. (4)

    E. (5)

56. Which of the following issues was one of the main causes for the split between the Roman Catholic and Orthodox churches after 1054?

    A. The Orthodox Church's lack of bishops
    B. The insistence of the patriarch of Constantinople on supremacy within church councils
    C. The segregation of monks within the Eastern Empire
    D. The Roman Catholic practice of requiring celibacy for its priests
    E. The Eastern emperor's insistence at making the church a part of the state bureaucracy

57. Starting with the first Ming ruler in 1368, what does this era of Chinese history resemble in one of the world's other great empires?

    A. Six centuries of growth for Japan
    B. Pax Romana for Rome
    C. Ottoman rule lasting through World War I
    D. The empire on which "the sun never set" in England
    E. Complete absolutism achieved by Louis XIV

58. Following the end of World War II, which of the following best describes Vietnam?

    A. It was not able to develop economically because it was plagued by wars.
    B. It became dominated politically by communist North Korea.
    C. It decided to adopt an economic model based on Japanese success before the war.
    D. It relied on the U.S.S.R. for subsidies and guidance.
    E. It created a British-style parliamentary system.

"If a man puts out the eye of a freed man, or breaks the bone of a freed man, he shall pay one gold mina."

"If a man puts out the eye of a man's slave, or breaks the bone of a man's slave, he shall pay one-half its value."

—Hammurabi's Code, Nos. 198 and 199

59. These laws from the Code of Hammurabi from ancient Babylonia reveal

    A. a relaxed, flexible society.
    B. a rigid class structure that was unequal.
    C. a rigid class structure that was equal.
    D. an attempt to organize society.
    E. laws that were tied to a strict religious order.

"I salute you all, sons of Mali…as long as I breathe, Mali will never be in thrall—rather death than slavery. We will live free because our ancestors lived free."

60. Which mid-13th century leader said this as he began to grow Mali's imperial power in Africa?

    A. Mansa Musa
    B. Sundiata
    C. Sahel
    D. Niani
    E. Nubia

"One should always speak the truth and tread incessantly on the path of righteousness."

"Only that person is preferred as a leader, who adheres by laws and rules."

"One should always help the weak, the destitute, and the impoverished."

—The Vedas

61. Why would these selections of the ancient Aryan Vedas be important to modern scholars?

A. They form a mirror image of the *Epic of Gilgamesh*.

B. They give us insight into what was important to the ancient Indians and form the basis of modern Indian society.

C. They explain the *Mahabharata*.

D. They explain what happened to the original Indian civilization.

E. They form the pattern that allows modern scholars to decipher the ancient Aryan alphabet.

62. The central theory of mercantilist economics was which of the following?

A. The world was full of limitless resources.

B. The world was bound by a scarcity of resources.

C. Spain should quickly form a transatlantic monopoly.

D. Always take into account the economic needs and wants of the colonists.

E. Colonies should extract raw materials to be provided for the motherland.

"I began the revolution with 82 men. If I had to do it again, I would do it with 10 or 15 and absolute faith. It does not matter how small you are if you have faith and a plan of action."

63. When this statement was issued, Cuban revolutionaries had just overthrown the government of which leader in 1959?

A. Fidel Castro

B. Simón Bolívar

C. Fulgencio Batista

D. Daniel Ortega

E. Pablo Escobar

64. Mughal Dynasty leader Akbar the Great wanted to unify his empire through which of the following?

A. Reforming the central and provincial government

B. Patronizing the arts and creating a "New India"

C. Governing through religious toleration

D. Reforming the unequal tax system

E. Islamic religious uniformity throughout India

"I came to office with one deliberate intent: to change Britain from a dependent to a self-reliant society.... This means creating a new culture—an enterprise culture—which accords a new status to the entrepreneur and offers him the rewards to match; which breeds a new generation of men and women who create jobs for others instead of waiting for others to create jobs for them."

65. Which British Conservative Party leader gave this speech?

   A. Queen Elizabeth
   B. Simone de Beauvoir
   C. Margaret Thatcher
   D. David Lloyd George
   E. John Keynes

66. Emperor Trajan's decision to conquer territory and tribes north of the Danube River had which of the following results for Rome?

   A. It enlarged the empire, gaining resources to sustain its growth.
   B. It overextended the ability of Rome to defend its borders, further weakening the empire.
   C. It created a new trade route and gained a new outlet for European traders.
   D. It angered the native Goths, who began to migrate into Roman territory.
   E. It allowed Diocletian to split the empire in half, keeping the Eastern Empire for himself, which limited Rome's access to the Eastern markets.

67. How did the spread of Islam differ in East Africa from that in Central and West Africa?

   A. East Africa was Islamized by overland routes, whereas West Africa was converted by sea routes.
   B. East Africa was Islamized by sea routes, whereas West Africa was converted by overland routes.
   C. West Africa was never Islamized as was East Africa.
   D. East Africa was converted by force and West Africa, by choice.
   E. West Africa was converted by force, whereas East Africa never converted.

68. How was the Revolution of Brazil different from revolutions during the same time period?

   A. It was simple, peaceful, and easy as the Portuguese monarchs left Portugal and moved to Brazil.
   B. It was even more violent than the French Revolution with atrocities committed on both sides.
   C. It was only the Creoles that rebelled to keep their rank and titles.
   D. The Brazilian Revolution never developed as there was no popular support.
   E. Unlike Haiti and Mexico, the peasant class did directly benefit from independence.

69. From 1100 C.E. to 1185 C.E., which of the following reasons was the cause of a major turning point in Japanese history?

   A. The Mongol invasions were repulsed.
   B. Governing authority was transferred to the military shogun.
   C. The Ashikaga Bakufu collapsed.
   D. Minamato Yoritomo took control assuming full governmental power.
   E. The second and final dynasty came to power.

70. Which of the following was the most powerful ruler of the ancient world?

    A. Chinese emperor
    B. Chief vizier
    C. Pharaoh
    D. Priest-king
    E. Council elder

71. After World War II, the British government agreed to the independence of India. As independence was about to happen, the attempted unification of Hindu and Muslim interests in India resulted in spreading violence, forcing the British government to do which of the following?

    A. Call on Mahatma Gandhi to quell the violence
    B. Separate the two opposing sides by creating the Muslim state of Pakistan
    C. Maintain a political occupation until 1999
    D. Install Jawaharlal Nehru as a dictator
    E. Leave the opposing sides to find a solution by themselves and pull out of India, which resulted in the deaths of thousands

72. Which of the following represents a similarity between the Ming and Ottoman Dynasties in terms of leadership?

    A. Both emperors were seen as fathers of their people.
    B. Both emperors limited contact between their people and the outside world for fear of corruption.
    C. Both societies were organized under strict military guidelines.
    D. Both societies sent future governmental leaders and officials to train in the provinces to gain experience before tackling larger problems.
    E. Both emperors came to power through violence and bloodshed.

73. How are the concepts of Hinduism's dharma similar to the sharia in Islam?

    A. Both stressed loyalty to the emperor.
    B. Both allowed the emperor to further centralize the power in the state.
    C. Both governed an individual's social, political, commercial, and religious conduct.
    D. Both explained the remoteness of the emperor from his subjects.
    E. Both described laws and punishments for each society.

74. How did the profit margin of the slave trade compare to that of other business opportunities during the transatlantic trade period?

    A. The slave trade was less profitable on the whole than other business ventures because the high risks outweighed the potential return.
    B. The slave trade became increasingly dangerous due to acts of piracy.
    C. Profits from the slave trade in the 18th century were so lucrative that money generated from the trade made the risks worth it and laid the financial foundation for the Industrial Revolution.
    D. The slave trade was slightly more profitable than similar traditional artisan practices.
    E. The upfront cost of the slave trade began to outweigh its profitability.

75. The Fertile Crescent has been called the crossroads of the world because it was

    A. the first center of advanced civilization.

    B. often flooded by the Tigris and Euphrates Rivers.

    C. protected from invasion by deserts and mountains.

    D. on the routes that connected Africa, Asia, and Europe.

    E. a civilization that spread outward from Mesopotamia to other regions.

76. This hallmark of Western civilization has been fiercely defended in the West, but is completely different in the East.

    A. Separation of church and state

    B. The concept of the Corpus Juris Civilis

    C. Having Rome as the geographical center of the empire

    D. The use of a trained and literate bureaucracy to govern the empire

    E. Having a cathedral at the center of each town

77. Why do historians know much more about the Aztecs than any other Mesoamerican civilization?

    A. They developed a writing system that is easily decipherable.

    B. The paintings and sculpture on temples closely resemble hieroglyphics.

    C. They were the first Mesoamerican civilization to have European contact.

    D. They were direct descendants of the Mayas.

    E. Their language is still spoken in many parts of Mesoamerica to this day.

78. This location exemplifies the grandeur of Moorish Islamic architecture.

    A. Museo de Barcelona

    B. Alhambra Mosque

    C. Richard the Lionheart's castle in Antioch

    D. Pharos lighthouse in Alexandria

    E. Coliseum of Tunisia

79. The 2014 annexation of the Crimean Peninsula by the Russian Federation is reminiscent of which other country's annexation of territory in the early to mid-20th century?

A. Prussia's acquisition of Alsace and Lorraine
B. Austria's gaining Serbia
C. Germany's gaining the Sudetenland from Czechoslovakia
D. Japan's gaining territory in Manchuria
E. Soviet acquisition of the Baltic states

80. Which African kingdom began its ascent to power in 350 C.E.?

A. Nubia
B. Axum
C. Meroe
D. Sudan
E. Ghana

81. The Tennis Court Oath was taken for which of the following reasons?

A. After the Third Estate left, the Estates-General began forming the National Assembly.
B. The First Estate issued a response to the raise in taxes.
C. To peacefully meet to request that the king step down from the throne to avoid violence
D. The Catholic majority of rural people wanted to prevent rioting in Paris.
E. To unite the aristocracy against the military forces threatening revolution

82. Which of the following is the biggest threat to modern global security?

A. the World Wide Web
B. terrorism
C. poverty in Third World nations
D. large accumulations of national debt
E. global warming

83. For what purpose was the Cantonese system of Ming China developed?

A. To limit the contacts of Chinese citizens and European merchants
B. To train Confucian officials by letting them gain experience in the provinces
C. To establish a system of taxation where yields of each harvest are measured, and the most plentiful regions pay a higher tax percentage
D. To promote the traditional Chinese idea that the entire population is one big family with the emperor as the head
E. To show the Japanese that true Confucianists do not need a shogun

84. Pope Gregory VII decreed the practice of investiture invalid. What was the practice of investiture?

A. The practice where regional aristocrats dressed in bishop's robes and attempted to enforce their policies as members of the church

B. The practice of state appointments of bishops who were coming from a secular background

C. The practice of trying clerics in secular courts to allow the aristocrats to gain further control of the church

D. The state's power to tax the church and its officials

E. Loaning money at high rates of interest to poor peasants

85. Unlike Mesopotamia and Egypt, the Harappa civilization in the Indus River Valley

A. became a geographic center for a unified, continuous culture lasting for thousands of years.

B. has writings that have never been translated.

C. was completely secure from nomadic invasions.

D. never developed a military social class.

E. developed a monotheistic religion.

86. On what continent(s) were these paleolithic cave paintings found?

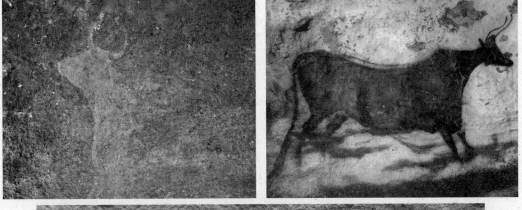

A. Australia

B. Africa and North America

C. Europe and Africa

D. Asia

E. All of the above

87. As Europe and North America became industrial powers, what was every other region of the world forced to do?

    A. Become suppliers of raw materials
    B. Become reactive and dependent economically and politically on the industrialized West
    C. Accept their positions as Second and Third World nations
    D. Become willing, active participants in the mercantilist system
    E. Industrialize as rapidly and completely as possible

88. Which was NOT a result of the Crusades?

    A. Religious and political success at freeing the Holy Land
    B. Creation of trade routes between East and West
    C. The creation of new industries and towns in new areas away from traditional towns and cities
    D. The creation of new religious military orders to combat the spread of Islam
    E. Exchanging of Western technological ideas to the population of Constantinople

"I have fulfilled the sacred promises which I made Peru…A numerous army, under the direction of warlike chiefs, is ready to march in a few days to put an end to the war. Nothing is left for me to do, but to offer you my sincerest thanks, and to promise, that if the liberties of the Peruvians shall ever be attacked, I shall claim the honor of accompanying them to defend their freedom like a citizen."

89. Who said this prior to the liberation of Peru from Spanish control?

    A. Simón Bolívar
    B. José de San Martín
    C. Bartolomé de Las Casas
    D. Maximilien Robespierre
    E. Francisco Pizarro

"If we have rice, we have everything; our people can eat their fill and we can export it for hard currency…The more we export, the better we can afford to buy equipment, machines, and other instruments necessary for building our industry…and for rapidly changing our agriculture."

—Pol Pot

90. Based on statements like this, Pol Pot became an internationally known figure because he

    A. was thrown out of power by the Vietnamese communist government.
    B. gained unlimited support from China.
    C. became the leader of the Khmer Rouge.
    D. became the first Asian leader to accept subsidies from the Soviet Union.
    E. worked to bring peace in Vietnam and Korea between U.S. and communist forces.

91. The great European "scramble for Africa" was largely over by

    A. 1840.
    B. 1805.
    C. 1914.
    D. 1900.
    E. 1945.

92. In which of the following ways were the Byzantine bureaucracy and the Chinese Confucian bureaucracy similar?

    A. There was an extensive state exam system in both empires.
    B. Emperors played a small role in government as they became mere figureheads.
    C. There was no link between the central bureaucracy and the local governmental administration.
    D. Both bureaucracies were open to talented commoners and men of ability, not just powerful aristocrats.
    E. They were subservient to the authority of the church.

93. In river valley societies, priests developed considerable power because they

    A. controlled agriculture.
    B. dominated government.
    C. owned the land.
    D. claimed to be able to interpret the gods' wishes and placate the gods.
    E. regulated trade between cities and regional centers.

94. The English Factory Act of 1833 was created to address which of the following problems?

    A. The 10-hour work day for children
    B. The lack of education in child workers
    C. The damage caused by the breakdown of traditional family structures
    D. The nurturing, discipline, and education of children almost exclusively in the hands of teachers and not the parents at home
    E. All of the above

95. The Sandinistas overthrew which U.S.-backed Nicaraguan regime in 1979?

    A. Ralul
    B. Somoza
    C. Mujahideen
    D. Escobar
    E. Contras

ANSWER KEY
Practice Test 1

1. B	25. E	49. A	73. C
2. A	26. C	50. B	74. C
3. C	27. B	51. C	75. D
4. C	28. B	52. A	76. A
5. B	29. D	53. B	77. C
6. E	30. B	54. B	78. B
7. E	31. C	55. E	79. C
8. B	32. A	56. D	80. B
9. A	33. D	57. B	81. A
10. D	34. D	58. A	82. B
11. E	35. A	59. B	83. A
12. B	36. D	60. B	84. B
13. D	37. E	61. B	85. B
14. D	38. D	62. E	86. C
15. C	39. C	63. C	87. B
16. B	40. B	64. C	88. D
17. B	41. A	65. C	89. B
18. A	42. D	66. B	90. C
19. D	43. B	67. B	91. C
20. B	44. D	68. A	92. D
21. C	45. A	69. B	93. D
22. E	46. D	70. C	94. E
23. B	47. E	71. B	95. B
24. B	48. D	72. D	

ANSWER EXPLANATIONS

1. **(B)** Both Confucius and Socrates felt that they were just transmitters of tradition and were not offering anything new.

2. **(A)** Northwestern Europe fell into a period of isolation during the Dark Ages. During this time, they formed a new, distinct culture. The period was also dominated by feudalism, which used the same social hierarchy seen in the historical development of Japan.

3. **(C)** Latin America became embroiled in the war of influence between the United States and U.S.S.R. Every country in Latin America was solicited by the opposing ideological rivals.

4. **(C)** The finding of King Tut's tomb revealed a wealth of archeological evidence as it is the only pharaoh's tomb ever found intact. It let us have an insight into what the world of a pharaoh was like.

5. **(B)** The unification of Germany proved to be the most important factor as Germany would shape many world events up to the beginning of the Cold War.

6. **(E)** By looking at the pyramids and ziggurats that have maintained structural integrity considering the necessary ability to organize the building materials and workers needed for such large-scale projects, it is easy to see the knowledge of complex mathematics and evidence of strong central authority in these ancient societies.

7. **(E)** The Shogunate of Tokugawa developed a policy of strict seclusion, cutting Japan off from the rest of world. The Meiji wanted to open up Japan and learn from the Western powers to adapt what they learned to fit a specific Japanese need.

8. **(B)** The city of Timbuktu became a leading cultural and intellectual center after the Hajj of Mansa Musa and other Malinke kings, who welcomed Islamic influence into West Africa.

9. **(A)** The city-state of Athens is associated with the concept of the polis, a city that acts as its own independent government. The creation of democracy occurred in Athens based on the concept of the polis.

10. **(D)** India depended on water coming from the spring monsoons, or seasonal winds, which brought much-needed rain to India.

11. **(E)** The finding of the New World by Spain spelled doom for millions of Native Americans and led to Spain being involved in the New World longer than any other European nation.

12. **(B)** Following the destruction caused by World War II, the United States wanted to eliminate the Japanese military command structure and military forces in order to bring democracy to the former empire of Japan by introducing a constitutional monarch.

13. **(D)** The civilization of Zimbabwe, including the Great Zimbabwe, was laid out with an acropolis in the middle. The acropolis was surrounded by a defensive wall and included temples to the main gods and granaries. Outside of the acropolis was the main city surrounded by another wall, and then outside the fortress were the

dwellings of the villagers. The Great Zimbabwe hilltop acropolis with its many smaller cities spread out over a wide area is similar, but not exactly identical to, the ancient Greek city-states and the layout of the Mayan Empire.

14. **(D)** Because China depended on an agricultural economy for centuries, both the nobles and the commoners depended on food and cash crops for survival as well as the chief economic enterprise.

15. **(C)** While Europe had changed dramatically beginning with the Renaissance, China and Japan had kept their traditional societies and had not modernized, giving them a look of slow-moving progress at best.

16. **(B)** A madrasa is the Islamic equivalent of a European college. Students were taught by a master who personally certified that their students had mastered their content.

17. **(B)** The people of Mesoamerica never developed the wheel because they did not have large beasts of burden, so everything was done by pure human labor.

18. **(A)** The Egyptian civilization was isolated for many years and had three main periods of history where dynastic rulers provided stability. In Mesopotamia, there were many different civilizations at war with each other, creating a turbulent atmosphere of instability with many rulers.

19. **(D)** Ram wanted to learn modern techniques and technology from England and then use them to be self-sufficient. It would remove India from British imperial control.

20. **(B)** The war in Russia between the Red Communists and the White Traditionalists turned quickly into a civil war.

21. **(C)** The great thinkers and scientists studied at the House of Muses, created by Alexander the Great in Alexandria, Egypt.

22. **(E)** The civilizations of the Americas all practiced pyramidal or advanced monumental architecture, all were polytheistic (with the sun god being dominant), all practiced human sacrifice (with the Aztecs using it daily to power the sun and the Incas using it the least), and all had some variation of a soccer/basketball/rugby match for both entertainment and religious purposes.

23. **(B)** The weakening of the Soviet Union was displayed to the world in May 1989 during the Tiananmen Square protest for greater democracy in China. In November 1989, East German and West German citizens celebrated the tearing down of the Berlin Wall, allowing them to freely travel once again.

24. **(B)** Emperor Justinian reigned during the early Byzantine Empire, which was experiencing its Golden Age. The fall of Rome was not forgotten, and Justinian had visions of becoming emperor of a united empire and restoring the greatness of the empire.

25. **(E)** The Bantu migrations took place over thousands of years. West African farmers migrated to the central and eastern coasts of Africa while working their way south. Along the way, they displaced other smaller groups of people, while spreading their technology and root language dialect.

26. **(C)** Emperor Justinian wanted to centralize his power as well as create religious and legal conformity within his empire. Using the "one god, one religion, one empire" philosophy, Justinian had his scholars revise centuries of Roman law into the Corpus Juris Civilis, or body of common law. Corpus Juris Civilis streamlined and got rid of contradictory laws but kept those that helped Justinian.

27. **(B)** The effects of the Great Depression were felt around the world, but the impact was less severe in Japan. They had gone off the gold standard of backing a paper currency and were devoted to self-sufficiency when it came to industrialization and a viable economy.

28. **(B)** The Muslim occupation of the Byzantine Empire, and subsequent cutoff of information and technology, forced Western Europe to look at its own resources to survive. They combined classical Roman culture and Germanic traditions to survive and create a new culture to replace what was lost during the collapse.

29. **(D)** Peter went abroad to learn and copy manufacturing ideas of the Western powers so he could build industries devoted to a strong military that would be loyal to him.

30. **(B)** The troubles experienced by the developing African states are the result of colonial empires extracting wealth and raw materials at the expense of the native Africans, who were not taught how to run any business other than to provide cheap labor. When the colonial powers left after World War II, the countries began to deteriorate because they did not have the education or knowledge to make the systems run.

31. **(C)** As the Muslim army moved eastward, the indigenous Indian religion of Buddhism was nearly erased as Hinduism and Islam came to dominate and move further eastward into China.

32. **(A)** After the Bering Strait melted, the land bridge between Asia and North America was broken. As a result, the Americas were cut off from cultural diffusion and remained behind in technology.

33. **(D)** This was the high point of President Carter's presidency as the former antagonists—Islamic Egypt and Israel—formed peaceful relations, which was a groundbreaking historic achievement.

34. **(D)** Each king or emperor limited his bureaucracy to a few ministers or offices so they could remain hands-on. They knew exactly what was happening throughout their empire by meeting daily with a few key advisors.

35. **(A)** John Locke was a philosopher who believed that people were basically good and moral. According to Locke, they were also entitled to natural rights, which were things that everyone has from the time they are born.

36. **(D)** The Indus and Ganges Rivers were fed by the monsoon rains that flooded and gave life to northern and eastern India, where the largest parts of the population lived in the ancient civilization.

37. **(E)** With no strong leader to keep the tribes united, European rulers retreated to the castle mentality of self-sufficiency. They stayed unnoticed in their castles, only looking out for themselves, and they did not want to be part of an empire as a whole.

38. **(D)** The Soviet invasion of Afghanistan made all the promises of goodwill and cooperation seem hollow as Cold War tensions once again began to rise when the Soviets invaded in 1979.

39. **(C)** The European colonization proved to be destructive to the people. They had their natural resources extracted from the land and were forced into a system of governmental and labor subservience to their colonial rulers, who gave no profits or benefits to the native populations.

40. **(B)** Tenochtitlan was the center of the Aztec civilization and became the most populous city in Mesoamerica. It was built on islands in the center of a lake.

41. **(A)** Due to the greater distance needed to travel and the geography to cross, China probably developed later than Egypt or Mesopotamia.

42. **(D)** These three Central/Eastern European powers had large Polish populations as well as members of other groups who thought their own interests were more important than the interests of the larger empire. As a result, they had their traditional governments overthrown.

43. **(B)** Czar Nicholas I of Russia was after a warm water port on the Crimean peninsula, so Russia fought for the port against the Ottoman Empire and its new allies: England and France.

44. **(D)** When Minamoto Yoritomo decreed that Japan had learned all it could from China, Japan decided to turn inward and focus on Japanese interests alone.

45. **(A)** Just like Confucian scholars, Japanese officials were to be seen as role models to the people and, as a result, were held to a higher standard.

46. **(D)** Pope Leo III wanted to demonstrate the supremacy of the Church by creating and crowning the Holy Roman emperor. On the other hand, having the pope crown him added credibility and validity to Charlemagne's title as emperor, so it helped both parties.

47. **(E)** Even though China maintained a communist dictatorship, it began to move increasingly toward a market economy because of its natural resources and cheap labor force.

48. **(D)** The first writing system was developed in ancient Sumeria around 3000 B.C.E.

49. **(A)** Confucian social relationships were meant to build a chain of unity from the emperor to the poorest peasant by giving most people a "superior and inferior" relationship responsibility where they have to teach and listen. By following these rules, society will create harmony.

50. **(B)** The English Bill of Rights gave basic rights to the aristocracy and limited the power of the monarchy.

51. **(C)** Roughly 600 years passed from the fall of Rome in 476 C.E. to the First Crusade, which was launched in 1092. During this time, Western Europe experienced little, if any, cultural diffusion.

52. **(A)** Ancient Rome left behind a great deal of easily seen physical remains. Some examples are the city of Pompeii, the Pont du Gard bridge near Nimes, France, and

aqueducts that still bring water to cities in Spain. These physical remains allow scholars and historians to easily study Roman culture and civilization as they can easily touch it and see it during their research.

53. **(B)** Churchill's speech at Westminster College in Missouri is seen as the beginning of the Cold War, which affected the world for most of the late 20th century.

54. **(B)** Both the caste system and filial piety placed specific roles on people in society in a rigid hierarchical system.

55. **(E)** Magellan entered a small bay in November 1520 at the tip of South America, and despite strong winds and cross-currents in the ocean, he and his men rounded the Horn of South America to continue their legendary voyage around the globe.

56. **(D)** One of the three main disputes was the Roman Catholic policy of having its priests married to the church, so it remained the center of their focus during this troubled time. Catholic priests were not allowed to marry, whereas in the Byzantine Empire, they were. However, Byzantine bishops and monks were not allowed to marry.

57. **(B)** The start of the Ming Dynasty brought nearly 600 years of continued growth for China, resembling Pax Romana in ancient Rome.

58. **(A)** Indochina/Vietnam was not able to build any type of economy as it was engaged in nearly 30 years of war, first against the French and then against South Vietnam and the United States, who were fighting against communist North Vietnam.

59. **(B)** Hammurabi's Code displays harsh penalties for crimes, which are even harsher on poor people and women. This shows an unequal class structure.

60. **(B)** Sundiata reigned from 1230 C.E. to 1255 C.E. During this time, the kingdom of Mali experienced a large population growth. Sundiata used his resources of agricultural wealth and commercial skill to build the magnificent city of Timbuktu, which bound together the large, diverse Malian Empire.

61. **(B)** The Vedas tell us what was important to the ancient Aryans in terms of society and laws. The Vedas formed the basis of the Hindu religion.

62. **(E)** Colonies were areas of plentiful resources that should be extracted for the specific purpose of increasing the wealth of the mother country.

63. **(C)** On New Year's Eve 1959, Fidel Castro uttered these words as he and his revolutionaries overthrew the corrupt U.S.-backed government of Fulgencio Batista.

64. **(C)** Unlike many of his contemporaries, Akbar went to great lengths to understand what religions had in common rather than what separated them. He held conversations with religious leaders and recognized the different faiths in his kingdom.

65. **(C)** Margaret Thatcher became the first female prime minister of England. She sought to halt the economic decline of her country by cutting back on governmental bureaucracy, allowing the privatization of governmental business. Thatcher was never able to revive the economy to her expectations.

66. **(B)** Trajan overextended the empire as the army did not have enough men to control the entire border. The attacks provoked war with a new group of barbarian invaders that kept slipping through holes in the massive border to attack and disrupt the Roman Empire, eventually leading to its fall.

67. **(B)** East Africa was converted mainly by sea traders due to its proximity to the Middle East. West and Central Africa were converted by warriors and merchants who came to West Africa over the trans-Sahara trade routes.

68. **(A)** The Portuguese monarchy, fleeing from Napoleon, came to their colony in Brazil and set up their kingdom in Brazil with no violence at all.

69. **(B)** The emperor became a figurehead as a shogun (military general) began to run the day-to-day operations of governing Japan.

70. **(C)** Because Egypt was isolated and the pharaoh was seen as a living representation of the sun on Earth, the Egyptian pharaoh was the most powerful monarch of the ancient world. The pharaoh owned all of the land and resources and was able to command the entire empire.

71. **(B)** The British government decided to divide, or partition, the subcontinent of India in 1947. The Hindu majority received a larger portion of India, and Muslim Pakistan received less. Thousands of people crossed the border in both directions for safety as coexisting proved to be difficult.

72. **(D)** Both the Confucian scholars of China and the royal sons of the sultan had to learn in the provinces. They governed small villages and towns, gaining the skills necessary to run a large empire. Only then would they move up in position after they proved themselves.

73. **(C)** Dharma and the sharia are meant to be guides, or rulebooks, on how you should live your life not just publically, but privately as well.

74. **(C)** The slave trade was so lucrative that if a slave ship made one successful round trip to Africa and back, the profits for investors was immense. The slave trade provided the capital for the upcoming Industrial Revolution.

75. **(D)** The Fertile Crescent was the place where many trade routes that connected Africa, Asia, and Europe came together. You could not leave one continent and get into another without going through this region.

76. **(A)** When Rome collapsed, only the church retained the governmental structure of the old empire due to the absence of any central government to fill that role in the West. However, in the Eastern Empire, the church served as the government. Along with its primary mission to save souls during this troubled time period, the church had the power to remain separate from secular political authority.

77. **(C)** They were the first to encounter a large European contingent. Historians have many accounts of the Spanish descriptions of the Aztecs and their society. Even with the heavy Spanish bias, historians know much more about them as a result.

78. **(B)** The famous Alhambra Mosque in Cordoba, Spain, was built by Abd al-Rahman I. Both Muslim and Christian students studied at Alhambra together for many years until the Reconquista of Spain started after the death of Abd al-Rahman III.

79. **(C)** The annexation of the Crimea, because it held Russians in a traditionally Russian-cultured area, is eerily reminiscent of what Hitler did during his rule in Germany with the acquisition of the German-culture-dominated Sudetenland in 1938.

80. **(B)** The East African kingdom of Axum began its ascent to power in 350 C.E. because of its access to the Red Sea and its military power.

81. **(A)** The Third Estate left with sympathetic members of the First and Second Estates to begin forming a new legislature called the National Assembly.

82. **(B)** Because of the differing forms of terrorism, from physical acts of terror to cyber-terrorism, it is difficult to combat at times, making it the biggest threat to modern global security.

83. **(A)** After European sailors demonstrated poor behavior, the Ming emperors restricted foreign sailors to one port in Canton. They isolated a spit of land to prevent them from entering China proper.

84. **(B)** Nobles were naming their friends and relatives to high positions within the church to increase their power and control in local areas.

85. **(B)** The Rosetta Stone in Egypt and the Bahistan rock in Mesopotamia allowed us to translate writings in Egypt and Mesopotamia. There has been no decoding device found in the earliest civilization of India, so their writing remains a mystery.

86. **(C)** One of the most common misconceptions in world history is that people on different continents were cut off from one another throughout much of world history. This is simply not true. Evidence of interaction is seen in cave paintings in North Africa and the southern coast of Spain and France. The paintings show amazing similarities of humans hunting large animals.

87. **(B)** Other areas of the world provided necessary raw materials and became dependent on the industrialized West.

88. **(D)** The pope sent knights to give war-ravaged Europe a break, and no new orders of religious knights were created.

89. **(B)** Peru, and much of southern South America, was liberated by José de San Martín.

90. **(C)** Pol Pot became the totalitarian leader of the Khmer Rouge in Cambodia during the Vietnam War. He was determined to bring about agriculture-based socialism and forced thousands of urban-dwelling citizens to relocate to the countryside to undergo massive labor projects.

91. **(C)** By the outbreak of World War I, the scramble for Africa had ended as only Ethiopia and Liberia remained untouched by European imperial powers.

92. **(D)** Both the Byzantine and Chinese empires created exams and opened governmental jobs to men of ability. *What* a man knew became more important than *whom* he knew. This ensured a better and more efficient governmental administration.

93. **(D)** Priests and priest-kings gained control over early cities because of the claim that they could speak to the gods, interpret their messages, and know how to please them.

94. **(E)** The English Factory Act required an eight-hour workday for children, followed by two hours of education paid for by the factory owner. This was done as a way to rebuild the loss of family time as nearly all the family was involved in the industrial process in some way.

95. **(B)** The Sandinistas overthrew the Somoza family, who had held power since 1936. The Somozas had been backed by the United States due to a strong anticommunist stance after World War II. However, after the Somoza family stole much of the country's wealth, many smaller groups unified under the title of Sandinista (named after a 1930s revolutionary leader) and won victory in 1979.

ANSWER SHEET
Practice Test 2

1. Ⓐ Ⓑ Ⓒ Ⓓ Ⓔ   25. Ⓐ Ⓑ Ⓒ Ⓓ Ⓔ   49. Ⓐ Ⓑ Ⓒ Ⓓ Ⓔ   73. Ⓐ Ⓑ Ⓒ Ⓓ Ⓔ
2. Ⓐ Ⓑ Ⓒ Ⓓ Ⓔ   26. Ⓐ Ⓑ Ⓒ Ⓓ Ⓔ   50. Ⓐ Ⓑ Ⓒ Ⓓ Ⓔ   74. Ⓐ Ⓑ Ⓒ Ⓓ Ⓔ
3. Ⓐ Ⓑ Ⓒ Ⓓ Ⓔ   27. Ⓐ Ⓑ Ⓒ Ⓓ Ⓔ   51. Ⓐ Ⓑ Ⓒ Ⓓ Ⓔ   75. Ⓐ Ⓑ Ⓒ Ⓓ Ⓔ
4. Ⓐ Ⓑ Ⓒ Ⓓ Ⓔ   28. Ⓐ Ⓑ Ⓒ Ⓓ Ⓔ   52. Ⓐ Ⓑ Ⓒ Ⓓ Ⓔ   76. Ⓐ Ⓑ Ⓒ Ⓓ Ⓔ
5. Ⓐ Ⓑ Ⓒ Ⓓ Ⓔ   29. Ⓐ Ⓑ Ⓒ Ⓓ Ⓔ   53. Ⓐ Ⓑ Ⓒ Ⓓ Ⓔ   77. Ⓐ Ⓑ Ⓒ Ⓓ Ⓔ
6. Ⓐ Ⓑ Ⓒ Ⓓ Ⓔ   30. Ⓐ Ⓑ Ⓒ Ⓓ Ⓔ   54. Ⓐ Ⓑ Ⓒ Ⓓ Ⓔ   78. Ⓐ Ⓑ Ⓒ Ⓓ Ⓔ
7. Ⓐ Ⓑ Ⓒ Ⓓ Ⓔ   31. Ⓐ Ⓑ Ⓒ Ⓓ Ⓔ   55. Ⓐ Ⓑ Ⓒ Ⓓ Ⓔ   79. Ⓐ Ⓑ Ⓒ Ⓓ Ⓔ
8. Ⓐ Ⓑ Ⓒ Ⓓ Ⓔ   32. Ⓐ Ⓑ Ⓒ Ⓓ Ⓔ   56. Ⓐ Ⓑ Ⓒ Ⓓ Ⓔ   80. Ⓐ Ⓑ Ⓒ Ⓓ Ⓔ
9. Ⓐ Ⓑ Ⓒ Ⓓ Ⓔ   33. Ⓐ Ⓑ Ⓒ Ⓓ Ⓔ   57. Ⓐ Ⓑ Ⓒ Ⓓ Ⓔ   81. Ⓐ Ⓑ Ⓒ Ⓓ Ⓔ
10. Ⓐ Ⓑ Ⓒ Ⓓ Ⓔ   34. Ⓐ Ⓑ Ⓒ Ⓓ Ⓔ   58. Ⓐ Ⓑ Ⓒ Ⓓ Ⓔ   82. Ⓐ Ⓑ Ⓒ Ⓓ Ⓔ
11. Ⓐ Ⓑ Ⓒ Ⓓ Ⓔ   35. Ⓐ Ⓑ Ⓒ Ⓓ Ⓔ   59. Ⓐ Ⓑ Ⓒ Ⓓ Ⓔ   83. Ⓐ Ⓑ Ⓒ Ⓓ Ⓔ
12. Ⓐ Ⓑ Ⓒ Ⓓ Ⓔ   36. Ⓐ Ⓑ Ⓒ Ⓓ Ⓔ   60. Ⓐ Ⓑ Ⓒ Ⓓ Ⓔ   84. Ⓐ Ⓑ Ⓒ Ⓓ Ⓔ
13. Ⓐ Ⓑ Ⓒ Ⓓ Ⓔ   37. Ⓐ Ⓑ Ⓒ Ⓓ Ⓔ   61. Ⓐ Ⓑ Ⓒ Ⓓ Ⓔ   85. Ⓐ Ⓑ Ⓒ Ⓓ Ⓔ
14. Ⓐ Ⓑ Ⓒ Ⓓ Ⓔ   38. Ⓐ Ⓑ Ⓒ Ⓓ Ⓔ   62. Ⓐ Ⓑ Ⓒ Ⓓ Ⓔ   86. Ⓐ Ⓑ Ⓒ Ⓓ Ⓔ
15. Ⓐ Ⓑ Ⓒ Ⓓ Ⓔ   39. Ⓐ Ⓑ Ⓒ Ⓓ Ⓔ   63. Ⓐ Ⓑ Ⓒ Ⓓ Ⓔ   87. Ⓐ Ⓑ Ⓒ Ⓓ Ⓔ
16. Ⓐ Ⓑ Ⓒ Ⓓ Ⓔ   40. Ⓐ Ⓑ Ⓒ Ⓓ Ⓔ   64. Ⓐ Ⓑ Ⓒ Ⓓ Ⓔ   88. Ⓐ Ⓑ Ⓒ Ⓓ Ⓔ
17. Ⓐ Ⓑ Ⓒ Ⓓ Ⓔ   41. Ⓐ Ⓑ Ⓒ Ⓓ Ⓔ   65. Ⓐ Ⓑ Ⓒ Ⓓ Ⓔ   89. Ⓐ Ⓑ Ⓒ Ⓓ Ⓔ
18. Ⓐ Ⓑ Ⓒ Ⓓ Ⓔ   42. Ⓐ Ⓑ Ⓒ Ⓓ Ⓔ   66. Ⓐ Ⓑ Ⓒ Ⓓ Ⓔ   90. Ⓐ Ⓑ Ⓒ Ⓓ Ⓔ
19. Ⓐ Ⓑ Ⓒ Ⓓ Ⓔ   43. Ⓐ Ⓑ Ⓒ Ⓓ Ⓔ   67. Ⓐ Ⓑ Ⓒ Ⓓ Ⓔ   91. Ⓐ Ⓑ Ⓒ Ⓓ Ⓔ
20. Ⓐ Ⓑ Ⓒ Ⓓ Ⓔ   44. Ⓐ Ⓑ Ⓒ Ⓓ Ⓔ   68. Ⓐ Ⓑ Ⓒ Ⓓ Ⓔ   92. Ⓐ Ⓑ Ⓒ Ⓓ Ⓔ
21. Ⓐ Ⓑ Ⓒ Ⓓ Ⓔ   45. Ⓐ Ⓑ Ⓒ Ⓓ Ⓔ   69. Ⓐ Ⓑ Ⓒ Ⓓ Ⓔ   93. Ⓐ Ⓑ Ⓒ Ⓓ Ⓔ
22. Ⓐ Ⓑ Ⓒ Ⓓ Ⓔ   46. Ⓐ Ⓑ Ⓒ Ⓓ Ⓔ   70. Ⓐ Ⓑ Ⓒ Ⓓ Ⓔ   94. Ⓐ Ⓑ Ⓒ Ⓓ Ⓔ
23. Ⓐ Ⓑ Ⓒ Ⓓ Ⓔ   47. Ⓐ Ⓑ Ⓒ Ⓓ Ⓔ   71. Ⓐ Ⓑ Ⓒ Ⓓ Ⓔ   95. Ⓐ Ⓑ Ⓒ Ⓓ Ⓔ
24. Ⓐ Ⓑ Ⓒ Ⓓ Ⓔ   48. Ⓐ Ⓑ Ⓒ Ⓓ Ⓔ   72. Ⓐ Ⓑ Ⓒ Ⓓ Ⓔ

Practice Test 2

"It is my fervent hope that, once Your Highness perceives the extent of the injustices suffered by these innocent peoples and the way in which they are being destroyed and crushed underfoot, unjustly, and for no other reason than to satisfy the greed and ambition of those whose purpose it is to commit such wicked atrocities, Your Highness will see fit to beg and entreat His Majesty to refuse all those who see royal license for such evil and detestable ventures…"

—Bartolomé de Las Casas

1. Based on this passage, what was the primary purpose of *The Black Legend*?

   A. Reveal the true Spanish treatment of Native Americans as being inhumane
   B. Condemn exploitation of Native Americans by the Roman Catholic Church
   C. Provide a history of the English traders who were trying to capture Spanish territory
   D. Describe the European diseases that decimated Native American tribes
   E. Exploit people who were better able to endure hard physical labor because of their adaptability to geography

"Fight them with your faith in God, fight them in defense of every free honorable woman and every innocent child, and in defense of the values of manhood and the military honor…. Fight them because with their defeat you will be at the last entrance of the conquest of all conquests. The war will end with… dignity, glory, and triumph for your people, army, and nation."

—Saddam Hussein, January 19, 1991

2. Which oil-producing country in the Persian Gulf had Saddam Hussein already invaded when he made this speech?

   A. Saudi Arabia
   B. United Arab Emirates
   C. Bahrain
   D. Kuwait
   E. Yemen

3. The Han Dynasty was the contemporary of what other great world civilization?

   A. Classical Greece
   B. Classical Rome
   C. The spreading of Islam
   D. Europe in the Middle Ages
   E. Feudal Japan

4. The view that has been perpetuated that the region of Africa south of the Sahara as being isolated from civilization until it was "discovered" by Europeans

   A. has largely proved true.
   B. badly distorts reality.
   C. is substantiated by recent archeological research.
   D. is backed up by written documents from several different sources.
   E. is just a theory.

5. Who was the scholar hired by Charlemagne to organize and create his palace school to create better administrators?

   A. Einhard
   B. Angilbert
   C. Alcuin of York
   D. Theodoric
   E. Francis

6. British expansion and involvement into the economic way of life of the rural Indian countryside had which effect on most Indians?

   A. It brought about famine, which forced many Indians into indentured servitude.
   B. It forced them to accept the laws of the British East India Company.
   C. It caused the destruction of traditional farming methods and techniques.
   D. It allowed the crown to enforce their system of direct rule.
   E. It forced rural Indians to pay more lagan, or taxes, to the British colonial government.

7. What is the primary drawback to accepting the written descriptions of outside sources as valid evidence for African history?

   A. They only give us reliable access to relatively recent history.
   B. There are very few accounts available.
   C. They are often riddled with strong biases.
   D. They only focus on the larger African societies.
   E. The language of the era is still undecipherable.

8. Which of the following combinations made up the Triple Alliance in World War I?

   A. France, Germany, and Russia
   B. Italy, Russia, and Austria-Hungary
   C. Germany, Austria-Hungary, Ottoman Empire, and Italy
   D. England, France, and the United States
   E. France, Ottoman Empire, and Russia

9. Why did Pope Urban II launch the First Crusade?

   A. To possibly begin the process of the reunification of the church
   B. To get the warring Christian knights out of Europe and focus on an external enemy
   C. The Eastern emperor asked him for help, thus acknowledging his authority
   D. To help the peasants enjoy a period of peace
   E. All of the above

10. Teotihuacan's influence on the surrounding territory waned about 500 C.E. because of

    A. an invasion by the Aztecs.

    B. the Spanish presence in the region.

    C. a massive fire destroying much of the city.

    D. factors that are still poorly understood.

    E. an earthquake that killed most of the civilization.

11. Which religion played a key role in the transmission of several aspects of Chinese civilization to Japan?

    A. Buddhism

    B. Daoism

    C. Judaism

    D. Christianity

    E. Hinduism

12. Otto von Bismarck was a key figure in mid-19th century political events for accomplishing which of the following?

    A. Orchestrating the unification of Germany

    B. Writing the Treaty of Versailles after World War I

    C. Becoming a vocal critic of several European monarchies and hastening their overthrow

    D. Dealing two decisive blows to two major European powers

    E. Both A and D

13. The two main factors that determined the strictness and authoritarian aspects of Spartan society were

    A. the conquest of Persia and the beginning of trade with foreigners from Asia.

    B. the conquest of Messina and the enslavement of the helots.

    C. the rigorous training to win individual glory and their dislike for Athens.

    D. the Spartan mistrust of Athens and of their desire to compete with them.

    E. the Spartan ideals of isolation and self-sufficiency.

14. Which foreign power was able to exercise and maintain a strong influence over Latin America in the early decades of the 19th century?

    A. Germany

    B. The United States

    C. Britain

    D. Portugal

    E. France

15. By 1600, which of the following empires controlled a vast territory and was as strong as any other empire in Western Europe and China?

    A. Safavid

    B. Ottoman

    C. Mughal

    D. Seljuk

    E. Fatimid

16. When it is compared to modern American ideals about democracy, the form of democracy practiced in ancient Athens was different as it was designed to do which of the following?

    A. Urge the aristocratic assembly to allow plebeians to enter the assembly
    B. Separate foreign residents from natural-born native Athenians
    C. Require experienced generals to serve as governors to the districts they conquered
    D. Have all citizens participate directly in law and governmental policy making
    E. Expand and extend citizenship to those who could benefit the city-state of Athens

17. The Tang and Song Dynasties depended on which of the following institutions or groups to help them govern the Chinese empire?

    A. Aristocratic landlords
    B. Confucian scholar officials
    C. Widespread merchant guilds
    D. Buddhist monasteries
    E. Family members appointed by the emperor

18. Which two monarchies became governed by a code of written law that was proactive and preventative in nature?

    A. Ottoman and France
    B. Ottoman and Tokugawa
    C. Tokugawa and Ming
    D. Stuart and Ottoman
    E. Romanov and Ottoman

19. "Soldiers, Sailors, and Airmen of the Allied Expeditionary Force! You are about to embark upon the Great Crusade, toward which we have striven these many months. The eyes of the world are upon you." To which event is this quote referring?

    A. D-Day
    B. Pearl Harbor
    C. Surrender of Japan
    D. Berlin Airlift
    E. Armistice ending World War I

Legalist arguments: "When the revenue for the defence of the frontier fell short, the salt and iron monopoly was established…and the system of equitable marketing introduced…and wealth increased so as to furnish frontier expenses…A Receiving Bureau has been established…to monopolize all the commodities…known as the balancing standard. With the balancing standard, people are safeguarded from unemployment…"

Confucian arguments: "It is our humble opinion that the principle of ruling men lies in…discouraging mercantile pursuits….But now, with the system of salt and iron monopolies…the Government has entered into financial competition with the people…sanctioning selfishness and greed. The establishment of the salt and iron monopoly…to supply the army needs were not permanent schemes; it is therefore desirable that they now be abolished."

20. Based on your knowledge of the Han Dynasty, use the above passages to determine the outcome of the Salt and Iron Debates between Confucian and legalist scholars:

   A. Legalists were able to claim victory, saying that the state could legally enjoy profits from the sale of monopolized products.
   B. Confucian scholars were able to claim victory, saying that resources should be left in private hands because the moral purity of officials would be corrupted as they would be nothing more than lowly merchants.
   C. Merchants claimed victory as their status would rise in society when they were able to make vast sums of money.
   D. Neither side could claim victory as the Han economic reforms made the country so economically powerful that the emperor chose not to listen to either side.
   E. The emperor said, "I will institute a policy of ever-level granaries for the good of all China," and "I will do as I please as I am the emperor."

21. Which of the following groups formed the core population of the Mali state?

   A. Keita
   B. Malinke
   C. Askia Dawud
   D. Bilal
   E. Funji

22. Which event finally prompted Czar Alexander II to make long overdue necessary reforms?

   A. The request of his father, Nicholas I
   B. The Russian loss in the Russo-Japanese War
   C. The Russian loss in the Crimean War
   D. Russia gaining its long sought-after warm water port in Vladivostok
   E. The final conquest of the Russian boyars and the elimination of their ability to impact the government

23. Muslim orthodoxy can be best defined as

    A. a set of rigid theological controls imposed by the Qur'an.
    B. terms of what Muslims *do* rather than what they *believe*.
    C. intolerance within the Muslim ulama.
    D. "prophet-dominated" rather than "idea-dominated" theology.
    E. terms of domination and subservience.

24. Which of the following are similarities between Mesoamerica and other early civilizations and their cultures?

    A. Pyramid building
    B. Governmental forums
    C. Guilds for merchants
    D. Accurate calendars
    E. All of the above

"The seeds of totalitarian regimes are nurtured by misery and want. They spread and grow in the evil soil of poverty and strife. They reach their full growth when the hope of a people for a better life has died. We must keep that hope alive. The free peoples of the world look to us for support in maintaining their freedoms. If we falter in our leadership, we may endanger the peace of the world—and we shall surely endanger the welfare of our own nation. Great responsibilities have been placed upon us by the swift movement of events."

25. Which strategy did the United States employ toward communism following this 1947 address presented to a joint session of the United States Congress?

    A. The policy of containment, known as the Truman Doctrine, of preventing the spread of communism
    B. Halting the swift and immediate destruction of communism to a policy of acceptance and unity
    C. Ending the war with North Korea but continuing into China
    D. Promoted a policy of patience and vigilance until the threat died out on its own
    E. Working to achieve unification of the Korean Peninsula

26. After the Portuguese came to Africa, the major African kingdom that they developed agreements with was

    A. Senegambia.
    B. Liberia.
    C. Congo.
    D. Gold Coast.
    E. Ethiopia.

27. Based on the following map, which country became home to the terrorist group al-Qaeda and the Taliban between 1980 and 2008?

A. Pakistan
B. Iraq
C. Iran
D. Afghanistan
E. Sudan

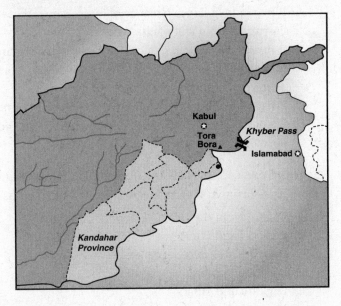

28. The Delian League quickly became an Athenian empire after the Persian wars because of which of the following reasons?
    A. Because of the devastating effects of the Persian wars and the unwillingness of the allies to defend themselves, the Ethenian Empire no longer saw a threat.
    B. The Persian threat was becoming more dangerous once again.
    C. The attack on the city of Syracuse on Sicily cost the League most of its navy.
    D. The city-state of Delos did not like being responsible for the treasury.
    E. Athens stood alone as the single most militarily powerful city-state so they claimed leadership.

29. How did the spreading of Islam differ in Eastern Africa from that of its spread in Western Africa?

    A. East Africa was Islamized by Muslims using overland routes, whereas West Africa was converted mostly by sea routes.
    B. East Africa was Islamized by sea routes due to its proximity, whereas West Africa was converted by Muslims using overland routes.
    C. West Africa was never Islamized as it was too far to travel through the Sahara.
    D. East Africa was converted by military force, and West African leaders chose conversion.
    E. West Africa was converted by force, whereas East Africa never converted as Christianity had a deep hold on the region.

30. By 1991, two decades of peace after nearly three decades of war in Vietnam had which of the following effects on the unified Vietnamese economy?

A. It began to collapse because of fears of instability within the government and corruption that still plagued the country.

B. It finally was able to gain self-sufficiency in a manufacturing-based economy.

C. It began to achieve a high rate of growth due to an influx of, and steadily growing, sources of foreign investment.

D. It became increasingly militarized to prevent outside capitalist influences.

E. It isolated itself from participating in the global economy to focus on domestic development.

31. Which two countries experienced similar circumstances and positions when industrializing in their respective geographic regions?

A. England and the United States

B. England and France

C. United States and Germany

D. Japan and Korea

E. England and Japan

32. Without metal, which of the following materials was used to make weapons and tools in early Mesoamerica?

A. Flint

B. Gold

C. Obsidian

D. Copper

E. Bronze

"Good people do not need laws to tell them to act responsibly, while bad people will find a way around the laws."

"When there is an income tax, the just man will pay more and the unjust less on the same amount of income."

"The curse of me and my nation is that we always think things can be bettered by immediate action of some sort, any sort rather than no sort."

—Plato

33. To what governmental concept is Plato referring to in these selections?

A. Democracy

B. Justice

C. Castes

D. Dictatorship

E. Monarchy

34. In comparing independence movements across Africa, Asia, and Latin America after World War II, which country had the most peaceful transition to independence?

A. Zaire

B. India

C. Brazil

D. Kenya

E. Cuba

35. Which definition would best describe a *Sepoy*?

   A. A lower caste individual who would be a servant to the British elite
   B. Hindu and Muslim Indian troops in the British Army serving in India
   C. Indian employees sent to govern the outer reaches of the British empire
   D. An elite Muslim division of the British army
   E. Radical separatists who wanted immediate revolution against the British rulers

36. The three constants in society during the Middle Ages were

   A. famine, disease, and invasion.
   B. invasion, lack of justice, and corrupt officials.
   C. famine, disease, and heavy taxation.
   D. famine, disease, and civil war.
   E. civil war, Muslim invasion, and disease.

37. One of the primary objectives of the Indian National Congress was

   A. to publically support Hindu and Muslim separation.
   B. to begin the process for Indian independence.
   C. to promote Indian culture and nationalism.
   D. to ask for immediate removal from Muslims in the government.
   E. to heal India's economy from the 22-year civil war between Hindus and Muslims.

38. The Portuguese brought which new condition to the East Coast of Africa?

   A. A sharp increase in economic prosperity
   B. A drastic economic decline
   C. Contempt for internal unity among Africans in the interior of Africa
   D. An increase in the gold trade with Europe
   E. General population growth

39. From which early river valley civilization would the following artifact and writing style have been found?

   A. Egypt
   B. Mesopotamia
   C. Olmec
   D. India
   E. China

"When one makes a Revolution, one cannot mark time; one must always go forward—or go back. He who now talks about the 'freedom of the press' goes backward, and halts our headlong course towards Socialism."

"Give us the child for 8 years, and it will be a Bolshevik forever."

"The oppressed are allowed once every few years to decide which particular representatives of the oppressing class are to represent and repress them in Parliament."

—Vladimir Lenin

40. These statements mark the beginning of which Russian conflict?

   A. Cold War
   B. Russian Civil War
   C. World War I
   D. Russo-Japanese War
   E. World War II

41. The first major Turkish dynasty of Islam was the

   A. Ottoman.
   B. Mamluk.
   C. Seljuk.
   D. Almoravid.
   E. Sufi.

42. Which Enlightenment philosopher said, "In order to have liberty, it is necessary that the powers of government be separated"?

   A. Voltaire
   B. Thomas Hobbes
   C. Jean-Jacques Rousseau
   D. Baron de Montesquieu
   E. John Locke

"It is accordingly our wish and command that the English Church shall be free, and that men in our kingdom shall have and keep all these liberties, rights, and concessions, well and peaceably in their fullness and entirety for them and their heirs, of us and our heirs, and in all things and all places for ever."

43. The text comes from which of the following documents, written in 1215, which allowed more people access to government since the Republic of Rome?

   A. *Summa Theologica*
   B. Concordat of Worms
   C. Doctrine of Papal Primacy
   D. Magna Carta
   E. English Bill of Rights

44. The concept of the samsara/transmigration refers to

    A. the endless cycle of death and rebirth.

    B. the Buddhist concept of permanence in a changing world.

    C. the primary book of Confucius and his teachings.

    D. Siddhartha Gautama's transformation into the Buddha, or Enlightened One.

    E. The resetting of the Dynastic Cycle for a new dynasty in China.

"The first wall to fall was pushed over in 1980 in the…shipyards. Later, other symbolic walls came down, and the Germans, of course, tore down the literal wall in Berlin. The fall of the Berlin Wall makes for nice pictures. But it all started in the shipyards."

—Lech Walesa

45. To which independence movement is Lech Walesa referring to in this quote?

    A. Solidarity in Poland

    B. Final success of the Hungarian Revolution

    C. The Baltic States reasserting their independence

    D. The division of the Czech Republic and Slovakia

    E. Ukrainian independence, which had been a struggle since Breshnev came to power

46. After conquering a new village or territory, how did the Aztecs treat their new acquisition?

    A. Destroyed their enemy's cities

    B. Did not demand tribute in goods or labor

    C. Left the local elite in power and ruled indirectly

    D. Enslaved the entire population

    E. Assimilated the local elite into their society

47. What trademark of all Chinese dynasties was set by the early Han Dynasty and Wu Ti?

    A. Strong dynasties expanded the borders of China.

    B. Strong dynasties should forcibly relocate part of the peasant population to prevent rebellion.

    C. They built a canal linking the two strongest economic parts of China.

    D. They said that Confucian classics should be the standard for education to create and maintain good government.

    E. They felt that a good advisor had to be fired at least two times before being worthy to serve the emperor.

48. What was the main accomplishment of the Congress of Vienna?

    A. It put an end to Napoleon's invasions.

    B. It created a balance of power in Europe, assuring that no one could become vastly more powerful than the others.

    C. It forced Napoleon III to call King William I "Kaiser Wilhelm" in the Hall of Mirrors.

    D. It sent a secret communiqué, intercepted by Bismarck, to start the Franco-Prussian War.

    E. It was a performance given by Mozart at the Vienna Opera House.

49. The most difficult problem facing African nations and the work of the United Nations in Africa from the time of decolonization to the present would be which of the following?

A. Prevalent civil wars
B. Religious intolerance
C. Lack of necessary infrastructure
D. Unstable and ineffective governmental regimes
E. Epidemic and communicable sicknesses and diseases such as AIDS, malaria, and Ebola

50. The creation of the Internet, or World Wide Web, was a leap forward in technology in terms of conducting business and diffusing culture. Which country had its own Great Leap Forward by emphasizing traditional methods and techniques of business and cultural retention during the height of the Cold War?

A. Japan
B. Russia
C. China
D. Cuba
E. India

51. Which three countries built their nationalist movements on three pillars?

A. Russia, China, and Japan
B. Japan, Austria, and Russia
C. Austria, Germany, and Japan
D. China, Austria, and Germany
E. Germany, Japan, and China

52. Which of the following is the name given to the form of Christianity that emerged in the Byzantine Empire?

A. Roman Catholicism
B. Zoroastrianism
C. Orthodox Christianity
D. Sufi Piety
E. Coptic Christianity

53. During the time period from 500 C.E. to 1450 C.E., empires and regional societies in the Americas

A. remained entirely separate from those of the Old World.
B. experienced the initial contact that led eventually to European invasion of the New World.
C. failed to develop imperial forms of government—a failure that mirrored European society.
D. were united under a single government and emperor.
E. abandoned Central America and migrated in eastern North America.

"It is not a liberty of circumstance, conceded to us alone, that we wish; it is the adoption absolute of the principle that no man, born red, black, or white, can be the property of his fellow man."

54. Which revolutionary uttered this quote while leading a revolution on the island of Haiti to gain freedom from France?

A. Toussaint L' Ouverture
B. Baron de Montesquieu
C. José de San Martín
D. Agustín de Iturbide
E. Simón Bolívar

55. Under the reign of Mansa Musa, the city of Timbuktu

A. declined as an administrative center.
B. was founded as the capital of the Mali Empire.
C. became known as an intellectual, cultural, and economic center.
D. was taken over by the Berber Tuaregs.
E. fell into a deep economic recession.

56. Conversion to Islam and the absorption of Islamic cultural and religious influences came most often at the hands of which of the following?

A. Sufi missionaries
B. Traders along the Silk Road traveling to and from the Middle East into Asia
C. The Gunpowder Empires
D. The Golden Horde of the Khans
E. Tamerlane's crusade of conquest toward Southeast Asia

"That the pretended power of suspending laws, or the execution of laws, by regal authority, without consent of parliament if illegal.... That it is the right of the subjects to petition the king, and all...prosecutions for such petitioning are illegal.... That election of the members of parliament ought to be free..."

—The English Bill of Rights, 1689

57. Following the Glorious Revolution in 1688, William of Orange recognized this Bill of Rights, which was written to accomplish which of the following?

A. It limited the powers of the monarchy and prohibited Roman Catholics from serving as the king of England.
B. It guaranteed civil liberties for all Englishmen.
C. It became a major source of resistance for him during the rest of his reign as king.
D. It allowed the king to remain above the laws that governed the rest of the population.
E. It allowed him to hand-pick his cabinet ministers.

58. When Adolf Hitler became the German chancellor and began to show aggression toward the Treaty of Versailles and its provisions, which policy did the Western European leaders adopt in dealing with Hitler?

   A. The policy of appeasement
   B. Rearmament and military build-up
   C. Annual meetings geared to include Germany in European affairs
   D. Alliance building to prevent war
   E. Rewriting of the Treaty of Versailles to meet some of Hitler's requests

   "To save a family, abandon a man; to save the village, abandon a family; to save the country, abandon a village; to save the soul, abandon the earth."

59. Based on this quote, identify the epic Indian poem that combines mythology, history, and religion as characters fight to regain their kingdom.

   A. *The Legend of Yu*
   B. Arjuna
   C. *Mahabharata*
   D. Krishna
   E. *The Tale of the Rajahs*

60. Which of the following best describes Japan during the Nara and Heian period of Japanese history?

   A. Japan made contact with China and adopted their culture.
   B. Japan became isolationist and turned away from the world.
   C. Japan became culturally divided as it was in a state of constant civil war.
   D. Warlords fought each other for control of the Japanese provinces.
   E. Japan focused on developing a system of agriculture to fit their specific needs.

61. Under Philip II, why did Spain grow to be the most powerful country in Europe?

   A. Spain enjoyed a massive trading fleet that brought in riches from all over the world.
   B. The Spanish people loved and respected King Philip.
   C. The Spanish monarchs controlled an empire in Europe larger than any other since the Roman Empire.
   D. The Spanish Armada was thought to be invincible.
   E. Philip was able to achieve religious uniformity inside Spain and formed a close relationship with the pope.

62. The caste system of early India served, in part, as a political institution by

   A. creating a uniform system of worship.
   B. unifying the diverse population under a single government.
   C. creating widespread interest in government and politics in the rural areas.
   D. promoting a belief in ancient tribal rights.
   E. enforcing rules about behavior.

63. Why was Mao successful in unifying China where Chiang had failed?

   A. Chiang was too violent in dealing with rival political parties.

   B. Members of the CCP were angry at Chiang's policies of subordinance to the Western powers.

   C. Mao started his movement with respect for peasants and built on a grassroots base where Chiang ruled through landlords and officials.

   D. Chiang chose the German "Bismarckian" model for his bureaucracy, giving him most of the power in the Chinese government.

   E. The CCP had a larger military and was better equipped to fight imperial Japan.

64. Why do historians know much more about the Aztecs than any other Mesoamerican civilization?

   A. They developed a writing system that is easily decipherable.

   B. The paintings and sculpture on temples closely resemble Egyptian hieroglyphics.

   C. They were the first Mesoamerican civilization to have European contact on a large scale.

   D. They were direct descendants of the Mayas, so the writing systems are easy to match.

   E. Their language is still spoken in many parts of Mesoamerica to this day.

65. The two nationalist groups that believed in the movement of populism were

   A. KMT and CCP.

   B. CCP and Land & Freedom.

   C. People's Will and KMT.

   D. CCP and People's Will.

   E. CCP and Black Hand.

66. Who is the Frankish king directly responsible for the conversion of his people to Christianity in order to gain an initial semblance of unity over the Frankish tribes?

   A. Charles Martel

   B. Clovis

   C. Charlemagne

   D. Pepin III

   E. Louis IX

67. Which of the following closely describes the mita system used by the Incas?

   A. A population count and land survey for tax purposes

   B. A method of recording time and an ancient abacus-like device for mathematical calculation

   C. A system of service to empire required by all citizens

   D. A technique used in building the 14,000 miles of road throughout the Incan Empire

   E. A defensive network that prevented them from being overrun by the Aztecs and Spanish

68. The Neolithic Revolution occurred first in which of the following early river valley civilizations?

    A. Egypt
    B. The Middle East
    C. Central America
    D. China
    E. India

69. Which factor was primarily responsible for splitting India into two nations when Pakistan became a country in 1948?

    A. The defeat of imperial Japan
    B. Religious conflicts between Hindus and Muslims
    C. India's choice to join the NATO alliance system headed by the United States
    D. Overpopulation and deforestation in India, which reduced its primary pastureland
    E. The desire of many to become political isolationists in politics, which was the platform of the Pakistani separatist group

70. The Meiji leaders decided to develop a constitution along the lines of which European model that gives great powers to the emperor/king?

    A. Germany
    B. Russia
    C. France
    D. Austria-Hungary
    E. Ottoman

71. The capital of the Byzantine or Eastern Empire and its commercial headquarters was located in which of the following ancient trading cities?

    A. Rome
    B. Ephesus
    C. Constantinople
    D. Baghdad
    E. Athens

72. What similarity exists between the city-states of the Mayas and Japan?

    A. They both had a feudalism style of government with a code of warrior ethics among the aristocracy.
    B. The economy was run through a confederation of city-states.
    C. All cities were governed by a single dynastic family.
    D. Rule was passed matrilineally.
    E. Both looked inward after copying all they could use from a more advanced neighbor.

"Without glasnost there is not, and there cannot be, democratism, the political creativity of the masses and their participation in management."

"Without perestroika, the cold war simply would not have ended. But the world could not continue developing as it had, with the stark menace of nuclear war ever present."

73. Which leader of the Soviet Union hastened the end of communism with these statements?

    A. Nikita Khrushchev
    B. Mikhail Gorbachev
    C. Leonid Brezhnev
    D. Boris Yeltsin
    E. Vladimir Putin

74. Japanese society quickly gained worldwide attention during the late 19th and early 20th centuries for their ability to

    A. quickly adapt for invasion.
    B. handle rapid industrial growth and territorial expansion.
    C. stay out of World War I and focus on their own internal problems.
    D. sacrifice short-term success for long-term gains.
    E. both A and D

75. Which Islamic conqueror spread Islam while leaving a path of destruction behind him, and then brought Islam to India, beginning a long period of Hindu and Muslim tension on the subcontinent of India?

    A. Tamerlane
    B. Hulagu Khan
    C. Berke
    D. Saladin
    E. Akbar the Great

76. The rise of the great empires during the ancient river valley civilizations had which of the following common features?

    A. dependency on flooding rivers
    B. large mobilized armies
    C. agriculture-based economies
    D. dominant centralized monarchies
    E. well-organized bureaucracies

77. Why did the pharaohs of ancient Egypt have such an absolute form of power over their civilizations?

    A. They were able to accurately predict when the Nile would flood.
    B. Pharaohs interpreted the will of the ancestors.
    C. Pharaohs were seen as living gods.
    D. The pharaohs were responsible for placating the various different Egyptian gods.
    E. The pharaohs were able to conqueror a vast territory, the control of which gave the pharaohs a large increase in power.

78. Which event motivated the United States to adopt a policy of isolationism during the 1920s?

   A. The creation of the League of Nations
   B. U.S. refusal to pay the high trade tariffs to European countries
   C. The enormous amount of casualties suffered in World War I
   D. The controversial provisions of the Treaty of Versailles and the secret agreements between Britain and France during World War I
   E. The retaking of Alsace and Lorraine by Germany

79. When comparing the thoughts of a Confucian-run government in China with the government of Japan, which of the following is seen as a problem with the description?

   A. There is no place in Confucian thought for a shogun.
   B. Japanese emperors were seen as living gods of the sun, so there could be no Dynastic Cycle.
   C. China was a centralized government, whereas Japan maintained a delicate balance between centralized control and independent provinces.
   D. Japan lacked an examination system to pick qualified officials.
   E. All of the above

80. How did the brothers Tiberius and Gaius Gracchus fundamentally change the way Roman politics were practiced?

   A. The Gracchi brothers took their appeal directly to the people instead of keeping everything to the Senate.
   B. They were able to restructure the government in the Roman provinces.
   C. They used their family name to challenge traditional senatorial rule.
   D. Political issues began to be resolved by verbal commitment and honor rather than by voting.
   E. They wanted to greatly expand city revenue by granting blanket citizenship to all within Rome's sphere of influence.

81. In Raphael's painting *The Marriage of the Virgin*, what Renaissance creation or invention does the painting display?

   A. Humanism
   B. Spiritualism
   C. Patronage
   D. Anatomy
   E. Perspective

82. Since the end of World War II, the Middle East has experienced all of the following obstacles or difficulties EXCEPT

    A. the creation of new states and disputed international borders.

    B. the state of conflict between Israel and Palestine.

    C. the decrease in oil production.

    D. the resurgence of religious, political, and social reform movements geared to create a strict adherence to Islam.

    E. recurring difficulties with the decolonization process, along with competing ethnic and tribal minority groups trying to coexist in the same territory.

83. The Hopewell Native Americas of the Midwest and South are most known for their

    A. extensive trade networks.

    B. belief in a sun god that resembled Quetzalcoatl.

    C. building of large earthen mounds.

    D. forming the Iroquois League.

    E. unifying the city-states of the Mississippi River Valley.

84. Which African empire captured neighboring tribes and used them as plantation laborers for sugarcane and bananas, and became the model for slavery in the New World?

    A. Ghana

    B. Mali

    C. Songhai

    D. Afrikaner

    E. Ashkia

"Love turns back toward the lover, unkindness brings evil return. It is for no good deed or good purpose that you bring back a sorrow among us, our sorrows mount up without end."

                               —Selection from *Awoi No Uye*

85. What ancient civilization's theater performances bear many similarities to the Japanese Noh play selection above?

    A. Korea

    B. China

    C. Greece

    D. Rome

    E. India

86. The primary goal of Julius Caesar's reforms as he became dictator was geared toward

    A. repealing the reforms of Sulla.

    B. bringing organization, stability, and efficiency to the Roman Empire.

    C. gaining support from the public in regard to his appointment as dictator.

    D. assuming full control of all Roman military forces.

    E. allowing more of his supporters to gain access to the Senate to vote for his reforms.

87. As Pakistan separated from India to form a new country, which densely populated country broke off from Pakistan to become an independent country of its own?

    A. Sri Lanka
    B. Burma
    C. Tibet
    D. Myanmar
    E. Bangladesh

    "You can kill ten of our men for every one we kill of yours. But even at those odds, you will lose and we will win."

88. Which Soviet-backed leader of the Vietcong communist government in North Vietnam made this statement?

    A. Chiang Kai-shek
    B. Ho Chi Minh
    C. Ngo Dinh Diem
    D. Sun Yet-sen
    E. Pol Pot

89. Why did the Chinese refer to themselves as the Middle Kingdom?

    A. They were the farthest removed of the ancient river valley civilizations.
    B. They had no access to cultural diffusion because of geography.
    C. They were conquered by barbarians from Mongolia.
    D. They were located along the Yellow River.
    E. It was the name picked by the early Shang emperors to demonstrate their power.

90. How did the series of inventions from the spinning jenny, the steam engine, and Henry Cort's steel process create the biggest change in human history since the Neolithic Revolution?

    A. Allowed industry to grow at an unprecedented rate with the adaptability of industrial machines
    B. Further defined gender roles, regulating women to a secondary status
    C. Allowed more people than ever before to become employed and participate in the economy
    D. Finally enabled the West to open up China and Japan after centuries of seclusion
    E. Allowed more women to enter the workforce than ever before

91. The end of the leadership of Maximilien Robespierre was in response to

    A. his hatred of the sans-culottes.
    B. the reaction of the surviving aristocracy who were living abroad and who called for international intervention to stop the bloodshed.
    C. asking the legislature to pass a law allowing him to execute leaders of the government for being counterrevolutionaries.
    D. the sheer violence of the Reign of Terror.
    E. the French losing wars on the continent and abroad in North America to Great Britain.

92. These men participated in this key 1923 event staged by Adolf Hitler, which helped him to promote the Nazi Party throughout Germany.

    A. The Beer Hall Putsch in Munich
    B. The Nuremberg rally
    C. During Kristallnacht
    D. The invasion of Poland
    E. The annexation of Austria

93. During the Middle Kingdom of Egyptian history, which catastrophe caused a fundamental change in Egyptian behavior and ushered in the New Kingdom?

    A. Mesopotamian tribes such as the Hebrews were taken as slaves.
    B. A massive famine forced the Egyptians to seek assistance from nearby Sumeria.
    C. The Nile began to flood at irregular levels.
    D. The Hyksos invaders conquered Egypt with superior weapons and assumed control of Egypt.
    E. African tribes from Nubia and the Sudan began to divert the Nile River, causing the Egyptians to take an aggressive stance toward their southern neighbors.

94. Which of the following is responsible for creating the first tent government, or bakufu?

    A. Kamakura
    B. Fujiwara
    C. Yoritomo
    D. Joei
    E. None of the above

95. When compared to the political situation of continental Europe, the system in England could be seen as

    A. unresponsive to political ideas of the majority of its population.
    B. ideal as there were very few opposing opinions because of similar views among the nobility.
    C. more free and responsive to public opinion due to England's separation from continental Europe.
    D. a rigidly controlled set of laws put in place by the dominant Stuart Dynasty.
    E. a country unified along economic and religious lines, thereby enabling it to create its world empire.

ANSWER KEY
Practice Test 2

1. A	25. A	49. E	73. B
2. D	26. C	50. C	74. E
3. B	27. D	51. A	75. A
4. B	28. A	52. C	76. D
5. C	29. B	53. A	77. C
6. A	30. C	54. A	78. D
7. C	31. E	55. C	79. E
8. C	32. C	56. A	80. A
9. E	33. A	57. A	81. E
10. C	34. C	58. A	82. C
11. A	35. B	59. C	83. C
12. E	36. A	60. A	84. B
13. B	37. C	61. A	85. C
14. C	38. B	62. E	86. B
15. B	39. B	63. C	87. E
16. D	40. B	64. C	88. B
17. B	41. B	65. B	89. A
18. B	42. D	66. B	90. A
19. A	43. D	67. C	91. C
20. B	44. A	68. B	92. A
21. B	45. A	69. B	93. D
22. C	46. C	70. A	94. C
23. B	47. A	71. C	95. C
24. E	48. B	72. C	

ANSWER EXPLANATIONS

1. **(A)** *The Black Legend* told those back in Spain what was really happening to the natives in the New World, causing some token reforms to be made in the treatment of natives.

2. **(D)** Saddam Hussein's invasion of Kuwait in 1990 led to a world coalition, led by the United States, to expel Hussein's forces from Kuwait. This is commonly known as the Persian Gulf War I.

3. **(B)** The Han Dynasty was a contemporary of ancient Rome. When Rome was reaching the high point of its power and civilization, the Han Dynasty was as well.

4. **(B)** Many civilizations south of the Sahara Desert, such as Ghana, Songhai, and Zimbabwe, thrived before Europeans arrived. They built great empires and civilizations while Europeans were trapped in the Dark Ages. Civilizations in Africa often progressed faster and were more advanced than their European counterparts through much of this period.

5. **(C)** Alcuin of York was hired by Charlemagne, in his new city of Aachen, to build a school to reintroduce learning. Charlemagne wanted to have more efficient administrators for his Holy Roman Empire.

6. **(A)** The British intrusion into the delicate economic balance in India brought about widespread famine, forcing many Indians into indentured servitude just to survive.

7. **(C)** Since many African civilizations did not develop writing and relied on an oral tradition, much of what we know comes from the perspective of outside sources who looked at Africa through their eyes, resulting in stereotypes.

8. **(C)** The Triple Alliance in World War I was created by the central empires of Europe: Germany, Austria-Hungary, Italy, and Austria's southern neighbor, the Ottoman Empire, with whom Austria shared a border.

9. **(E)** Pope Urban II was asked by the Byzantine emperor to aid in pushing the Muslims back from the gates of Constantinople. This validated the office of the pope within the Eastern Empire, while giving the peasants in the west a time of peace. The Christian knights focused on an external enemy instead of fighting each other.

10. **(C)** A fire broke out that destroyed the religious center and much of the housing for the upper classes. As a result, Teotihuacan was never able to return to its height of power and influence.

11. **(A)** The adaptability of Buddhism, its openness, and its easy-to-follow, consistent guidelines allowed its influence to help the ideals of higher Chinese culture to be transmitted to Japan.

12. **(E)** As the prime minister of Prussia, Bismarck was the force behind the unification of Germany as Prussia defeated first Austria-Hungary and then Napoleon III in France.

13. **(B)** When Sparta conquered the city-state of Messina, they quickly realized that they were outnumbered by their slaves, so they created a society to keep the slaves under control and their citizens safe.

14. **(C)** With the supremacy of the Royal Navy, extensive British-held territory in the Caribbean Sea, and flourishing trade in India and China, England was able to exert pressure over much of Latin America.

15. **(B)** By 1600, the Ottomans controlled territory from southeastern Europe to Arabia to the heart of Mesopotamia. Their military and economic strength was a match for any other empire in the world at the time, but it began to quickly diminish due to the rapid rise in technology from Western Europe.

16. **(D)** Pericles said that a man who does not participate in government is not only harmless but useless. Athenians believed that all men should be involved in creating and enforcing of laws for the city-state of Athens. Democratic citizenship came at the price of civic involvement.

17. **(B)** To help govern their growing empire, the Tang and Song relied heavily on the scholar officials to help maintain governing quality and efficiency.

18. **(B)** The Ottoman Qunname and the governing ideals of Tokugawa were written to prevent crimes before they happened. They established laws and punishments that would be known by everyone, rather than creating them as problems arose.

19. **(A)** This is the order of the day given by the supreme commander of the Allied Expeditionary Force Dwight D. Eisenhower as the Allied troops began Operation Overlord, which took place on June 6, 1944, otherwise known as D-Day.

20. **(B)** Confucian scholars won the argument by comparing the government to merchants. However, the government still maintained a monopoly on certain products.

21. **(B)** The Malinke people were the largest tribe in the Malinke Empire and formed the heart of the Malian state.

22. **(C)** After the death of his father during the Crimean War (which Russia lost), Czar Alexander II realized that reforms were not only necessary but possible.

23. **(B)** Orthodoxy, or what you believe, defines Muslims. Whether Shiite or Sunni, the basic core belief is the same. The only difference is who they believe should be the leader or caliph.

24. **(E)** While Mesoamerica was slightly behind in terms of technology, they were able to accomplish similar feats of engineering and technology that other early civilizations also completed: large pyramids of the Maya along with the Mayan calendar, large merchant guilds of the Aztecs and Incas, and governmental forums from all Mesoamerican civilizations.

25. **(A)** As a result of the growing fear of communism at home and abroad, President Harry Truman spoke before Congress and ushered in the United States policy of containment. It was created to hold communism where it currently existed but not letting it spread to other regions.

26. **(C)** The kingdom of the Congo made elaborate concessions to the Portuguese in return for European trade goods. The king of the Congo also allowed the Portuguese to capture slaves from within his territory.

27. **(D)** Afghanistan was home to Osama bin Laden's al-Qaeda and was governed by the Taliban until U.S. intervention removed them from power.

28. **(A)** With other city-states just paying in to protect the treasury and their unwillingness to provide troops, this left Athens to supply the naval force and manpower for the defense of the League. Thus, Athens began to dominate.

29. **(B)** Due to the proximity to the Middle East, East Africa was converted by sea routes as the small distance across the Red Sea made sea trading and cultural diffusion easy.

30. **(C)** Years of peace and the recruitment of foreign investment helped to spur the economy of Vietnam to achieve higher rates of growth than had ever been experienced throughout Vietnamese history.

31. **(E)** England and Japan were the first to industrialize from scratch on their respective continents and spheres of influence.

32. **(C)** With large veins of obsidian throughout Mesoamerica, obsidian was the material of choice for both tools and weapons.

33. **(A)** After the sentencing and death of his teacher and mentor Socrates, Plato became disillusioned with democracy and went in search of the best form of government.

34. **(C)** Brazil did not have a violent civil war or long period of instability when it came to declaring its independence. It was quick and peaceful compared to the other independence movements across the world after World War II.

35. **(B)** Sepoys were Native Indian troops of both Hindu and Muslim faith who served in the British army in India.

36. **(A)** The Middle Ages marked a period of unrest for the people due to constant warfare, coupled with poor agriculture practices leading to famine. The constant threat of outside invasion from warring clans made life difficult (and short) during this time.

37. **(C)** The Indian National Congress peaceably and openly supported Indian nationalism to remind Indians of their heritage and importance.

38. **(B)** With the destruction of the Islamic sea trade and the Portuguese Prazeros that stayed in Africa, the Portuguese left behind massive economic decline.

39. **(B)** The writing style and tablet are examples from ancient Sumer in Mesopotamia.

40. **(B)** Russia collapsed into a civil war between Red, or communist, Russians and White Russians, who were loyal to the monarchy and wanted to initiate wider democratic changes in the Russian government.

41. **(B)** The Mamluks were the first dynasty to withstand a Mongol invasion. They laid the foundation for a Turkish caliphate, which eventually became the long-lasting Ottoman Empire.

42. **(D)** Baron de Montesquieu believed in protecting the liberties of the people. In order to keep the government from growing too powerful, the powers of the government should be spread out among different branches.

43. **(D)** The Magna Carta, signed in 1215, put limits on the power of the English monarchs and gave basic rights and privileges to the aristocracy, allowing a greater voice in government. This was the first step toward democracy that the world had seen since the end of the Republic of Rome.

44. **(A)** Samsara is the endless cycle of death and rebirth that followers of Hinduism go through as they try to achieve union with Brahman, the all-powerful cosmic order of the universe to which all beings are connected.

45. **(A)** Lech Walesa began the Solidarity Movement in Poland in 1980. However, Solidarity was banned by the Polish government, and the government declared martial law to keep the Communist Party in power. In 1989, Solidarity made a giant leap forward as it was finally accepted as a political party.

46. **(C)** The Aztecs left the local leaders in place to maintain stability and instead extracted resources in the form of heavy tribute. They allowed the city to survive as a source for more potential sacrifice captives, which were needed to power the sun god.

47. **(A)** From the point of view of the Han Dynasty, the hallmark of all strong dynasties was the ability to increase the size of the Chinese empire.

48. **(B)** The Congress of Vienna was held to promote the stability of European monarchies and to keep a balance of power in Europe so a time of peace could be enjoyed.

49. **(E)** With poor hygiene and lack of adequate medical facilities, diseases such as malaria, the AIDS epidemic of the 1980s and 1990s, and the Ebola outbreak of 2014 are constant problems facing Africans and the United Nations.

50. **(C)** Mao Tse-tung's Great Leap Forward started in 1958 and was designed to stamp out Western influence in China. The resulting economic policies led to the deaths of millions of people due to starvation.

51. **(A)** Russia, China, and Japan had different goals but all adhered to a small number of goals that each thought it could realistically accomplish to strengthen their country; thus, they each built their nationalist movements on three pillars.

52. **(C)** Eastern Orthodox Christianity differed from Catholicism by following the Arian Creed, in which the Father and Son are one being while the Holy Spirit is a separate entity. There were other differences, such as allowing priests to marry and using leavened bread for communion.

53. **(A)** Civilizations in the Americas remained separated from those in Europe, Africa, or Asia until the Age of Exploration and the voyage of Christopher Columbus.

54. **(A)** Haitian independence was inspired and led by Toussaint L'Ouverture.

55. **(C)** When Mansa Musa returned from his Hajj, he brought back many Muslim scholars and officials. As a result, Mansa Musa was able to turn Timbuktu into a leading cultural and trading center.

56. **(A)** The ability of the Sufis to be adaptive and tolerant of other religions helped to spread the acceptance of Islam.

57. **(A)** The English Bill of Rights forever limited the power of the English monarchy and gave certain rights to the upper classes. It also legally prevented Roman Catholics from sitting on the throne of England.

58. **(A)** English Prime Minister Neville Chamberlin was the leader of the appeasement policy as many thought Hitler's terms were limited and acceptable.

59. **(C)** The *Mahabharata* is India's longest poem at nearly 100,000 verses long. It was passed down orally for centuries before being written down. It is still being published today and is being turned into a movie series in India's Bollywood.

60. **(A)** During the Nara and Heian period, young, aristocratic Japanese men traveled to China as did merchants and scholars. They saw China as the mother country. They studied there and returned to Japan with all of the information they acquired. They modified and adapted Chinese ideas to meet Japanese needs.

61. **(A)** The mighty Spanish Armada brought wealth to Spain from its overseas empires: gold and silver from Mexico, spices from Peru, and textiles from Naples.

62. **(E)** The caste system enforced rules on what you could do, where you could go, and who you could interact with, forming a set system of rules that everyone had to follow.

63. **(C)** Mao worked among the peasants, educating and establishing village councils. He gave people a seemingly greater role in government, thus earning their support, whereas Chiang was cut off from his power base while fighting the Japanese.

64. **(C)** When Cortez conquered the Aztecs and took their gold, the conquistadors began to write and report what they had seen in the Aztec capital of Tenochtitlan. They were awestruck at many of the things they saw, not only the amount of gold but things such as the marketplace and other aspects of Aztec society.

65. **(B)** Both of the movements, Mao's Communist Peoples Party and Russia's Land & Freedom, believed in populism, which targeted the grassroots peasants as the way to achieve change in their respective countries.

66. **(B)** Near the time of the fall of the western Roman Empire, Clovis founded the kingdom of the Franks and the Merovingian Dynasty. He began to build unity among the Frankish tribes in Central Europe.

67. **(C)** The mita system was a form of taxation where all Incan citizens were required to work a set number of days per year on public works projects for the good of the Incan Empire.

68. **(B)** The Neolithic Revolution first took place in ancient Mesopotamia, where there is the earliest evidence of civilization.

69. **(B)** India split to become the new nation of Pakistan as a result of increasing religious tension. The majority of Indian people were Hindu, but a large minority of India's citizens were practitioners of Islam. Many of these citizens relocated to Pakistan, which was created to be governed by an Islamic practicing government.

70. **(A)** The Japanese government adopted a constitution along German lines. The Japanese were heavily influenced by the constitution written by Otto von Bismarck.

71. **(C)** The city of Constantinople was previously called Byzantium before it was set up to bring tribute and trade into Rome. Constantinople formed the Eastern sector of the Eastern Empire. Along with its key location near the intersection of three continents, its harbor was good for both trade and defense.

72. **(C)** As Japan is governed by a single dynasty, so were the city-states of the Mayas during the duration of the Mayan civilization.

73. **(B)** In 1985, Mikhail Gorbachev hoped to cure the inefficiency of the Soviet economic and governmental bureaucracies by instituting the policies of glasnost and perestroika, which eventually would be factors in the collapse of the Soviet Union.

74. **(E)** The Japanese people were able to sacrifice short-term gratification for long-term gain, and as a result, they were able to become an industrialized society faster than any other country.

75. **(A)** In 1398, Tamerlane entered northern India and sacked the city of Delhi, enslaving many people and fragmenting the empire. It ended the rule of sultans, who had controlled the region for hundreds of years.

76. **(D)** All of the river valley civilizations had dominate centralized monarchies: Egyptian pharaohs, Mesopotamian kings, Chinese emperors, and a leader of the Harappa and Mohenjo-daro civilizations.

77. **(C)** The pharaohs had complete control of the civilization as they were seen as living representations of the sun god on Earth.

78. **(D)** The harsh provisions of the Treaty of Versailles and the reluctance to get involved in European affairs after President Woodrow Wilson was ridiculed in Europe encouraged the United States to adopt the isolation policy.

79. **(E)** Since the emperor of China was the father of his people, China did not need a shogun. Since Japan only had one single dynasty, there was no Dynastic Cycle to run through. In Japan, governmental jobs were handed out with an examination system, and China was governed by a strong central government.

80. **(A)** By taking their ideas to the middle class, the Gracchi brothers changed Roman political behavior as debates and discussions were removed from the Senate and taken to the people, whose support was necessary to determine outcomes.

81. **(E)** Raphael used a grid in the courtyard pavement behind the wedding party and an arch in the background to draw the viewer's eye to the back, giving the painting the illusion of depth and distance to make it more life-like.

82. **(C)** As a result of growing industrial economies and a larger world population, oil production has only increased since World War II.

83. **(C)** The Hopewells left large mounds circa 700 B.C.E. Some mounds took the shape of animals, like the Great Serpent Mound in Ohio. The earthen mounds demonstrated strong central leadership, engineering sophistication, and skilled craftsmanship.

84. **(B)** The kingdom of Mali controlled the lush farmland along the Niger River. They began to use captured prisoners of war to work the sugarcane fields and became the model for the Portuguese and Spanish colonies of the New World.

85. **(C)** The Noh play was performed outdoors by male actors who wore elaborate and colorful costumes and masks to display emotion. The Noh plays told stories that taught morals to the public.

86. **(B)** Julius Caesar's main reforms were geared at ending corruption and disorganization in the city of Rome and throughout all parts of the empire.

87. **(E)** After being excluded from politics and suffering ethnic discrimination, citizens of eastern Pakistan separated from western Pakistan after a period of protests. After a brief civil war, Bangladesh gained independence in 1971.

88. **(B)** Ho Chi Minh was a Vietnamese leader who fought in World War I and led a successful guerrilla war against the Japanese in World War II. He turned to communism to help unify his country and end French imperial control.

89. **(A)** The Chinese river valley civilization was so far removed from any of the other river valleys that they did not see anyone else. Thus, they believed that they were the center of the universe.

90. **(A)** It allowed for the industry to grow at an unprecedented rate, creating jobs and higher income. More labor-saving innovations were created, radically changing the traditional world framework.

91. **(C)** Robespierre went too far in asking the legislature to pass a law allowing him to execute the legislature! He had become corrupted with power.

92. **(A)** Hitler became a national figure after his arrest for leading the Beer Hall Putsch in Munich in 1923. He used the trial to promote his name and platform.

93. **(D)** In 1700 B.C.E., the Hyksos invaded in the turbulent Middle Kingdom. Their iron weapons and wheeled chariots overwhelmed the Egyptians. As a result, the Egyptians in the New Kingdom began to conquer the Middle East to form a buffer against invading tribes.

94. **(C)** Yoritomo, the emperor's supreme military leader, put down a rebellion of dissatisfied samurai and then assumed control of the government.

95. **(C)** Due to being an island nation, with people who received some freedom of speech and a greater unity, plus a working infrastructure with no tolls or tariffs, England was seen as more free than continental Europe.

ANSWER SHEET
Practice Test 3

PRACTICE TEST 3

1. Ⓐ Ⓑ Ⓒ Ⓓ Ⓔ	25. Ⓐ Ⓑ Ⓒ Ⓓ Ⓔ	49. Ⓐ Ⓑ Ⓒ Ⓓ Ⓔ	73. Ⓐ Ⓑ Ⓒ Ⓓ Ⓔ
2. Ⓐ Ⓑ Ⓒ Ⓓ Ⓔ	26. Ⓐ Ⓑ Ⓒ Ⓓ Ⓔ	50. Ⓐ Ⓑ Ⓒ Ⓓ Ⓔ	74. Ⓐ Ⓑ Ⓒ Ⓓ Ⓔ
3. Ⓐ Ⓑ Ⓒ Ⓓ Ⓔ	27. Ⓐ Ⓑ Ⓒ Ⓓ Ⓔ	51. Ⓐ Ⓑ Ⓒ Ⓓ Ⓔ	75. Ⓐ Ⓑ Ⓒ Ⓓ Ⓔ
4. Ⓐ Ⓑ Ⓒ Ⓓ Ⓔ	28. Ⓐ Ⓑ Ⓒ Ⓓ Ⓔ	52. Ⓐ Ⓑ Ⓒ Ⓓ Ⓔ	76. Ⓐ Ⓑ Ⓒ Ⓓ Ⓔ
5. Ⓐ Ⓑ Ⓒ Ⓓ Ⓔ	29. Ⓐ Ⓑ Ⓒ Ⓓ Ⓔ	53. Ⓐ Ⓑ Ⓒ Ⓓ Ⓔ	77. Ⓐ Ⓑ Ⓒ Ⓓ Ⓔ
6. Ⓐ Ⓑ Ⓒ Ⓓ Ⓔ	30. Ⓐ Ⓑ Ⓒ Ⓓ Ⓔ	54. Ⓐ Ⓑ Ⓒ Ⓓ Ⓔ	78. Ⓐ Ⓑ Ⓒ Ⓓ Ⓔ
7. Ⓐ Ⓑ Ⓒ Ⓓ Ⓔ	31. Ⓐ Ⓑ Ⓒ Ⓓ Ⓔ	55. Ⓐ Ⓑ Ⓒ Ⓓ Ⓔ	79. Ⓐ Ⓑ Ⓒ Ⓓ Ⓔ
8. Ⓐ Ⓑ Ⓒ Ⓓ Ⓔ	32. Ⓐ Ⓑ Ⓒ Ⓓ Ⓔ	56. Ⓐ Ⓑ Ⓒ Ⓓ Ⓔ	80. Ⓐ Ⓑ Ⓒ Ⓓ Ⓔ
9. Ⓐ Ⓑ Ⓒ Ⓓ Ⓔ	33. Ⓐ Ⓑ Ⓒ Ⓓ Ⓔ	57. Ⓐ Ⓑ Ⓒ Ⓓ Ⓔ	81. Ⓐ Ⓑ Ⓒ Ⓓ Ⓔ
10. Ⓐ Ⓑ Ⓒ Ⓓ Ⓔ	34. Ⓐ Ⓑ Ⓒ Ⓓ Ⓔ	58. Ⓐ Ⓑ Ⓒ Ⓓ Ⓔ	82. Ⓐ Ⓑ Ⓒ Ⓓ Ⓔ
11. Ⓐ Ⓑ Ⓒ Ⓓ Ⓔ	35. Ⓐ Ⓑ Ⓒ Ⓓ Ⓔ	59. Ⓐ Ⓑ Ⓒ Ⓓ Ⓔ	83. Ⓐ Ⓑ Ⓒ Ⓓ Ⓔ
12. Ⓐ Ⓑ Ⓒ Ⓓ Ⓔ	36. Ⓐ Ⓑ Ⓒ Ⓓ Ⓔ	60. Ⓐ Ⓑ Ⓒ Ⓓ Ⓔ	84. Ⓐ Ⓑ Ⓒ Ⓓ Ⓔ
13. Ⓐ Ⓑ Ⓒ Ⓓ Ⓔ	37. Ⓐ Ⓑ Ⓒ Ⓓ Ⓔ	61. Ⓐ Ⓑ Ⓒ Ⓓ Ⓔ	85. Ⓐ Ⓑ Ⓒ Ⓓ Ⓔ
14. Ⓐ Ⓑ Ⓒ Ⓓ Ⓔ	38. Ⓐ Ⓑ Ⓒ Ⓓ Ⓔ	62. Ⓐ Ⓑ Ⓒ Ⓓ Ⓔ	86. Ⓐ Ⓑ Ⓒ Ⓓ Ⓔ
15. Ⓐ Ⓑ Ⓒ Ⓓ Ⓔ	39. Ⓐ Ⓑ Ⓒ Ⓓ Ⓔ	63. Ⓐ Ⓑ Ⓒ Ⓓ Ⓔ	87. Ⓐ Ⓑ Ⓒ Ⓓ Ⓔ
16. Ⓐ Ⓑ Ⓒ Ⓓ Ⓔ	40. Ⓐ Ⓑ Ⓒ Ⓓ Ⓔ	64. Ⓐ Ⓑ Ⓒ Ⓓ Ⓔ	88. Ⓐ Ⓑ Ⓒ Ⓓ Ⓔ
17. Ⓐ Ⓑ Ⓒ Ⓓ Ⓔ	41. Ⓐ Ⓑ Ⓒ Ⓓ Ⓔ	65. Ⓐ Ⓑ Ⓒ Ⓓ Ⓔ	89. Ⓐ Ⓑ Ⓒ Ⓓ Ⓔ
18. Ⓐ Ⓑ Ⓒ Ⓓ Ⓔ	42. Ⓐ Ⓑ Ⓒ Ⓓ Ⓔ	66. Ⓐ Ⓑ Ⓒ Ⓓ Ⓔ	90. Ⓐ Ⓑ Ⓒ Ⓓ Ⓔ
19. Ⓐ Ⓑ Ⓒ Ⓓ Ⓔ	43. Ⓐ Ⓑ Ⓒ Ⓓ Ⓔ	67. Ⓐ Ⓑ Ⓒ Ⓓ Ⓔ	91. Ⓐ Ⓑ Ⓒ Ⓓ Ⓔ
20. Ⓐ Ⓑ Ⓒ Ⓓ Ⓔ	44. Ⓐ Ⓑ Ⓒ Ⓓ Ⓔ	68. Ⓐ Ⓑ Ⓒ Ⓓ Ⓔ	92. Ⓐ Ⓑ Ⓒ Ⓓ Ⓔ
21. Ⓐ Ⓑ Ⓒ Ⓓ Ⓔ	45. Ⓐ Ⓑ Ⓒ Ⓓ Ⓔ	69. Ⓐ Ⓑ Ⓒ Ⓓ Ⓔ	93. Ⓐ Ⓑ Ⓒ Ⓓ Ⓔ
22. Ⓐ Ⓑ Ⓒ Ⓓ Ⓔ	46. Ⓐ Ⓑ Ⓒ Ⓓ Ⓔ	70. Ⓐ Ⓑ Ⓒ Ⓓ Ⓔ	94. Ⓐ Ⓑ Ⓒ Ⓓ Ⓔ
23. Ⓐ Ⓑ Ⓒ Ⓓ Ⓔ	47. Ⓐ Ⓑ Ⓒ Ⓓ Ⓔ	71. Ⓐ Ⓑ Ⓒ Ⓓ Ⓔ	95. Ⓐ Ⓑ Ⓒ Ⓓ Ⓔ
24. Ⓐ Ⓑ Ⓒ Ⓓ Ⓔ	48. Ⓐ Ⓑ Ⓒ Ⓓ Ⓔ	72. Ⓐ Ⓑ Ⓒ Ⓓ Ⓔ	

Practice Test 3

1. In which country did the Leakey family discover the oldest human remains?

   A. Kenya
   B. Ethiopia
   C. Tanzania
   D. Somalia
   E. Zaire

2. What small shift did Vladimir Lenin make in his Marxist views, which caused criticism of his leadership throughout Russia?

   A. Collectivization
   B. Institution of glasnost
   C. Belief in détente
   D. Use of the gulag system
   E. New Economic Plans

3. As the political structure of the Tokugawa state was completed, which part of Japan was going through unwilling changes as reflected in the phrase, "Reason may be violated in the name of the law."

   A. The economy
   B. The legislature or "Diet"
   C. Japanese society
   D. Japanese social hierarchy
   E. Role of the castle town

4. As the 7th century began, which groups would have posed the greatest threat to the eastern borders of the Byzantine Empire?

   A. The Persian Sassanid Empire
   B. The Mongols
   C. The Huns
   D. The Arabic Muslims
   E. The Franks

5. Which Mexican revolutionary leader of the late 1800s/early 1900s was similar to the Gracchi brothers of Rome, as they all used their wealth and social influence to bring about positive governmental changes, and they were all assassinated?

   A. Miguel Hidalgo

   B. Antonio López de Santa Anna

   C. Jorge Miguel

   D. Francisco Madero

   E. Porfirio Díaz

6. What was the MAIN cause that resulted in the Ch'in Dynasty falling so quickly?

   A. They heavily taxed the people to build the roads.

   B. They changed society too quickly, giving the people little time to adapt.

   C. They burned books on all opposing thoughts and philosophies.

   D. The massive building project required to connect the Great Wall was too much for the dynasty to maintain.

   E. Shi Huang Di had no adequate successors.

7. Who pushed Austria-Hungary very hard in dealing with Serbia after the assassination of the archduke?

   A. Russia

   B. England

   C. Germany

   D. United States

   E. Ottoman Turkey

"A government must not waiver once it has chosen its course. It must not look to the left or right but go forward."

"The secret of politics? Make a good treaty with Russia."

"Politics is the art of possible."

"Anyone who has ever looked into the glazed eyes of a soldier dying on the battlefield will think hard before starting a war."

—Otto von Bismarck

8. Based on these quotes, why do you think Bismarck was able to unify Germany when so many others dating back to Charlemagne had failed?

   A. Bismarck had spent many years as a diplomat to France and Russia, assessing their abilities.

   B. Bismarck possessed the ability to make ruthless decisions, regardless of the consequences.

   C. Bismarck possessed the ability to manipulate others.

   D. Bismarck understood the needs of what the state actually needed, and he was able to focus his willpower on accomplishing them.

   E. All of the above

"We no longer live in a world where only the actual firing of weapons represents a sufficient challenge to a nation's security to constitute maximum peril. Nuclear weapons are so destructive... that any substantially increased possibility of their use... may well be regarded as a definite threat to peace."

—President John F. Kennedy

9. Based on your knowledge of the Cold War, to which event is President Kennedy referring?

   A. Cuban Missile Crisis
   B. Bay of Pigs Invasion
   C. Fulgencio Batista fleeing Cuba in 1959
   D. Establishment of the Truman Doctrine
   E. The shooting down of a United States U-2 reconnaissance plane by the Soviet Union

10. Which of the following is NOT one of the five pillars of Islam?

   A. Paying of a tithe
   B. Sharia
   C. Participating in the Hajj
   D. Exercising of Ramadan
   E. Praying five times a day

11. As Egypt began to assert its independence from Ottoman rule and build the Suez Canal, which European power used nebulous tactics to gain control of the Canal and Egypt?

   A. Great Britain
   B. France
   C. Belgium
   D. Germany
   E. Spain

12. What necessary survival event in India does this map demonstrate?

   A. Hurricane
   B. El Niño
   C. Monsoon
   D. Tornadic flow
   E. Tsunami

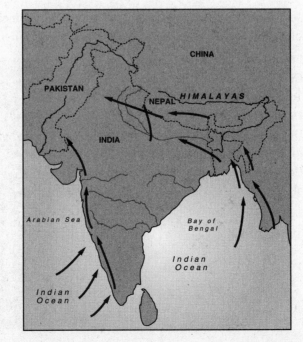

13. The May Fourth Movement in China can best be described as

   A. a central desire to return to the traditional ways of the Dynastic Cycle.
   B. a nationalist movement motivated by foreign control.
   C. a concentrated attempt to introduce Westernization to China.
   D. a student-led attempt to free political prisoners.
   E. providing an international stage for the Japanese to suppress rebellion.

14. This is the secondary class of Roman citizens who made up the majority of the population.

   A. Plebeian
   B. Tribune
   C. Clients
   D. Censor
   E. Patrician

15. What proved to be the major source of wealth for the Songhai Empire?

   A. Trade in spices from the interior of Africa
   B. Expansion of the caravan trade across the Sahara
   C. Maritime trade with the east coast of Africa
   D. The slave trade and gold trade with Europeans
   E. Wealth inherited from their ancestors

16. Which two countries that practiced self-isolation were directly responsible for forcing each other to once again become involved in international world affairs?

   A. Germany and Russia
   B. Russia and France
   C. Germany and the United States
   D. Great Britain and Japan
   E. Japan and United States

17. In Gerardus Cremonensis "Recueil des traités de médecine" (1250–1260), Islamic scholar Muhammad al-Razi is depicted as a practitioner of which area of study?

   A. Bacteria and medicine
   B. Geography of the Middle East
   C. Trade and travel throughout Dar al-Islam
   D. Development of sailing technology for trade on the Indian Ocean
   E. Creation of Arabic numerals and algebra

18. The different religions and political philosophies of Confucianism, legalism, Taoism, Judaism, Buddhism, and Hinduism

    A. were officially sanctioned doctrines of Ch'in and Han emperors.
    B. are religions that developed in classical age China.
    C. emphasized the needs of the individual over the welfare of the state.
    D. had little to no influence upon China and Chinese society.
    E. originated as responses to societal problems during times of disruption.

19. In which Mesoamerican civilization did women have a high amount of rights and privileges, such as owning property, conducting business, and entering the priesthood?

    A. Incas
    B. Mayas
    C. Olmecs
    D. Aztecs
    E. Teotihuacan

20. In order to be on equal terms with the rest of the world, Japan felt it needed to possess what two important international credentials?

    A. A military victory and a large navy
    B. A military victory and a warm water port
    C. A military victory and secular control over the church
    D. A military victory and colonies abroad
    E. A military victory and large industrial complexes

21. Paul's major contribution to the growing movement of Christianity was

    A. his insistence that through Christ everyone can be saved.
    B. spreading the Gospel.
    C. introducing the sacrament of communion.
    D. writing letters to motivate early Christians.
    E. convincing the Roman government to accept Christians.

22. Which traditional European power dominated Southeast Asia until 1955?

    A. Germany
    B. France
    C. Great Britain
    D. Spain
    E. Austria-Hungary

23. What was accomplished by the Treaty of Verdun in 843?

    A. Partitioned the Carolingian Empire
    B. Established peace between the Franks and Muslims
    C. Created the Papal States
    D. Stopped the fighting of the First Crusade
    E. Made peace between the Western and Eastern churches

24. Which two European leaders wanted to form societies governed by strict discipline and work ethic, and then set their governments or communities to operate this way?

    A. Martin Luther and Thomas Hobbes
    B. Oliver Cromwell and Peter the Great
    C. John Calvin and Lorenzo de Medici
    D. Prince Clemens von Metternich and Napoleon
    E. John Calvin and Oliver Cromwell

25. How is the writing of the ancient Indus River Valley different from that of Egypt, Mesopotamia, and China?

    A. We are still unable to decipher their style.
    B. It is written in a very elegant style that has become an art form.
    C. It cannot be matched with any known Western alphabet.
    D. They did not develop the ability to write.
    E. They were the first to write on paper.

26. Which country was NOT a former satellite of the Soviet Union when the breakup of the Soviet Union began in 1990?

    A. Poland
    B. Czechoslovakia
    C. Romania
    D. West Germany
    E. Hungary

27. After witnessing 100,000 dead soldiers, which Maurya emperor converted to Buddhism and issued the following quote on caring for his people, "All people are my children, and just as I desire for my children that they should obtain welfare and happiness"?

    A. Chandragupta
    B. Ashoka
    C. Tamil
    D. Shah Jahan
    E. Theravada

28. A Japanese *zaibatsu* would be best described as which of the following?

    A. A Japanese corporation
    B. Original Japanese business
    C. The accumulation of industrial capital
    D. Foreign banks that heavily invested in Japanese industry
    E. A political party formed to combat the elimination of the samurai

29. Which two religious leaders wanted to reform the church after decades of corruption?

    A. John Calvin and Benedict of Nurisa
    B. Martin Luther and Pope Gregory VII
    C. Pope Urban II and Oliver Cromwell
    D. Henry VIII and Catherine of Aragon
    E. St. Theresa of Avila and Ignatius of Loyola

30. How many people maximum existed in Paleolithic clans?

    A. 30–40
    B. 20–30
    C. 10–15
    D. 30–60
    E. 60–80

31. Which two African nations followed two very different routes to independence?

    A. Algeria and Libya
    B. Egypt and the Sudan
    C. Ethiopia and Zaire
    D. Congo and Rhodesia
    E. Ghana and Kenya

32. Which best describes the process of proletarianization?

    A. The education of workers paid by the owner of a factory
    B. The eventual loss of safe working conditions in a factory
    C. The loss of artisans having the ability to claim ownership over the production of their products, meaning a loss of control over the price and quality of items produced
    D. The growing discontent of upper classes caused by the increase in rural workers moving into cities looking for work
    E. The final defeat of feudalism

33. In which of the following ways were the medieval ages of Western Europe NOT like other civilizations?

    A. The Middle Ages finally saw the spread of civilization outside the Mediterranean region to new areas in Northern and Eastern Europe.
    B. Several new religious ideas helped the spread of Western civilization.
    C. Western Europe during the Middle Ages remained culturally backward and isolated.
    D. Western Europe was integrated into the new international trading networks.
    E. Western Europe was plagued with a succession of epidemic diseases.

34. Peter the Great's economic policy was geared toward

    A. making Russia a major commercial power in Europe to rival that of the West.
    B. increasing the power and size of his armed forces.
    C. stripping the boyars of their traditional power.
    D. removing the streltsy from their position of power.
    E. Both A and C

35. Which of the following countries experienced the most rapid industrialization and recovery from recession periods in relation to the other industrial powers in the world?

    A. United States
    B. England
    C. Portugal
    D. Japan
    E. France

"Neither a life of self-indulgence, nor one of self-mortification can bring happiness. Only a middle path, avoiding these two extremes, leads to peace of mind, wisdom, and complete liberation from the dissatisfactions of life."

—Bhante Gunaratana, "Eight Mindful Steps to Happiness"

36. Which religion/philosophy is closely associated with these ideals?

    A. Hinduism
    B. Buddhism
    C. Judaism
    D. Islam
    E. Monotheism

37. The armies of Genghis Khan that spread across Asia and Europe, attacked the Russian town of Kiev, and settled in Russia became known as

    A. Orthodox Mongols.
    B. the Golden Horde.
    C. Boyars.
    D. Cossacks.
    E. Tartars.

38. The Cape Society of South Africa in the 18th century included all of the following EXCEPT

    A. Portuguese.
    B. Afrikaners.
    C. English.
    D. Khoikhoi.
    E. Prazeros.

39. Which two countries were left out of the signing of the Treaty of Versailles, which led to conflict throughout the remainder of the 20th century?

    A. Russia and Germany
    B. Germany and Austria
    C. Italy and Russia
    D. Russia and Japan
    E. Japan and Belgium

40. Which of the following occupied the lowest place in the official Chinese society hierarchy?

    A. Students
    B. Merchants
    C. Peasants
    D. Artisans
    E. Soldiers

41. Why can President Corazon Aquino of the Philippines be compared to President George Washington of the United States?

    A. They went from being general to president.
    B. They became the first president of a new independent country.
    C. They set presidential term limits.
    D. They took over the government after British rule.
    E. They endured harsh criticism during the formative years of their presidencies.

42. Louis XIV's mastery of propaganda and his palace at Versailles were created to

    A. overtly display his grandeur to the people.
    B. slowly exert his control over the nobility as he was the chief source of patronage.
    C. give Louis massive political dividends, even while it cost nearly half of his yearly revenue.
    D. organize his court around his personal routine.
    E. All of the above

43. As a result of the formation and recognition of Israel, this group has been defiant of Israeli rule ever since the country's founding in 1964?

    A. Hamas
    B. Al-Qaeda
    C. Palestinian Liberation Organization
    D. Hezbollah
    E. Intifada

44. Which step is out of proper chronological order according to the Dynastic Cycle of the Mandate of Heaven?

Six Steps of the Chinese Dynastic Cycle

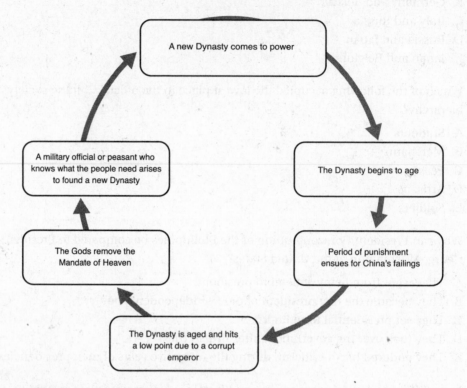

A. A new Dynasty comes to power.

B. The Dynasty begins to age.

C. Period of punishment ensues for China's failings.

D. The Dynasty is aged and hits a low point due to a corrupt emperor.

E. The Gods remove the Mandate of Heaven.

45. What type of engineering and technology used in Mesoamerica is pictured here?

A. Terracing for agriculture

B. Using a mountaintop acropolis for defense

C. Pyramid building

D. Large towers for defensive lookouts

E. Water storage and filtrations system

46. What is the similarity between the unification of Germany and the unification of Italy during their nationalist movements?

  A. Both had to win victories over France.
  B. Both had support of the pope and the church.
  C. Both were led by conservative monarchists trying to increase the power of their king.
  D. Both were accomplished by grassroots leaders.
  E. Both were achieved after long and bloody civil wars.

47. Why was the capital of the Roman empire moved eastward to what became Constantinople?

  A. It could easily protect the Danube and western frontier.
  B. It could control trade in the Caspian Sea.
  C. It was easily defensible.
  D. It was close to the Silk Road of China, old Roman trade routes, and the meeting points of three continents giving it easy access for trade and traders coming and going between the areas.
  E. All of the above

48. Since 1995, a major trade dispute between the United States and China has been over the

  A. pirating of U.S. movies, CDs, and computer software.
  B. presence and success of the Coca-Cola Corporation.
  C. refusal of the Chinese to open markets to American automobile manufacturers.
  D. documented human rights violations.
  E. limiting of Google applications and the refusal to set up cell phone and satellite relay stations.

49. The sole responsibility of the Casa de Contratación was to

  A. protect the Spanish sea lanes.
  B. regulate trade with the New World.
  C. serve as a training school for the governing executives.
  D. act as a supreme court for the New World.
  E. collect one-fifth of all silver mining revenue for the Spanish crown.

50. After conquering this North African empire, Rome controlled land on three continents and called the Mediterranean Sea *Mare Nostrum*, meaning "Our Sea."

  A. Nubia
  B. Ghana
  E. Byzantium
  D. Sardinia
  E. Carthage

51. The Song Dynasty in China took which invention, originally made for entertainment, and adapted it for use during warfare?

    A. Movable type for propaganda
    B. Chain link armor
    C. Gunpowder
    D. Smallpox vaccine to inoculate troops
    E. Crossbows

52. Which of the following best describes the result of the conflict over the use of religious images or icons in the Eastern Orthodox Church?

    A. The Orthodox Church banned the use of religious images, most likely due to Islamic influence.
    B. Because of the popular practice of having and using icons, the Orthodox Church promoted their usage.
    C. After a long and complex battle, icon use was gradually restored, while the tradition of state control over church affairs was also reasserted.
    D. Because of the strong resistance of the monks, icon use was restricted to those regions of the empire where the monasteries were located.
    E. The use of icons was a widely accepted practice with both the Eastern and Western churches.

53. Which is the main difference between the fascist and communist ideologies?

    A. Communism focuses on unification and nationalism, whereas fascism revolves around a theory of equality within the state.
    B. Fascism is an ideology of aggressive nationalism, whereas communism is an economic theory of equality.
    C. Communism exercises self-sufficiency, whereas fascism deals with each according to his needs.
    D. Fascism was geared for the long haul, whereas communism was seen as a drastic, but necessary, quick fix.
    E. Fascism was an exportable concept, whereas communism was conceptually an internal ideology.

"When anyone studies a little or pays a little attention to the rules of Islamic government, Islamic politics, Islamic society, and Islamic economy, he will realize that Islam is a very political religion. Anyone who will say that religion is separate from politics is a fool; he does not know Islam or politics."

—Ayatollah Khomeini

54. Based on this statement, why did the Ayatollah Khomeini lead an Iranian governmental revolution in 1979?

    A. To reduce the influence of the Kurds and other minority groups
    B. To remove Iran from being sought by both sides in the Cold War
    C. To get rid of governmental corruption and abuses of power
    D. To separate the church and the state from becoming intertwined
    E. To respond to the creation of Israel

55. What is the difference of the vision for Latin American independence between Simón Bolívar and José de San Martín?

    A. San Martín wanted democratic republics, and Bolívar wanted newly independent countries to be governed by Latin American monarchies.
    B. Bolívar hoped for a grassroots citizen-led government, whereas San Martín wanted a rule by land aristocracy.
    C. Bolívar wanted to use a governing model based on Spanish peninsular rule, whereas San Martín favored a Creole, or local authoritarian rule.
    D. San Martín wanted newly independent countries to be governed by Latin American monarchies whereas Bolívar wanted democratic republics.
    E. Bolívar wanted to open trade with the United States and Great Britain, whereas San Martín wanted to remain isolated and become self-sufficient.

56. The new merchant class in Europe that arose after the Crusades was composed of which of the following social classes?

    A. Landed nobility
    B. Vassals of the king
    C. Poor, landless adventurers
    D. Middle class
    E. Second- and third-class knights who had no better option

57. Who took over the leadership of Russia when Vladimir Lenin died?

    A. Nikita Khrushchev
    B. Leon Trotsky
    C. Leonid Brezhnev
    D. Joseph Stalin
    E. Mikhail Gorbachev

58. Between 1300 and 1800, which Islamic empires were known as the Gunpowder Empires?

    A. Ottoman, Mughal, and Sassanid
    B. Abbasid, Umayyad, Mughal
    C. Mamluk, Sassanid, Ottoman
    D. Sassanid, Fatimid, Abbasid
    E. Fatimid, Ottoman, Seljuk

59. The decolonization of Mexico and Central America was responsible for which new type of conflict?

    A. Illegal immigration/border war
    B. Drug wars
    C. Contra Affair
    D. Latin American Cold War
    E. Economic warfare between multinational corporations

60. England used which area of the world as a penal colony?

    A. Falkland Islands

    B. Virginia

    C. South Africa

    D. Australia

    E. Mosquito Coast

61. How did the introduction of a feudal monarchy in England compare to that of the government in France?

    A. The English feudal monarchy developed more gradually and slowly in response to its rapidly improving economy.

    B. The English feudal monarchy was introduced quickly in 1066, whereas the French feudal monarchy developed slowly over several hundred years due to conflicts among the French aristocracy.

    C. The French feudal monarchy arose almost immediately as a result of the defeat of the Viking invaders of Paris.

    D. France failed to develop a feudal monarchy until the 15th century.

    E. As a result of William the Conqueror's victory, England never developed a strong feudal monarchy.

62. Following the breakup of the Soviet Union, Slobodan Milosevic began an ethnic cleansing of Muslims from which country?

    A. Serbia

    B. Bosnia and Herzegovina

    C. Yugoslavia

    D. Ukraine

    E. Macedonia

63. Which river valley civilization had the most diverse and deep social class system, consisting of eight distinct classes of society?

    A. Mesopotamia

    B. China

    C. Rome

    D. Egypt

    E. India

64. Which two U.S. presidents were directly responsible for the development and execution of the atomic bomb project?

    A. Harry S. Truman and John F. Kennedy

    B. Franklin D. Roosevelt and Harry S Truman

    C. Franklin D. Roosevelt and Dwight D. Eisenhower

    D. J. Edgar Hoover and Franklin D. Roosevelt

    E. Harry S Truman and Richard Nixon

"Every man has a property in his own person. This nobody has a right to, but himself."

"During the time men live without a common power to keep them all in awe, they are in that condition called war; and such a war, as if of every man, against every man."

65. Which two Enlightenment thinkers voiced these opposing views on the role of government?

A. Locke and Voltaire
B. Voltaire and Montesquieu
C. Montesquieu and Hobbes
D. Hobbes and Locke
E. Rousseau and Diderot

66. Under which Mughal Dynasty ruler did the British East India Company gain access to India's coastal ports and begin the process of dominating India?

A. Akbar
B. Ram Mohun Roy
C. Babar
D. Jahangir
E. Shah Jahan

"And so we are going to establish a school for the service of the Lord. In founding it, we hope to introduce nothing harsh or burdensome. But if a certain strictness results from the dictates of equity for the amendment of vices or the preservation of charity, do not be at once dismayed and fly from the way of salvation, whose entrance cannot but be narrow."

67. Which organizer of western Monasticism wrote this passage?

A. John Calvin
B. Benedict of Nurisa
C. Anthony of Egypt
D. Martin of Tours
E. Charles Martel

68. Which two world leaders allowed hubris to bring about the "beginning of the end" of their dominance by attacking Russia during the brutal winter season?

A. Genghis Khan and Otto von Bismarck
B. Napoleon Bonaparte and Charlemagne
C. Maximilien Robespierre and Adolf Hitler
D. Clemens von Metternich and King Louis XIV
E. Napoleon Bonaparte and Adolf Hitler

69. Which invention allowed Islamic traders to spread civilization and expand trade through the Indian Ocean?

    A. Lateen sail

    B. Junk

    C. Trireme

    D. Square sail

    E. Mercury compass

"When I make myself imagine what it is like to be one of those women who live at home, faithfully serving their husbands—women who have not a single exciting prospect in life yet who believe that they are perfectly happy—I am filled with scorn…I cannot bear men who believe that women serving in the Palace are…frivolous and wicked. Yet I suppose their prejudice is understandable."

—Sei Shonagon, *The Pillow Book*

70. What part of Japanese culture is the author describing in this passage?

    A. Satirical essays about courtly life

    B. The feelings of an imperial concubine and her long lost love

    C. The harsh life of peasants and slaves

    D. A history of previous dynasties

    E. The difficulty in modifying Chinese culture to Japan

71. For which of the following reasons was the Opium War fought?

    A. France and Britain were competing for control of the opium trade with China.

    B. Since China banned the use of opium, it threatened a key part of British trade.

    C. Chinese citizens and the Chinese government differed in their ideas on how to rid the nation of foreigners.

    D. They allowed China to reestablish the tribute system.

    E. The Chinese government wanted to adopt a Ch'in Dynasty-like monopoly on opium.

Dividend = Divisor x quotient + remainder

$a^2 + b^2 = c^2$

Volume of a sphere = $\frac{4}{3}\pi r^3$

72. Near the end of the Greek era of dominance, at which location were these scientific and mathematical equations discovered?

    A. Athens

    B. Persepolis

    C. House of Muses

    D. Delos

    E. Delphi

73. Who was responsible for the development of a steam engine that could be applied to industrial production?

    A. James Watt

    B. Eli Whitney

    C. James Arkwright

    D. Robert Morse

    E. Robert Fulton

74. Which Native American tribe would have lived in the dwellings pictured here in order to stay safe from warring tribes?

    A. Hopewell

    B. Pueblo

    C. Nez Perce

    D. Huron

    E. Cherokee

75. What region of Africa was first converted to Islam by 700 C.E.?

    A. East Africa

    B. Central Africa

    C. West Africa

    D. North Africa

    E. South Africa

76. Who was responsible for bringing the written word to a mass population in Europe, helping to further the growing movement of the Renaissance?

    A. Voltaire

    B. Johannes Gutenberg

    C. Cervantes

    D. Denis Diderot

    E. Jean-Jacques Rousseau

77. During the High Middle Ages after the Crusades, who did towns tend to ally themselves with in terms of the political structure of the age?

    A. Kings against the middle class and the lower classes

    B. Kings against feudal lords

    C. Feudal lords against the kings and the newly created guild system

    D. The church against the feudal lords

    E. Local bishops to protect them from greedy nobles

78. The Hindu concept of karma can best be defined as

A. matter that attaches itself to your soul.

B. the acceptance of your caste, gender, and class.

C. work.

D. always being subject to change.

E. insubstantial as all things are subject to change.

79. What area of the world is home to the three monotheistic faiths?

A. Southeastern Europe

B. China

C. Southeast Asia

D. The Middle East

E. India

"The boundary rejoins the Tiberias sub-district boundary at a point on the Nazareth-Tiberias road south-east of the built-up area of Tur'an..."

—Resolution 181, General Assembly of the United Nations, 1947

80. After the Holocaust in World War II, this document created which new homeland, causing tension in the region ever since?

A. Israel

B. Pakistan

C. Bangladesh

D. Lebanon

E. Bosnia

81. During the era of the Triangle Trade, what was the leg of triangle that dealt with the African slave trade coming from Africa known as?

A. Transatlantic

B. Middle Passage

C. Indian Passage

D. Tobacco Route

E. Rum Runner

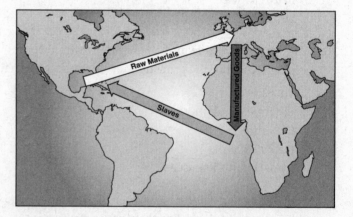

82. Which international movement is specifically designed to combat problems such as global warming and overpopulation?

A. Green Revolution

B. Globalization

C. International Environment Foundation

D. Pan-Africanism

E. Green Peace

83. How should a perfect sage king treat his people?

    A. As a perfectly moral people
    B. As low creatures who will transform only with strict governmental guidelines
    C. With responsibility as the head Confucian role model
    D. As straw dogs who will transform on their own naturally
    E. Morally with upmost righteousness

84. Which policy of the Han Dynasty did the emperors of the Tang Dynasty intentionally choose to keep?

    A. Landscape painting
    B. Printing edicts with movable type
    C. Restricting the number of Confucian scholars
    D. Expansion of the empire
    E. Governmental patronage of technological invention

85. In what way were these works of art by northern Renaissance painters Jan and Hubert van Eyck influential during the Renaissance?

    A. They used oil paints to make their paintings more durable and life-like.
    B. They influenced other Flemish artists.
    C. They were the original humanists.
    D. They painted scenes of ancient Greeks.
    E. They depicted scenes of the Black Death.

"During my lifetime I have dedicated myself to this struggle of the African people. I have fought against white domination, and I have fought against black domination. I have cherished the ideal of a democratic and free society in which all persons live together in harmony and with equal opportunities. It is an ideal which I hope to live for and to achieve. But if needs be, it is an ideal for which I am prepared to die."

—Nelson Mandela

86. Which other African leader's fight for independence mirrored that of Nelson Mandela?

A. Kwame Nkrumah
B. King Afonso
C. Jomo Kenyatta
D. Mobutu Sese Seko
E. Robert Mugabe

87. Which modern-day invention has accelerated cultural diffusion faster than ever before in human history?

A. The first communication satellites
B. Advanced medical technology
C. Expansion of free trade to former isolated areas
D. The World Wide Web (Internet)
E. The Green Revolution

88. Pope Innocent III stated that "the relationship between Pope and Emperor is like the sun to the moon" and further demonstrated this high point of papal power by

A. excommunicating Prince John in England.
B. excommunicating Philip Augustus and placing the people of France under interdict.
C. making an alliance with Philip against Otto of Germany.
D. All of the above
E. forcing King Louis XIV to admit his subservience.

89. How was the French relationship with native groups in the New World different from that of England and Spain?

A. The French let numerous settlements on the frontiers characterize their efforts.
B. The French crown gave complete support to Jesuit missionary efforts.
C. The French had a sparse presence, seen only on the Atlantic Coast.
D. The French were not extractive in terms of permanent damage to the land; they just wanted fur.
E. The French let trade, not settlement, define their peaceful interactions with Native Americans.

90. This leader's assassination put an end to violence during the Pakistan-India split?

A. Franz Ferdinand
B. Jawaharlal Nehru
C. Ram Mohun Roy
D. Mahatma Gandhi
E. Rajiv Gandhi

91. Under whose leadership did a direct democracy grow and the freest government the world had ever known exist?

    A. Draco
    B. Pericles
    C. Pisistratus
    D. Cleisthenes
    E. Themistocles

92. Which Latin American country waged a war on its own citizens while trying to achieve independence, similar to Robespierre during the French Revolution?

    A. Brazil
    B. Venezuela
    C. Argentina
    D. Colombia
    E. Uruguay

"I have determined to write you this letter to inform you of everything that has been done and discovered in this voyage of mine....All of these island are very beautiful... The inhabitants...manifest the greatest affection towards all of us, exchanging valuable things for trifles...I gave them many beautiful and pleasing things, which I had brought with me...that they might become Christians and inclined to love our King and Queen and Princes and all the people of Spain..."

93. Which explorer wrote and delivered this letter to his sponsors upon returning from his voyage in 1493?

    A. Henry the Navigator
    B. Amerigo Vespucci
    C. Vasco de Gama
    D. Ferdinand Magellan
    E. Christopher Columbus

94. The Yamato family was able to unify Japan because of this Korean ally, who gave them the knowledge and ability to smelt iron and served as a bridge between Japan and China?

    A. Silla
    B. Koguryo
    C. Paekche
    D. Kiyamori
    E. Sui

95. In which river valley civilization was your heart weighed in the Underworld to determine if you went to the Happy Valley of Food?

    A. India
    B. Japan
    C. Mesopotamia
    D. Egypt
    E. Athens

ANSWER KEY
Practice Test 3

1. C	25. A	49. B	73. A
2. E	26. D	50. E	74. B
3. C	27. B	51. C	75. D
4. D	28. A	52. C	76. B
5. D	29. B	53. B	77. B
6. B	30. B	54. C	78. C
7. C	31. E	55. D	79. D
8. E	32. C	56. C	80. A
9. A	33. C	57. D	81. B
10. B	34. E	58. A	82. A
11. A	35. D	59. B	83. D
12. C	36. B	60. D	84. D
13. B	37. B	61. D	85. A
14. A	38. E	62. B	86. C
15. D	39. A	63. B	87. D
16. E	40. B	64. B	88. D
17. A	41. C	65. D	89. E
18. E	42. E	66. E	90. D
19. D	43. C	67. B	91. B
20. D	44. C	68. E	92. C
21. B	45. A	69. A	93. E
22. B	46. C	70. A	94. C
23. A	47. E	71. B	95. D
24. E	48. A	72. C	

ANSWER EXPLANATIONS

1. **(C)** In the Olduvai Gorge in Tanzania, Africa, scientists Louis and Mary Leakey found the oldest human remains in 1960.

2. **(E)** To improve the Soviet economy, Lenin began to use New Economic Plans, or NEPs, in 1921. NEPs allowed private ownership of nonessential businesses and allowed farmers to sell surplus products for profit.

3. **(C)** While Japan was transitioning, many people were still rooted in their traditional feudal behaviors.

4. **(D)** After Muhammad's vision in 622 C.E., Islam began to spread rapidly. After Muhammad's ascension, the next five caliphs expanded the religion and Islamic empire to the north, west, and east, reaching all parts of the Byzantine Empire.

5. **(D)** Francisco Madero was from a wealthy landowning family. He was an advocate of social justice and greater democracy and used his wealth to try to bring about change in Mexico. He was assassinated in 1913 by angry members of the previous regime.

6. **(B)** The Ch'in radically changed traditional society and forced people to follow a strict and orderly set of laws with little time to react, bringing about their quick downfall.

7. **(C)** Kaiser Wilhelm II issued his famous "blank check of support" for Austria, promising to back them with whatever they needed as an attack on one European royal was an attack on them all.

8. **(E)** Bismarck had been ambassador to both France and Russia and understood their capabilities. He was able to apply that knowledge by understanding what the Prussian state needed. In carrying out his goals, he had the ability to focus on these objectives and manipulate others to do what he wanted, no matter the consequences.

9. **(A)** The Cuban Missile Crisis of 1962 brought the world close to nuclear war as the Soviet Union began placing nuclear missiles in Cuba, 90 miles from the U.S. coast. President John F. Kennedy placed a blockade of ships around Cuba until the missiles were removed.

10. **(B)** The sharia is not one of the five pillars of Islam. Instead, it is the governing code of Islamic behavior—religious, social, political, and commercial—dictating how you act in public and how you act in private.

11. **(A)** British Prime Minister Disraeli purchased the majority of stock in the Suez Canal, which the Egyptian government was selling to pay back international loans. When Great Britain took control of the canal, they slowly exerted their power and influence over all of Egypt.

12. **(C)** The life-giving monsoons bring vital water to India during the spring/summer as the winds blow southwest to northeast off the Indian Ocean. In summer/fall, the winds change course and blow hot drying air from northeast to southwest.

13. **(B)** The May Fourth Movement was a nationalist movement spurned by the treatment that China was experiencing at the hands of colonial powers, such as Britain and Japan.

14. **(A)** The plebeian class, or second-class citizens, made up the majority of the population of ancient Rome. They fought long and hard for political representation.

15. **(D)** The kingdom of Songhai used slaves in their gold mining operations. They also traded slaves and gold with the Portuguese and other European empires until the 1700s.

16. **(E)** The Japanese imposed self-isolation under the reign of Tokugawa Ieyasu in 1639 and remained isolated until U.S. Commodore Perry entered Japan in 1853. The United States isolated itself from the world after World War I and further isolated itself during the 1930s during the onset of the Great Depression. The United States remained isolated until December 7, 1941, when Japan bombed Pearl Harbor.

17. **(A)** Muhammad al-Razi began his groundbreaking research and study in the area of bacteria and medicine when developing medical treatments and building hospitals circa 900 C.E.

18. **(E)** All of these religions and political philosophies were created to solve problems and restore order during times of instability or disruptions caused by the growing complexities and advances of civilization.

19. **(D)** The Mayan city of Palenque had two women rulers; however, it was the Aztec civilization where women had the highest amount of rights and privileges.

20. **(D)** Following the example of the Western powers, Japan wanted to create a large, powerful, modern military and capture colonies overseas for resources. This is similar to what Great Britain, France, and other Western countries had done.

21. **(B)** The spreading of the Gospel to Gentiles (non-Hebrews) around the Mediterranean Sea is the major accomplishment of the apostle Paul.

22. **(B)** France colonized Indochina in 1887 and remained a presence there until 1956, when the French gave up colonial control after tiring of fighting Ho Chi Minh and his communist guerrilla forces.

23. **(A)** It ended the brief unification of the Holy Roman Empire as Charlemagne's grandsons fought their oldest brother for land. The treaty stopped the fighting and split Europe once again into three separate kingdoms.

24. **(E)** John Calvin and Oliver Cromwell were leaders of their community and country who believed in governing through strict religious lines, discipline, and work ethic to cure corruption and abuses that had been prevalent in society.

25. **(A)** As a result of the unexplained disappearance of the people of the Indus River Valley, historians have not been able to recover a method of interpreting or translating the writing of the ancient Indus Valley.

26. **(D)** West Germany was a member of NATO and a democratic country since its founding in 1949.

27. **(B)** In 268 B.C.E., after conquering the Deccan Plateau, Emperor Ashoka converted to Buddhism and set pillars across India promising good government.

28. **(A)** A zaibatsu is best defined as a Japanese corporation, like Iwasaki Yataro's Mitsubishi Bank.

29. **(B)** In 1073, Pope Gregory VII extended the Cluniac Reforms, which began in the 900s and were devoted to religious purity within the church. In 1517, Martin Luther wrote his *95 Theses*, identifying problems within the church, like the selling of indulgences and relics.

30. **(B)** Paleolithic clans maxed out between 20 and 30 members because after that point, it became too difficult to feed and support a population larger than that on a daily basis.

31. **(E)** Ghana and Kenya achieved independence but followed two different routes. Ghana peacefully won independence in 1957. Kenya fought a bloody war against the British, and it was not until 1963 that Britain recognized Kenyan independence with the election of Jomo Kenyatta as the first president.

32. **(C)** As products became mass-produced and the demand in quantity increased, a cheaper product was produced. It was more readily available than those handcrafted by artisans, who eventually were put out of business.

33. **(C)** Unlike other civilizations around the world, medieval Europe regressed in education and culture during the Middle Ages. They were cut off from cultural diffusion during the period from 500 C.E. to 1000 C.E.

34. **(E)** Peter wanted to get rid of the boyars who had long stood in the way of Russian reforms. He also wanted to harness the tremendous natural resources of Russia to make them an industrial power.

35. **(D)** Japan, considered to be the gold standard of industrialization, was determined to be self-sufficient and recovered more quickly than anyone else.

36. **(B)** By becoming the Enlightened One, the Buddha wanted to teach everyone the secret to achieving nirvana to escape from mortal existence. He gave a series of instructions to his followers—his Middle Path—to help the followers achieve nirvana.

37. **(B)** The Golden Horde attacked Kiev in 1236. They were known as the Golden Horde due to the color of their yurts (tents).

38. **(E)** Prazeros were Portuguese sailors and merchants who settled in East Africa after the destruction of East African and Islamic trading cities and trade routes.

39. **(A)** Leaving out the major Central and Eastern powers—Germany and Russia—from the Treaty of Versailles caused problems throughout World War II as anger erupted from both countries.

40. **(B)** The Chinese valued hard work, whereas merchants, albeit necessary, were seen as those who made money from other people's labor. They were not respected.

41. **(C)** Corazon Aquino set a one-term, six-year limit for the position of president in the Philippines, similar to George Washington, who set the precedent of serving no more than two terms for eight years in the United States.

42. **(E)** Louis used Versailles to provide his people with a visual of his power and as a vehicle to manipulate and subjugate his rivals.

43. **(C)** The Palestinian Liberation Organization (PLO) led by Yasser Arafat has waged guerrilla war or resistance movements against Israeli rule, bringing about a conflict that has seen only brief periods of peace or cease-fire.

44. **(C)** The period of punishment—floods, famine, and invasion—comes after the Mandate is removed. The chaos exists until a new emperor proves himself and starts the Dynastic Cycle once again.

45. **(A)** The image shows terraced agriculture used throughout Mesoamerica and the Incan Empire. Terraced farming used flat lands carved into a mountainside to maximize agricultural space and to prevent soil and crop erosion on the steep hillsides.

46. **(C)** Both Count Camillo Cavour and Otto von Bismarck were appointed prime ministers by their kings. Both men were also conservative monarchists who knew as their king grew in power, they would reap the benefits. Thus, they orchestrated the unification of their countries.

47. **(E)** Constantinople became the new capital as it was closer to the trade routes in the Middle East and east Asia, and its location made it easy to defend and gave them easy access to the Mediterranean and Black Sea.

48. **(A)** A major trade dispute arose when China stopped U.S. shipments and copied entertainment items and software. China then resold it under a Chinese governmental label, causing President Clinton to threaten to revoke China's "most-favored nation" clause.

49. **(B)** The Casa de Contratación, or House of Trade, was created specifically to control and regulate trade with the New World.

50. **(E)** Following the defeat of Carthage in 146 B.C.E., Rome won an empire that spanned parts of three continents and virtually all land touching the Mediterranean Sea.

51. **(C)** Circa 960 C.E., the Song dynasty adapted gunpowder used for firework displays so it could be used in movable cannons to be used in warfare.

52. **(C)** Emperor Leo III banned their use, possibly to make peace with advancing Islamic armies. However, due to their use and popularity with the people, icons were restored but were heavily regulated by the government, which maintained control of the church.

53. **(B)** Fascism is a political ideology extolling the glory of the state, past glory, and aggressive nationalism. Communism is an economic theory based on equality and public ownership of the means of production where each worker is paid according to his or her needs and abilities.

54. **(C)** The Revolution of 1979 was led by Khomeini as he accused the Shah of violating the sharia, becoming too corrupt, and giving into Western influences.

55. **(D)** After helping many Latin American nations achieve independence from Spanish rule, José de San Martín wanted monarchs to rule the new countries, whereas Simón Bolívar wanted the new countries to become democratic republics.

56. **(C)** Unskilled laborers who had little to lose formed the new merchant class. They were willing to risk their lives in order to get off the manors where they were subject to the whims of their lord and to increase their wealth.

57. **(D)** After the death of Vladimir Lenin, Joseph Stalin, head of the Communist Party, placed his supporters in positions of power while slowly isolating Leon Trotsky. Then, he assumed leadership of the Soviet Union.

58. **(A)** The Ottoman, Mughal, and Sassanid empires were known as the Gunpowder Empires because their mastery of gunpowder and firearms allowed them to form dominant empires from Europe to Southeast Asia.

59. **(B)** Countries such as Colombia have been growing drugs for years, and criminal gangs began smuggling illegal drugs to other countries in the 1970s. The U.S. government declared a "War on Drugs" in 1980.

60. **(D)** England sent a colonization party of convicts to Australia in 1788. They landed in Botany Bay and began to set up a permanent colony.

61. **(D)** Without a strong, dominant family or noble, France was dominated by several regional rulers of near-equal strength. This prevented anyone from claiming to be the king of France until the 1400s.

62. **(B)** Slobodan Milosevic was the president of Serbia during a cleansing of Muslims in Bosnia and Herzegovina, which took place between 1992 and 1995. Milosevic died during his international war crimes trial at The Hague in 2006.

63. **(B)** China is recognized as having the widest gap in social classes. The upper classes lived a life of luxury in the palaces; in many places, peasants lived in earthen holes in the ground covered with bamboo. This disparity was visually demonstrated by the extremes between social classes.

64. **(B)** President Franklin Roosevelt was a major force behind the Manhattan Project and the development of the atomic bomb. President Harry Truman was made aware of the project after the death of President Roosevelt and gave the approval to drop atomic bombs on Hiroshima and Nagasaki.

65. **(D)** John Locke believed that all people have the right to life, liberty, and property, and it is the job of a government to protect those rights. Any government that does not do so should be changed. Thomas Hobbes believed that people were selfish and greedy, and existed in a state of nature. He said that if people were not controlled, they would repress each other, so people should give up freedoms to a powerful government that could organize and maintain order.

66. **(E)** Under the leadership of Shah Jahan, the British East India Company gained initial access to Indian trading ports from which the British would slowly begin to extend their power in India.

67. **(B)** Benedict wrote the Benedictine Order, which regimented the life of a monk into four equal periods: three hours each of praying, working, studying, and sleeping. Keeping monks in this routine made it easy to resist temptation and focus on the work of the church.

68. **(E)** Both Napoleon Bonaparte, who invaded Russia in June of 1812, and Adolf Hitler, who invaded Russia in June of 1941, attacked in the summer after enjoying tremendous success on land. Due to the vastness of Russia and the fight put up by its citizens, both attacks stalled. Their armies were brutalized and decimated by the Russian winter. As a result of their failed invasions, both Napoleon and Hitler saw the beginning of the end of their empires.

69. **(A)** The Arab use of the lateen sail greatly aided long distance trade and travel across the Indian Ocean to East Africa.

70. **(A)** Sei Shonagon wrote essays on how life in the palace was glamorous and exciting when viewed from the outside. However, from the inside, it was an endless, boring routine of doing the same thing day after day. *The Pillow Book* also talked about how women were treated at night by the members of the imperial court.

71. **(B)** China's banning of opium removed a highly lucrative part of British overseas trade with Asia. They sold the consumable narcotic to the Chinese in exchange for tea, which Britain sold on the world market for a high price.

72. **(C)** The House of Muses was founded by Alexander the Great in Alexandria, Egypt. It became one of the world's first universities with a library, lecture hall, and laboratories. This attracted scholars from around the ancient world. Euclid, Pythagorus, and Archimedes all studied at the House of Muses.

73. **(A)** James Watt's steam engine is the single most important improvement of the Industrial Revolution.

74. **(B)** The Anasazi Indians built dwellings among the cliffs of the Southwestern United States between 900 C.E. to 1350 C.E. They were later named the Pueblo by the Spanish conquistadors. Some pueblo dwellings can still be seen today in Colorado and New Mexico.

75. **(D)** North African Berbers became some of the first in Africa to be converted to Islam in the 700s C.E. as Islamic expansion broke out from the Middle East and began to expand outside of the Arabian Peninsula. North Africa and Berber traders were easily accessible due to the existing trade routes.

76. **(B)** In 1456, Johannes Gutenberg of Germany printed the Bible with movable type. The movable type printing press became one of the most important inventions in human history. Books were cheaper and easier to produce; as a result, they became accessible to more and more people who began to learn to read and write, vastly increasing literacy.

77. **(B)** Towns sided with kings, who chartered the towns so people would have the freedom to work and make a profit. It was a chance for the people to work for themselves and not a feudal lord.

78. **(C)** Karma is the work that you do. Good actions have good effects, and bad actions act as a weight holding you down in the next round of rebirth. Karma is the total sum of an individual's actions in his or her current or former lives.

79. **(D)** The Middle East—with Israel and Saudi Arabia—is home to the three monotheistic faiths: Judaism, Christianity, and Islam.

80. **(A)** Great Britain's creation of Israel and the U.S. recognition of Israel in 1948 as a homeland for Jewish refugees after World War II has created a state of warfare or tension ever since.

81. **(B)** This brutal leg of the journey was known as the Middle Passage. Slaves were loaded into cargo holds, subjected to brutal conditions, and taken to the Caribbean and the Americas.

82. **(A)** The Green Revolution is the use of new seeds, fertilizers, and hybrid crops to increase food production in India and other countries with food production problems.

83. **(D)** The sage king should treat his people as straw dogs because if he did anything to help them, then the people would always expect his help. A sage king must do nothing, and the people would learn and transform on their own.

84. **(D)** The Tang Dynasty kept up the policy of increasing China's borders in order to be a strong successful dynasty. The Tang pushed the borders west to Afghanistan and south to Vietnam.

85. **(A)** The van Eycks developed and painted with oil paints, making their scenes much richer in detail and bringing realism to their art.

86. **(C)** As World War II ended, Jomo Kenyatta began to speak of an independent Kenya. As Mau Mau guerrillas began to attack settlers and other Africans, Kenyatta was arrested. He was released in 1963 and was elected prime minister.

87. **(D)** The World Wide Web places information sharing, business transactions, photos, and videos in the hands of people across the globe almost instantaneously.

88. **(D)** Pope Innocent III, at one time or another, excommunicated and placed under interdict the monarchs of England, France, and Germany for the individual actions at home and during the war of rightful succession for title of Holy Roman emperor.

89. **(E)** The French were not after permanent territorial acquisition like the English and Spanish. They peaceably interacted with the natives.

90. **(D)** The assassination of Mahatma Gandhi in 1948 discredited violent extremists who were upset at the Muslim and Hindu partitioning of India.

91. **(B)** Under the leadership of general statesman Pericles at the end of the Persian Wars, Athens created a direct democracy where political participation was encouraged. Pericles believed that a man who does not take part in the governing of his city was not harmless but useless. Pericles ruled during a period known as the Golden Age of Athens.

92. **(C)** In 1976, after the death of Juan Perón, the Argentinian military took over to defeat the Argentinian guerrillas. The army waged a campaign of terror and killing, resulting in the deaths of an unknown number of its own civilians in the process.

93. **(E)** Columbus's voyage was sponsored by Ferdinand and Isabella in 1492. That same year, Columbus launched the first of his four voyages to the Americas, discovering a new land. However, till the end of his life, Columbus was convinced he was in Asia.

94. **(C)** The Paekche Dynasty of southeast Korea was the closest to Japan and gave the knowledge of iron smelting to the Yamato family. This allowed them to defeat their rivals with stronger weapons. The Paekche Dynasty also introduced Japan to China.

95. **(D)** Ancient Egyptians believed that a dead soul placed its heart on a scale in front of Osiris, God of the Underworld. If you were pure and good of heart, you went to the Happy Valley of Food, where you did not have to labor to get food.

Index

creoles, 276
Crimean War, 291, 297, 318
Cromwell, Oliver, 234–235
Crow Indians, 190
crusades, 145, 152–153, 158
Cuba, 379–380
Cuban Missile Crisis, 379–380, 408
cultural diffusion
  in Africa, 166, 168, 173
  in Asia, 51
  in China, 195, 207
  in Europe, 153
  in India, 80
  in the New Kingdom (Egypt), 33
  of Japan, 111
  with Paleolithic and Neolithic people, 28–29
  with Phoenicians, 39
  in the Americas, 23, 25–26, 179
Cultural Revolution, 403
cuneiform, 37
cyberterrorism, 447
Cyrus the Great, 38–39

D
da Gama, Vasco, 225
da Vinci, Leonardo, 214
daimyo, 246–247
"Dar al-Islam," 204
Darius (emperor), 39
Darius III, 78
Darius (king), 73–74
Dark Ages, 69, 109, 115, 122, 126, 128, 132, 145, 153–154, 170, 186, 204, 225, 246
David (Michelangelo), 214
Dawes Plan, 350
D-Day, 370
de Clerk, F. W., 393
de Pisan, Christine, 214
Declaration of Independence, 270
Declaration of the Rights of Man and of the Citizen, The, 273
decolonization, 387
Delian League, 75
demilitarized zone (DMZ), 336, 364, 396
Deng Xiaoping, 403–404, 437
Descartes, René, 220
De-Stalinization, 417
détente, 420
Dharma, 56–57
Diaz, Porfiro, 410
Diderot, Denis, 262
Diem, President, 380–381
Diet, 305, 395
Diocletian, 94
Directory, The, 275
Dirty War, 407
Discobolus, 77
Disraeli, Benjamin, 318
Doctrine of Papal Primacy, 132
Don Quixote (de Cervantes), 216, 240
Donatello, 214
Doomsday book, 157
Dorians, 69
Draco, 72

Drake, Francis, 240
Dual Alliance, 330
Dukkha, 59
Duma, 339–340
Dutch Communist Party, 351
Dutch East India Trading Company, 175–176, 226
Duvalier, Francois, 412
Duvalier, Jean-Claude, 412
Dynastic Cycle, 45–46, 99

E
Eastern Orthodox Christianity, 144–145
"Economic Consequences of Peace, The" (Keynes), 337
Edict of Nantes, 238
Egypt, 31, 33, 318
eightfold path, 59
Eisenhower, Dwight D., 370, 378
Eleanor of Aquitaine, 157–158, 160
Elements, The (Euclid), 79
Elizabeth I (queen), 233, 239–240
Emmanuel, Victor (king), 292–293, 330, 336
Emmanuel III, Victor (king), 355
Empress Amida, 114
Empress Wu Zetian, 194
Ems Dispatch, 295
encomienda, 255
Engels, Friedrich, 286
English Civil War, 234
English factory act, 285
enlightenment, 261–264
Enola Gay (bomber plane), 371
Entent Cordiale, 331
Epic of Gilgamesh, The, 43
Erasmus, 215
Escobar, Pablo, 445
Estates General, 271–272
Euclid, 79
Euphrates River, 35, 89, 205
Euripides, 78
European Community (EC), 443
European Economic Community (EEC), 443
European Union (EU), 443
ever-level granaries, 99–100

F
Facebook, 447–448
Farm Credit Act, 346
farming, 26
fascism, 354–355
Fatima, 125
Fatimid Dynasty, 205
Ferdinand, Franz, 332
Ferdinand (king of Spain), 224
Ferdinand VII (king), 279
Fertile Crescent, 35, 38
Feudalism, 46, 112–114, 134–136
Filial Piety, 53
"Fireside Chats," 346
First Continental Congress, 269
First Crusade, 145, 152–153
First Triumvirate, 87–88
five pillars of Islam, 122
Five-Year Plans, 353, 402
Flavian Dynasty, 91

foot binding, 196
Forbidden City, 249
Ford, Henry, 345
Four Modernizations, 403, 437
four river valley civilizations, 29
Fourteen Points Plan, 335
Fox, Vicente, 412
France, 258
Francis I (emperor), 296
Franco, Francisco, 364–365
Franco-Prussian war, 336
Frank, Anne, 370
Franklin, Benjamin, 269
Franks, 131
Frederick Barbarossa (emperor), 155, 158–159
Frederick II, 159
Frederick William II (emperor), 273
French Revolution, 271–275
"From Stettin in the Baltic to Trieste in the Adriatic"
    (Churchill), 376
Fujiwara family, 113

G
Galileo, 219
Gandhi, Indira, 398
Gandhi, Mahatma, 315–316, 397–398
Gandhi, Rajiv, 398–399
Garibaldi, Giuseppe, 292–293
genocide, 369–370, 394
geography
    Africa, 165–166, 171, 174, 312
    Australia, 47
    Byzantine Empire, 143
    China, 43
    defined, 23
    Egypt, 31, 33
    Greece, 70
    Incas, 187
    India, 40
    Japan, 110
    Korea, 109
    Mesoamerica, 179
    Mesopotamia, 35
    Persia, 73
    prehistory/Paleolithic to human civilization emergence,
        23
    Rome, 83
    Russia, 145–146
George I (king), 235–236
Germany, 152, 158–159, 293–295
Ghana, Kingdom of, 167–168
Glasnost, 421
Glorious Revolution, 235–236
Goddess of Democracy, 437
Godwinson, Harold, 157
Gold Coast, 170
Golden Horde, 146–147
Goldman Sachs, 46
Good Neighbor Policy, 411
Gorbachev, Mikhail, 420–422
Gosplan, 353
government
    ancient Greek, 70–71
    Aztecs, 185–186

caste system of, 42, 55, 62
creation of, 27
first unified code of law, 38
Han, 101–102
Ieyasu, Tokugawa (Japan), 247–248
Mayan civilization, 183
Mesopotamia, 36
Neolithic Revolution, 27
Olmec, 181
Peter the Great (Russia), 242
republic, 83
Suleiman the Magnificent, 244–245
Tang Dynasty, 194
Teotihuacan, 181
Zhou Dynasty, 46
Gracchus, Gaius, 86–87
Gracchus, Tiberius, 86–87
granaries, ever-level, 99–100
Grand Canal, 194
Great Depression, 306, 325, 345–357, 363–364, 407
Great Leap Forward, 402–403
Great Proletarian Cultural Revolution, 402
Great Royal Road, 39
Great Schism, 145
Great Scramble, The, 312
Great Zimbabwe, 174–175
Greece, 34, 39, 61–62, 69–81, 89–90
Green Revolution, 398, 440–441
Gregory (pope), 156
Gregory VII (pope), 151–152
gunpowder empires, 207–208, 223, 244, 317
Gupta Dynasty, 96
Gutenberg, Johannes, 216

H
Habsburg Dynasty, 238–240
hacienda, 255
Hadrian (emperor), 91
Haiti, 276–277
Hamas, 432
Hamilcar, 85
Hammurabi (Babylonian king), 38
Han Dynasty, 99–104
Han Fei Tzu, 51
Han Wu Ti, 99–102
Hanging Gardens of Babylon, 38
Hangul language, 110
Hannibal, 85
Harappa (India), 41
Harding, Warren G., 345
Hatshepsut (queen), 33–34
Hausa, 390
Heian Dynasty, 112
heliocentric theory of the universe, 219
Hellenistic culture, 79, 145
Helsinki Accords, 442
Henry II (king), 158
Henry IV (emperor), 151–152
Henry of Portugal (Henry the Navigator) (prince), 224, 253
Henry VI, 159
Henry VIII (king), 218, 233
Herodotus, 78
Hidalgo, Miguel, 279
hieroglyphics, 34–35, 187

Lashkar-Taiba, 445
latifundia, 86
lay investiture, 151–152
League of Nations, 335–337, 363–364
Leakey, Louis and Mary, 23
legalism, 51–52
Lenin, Vladimir, 340–343, 352
Leonidas (king), 74
Leopold II (emperor), 273
Leopold II (king), 312
Lepidus, Marcus, 88
Leviathan (Hobbes), 261
Li Bo, 96
Liberal Party, 347
Lloyd-George, David, 336
Locarno Accords, 350–351, 363
Locke, John, 261, 270–271
Long Count calendar, 183
Louis XIV (king), 235–238
Louis XVI (king), 271–274
Louis XVIII (king), 275–276
L'Ouverture, Toussaint, 277
Ludendorff, Prime Minister/General, 335
Lumumba, Patrice, 391
Lusitania (British ship), 334
Luther, Martin, 217
Lutheranism, 217

M
MacArthur, Douglas, 378, 395, 402
Madero, Francisco, 410
madrasa, 203–204
Magellan, Ferdinand, 225
Magna Carta, 158
magnetic compass, 223
Mahabharata, 43
Mahavira, 57–58
Mali, Kingdom of, 168–169
Malinke people, 168
Mamaconas, 188
Mamluk Dynasty, 205
Mandate of Heaven, The, 45–46
Mandela, Nelson, 390, 393–394
Manhattan Project, 371
Mansa Musa (Malinke), 169–170
Mao Tse-tung, 94, 303–304, 307, 378, 382, 400–403
Marcos, Ferdinand, 400–401
Marriage of the Virgin, The (Rafael), 214
Marshall Plan, 376
Martel, Charles (Charles the Hammer), 133
Marx, Karl, 286–287, 298, 340–342
mathematics, 35, 37–38, 79, 95, 127–128, 183, 219
Mau Mau, 389
Maurya, Chandragupta, 80
May Fourth Movement, 301–302
Mayan civilization, 182–184
Mazarin, Chief Minister, 236
Mazzini, Giuseppe, 292
McVeigh, Timothy, 445
Mecca, 119–120
Medici family, 213
Mehmed II, 145
Meiji Restoration, 323–324, 363, 395
Mein Kampf (My Struggle) (Hitler), 350

Meir, Golda, 432
Mencius, 54
Menes (king), 31
mercantilism, 253
Merovingian Dynasty, 133
Mesoamerica, 179–182
Mesopotamia, 35–40, 59–61
Metternich, Clemens von, 276, 291, 296–297, 330–331
Meuse Argonne, 335
Mexico, 279, 410
Michelangelo, 214
Middle Ages, 151–162
Middle Kingdom, 33
Middle Path, 58
militarism, 329
Milosevic, Slobodan, 424, 442
Ming Dynasty, 248–251
Minoans, 69
missionaries, 254
mita system, 188
Mitsubishi Corporation, 324
Mobutu, Joseph, 391
Mobutu Sese Seko, 391
Moche, 186–187
Mohammed, Khalid, 445
Mohenjo-daro (India), 41
Moksha, 57
Mona Lisa (da Vinci), 214
monasteries, 132–133
Mongols, 92–93, 100, 102–103, 146–147, 205–206
monotheism, 59
Monroe, James, 279
Monroe Doctrine, 279
monsoons, 40–41
Monte Albán, 181
Montesquieu, Baron de, 261–262
Montgomery, Bernard Law, 370
Moorish culture, 204
More, Thomas, 216
Mosaddeq, Mohammad, 430
Moscow, 147–148
Moses, 60
Mu'ayina, 124
Mubarak, Hosni, 429
Mugabe, Robert, 392
Mughal Dynasty, 207–208, 243–244, 314
Muhammad, 119–122, 208–209
Muhammad, Ali Mahdi, 441
mujahideen, 399, 433
mummification, 34–35
Muslims, 120–121, 125–126, 396–397, 434
Mussolini, Benito, 354–356, 363, 365, 367
Mycenaeans, 69

N
Nagy, Imre, 419
Napoleon, 316, 318
Napoleon III, 292, 294–295
Nasca people, 187
Nasser, Gamal Abdel, 428–429
Natchez Indians, 191
National League for Democracy, 400
National Socialist Workers' Party, 348

Q

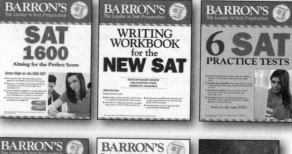